Paul Heger
The Three Biblical Altar Laws

1749
Walter de Gruyter
250
Berlin · New York
1999

Beihefte zur Zeitschrift für die alttestamentliche Wissenschaft

Herausgegeben von
Otto Kaiser

Band 279

Walter de Gruyter · Berlin · New York
1999

Paul Heger

The Three Biblical Altar Laws

Developments in the Sacrificial Cult
in Practice and Theology

Political and Economic Background

Walter de Gruyter · Berlin · New York
1999

Die Deutsche Bibliothek — Cataloging-in-Publication-Data

[Zeitschrift für die alttestamentliche Wissenschaft / Beihefte]
Beihefte zur Zeitschrift für die alttestamentliche Wissenschaft. —
Berlin ; New York : de Gruyter
   Früher Schriftenreihe
   Reihe Beihefte zu: Zeitschrift für die alttestamentliche Wissenschaft
   Bd. 279. Heger, Paul: The three biblical altar laws. — 1999

Heger, Paul:
The three biblical altar laws : developments in the sacrificial cult in
practice and theology ; political and economic background / Paul
Heger. — Berlin ; New York : de Gruyter, 1999
   (Beihefte zur Zeitschrift für die alttestamentliche Wissenschaft ; Bd.
   279)
   ISBN 3-11-016474-4

ISSN 0934-2575

Printed in Germany
Printing: Werner Hildebrand, Berlin
Binding: Lüderitz & Bauer-GmbH, Berlin

Acknowledgements

It is my pleasant duty to acknowledge the encouragement and counsel I received during the research and preparation of this book. I am deeply indebted to my mentor, Professor Harry Fox, of the Department of Near and Middle Eastern Civilizations, University of Toronto, who has graciously read the entire manuscript and extended advice and valuable suggestions. My profuse thanks are also due to Professor John Revell, who read the entire manuscript and made valuable comments, which I have incorporated in the final edition of the book. I have also had the good fortune to discuss a great number of issues with Professor John W. Wevers, and am grateful for his helpful recommendations. My deep appreciation is also due to Professor Otto Kaiser, for the most pleasant and beneficial conversation that took place last year about the topic of the book, and for his reassuring perspective. I am most thankful to Ms. Diane Kriger, for her extremely conscientious work in the important phase of editing and correction of the text. Last but not least I express my gratitude to all the Professors of the Department of Near and Middle Eastern Civilizations at the University of Toronto, from whose teachings I have benefited during my studies.

Toronto, Ontario, December, 1998

Contents

9.   Developments in the Sacrificial Cult in Practice and Theology   321

10. Conclusion   391

Appendices

Introduction

Scope and Methodology of Study

The cult and its rituals have been a decisive element in the culture of every society from the onset of social interaction between humans, and have had a dominant influence on almost every aspect of human life and development. In Israelite civilization one may affirm that these circumstances are even more emphasized, since through its mythology Israel retrojects its own creation to the divine selection of Abraham, its founding father, for a particular relationship with the Deity.[1] This special relationship is Israel's raison d'être, and dictates a continual intercourse,[2] achieved through cult and rituals.[3] The external pattern of the ceremonials underwent changes, but the

---

1   We read: והקמתי את בריתי ביני ובינך ובין זרעך אחריך "I will establish my covenant as an everlasting covenant between me and you and your descendants after you [Gen. 17: 7]"; רק באבתיך חשק ה' לאהבה אותם ויבחר בזרעם "Yet the Lord set his affection on your forefathers and loved them, and he chose you, their descendants [Deut. 10: 15]"; ובך בחר ה' להיות לו לעם סגלה "the Lord has chosen you to be his treasured possession [Deut. 14: 2]"; ושכנתי בתוכם לעולם "and I will live among them for ever [Eze. 43: 9]"; ועשו לי מקדש ושכנתי בתוכם "and I will dwell among them [Exod. 25: 8]"; תמיד עיני ה' אלהיך בה "the eyes of the Lord your God are continually on it [on your land] [Deut. 11: 12]," among many other biblical citations with the same message.

2   As the complement to the divine attitude, we encounter the reciprocal Israelite response; we read in Jos. 24: 22: כי אתם בחרתם לכם את ה' לעבד אותו "you have chosen to serve the Lord, " and in Ps. 16: 8: שויתי ה' לנגדי תמיד "I have set the Lord always before me."

3   Moses asked Pharaoh to liberate the people: לעבד את ה' אלהינו "to worship the Lord our God [Exod. 10: 26]"; God commanded the Israelites in the early Book of the Covenant: ועבדתם את ה' אלהיכם "Worship the Lord your God [Exod.23: 25]"; in Deut. 11: 13, they were again exhorted: לאהבה את ה' אלהיכם ולעבדו בכל לבבכם ובכל נפשכם "to love the Lord your God and to serve him with all your heart and with all your soul." The concept עבודה pertains to sacrificial offerings, as is obvious from Moses' dialogues with Pharaoh (Exod. 8: 21, 23, 24; 10: 25). Though in Deut. and Num. the actual sacrificial worship is delegated to the priests and Levites, the concepts עבדת ה', עבדת המשכן, עבדת הקדש relating to the sacrificial cult are found frequently throughout the Bible. After the destruction of the Temple and the cessation of the sacrificial ritual, the Sages interpreted the concept עבודה as referring to another type of ritual. We read in Mekhilta d'Rabbi Simeon bar Johai 23: 25: איזו היא עבודה שבלב

basic underlying theology of a people dedicated to the performance of religious service[4] has remained unchanged even to this day.[5] R. Rendtorff [6] writes that "the significant events in the history of Israel are meaningful in the history of the cult." I wish to add that there is a reciprocal relationship between historical events and the developments in the cult, and one influences the other; as historical circumstances affect the cult, shifts in theology and in the nature of the cult influence the conduct of the people, and in consequence the course of its history.

Research on the development of the sacrificial ritual in Israel is therefore most interesting and rewarding, since it reveals the shifts in both concrete rituals and the underlying theologies from ancient times until today. The plethora of Israelite texts extending over an extremely long period offers an excellent prospect of research. In contrast to other ancient cultures, whose texts pertain to their own limited period of existence and thus usually grant us only a "snapshot" of the relevant society frozen in time, the Israelite texts offer us a "moving picture" with a continuous flow of changing patterns of rituals, and opportunities to observe the corresponding shift of ideas. Offerings to the Deity in various forms, whether presentation of food and gifts or sacrifices of living subjects, are the most ancient type of worship, and therefore it is only natural to begin the study with the Israelite altar laws, the primary requirement of a dedicated locus for the presentation of offerings. The textual evidence of the developmental stages of the altar law, assistance from the material archeological findings, and the biblical historical narratives guide us in our quest to deduce the theological shifts during the entire span of the sacrificial cult history - that is, from the early nomadic period until the replacement of sacrifice with recitation, another type of ritual.

The study will thoroughly examine the relevant biblical texts of the altar laws in all their minutiae, will search for inconsistencies in each text, and will attempt to reveal their basis or original intent. It will then contrast these laws, and from the comparison of their ritual character and historical setting

---

הוי אומר זו תפלה "What type of 'work' / 'service' [can be performed with] the heart? You must say: It is prayer."

[4]   In the sense of λειτουργέω, in the New Testament. The dictum in Exod. 19: 6 ואתם תהיו לי ממלכת כהנים וגוי קדוש "You will be for me a kingdom of priests and a holy nation" refers to all Israelites.

[5]   A plaque with the phrase שויתי ה' לנגדי תמיד "I have set the Lord always before me [Ps. 16: 8]" is an established furnishing of every synagogue. This attitude is also reflected in the rituals of daily life in all its aspects, from the moment a Jewish person awakens until he sleeps, and to some extent even when he is asleep.

[6]   R. Rendtorff, "Der Kultus in Alten Israel," in *Gesammelte Studien zum Alten Testament* (München, 1975), writes on p. 90: "...die Haupteinschnitte in der Geschichte Israels zugleich Einschnitte in der Geschichte seine Kultus bedeuten."

establish their chronological order, and attempt to reveal the shifts in their underlying theology. I shall obviously gain assistance in this assignment from the customary tools of research: the different ancient translations such as the LXX, Onkelos and Jonathan, the New Testament, the apocryphal works and ancient historical and philosophical writings such as those of Josephus and Philo, and the results of modern scholarly research. In addition, I shall juxtapose the relevant questions and solutions of the rabbinic and traditional commentators to the inconsistencies and contradictions revealed in the biblical texts. As I have written elsewhere, the Sages and their followers were aware of these problems; sometimes they asked them explicitly, and in other occasions one can deduce from their particular interpretation that they implicitly tried to resolve an inconsistency that they observed in the text. One perceives that in some instances they were sensitive to discrepancies which modern scholars have overlooked; in other instances, it is rather fascinating to scrutinize their proposed solutions.

In addition to such philological, textual and literary examination of the various texts and the archeological evidence, I have analyzed the political and economic circumstances of each period and postulated their logical impact on the manner of performance of the cult and its underlying theology. One should not underestimate the significance of these factors on radical changes in the cult, often hidden under a veneer of pious, religiously-conditioned motives.

I shall therefore dedicate a chapter at the end of the study to the examination of the changes in the sacrificial cult in practice and theology, from the inception of the relevant Israelite texts until the replacement of the sacrificial cult with another type of ritual after the destruction of the Temple. I shall investigate the primary events along this extended path, namely the political circumstances and the consequential cult reforms of Ahaz, Josiah, Ezra and Nehemiah, the Maccabees, and Rabban Johanan ben Zakkai, the rabbinic leader after the Temple's destruction. I shall attempt to reveal and understand in this chapter the enigma of how the Sages succeeded in a short period of time in maintaining on the one hand the emotional yearning of the people for the renewal of the sacrificial cult, and in inculcating at the same time the perception that the spiritual surrogate was equivalent in religious excitement and fulfillment of God's precept to the original sacrifice. The study will critically examine the common conception that the sacrifices were replaced by prayers, and explore a different approach to this assumption, with an attempt to reach an hypothesis which may assist us in unveiling the reasons behind the establishment of this unique institution of fixed prayers. I shall proceed with an examination of these topics in their chronological order, starting with the biblical pericopes containing the laws relating to the construction of the altars.

Outline

In the Pentateuch we find three pericopes commanding the construction of an altar. In the Book of the Covenant, assumed to be an independent book of law inserted into the Pentateuchal narrative, we read in Exod. 20: 21- 23:[7]

מזבח אדמה תעשה לי וזבחת עליו את עלתיך ואת שלמיך את צאנך ואת
בקרך בכל המקום אשר אזכיר את שמי אבוא אליך וברכתיך. ואם מזבח
אבנים תעשה לי לא תבנה אתהן גזית כי חרבך הנפת עליה ותחללה. ולא
תעלה במעלת על מזבחי אשר לא תגלה ערותך עליו.

Make an altar of earth for me and sacrifice on it your burnt offerings and fellowship offerings, your sheep and goats and your cattle. Wherever I cause my name to be honoured, I will come to you and bless you. If you make an altar of stones for me, do not build it with dressed stones, for you will defile it if you use a tool on it. And do not go up to my altar on steps, lest your nakedness be exposed on it.[8]

In Deut. 27: 2- 8, we find a similar, but certainly not an identical, command to build an altar. The pericope starts by setting out when and where this command was to take effect. Contrary to the above rule in the Book of the Covenant, which is not specific with regard to place and time, the command in Deut. specifies both date and location. We read there in vv. 2 - 3:

והיה ביום אשר תעברו את הירדן אל הארץ אשר ה' אלהיך נתן לך והקמת
לך אבנים גדלות ושדת אתם בשיד. וכתבת עליהן את כל דברי התורה
הזאת בעברך למען אשר תבא אל הארץ אשר ה' אלהיך נתן לך ארץ זבת
חלב ודבש כאשר דבר ה' אלהי אבתיך לך.

When you have crossed the Jordan into the land the Lord your God is giving you, set up some large stones and coat them with plaster.[9] Write on them all the words of this law when you have crossed over to enter the land the Lord your God is giving you, a land flowing with milk and honey, just as the Lord, the God of your fathers, promised you.

A doublet with seemingly divergent instructions appears in vv. 4 - 8:

והיה בעברכם את הירדן תקימו את האבנים האלה אשר אנכי מצוה אתכם
היום בהר עיבל ושדת אותם בשיד. ובנית שם מזבח לה' אלהיך מזבח
אבנים לא תניף עליהם ברזל. אבנים שלמות תבנה את מזבח ה' אלהיך
והעלית עליו עולת לה' אלהיך. וזבחת שלמים ואכלת שם ושמחת לפני ה'
אלהיך. וכתבת על האבנים את כל דברי התורה הזאת באר היטב.

---

[7]   In the KJV, these verses are numbered 24 - 26 in chapter 20.

[8]   This is the NIV translation, which is an interpretation, and not true to the text. In the following discussion and exegesis of this and the other pericopes, I shall discuss the underlying intentions of the passages.

[9]   Here too the NIV interpreted the beginning of the verse, and avoided the literal translation of the KJV: "And it shall be on the day when ye shall pass over Jordan." I shall quote the postulates of the traditional Jewish sources on this issue.

And when you have crossed the Jordan, set up these stones on Mount Ebal, as I command you today, and coat them with plaster. Build there an altar to the Lord your God, an altar of stones. Do not use any iron tool upon them. Build the altar of the Lord your God with fieldstones [10] and offer burnt offerings on it to the Lord your God. Sacrifice fellowship offerings there, eating them and rejoicing in the presence of the Lord your God. And you shall write very clearly all the words of this law on these stones you have set up.

In complete contrast to these commands to build altars of earth and stone, the altar of the Tabernacle was to be made of wood and covered with bronze. We read the relevant command in Exod. 27: 1- 8:

ועשית את המזבח עצי שטים חמש אמות ארך וחמש אמות רחב רבוע
יהיה המזבח ושלש אמות קמתו. ועשית קרנתיו על ארבע פנתיו ממנו תהיין
קרנתיו וצפית אתו נחשת. ועשית סירתיו לדשנו ויעיו ומזרקתיו ומזלגתיו
ומחתתיו לכל כליו תעשה נחשת. ועשית לו מכבר מעשה רשת נחשת
ועשית על הרשת ארבע טבעת נחשת על ארבע קצותיו. ונתתה אתה תחת
כרכב המזבח מלמטה והיתה הרשת עד חצי המזבח. ועשית בדים למזבח
בדי עצי שטים וצפית אתם נחשת. והובא את בדיו בטבעת והיו הבדים על
שתי צלעת המזבח בשאת אתו. נבוב לחת תעשה אתו כאשר הראה אתך
בהר כן יעשו.

Build an altar of acacia wood, three cubits high; it is to be square, five cubits long and five cubits wide. Make a horn at each of the four corners, so that the horns and the altar are of one piece, and overlay the altar with bronze. Make all its utensils of bronze - its pots to remove the ashes, and its shovels, sprinkling bowls, meat forks and firepans.. Make a grating for it, a bronze network, and make a bronze ring at each of the four corners of the network. Put it under the ledge[11] of the altar so that it is halfway up the altar.. Make poles of acacia wood for the altar and overlay them with bronze. The poles are to be inserted into the rings so they will be on two sides of the altar when it is carried. Make the altar hollow, out of boards. It is to be made just as you were shown on the mountain.

An additional relevant passage in I Kings 5: 29 (5: 15 in KJV) concerns the stones of Solomon's Temple: ויהי לשלמה שבעים אלף נשא סבל ושמנים אלף חצב בהר "Solomon had seventy thousand carriers and eighty thousand stonecutters in the hills."

The inconsistencies and contradictions among these three commands are obvious on first sight, and many more will come to light in the study through a punctilious critical examination of each pericope, separately as well as in juxtaposition with the others.

Certain scholars detect a relationship between the altar law of Exod. 20 and that of Deut. 27, because of the apparent similarity with respect to the

---

[10] I have quoted the NIV translation, but I shall discuss the interpretation of this term, and propose the phrase "whole-perfect stones" as the correct implication of the concept אבנים שלמות. The KJV translates "whole" stones.

[11] This too is the NIV translation, and I shall use this term, except when noting other interpretations. In the course of the study I shall discuss the perplexities raised by this term and its various interpretations.

prohibition לא תבנה אתהן גזית "do not build it with dressed stones," in Exod. 20: 22 and אבנים שלמות תבנה את מזבח "with 'whole-perfect' stones you should build the altar," in Deut. 27: 6. The positive command to use אבנים שלמות appeared to these scholars to be the parallel of the prohibition against using dressed stones for the altar. This correlation was probably strengthened by the term נוף which appears in both pericopes: the explicative phrase כי חרבך הנפת עליה "because you wielded your sword upon it," in Exod. 20: 22, and the interdiction in Deut.27: 5, לא תניף עליהם ברזל. The rabbinic literature, in its usual quest for harmonization of all biblical pericopes, goes even further and attempts to amalgamate into one thesis the three altar laws, and also the record in I Kings 6: 7 והבית בהבנתו אבן שלמה מסע נבנה ומקבות והגרזן כל כלי ברזל לא נשמע בבית בהבנתו "In building the Temple, it was built only of 'whole-perfect', carried stones, no hammer or pick or any other iron tool was heard in the Temple when it was built." The terms אבן שלמה and ברזל which appear in Deut. and in I Kings seemed an adequate basis on which to associate the two pericopes; and the other identical terms in Deut. and Exod., as cited above, sufficed to link all three together. This equation is based on a common type of talmudic logic: if A has similarities to B, and B has similarities to C, then A is similar to C. Overlooked was the fact that although Exod. specifically prohibits the use of גזית, I Kings explicitly reports its use in 5: 31: אבני גזית.

Though the two disparate altar laws were seen as connected, scholars had difficulty revealing the common principle behind the two laws, and various hypotheses were offered to resolve this intricate topic. The rabbinic connection of the three different altar laws with the narrative about the construction of the Temple, an entirely extraneous theme, also necessitated various solutions to bridge the gap between them. This study critically examines the scholarly propositions as well as the rabbinic explanations. Substantial attention will be dedicated to a recent publication by S. M. Olyan[12] regarding his interpretation of the term אבנים שלמות in Deut. 27: 6, and consequently the motive of the biblical command. The study will analyze the terms שלם and חלל in our pericopes, and compare them with their ranges of meaning in other biblical texts; it will also examine the term תמים, cited by Olyan in his study as designating the same characteristic as שלם. Olyan's hypothesis of the biblical motive for the use of אבנים שלמות will also be critically investigated, and the study will attempt to offer a more appropriate explanation of the meaning of this phrase. It will also explore the disparate terms which occur in our pericopes. Two terms found in the motive

---

[12] Saul M. Olyan, "Why an Altar of Unfinished Stones? Some Thoughts on Exod. 20,25 and Dtn 27,5 - 6," *ZAW* 108 (1996), pp. 161 - 171

for the prohibition in Exod., חרב "sword" and ותחללה regarding the defilement of the altar, are absent in Deut.; on the other hand, in Deut. we find the term ברזל, an indeterminate "iron tool".

The study will emphasize the significant variations, literary and structural, between the two pericopes, and will attempt to demonstrate their origins in two different periods and disparate historical settings. It will relate the relevance of each law to the distinct circumstances of life in Israelite society, and to the different philosophical and theological environments in the particular periods. The study will also avail itself of a comparison between the early conditions of Israelite society and Arab nomadic custom.

The study will then examine the correlation between the pericope in Deut., concerning the requisite stones of the altar, and the various narratives in I Kings chaps. 5 - 7, in which a number of similar terms are used regarding the stones used for the building of Solomon's Temple and palace.[13] It is obvious that there could be no relation between these narratives and the pericope in Exod. 20; the latter refers to the stones of the altar while the former record the type of stone used in building the Temple. Moreover, Solomon certainly used אבני גזית for the foundations,[14] a type explicitly prohibited in Exod. 20. The study will therefore concentrate on the correlation between the relevant phrases in Kings and Deut., and will critically analyze the rabbinic perception of an affinity among all the passages, and their solution to the oddities of the text. I shall examine the scholarly opinion that the decree of Exod. 20 to use only stones "in their natural state" was extended to include the stones for the Temple building, and that the Kings narrative implies a mandate to use stones in their natural state for both the building of the Temple and for the altar, propositions which would implicitly link the pericopes in Exod. 20 and Deut. 27 to the Kings passages through a common motif. The study will also demonstrate the irrationality of the rabbinic solution in reconciling the evident contradiction between Exod. 20 and Kings regarding the use of גזית by Solomon; that is, that the prohibition of iron tools for the preparation of

---

[13] אבנים גדלות אבנים יקרות "Great stones, costly stones [I Kings 5: 31 in MT, 5: 17 in KJV, 6: 1a in LXX]"; והבית בהבנתו אבן שלמה מסע נבנה "In building the Temple, of [exclusively] whole-perfect, carried stone it was built [I Kings 6: 7]"; כל אלה אבנים יקרת כמדות גזית מגררות במגרה מבית ומחוץ...אבנים יקרות אבנים גדלות "All אבני עשר אמות ואבני שמנה אמות ומלמעלה אבנים יקרות כמדות גזית costly stones, in the size of dressed [hewn/ squared] stone, levelled with a plane, in and outside...costly stones, large stones, stones of ten cubits and stones of eight cubits and above costly stones in the size of dressed [hewn/ squared] stones [I Kings 7: 9 - 11, 46 - 48 in LXX]."

[14] I Kings 5: 31. We encounter again the expression כמדות גזית in I Kings 7: 11 relating to the walls, and one must assume that it refers to dressed stones, but I limited the expression "certainly" to the foundations.

the stones for the Temple building was limited to the Temple precinct, but was sanctioned outside it. Finally, I shall attempt to postulate a reasonable explanation of the apparently odd report in Kings 6: 7 that "no [noise] of iron tools was heard at the Temple site."

The study will then discuss the utilization of archeological evidence to ascertain the actual types of altars built and used in ancient Israel. It will identify the problems which impede the indisputable identification of the altars and the correlation of archeological evidence with the biblical texts, quoting a number of debates among eminent archeologists with respect to the identification of altars at prominent sites. In particular, the noted dispute between Yadin and Aharoni regarding the Beer Sheba excavation will be thoroughly debated, and their use and interpretation of biblical texts to support their identifications will be critically analyzed. The study will also examine the broad difference of opinion between Zertal and Shanks regarding the identification of an altar at Mt. Ebal, and that between Ussishkin and Stern with respect to the excavation at Meggido. Zertal's reliance on "biblical tradition" for his classification of the site will be critically analyzed.

The text of the command to make a bronze altar in Exod. 27: 1 - 8 will be minutely analyzed. The difficult passages in the text will be indicated and thoroughly examined, also with the help of the various ancient translations such as the Targums and the LXX. The evident contradictions as to type and size between this altar and that described in Eze. 43: 13 - 17 and II Chr. 4: 1 will similarly be emphasized. The study will quote the rabbinic attempts to harmonize all these pericopes, and attempt to demonstrate the impossibility of this Sisyphean task. The appearance of such odd items as סירת "cooking pots" and מזלגת "forks" among the altar accessories for the burning of fat or of the entire carcass of an animal is another bizarre phenomenon, and a comparison with other biblical citations regarding this altar and its accessories will be effected.

A fundamental problem regarding the issue of the bronze altar is the meaning of the terms מכבר and כרכב, רשת, described as essential elements in the altar's construction in vv. 4 and 5, and their nature, application and function in the structure and use of the altar. We must also add the term מחתתיו in v. 3, which indicates an affinity with incense; this affinity is suggested in the Samaritan Targum, while the LXX translates πυρεῖον, in singular, in contrast to the MT text in plural. This peculiar translation of the LXX hints at the probability that the translator had something in mind other than firepans, perhaps some essential element of the altar located on its top. Such an assumption, supported by the entirely different text of this pericope in the LXX, further complicates the understanding of the MT text regarding the structure and appearance of the altar that the editor intended to portray.

I shall critically analyze the propositions of Haran and Cassuto, who attempted to solve the riddle within the confines of the MT text and its traditional interpretations, and indicate the deficiencies of their arguments. I shall then postulate a reasonable representation of the altar based on the LXX rendition, which deviates from the MT text, and explore the probability that invention, or a vague reminiscence of some similar cult furnishing, rather than a concrete model, was the basis for the portrayal of the bronze altar by the author or editor. I shall examine the term בדים, used for the carrying poles of the altar rather than the more appropriate term מוט, utilized elsewhere in the Pentateuch (Num. 13: 23) precisely to describe two people carrying a load on their shoulders with poles; I shall then propose an hypothesis to justify the apparently odd use of the term בדים for all the Tabernacle's furnishings, including the bronze altar.

The significance of the altar's קרנים "horns" is an issue much debated among scholars; various propositions in this respect will be assessed. The semantic range of the term קרן in its many concrete and metaphorical meanings will be scrutinized, with the aim of dissociating the קרנים of the altar from the simplistic assumption of "animal horns" attached to its corners, and considering them merely as projections. The study will discuss the distinction between the dual form קרנים and the plural קרנות, and the association of these forms with different concrete and metaphorical meanings. The suggestion by some scholars that the horns on the Israelite altar symbolize bull's horns is not confirmed in Israelite mythology; nor do the styles of altars found at archeological sites show any similarity to animal horns. The study will therefore propose a different metaphorical interpretation of the protruding elements on the four corners of the altar, and a plausible explanation for their presence on the permanent stone altars.

Scholarly opinion rejects the entire narrative of the Tabernacle and its complex furnishings as portrayed in Exod. 25 - 30. The absence in Kings of a bronze altar among the bronze furnishings made by Solomon, and in the list of the bronze objects seized by Nebuzaradan, intensifies doubt as to the existence of such an altar, and the study will endeavour to add further questions concerning this dilemma. The editor of Chr. adds a bronze altar to the inventory of Solomon's Temple, with different dimensions than those of the Exod. altar but without its perplexing structural description; this attempt to correct the deficiency in Kings in turn raises its own questions. The rabbinic effort to harmonize the inconsistencies will be critically analyzed and its flaws revealed. The study will highlight additional oddities encountered with respect to the bronze altar: its absence in numerous biblical passages in which we would absolutely expect its presence; the fact that the poles of the ark were never to be removed, but the poles of the bronze altar as well as those of the other furnishings such as the golden altar and the table were not subject to such a decree. It would be convenient to conclude that such a bronze altar never actually existed, but we cannot ignore the narrative in II Kings 16 about a bronze altar removed by King Ahaz from its central location in the Temple's court. The study will venture to reveal whether Ahaz effected a cult reform, hidden beneath the biblical narrative concerning this altar. The affinity between שלחן "table" and מזבח "altar", both in practice and in the biblical language of a particular period, points the way to a solution of this issue of the bronze altar.

There is basic scholarly agreement on the fact of Josiah's reform of the sacrificial cult, including its goal of centralization in Jerusalem and the obstacles to be expected as a result of this drastic change. The motives that induced Josiah to undertake this unique and exceptional measure are, however, the subject of debate. Josiah's course of action, so alien to the custom of the surrounding cultures, elicits our amazement and demands a thorough examination of all relevant texts as well as the political and economic circumstances in that period. The study will focus in particular on the problem of the almost identical language in the two passages recording repairs of the Temple, by Joash in II Kings 12 and by Josiah in II Kings 22, and will critically analyze various scholarly opinions on this topic. It will also examine the expressions used by the Kings editor in connection with the issue of the cult in Jerusalem versus the worship at the *bamoth*.

This research will enable us to conclude which king actually repaired the Temple, as an indication of his particular concern for the cult centralization in Jerusalem. We shall then minutely examine Josiah's activities in Judah and Samaria as recorded in Scripture, the political circumstances in the area, and Josiah's presumed political objectives. We shall also investigate the deuteronomic ordinances proclaimed during Josiah's period relevant to the newly-created status of Jerusalem, in order to detect the practical purpose concealed under the guise of a divine selection. Thus we shall reveal the background of Josiah's reform, his ultimate objective and the impact of this reform on the future character of the Israelite sacrificial cult.

The replacement of sacrifices with recitation and prayers after the destruction of the Temple in 70 C. E. constituted the last step in the developmental stages of the Israelite sacrificial cult. Such changes must have been accompanied by modifications in the theological foundation, which either generated the shifts in the manner of performance of the cult or were themselves caused by such shifts. The study will examine the interaction between these two cardinal elements based on a scrutiny of the available texts as well as logical speculation and comparison with other sources. As the nature of sacrifice changed from the initial offering of food to the gods to the burnt offerings effected by Ahaz, so a corresponding shift in the theology underlying the sacrifices occurred. The study will explore the correlation between Ahaz' reform and the development and expression of monotheism and its doctrines; as the relationship between God and man was rethought, there was a corresponding influence upon the practice and theology of sacrifices. Prophetic utterances of this period will be analyzed in light of these changes.

The study continues by investigating the sequence of events in Israelite history from Ahaz until the destruction of the Second Temple, with respect to their impact on the sacrificial cult, in order to detect whether there is a continuous line of development, with each stage conditioned by the last until the ultimate disappearance of sacrifice. This investigation will involve a thorough analysis of the religious and political activities of Ezra and Nehemiah, the most significant innovators in Israelite faith and law after the return from the exile. It will examine the impact of their modifications in the interpretation and application of the law in general, and their novel organization of the cult and its financing, as well as the impact of their reforms on the subsequent development of the sacrificial cult. The relationship between the public financing of sacrifices and the underlying theology will be explored, as well as the question of whether Ezra and Nehemiah had political goals concealed in the cult reform in addition to the practical requirement of a constant and secure endowment for the maintenance of the Temple and the sacrificial ceremonies. The study will address the correlation between their reform and the creation of the priestly hegemony, the shift of political power to the High Priest, and the edition of the P stratum of the Pentateuch, which established and institutionalized the sacrificial ceremonial and perfected the corresponding creed. Analysis of scriptural narratives forms the foundation of this chapter, but for later developments, such as the circumstances which provoked the unusual disregard of the sacrifices by the priests before the Maccabean revolt, we will have to rely on the Apocrypha, the New Testament, historical writings and other post-biblical literature.

The Maccabean revolution, as we know, reinstated sacrifices to their position of significance. The study will conclude by examining the final stage in the development of the sacrificial system, its replacement. It is generally assumed that sacrifice was replaced with prayer, based on a number of rabbinic declarations. We will first determine whether sacrifices in fact ceased after the Temple's destruction, as suggested by some scholars, and whether any cessation was due to a deliberate decision of the Rabbis or was a result of hindrance by the Roman authorities. Considering the utmost significance bestowed on sacrifice before the Temple's destruction, one must wonder at how quickly and successfully it was replaced in Israelite society by recitation and prayer. The study will probe the possibility that this unlikely change was facilitated by the theological shifts initiated by Ahaz and followed by Josiah, Ezra and Nehemiah, leaders who established a precedent of revision and amendment, which adapted itself to further development in response to the requirements of changed circumstances. Rabbinic declarations with respect to the replacement of sacrifices will be examined, along with the preceding theological changes which may have facilitated this transformation between two so disparate cult elements. The study will endeavour to illuminate why the unique rite of fixed public prayers was instituted and will assess its overwhelming effect on both the Israelite cult and its cognate religions.

Sources

Quotations from post-biblical sources have generally been taken from the common printed editions; variations are insignificant and do not affect the essence of our quotations. For the Septuagint quotations, I relied on Wevers' critical edition of the Pentateuch, on Ziegler's edition for the available prophets and on Rahlf's edition for the remaining scriptural books. For the Greek New Testament, the edition published by the United Bible Societies was used. Quotations from Onkelos were taken from the Yemenite Taj edition; difficult readings were also compared with Sperber's critical edition. Quotations from the Samaritan Targum were based on manuscripts J and A of A. Tal's edition. Translations have been provided for each of the biblical verses cited; these have generally been based on the NIV translation of the Bible, and in some cases complemented with my own interpretation. I hasten to emphasize that such translations were provided as a convenience for the reader, and not as evidence of a particular postulate. I also set out my own translations for the quotations from traditional Hebrew writings, and for citations from contemporary scholarly publications in Hebrew, German and French, as a convenience to the reader.

Limitations

I would like to reiterate what I have hinted throughout this introduction and explicitly pronounced at the conclusion of my previous book with respect to the investigation of the ancient Israelite cult and its developmental stages, and that is the limitations of such a study. Unlike the physical sciences, it is impossible to test and verify the results of research in this field. I believe that the diligent and meticulous interpretation of primary sources and rational reflection on the results of such analysis, together with the examination of a variety of secondary sources, provide the intellectual resources necessary to postulate reasonable solutions and to formulate a thesis that comes as close to the truth as possible, considering the above limitations.

As is well known, the investigation of biblical texts is an intricate task; one topic leads to another, and each study extends far beyond what was originally anticipated. My examination of the altar laws is no exception. I have attempted to elaborate on most of the interconnected issues in the footnotes rather than in the text, to enable a continuous reading and perception of the main thesis. The footnotes either explain more thoroughly the topics quoted in the text, or indicate different and sometimes opposing interpretations. Three related issues I have concluded were better reviewed within the framework of separate Appendices: "1 Kings 6: 17 - 22: A Comparison Between the MT and LXX Texts," on the golden altar, the literary difficulties in the MT text, and the attempt of the LXX to remedy these difficulties through radical changes; "The Hermeneutic Method of Ezra and Nehemiah with Respect to the Labour Restrictions on Sabbath and the Prohibition against Intermarriage"; and "The Priesthood of Jehoiada."

1. The Relationship between the Altar Laws in Exod. 20 and Deut. 27

1.1 Biblical Passages Concerning the Construction of Altars

There are three pericopes in the Pentateuch commanding the construction of an altar. As these have been cited in full in the Introduction, I shall now quote only the relevant passages in English.

In the Book of the Covenant, we read in Exod. 20: 21- 23:[1]

Make an altar of earth for me and sacrifice on it....If you make an altar of stones for me, do not build it with dressed stones, for you will defile it if you use a tool on it. And do not go up to my altar on steps, lest your nakedness be exposed on it

In Deut. 27: 2 - 8, we encounter another command to build an altar:

Build there an altar to the Lord your God, an altar of stones. Do not use any iron tool upon them.

Exod. 27: 1 - 8 contains a command to build an altar of wood, covered with bronze:

Build an altar of acacia wood....Make a horn at each of the four corners...and overlay the altar with bronze. Make a grating for it, a bronze network...Put it under the ledge of the altar....Make poles of acacia wood for the altar and overlay them with bronze....Make the altar hollow.

The inconsistencies and contradictions among these three commands of the altar are obvious on first sight, and many more will come to light through a punctilious critical examination of each pericope, separately as well as in juxtaposition with the others. I shall than compare these Pentateuchal commands with other scriptural passages concerning the Altar of Burnt Offerings. This latter altar is called by the term מזבח העלה in the P stratum of the Pentateuch and in Chronicles, but in all other scriptural writings it is generally called by the neutral term "the altar," or "the altar of God"; on a few occasions (which shall be discussed in depth in sections 1.2.3.1, 1.2.3.2 and 7.1.2) it is called מזבח הנחשת, the bronze altar.

1.1.1 Is There a Correlation Between Exod. 20 and Deut. 27?

The obvious similarity of the pericopes in Exod. 20 and Deut. 27 has naturally induced both the traditional commentators and modern scholars to consider them together and to attempt a harmonization between them. Although the simple, straightforward translation of the phrase in Exod. 20: 21b, בכל המקום אשר אזכיר את שמי "wherever I will remember my

---

[1]   In the KJV, these verses are numbered 24 - 26 of chapter 20.

name," demonstrates a clear contradiction to the deuteronomic centralization of the cult, it seems to me that the similarity of the regulations in both pericopes regarding the type and preparation of the altar was the main basis of the quest for harmonization. In his commentary to Exodus 20: 22,[2] N. Sarna writes: "This prohibition is reiterated in Deuteronomy 27: 5-6 in regard to the instructions for the altar to be erected on Mount Ebal, and Joshua strictly enforced it." He then adds: "We are told that in the construction of Solomon's Temple 'only finished stones cut at the quarry were used,'" connecting the description of the Temple building in I Kings 6: 7 to the prohibition against using hewn stones in Exod. 20: 22. I shall revert to this issue in chap. 3.

A. Dillmann[3] in *Die Bücher Exodus und Leviticus* also considers the prohibition against using "hewn stones" of Exod. 20: 22 to be identical with the command to use "whole stones" unsullied by "an iron tool on them" in Deut. 27: 5 - 6. He writes on p. 248: "Die Vorschrift findet sich wieder Dt 27, 5f." ("This regulation [not to use hewn stones in Exod. 20: 22] appears again in Deut. 27: 5.") Though Dillmann links the two pericopes, he observes a contradiction between the deuteronomic centralization of the cult and what he considers the probable original version of the phrase בכל המקום אשר אזכיר את שמי; in his opinion, the phrase was later amended to soften the blatant divergence between the two texts. In his commentary[4] to Deut. 27: 6, he translates אבנים שלמות as ganzen ("whole") and vollständigen ("perfect"), two terms that could be compatible with hewn stones.

H.W. Hertzberg[5] also connects the two pericopes, in his commentary and translation to Joshua 8: 31, but not in a direct way. He simply suggests that the regulation for the building of the altar in Deut. 27: 5 is old and also appears in the Book of the Covenant in Exod. 20: 22. S. R. Driver[6] also links both pericopes; although he correctly translates אבנים שלמות as "whole stone," he adds: "It is to be built, according to the ancient law of Exod. 20: 22 (JE), in simple fashion ... i.e. of unhewn stones, upon which no tool has been used." I wish to comment at this stage that I do not observe in Deut. any hint of a simple altar construction. On the contrary, the command to build the

---

[2] N. Sarna, *Exodus* שמות, *The JPS Torah Commentary* (Philadelphia, 1991).

[3] A. Dillmann, *Die Bücher Exodus und Leviticus,* Kurzgefasstes exegetisches Handbuch zum Alten Testament, XII, 3rd ed. (Leipzig, 1897).

[4] A. Dillmann, *Die Bücher Numeri, Deuteronomium und Joshua,* Kurzgefasstes exegetisches Handbuch zum Alten Testament, XIII, 2nd ed. (Leipzig, 1886).

[5] H.W. Hertzberg, *Die Bücher Joshua, Richter, Ruth,* 3rd ed. (Göttingen, 1965).

[6] S.R. Driver, *Deuteronomy, The International Critical Commentary on the Holy Scriptures of the Old and New Testaments,* 2nd ed. (Edinburgh, 1896).

altar of great stones and of whole stones demonstrates a requirement that the builders be seriously concerned with its structure. This is all the more evident when the text is juxtaposed to that in Exod. 20: 21 which seems to commend the simplicity of the altar and stresses the insignificance of the choice of construction material and site.

Von Rad,[7] in his commentary to Deut. 27, does not express an explicit opinion concerning the linkage between the two pericopes; he merely writes: "On the command not to use an iron tool on the stones for the altar, see Exod. 20: 22," without further comment. M. Noth does not mention any connection to Deut. 27: 5 - 6 in his commentary to Exod. 20: 21 - 23. One may assume that he considers these two pericopes unrelated, at least in their original unamended versions; however, he interprets the motive behind this prohibition as being that "...the stones must remain unworked, as working with human tools would do away with their original condition." Keil and Delitzsch[8] elaborate on the symbolic significance of the command regarding the construction of the altar in Exod. 20: 21 - 23, and they too connect the two pericopes in their comments on Deut. 27: 5 - 6. They assume that the law was not written on the unhewn stones of the altar, which would be inappropriate for such writing.

M. Anbar[9] observes the difference between the commands in Exod. 20: 22 and Deut. 27: 5 - 6 concerning the type of stones. He considers the verses in Deut. an interpolation, consisting of "a Deuteronomic adaptation of the law of the altar in Exod. 20: 21 - 22." He thus assumes that the intention of the deuteronomic editor was to harmonize the two pericopes, and writes: "The aim of this interpolation was to compare the ceremony of Mount Sinai (Exod. 24: 4 - 5) with that of Mount Ebal." M. Weinfeld,[10] on the other hand, observes a clear and distinct contradiction between the deuteronomic tradition, which emphasizes the establishment of the people of Israel in the Plains of Moab as a preparation for the ceremony at Gerizim and Ebal, and the Sinai tradition of Exodus. He writes: "This conception [the deuteronomic] contradicts the traditions in Exodus, according to which the foundation of the

---

[7]   G. von Rad, *Deuteronomy, A Commentary,* The Old Testament Library, translated by D. Barton (Philadelphia, 1966).

[8]   Keil & Delitzsch, *Commentaries to the Old Testament,* translated from German by J. Martin, Vol. II and Vol. III.

[9]   M. Anbar, "The Building of an Altar on Mount Ebal," in *Das Deuteronium. Entstehung, Gestalt und Botschaft,* Bibliotheca Ephemeridum Theologicarum Lovaniensiensium LXVIII, pp. 304 - 309, ed. N. Lohfink (Leuven, 1985).

[10] M. Weinfeld, "The Deuteronomic Movement," in *Das Deuteronium. Entstehung, Gestalt und Botschaft,* Bibliotheca Ephemeridum Theologicarum Lovaniensium LXVIII, pp. 76-98, ed. N. Lohfink, (Leuven, 1985).

people of Israel - also involving erecting pillars, building an altar and writing the Laws (Exod. 24: 3-8) took place at Sinai." Weinfeld does not explicitly dissociate the two commands based on the type of stones, but from his forthright declaration of the incompatibility of the two passages, we may deduce that he assumes no relation between the specific commands regarding the construction of the altar. Finally, it is obvious that the rabbinic tradition attempts to harmonize these two pericopes, as well as many other passages related to the stones of the altar and Solomon's Temple.

1.2 Critical Analysis of the Biblical Passages

1.2.1 Methodology

Before I further expose these traditional views, and suggest a different hypothesis, I wish to analyze the biblical texts through a close reading regarding their literary and structural form and the historical circumstances which might have influenced their conception. In addition to the use of Wellhausen's *Literarkritik* "literary criticism" and Gunkel's *formgeschichtliche Schule* "form criticism," which do not contradict each other, we must complement our biblical research with the historical particulars of the cult evolution, as far as we know it or are able to deduce it from the study of other sources. The various known stages of the cult development, and their application to the analysis of biblical texts, may reliably assist in identifying the period in which a pericope, or parts of it, originated in its primeval state.

To emphasize the importance of the *kulturgeschichtliche* "cult history" examination method, I would like to present some examples of its application. The scholarly discussion regarding the issue of chronological priority between Ezra and Chronicles is well known, but the critical analysis was based mainly, if not exclusively, on concepts of literary criticism, without consideration of specific details of customs and events which can be historically assessed in their relative periods. The conclusions of Albright,[11] among others, regarding the dates and personalities of the editors of Chronicles and Ezra, are based exclusively on philological and literary comparison between the two books, without an examination of the differences in the way cult phenomena are described in these books. For example, there is no mention of a daily incense celebration in Ezra, whereas

---

[11] W.F. Albright, "The Date and Personality of the Chronicler," *JBL* 40 (1921), pp. 104 - 124.

the incense ceremonies are overwhelmingly emphasized in Chronicles.[12] This fact would demonstrate the later date of Chr., or at least of the many references there to the incense celebration.

This relative dating of the texts is important with respect to another issue related to our subject, the building of the holocaust altar as narrated in Ezra 3: 2: ויבנו את מזבח אלהי ישראל להעלות עליו עלות " ...[they] began to build the altar of the God of Israel to sacrifice burnt offerings on it." As the term בנה attests,[13] this was certainly an altar built of earth or stones, in conformity with the regulations in Exod. 20: 21 - 22, and not a bronze altar, as the command in Exod. 27: 1 - 8 requires. One must ask why Ezra did not adhere to this latter biblical law, if this specific rule were already known in his period. The law appears in the late P stratum, and was known to the compiler or editor of Chronicles; according to II Chr. 4: 1, Solomon did construct a bronze altar for the Temple: ויעש מזבח נחשת. This distinct difference between the Ezra and Chronicles narratives concerning a significant cult phenomenon offers a reliable criterion on which to evaluate whether the two books originate from identical or different sources, and to determine which is of prior date. It seems to me that the importance of investigating cult phenomena in the biblical narratives, as part of the general analysis, cannot be overestimated. It makes no difference whether we consider the narratives as composed of authentic facts, or whether we comprehend them as information shaped and transmitted for specific purposes. In the latter case, we must not consider the text as a deliberate falsification of the facts, but as reflecting a genuine belief of the writer that according to his credo and insight events must have been so; thus his report serves as authentic testimony to the opinions and facts existing in his period. In our example, we may declare without hesitation that the passage in II Chr. 4: 1 attesting to the

---

[12] See further P. Heger, *The Development of the Incense Cult in Israel* [hereinafter *Incense*], pp. 172ff.

[13] The Talmud also attests that Ezra did not build a bronze altar. We read in B. T. Zebahim 62a: אמר רבה בר בר חנה א"ר יוחנן שלשה נביאים עלו עמהם מן הגולה אחד שהעיד להם על המזבח ואחד שהעיד להם על מקום המזבח ואחד שהעיד להם שמקריבין אף על פי שאין בית במתניתא תנא ר"א בן יעקב אומר שלשה נביאים עלו עמהן מן הגולה אחד שהעיד להם על המזבח ועל מקום המזבח ואחד שהעיד להם שמקריבין אף על פי שאין בית ואחד שהעיד להם על התורה שתכתב אשורית "Three prophets came up with them [the exiles] from the exile: one gave witness to them as to the [size] of the altar, one gave witness as to the place of the altar and one attested that one may offer sacrifices although there is no Temple [yet built]...." A discussion then follows about the size of the altar and its construction details; the details correspond to the altar's description in Ezek. 43, rather than to a bronze altar.

construction of a bronze altar by Solomon was written after the redaction of the P stratum of the Pentateuch, and that we cannot say the same of Ezra 3: 2.

A passage in Ezra 3: 4 - 5 offers another example of a cultic narrative which assists in dating the passage relative to the final redaction of the P stratum. We read there:

ויעשו את חג הסכות ככתוב ועלת יום ביום במספר כמשפט דבר יום ביומו.
ואחרי כן עלת תמיד ולחדשים ולכל מועדי ה׳

Then in accordance with what is written, they celebrated the Feast of the Tabernacles with the required number of burnt offerings prescribed for each day. After that,[14] they presented the regular burnt offerings, the New Moon sacrifices and the sacrifices for all the appointed sacred feasts of the Lord....

Only the עולה, the holocaust offering, is reported here, but in Num. 29: 16 a sin offering is required every day of the Feast of Tabernacles: ושעיר עזים אחד חטאת מלבד עלת התמיד "...one male goat as a sin offering, in addition to the regular burnt offering...." It seems that in the time of Ezra this daily sin offering during the Feast of Tabernacles was not yet established.[15]

---

[14] The expression "after that" is odd, since it is not clear to what time it refers. In the Codex in Num. 29 setting out the fixed sacrifices for each day and holy days, we read in v.16: מלבד עלת התמיד "in addition to the regular burnt offering"; that is, the daily perpetual burnt offerings are to be brought in addition to the special burnt offerings of the holiday. This verse could, therefore, refer to this daily perpetual offering, but then it would contradict the rabbinic order of the sacrifices (B. T. Yoma 33a), which requires the daily holocaust to be offered before the special holiday offerings, and not after them. Rashi and Ibn Ezra were aware of this problem, and emphasize that "after that" means that after the holidays they offered the daily perpetual holocaust offering, mornings and evenings. They attempted to harmonize the text in Ezra with Num. 29: 16 and its rabbinic interpretation, but not, in my opinion, very successfully; the expression " after that", and a statement that they offered the daily perpetual sacrifice after the holiday, would be superfluous, since this fact is already clearly stated in the antecedent verse 3 in Ezra 3: ויעל עליו עלות לה׳ עלות לבקר ולערב "...and sacrificed burnt sacrifices on it to the Lord, both the morning and evening sacrifices."

[15] In Ezra 6: 17 we read: וצפירי עזין לחטיא על כל ישראל תרי עשר למנין שבטי ישראל "and as a sin offering for all Israel, twelve male goats, one for each of the tribes of Israel." It is possible that a regular sin offering was already celebrated in Ezra's period, but this cannot be deduced from this verse. First, the MT text "Ketib" is peculiar, and should have been לחטאת, instead of לחטיא. Second, we read in Ezra 8: 35, after a list of holocaust offerings of various animals: צפירי חטאת שנים עשר הכל עלה לה׳ "and as a sin offering, twelve male goats; all this was a burnt offering to the Lord." We see that these twelve male goats "for sin" are explicitly described as holocaust offerings; hence, we may assume that the same applies to the "sin offering" mentioned in 6: 17. The holocaust offering was initially considered - before the priestly establishment instituted the rule that the priest would receive the meat of the sin offering - as an atonement offering. We read in Lev. 1: 4, an early pericope concerning the sin offering, ונרצה לו לכפר עליו "and it will be accepted on his behalf to make atonement for him." Sifra on

Leviticus דבורא דנדבה פרשה ג ד"ה פרק ד interprets this verse and tells us which transgressions are atoned for by the holocaust sacrifice: על מצות עשה ועל מצות לא תעשה שיש בה קום ועשה "...for failing to perform an obligatory precept, and on a transgression that is redressed by an affirmative action." (For example, the command in Deut. 22: 7, שלח תשלח את האם "Let the mother go," is the affirmative decree for the negative transgression in v. 6, לא תקח האם על הבנים "Do not take the mother with young [birds].")

Similarly, the male goats in Ezra 6: 17 and 8: 35 were considered holocaust offerings for atonement, and the other animal offerings were considered regular holocaust offerings. At any rate, the use of twelve male goats as sin offerings is not consistent with the rules of the P stratum of the Pentateuch. At the consecration of the Tent of Meeting, only one male goat was offered for the people of Israel, according to Lev. chap. 9. Moreover, a sin offering could not be offered voluntarily, but only if specifically commanded, or as atonement for an involuntary sin, as prescribed in Lev. chap. 4. The traditional commentators Rashi and Mezudath David were aware of the inconsistency in this text, and in the dicta in B.T. Zebahim 8b that sin and guilt offerings could not be offered voluntarily, and attempt a solution by declaring that it was הוראת שעה "a special ordinance." A. Kahana, in his תנ"ך עם פירוש מדעי, ספרי עזרא ונחמיה (Tel Aviv, 1930), p.40, tries to solve this issue by comparing the twelve male goats of the sin offering of the princes at the consecration of the altar, in Num. 7: 87. However, the Ezra passage reports on the consecration of the Temple, חנכת בית אלהא (6:16), whereas the pericope in Num. specifically concerns the altar: זאת חנכת המזבח ביום המשח אתו "the dedication of the altar on the day of its anointing [Num. 7: 84]." Moreover, Ezra 8: 35 again refers to twelve male goats - and this verse does not repeat the same event as Ezra 6: 17, since the other offerings are in different amounts - and here it is obvious that they were voluntary offerings, having no relation to the consecration of the Temple. At the dedication of Solomon's temple, Solomon offered enormous quantities of sacrifices (I Kings 8: 63 - 64), but no sin offerings. In Ezek. we do find, again at the consecration of the altar, seven male goats, one each day of the week as sin and purification offerings. From the text in Ezra 6: 17, one may also assume that all twelve goats were offered in one day; there is no mention of the number of days for the consecration celebration, as in Lev. and Ezekiel. Ezekiel also lists a daily offering of male goats as a sin offering during the seven days of Passover, but he does not mention a similar offering for the Feast of Tabernacles; further, the sacrificial canon of Ezekiel does not correspond to the regulations in the P stratum of the Pentateuch. The sin offering underwent many changes from its inception until the organization of its final rules, and we have no precise indications of its initial character. II Kings 12: 17 (v. 16 in KJV), כסף אשם וכסף חטאות לא יובא בית ה' "The money from the guilt offerings and sin offerings was not brought into the Temple of the Lord," is a peculiar statement, in that it implies a money offering, not the animal sacrifice indicated in Lev. chap. 4. Even in the priestly regulations we observe different phases in the development of this late offering. Lev. 4 refers to sin offerings for transgressions of the High Priest and of all the people (a later expansion of the sin offerings according to K. Elliger, *Handbuch zum Alten Testament, Leviticus* [Tübingen, 1966, p. 54]); these are totally burned. The subsequent sin offerings for the prince and for individuals refer only to the fat burned on the altar; there are no indications as to the use of the remainder of the animal. One might assume either that the flesh was eaten by the offerer, similar to the שלמים, or was entirely burned, similar to the antecedent sin offerings. It is only in the later pericope of Lev. 6: 18 - 23 that the matter is

In Ezra 3: 2, we have an additional corroboration of this postulate; the purpose of the altar is explicitly stated to be ויבנו את מזבח אלהי ישראל להעלות עליו עלות ככתוב בתורת משה "they built the altar of the God of Israel to sacrifice burnt offerings on it, in accordance with what is written in the Law of Moses."

1.2.2 Exod. 20: 21 - 23

1.2.2.1 Literary and Structural Analysis

Scholars[16] have questioned whether these three verses were originally in their current position, or were interpolated here before the Book of the Covenant. There are a number of irregularities. The verbs in the antecedent verses 19 and 20, which the redactor put as a preamble before verses 21 - 23, are expressed in plural, whereas the verbs in verses 21 - 23 are in singular, as in the main body of laws in the Book of the Covenant which follows. (Targum Neophyti has in fact changed all the verbs in verse 21 into plural, whereas the LXX puts the first part of the verse in plural and the second half in singular.) One would therefore have expected these cult regulations to appear in the pericope 23: 10 - 19 together with the remaining cult rules. Noth speculates that these regulations were deemed of such importance that they were "put at the beginning of the book at a later date," and, remarkably, before the heading in chap. 23 of the Book of the Covenant, "These are the Laws."

A further inconsistency lies in the fact that the command in v. 21, the core of the regulation, is apodictic, contrary to the casuistic style of the Book of the Covenant. Verse 22, on the other hand, is casuistic, a fact which raises the question whether the two verses are from the same period and origin, or whether the whole pericope in vv. 21 - 23 is an amalgamation of rules from different sources, or underwent changes before reaching us in its current

---

settled; this pericope complements chap. 4 with ritual details that were probably not yet finalized earlier, and assigns the priest's remuneration; we read in 6: 19 (26 in KJV): הכהן המחטא אתה יאכלנה "The priest who offers it shall eat it." The gradual development of the cult of the sin offering and its separation from the ancient holocaust are thus evident; see also chap. 9 n. 43 regarding the inconsistency between the rules of the sin offering in Lev. 4: 13 - 21, in which an ox for a חטאת is required, and Num. 15: 22 - 26, in which an ox for an עולה and a male goat for a חטאת are specified. Cf. R. Rendtorff, *Studien zur Geschichte des Opfers im Alten Israel* (Neukirchen, 1967), p. 240, regarding the changes in the character of the sin offering.

[16] See N. Sarna, *Exodus* שמות and M. Noth, *Exodus, A Commentary*, transl. J.S. Bowden (Philadelphia, 1962).

form.[17] There is also the odd mix of singular and plural in v. 22. The pronoun אתהן may refer to the אבנים, stones, in plural, but then we have in the continuation of the verse the pronoun עליה and the verb ותחללה, in singular form.[18]

Y. Osumi[19] quotes a great number of imperfections and examples of unevenness in these verses, observed by various scholars. Nonetheless, Osumi considers the unit a compact, unified pericope, and debates the view that there are primary and secondary parts in these verses. I do not consider it essential to add to the abundant comments on these literary issues, or to take sides in the discussion. It suffices for my purpose to demonstrate the literary oddities in these verses; but I shall concentrate in due course on an examination of these verses within the context of the commonly accepted history of cultic development. Such an approach should decisively indicate whether the origins and periods of these verses are common or different.

1.2.2.2 Exod. 20:21

We may now undertake a phrase by phrase analysis. We find in Exod. 20: 21 the phrase וזבחת עליו את עלתיך ואת שלמיך את צאנך ואת בקרך "and sacrifice on it your burnt offerings and fellowship offerings, your sheep and goats and your cattle." This is considered by some scholars to be an entirely secondary addition, since in the chronological order of events and ordinances, there is as yet no command to offer sacrifices, and certainly no details concerning the types of offerings. Even in the verses of the Book of the Covenant which explicitly refer to cult matters, such as Exod. 23: 14 - 19, there is no mention of the particular sacrifices עולה or שלמים. There is indeed no explicit general command to offer sacrifices, and one has the

---

[17] Cf. L. Schwienhorst - Schönberger, *Das Bundesbuch*, BZAW 188 (Berlin, 1990), pp. 30 ff., "Strukturanalyse", with respect to the many scholarly opinions concerning the structural analysis of the Book of the Covenant.

[18] K. Koch states: "...where a long history of transmission can be assumed, the final result which the text under study offers usually contains many irregularities": *The Growth of the Biblical Tradition*, translated from the second German edition by S. M. Cupitt (New York, 1969), p. 52. Onkelos translates עלה in singular, following the MT, but the LXX corrects the text with αὐτου, "them", in plural. The Samaritan Pentateuch has the pronoun and the verb in singular, but casts the two words in the masculine gender, making their referent the מזבח, not the stones. We read there: הנפת עליו ותחללהו; thus it is the altar which is defiled by the use of a sword in its construction. The Samaritan Targum, in both MSS, also has these terms in singular masculine.

[19] See Y. Osumi, *Die Kompositionsgeschichte des Bundesbuches Exodus 20,22b - 23, 33*, Orbis Biblicus et Orientalis 105 (Göttingen, 1991), pp. 80ff.

impression that verse 23: 18,[20] the only one which mentions an offering and its corresponding rules, refers to the previously decreed Passover ritual. This pericope, similar to our pericope in Exod. 20: 21 - 23, reveals a spontaneous style of cult and not an exact and established ritual. In our verse, the words וזבחת עליו...את צאנך ואת בקרך, which contain no distinct cultic nomenclature, might be appropriate to a plebeian cult, but the rest of the phrase bears witness to a regulated, established cult. Moreover, the words את עלתיך ואת שלמיך seem in apparent contradiction to the following element את צאנך ואת בקרך, or at least superfluous, and may have been a later interjection, to comply with the deuteronomic pericope 27: 6 - 7.[21]

Another oddity of this doublet also leads us to consider the passage את עלתיך ואת שלמיך as a later interjection.[22] The expression וזבחת עליו את עלתיך ואת שלמיך contains the only linkage of the term זבח with the holocaust sacrifice עולה. The usual phrase, which seems to be a *terminus technicus*, links some form of the verb עלה with the sacrifice עולה, while the

---

[20] לא תזבח על חמץ דם זבחי ולא ילין חלב חגי עד בקר "Do not offer the blood of a sacrifice to me along with anything containing yeast. The fat of my festival offerings must not be kept until morning."

[21] In fact, the traditional commentator Ramban also remarks in his commentary to Exod. 20: 23 that this pericope refers not to sacrifices, but exclusively to the Law of the Altar. He expresses surprise that the prohibition against climbing on steps to the altar is contained in this pericope, since it is not related to the building of the altar but is rather a law directed at the offerer on his conduct. Ramban suggests that since the pericope starts with the altar law, it is completed with a related rule, but emphasizes that the rules of the sacrifice occur only in Leviticus. Professor Fox has drawn my attention to the proposition that according to the general rules of syntax for a parallel doublet, which is unmistakably the form here, the shorter version comes first. In this case, the shorter את צאנך ואת בקרך should have preceded the longer את עלתיך ואת שלמיך. The fact that the order is reversed may also hint, therefore, at a later interjection. For a discussion of the relationship between repetition and editorial activity, see, e.g., E.J. Revell, "The Repetition of Introductions to Speech as a Feature of Biblical Hebrew," *VT* 47 (1997), pp. 91-110.

[22] It is not unusual that such interjections were effected in a sloppy way, and we encounter many such occurrences through a critical analysis of biblical texts. It seems that the emendators were concerned rather with the "correct" theological or cult issues pertaining to their period than with the exact definition of the applicable terms. Cf. L. Schwienhorst - Schönberger, *Das Bundesbuch*, BZAW 188, pp. 412 ff. with respect to the redaction of the Book of the Covenant. He postulates a late deuteronomic redaction (p. 412) for the phrase את עלתיך ואת שלמיך. The linkage of the Horeb Decalogue to the Sinai narrative is attributed to a P redactor. Schwienhorst does not explain the oddity of the terms עלה and זבח to which I refer in the text; he does not consider the terms פרים and שלמים in Exod. 24: 5 to be of deuteronomic origin.

verb זבח is linked with שלמים.[23] In some cases the two sacrifices are described with one verb עלה, possibly for stylistic reasons,[24] be it the עולה with or with שלמים, but nowhere except in our verse is the term זבח applied to עולה; in its various grammatical forms זבח is always linked with שלמים.[25] If, on the other hand, we delete the phrase את עלתיך ואת שלמיך, we have a verse complete in itself without a rival doublet, and also a command appropriate to a popular, unsophisticated sacrificial worship without specific rules. There is no indication of a distinct classification of sacrifices, nor any regulation concerning the sex and age of the animals, as precisely detailed in the later P stratum of the Pentateuch. Such an elementary approach to sacrifice conforms to the simplistic regulations in our verses for the construction of the altar, which contain no measurements and no specific location (in contrast to the complex rules of the altar in Exod. 27: 1 - 8, as we shall see further on). The reading וזבחת עליו את צאנך ואת בקרך בכל המקום would fit perfectly within this pericope, which would then consist of a complete and independent command concerning a simple sacrificial cult: to build an altar and to slaughter upon it sheep and cattle. Both commands, the building of the altar and the slaughter, are expressed in a future hortatory mood; each command is an independent full-fledged ordinance necessitating no additional regulation. Though there are no precise rules as to the size and locus of the altar, there are limits on the animals to be slaughtered - only sheep and cattle, no fowl or fish as in the surrounding cultures. The pericope is therefore a compact description of the entire

---

[23] In the parallel pericope, Deut. 27: 6-7, we find: והעלית עליו עולת לה׳ אלהיך וזבחת שלמים "...and offer burnt offerings on it [the altar] to the Lord your God. Sacrifice fellowship offerings..."; in Exod. 24: 5: ויעלו עלת ויזבחו זבחים "...and they offered burnt offerings...and sacrificed fellowship offerings...: in Jos. 8:31, the parallel verse to Deut. 27: ויעלו עליו עלות לה׳ ויזבחו שלמים "On it they offered to the Lord burnt offerings and sacrificed fellowship offerings."

[24] For instance, אשר יעלה עלה או זבח "... who offers a burnt offering or sacrifice [Lev. 17: 8]"; ויעלו עלות ושלמים לפני ה׳ "...presented burnt offerings and fellowship offerings to the Lord [Jud. 20: 26]"; וכי יעלו עלה ומנחה "...though they offer burnt offerings and grain offerings [Jer. 14: 12]"; להעלות עליו עולה ומנחה "...to offer burnt offerings and grain offerings...on it [Jos. 22: 23]."

[25] In addition to the examples in n. 24, we find: ואת האיל יעשה זבח שלמים "He is...to sacrifice the ram as a fellowship offering [Num. 6: 17]"; זבחי שלמיכם "your...fellowhip offerings [Num. 10: 10]"; זבחי שלמים "...fellowship offerings [Jos. 22: 23 and I Sam. 10: 8]." In some instances other terms are used in connection with the offering of שלמים, such as עשה or נגש, as for example ויעש שלמים (I Kings 3: 15) and ויגשו שלמים (Exod. 32: 6); but in both these cases the offering of the עולה occurs with the typical term עלה.

sacrificial cult,[26] appropriate to the conditions obtaining in the period of its probable inception

We must also consider the expression וזבחת עליו, which means literally to slaughter "upon it." This is contrary to the rules of Leviticus, which prescribe the slaughtering of the animal on the ground near the altar;[27] only

---

[26] This postulate contradicts Ramban's opinion cited above that this pericope does not deal with sacrifices, a matter dealt with only in Leviticus.

[27] This is the conclusion of the rabbinic interpretations of the texts in Leviticus, although even in the Leviticus rules one may observe some uncertainty, and possibly traces of different traditions regarding the place of slaughter. In Lev. 1: 2 - 9, the first rules regarding the holocaust, one may assume from the context that the slaughtering of the bull is to be done on the ground, but the text itself, ושחט את בן הבקר לפני ה' "He is to slaughter the young bull before the Lord [v. 5]," certainly does not preclude slaughter on the altar. The indeterminate expression לפני ה' is also mentioned as the place where the sin sacrifices of the High Priest and the whole community should be slaughtered (Lev. 4: 2- 21). However, these verses offer us no clear definition of the correct locus; nor do the inconclusive rules of the other sin offerings ושחט אתו במקום אשר ישחט את העלה לפני ה' "and slaughter it at the place where the burnt offering is slaughtered before the Lord [Lev. 4: 24, with similar words in vv. 29 and 33]. " One would almost be tempted to speculate that the writer of these equivocal rules elegantly disentangled himself from this tricky issue of the place of the slaughter. Only regarding the peace offerings do we find a precise locus: ושחטו פתח אהל מועד "and slaughter it at the entrance of the Tent of Meeting [Lev. 3: 2]" and לפני אהל מועד "in front of the Tent of Meeting [3: 8, 13]." On the other hand, we have a contrasting rule in Lev. 1: 11, concerning the sheep and goat holocaust: ושחט אתו על ירך המזבח צפנה לפני ה' "He is to slaughter it at the north side of the altar before the Lord." The plain interpretation of this rule requires the slaughter upon the altar, and not at its side, and so it was understood by the Sages and traditional commentators. We read in Mishnah Zebahim 6: 1: קדשי קדשים ששחטן בראש המזבח רבי יוסי אומר כאילו נשחטו בצפון "The most holy sacrifices which were slaughtered on the top of the altar, Rabbi Jose says [they are faultless since] they are considered as having been slaughtered on the north side of the Temple." In Tosefta Korbanoth 7: 1, we find Rabbi Jose's justification for his decision. We read there: רבי יוסי אומר מזבח כולו צפון שנאמר ושחט אתו על ירך המזבח צפנה "Rabbi Jose says the entire altar is [considered to be on] the north, since it is written 'He is to slaughter it at the north side of the altar before the Lord.'" Rabbi Judah, who opposes Rabbi Jose, and declares: מחצי המזבח ולדרום כדרום מחצי המזבח לצפון כצפון "the southern half of the altar is considered as the south and the northern half of the altar as the north." does not invalidate slaughter on the altar; he merely requires that the slaughter be on the north side of the altar, since these sacrifices are required to be slaughtered on the north side. The dispute refers exclusively to the issue of whether the entire surface, or only the north side of the altar, is considered to be "the north side." In the Mekhilta of Rabbi Ishmael, Jethro *Parshah* 11, we have further clear confirmation that the plain interpretation of our verse refers to slaughter upon the altar. We read there: רבי יוסי אומר אף לשחוט בראש המזבח והכתוב מסייעו שנאמר מזבח אדמה תעשה לי וזבחת עליו "Rabbi Jose says also to slaughter on the top of the altar, and the verse [in the Torah] supports [his opinion], since it is said 'Make an altar of earth for me and

the burning of the dissected pieces of the holocaust and the fat of the peace offering takes place on the altar. This is the simple meaning of Exod. 20: 21, and we must therefore assume that it represents a period in which the custom was to slaughter the animals on the altar. I shall elaborate on this issue using comparative sources, but I would only mention at this stage that we also have such evidence from another biblical source. We read in Gen. 22: 9 – 10: ויעקד את יצחק בנו וישם אתו על המזבח ממעל לעצים. וישלח אברהם את ידו ויקח את המאכלת לשחט את בנו "He bound his son Isaac and laid him on the altar, on top of the wood. Then he reached out his hand and took the knife to slay his son." The unusual feature of the narrative, the binding of the intended sacrifice on top of the altar before the slaughter, originates

---

slaughter upon it.'" Yet further confirmation of the postulate that the plain meaning of our verse indicates slaughtering upon the altar is found in the antecedent deliberation in the Mekhilta. We read there: וזבחת עליועליו כנגדו אתה אומר עליו כנגדו או אינו אלא עליו כמשמעו "'Slaughter on it,' 'on it' [means] 'opposite'; you say that 'on it' [means] 'opposite it', but perhaps it really means 'upon it', as is its plain meaning?" The deliberation proceeds without conclusion, until another verse is cited to confirm the decision that in Exod. 20: 21 עליו must indicate "on its side." However, in Deut. 12: 27 we read: ועשית עלתיך הבשר והדם על מזבח ה' אלהיך "Present your burnt offerings on the altar of the Lord your God, both the meat and the blood"; according to the Mekhilta's interpretation this indicates that only the meat and the blood should be placed on the altar, but the slaughtering should not be done upon the altar: הבשר והדם בראש המזבח ואין שחיטה בראש המזבח. Though the plain meaning of our verse is unmistakably "slaughter upon the altar," it is due to the contradiction with the interpretation of another verse that the Sages decide to interpret it "on the side." The Talmud generally interpreted the disparate commands in Leviticus regarding the place of slaughter as indicating the sides of the Temple court; the holocaust and the sin sacrifices are to be slaughtered on the north side, and the peace offering anywhere in the court. With respect to the bird offering, where it is written והקריבו הכהן אל המזבח ומלק את ראשו "The priest shall bring it to the altar, wring off the head [Lev. 1: 15]," it is obvious that the slaughter must be upon the altar; only here does the Mishnah declare, in Zebahim 6: 5: עולת העוף כיצד היתה נעשית עלה בכבש ופנה לסובב בא לו לקרן דרומית מזרחית היה מולק את ראשה "How was the bird holocaust performed? He [the priest] went up the ascent and turned to the gallery and came to the south-eastern corner and twisted its head." The Talmud has generally ignored the plain meaning of Lev. 1: 11, and the traditional commentators attempted to balance the plain meaning with the talmudic decisions. Rashi explains the term ירך as צד על, "on the side." Ibn Ezra too emphasizes the idea of מחוץ, "outside [the altar]." Onkelos translates על צדא דמדבחא "on the side of the altar," a term which exactly follows the Hebrew text without any indication of its precise meaning. Jonathan uses על שיפולי מדבחא "at the lower part of the altar"; שיפולי is a term that is used to express the foot of a mountain, that is, apart from the mountain. For the translation of על, the LXX uses the preposition ἐκ, which has a nuance of "from"; על usually means "on", and is translated by the LXX in all other occurrences in this chapter as ἐπι.

unmistakably from a period in which the altar served for the slaughtering of the animals. The term מזבח itself, based on its etymology, was originally a place of slaughter, as was the Aramaic מדבחא.

The use of the definite article in the phrase בכל המקום in v. 21 seems odd and a contradiction in terms;[28] this issue was approached in diverse ways by the various interpreters and commentators. Onkelos follows the MT strictly and translates with בכל אתרא, with the definite article, as does the Targum Neophyti. Jonathan, on the other hand, corrects the text to בכל אתר with no definite article. The Samaritan Pentateuch has a completely different text - במקום אשר אזכרתי - without the indefinite בכל, and thus avoids the problem; both Samaritan Targum MSS translate with ובאתרא, with a definite article. The LXX also has a different structure of this phrase, οὗ ἐὰν ἐπονομάσω τὸ ὄνομά μου ἐκεῖ, thus escaping the problem of the MT. The KJV translates "In all places where I record" with the noun indefinite, and the NIV avoids the problem by eliminating the term "place", using the indefinite "wherever I cause my name...." Dillmann[29] quotes Merx in his comments on this verse, saying that the original text was actually בכל מקום with an indefinite noun, but was later changed for doctrinal reasons to refer to "the well-known place," the Temple in Jerusalem. In fact, certain of the traditional commentators, aware of the irregularity in this expression, interpreted "the place" as referring to Jerusalem, basing their postulate on talmudic[30] quotations.

---

28 The use of the definite article after כל is attested elsewhere (e.g. Gen. 1: 21). See Joüon, *A Grammar of Biblical Hebrew* (Rome, 1993), Vol. II, p. 445, s. 125h.

29 p. 248.

30 We read in B.T. Sotah 38a: רבי יאשיה אומר אינו צריך הרי הוא אומר בכל המקום אשר אזכיר את שמי אבוא אליך בכל מקום ס״ד אלא מקרא זה מסורס הוא בכל מקום אשר אבוא אליך וברכתיך שם אזכיר את שמי והיכן אבוא אליך וברכתיך בבית הבחירה, שם אזכיר את שמי בבית הבחירה "R. Jashia says:...it is said [Exod. 20: 21] 'In every place in which I shall make my name remembered, I shall come to you.' Is it possible in every place? [We must say] that this verse is corrupt. [It should read]: In every place where I will come to you and bless you, I shall make my name remembered; and where will I come to bless you? In the house I shall choose [the Temple], there I shall make my name remembered." A similar Midrash is found in Sifrei on Numbers *Pisqa* 39: ר' יונתן אומר הרי הוא אומר בכל המקום אשר אזכיר את שמי זה מקרא מסורס בכל מקום שאני נגלה עליך שם תהא מזכיר את שמי והיכן אני נגלה עליך בבית הבחירה אף אתה לא תהא מזכיר את שמי אלא בבית הבחירה מיכן אמרו שם המפורש אסור לאומרו בגבולים. "R. Jonathan says: It is written [Exod. 20: 21]: 'In every place where I shall make my name remembered'; this is a corrupt phrase. [It should read]: In every place where I shall appear to you, there you should remember my name; and where shall I appear to you? In the place I shall choose [the Temple], [therefore] you

The next irregularity is encountered in the last part of verse 21: אשר אזכיר את שמי, whose simple translation is "where I shall remember my name."[31] This does not make sense in the context. One would expect after the command to build a simple earthen altar the Deity's declaration that the place of worship is not important, and wherever you (the Israelite) will call upon and adore God, there He will respond and bless you. The redactor of this pericope has deliberately contrasted the gold and silver idols[32] in 20: 23 with

---

should not say my name [the Tetragramaton] except in the Temple." On the other hand, we find a talmudic dictum which demonstrates that certain Sages understood the term בכל המקום to indicate "everywhere". We read in Y.T. Berakhoth 4: 4, 4b: ר' אבא ר' חייא בשם רבי יוחנן צריך אדם להתפלל במקום שהוא מיוחד לתפלה ומה טעם בכל המקום אשר אזכיר את שמי אשר תזכיר את שמי אין כתוב כאן אלא בכל מקום אשר אזכיר "[Said] R. Abba [son] of R. Hiya in the name of R. Johanan: A man should pray in a place dedicated to prayer. But what about 'In every place where I shall make my name remembered [which demonstrates that every place is right]'? [A.] It is not written in [every place] in which you will remember [my name], but rather in every place I shall make it to be remembered." It is evident that the expression בכל המקום is being interpreted here as "everywhere".

Further on the issue of בכל מקום, we find a Midrash in B.T. Zebahim 117b: והנה אומר ויתן דוד לארנן במקום שקלי זהב, ר"ל בכל המקום כי בגרן היה המזבח והשדה כלו נבנה בו הבית "It is said [in I Chr. 21: 25] 'So David paid Araunah six hundred shekels of gold for the site' [the term במקום is vocalized here so as to be read with a definite article] and this means that [David paid for] the whole site [בכל המקום, the same term as in Exod. 20:21], since on the site of the barn [he built] the altar, and on the site of the entire field, the Temple was built." This Midrash refers to an issue of contrasting citations, the first in II Sam. 24: 24, where we read: "So David bought the threshing floor and the oxen and paid fifty shekels of silver for them," and the second in I Chr. 21: 25, where we read: "So David paid Araunah six hundred shekels of gold for the site." The purchase of the site is not mentioned in II Sam. and only fifty silver shekels were paid for the threshing floor and the oxen, whereas according to Chr., David also bought the site and paid six hundred shekels of gold. The Rabbis attempted, as usual, to harmonize the contradicting quotations and connected the site bought by David for the Temple with the determined term המקום in Exod. 20: 21. Thus, they also succeeded in solving the semantic irregularity of the term בכל המקום with the definite article.

[31] Because of the הפעיל construction, it was translated as "I will cause my name to be remembered."

[32] This is the only place in the Pentateuch in which a prohibition against making idols refers to false gods of gold and silver. In other occurrences we have: לא תעשה לך פסל וכל תמונה ("You shall not make for yourself an idol in the form of anything...[Exod. 20: 4])"; לא תעשו ("Do not set up...any *Asherah*...[Deut. 16: 21])"; לא תטע לך אשרה ("Do not make idols or set up an imaage or a sacred stone for yourselves, and do not place a carved stone in your land...[Lev. 26: 1])"; ואלהי מסכה לא תעשו לכם ("Do not...make gods of cast metal for yourselves [Lev. 19: 4])"; פן תשחתון ועשיתם לכם

the simplicity of the earthen altar which could be built everywhere. No elaborate figures or temples are necessary to receive God's blessing; man's call to God is the only requisite for His response and blessing. The simple meaning "where I (God) will cause my name to be remembered" is contrary to the context of this pericope and to the general biblical idea of worship.[33]

Onkelos changed the effect of this phrase and interpreted it as בכל אתרא דִי אשרי שכינתי לתמן אשלח ברכתי לך "In every place where I shall dwell, there I shall grant you my blessing." Jonathan's interpretation is in the same style and conveys the identical message, but he adds after "I shall dwell" ואנת פלח קדמי "and you will worship before me." Both interpret the verse to refer to Jerusalem, God's dwelling. As noted above, the Samaritan Pentateuch has במקום אשר אזכרתי, "where I remembered [my name]." The reference here is to the tenth commandment in the Samaritan Pentateuch, which decrees the building of the Temple on Mount Gerizim. The Samaritan Targum MS J follows the Samaritan Pentateuch and translates דאדכר in the perfect tense, whereas MS A has דתדכר, in the second person imperfect, which makes more sense in the context, as elaborated above. The Peshitta also has this verb in second person, as does the Targum Neophyti, with תדכרון "you will remember," in second person imperfect.[34] The latter Targum changes the entire verse into plural to conform with the antecedent verses, although the MT has this verse in singular (as I have discussed

---

פסל תמונת כל סמל תבנית זכר או נקבה. תבנית כל בהמה אשר בארץ תבנית כל צפור כנף אשר תעוף בשמים ("So that you do not become corrupt and make for yourselves an idol, an image of any shape, whether formed like a man or a woman, or like any animal on earth or any bird that flies in the air [Deut. 4: 16-17])." Though we do have in Deut. 29:16: ותראו את שקוציהם ואת גלליהם עץ ואבן כסף וזהב אשר עמהם "You saw among them their detestable images and idols of wood and stone, of silver and gold," and in Deut. 7: 25: לא תחמד כסף וזהב עליהם "Do not covet the silver and gold on them....," both cases refer to the idols of the people and are not direct prohibitions, as in our verse. In a Midrash in B.T. Yoma 86b, R. Jannai links an abundance of gold and silver with idolatry: אמר משה לפני הקדוש ברוך הוא רבונו של עולם כסף וזהב שהרבית להם לישראל עד שאמרו די גרם להם שיעשו אלהי זהב "Moses said to the Almighty: ['They have made themselves gods of gold' (Exod. 32: 31)] - the silver and gold you have amassed for Israel [at the exodus from Egypt], until they said 'Enough', caused them to make idols of gold."

[33] N. Sarna writes in his commentary to Exodus, "This construction, with both subject and object referring to God, is unparalleled. God would not be expected to call on Himself or evoke His own name in worship." Sarna then quotes the traditional interpretations to the effect that the verb is in a causative construction, and that the verse refers to Jerusalem.

[34] This Targum adds to its interpretation: בכל אתרא די תדכרון ית שמי בצלו אתגלי במימרדה עליכון "In every place you will remember my name with prayer, I shall reveal myself to you with my *logos*."

above). The LXX has the verb in the first person, but has used the unique term ἐπονομάζω "to be named," to render the Hebrew Hiph'il.[35] The other occurrences in the Pentateuch of the Hiph'il of this verb[36] are not translated with this term. The LXX meaning corresponds to the structure of a causative Hiph'il, "I will cause my name to be remembered," and seems to be a deliberate attempt to solve the above-mentioned textual difficulty. Noth has elaborated on this interpretation and writes: "Verse 21b contemplates a number of holy places. In fact holy places with altars could not be founded at whatever place men wished, but only where God 'caused his name to be remembered.'" Such an interpretation might be an appropriate solution for the difficult MT text, but it seems to me that we should attempt to reconstruct the simple meaning of the "original" text, which intends to say that at every place from which the Israelite calls upon God, He will respond. The context endorses such an interpretation, if we read תזכיר in second person.

Noth, as we have seen, does not interpret the second part[37] of this verse as specifying one exclusive place for the building of an altar; however, earlier scholars attempted to reconcile this verse with the mandate for cult centralization. Dillmann[38] interprets this phrase more elaborately, though still in a causative sense, and adds "where I shall make my name remembered, i.e., by some announcement to inform that there my name should be remembered, or a memorial to be erected." Keil and Delitzsch[39] go a step further and write: "הזכיר שם does not mean 'to make the name of the Lord remembered,' i.e., to cause men to remember it; but to establish a memorial of His name, i.e., to make a glorious revelation of His divine nature etc.''; that is, there is a definite intention to indicate the Temple in Jerusalem. Cassuto[40] interprets this ambiguous expression in another way, suggesting that the phrase refers to and complements the previous narrative of the revelation at Sinai, and not the specific altar law; the intent is to emphasize that the Deity is everywhere - not only on God's mountain - and therefore can be worshipped בכל המקום. The Talmud, not surprisingly, has also harmonized

---

[35] See J. W. Wevers, *Notes on the Greek Text of Exodus*, Septuagint and Cognate Studies 35 (Atlanta, 1990), p. 319.

[36] See Gen. 40: 14 and Exod. 23: 13.

[37] If I understand Noth's interpretation correctly, he also considers the first part of this verse to indicate that places to build an altar may be chosen freely. He writes: "...they do not mean sanctuaries in places with fixed settlements, but altars erected in free land." Such a rule, he adds, is appropriate for a nomadic society.

[38] *Die Bücher Exodus und Leviticus.*

[39] Vol. II, p. 128.

[40] M. D. Cassuto, פירוש על ספר שמות (Jerusalem, 1952), p. 177.

this verse with the idea of cult centralization at the Temple. In addition to a Midrash in B.T. Sotah 38a, we find an interesting Midrash on this verse by Hillel the Elder in Tosefta Sukkah 4: 3:

הלל הזקן או׳ למקום שלבי אוהב לשם רגליי מוליכות אותי אם אתה תבוא
לביתי אני אבא לביתיך אם אתה לא תבוא לביתי אני לא אבוא לביתיך שנ׳
בכל המקום אשר אזכיר את שמי אבא אליך וברכתיך

Hillel the Elder says: My legs bring me to the place my heart loves. If you shall come to my place, I shall come to your place, if you shall not come to my place, I shall not come to your place, because it is said: 'In every place in which I shall have my name remembered, I will come to bless you.'

However, whether the traditional sources interpret the verse as allowing building in every place, or believed it to be restricted to a designated locus, they must still wrestle with the problem of the "earthen" altar. The command to construct an altar in Exod. 27: 1 - 8 prescribes a bronze altar for the Tabernacle, not an earthen one, and in Deut. 27: 2 - 6 a stone altar is to be built. The command to build an earthen altar is also in contradiction to both the talmudic description[41] and the historical record regarding the material of the Second Temple altar; both sources assert that this altar was of stone. The Rabbis' solution was therefore to interpret the term מזבח אדמה figuratively. We read in Mekhilta deR. Simeon bar Johai 20: 21:

מה נא׳ לך מזבח אדמה תעשה לי יכול אדמה ודאי ת״ל אבנים שלמות
תבנה את מזבח ה׳ אלהיך כשתכנס לארץ עשה לי מזבח המחובר באדמה
דברי ר׳ יהודה ר׳ מאיר אומר תחת עזרות היה חלול והמזבח היה מחובר
באדמה

What does it mean 'Make an altar of earth for me' ? Does it really mean of earth? [This could not be] since it is written [Deut. 27: 6] 'of whole stones you should build God's altar.' [It means,] 'When you enter the land [of Israel] make for me an altar connected with the earth,' these are the words of R. Jehudah....

In B. T. Zebahim 58a we read: מזבח אדמה תעשה לי שיהא מחובר "Make an altar of מאדמה שלא יבננו לא על גבי מחילות ולא על גבי כיפין

---

[41] We read in Mishnah Midoth 3: 4: אחד אבני הכבש ואחד אבני המזבח מבקעת בית
כרם "Both the stones of the ascent [to the altar] and of the altar [come] from the Valley of Beth Kerem." I Macc. 4: 47 tells us that the Maccabees took "whole stones, according to the Law [the אבנים שלמות of Deut. 27: 6] and built a new altar like the former one." We may deduce therefore that both the previous altar desecrated by the Seleucids and the new one built by the Maccabees were of stone. I Macc. also states that the previous altar was of stone, and that the desecrated stones were kept in a special place, since they were originally sacred as altar stones. This account is confirmed in a talmudic source. We read in Mishnah Midoth 1: 6: ארבע לשכות היו בבית המוקד "Four chambers were in the House of the Flame," and in the north-eastern chamber גנזו בני חשמונאי את אבני המזבח ששקצום מלכי יון "the Hasmoneans hid the altar's stones desecrated by the Hellenistic kings."

earth for me,' [what does it mean?] That it should be connected to the earth, not built over tunnels or on arches." Following these talmudic homilies, Targum Yerushalmi[42] interprets מזבח אדמה as מדבח קביע בארעא "an altar fixed on the ground."[43] I shall elaborate further on whether the Rabbis succeeded in solving the various inconsistencies in the biblical altar laws.

1.2.2.3 Exod. 20:22

The rule for the building of a stone altar in Exod. 20: 22 starts with a casuistic form ואם "And if", in contrast with the apodictic command to build an earthen altar in verse 21. On the other hand, the conjunction "and" demonstrates that the redactor clearly intended to connect the two verses, even if they were originally from two different sources. We must interpret the redactor's intention as indicating that the usual or even preferred type of altar is the "earthen", and while one is allowed to build an altar of stone, there are certain limitations. Most of the commentators do not elaborate on the hermeneutics of this expression and simply translate the term ואם as "And if". However, Dillmann[44] writes: "Die Altäre dürfen auch aus Steinen gemacht werden" ("The altars may [the German term *dürfen* implies that one is allowed to do something] be built of stones"), which corresponds to the sense of this verse which I have discussed. A critical approach to biblical exegesis would have no difficulty with the fact that the origin of this pericope seems to be in the early nomadic period,[45] when the earthen altar was the

---

[42] It is remarkable that in this instance Jonathan does not follow the talmudic homily and translates literally מדבח אדמתא "an earthen altar," as does Onkelos. Targum Neophyti follows the Targum Yerushalmi, and interprets מדבח קביע על ארעא "an altar fixed on the ground."

[43] We must note that according to these talmudic homilies, the biblical command to build an altar attached to the earth refers to the stone altar, the subject of the law in Exod. 20: 22-23. In B. T. Hagigah 27a, the same homily on Exod. 20: 21 requiring the altar to be attached to the earth refers to the bronze altar, the subject of Exod. 27: 1-8. Tosafoth ponder on this apparent contradiction, and offer an interesting solution: since Solomon's stone altar replaced the bronze altar, the verse decreeing the altar's attachment to the earth refers to both the stone and the bronze altars. We may again observe how the complicated solutions attempting to harmonize between conflicting pericopes provoke further dilemmas and require supplementary rhetorical justifications.

[44] *Exodus und Leviticus*, p. 248.

[45] I shall elaborate subsequently on this postulate. I shall only quote here M. Noth who writes on this verse, "The law itself is of course old, as it presupposes very simple conditions....We must therefore suppose this ordinance to originate perhaps from communities of nomadic herdsmen" (*Exodus*, p. 176). I would like to add here that Noth writes in his *Exodus*, p. 175 that there seems to be an inconsistency concerning God's

common custom, whereas the commands in Deut. 27: 2 - 6 to build a stone altar stem from a later period. However, the Talmud with its harmonistic conception of the Bible has difficulties with the apparent contradictions. We read in Mekhilta d'Rabbi Ishmael Jethro *Parshah* 11: ואם מזבח אבנים תעשה לי רבי ישמעאל אומר כל אם ואם שבתורה רשות, חוץ משלשה "Rabbi Ishmael said, Every אם ['if'] in the Torah implies 'you may' except in three occurrences [where it implies a command]." One of them is our verse: כיוצא בו ואם מזבח אבנים תעשה לי חובה "'And if you build an altar of stone' implies a command to build an altar." ומה ת"ל ואם מזבח אבנים אלא רצה לעשות של אבנים יעשה של לבנים יעשה "And what does the [casuistic] ואם imply? It means if one wishes to build [an altar] of stones, one may; of bricks, one may."

The first limitation on the stone altar is לא תבנה אתהן גזית. We must ask what the term גזית really implies. The KJV translates it as "hewn stone," as do Sarna and Noth; the NIV has "dressed stones." Onkelos translates with פסילן "cut stones," Jonathan has חציבין "hewn stones," and the LXX translates τμητούς "cut, cleaved." This is the only occurrence of the term גזית in the Pentateuch, as well as of the verb גזז, referring to stones; all other occurrences of this verb in the Pentateuch refer to the shearing of sheep. In the other biblical books, the term also refers for the most part to the shearing of sheep, but in some occurrences it is applied to building stones. We cannot be sure whether the term in our verse implies "hewn" stones and the rule thus prohibits the cutting of stone out of solid rock, or whether the restriction also applies to the process of leveling natural, unhewn stones. The precise answer to this issue is important for the purpose of contrasting the rule in our verse with the regulations in Deut. 27: 5 - 6; though they seem similar, they are certainly not identical. I shall discuss this matter in chap. 3.

The motive behind the rule in our verse is stated to be כי חרבך הנפת עליה ותחללה "because you lifted your sword upon it and defiled it." This might imply a prohibition against use of metal implements on the altar stones, whether for splitting the stones from the rock or for leveling them, because metal is the substance of which homicidal instruments are made. I would suggest, however, that from textual analysis alone one is not compelled to interpret the phrase in this way. The expression הנפת חרב implies the raising of a sword, as the verb נוף itself indicates "to raise." The LXX translates הנפת as ἐπιβέβληκας from the verb ἐπιβάλλω "to throw or cast upon" (Liddell and Scott), thus implying the wielding of a sword to hit someone. On the other hand, the term הניף אהרן in Lev. 9: 21, describing

---

speaking from heaven in 20: 22, which supposes heaven to be the divine realm, and the notion that God descended on Mount Sinai in 19: 18.

the breast which Aaron waved, is translated by the LXX as ἀφεῖλεν, from the verb ἀφαιρέω "to take off, to remove." The same term ἀφαιρέω is used by the LXX for the translation of the cultic terms סור, regarding the removal of the lobe of the liver (יסירנה) in Lev. 4: 9, and רום, regarding the removal of the fat of the entrails (ירים) in Lev. 4: 8. We observe that in our case the LXX translator understood the expression הנפת חרב to apply to the specific action of raising a metal tool in a particular manner identical to the wielding of a sword to hit someone.

It is noteworthy that the term נוף is used in the Bible either in connection with the cultic practice of raising - interpreted as "waving" the sacrificial parts - or as related to aggressive, violent conduct with a wide variety of semantic associations.[46] It seems that the biblical language has no different terms for these two types of "raising", and either the direct object of the verb or the context suggests the particular meaning in each case. The context of the phrase כי חרבך הנפת עליה may therefore imply an action similar to the wielding of a sword, that is the splitting of a slab of stone from a rock, but not a smooth leveling of a natural stone. It is evident that the defilement of the stone results from a connection with a homicidal implement,[47] but it is

---

[46] The verb נוף and the noun תנופה abound in the P stratum of the Pentateuch, where they refer to the cultic practice of "raising - waving". Most of the other occurrences suggest an aggressive violent action. See Isa. 10: 15, 32; 11: 15; 19: 16; 30: 28, 32; Zech. 2: 13; Job 31: 21, which all suggest overt aggression. II Kings 5: 11 has והניף ידו אל המקום ואסף המצורע "wave his hand over the spot and cure me of my leprosy," which implies that Elisha will with the raising of his hands attack and chase away the illness. The phrase וחרמש לא תניף על קמת רעך "you must not put a sickle to your neighbour's standing grain [Deut. 23: 26, 25 in KJV]," refers to the forceful action of cutting grain. There are two unusual occurrences: גשם נדבות תניף "You gave abundant showers [Ps. 68: 10, 9 in KJV]" and נפתי משכבי "I have perfumed my bed [Prov. 7: 17]"; but we must consider these as a semantic development through association. Abundant showers come down with a force, sometimes called יורה "the shooting rain", and therefore the powerful term נוף is appropriate. The same applies to the sprinkling of a liquid perfume that is vapourized through a forceful dispersion. The talmudic and modern Hebrew term נפה "sieve" also originates from the fact that the grain is violently waved in order to separate the pure flour from the bran. In fact we find this expression in the above-mentioned Isa. 30: 28: להנפה גוים בנפת שוא "He shakes the nation in the sieve of destruction." There is only one occurrence in which the raising of the hand does not clearly reveal an aggressive action, in Isa. 13: 2: הניפו יד "beckon to them" (NIV) or "shake the hand" (KJV). However, Radak, the noted traditional commentator, does interpret this as a hostile expression; they should raise their hand to call the armies of Persia and Media to hurry and destroy Babylonia.

[47] M. Noth does not consider the simple and plain motive stated in the text, that is, the connection with a homicidal implement, as the basis of the prohibition; he writes: "An altar erected of stones is permitted, but the stones must remain unworked, as working with

not certain whether this applies exclusively to an aggressive action, as the expression חרבך הנפת would suggest, or simply the touch of such an implement, or even the touch of any tool of the same material of which weapons are made.[48]

The Rabbis decided to interpret this prohibition restrictively and literally,[49] and ruled that the stones of the altar must not come into any contact with iron. We read in Mishnah Midoth 3: 4:

אחד אבני הכבש ואחד אבני המזבח מבקעת בית כרם וחופרין למטה
מהבתולה ומביאים משם אבנים שלמות שלא הונף עליהן ברזל שהברזל
פוסל בנגיעה

---

human tools would do away with their original condition and integrity and hence their requisite holiness" *(Exodus,* p. 176). I assume that Noth developed this exegesis on the basis of Deut. 27: 6 where the concept of אבנים שלמות (whole-perfect stones) is utilized, assuming perhaps that at least concerning the motive for the prohibition, the pericopes are interrelated. As I already hinted, I propose to disconnect the two commands, and to take the motive of the prohibition offered in verse Exod. 20: 22 in its simple and plain meaning, as evidently referring to an homicidal implement. I shall discuss the similarities and contrasts between this pericope and Deut. 27: 6 in section 1.3. As we have seen, the Talmud, which certainly connects the two pericopes and which cannot admit, for theological reasons, any dichotomy between two biblical dicta, also interprets the motive for the prohibition according to its plain meaning, that is, the association with an homicidal device.

[48] Although I do not extend the Law of the Altar to the building of the Temple, an issue discussed in chap. 3, I wish to draw attention here to chap. 3 n. 19 where I distinguish between wielding an implement for splitting, and dragging a stone through a mechanical device to smooth and level it.

[49] Occasionally the Rabbis decided to apply the literal meaning of the text in their decisions, even though it led to difficulties in practice, or was even opposed to the purpose of the law. We read in Mishnah Eirubin 5: 4: אין מודדין אלא בחבל של חמישים אמה לא פחות ולא יותר ולא ימדוד אלא כנגד לבו "[For the purpose of measuring the extent of a town's *eirub*, that is, a two thousand cubit extension within which one may go on Sabbath] one must measure with a cord of fifty cubits, not more and not less, and one must measure at the height of his heart [that is both people who hold the cord must keep it at the same height to avoid an incorrect measurement due to a slope of the cord]." The Mishnah then indicates further punctilious rules on how to perform the measurement in order to avoid any minute inaccuracy. In B. T. Eirubin 58a, we read: אמר רבי יהושע בן חנניא אין לך שיפה למדידה יותר משלשלאות של ברזל אבל מה נעשה שהרי אמרה תורה ובידו חבל מדה "Said Rabbi Joshua ben Hanania: No device is more appropriate than an iron chain, but what can we do, since the Torah said 'And in his hand a measuring line [Zech. 2: 5, 2: 1 in KJV].'" We observe that although an absolutely accurate measure is required, and in practice this would be facilitated with an iron chain which does not expand, the Mishnah requires a cord, which does expand and does not offer the same accuracy, because of a verse in Scripture which implies that measuring is done with a cord. The literal application of a text has here subverted the obvious intent of a regulation. See also n. 110.

Both the stones of the ascent [to the altar] and of the altar [come] from the Valley of Beth Kerem; one digs below the untouched soil and one brings up from there whole stones on which no iron was wielded, since iron defiles by contact.

It is remarkable that the Rabbis base their conclusion not on our verse in Exod. but on the similar verses Deut. 27: 5 - 6. This demonstrates that, even according to the rabbinic conception, our verse does not require an interpretation prohibiting any contact with iron. We read an interesting homily in the Mekhilta of Rabbi Simeon bar Johai on Exod. 20: 22:

לא תבנה אתהן גזית מכלל שנ׳ כי חרבך הנפת [יכול ל]א יהו פסולות אלא
אם כן נתגזזו בחרב תל׳ לו׳ לא תניף [עליהם בר]זל הרי ברזל כחרב אם
סופינו לעשות ברזל כחרב מה] תל׳ לו׳ כי] חרבך זו היא שרבן יוחנן בן זכאי
או׳ מה ראה ברזל ליפסל [מכל מ]יני מתכות] כולן] מפני שהחרב נעשת
ממנו וחרב [סימן] פורענות ומזבח סימן כפרה מעבירין דבר שהוא סימן
פורענות מפני דבר שהוא סימן כפרה

'Do not build it with dressed stones' [Exod. 20: 22]. Since it says 'because you wielded your sword upon it' [we might perceive] that they are defiled only when cut with a sword? [A.] It says ' do not wield iron upon them' [Deut. 27: 5]; iron is equivalent to a sword. [Q.] If iron is equivalent to a sword then why is it written 'because you wielded your sword upon it' [Exod. 20: 22]? [A] As Rabbi Johanan ben Zakkai said: Why does iron, out of all metals, render something unfit? Because a sword is made of it and a sword is a symbol of castigation, whereas the altar is a symbol of atonement; one overrides a symbol of castigation on account of a symbol of atonement.

It seems that the strict rule of the rabbis on this issue prevailed during the later period of the Second Temple, in practice, or at least in theory. However, I have doubts as to the authenticity of these rabbinic reports concerning details of the Temple, because we encounter debates and disputes regarding important items of the Temple structure, as well as admissions of early Tannaim who lived close to the time of its destruction that they did not remember significant details. One must therefore question whether the Rabbis described details of the Temple as they actually were, or as they ought to have been according to their interpretation of the biblical commands.

I shall quote a few examples. We read in Mishnah Midoth 1: 3: חמשה שערים היו להר הבית "The Temple Mount had five gates," and in 1: 4: שבעה שערים היו בעזרה "Seven gates were in the Holy Precinct," constituting twelve gates. But in Mishnah Sheqalim 6: 3 we read that there were thirteen genuflections in the Temple, כנגד שלשה עשר השערים "opposite the thirteen gates"; and in Midoth 2: 6 we read: ושלש עשרה השתחויות היו שם אבא יוסי בן חנן אומר כנגד שלשה עשר שערים "There were thirteen genuflections there [in the Temple]. Abba Jose ben Hanan says: They were opposite the thirteen gates." We thus see a controversy concerning such an important issue as the number of gates in the Temple. Moreover, we must observe the connection between the number of genuflections, a symbol of piety, and the number of gates, a purely architectural and practical issue.

We must also consider the sacred symbolism of the number thirteen, as we learn from Mishnah Sheqalim 6: 1: שלשה עשר שופרות שלשה עשר שולחנות שלש עשרה השתחויות היו במקדש "Thirteen horns, thirteen tables, thirteen genuflections were in the Temple." The symbolic and sacred importance of the number thirteen may therefore have given rise to the declaration that there were thirteen gates, similar to other artifacts in the Temple; that is, it was a metaphorical number unrelated to the actual count of the gates or other artifacts.

Further evidence of a questionable statement concerning practical details of the Temple is found in Mishnah Midoth 2: 5: אמר רבי אליעזר בן יעקב שכחתי מה היתה משמשת אבא שאול אומר שם היו נותנין יין ושמן היא היתה נקראת לשכת בית שמניה "Said Rabbi Eleazar b. Jacob: I have forgotten the use of the [south-western chamber in the Temple precinct]; Abba Shaul says: There one would store wine and oil and it was called the Oil Chamber." Rabbi Eleazar b. Jacob lived at the time of the Temple, as we gather from Midoth 1:2: רבי אליעזר בן יעקב אומר פעם אחת מצאו את אחי אמא ישן ושרפו את כסותו " Rabbi Eleazar b. Jacob said: Once they [the supervisors] found my uncle sleeping [on duty], and they burned his clothes." Nevertheless, he admits that he does not remember the name and the use of an important chamber. We have another example, regarding knowledge of dimensions. Mishnah Midoth 5: 2 imparts the measurements of the width of the Temple yard, מן הצפון לדרום מאה ושלשים וחמש "from north to south one hundred thirty-five cubits," and then lists the sizes of the different accoutrements and the distances between them. When these sum up to one hundred and ten cubits, the Mishnah does not know how to divide the remaining twenty-five cubits between the distance from the altar's ascent and the wall, and the surface of the *nanasin* - small columns on which the slaughtered animals were tied for flaying; the Mishnah simply says והמותר בין הכבש לכותל ומקום הננסין "and the remaining [twenty-five cubits were divided] between the distance from the altar's ascent and the wall, and the surface of the *nanasin*."

To recapitulate, there may actually have been in force during the last period of the Second Temple a strict rule that iron defiled the stone of the altar solely by contact, as the Talmud recounts; but in light of the above examples, one may doubt the authenticity of this rule.

Josephus records in *War* V: 225: κατεσκευάσθη δ' ἄνευ σιδήρου καὶ οὐδέποτ' ἔψαυεν αὐτοῦ σίδηρος "No iron was used in its [the altar's] construction, nor did iron ever touch it."[50] In *Against Apion* I: 198 he

---

[50] Josephus, *The Jewish War*, The Loeb Classical Library, Vol. III, transl. H. St. J. Thackeray (London, 1928).

confirms again that the altar consisted of ἀτμήτων συλλέκτων ἀργῶν λίθων οὕτω συγκείμενος "heaped up stones, unhewn and unwrought."[51] However, his records must also be used with caution; it is to be noted that in the above-cited verses, Josephus also gives two conflicting accounts of the size of the altar. In *War* he writes: ὁ βωμὸς πεντεκαίδεκα μὲν ὕψος ἦν πήχεων εὖρος δὲ καὶ μῆκος ἐκτείν ων ἰσαν ἀνὰ πεντήκοντα πήχεις τετράγωνος ἵδρυτο "the altar fifteen cubits high, and with a breadth and length extending alike to fifty cubits, in shape a square." In *Against Apion* he indicates quite different measurements: πλευρὰν μὲν ἐκάστην εἴκοσι πηχῶν ὕψος δὲ δεκάπηχυ "each side is twenty cubits long and the height ten cubits." That is, we have a measurement of 50 x 50 x 15 cubits as against 20 x 20 x 10 cubits. Given this great inconsistency, it is difficult to rely on any of the statements of Josephus concerning the construction of the altar.

Thus the evidence concerning the issue of defilement by iron in the Second Temple period is quite vague. I shall return to this issue in section 2.2, specifically with respect to the larger issue of whether the altar laws in Exod. and Deut. are related.

1.2.2.4 Exod. 20:23

I shall not proceed here with the literary and textual analysis of verse 23, since it has no direct impact on the main subjects of our study: the different commands concerning the structure of the holocaust altar and the question of whether a bronze altar was ever in use. However, I shall revert to this verse in section 1.3.

1.2.3 Deut. 27: 1 - 8

1.2.3.1 Literary and Structural Analysis: Scholarly Opinion

The textual problems of this pericope are all too evident, and much has been written on them by various scholars, and from different perspectives. I shall therefore concentrate most of my analysis on the verses which deal specifically with the altar. As well, the apparent mixing of the stones of the altar with "other" stones, and the seemingly clumsy duplications in this pericope, require discussion, and necessitate a presentation of certain scholarly criticism to serve as background. I shall also set out various

---

[51] Josephus, *Against Apion*, The Loeb Classical Library, transl. H. St. J. Thackeray (London, 1926).

talmudic and midrashic citations to demonstrate a similar rabbinic perplexity with these verses and the attempted solutions. The present case provides a particularly interesting example of the sometimes spectacular homiletic 'acrobatics' in which the Rabbis engaged in order to harmonize apparently contradictory biblical statements.

Dillmann[52] assumes vv. 1 - 8 are a later interpolation into the original deuteronomic source; from the redactional aspect, these verses are out of context here and interrupt the logical sequence between 26: 19 and 27: 9. G. von Rad[53] perceives this pericope as extraneous, on the basis of both style and substance. The text from chap. 6 of Deuteronomy onwards takes the pattern of a single hortatory speech by Moses to Israel. From this point of view, it is extremely odd to find phrases which introduce Moses in the third person, such as ויצו משה and וידבר משה. Such expressions occur three times in chap. 27, in verses 1, 9 and 11, in which a narrator speaks of Moses in the third person, in past tense. The last occurrence of such a form prior to the beginning of the speech in chap. 6 is found in Deut. 5: 1; in fact, Moses is not often mentioned in Deuteronomy, except in introductory headings or in secondary additions. The occurrence of such an expression in our pericope would demonstrate a later interjection. Concerning the subject of the pericope, von Rad draws attention to the fact that whereas Deuteronomy generally promulgates universal and timeless values and ways of life, this pericope deals with a temporary cultic issue. He also perceives a contradiction between the command in our pericope to construct an altar on Mount Ebal after entering the land and to offer there holocaust and peace sacrifices, and the instruction to bring such offerings to an as yet unknown location, המקום אשר יבחר "to the place the Lord your God will choose [Deut. 12: 11]."[54] I may add that chapters 11 and 12 are parallel to chap. 27

---

[52] pp. 364ff

[53] G. von Rad, *5. Buch Moses*, 2. Auflage (Göttingen, 1968), p. 118.

[54] The traditional scholar D. Hoffmann, in his comments in *Deuteronomy* (Berlin, 1922), attempts to solve this inconsistency by arguing that an exclusive locus for the sanctuary did not apply to the period before Israel "reached the resting place and the inheritance" as written in Deut. 12: 9: כי לא באתם עד עתה אל המנוחה ואל הנחלה. Therefore, he contends, an appropriate location had to be designated for temporary use during the ceremony at Mount Ebal. Hoffmann does not address the fact that the text does not specifically designate this altar exclusively for the blessing and curse ceremony. On the contrary, from the context one must assume that the construction of the altar on Mount Ebal and the command to offer sacrifices there was not limited to the ceremony; there is no mention of a sacrificial offering at the ceremony itself, as one would expect if the sacrifices and ceremony were interrelated. In the parallel pericopes concerning the blessing and curse ceremony at Mounts Ebal and Gerizim in Deut. chaps. 11 and 12, there is no command to build an altar, or to offer sacrifices at that ceremony. We must therefore

in that both address the same issue of the blessings and curses on Mounts Gerizim and Ebal; hence the discrepancy concerning the place of the altar is heightened. Von Rad suggests that verses 27: 1 - 8 and 11 - 26 originate from a pre-deuteronomic tradition, possibly from Shekhem, clothed in a deuteronomic phraseology. Further, since the command is to construct the altar and offer sacrifices right after crossing the Jordan, it seems to have referred originally to the Gilgal sanctuary; it is thus aetiological in nature, serving as a justification for the holiness of this ancient sanctuary.

M. Anbar compares verses 2 - 8 of our pericope with the corresponding pericope in Jos. 8: 30 - 32, which narrates the fulfillment of the command to construct the altar after the crossing of the Jordan. Anbar "dissects" the structure of these verses and demonstrates the obvious doublets and repetitions, which suggest the original existence of two commands and the interpolation of rules to harmonize our verses with the instructions in Exod. 20: 21 - 22. He writes: "The aim of this interpolation was to compare the ceremony of Mount Sinai (Exod. 24: 4 - 5) with that of Mount Ebal, as the covenant of Sinai (Exod. 19 – 24) is parallel to the covenant of Shekhem (Jos. 24)." I do not contest Anbar's general proposal that there was an attempt of the redactor to harmonize the Sinai and Shekhem traditions, a procedure also proposed by M. Weinfeld based on different aspects and considerations; however, as previously noted, I perceive a distinct difference between the rules concerning the stones of the altar in Exod. 20: 22 and those in Deut. 27: 5 - 6, upon which I shall elaborate in sections 1.3 and 2.2.

Our pericope begins with והיה ביום אשר תעברו את הירדן "On the day when you shall pass the Jordan [Deut. 27: 2]," and the literal understanding is "on the same day that you cross the Jordan." Onkelos thus translates ויהי ביומא די תעברון, as do Jonathan, Neophyti and the Samaritan Targum, and the LXX similarly translates ἡμέρα. If we assume an amalgamation of various verses from different sources, this command refers to the stones of Gilgal, as we read in Jos. 4: 20: ואת שתים עשרה האבנים האלה אשר לקחו מן הירדן הקים יהושע בגלגל "And Joshua set up at Gilgal the twelve stones they had taken out of the Jordan." However, if the harmonization theory requires us to consider the pericope as a uniform, uninterrupted narrative referring to the setting up of the stones and the construction of the altar on Mount Ebal, we face great difficulties. The Israelites had just crossed the Jordan, they had not yet fought their way into the western part of the land, and Mounts Gerizim and Ebal are quite far from the Jordan, near the city of

conclude that this ceremony did not require an offering of sacrifices, and the command to build an altar on Mount Ebal in Deut. 27: 2 - 8 does not refer specifically to the ceremony, but has a more universal aspect.

Shekhem.[55] How could the Israelites have accomplished all this in one day? The Rabbis were aware of the problem, and we find two contrasting solutions. In B.T. Sotah 36a, Rabbi Simeon says:

בא וראה כמה נסים נעשו באותו היום עברו ישראל את הירדן ובאו להר
גריזים ולהר עיבל יתר מששים מיל ואין כל בריה יכולה לעמוד בפניהם

Come and see how many miracles occurred on that day: Israel crossed the Jordan, they reached Mount Gerizim and Mount Ebal sixty miles away, and no-one could stand against them.

Another opinion in Y. T. Sotah 7: 3, 21c concerns the location of Mounts Gerizim and Ebal, apparently in response to the textual difficulties in Deut. 11: 30.[56] In this verse the directions to the mountains for the blessing and curse ceremony are indicated in an apparently convoluted way. The first direction is אחרי דרך מבוא השמש, literally "after the western road," and then בארץ הכנעני הישב בערבה מול הגלגל אצל אלוני מרה "in the territory of the Canaanites living in the Arabah in front of [or opposite] Gilgal at [in the vicinity of] the trees of Moreh." The expression אחרי דרך מבוא השמש is already somewhat peculiar, and Rashi as well as Ibn Ezra demonstrate notable efforts to channel the exegesis of this phrase into the appropriate direction according to their predetermined opinions. Rashi interprets this phrase להלן מן הירדן "away from the Jordan," to conform with the fact that the mountains are far from the Jordan. However, a difficulty is then raised with the expression מול הגלגל, which gives the impression that the mountains are near Gilgal, which is close to the Jordan. Therefore, Rashi must interpret this latter phrase contrary to its plain meaning, and says רחוק

---

[55] It is interesting to note here the talmudic tendency to find support from the Bible for well-known facts, for which verification would appear to be superfluous. The location of the mountains Gerizim and Ebal was established, but the Rabbis attempted to find biblical phrases supporting their locations. We read in Mishnah Sotah 7: 5 that the Israelites came for the blessing and curse ceremony to Mount Gerizim and Mount Ebal in Samaria, near Shekhem, which is at Alonei Moreh. This statement is based on Deut. 11: 30, cited in the text, but the city of Shekhem is not mentioned in the biblical verse. Therefore, the Mishnah proceeds to confirm its declaration: שנאמר הלא המה...אצל אלוני מרה ולהלן הוא אומר ויעבר אברם בארץ עד מקום שכם עד אלון מורה מה אלון "...as it is said 'near מורה האמור להלן שכם אף אלון מרה האמור כאן שכם Alonei Moreh [Deut. 11: 30]' and in another place it is said 'Abram travelled through the land as far as the location of Shekhem up to Alon Moreh [Gen. 12: 6]'; just as there Alon Moreh is identical to Shekhem, so here it is Shekhem."

[56] G. Seitz, in *Redaktionsgeschichtliche Studien zum Deuteronomium* (Stuttgart, 1971), writes on p. 88 that it is impossible to understand the geographical data in this verse. He quotes Eissfeldt's opinion that the phrase בארץ הכנעני הישב בערבה מול הגלגל is a later interjection, effected with the intention of blending the original Shekhem narrative with the Gilgal episode.

מן הגלגל "far from Gilgal." Ibn Ezra offers a more elegant solution, stating "in the direction of Gilgal"; that is, since the mountains run from north to south, the verse pinpoints the location of Gerizim and Ebal: at the intersection of a straight line leading from Gilgal with the north-south line of the mountains.

Y.T. Sotah, 7: 3, 21c cites another opinion. Rabbi Eliezer considers the difficulties of the previous interpretation and declares: שתי גבשושיות עשו וקראו זה הר גריזים וזה הר עיבל "They made two piles [of earth or stones] and called one Mount Gerizim and the other one Mount Ebal." The Talmud then elaborates: על דעתיה דרבי יהודה מאה ועשרים מיל הלכו באותו היום על דעתיה דרבי אליעזר לא זזו ממקומן "In the opinion of R. Judah they travelled 120 miles in one day; in the opinion of R. Eliezer, they didn't move at all." Rabbi Eliezer does not consider the geographic realities, and Rabbi Judah of the Mishnah disregards the practical realities, which would require, as we have seen, a miraculous trek of 120 miles in one day.

Another textual problem arises due to the repetition of instructions regarding the stones. In Deut. 27: 2 we read: והקמת לך אבנים גדלות "Set up large stones"; from the context it seems that this was to be done at the crossing of the Jordan, as set out in the beginning of the verse: והיה ביום אשר תעברו את הירדן "And on the day when you shall cross the Jordan."[57] In v. 4 we read: תקימו את האבנים האלה...בהר עיבל "Set up these stones on Mount Ebal"; it is not clear whether these are the same stones, or whether the two verses refer to different stones. The issue is rendered even more

---

[57] As we have seen from the previous citations, the Talmud and the traditional commentators do take this expression literally, that is, on the day of the crossing of the Jordan,. Therefore, they run into difficulties with the narrative in Jos. 8: 30 - 31, where we read אז יבנה יהושע מזבח לה' אלהי ישראל בהר עיבל כאשר צוה משה "Then Joshua built an altar to the Lord, the God of Israel, on Mount Ebal. As Moses commanded...." The building of the altar on Mount Ebal refers unmistakably to the command in Deut. 27: 2; but according to the text this was accomplished by Joshua after the destruction of Ai, not on the day of the Jordan crossing. Rashi and Radak therefore rely on the talmudic statement אין מוקדם ומאוחר בתורה, "there is no order in the biblical narrative"; thus an event which occurs later in the text did not necessarily occur later in reality, an approach which avoids any question about chronological inconsistency in the Bible. Rashi and Radak affirm the literal interpretation of Deut. 27: 2 that the altar was built on the day of the crossing, and retroject the narrative in Jos. 8: 30 to an earlier spot in Joshua, right after the Jordan crossing. In the LXX this pericope appears in 9: 2, which is also out of place if the altar was built on the day of the Jordan crossing; this may indicate a later interjection into the text, to adapt it to the deuteronomic pericope. The Anchor Bible notes that Jos. 22: 1 also starts with the characteristic term אז. This chapter records the building of an illegal altar, and the aetiological purpose of promoting the deuteronomic cult centralization is obvious in this pericope; the use of the same opening term demonstrates a common principle underlying both pericopes.

confusing when we consider the narrative at the crossing of the Jordan. We read in Jos. 4: 8: וישאו שתי עשרה אבנים מתוך הירדן...ויעברום עמם אל המלון וינחום שם "They took twelve stones from the middle of the Jordan...and they carried them over with them to their camp, where they put them down." But in v. 9 we read another description of twelve stones: ושתים עשרה אבנים הקים יהושע בתוך הירדן תחת מצב רגלי הכהנים נשאי ארון הברית ויהיו שם עד היום הזה "Joshua set up the twelve stones that had been in the middle of the Jordan at the spot where the priests who carried the ark of the covenant had stood. And they are there to this day."

Apparently the Rabbis could not accept that the stone altar erected on Mount Ebal remained there permanently, as this would violate the prohibition against *bamoth*.[58] We read in Mishnah Sotah 7: 5, subsequent to the description of the blessing and curse ceremony:

---

[58] Even a temporary construction of such an altar would be a contravention of the *bamoth* prohibition, according to the talmudic opinion that the *bamoth* were only allowed when there was no Tabernacle. We read in Mishnah Zebahim 14: 4: עד שלא הוקם המשכן היו הבמות מותרות ועבודה בבכורות, משהוקם המשכן נאסרו הבמות ועבודה בכהנים "Before the erection of the Tabernacle [offerings on] the *bamoth* were permitted, and the celebrations [were performed] by the first-born; after the erection of the Tabernacle [offerings on] the *bamoth* were prohibited and the celebrations [were performed] by the priests." According to this Mishnah, the construction of an altar other than the one in the Tabernacle was prohibited; yet we find in the following Mishnah 5: באו לגלגל הותרו הבמות "when they came to Gilgal the [sacrifices on the] *bamoth* were permitted," in flagrant contradiction to the previous Mishnah. This difficulty was also recognized by the Talmud, in B.T. Zebahim 117a: מה בין אהל מועד שבמדבר מותרות אהל מועד לבין אהל מועד שבגלגל אהל מועד שבמדבר לא היו במות שבגלגל היו הבמות מותרות "What is the difference between the Tabernacle of the desert and the Tabernacle of Gilgal? At the Tabernacle of the desert the *bamoth* were not permitted, at the [time of] the Tabernacle at Gilgal the *bamoth* were permitted." The reason for this apparently illogical statement is found in Zebahim 119a, based on Deut. 12: 1ff., according to what one is allowed to do "here", in the desert, and "there", after the Jordan crossing: כי לא באתם עד עתה אל המנוחה ואל הנחלה אל המנוחה זו שילה נחלה זו ירושלי' למה חלקן כדי ליתן היתר בין זה לזה "Since you have not yet reached the resting place and the inheritance [Deut. 12:9]' - the resting place is Shilo and the inheritance is Jerusalem; why has the Bible differentiated them? In order to permit [worship at *bamoth*] between them [in the periods when the Tabernacle was neither in Shilo nor in Jerusalem]." Hence at the period of the Tabernacle in Gilgal, the *bamoth* were permitted. The Talmud also offers a reason for the permission at Gilgal, in another homily in Zebahim 118b: ימי אהל מועד שבגלגל ארבע עשרה ז' שכבשו וז' שחלקו "The Tabernacle was in Gilgal fourteen years, seven [years] for the duration of the conquest and seven [years] for the division [of the conquered land]." Hence when the Tabernacle stood at Gilgal, the land was not yet completely divided; the Israelites had not yet received their inheritance, the juncture for their change in status. But it seems that not all the Sages were satisfied with these solutions, and other midrashic sources suggest that the permission to build an altar on Mount Ebal was a unique concession pronounced by a

ואחר כך הביאו את האבנים ובנו את המזבח וסדוהו בסיד וכתבו עליו את
כל דברי התורה בשבעים לשון שנאמר "באר היטב" ונטלו את האבנים
ובאו ולנו במקומן

And after that [the ceremony] they brought the stones and built the altar and whitewashed it
with lime, and wrote upon it the whole Torah in seventy languages, since it is said 'very
clearly'[Deut. 27: 8]; and [having dismantled the altar] they took the stones and carried them
back to their place [Gilgal, according to Jos. 4: 8: ויעברום עמם אל המלון וינחום
שם 'and they carried them over with them to their camp/ lodge, where they put them
down.'[59]]

The repetitions in this pericope cause yet another difficulty. In Deut. 27: 2
and 3, the Israelites are commanded to set up large stones on the day they
cross the Jordan, to whitewash them, and to write on them all the words of
the Law. In verse 4 they are commanded to set up האבנים האלה when they
cross the Jordan, and to whitewash them. In verse 5, they are commanded to
build an altar of stones, with no indication as to whether this refers to the
previously mentioned stones, or to others. In verse 8, the closing verse of this
pericope, there is again a command to write all the words of the Law on the
stones, again with no indication as to the stones referred to. It is little wonder,
then, that even the Rabbis held contradictory opinions as to whether the
writing of the Law should be rendered on the set-up stones, or on the stones
of the altar. We have seen that the Mishnah in Sotah 7: 5 declares that the
Israelites wrote the Law on the stones of the altar and then dismantled it, but
in Y. T. Sotah 7: 5, 21d, we encounter a conflict between two Rabbis on this
point: על אבני המלון נכתבו דברי רבי יודה רבי יוסי אומר על אבני מזבח
נכתבו "[The Law] was written on the stones which were taken to the camp,
said Rabbi Judah; Rabbi Jose says, They were written on the stones of the
altar." It is obvious that the point at issue in the Gemara is that if the Law
were written on the stones of the altar, which was dismantled on the same

---

prophet. We read in Y. T. Megilah 1: 12, 72c: אין הבמה אמר ר' יוסי בן חנינא אומר
ניתרת אלא על ידי נביא "... permission [to present offerings] on a *bamah* could only
be declared by a prophet." Rabbi Johanan bar Marieh supports this declaration from the
example of Joshua, who according to Jos. 8: 30, built an altar on Mount Ebal.

[59] Rashi explains the Mishnah based on the text in B. T. Sotah 36a, which complements this
Mishnah: וקפלו את האבנים ובאו ולנו בגלגל שנאמר והעברתם אותם עמכם
והנחתם אותם במלון יכול בכל מלון ומלון ת"ל אשר תלינו בו הלילה "And they
peeled the [writing from the] stones [this is the traditional translation, based on a
transposition of the letters to form קלף 'to peel', but one may also consider the term to be
קפל 'to fold', to pack one on top of the other, a common system of transporting stones in
layers], and returned to stay overnight in Gilgal, since it is said 'to carry them over with
you and put them down at the lodge where you stay tonight [Jos. 4: 3]'; would it mean to
put them in any camp? [No], since the verse says in the lodge 'where you stay tonight,'"
hence in Gilgal.

day, how could one learn from it? The answers in turn bring new questions, and so on. I have quoted extensively from the talmudic discussions on this pericope to demonstrate the Sisyphean task the Rabbis undertook in harmonizing the difficulties of the pericope, both within the verses and in their relation to other pericopes. It is a twist of fate that the deuteronomic redactor's attempt to harmonize this pericope with the Joshua narrative created such a troublesome task for the Rabbis, who were compelled to smooth out the results of his untidy work.

On the issue of the identification of the stones, there are various scholarly views. I have already mentioned the critical analysis by M. Anbar, who offers his opinion on how to divide this pericope into different parts, and various other proposals concerning the development of the pericope. He affirms, at the same time, that many questions remain without a logical answer. Keil and Delitzsch[60] are not much concerned with the repetitions in the text. They affirm that the writing had to be effected on the stones, and not upon the altar; this is based on the practical reason that the altar had to be constructed of unhewn stones,[61] on which it would be impossible to write. M. Weinfeld [62] does not discuss the textual irregularities of the pericope, but in the course of his exegetical analysis contends that verses 5 - 7 concerning the altar are an "anomalous feature of the text" disrupting the continuity between verses 4 and 8. Hence it is clear that in his opinion the writing of the Law was carried out on the stones. The traditional scholar D. Hoffmann[63] also affirms that the Law was written on the erected stones, and not on the altar. He concludes this from both a textual and a practical standpoint. The expression מזבח אבנים in verse 5 confirms, in his opinion, that these stones are different than האבנים האלה to be set up in verse 4. He also considers that it would be impossible to write on unhewn stones, for practical reasons.

A comment may be made here on the issue of the altar on Mount Ebal. As is well known, the Pentateuch of the Samaritans commands the altar to be built on Mount Gerizim, their holy mountain. I would suggest that originally an ancient sanctuary was situated on Mount Gerizim,[64] and therefore the later

---

[60] pp. 430 ff.

[61] They do not consider that in this pericope there is no prohibition against using hewn stones, as in Exod. 20: 22.

[62] *Deuteronomy and the Deuteronomic School* (Oxford, 1972), p. 166.

[63] p. 90.

[64] The fact that the remains of an ancient altar have been found on Mount Ebal does not refute my postulate. The Samaritan Temple on Mount Gerizim was totally destroyed by the Hasmoneans; see *Ant.* XIII: 256. In addition, the assumption of A. Zertal, "Has Joshua's Altar Been Found on Mt. Ebal?" *BAR* 11/1 (Jan/Feb. 1985), pp. 26-43 that the

text provided an aetiological reason for its presence on that location. It may be inferred from the MT that these mountains had a sacred history, and therefore the important ceremony of the blessings and curses had to take place upon them. Following this logic, one would expect the altar to be built on Mount Gerizim, where the blessings were proclaimed, and not on Mount Ebal, the site of the curses.[65] We also observe the ancient holiness of Mount Gerizim reflected in the story of Jotham, who climbed this mountain to announce his solemn declaration, although Mount Ebal is the higher

---

archeological remains are those of an altar was questioned by H. Shanks, "Two Early Israelite Cult Sites Questioned," *BAR* XIV/I (Jan./Feb. 1988), pp. 48-52.

[65] It seems that certain traditional commentators were sensitive to this question, and we find an interesting response in Midrash Tanhuma (Buber), *Parshah* Veyera, *siman* 29: הכותים עתידים לומר הר גריזים שלנו הוא ששם ניתנו הברכות ואינן יודעים ששם נותנין הקללות האיך הוא הדבר אלא שאותן שהיו עומדין בהר עיבל ומקללין למי היו מקללין לא לאלו שעומדין כנגדן ואלו שמברכין למי היו מברכין לא לאלו שכנגדן נמצאו הקללות באות על הר גריזים והברכות על הר עיבל "The Kutim [Samaritans] will say Mount Gerizim is ours [the Holy Mountain] since there the blessings were given, but they do not know that [actually] the curses were given there. How is that? Those who stood on Mount Ebal and cursed, whom did they curse? Was it not those who stood opposite? And those who blessed, whom did they bless? Was it not those who stood opposite? Hence the curses are directed to Mount Gerizim and the blessings to Mount Ebal." But the Midrash did not consider that based on the text, especially Jos. 8: 33, it may be inferred that the priests and Levites who pronounced the blessings and the curses stood in the middle, in the valley between the two mountains, and from there proclaimed the blessings and curses towards the people who stood on the mountains. Mishnah Sotah 7: 5 also understood the text in this way. We read there: ששה שבטים עלו לראש הר גריזים וששה שבטים עלו לראש הר עיבל והכהנים והלוים והארון עומדים למטה באמצע הכהנים מקיפין את הארון והלוים את הכהנים וכל ישראל מכאן ומכאן שנאמר וכל ישראל וזקניו ושטרים ושופטיו עומדים מזה ומזה לארון וגו' הפכו פניהם כלפי הר גריזים ופתחו בברכה הפכו פניהם כלפי הר עיבל ופתחו בקללה "Six tribes went up to the top of Mount Gerizim and six tribes went up to the top of Mount Ebal, and the priests and the Levites and the ark stood below, in the middle, the priests surrounding the ark, and the Levites the priests, and all Israel [stood] on both sides, as it is written 'And all of Israel and its elders and their officials and their judges stood on both sides of the ark' [Jos. 8: 33]; they [the Levites, according to Deut. 27: 14; Joshua, according to Jos. 8: 34] turned their faces toward Mount Gerizim and commenced with the blessing... [then] turned their faces toward Mount Ebal and commenced with the curse...." We observe that the curse was directed toward Mount Ebal, contrary to the assumption of Midrash Tanhuma. I may also refer to Deut. 11: 29, where we observe a clear association of the blessing with Mount Gerizim and the curse with Mount Ebal: ונתתה את הברכה על הר גרזים ואת הקללה על הר עיבל "Confer the blessing on Mount Gerizim and the curse on Mount Ebal." This text invalidates Tanhuma's solution to the issue.

mountain. M. Weinfeld[66] states in his discussion of the blessing and curse ceremony at Mounts Gerizim and Ebal in Deut. 11: 29 - 32 and Deut. 27: 1 - 26: "Deuteronomy preserved then a very old tradition about the establishment of the nation at Shekhem, the capital of the house of Joseph." One would therefore expect that the Samaritan belief that Mount Gerizim is the holy place originally prevailed in this pericope, since the Samaritans consider themselves to be the successors of the house of Joseph and the legitimate guardians of its true heritage. There on Mount Gerizim, not on Mount Ebal, would the altar be built at this important ceremony. It seems to me, therefore, that the change requiring the altar to be built on Mount Ebal instead of on Mount Gerizim was effected by the MT redactors.

I shall not further analyze verses 2 - 4 and 7 - 8 of our pericope, which are not pertinent to the main subject of our research; it has sufficed to demonstrate the literary potpourri constituted by the verses from different sources and periods which make up the pericope. I shall analyze only the relevant rules of the altar in verses 5 and 6.

The first command, in apodictic form, is to build a מזבח אבנים "an altar of stones." We note immediately the conflict with Exod. 20: 22. It is not simply that the latter verse seems to prefer an earthen altar, but that the building of an earthen altar would be in direct violation of the explicit command in Deut. 27:5 to build an altar of stones. Verse 5 starts with a general command to build an altar, ובנית שם מזבח "Build there an altar," but repeats the term "altar" to stress the specific type of altar to be built: מזבח אבנים "an altar of stones." This emphasis on the particular technical description of the altar demonstrates that this rule is unquestionably in plain contradiction to the Law of the Altar in Exod. 20: 22. We must therefore start by rejecting any attempt to harmonize between the two entirely conflicting rules for the construction of the altar.

I refer to my exegetical analysis above of the term נוף with respect to Exod. 20: 22, and reiterate the significance of this interpretation in the context of Deut. 27: 5. The specific and restricted meaning of this term, which refers only to an action in which an iron implement is swung from above to hit something, is in my opinion crucial to the correct understanding of this rule. It is also necessary for an understanding of I Kings 6: 7, which has been related to Deut. 27: 5 - 6 by both the Talmud and the traditional commentators, as well as by modern scholars. We read there: והבית בהבנתו אבן שלמה מסע נבנה ומקבות והגרזן כל כלי ברזל לא נשמע בבית בהבנתו

---

[66] "The Emergence of the Deuteronomic Movement: The Historical Antecedents," in *Das Deuteronium, Enstehung, Gestalt und Botschaft,* ed. N. Lohfink (Leuven 1985), p. 79.

"In building the Temple, it was built only of 'whole-perfect' carried[67] stones,
no hammer or pick or any other iron tool was heard in the Temple when it

---

[67] The exact translation and interpretation of the term מסע in this context is a debated issue,
since the root נסע from which it derives usually means "to move", with all its
ramifications. Mandelkern indicates for the term מסע *lapicidina*; *genus telorum*; *hasta*;
and various types of cutting tools and arms, but then he explains that in our verse it refers
to אבנים שהסיעו, which seems to imply "carried" stones. The LXX translates λίθοις
ἀκροτόμοις ἀργοῖς "stones cut-off sharply, unworked," and it is difficult to match this
translation literally with the Hebrew term; we must consider it an interpretation, rather
than a translation. It is difficult to know exactly what the translator really intended to
imply by the term ἀργοῖς. It could mean "shining, bright, glistening" (Liddell and Scott),
implying something of quality, or it could be a contraction of α-εργος, "left undone," just
the opposite. From the context, if ἀκροτόμοῖς is translated as "cut-off sharply," the
translation "glistening" would be appropriate in the context. On the other hand, Josephus
uses this term in *Against Apion* I: 198 to describe the stones of the altar: ἀτμήτων
συλλέκτων ἀργῶν, which in the context must be translated " compiled, uncut,
unworked." We must bear in mind that the two descriptions are conflicting: the LXX
reports "cut stones" and Josephus records "uncut stones." Therefore, the interpretation of
the term ἀργοῖς could also be different. The Targum translates אבנין שלמין מטקס
"whole stones 'closely fitted' (Jastrow, pass. participle of טקס, possibly from the Greek
τασσω)." The Vulgate also translates the phrase as worked stones. *lapidibus dolatis atque
perfectis* "stones cut to perfection." The KJV has "stone made ready before it was
brought," and the NIV states "blocks dressed at the quarry," but it is obvious that both are
interpretations based on the traditional homilies, as we shall see in section 3.2. In B. T.
Sotah 48b, we find a debate between two Tannaim, from which we may infer that מסע is
understood to derive from the root נסע "to move". We read there: ת"ר שמיר שבו בנה
שלמה את בהמ"ק שנא׳ והבית בהבנתו אבן שלמה מסע נבנה הדברים ככתבן
דברי ר׳ יהודה אמר לו ר׳ נחמיה וכי אפשר לומר כן והלא כבר נאמר כל אלה
אבנים יקרת וגו׳ מגררות במגרה אם כן מה ת"ל לא נשמע בבית בהבנותו שהיה
מתקין מבחוץ ומכניס מבפנים אמר רבי נראין דברי רבי יהודה באבני מקדש
ודברי ר׳ נחמיה באבני ביתו "The Sages taught: The 'Shamir' [a legendary worm,
which cuts stones] with which Solomon built the Temple, as it is written [I Kings 6: 7]:
'In building the Temple, it was built only of whole-perfect carried stones,' [was
withdrawn after its destruction], said Rabbi Judah; Rabbi Nehemiah said to him: How is
it possible to assert this since it is said [I Kings 7: 9]:'High grade stones cut to size and
trimmed with a plane ['saw' in KJV and NIV]'? What do we understand from the phrase
'[no hammer etc.] was heard in the Temple when it was built'? [This phrase states] that
one dressed the stones outside the Temple and brought them in[to the Temple already
dressed]." Rabbi said: The words of R. Judah are to be preferred regarding the stones of
the Temple, and those of R. Nehemiah are to be preferred regarding the stones of his
[Solomon's] house." This seems to me a totally illogical solution, and I shall elaborate
upon it in section 3.2. It is natural that the traditional commentators follow this line of
harmonization between the two conflicting verses, and must also reconcile the difficulty
arising from the term אבני גזית "cut stones" in I Kings 5: 31 with reference to the
building of the Temple. But even they translate מסע as referring to "moving", not
"cutting". Rashi explains מסע. כמו שהסיעוה מן ההר " "...as it was carried from the

was built." This narrative does have an affinity with Deut. 27: 5 - 6, and I shall elaborate upon this further. However, the talmudic Sages and their followers, as well as certain modern scholars, have also brought Exod. 20: 22 into the relation since it too contains the term נוף, and the resulting tangle of dissimilar texts, sources and motives must be carefully picked apart.

David Weiss Halivni asserts in his book Midrash, Mishna and Gemara [68] that biblical laws are vindicatory and justified, and I think we can fully agree with his postulate. If we consider the structure of our pericope in Deut. 27: 5 - 7, we may identify the following elements:

the command: to build an altar
the place: on Mount Ebal
the type: an altar of stones, on which no iron tool was to be wielded
the motive: because you should build it of whole-perfect stones
the purpose: to offer whole-burnt sacrifices and eat peace offerings there.

Exod. 20: 21 - 22 has the same general style, but the structure is different, constrained by the fact that the pericope concerns two types of altars. In verse 21 the elements are:

---

mountain"; Radak is more specific and explains: כמו שהסיעו אותן מן ההר ושם היו פוסלין אותן במדות גזית אבל משהביאו האבנים לבית לא היו פוסלין מהן דבר "as they were brought from the mountain and there they were hewn in the sizes of 'Gazit' [a well-known dimension], but when brought into the Temple, nothing was chopped off from them." A. S. Hartom, following Cassuto's method, translates מסע. כפי שהוסעו מההר "...as they were transported from the mountain."

Surprisingly, M. Noth, in Könige, Biblischer Kommentar Altes Testament, IX/1 (Neukirchen, 1968), translates מסע as "brechen" "to split (stones)," and the term refers either to the quarry, or the hewing. The term מסע is to be understood as a description of שלמה. Noth establishes his translation based on the words ויסעו אבנים גדלות "They removed from the quarry large blocks [NIV, I Kings 5: 31]," and מסיע אבנים יעצב בהם "Whoever quarries stones may be injured by them [NIV, Eccl. 10: 9]." I see no reason to translate the term מסע in these two verses in any way other than their usual meaning of "moving", not "hewing". It is true that Rashi and Radak translate the term ויסעו in I Kings as ועקרו "they cleft," following the Targum translation ועקרו, a term which might support Noth's translation. However, both Rashi and Ibn Ezra interpret the term מסע in Eccl. as the usual "move or remove." The LXX translates there ἐξαίρων, a term which expresses a similar idea of raising and carrying away. I Kings 5: 31 is missing in LXX and this fact may hint at a later interjection. At any rate, the following verse I Kings 5: 32 states ויפסלו, "they sculpted" stones, and this confirms that the builders used metal tools to hew, carve and prepare the stones for the building of the Temple. Noth asserts that I Kings 6: 7 records that the stones were not cut at the site of the Temple, but were prepared at the site of the quarry; he would then be forced to accept the talmudic assertion that the prohibition against using iron tools applied only inside the Temple precinct. This is illogical, as I shall show.

[68] David Weiss Halivni, *Midrash, Mishna and Gemara* (Cambridge, 1986).

the command: to build an altar

the type: an earthen altar

the purpose: to offer sacrifices of your flock and cattle

the place: anywhere

the motive: I will come everywhere to bless you.

One may deduce from the structure of the verse that the permission to build a stone altar originates from a different source than that of the earthen altar, and was added later to the Law. The stated purpose, "to offer sacrifices anywhere," concludes the law of the earthen altar; this law is complete in itself. Only then is permission to build a stone altar added. There is no indication of purpose or place, since the redactor evidently intended these to be the same as for the earthen altar. However, the structure follows the same pattern as above:

the permission: to build an altar of stones

the type: of unhewn stones

the motive: the use of an homicidal implement defiles the stone.

The two pericopes, as we have seen, set out precise explanations for their specific details, though the two are entirely different, both in their requirements and in their motives. Our pericope in Deut. 27 prohibits the wielding of iron implements on the stones to split them, because the altar demands whole-perfect stones; the pericope in Exod. 20 prohibits the use of any tool which could be used as an homicidal implement, because such an act, equivalent to a violent action, would defile the stones, making them unfit for an altar.

Statutes and regulations are usually incomplete and inadequate and cannot offer precise rules for every eventuality. Examination of the motive behind the statute, set out in its preamble, allows us to comprehend the intention of the lawgiver, and enables us to adapt the principle of the law to actual circumstances. By similarly examining the explanation for the requirement not to wield "iron" on the stones, that is, because whole-perfect stones are required, we may discern the intent of the "statute", correctly interpret its purpose, and define its exact applications and limits. We must therefore analyze the term שלם in connection with stones. A comparison with the similar requirements in Exod. 20: 22 will then assist us in the verification of our interpretation.

1.2.3.2 The Interpretation of אבנים שלמות

I do not think that the requirement to build the altar of אבנים שלמות should be interpreted as requiring untouched fieldstones in their natural state, because the term שלם does not imply the idea of "untouched"; it implies only "whole - complete - unbroken - perfect." Onkelos, Jonathan and the Samaritan Targum translate שלמן, which does not help us with the precise meaning, but the Neophyti Targum elaborates: אבנין טבין שלמן מן מום "good [quality -perfect] stones without blemish." The LXX also translates as ὁλοκλήρους "complete in all parts, entire, perfect," a term which would not preclude a certain dressing of the stones to make them "perfect", without breaking them into parts. There are two other associations of אבן with שלם in the Bible in addition to our verse and I Kings 6: 7: אבן שלמה in Deut. 25: 15 and ואבן שלמה in Prov.11: 1. In both occurrences, the term indicates "perfect" or "whole", and certainly does not rule out any processing and modification by tools; on the contrary, the fact that the stones in these verses are weightstones would absolutely necessitate such preparation to make them true to weight.

The term שלם occurs frequently in the Bible, with the connotation of "perfect", "whole", "integral",[69] and so we must understand our verse as specifying "whole-perfect stones." It is interesting to note that both the Talmud and the Ramban, a traditional commentator, are willing to perceive the interpretation of אבן שלמה as "smooth", when this does not conflict with the interpretation of other biblical verses. We read in B. T. Zebahim 54b a rhetorical discussion on how it would be possible to demolish a section of the altar, since אבנים שלמות כתיב, "it is written whole-perfect [smooth] stones," and in a demolition the stones would not remain smooth. Similar evidence of the interpretation of אבנים שלמות is encountered in B. T. Abodah Zarah 52b. The Talmud refers to the storage of stones of the altar which were defiled by the Hellenistic occupation of the Temple, since they could not be used for legitimate sacrificial worship. The discussion proceeds: היכי נעביד ניתברינהו אבנים שלמות אמר רחמנא, ננסרינהו לא תניף עליהם ברזל אמר רחמנא

How should we proceed [with the stones]? Should we break them? Scripture says [the altar should be made of] 'whole-perfect stones [Deut. 27: 5].' Should we cut them with a saw? Scripture says, 'You must not wield on them an iron [tool]' [Deut. 27: 6].'

---

[69] See Gen. 34: 21: האנשים האלה שלמים הם אתנו "These men are friendly toward us..."; I Kings 8: 61: והיה לבבכם שלם "But your hearts must be fully committed..."; Isa. 38: 3: באמת ובלב שלם "...faithfully and with wholehearted devotion"; I Chr. 29: 9: בלב שלם התנדבו "...they had given freely and wholeheartedly"; and others. The term גלות שלמה in Amos 1: 6, 9 also means "complete/ integral / comprehensive."

We observe that in this case the antonym of שלמות is "broken", hence שלמות means "whole".[70] We also read in Ramban's commentary to Exod. 20: 21:

וזהו שאמר אבן שלמה מסע נבנה לא שהיא שלימה לגמרי רק שהיא
שלימה שאין בה פגם כדי שתחגור בה צפורן[71] אבל היא חלקה ושוה (ס״א
ונאה) ופירוש ״מסע״ שהיא גדולה כאשר הסיעו אותה מן ההר לא חלקו
הסלע לאבנים מרובות כמנהג הבונים

The statement there [I Kings 6:7] 'built of whole-perfect carried stone' does not mean that the stone was literally whole, only that there was no blemish in it [large enough] to catch a fingernail passed over it, but it was smooth and uniform [another MS: 'and elegant']. And the interpretation of מסע is that the stone [was kept] large as it was brought from the mountain, and was not split into many parts, according to the fashion of the builders.

On the other hand, S. R. Driver[72] connects our passage with the rule in Exod. 20: 21 - 22 and asserts: "It is to be built in simple fashion, of whole, i.e., of unhewn stones, upon which no tool has been used." A. Dillmann[73] also links the deuteronomic pericope with Exod. 20: 22, and although he translates אבנים שלמות as "ganzen oder vollständigen" "entire (whole) or complete," he adds his interpretation, "d.h. unbehauenen Steinen," "unhewn stones," presumably because of his association of the verse with Exod. 20: 22. He does not consider that the term גזית, employed in Exod. 20: 22 to describe the type of stones prohibited in the construction of the altar, is not mentioned in Deut. 27: 5 - 6.

In contrast to Exod. 20: 22, where the tool is indicated as a "sword", or something which could be used as such, Deut. 27: 5 specifies only the generic material ברזל "iron", and there is no indication whether this prohibits contact with anything made of iron, or prohibits only the use of specific tools made of iron. We also do not know whether it is only tools of iron which are prohibited, or whether the ban includes similar types of tools made of other materials, such as bronze. If we avoid harmonizing this pericope with Exod. 20: 22, we seem to be left with no understanding of this interdiction. I

---

[70] The talmudic statement that the command not to wield an iron implement on the stones serves as the basis for the prohibition against sawing the stones does not invalidate my thesis. Sawing might be prohibited simply on the basis of the apodictic command to use "whole- perfect" stones, and a stone cut into pieces by a saw would not meet this requirement.

[71] Ramban's statement derives from a talmudic discussion in B. T. Hulin 18a: וכמה פגימת המזבח כדי שתחגור בה צפורן "When is the altar defective [how great must the notch be]? Deep enough to catch a fingernail passing over."

[72] S. R. Driver, ed., *The International Critical Commentary on the Holy Scriptures of the Old and New Testaments, Deuteronomy*, 2nd edition (Edinburgh, 1896), p. 297.

[73] p. 366.

suggest, therefore, that we deduce the correct interpretation from the motive which follows the prohibition, that is אבנים שלמות תבנה "build of whole - perfect stones." Such an interpretation would imply a prohibition against any kind of working of the stones, which would change their "wholeness" or "perfection", regardless of the type of tool or its material.

On the other hand, an attempt to harmonize the two pericopes leads to illogical conclusions, as we may see from the following discussion in Mekhilta d'Rabbi Ishmael, Jethro, *Parshah* 11:

כי חרבך הנפת עליה וכו׳ מכאן היה רבי שמעון בן אלעזר אומר המזבח
נברא להאריך שנותיו של אדם והברזל נברא לקצר

[It is written] 'You have wielded your sword upon it [Exod. 20:22].' From this Rabbi Simeon ben Eleazar says, The altar was created to prolong the life of man, and iron was created to diminish it.

We observe that the linkage between the two pericopes has shifted the emphasis from the concept of "sword", and what it represents, to the concept of the material, "iron". We may also note the more explicit homily, cited above, in Mekhilta d'Rabbi Simeon bar Johai, chap. 20:

שנ׳ כי חרבך הנפת [יכול ל]א יהו פסולות אלא אם כן נתגזזו בחרב תל׳ לו׳
לא תניף [עליהם ברזל] הרי ברזל כחרב אם סופינו לעשות ברזל כחרב מה
תל׳ לו׳ כי] חרבך זו היא שרבן יוחנן בן זכאי או׳ מה ראה ברזל ליפסל
[מכל מ[יני מתכות]כולן[מפני שהחרב נעשית ממנו וחרב [סימן] פורענות
ומזבח סימן כפרה

[It is written] 'You have wielded your sword [Exod. 20: 22].' Could this indicate that only if cut by a sword [it is defiled]? We learn from 'You should not wield iron [upon them] [Deut. 27: 5]' that 'iron' is equivalent to 'sword'. If 'iron' is considered as equivalent to 'sword', why is it written 'You have wielded your sword'? This is what Rabbi Johanan ben Zakkai said: 'Why does iron out of all other metals [defile the stones]? Because the sword is made of iron, and iron is a symbol of castigation and the altar is a sign of atonement.

This harmonization process leads to the inevitable conclusion that the touch of iron in any form and manner defiles the stones, whereas the cutting of the stones with tools made of any other metals is permissible and does not defile them. This seems to me a complete reversal of the original intent of the biblical altar rules.

In a recently published study[74] S. M. Olyan suggests comparing the terms תמים and אין בה מום, indicating the requirement that the animals for sacrifice should be "unblemished", with the requirement that the altar stones be similarly "perfect, without any kind of defiling adulteration." While I agree with his definition, I do not agree with his conclusion that according to

---

[74] Saul M. Olyan, "Why an Altar of Unfinished Stones? Some Thoughts on Exod. 20,25 and Dtn 27,5 - 6," *ZAW* 108 (1996), pp. 161 - 171.

Deut. 27: 5 the altar was to be built with "unfinished stones", and that "any physical alteration" defiles the stones.

1.2.3.3 Discussion of S. M. Olyan's Theory

I distinguish between human interventions which defile, and are prohibited, and those which improve, and are permitted. There is not much one can do to improve the natural perfection of an animal, but it is certainly possible to improve the appearance of a rough stone in its natural state. In fact, there seems to be some support for my postulate in a talmudic source, regarding the embellishment of a sacrificial animal. Mishnah Bikurim 3: 3 vividly describes the colourful public procession carrying the first fruits into Jerusalem, and we read there: והשור הולך לפניהם וקרניו מצופות זהב ועטרת של זית בראשו החליל מכה לפניהם "And the bull was marching before them and his horns were overlaid with gold and a crown of olive [branches] was on his head; the flute played before them." We then read in the Y.T. Bikurim 3: 1, 65c: פשיטא שהוא מקריב שלמים "Certainly he offers [the bull] as a peace offering." Another Rabbi contends that a holocaust was offered, but both agree that the bull with the gold-covered horns was offered as a sacrifice, and there was no objection to this "human intervention" in adorning it. We read further in the Y. T.: יחיד שנתעצל ולא בא מביא גדי וקרניו מצופות כסף "If a man was lazy and did not come [to participate in the public ceremony], he brings a kid with its horns overlaid with silver." This demonstrates that embellishments of sacrificial animals were common, and a human intervention of such an improving nature was not considered defiling.

Olyan has also connected in his study the two pericopes Exod. 20: 22 and Deut. 27: 5 - 6, and therefore analyzes the term חלל as an antonym to תמים/שלם. He does not consider the fact that the term שלם does not occur in the Exod. pericope, and the term חלל, a specific cultic term, does not occur in the deuteronomic passage. חלל is an abstract concept connoting sacrilege, applied mainly within the cultic system. The term usually does not refer to the result of an action, but to the manner in which the action was performed. A peace offering consumed in the first two days after its sacrifice, for instance, is a corr ect manner of worship, but if one eats it on the third day, חלל את קדש ה' "he profaned what is holy for the Lord [Lev. 19: 8]." A further example deals with the case of the common priest. He is not allowed to marry אשה זנה וחללה...ואשה גרושה "a prostitute and a defiled woman and a divorced woman [Lev. 21: 7],"[75] whereas he is allowed to marry a widow. There is no physical difference between a widow and a divorced woman; each is no longer a virgin. The only difference is how the woman was separated from her previous husband: by an act of God which did not defile her, or by being cast out by her husband, an act which was considered at that period a great humiliation with subsequent stigma attached; her civil status was therefore irremediably ruined. Similarly, the prohibition against marrying a חללה did not relate to her physical condition but to her status. The same type of distinction applies to most of the other uses of the term חלל in cultic practice.[76]

The term חלל is not the precise opposite of either תמים or שלם, philologically or conceptually. The antonym of שלם is חסר, and the antonym of תמים is בעל מום.[77] The change of status is conditioned in the first case by a particular physical interference resulting in bodily adulteration, which causes a material loss of such an extent as to affect its perfection, or cause its diminution, and in the second case by a damaging, corrupting action. The stones, however, are "profaned" ותחללה[78] by being cut with an

---

[75] The traditional commentators explain the concept of "defiled" as born of a prohibited marriage.

[76] For instance, the High Priest may make himself unclean for certain related persons, but not for others, lest he be profaned להחלו (Lev. 21: 4). וחללת (Lev. 19: 12) is applied to the swearing of a false oath, though this involves the same physical action as swearing truly. A sacrifice on the altar offered by a priest with a blemish is prohibited because it profanes the sanctuary: ולא יחלל את מקדשי (Lev. 21: 23).

[77] The term שלם "complete/perfect" may also be considered as a synonym of מלא "full/complete", and we find an interesting Midrash on this point concerning the Ephod, the oracle source. We read in B. T. Sotah 48b: שמיר למאי אתא מיבעי ליה לכדתניא אבנים הללו אין כותבים אותן בדיו משום שנאמר פיתוחי חותם ואין מסריטן עליהם באזמל משום שנאמר במלואתם אלא כותב עליהם בדיו ומראה להן שמיר מבחוץ והן נבקעות מאליהן כתאניה זו שנבקעת בימות החמה ואינה חיסרה כלום "For what was the 'Shamir' [a legendary worm] needed? It was needed because of what was taught: [The names of the tribes] were not written upon these stones [of the Ephod] in ink, because it is said [Exod. 28: 21] 'engraved like a seal,' and were not engraved with a chisel, because it is written 'in their fullness' [Exod. 28: 20]; but one writes on them with ink and displays the 'Shamir' externally and they [the stones] split on their own, like the fig which splits in summer and nothing is lost from it." We observe here that the stones of the Ephod had to be complete, that is, nothing taken away or lost.

[78] The LXX translates μ η μ ί α ν τ α ι from the root μ ι α ί ν ω, "to stain, dye", but utilized mainly metaphorically, as morally stained, defiled. Onkelos translates ותחלינה, using the same MT root חלל. The Samaritan Targum MS J also translates וחללתנה, but MS A has ותברלנה "you will break it." Targum Jonathan, on the other hand, translates ותחללה as אפיסתא from the term אפס "nothing", namely, unworthy for the purpose. It is

homicidal implement. They do not change their status from קדש "holy" to "common", as Olyan suggests (p. 164), with any kind of human alteration; Scripture's prohibition is limited to a particular kind of human intervention, the use of a specific implement. I perceive no basis in Scripture for Olyan's statement, "The condition of the stone, the animal body, or the human body - whole/complete versus altered - is of central importance, not the means by which it might become defiled or necessarily whether its 'natural state' is preserved." Blemishes in sacrificial animals or priests are disfiguring, and there is no difference whether the blemish is a birth defect or effected by human intervention. There is therefore a certain logic that such an animal should not be offered to the Deity, and such a disfigured person should not present Him with the offering. In Malachi chap.1, which denounces the offering of blemished animals, there is a clear rationalization of such offerings as insulting and disrespectful to God. The prophet deplores the contempt for God's name, בוזי שמי (v. 6), by the placing of defiled food on His altar מגישים על מזבחי לחם מגאל (v. 7), and then elucidates the precise nature of the wrongdoing: והבאתם גזול ואת הפסח ואת החולה "When you bring plundered, limping or diseased animals [v. 13][79]," or וכי תגישון עור לזבח "When you bring blind animals for sacrifice [v. 8]." The result of this behaviour is the "profanation" of God's name, ואתם מחללים אתו (v. 12), with the same term חלל as used in our pericope. There are two points in support of my postulate. We see that the offering of a plundered animal, which has no bodily alteration in contrast to the crippled, blind or diseased animal, is still מחלל and profanes God's name. It is the change of status which makes it inappropriate, not any physical alteration or divergence from the norm at birth. We also note that it is the corrupted or deteriorating status of blemished animals which makes them מחולל "profane". In contrast, smoothing a stone has no deteriorating effect upon it, and does not defile it. And as we have seen, the term חלל does not occur in Deut. 27: 5 - 6; there is a prohibition against the use of ברזל "iron" in a particular way, and an

---

interesting to note that certain traditional commentators considered the talmudic explanations for the prohibition against using גזית, "dressed stones", as mere homilies, and searched for other explanations. Rashbam suggests that since it is a common fashion to depict figures on dressed stones, an idolatrous practice, their use was forbidden. Ibn Ezra declares, first, that one should not search for motives for the laws, but then speculates that one may consider a logical reason for this prohibition. He then offers a rather convoluted motive: the rock out of which the slabs for the altar were hewn may be used for idolatrous or other sacrilegious purposes, and this would amount to a desecration.

[79] Inexplicably, the NIV translates here "injured, crippled, diseased." While the term פסח could mean "crippled", the term גזול cannot be translated as "injured". The LXX translates this term with ἁρπάγματα, which implies "plundered".

apodictic command requiring the use of אבנים שלמות "whole stones". I would only add that the term תמים in the sense of a physically perfect animal appropriate for sacrifice, which is used by Olyan in his equation, does not occur in Deuteronomy. We do find prohibitions against offering animals "defiled in body," but the term תמים occurs only as a metaphorical concept: תמים תהיה עם ה' אלהיך "You shall be 'perfect' with your Lord God [Deut. 18: 13]," and הצור תמים פעלו "His work is perfect [Deut. 32: 4]."[80]

Finally, I would like to propose a conceivable meaning for the vague term ברזל, employed in Deut. 27: 5. We have seen that the Talmud arrives at the illogical conclusion that the term refers literally to the material "iron", so that cutting the stone with an ax of another material would not have the same defiling effect. We read, however, in Deut. 19: 5: ואשר יבא את רעהו ביער לחטב עצים ונדחה ידו בגרזן לכרת העץ ונשל הברזל מן העץ ומצא את רעהו ומת "A man may go into the forest with his neighbour to cut wood, and as he swings his ax to fell a tree, the "iron" [head of the ax] may fly off and hit his neighbour and kill him." We observe that the indeterminate term "iron", used here in connection with an instrument as in our expression לא תניף עליהם ברזל, refers to an ax, an iron implement for cutting wood or stone. In Deut. ברזל "iron" is considered a useful and worthy substance; in 8: 9, for example, it is indicated among the wealth and boon of the promised land: ארץ אשר אבניה ברזל ומהרריה תחצב נחשת "A land where the rocks are iron and you can dig copper out of the hills." No pejorative notion is attached to the term ברזל,[81] nor to the material itself. Only the term חרב bears in Scripture a connotation of doom, as a man-made homicidal weapon. This contrast is expressed in exhilarating poetic style in the well-known prophetic statement of eschatological expectation: וכתתו חרבותם לאתים וחניתותיהם למזמרות "They will beat their swords into plowshares and their spears into pruning hooks [Isa. 2: 4 and Micah 4: 3]." The plowshares and the pruning hooks are of "iron", just like the swords and the spears; but the first are the symbols of peace and well-being, and the latter of war and ruin, and thus to be kept from any association with the altar, the Deity's dwelling. [82]

---

[80] The LXX translates here ἀληθινὰος "truthful, trusty."

[81] The use of the term בכלי ברזל "an iron object" in Num. 35: 16 to describe a homicidal implement does not contradict my statement. In this case Scripture is attempting to emphasize the principle that in a case of murder the material of which the killing instrument was made is irrelevant. The iron object is mentioned among stone and wooden implements to make them all equivalent in this respect.

[82] It is remarkable that the reverse situation, that is, the shift from peace to war, is expressed with the same symbolism. We read in Joel 4: 10: כתו אתיכם לחרבות ומזמרתיכם לרמחים "Beat your plowshares into swords and your pruning hooks into spears."

1.3 Comparison and Contrast Between Exod. 20: 21-23
and Deut. 27: 5–6

This comparison of the pericopes must necessarily involve a certain repetition and overlapping of ideas and comments already considered, and I beg the reader's indulgence. In addition, I shall include in the criteria of comparison the pragmatic concept of *Sitz im Leben*,[83] which it seems to me can offer important clues for the establishment of the chronological order of the various pericopes. In chap. 3 I shall extend the range of the examination to the issue of the stones used for the building of Solomon's Temple, and attempt to determine whether there is a connection between the building of the Temple and either of our two pericopes.

The literary analysis of the two pericopes in Exod. and Deut. has demonstrated the points at which they diverge, and I shall only recapitulate the main points. In Exod. priority is given to the "formation" of an earthen altar, whereas in Deut. there is no longer any reference to such an altar; there is only a decree to "build" a stone altar. The Hebrew term עשה "make" in Exod. 20: 21 connotes some undetermined activity, but from the context we assume that the intention is to pile up a simple heap of earth and somehow elevate it. We may assume that if an altar of mud bricks were intended, the term used would have been מזבח לבנים. On the other hand, the command to erect a stone altar in Deut. 27: 5 and the prohibition in Exod. 20: 22[84] against building an altar of hewn stones contain the specific term בנה "to build". These differences are crucial to our understanding of the nature of the altars and the attitude toward the cult reflected in the pericopes, and consequently to a determination of the different periods in which each pericope may have been conceived.

---

[83] I do not restrict this term to the classical definition as coined by Gunkel, but intend by it its common meaning of historical setting. It thus comprises the conditions of life, and their philosophical- theological basis, so far as we can deduce them from biblical and non-biblical sources.

[84] The term עשה that occurs in this verse may indicate its affinity with the previously decreed earthen altar; that is, the words ואם...תעשה imply that one is allowed to make a simple altar of heaped-up stones, in contrast to the prohibited building of an elaborate altar of hewn stones, expressed with the appropriate term לא תבנה. One may, however, also consider that the use of עשה with respect to the stone altar is simply a repetition of this term in v. 21 with respect to the earthen altar, a common literary device, while for the specific rules for the construction of the stone altar the appropriate term בנה is utilized. It seems to me that we should opt for the second possibility, since for many of the occurrences of the term בנה with respect to the building of an altar in Scripture, we must assume that it refers to an *ad hoc* heap of natural stones. See chap. 7 n. 33 for a list of the terms used in Scripture for the construction of altars.

A common feature of both pericopes is the absence of any specifications and rules concerning the altar's dimensions[85] (length, width, and height) or form (round, square or oblong), whether the base and the top were of equal dimensions or there was a gradual decrease in size, and whether there were horns.[86] If we compare the lack of any technical description in these two

---

[85] Z. Zevit, "The Earthen Altar Laws of Exodus 20: 24-26 and Related Sacrificial Restrictions in their Cultural Context, in *Texts, Temples and Traditions, A Tribute to Menahem Haran* (Winona Lake, 1996), pp. 53- 62, extrapolates from the prohibition to climb up on steps upon the altar "that an individual would have to be on top of it" (p. 55), and "that the animal offerings be made on an unmistakably artificial surface raised significantly above its natural environs, so much that one might need two or three steps to ascend its top, and that this platform be made of earthen materials" (p. 57). I think that the text of this early command does not hint to any rule regarding the form and character of the altar, or its location, or the type of offerings. The phrase את עלתיך ואת שלמיך is generally assumed to be a later interjection, and this pericope reflects the utmost simplicity and lack of formalism. Furthermore, the issue of the steps is connected exclusively to the stone altar, and I cannot comprehend how it would result from the text that the platform should be made of earthen materials. Solomon's dedication (קדש) of the ground in order to offer sacrifices on it (I Kings 8: 64) indicates that it was the dedication - consecration of a site that made it apt for the cult, not its elevation. I therefore do not think it necessary to enter into a full debate on this rather stretched conjecture concerning the interpretation of the law, and the deduction reached by the author that the elevated altar was required as a measure against chtonic worship.

[86] The Talmud in fact wonders how the returnees from Babylon knew how to build the altar, which was of stone, given that there are no precise descriptions of the stone altar in the Pentateuch. The Rabbis were also aware of the discrepancies between Ezekiel's cultic canon and the Pentateuchal commands. B. T. Menahoth 45a contains a rhetorical discussion of the contradictions between Num. 28-29 and Ezekiel concerning the type and number of offerings; we then read: א"ר יוחנן פרשה זו אליהו עתיד לדורשה "Said Rabbi Johanan: This issue will be solved by Elijah [that is, at his return in the Messianic era]." Then another answer is given: אמר רב יהודה אמר רב זכור אותו האיש לטוב וחנינא בן חזקיה שמו שאלמלא הוא נגנז ספר יחזקאל שהיו דבריו סותרין דברי תורה "Said Rav Judah in the name of Rav: This man, Hanina son of Hizkiah, should be remembered for his excellence because if it were not for him, the book of Ezekiel would have been concealed, because his utterances invalidate commands of the Torah." Rashi explains what is evident from the talmudic text: שיש בסופו דברים בקרבנות שסותרין דברי תורה "Because there are in the last chapters of Ezekiel [those decreeing the cult rules] regulations concerning the sacrifices which invalidate commands of the Torah." Therefore, the Sages do not rely on Ezekiel's description of the altar, and we read in B. T. Zebahim 62a: אלא מזבח מנא ידעי "How did they [the returnees from Babylon] know how and where to build the altar?" After a number of answers, we read: ר"א בן יעקב אומר במתניתא תנא שלשה נביאים עלו עמהן מן הגולה אחד שהעיד להם על המזבח ועל מקום המזבח ואחד שהעיד להם שמקריבין אף על פי שאין בית ואחד שהעיד להם על התורה שתכתב אשורית "We have learned in the Mishnah, Rabbi Eliezer son of Jacob says: Three prophets came with them from the Exodus, one who attested concerning [the building of] the altar and the site of the altar [which had to

pericopes with the complex regulations for the construction of the altar in Ezek. 43: 13 -17 and Exod. 27: 1 - 8, we may grasp the fundamental shift in the concept of the altar and of the cult which must have occurred between the conception of these very divergent manners of sacrificial worship.

I have also drawn attention to the oddities in Exod. 20:21 in the phrase וזבחת עליו את עלתיך ואת שלמיך את צאנך ואת בקרך and my suggestion to consider the expression את עלתיך ואת שלמיך as a later interjection, a proposal which would address the irregularity of applying the term זבח to the offering of the holocaust sacrifice.[87] We would then have in Exod. 20 a portrayal of a non-specific slaughter of animals, in contrast to an established custom of distinct offerings, correctly expressed in Deut. with the technical terms עלה for the holocaust sacrifice and זבח for the peace offering.[88] In the Exod. pericope we find the expression וזבחת עליו "you should slaughter upon it," which demonstrates that the altar was to be used for slaughtering, not burning, and the archeological findings of the Iron Age II confirm this.[89] In Deut. we find an exact description of the two distinct purposes of the two offerings: the holocaust is to be brought up to the altar to be burned[90] והעלית עליו עולת, and the peace offering is to be eaten there, at the altar. The phrase ואכלת שם "eat it there" may also hint[91] at the theology behind this offering,

---

be on exactly the same spot as the previous one], and one who attested that one offers sacrifices even when there is no Temple [as it is recorded in Ezra 3: 2 that the people built the altar and began to bring offerings before the construction of the Temple], and one who attested that the Torah should be written in Assyrian [the new square alphabet, instead of the old Israelite writing]." We observe that the Sages were well aware of the problem that no dimensions for the stone altar are given in the Torah, but they could not conceive that it was built without any divine instruction, especially since in Exod. precise details are set out for each of the Tabernacle furnishings. We may deduce from this lack that before the establishment of a cultic canon in the P stratum of the Pentateuch, no importance was bestowed upon the form and dimension of the altar. The ancient attitude persisted in this regard.

[87] I disagree here with Osumi's doubt about the secondary character of the phrase את עלתיך ואת שלמיך. I believe I have sufficiently substantiated my postulate, and shall corroborate it further through the *Sitz im Leben* theory.

[88] The חטאת "sin offering" is not yet mentioned in this pericope; as scholars generally affirm, it was introduced much later into the sacrificial cult.

[89] See Zwickel, *Der Tempelkult in Kanaan und Israel, Palästinas von der Mittelbronzezeit bis zum Untergang Judas*, Forschungen zum Alten Testament 10 (Tübingen, 1994), p. 283, who states that in Strata X and IX at Arad the great altar was used only for the slaughtering of the animals, not for burning.

[90] Zwickel, ibid., p. 283: the 8th century altar at Tel Beer Sheba provides the oldest evidence of the use of an altar for burning offerings.

[91] It is not the purpose of this study to elaborate on the anthropological origins of the sacrificial cult; I have therefore expressed myself cautiously on this issue. The actual

as a meal of communion. If this is the real intention of the locative adverb,[92] it may offer additional evidence regarding the issue of the priority between the D and P sections of the Pentateuch.[93]

However we interpret the odd form of the verb אזכיר in the phrase בכל המקום in Exod. 20:21, the phrase attests unequivocally to the insignificance of the location, and evidently stresses the ability and in fact requirement to worship God in every place. Deut. 27, on the other hand, indicates a specific place at which to erect the altar and worship God. I have already cited von Rad's statement that the command to build an altar for offerings on Mount Ebal contradicts the reference in Deut. 12: 11 to a concealed location: המקום אשר יבחר ה' אלהיכם "to the place the Lord your God will choose." I have also cited certain rabbinic speculations concerning the prohibition of bamoth. However, a more fundamental issue is why an altar had to be built at all, when presumably the Tabernacle and its bronze altar were still extant.

---

history of the origin of sacrifice would not influence my postulate, one way or another; the purpose of the peace offering, its consumption at a sacred place, demonstrates its archaic origin. One must distinguish this rule from the rules in the P stratum, which in fact prohibit consumption at the altar. The command ואכלתם שם לפני ה' אלהיכם "You should eat there in the presence of the Lord, your God [Deut. 12: 7]" does not refer to the altar, but to the city which will be chosen for the building of God's sanctuary as His dwelling. We read in Mishnah Zebahim: 5: 7 שלמים קדשים קלים ...ונאכלין בכל העיר "Peace offerings - [of] low grade sanctity... are eaten in the entire city." In the other biblical pericopes concerning the peace offering, there is no indication as to where it is to be eaten.

[92] A narrative in B. T. Hagigah 4b may confirm the interpretation that שם in this verse refers to the altar. We read there: רב הונא כי מטי להאי קרא בכי וזבחת שלמים ואכלת שם עבד שרבו מצפה לאכול על שלחנו יתרחק ממנו דכתיב למה לי רב זבחיכם יאמר ה' "When Rav Huna reached this verse, he wept: 'You should slaughter peace offerings and eat there [Deut. 27: 7].' Would a servant whose master looks forward to eating at his table become estranged, as it is written 'What do I need the multitude of your offerings, says the Lord [Isa. 1: 11].'" Rav Huna interprets the term שם to indicate the table presented to the Deity, that is the altar.

[93] The same considerations apply to the absence of the other established sacrifices, such as the sin offering חטאת, which is not mentioned even in the Deuteronomy pericope. The Mekhilta of Rabbi Ishmael, Jethro *Parshah* 11 asks this question on Exod. 20: 21: וזבחת עליו את עלתיך אין לי אלא עולה ושלמים שאר כל הקדשים מניין "[It is written] 'Sacrifice on it your burnt offerings and fellowship offerings'; it would appear that only burnt offerings and fellowship offerings are meant; how do we know that other offerings [should also be offered there]?" The Midrash then applies various stylistic and textual comparisons to include all types of individual and public offerings. Our interest is to demonstrate that the Midrash too questioned why Scripture specifies only two types of sacrifice. The proposal that the sin offering was not yet established offers a straightforward solution, and aids in the establishment of the priority between biblical sections, and of the developmental stages of the sacrificial cult.

Midrash Numbers Rabbah פרשה יד ד״ה ביום השביעי in fact poses this question:

והלא המשכן היה שם וכתיב בתורה איש איש מבית ישראל אשר ישחט
וגו׳ אמר האלהים אני הוא שאמרתי לו שנא׳ ובנית שם מזבח לה׳ אלהיך
מזבח אבנים וגו׳

Was the Tabernacle not there, as it is written in the Torah: 'Any Israelite who sacrifices [...in the camp...instead of bringing it...in front of the Tabernacle...will be cut off from his people'- Lev. 17: 3-4] ? God said: I have ordered him [to build another altar] as it is said: 'Build there an altar to the Lord your God, an altar of stones [Deut. 27: 5].'

Though acknowledging this troublesome contradiction, the Sages could not offer a particularly logical solution;[94] I shall return to this apparently [95] insoluble question below.

Further significant differences in style and concept are evident in the comparison between Exod. 20: 22 and Deut. 27: 5. In Exod. the building of a stone altar is conditional, whereas in Deut. it is apodictic. In Exod. the use of גזית "hewn" or" cut" stones for the building of the altar is prohibited, but in Deut. the term גזית is not present; in fact, the term גזית occurs in the Pentateuch only in Exod. 20: 22. In Exod., the phrase כי חרבך הנפת עליה ותחללה serves as a rationalization for the preceding prohibition לא תבנה אתהן גזית, whereas in Deut. the apparently parallel phrase לא תניף עליהם ברזל represents the prohibition itself, and the justification for the prohibition is the following apodictic command אבנים שלמות תבנה. In Exod., we have a precise indication of the implement which defiles the stones, חרבך "your sword", which has as its justification the timeless ideal of the separation between the sacred (altar) and the profane (manslaughter). In Deut. the prohibition is against wielding ברזל,[96] the general term "iron", which gives no indication of the particular implement or the rationalization. As we have seen, the term חלל "to profane" or "to defile", a cultic concept utilized extensively in the P stratum of the Pentateuch, occurs in Exod. to describe the outcome of the prohibited action, and at the same time its ultimate motive. This cultic concept occurs nowhere in the Book of Deuteronomy.[97]

---

94 The solution offered in certain midrashim (cited above) was that a prophet could allow for such an exception; Joshua, who built the altar on Mount Ebal (Jos. 8: 31), was a prophet.

95 The Midrash answers the question of how it was permitted to build a *bamah* during the existence of the Tabernacle, but the more intriguing query is: why was it necessary to build an altar at all when the Tabernacle and all its furnishings were in use?

96 As we have seen, ברזל as a substance has no unfavourable connotation in Scripture; it is solely the implement and its application which are abominable, regardless of its material. See n. 81.

97 The verb חלל appears three times in Deut., in 20: 6 twice and in 28: 30, but in these occurrences it refers to enjoying the fruits of a vineyard.

We come now to Exod. 20: 23, the last verse in that pericope, which has no counterpart in the Deut. pericope. In addition to confirming the diversity between the two pericopes, the verse raises a further issue: does this last restriction in verse 23 refer to the earthen altar, to the stone altar, or to both? We have seen that the rules for the earthen altar constitute an independent pericope, complete with all relevant details, whereas the rules for the stone altar rely in great measure on the specifics expressed concerning the earthen altar, particularly with respect to purpose and location. Based on literary analysis, it would seem that verse 22 with its incomplete rules for the stone altar was a later addition to the text, whether incorporated during oral or written transmission. Literary analysis also confirms the common characteristics of verses 22 and 23. Both start with a negative: לא תבנה and ולא תעלה,[98] and each command is followed by the motive. Verse 21, with the rules concerning the earthen altar, has no negative, and consists only of an apodictic command. Following this line of thought, we may conclude that verse 23, which prohibits climbing on steps to the altar, refers to the stone altar. A practical consideration would also confirm this postulate: one may suppose that the earthen altar was a temporary, relatively low pile of accumulated earth; one could not stand on it, nor did one need to go up on steps to reach its peak, because of its low elevation. The fabrication of earthen steps would also seem to be a doubtful enterprise. These practical objections are elegantly answered if we assume that verse 23 refers exclusively to the stone altar. Verses 22 and 23 constitute an integral unit concerning this altar, and were subsequently added to the original Law of the Altar, which was based on rudimentary, archaic custom. We should also note the similarity of motive in verses 22 and 23. Although the outcome of the prohibition in v. 23 is not mentioned, we must assume that the exposure of nakedness would have the same effect as the prohibited act in v. 22, namely the profanation of the altar. The term ותחללה "you will profane it," applies to both prohibitions; it was not necessary to repeat it concerning the profanation of the altar by sexually inappropriate behaviour, as this was self-explanatory.[99]

---

[98] I do not rely on the conjunctive ו "and", since the previous verse 22 starts with the same conjunction; the form was utilized by the redactor to create a unified pericope, and does not bear witness to the separate origin of each of the verses.

[99] We read in the Mekhilta d'Rabbi Ishmael a homily on the prohibition against climbing upon the altar: מס׳ דבחדש יתרו פרשה יא ד״ה אשר לא: והרי דברים ק״ו ומה אם אבנים שאין בהן דעת לא לרעה ולא לטובה אמר הקדוש ברוך הוא לא תנהג בזיון בהן מנהג "We are to deduce [from this interdiction] *ad majorem*: If God has prohibited dishonourable behaviour with regard to the stones, which have no understanding of bad and good [all the more so should dishonourable behaviour be

Scholars have queried the prohibition against climbing up the altar on steps, a ban which would have been violated by the altar built by Solomon. There is no reference to an altar built by Solomon in Kings; the only such reference is in Chr.[100] Scholars also note the requirement that priests wear undergarments (Exod. 28: 42), which would invalidate the motive "lest your nakedness be exposed" and thus render the prohibition superfluous. Dillmann,[101] though he fails to consider the possibility that these apparently contradictory rules[102] derive from different periods and sources, offers an attractive solution. The Law of the Altar, he proposes, applies to all the people, and they are prohibited from going up on steps, whereas the requirement to put on undergarments is directed only to the priests. The bronze altar, three cubits high, certainly had steps, and this was the reason the priests were ordered to don undergarments. Dillmann further contemplates that the reason for the prohibition against building steps for the altar may have been originally similar to that for the ban against cutting the stones: a desire, he suggests, to use only materials in their natural state for the altar, with no man-made alterations. Sarna, in his commentary to Exodus, generally follows the same path, declaring "The instruction is clearly intended for the layman," but contrary to Dillmann suggests that this regulation was intended to oppose the ancient Near Eastern custom of officiating "in the nude." Sarna also cites Ezek. 43: 17, where the presence of steps to the altar is explicitly affirmed; he relies on the command that the priests wear breeches (Ezek. 44:

---

avoided in other situations]." We observe that the Sages understood the reason for this prohibition as avoidance of a dishonourable deed, hence a profanation.

[100] We read in II Chr. 4: 1: ויעש מזבח נחשת "He [Solomon] made a bronze altar," and in II Chr. 7: 7: כי מזבח הנחשת אשר עשה שלמה "...because the bronze altar Solomon had made...." In the parallel phrase to the second citation in I Kings 8: 64 we read: כי מזבח הנחשת אשר לפני ה' "...because the bronze altar before the Lord...," with no indication as to the builder.

[101] *Exodus und Leviticus*, p. 248.

[102] The Rabbis were, as usual, aware of this contradiction, and several midrashim attempt to reconcile this apparent inconsistency. We read in the Mekhilta of Rabbi Ishmael Jethro *Parshah* 11: ד"ה ולא תעלה: והלא כבר נאמר ועשה להם מכנסי בד לכסות בשר ערוה וגו' ומה ת"ל אשר לא תגלה ערותך עליו שלא יפסע בו פסיעה גסה אלא גודל בצד עקב ועקב בצד גודל "Since it was already said 'Make linen undergarments as a covering for the body [Exod. 28: 42]' why is the reason [for the prohibition against going up on steps to the altar] given as 'not to expose your nakedness'? [This teaches us] not to walk [on the altar] with large steps, but [slowly] heel after big toe [i.e. a symbol of piety and submission]." I thus understand the term פסיעה גסה as metaphorical, but Rashi explains in his commentary to Exod. 20: 23 that climbing on stairs requires a larger step than going up on a ramp, and such a large step is equivalent to "an exposure of nakedness."

18) to conclude that the prohibition against climbing up the altar on steps would be irrelevant for them. Noth[103] comments only that in Exod. 28: 42 "there is a later regulation of a different kind," that is, to put on undergarments. Osumi[104] puts in question the hypothesis of these and other scholars that the wearing of breeches excluded the priests from the prohibition against climbing up the altar, and proposes to consider the dictate in Exod. 20: 23 as a censuring and ridiculing of the ziggurat step-altar, and an indication of a conflict concerning the rules of the cult. Osumi asserts, therefore, that the Exod. altar law originates from the period of Amos.[105]

A question may be posed here. Scripture takes great care to expressly articulate the problem of the steps to the altar,[106] and also offers a justification for the restriction: to avoid the exposure of one's nakedness on the altar. The Rabbis concentrated on the word steps.[107] It seems that in fact the altar of the Second Temple had a sloping ramp to climb up. We find evidence of this in Mishnah Midoth 5: 2: מן הצפון לדרום מאה ושלשים וחמש הכבש והמזבח ששים ושתים "From the north to the south [the court was] one hundred and thirty [cubits], the altar and the ramp [had a dimension of] sixty-two [cubits]." In Mishnah 3: 1 we learn the dimensions of the altar itself: המזבח היה שלשים ושתים על שלשים ושתים "The altar [had dimensions of] thirty-two square [cubits]." Hence the ramp was thirty cubits long, the necessary length of a slope reaching to a height of ten cubits,[108] the

---

[103] *Exodus*, p. 177.

[104] p. 161.

[105] Zwickel, *Der Tempelkult in Kanaan und Israel*, p. 291 note 24, rejects Osumi's proposition for both textual and archeological reasons.

[106] We find interesting support for this assertion in אוצר המדרשים (Eisentstein), p. 194: כל מעלות במעלות מלאין בר מן א' לא תעלה במעלת חסר וי"ו ולמה שאפילו עלה מעלה אחת נפסלת "All the occurrences of מעלות [in the Bible] are written with a ו except the one in our verse [Exod. 20: 23], where it appears without a ו [orthography which suggests a singular form], and why? [This teaches us] that even going up one step is not allowed." We observe two important statements in this Midrash: a) that even one step up to the altar is not allowed, and b) that since Scripture promulgates in these verses the Law of the Altar, the prohibition does not refer to the officiant who transgresses the law by climbing on the altar; it is rather the altar which becomes blemished and disqualified.

[107] We read in the Mekhilta d'Rabbi Ishmael, Jethro, *Parshah* 11: ולא תעלה במעלת על מזבחי מכאן אמרו עשה כבש למזבח "'Do not go up on my altar on steps'; from this we learn: make a ramp for the altar."

[108] We read in B. T. Zebahim 59b: מה משכן י' אמות אף מזבח י' אמות "As the [posts in the court of the] Tabernacle [according to Rashi's explanation] are ten cubits high, so is the height of the altar." From Ezekiel's description of the construction of the altar (43: 13 -

height of the altar. There is also a confirmation from Josephus in War V: 225 that the altar had a sloping ramp. We read there: κερατοειδεῖς προανέχων γωνίας καὶ ἀπὸ μεσημβρίας ἐπ' αὐτὸν ἄνοδος ἠρέμα προσάντης ὑπτίαστο "...with horn-like projections at the corners, and approached from the south by a gently sloping acclivity."

The question is, therefore, whether one's nakedness is affected differently according to whether one climbs up on steps or on a ramp. If one wears breeches, there is no nakedness, but if one does not wear them and then stands on top of the altar, one's nakedness is still exposed, regardless of the way one reached the top. As we have seen,[109] the Mekhilta of Rabbi Ishmael is aware of this difficulty, and offers an answer, though a rather tenuous one.[110] It seems to me, therefore, that another reason must underlie this decree.

---

17), the altar would have a total height of ten cubits, including the base under the pavement and excluding the horns, or, taking into account the visible components, including the horns and excluding the base. Cf. Zimmerli, *Ezekiel 2, A Commentary on the Book of the Prophet Ezekiel, Chapters 25-48*, translated by J. D. Martin. (Philadelphia, 1983), p. 427, on 43: 13 - 17.

[109] See n. 102.

[110] I suggest that the ramp at the altar in the Second Temple period was not constructed as a practical solution to the problem of "exposing one's nakedness"; exposure occurs whether one climbs on a ramp or on stairs, and the problem obviously does not apply to the priests who wore linen breeches. This construction was merely the result of the people's strict adherence to the scriptural text: since Scripture prohibits climbing on stairs, they built a ramp. We find similar interpretations in rabbinic literature, and I shall quote some examples relating to the subject of our study. We read in Tosefta Sotah (Liebermann) 15: 1: והגרזן כל כלי ברזל לא נשמע... אלא מתקנין אותן מבחוץ ומכניסין אותן לפנים "'No ax and any other iron tool was heard [...at the Temple] [I Kings 6: 7],' and this verse contradicts another verse [I Kings 5: 31, 5: 17 in KJV], where we are told that אבני גזית dressed stones worked with iron tools were used for the Temple, and the answer is] they [the stones] were dressed outside the Temple precinct, and brought in afterwards." The prohibition against using iron tools, given its connection to the construction of the altar, was considered by the Rabbis to be limited in application only to the Temple precinct; this is illogical, as I shall discuss in section 3.2. Another such literal interpretation is found in Tosefta Baba Qama 7: 6: מזבח אבנים לא תניף עליהן ברזל וכי מה ראה הכתו' לפסול את הברזל יותר מכל מיני מתכות מפני שהחרב נעשית ממנו והחרב סימן פורענות "[Scripture says] 'Do not wield iron upon them [Deut. 27: 5].' Why has Scripture made a ban on iron out of all the metals? Because the sword is made of it, and the sword is a symbol of affliction." In fact, the Mekhilta of Rabbi Simeon bar Johai 20: 22 distinguishes between an iron tool which defiles the stone simply by touching and producing a scar, and other tools which defile only by chipping off a piece. Ramban, in his commentary to Exod. 20: 21, writes: ואם בא לסתת אותן בכלי כסף או בשמיר שהזכירו רבותינו (סוטה מח ב) הרי זה מותר "But if one uses a silver implement or the legendary worm to dress the stones, as our Sages mentioned (B.T. Sotah 48b), it is allowed." The rabbinic system of interpretation would probably

I propose a suggestion based on two disparate sources: the modern scholar Dillmann and a midrashic citation. Dillmann comments in one of his deliberations on the motive for the regulation in Exod. 20: 23 : "Der Altar soll also niedrig sein und ein allmählicher Aufgang hinaufführen"[111] ("The altar should be low and a sloping way should lead upwards.") I assume that Dillmann was influenced by the evidence in the Mishnah and Josephus that the altar in the Second Temple had such a sloping ascent, while his interpretation demonstrates his opinion that this verse implies that the altar was a low structure. I encountered a similar interpretation of this verse in the Mekhilta of Rabbi Simeon bar Johai, chap. 20, v. 23:

...הייתי אומר יכול יהא מזבח קטן ויעמוד בארץ ויקטיר ת״ל והעלה הכהן
את העלה ואת המנחה המזבחה אם כן למה נאמר במעלות שלא יעשה לו
מעלות

...I would have interpreted [this verse to imply] a small [= low] altar where the priest stands on the ground and offers, [but we cannot understand it in this way, because] it is written 'And the priest should bring up the holocaust and the *Minhah* upon the altar [Lev. 14: 20],' [and from this we learn that the altar had to be high];[112] what is then the meaning of [the prohibition not to go up] on steps? [The command implies] that one is not to make steps to the altar [but rather a sloping ascent].

---

have allowed the use of any other metal except iron, as Ramban deduces, if it were not for the parallel law of the altar in Exod. 20, which prohibits the use of a sword, and the usual rabbinic harmonization system. We read in the same chapter of the Mekhilta an explanation which Ramban seems to have overlooked: לא תבנה אתהן גזית מכלל שנ׳ כי חרבך הנפת [יכול ל]א יהו פסולות אלא אם כן נתגזזו בחרב תל׳ לו׳ לא תניף [עליהם בר]זל הרי ברזל כחרב "[It is written in Exod. 20: 22] 'Do not build them of dressed stones'; since it is said 'because you wielded your sword' we would have understood that the prohibition applies only when [the stones] were cut with a sword [but not with another tool]. Therefore it is written 'Do not wield iron upon them [Deut. 27: 5].' to compare iron to a sword." We observe that from the Exod. law alone, the Rabbis would have deduced that only the use of a sword is prohibited, as the literal prohibition in Scripture reads, but that the use of another tool is permitted. There are many such examples in the Talmud, but I think the above suffice to corroborate the proposition that the ramp of the altar in the Second Temple was constructed based on a literal interpretation of the prohibition against climbing on stairs: stairs are forbidden, but a ramp is permitted.

[111] p. 248

[112] In fact, we cannot deduce from this verse that the altar had to be high. Though a low altar is only an accumulation of one foot of earth and stones, one still has to put the offering on top, and therefore the use of the term והעלה הכהן "the priest should bring up / put upon" is appropriate. Moreover, there is nothing to exclude the priest standing on a low altar and celebrating the offering, slaughtering it, as was done in the earliest stage, or even burning it. This would also explain a phrase such as ויעל על המזבח....להקטיר "He went up on the altar...to offer [I Kings 12: 33]."

We observe that the Sages would have interpreted Exod. 20:23 as requiring a low altar,[113] if it were not for the apparently contradictory rule in Leviticus requiring the "bringing up" of the sacrifice upon the altar. It is not within the scope of this study to determine whether the use of the term עלה in the latter verse implies the "going up" of the priest, or merely the "bringing up" of the offering, without the necessity of the priest also climbing up on the altar. Other verses in Scripture do indicate such a procedure,[114] such as וירד מעשת החטאת "And [Aaron] stepped down after

---

[113] It is remarkable that a traditional commentator such as Radak also considered that the Israelite law of the altar required a low altar to be built. In his commentary to Ezek. 20: 29 מה הבמה אשר אתם הבאים שם "What is this high place you are going to?" he writes:.אמרתי להם מה הבמה מי צוה אתכם לעשות במה גבוה הלא צויתי אתכם מזבח אדמה תעשה לי אלא שאתם למדים ממעשה הגוים לעשות מזבח גבוה שנקרא במה "I said to them: What is the high place? Who commanded you to build a high place? I commanded you to build an earthen altar, but you learned from the gentiles to build a high altar, called *bamah*." As I have mentioned, traditional commentators sometimes interpreted biblical verses according to their plain meaning, when they did not take into account that an integrated view of all related verses might conflict with such an interpretation.

[114] I do not think that I Kings 12: 33 and 13: 1, narrating the story of Jeroboam's offerings, invalidates my postulate. We read twice in 12: 33: ויעל על המזבח, but as we know, the term עלה came to be a *terminus technicus* for the offering of the holocaust עולה. It is interesting that the traditional commentator Radak interprets the phrase ויעל על המזבח אשר עשה. העלה עליו עולות וזבחים "...he brought up on it holocausts and peace offerings." In 13: 1, on the other hand, we read וירבעם עמד על המזבח להקטיר "And Jeroboam stood on [or at] the altar." I suggest translating על as "at", as both the KJV and NIV have done, probably relying on the LXX, which has εἱστήκει ἐπὶ τὸ θυσιαστήριον "he put into place on the altar"; that is, there is no suggestion Jeroboam stood on the altar. The Targum translates the term מזבח as אגורא " a heathen altar," and consequently suggests that the verse does not reflect Israelite custom. I would also add that the prophecy against Jeroboam in chap. 13 announcing the birth of Josiah and the destruction of the altar, later fulfilled in II Kings 23: 16, is obviously a later aetiological addition, and does not bear witness to the size of the altar and the manner of offering in the period of origin of Exod. 20: 23. At any rate, even if we assume that in Jeroboam's period high altars were actually built, this would not contradict the fact that originally only low altars were the custom, and Exod. 20: 23 represents the archaic nomadic tradition. A further corroboration of my postulate may be deduced from II Sam. chap. 6, which describes the offerings performed at the transfer of the ark by David to the City of David. As I shall discuss more fully below, it is evident that no elaborate altars could have been built along the ark's route, and one must assume that the offerings were performed on the ground, or on simple, low *ad hoc* altars. There is no mention of an existing altar at the tent, and no record that an altar was built by David, though other such altars are recorded (for example, the altar at Araunah's threshing floor). Nevertheless, Scripture uses the technical term עלה for these celebrations. We read in vv. 17 - 18: ויעל דוד עלות

having offered the sin offering [Lev. 9:22]."[115] However, this concept appears in the P stratum of the Pentateuch, and dates from a period[116] in

---

ויכל דוד מהעלות העולה...'לפני ה' "And David sacrificed burnt offerings....After David had finished sacrificing the burnt offerings...."

[115] In fact, the text does not clearly require an interpretation that Aaron stepped down from the altar. One would expect for such an action וירד מן המזבח, as Targum Jonathan interprets the phrase ונחת מן מדבחא; Rashi too adds מעל המזבח "from the altar." Rashi's commentator שפתי חכמים explains that Rashi added this clarification so that we would not interpret that Aaron stepped down after having blessed the people. This would be the simple interpretation of the verse, and would imply that Aaron performed the blessing before the celebration of the offerings. We read in B. T. Megilah 18a: וירד מעשת החטאת והעלה והשלמים אימא קודם עבודה לא סלקא דעתך דכתיב וירד מעשת החטאת וגו' מי כתיב לעשות מעשת כתיב "It is written 'And he went down from performing the sin offering....' I might understand that it means before the offering? [No] that is unreasonable, since it is written 'from performing,' not 'to perform.'" Y. T. Ta'anith 4: 1, 67c actually confirms that the text is corrupted: וישא אהרן את ידו אל העם המקרא הזה מסורס הוא והלא לא צריך לומר אלא וירד מעשות החטאת והעולה והשלמים ואחר כך וישא אהרן את ידיו וגו' אלא מלמד שבירידתו למזבח היה נושא את כפיו ומברך את העם "And Aaron raised his hand [Lev. 9: 22].' This verse is misstated; it should have said first 'and he went down after having offered the sin offering, the burnt offering and the peace offering,' and afterwards 'and Aaron raised his hands,' but it teaches us that at his stepping-down from the altar he raised his hand and blessed the people." We note that the rabbinic interpretation, which seems logical, perceives that the blessing of the people was performed after the offerings were brought upon the altar. From Siracides we also learn that the blessing was performed after the offerings. In 50: 19 we read: καὶ τὴν λειτουργίαν αὐτου ἐτελείωσαν "and they finished their services," and in v. 20 we read: τότε καταβας ἐπῆρεν χεῖρας αὐτου "Then going down he raised his hands [for the blessing]." We read in Mishnah Tamid 7: 2 (6: 5 in another MS): באו ועמדו על מעלות האולם...וברכו את העם ברכה אחת...במדינה הכהנים נושאים את ידיהם "They came [after having accomplished their service] and stood on the steps of the *Ulam*...and blessed the people with one blessing ...in the provinces the priests raised their hands ...." There is an apparent contradiction between this Mishnah and Mishnah 5: 1 regarding the blessing; Maimonides and Tosafoth propose different solutions to reconcile the two mishnahs, but a detailed discussion is beyond the scope of our study. For our purpose, it suffices to demonstrate that the Sages also confirmed the oddity of this verse. Moreover, the association of וירד "he went down" with מעשת "from doing" is an uncommon expression. We may propose from the above arguments that the phrase has resulted from an alteration of the original text, either by accretion or eradication. The traditional interpretation "he went down from the altar" also raises some difficulties in logic. The bronze altar, which would seem to be the relevant altar in the context, was three cubits high, about the height of a man, and such an elevation would not require Aaron to climb upon the altar for the performance of the offering celebration. Ibn Ezra, in his straightforward fashion, seems to be aware of this oddity, and emphasizes the "going down," since the altar was three cubits high. We may agree that Aaron had to step down from such a height, but we still do not understand how he got up, or where he stood. There were no steps or ramp attached to the bronze altar, and there was no platform on its roof. We observe in Exod. 30: 3 that the golden altar had

a roof, גג, but the bronze altar had only a bronze net. The Talmud and the traditional commentators also address this problem. Rashi on Exod. 20: 20 cites the proposal in B. T. Zebahim 61b that the hollow space between the walls of the altar was filled with earth: שהוא אטום באדמה "solid with earth"; the Mekhilta d'Rabbi Ishmael, Jethro *Parshah* 11 states specifically: מזבח נחשת מלא אדמה תעשה לי "a bronze altar filled with earth...." But these homilies constitute dubious rhetoric, attempting to harmonize between the contradictory altar laws, and do not consider other practical issues. Aaron would not have been able to stand upon such a bronze net on top of the altar, because it would not offer him stability, and would be extremely hot due to the fire and burning coals upon it. The Second Temple altar was built of stones and had a gangway around it, where the priests stood and performed the offering celebrations, but there is nothing of this kind for the bronze altar, according to the simple and straightforward interpretation of Exod. 27: 1 - 8. The issue of where the priests stood at the performance of the offering celebrations at the Second Temple altar is also not very clear. Ezekiel's description of the step-altar does not elucidate where the priest stood. A Baraita cited in B. T. Zebahim 62b quotes a tannaitic dispute on this issue: אומר היה ר״ש בן יוחי אויר יש בין כבש למזבח אמר לו ואתה אי אתה אומר כן והלא כבר נאמר ועשית עלתיך הבשר והדם מה דם בזריקה אף בשר בזריקה אמר לו שאני אומר עומד בצד מערכה וזורק "Rabbi Simeon ben Johai said: There is an empty space between the ramp and the altar. He asked him [Rabbi Jose:] Don't you agree to that? Since it is written 'Present your burnt offerings, both the meat and the blood [Deut. 12:27],' just as the blood must be sprinkled, so the meat must be tossed [and therefore there must be a space between the ramp where the priest stood and the altar, so that the priest could toss onto an empty space]. He [Rabbi Jose] answered: I say he stood [on the top of the altar] at the edge of the burning site and threw [the pieces of flesh]." According to the opinion of one Tanna, the priest stood on the ramp and tossed the flesh from there, while the other maintained that the priest stood on the top of the altar itself. That the priests actually threw the pieces of flesh is corroborated in the *Letter of Aristeas* 93, where we read: ἀναρρίπτουσιν ἑκατέραις θαυμασίως ὕψος ἱκανὸν καὶ οὐχ ἁμαρτάνουσι τῆς ἐπιθέως "...and they throw each wonderfully sufficiently in height and do not miss the place." From the text we gather that they threw upward, and thus may conclude that the priests stood on the סובב "gangway" in the middle of the altar, or on the ramp at that height, and not on the top platform. Although we read in Mishnah Midoth 3: 1: מקום הילוך רגלי הכהנים אמה מזה ואמה מזה "The place where the priests walked was one cubit on each side [between the corners/ horns, that is, at the upper platform]," this may have been for other works, such as arranging the wood on the altar, ensuring all of the meat was burning, and cleaning the ashes; but for throwing the pieces of flesh, they stood on the lower platform. This method also allowed the priests to avoid the great fire on the top of the altar. They did go up to the top platform in the morning, when the fire was low, to ensure the burning of the pieces which were not burned during the night, as we read in Mishnah Tamid 2: 1: נטלו את המגריפות ואת הציונורות ועלו לראש המזבח האברין והפדרין שלא נתאכלו מבערב סונקין אותן לצדדי המזבח "They took the rakes and the hoes and went up on the top of the altar; the limbs and the inner parts from the evening, not yet burned, were pushed to the sides of the altar." Thus the method of throwing the flesh became an "official" command through appropriate midrashic interpretation of a scriptural verse, and the existence of an empty space between the ramp and the altar was conceived in order to comply with this method.

which the custom of building a low altar was no longer observed. The talmudic scholars were compelled to harmonize the different verses and adjust them to their particular circumstances, but we are free to interpret each verse on its own merit and reach a different conclusion. Hence, I suggest interpreting verse 23 as intending the construction of a simple low altar of unhewn stones, upon which the offerer does not have to climb to slaughter his animals. Remaining at the side and not on the top of the altar, his nakedness would not be exposed on the altar. Such an interpretation would be consistent with the antecedent command to build a simple altar of unhewn stones.

The custom of building a low altar, or of simply offering on a rock or on a large stone, is corroborated by I Kings 8: 64: ביום ההוא קדש המלך את תוך החצר אשר לפני בית ה׳ כי עשה שם את העלה ואת המנחה ואת חלבי השלמים "On that day the king consecrated the middle of the courtyard in front of the Temple of the Lord, and there he offered burnt offerings, grain offerings and the fat of peace offerings." Scripture does not specify the precise meaning of תוך החצר, but we must understand it as literally "on the ground," and J. Gray so interprets it.[117] He writes: "It is suggested that the famous rock under the present Dome of the Rock served as an altar."[118] The Talmud too remarks that the whole ground of the court was dedicated for the offering of sacrifices. In B. T. Zebahim 59a, Rabbi Judah comments on the above verse: דברים ככתבן "Matters are [to be understood literally] as written," and Rashi explains that Solomon consecrated the entire pavement of the court to offer sacrifices, because the altar was too small. Rabbi Jose argues with Rabbi Judah about the interpretation of the term קטן מהכיל "too small to hold the offerings [I Kings 8: 64]," but there is no controversy

---

Another verse may imply a high altar: I Kings 1: 53, וירדהו מעל המזבח "and he brought him down from the altar," a verse I shall discuss in connection with the issue of the "horns". It is interesting that Noth, *Könige*, p. 29 translates the verb as: "herunterholen" "to fetch down" and puts the word in quotation marks to stress its special interpretation; he adds that according to this expression, one must assume that Solomon's palace was lower than the sanctuary and the altar. Noth attempts to reconcile between v. 51, where we read that Adonijah clung to the horns of the altar, and v. 53 in which it is recorded that he was "taken down" from the altar. He interprets the verse to imply that Adonijah was fetched down to Solomon, and the verb refers to this move downward to Solomon's palace, and not to his being taken down from the altar. Rehm too translates וירדהו simply as "wegholen" "to fetch away," with no explanation for this apparently imprecise translation.

[116] The reference to the sin-offering also demonstrates the late origin of this verse.

[117] J. Gray, *I and II Kings,* Revised Edition, Old Testament Library (London, 1970), p. 233.

[118] Gray debates whether such an identification could be demonstrated, but it suffices for our purpose to establish that the sacrifices were offered on the ground.

between them concerning the fact that Solomon arranged for the offering on the ground.[119] Such a resolution to offer sacrifices on the ground[120] could only be conceived and performed if we assume that it was comparable to the archaic custom of bringing offerings on a simple pile of earth, in conformity with the rule in Exod. 20: 21.[121] Were the usual altars elaborate and of monumental proportions, such as for example the Babylonian ziggurat, or the lavishly adorned Mesopotamian presentation tables, it would have been contemptuous to present offerings to the Deity on the bare ground.

Further support for the proposition that the altar was a low structure may be deduced from the description of the altar in I Kings 18: 26. We read there of the behaviour of the prophets of Baal concerning their altar: ויפסחו על המזבח אשר עשה "And they hobbled up on the altar, which they had made."[122] From this verse we may deduce that the altar was low and thus the prophets could dance upon it.[123]

---

[119] There is explicit permission to offer on the ground in the Mekhilta d'Rabbi Simeon bar Johai 20: 21: מנ' לא יכולתה להקטיר על גבי המזבח הקטר על גבי אדמה תל' לו' מזבח אדמה תעשה לי "From where do we know that if you are unable to offer on the altar, you may offer on the earth? Because it is said 'Make for me an altar of earth.'"

[120] It is interesting to note that certain Sages still clung to the opinion that an altar was not indispensable for the offering of sacrifices, and a simple stone was also appropriate. Mishnah Zebahim 13: 3 records the prohibition against offering sacrifices outside the Temple: רבי יוסי אומר ...ואינו חיב עד שיעלה לראש המזבח. רבי שמעון אומר אפלו העלה על הסלע או על האבן חיב "Rabbi Jose says...he is only guilty when he lifts [the offering and places it] on top of the altar. Rabbi Simeon says: He is guilty when he merely lifts [the offering and places it] on a rock or a stone." The rhetoric in the relevant Gemara to explain the different opinions is even more interesting. We read in B. T. Zebahim 108b: מאי טעמא דרבי יוסי דכתיב ויבן נח מזבח לה'...מאי טעמא דר"ש דכתיב ויקח מנוח את גדי העזים ואת המנחה ויעל על הצור לה' ואידך נמי והכתיב ויבן מזבח לה' ההוא גובהה בעלמא "What is the reason for Rabbi Jose's [opinion that only by placing the offering upon an altar is he guilty]? Because it is written 'And Noah built an altar to the Lord [Gen. 8: 20].'...What is the reason for Rabbi Simeon's opinion? Because it is written 'Then Manoah took a young goat together with the grain offering and placed it on the rock to the Lord [Jud. 13: 19]' [hence the placing on a rock is a legitimate offering to the Lord, and an altar is not an absolute requirement]. What about the verse that Noah built an altar to the Lord? [A:] The altar [built by Noah] was just an [efficient] elevated platform, but not a prerequisite [to performing an offering]."

[121] It is not necessary for our purposes to elaborate on the issue of whether this verse is of deuteronomic origin in its entirety, as Noth suggests in *Könige*, p. 191; it seems to me that because of their distinct style, certain elements such as the phrase את העלה ואת המנחה ואת חלבי השלמים are a later priestly interjection.

[122] This is the translation of J. Gray, in *I & II Kings, A Commentary*, The Old Testament Library, Second Fully Revised Edition (London 1970). It also corrects the verb עשה,

which appears in singular in the MT text; Gray follows in this respect the LXX: καὶ διέτρεχον ἐπὶ τοῦ θυσιαστηρίου οὗ ἐποίησαν "and they run over [Liddell and Scott] the altar which **they** made." The LXX uses the preposition ἐπι, which, with the following noun in genitive, is to be translated as "on, upon". The parallel expression ἐπὶ Βωμου is common in Greek literature, and implies "upon the altar." I. Benzinger, in *Die Bücher der Könige*, Kurzer Hand-Commentar zum Alten Testament, Abt. IX (Freiburg i.B., 1899), suggests interpreting the biblical phrase as "'Umkreisen des Altars," that is, circling the altar, not dancing upon it. He refers to the term פסחים in II Kings 18: 21, but he does not consider that the LXX, on which he based his interpretation of that term, translates פסחים as χωλαίνω "to go lame," whereas in our verse the LXX uses the term διατρέξω "to run over, to cross." The KJV translates "They leaped upon the altar which was made," in order to avoid a direct contradiction to the MT text. Only the NIV, probably because of the difficulty in envisaging a low altar upon which one could dance, interprets "they danced around the altar they had made." The Targum translates על /ואשתטו/ ואשטטו אגורא דעבד "They engaged themselves in ecstatic exercises on the heathen altar [Jastrow]." Among the traditional commentators, Rashi and Radak quote the Targum's interpretation and affirm clearly that the action took place על המזבח "upon the altar." Only Ralbag interprets שהיו הולכים ושבים אצל המזבח "they were going back and forth at the altar." Ralbag also attempts to solve the issue of the singular form of the term עשה, and interprets it "which Ahab made."

One must admit that there is no indication in this pericope that the prophets of Baal made an altar; we might have expected a record of such a fact similar to the report that Elijah repaired the altar of the Lord (v. 30). There is evidence from other sources that a Canaanite Baal sanctuary and altar were present on the Carmel; we might assume that the compiler of the narrative knew of this fact, and thus attributed this particular altar to Ahab. Although Gray translated, as I have quoted above, "on the altar," he writes in his commentary on p. 397 that "the precise significance of the preposition על is uncertain here. It may indicate 'about', 'by the side of', or even 'before', or it may signify the ascent up to the altar by steps"; he does not deem the latter proposition applicable. Gray prefers de Vaux's interpretation of "a ritual dance about the altar." I do not see any reason to discard the simple interpretation of the phrase, that is, "upon the altar," as the LXX, the Targum and traditional commentators have translated it, if we assume that the altars in that period were of a simple and low construction. We must observe that both in v. 23 and in v. 33, we are told that the cut pieces of the ox were put on the wood, וישימו על העצים; the wood is in the foreground of the narrative and is granted the most significance. As in other occurrences, it is the importance of the wood in the sacrificial cult which is emphasized, and not the altar. We must compare this style with the numerous expressions in Leviticus where the altar is featured, such as Lev. 1: 8 and 12: על העצים אשר על האש אשר על המזבח "...on the burning wood that is on the altar," or v. 17: והקטיר...המזבחה על העצים אשר על האש "...shall burn it on the wood that is on the fire on the altar." The altar has prominence in these verses, and in other verses of the P stratum of the Pentateuch. In 33 instances, the term קטר is explicitly linked to the מזבח, and it is linked implicitly in two other verses. In sum, the text of I Kings 18: 30-32 is inconsistent regarding the altar, and the LXX has another version, a fact which indicates later changes to the text to adapt it to changed conditions; thus the passage cannot serve as definite evidence. I have, therefore, no hesitation in assuming that the altars were simple and low structures, which the Baal prophets could dance upon.

Yet another biblical narrative validates my thesis. We read in II Sam. 6: 13, at the transfer of the ark to the City of David: ויהי כי צעדו נשאי ארון ה' ששה צעדים ויזבח שור ומריא "When those who were carrying the ark of the Lord had taken six steps, he sacrificed a bull and a fattened calf." It is not clear from the text whether a bull and calf were sacrificed every six steps, or whether this was done only once, after the first six steps.[124] The Talmud interprets the verse to imply a sacrifice at every six steps.[125] Even with only

---

[123] We may also deduce from the fact of the trench dug around the altar for the absorption of the blood that the altar was the place of slaughter. It is remarkable that in the tradition of the sacrificial celebrations attributed to the primeval period, the Book of II Enoch also kept a recollection of slaughtering on top of the altar. See the discussion of Methuselah in 21: 16 ff. and of Nir in 22: 36.

[124] S. Bar-Efrat, שמואל ב, ed. M. Greenberg and S. Ahituv (Jerusalem, 1996), p. 69, considers the verbal form ויהי to imply a single act; a recurring act would require the form והיה. The LXX, however, translates with the compound ἦσαν αἴροντες which indicates an ongoing action. The Targum also interprets: והוה כד נטלו נטלי ארונא דה' שיתא זוגין ונכיס תור ופטים "And it happened when the carriers of the Lord's ark carried [it] six steps, they slaughtered a bull and a fatted calf."

[125] The parallel text in I Chr. 15: 26 differs from the one in II Sam., and we read there: ויהי בעזר האלהים את הלוים...ויזבחו שבעה פרים ושבעה אילים "Because God helped the Levites...they sacrificed seven bulls and seven rams." The phrase בעזר האלהים refers to the death of Uzziah, recounted in I Chr. chap. 13 as a punishment for touching the ark. It is interesting to note the different approaches in II Sam. and Chr. to the issue of the clerics, the Levites and Aaronites, and their relationship to the cult rites. There is no mention of Levites in II Sam. 6: 13; we read there נשאי ארון ה' "those who were carrying the ark of the Lord," with no indication that they had any special status. The narrative in Chr., on the other hand, starts in 15: 2 with a prohibition, specifically emphasizing who may carry the ark: אז אמר דויד לא לשאת את ארון האלהים כי אם הלוים כי בם בחר ה' לשאת את ארון ה' ולשרתו עד עולם "Then David said 'No one but the Levites may carry the ark of God, because the Lord chose them to carry the ark of the Lord and to minister before Him forever.'" The division between the clerics and the people was already established at that time, and the fear of approaching the holy artifacts was already inculcated in the minds of the people. We observe from v. 14 that even the priests and Levites had to consecrate themselves before approaching the ark: ויתקדשו הכהנים והלוים. Only the Levites carried the ark: וישאו בני הלוים את ארון האלהים "And the Levites carried the ark of God [v. 15]."
The Talmud observed the inconsistency in the two sources regarding the number of sacrifices: one bull and one calf every six steps in II Sam., and in I Chr. the offering of seven bulls and seven rams, with no indication whether this was a single offering or many. We read in B. T. Sotah 35b: אמר רב פפא בר שמואל על כל פסיעה ופסיעה שור ומריא על כל שש ושש פסיעות שבעה פרים ושבעה אילים אמר ליה רב חסדא אם כן מילאת את כל ארץ ישראל במות אלא אמר רב חסדא על כל שש ושש פסיעות שור ומריא על כל ששה סדרים של שש פסיעות שבעה פרים ושבעה אילים "Said Rav Pappa: A bull and a calf at each step, and seven bulls and seven rams at

one occurrence, there is no mention that an altar was built after the first six steps, and we must assume that the sacrifice was performed spontaneously, on a simple earth altar prepared ad hoc, or with no altar at all. If the sacrifices in fact took place every six steps, it would have been impossible to build elaborate altars at such short distances. We also read in 6: 17, after the placing of the ark in the tent: ויעל דוד עלות לפני ה׳ ושלמים "And David offered whole-burnt offerings before the Lord and peace offerings." There is again no indication in the verse that he built an altar; we must assume there was nothing significant to report about the construction of an altar. Concerning Solomon's transportation of the ark to Jerusalem, we again read in I Kings 8: 5: והמלך שלמה וכל עדת ישראל הנועדים עליו אתו לפני הארון מזבחים צאן ובקר אשר לא יספרו ולא ימנו מרב "And King Solomon and the entire assembly of Israel that had gathered about him before the ark, were sacrificing so many sheep and cattle that they could not be recorded or counted." The offerings were made "before the ark," but we read nothing of an altar which was already there or built for this specific purpose. This stands in contrast with the later record of offerings in v. 64 in the Temple precincts (a record which must have an aetiological purpose, as I shall discuss below). According to the text, at the bringing of the ark Solomon and the people offered sacrifices in such numbers that they "could not be recorded or counted"; this was evidently a larger amount than the offerings at the consecration of the Temple in v. 63, where the narrative indicates a finite number for each offering. Nonetheless, there is no mention of an altar for the offerings performed at the translocation of the ark.[126] We must, therefore, assume that the Israelites of the early monarchic period retained the archaic

---

every six steps. Said Rav Hisda: If so, you would fill up the whole country with *bamoth;* rather, Rav Hisda said: A bull and a calf at every six steps, and at every six successions of six steps (thirty-six steps) seven bulls and seven rams." Rav Hisda was sensitive to the issue of the myriad altars-*bamoth* which would be required to offer so many sacrifices, since he could not conceive of offerings on the ground or on a simple pile of earth and stones. In Y. T. Sanhedrin 10: 2, 29a a similar solution is offered for the discrepancy between the two pericopes, but there we encounter no question about the great number of required *bamoth:* רבי חנינה ורבי מנא חד אמר על כל צעידה וצעידה שור ומריא ובסוף שבעה פרים ושבעה אלים וחרנה אמר על כל צעידה וצעידה שבעה פרים ושבעה אלים ובסוף שור ומריא "Rabbi Hanina and Rabbi Mana disagree [on how to reconcile the conflicting pericopes]; one said a bull and a calf at every step, and at the end seven bulls and seven rams, and the other said seven bulls and seven rams at every step, and one bull and one calf at the end." The traditional commentators Rashi and Radak obviously follow the talmudic interpretation.

[126] There is also no mention of a translocation of an altar among the other artifacts mentioned in I Kings 8: 4: ויעלו את ארון ה׳ ואת אהל מועד ואת כל כלי הקדש אשר באהל "And they brought up the ark of the Lord and the Tent of Meeting, and all the sacred furnishings in it."

nomadic tradition of low, simple altars, made from an accumulation of earth or stones found in situ, and this custom corresponds to the early altar law in Exod. 20. There is in fact a paradoxical situation: on the one hand, we encounter in Scripture numerous records of the building of a מזבח "altar", a word obviously derived from the verb זבח "to slaughter", with no indication that slaughtering was performed there;[127] and on the other hand, as we have observed here, there are passages recording the slaughtering of offerings, with no indication that this was performed on a מזבח.

Both verses 22 and 23 also share a common philosophy or theology:[128] within the presence of a numinous spirit, the use of an homicidal tool would defile the altar, and the same violation of the holy would result from an exposure of the altar to the sexual parts of the body. These two concepts do not appear in Deut. 27: 5 - 6, and confirm the diversity of the two pericopes under discussion.

In conclusion, we have noted that although there is a similarity between the two pericopes, their resemblance is limited exclusively to:

a) the general subject of the stones appropriate for the building of an altar; however, there are distinct rules in each pericope for the stone altar, as well as the regulations for the earthen altar in Exod. 20:21;

b) the use of the term נוף to specify a prohibition against wielding something on the altar; however, the implement is different in each case.

The literary structure of both pericopes is totally dissimilar: in their prohibitions, in their positive commands, and in their rationalizations. The concepts, the materials and the regulations are equally distinct in each pericope, and therefore we must consider them to be independent narratives with different purposes and consequences.

---

[127] Gen. 12: 7, 8; 13: 4, 18; 26: 25; 33: 20 (which might have been a מצבה, as discussed elsewhere); 35: 1-7; Exod. 17: 15. In Jud. 6: 24 and I Sam. 7: 17 the building of altars is recorded, with no mention of their purpose. From the context in Jud. 6: 24, it seems that Gideon did not built the altar for the purpose of offering sacrifices, because Scripture emphasizes ויקרא לו ה' שלום "and called it the Lord is peace"; this type of act is also found with respect to certain patriarchal altars and Moses' altar in Exod. 17:15, where it is evident that the altar's erection was a devotional deed for remembrance of a miraculous event, and not for sacrificial celebrations.

[128] It is interesting that Keil & Delitzsch, who do not investigate the probability that the three verses of the Law of the Altar are not in their original location, connect the antecedent verses theologically with the Law of the Altar; the command to make a simple earthen altar for the worship of the God of Israel stands in contrast to the antecedent verses which censure the shaping of gold and silver gods. They write (*Biblical Commentary on the Old Testament*, p.127): "Israel needed only an altar, on which to cause its sacrifices to ascend to God."

1.3.1 Analysis of the Two Pericopes According to the *Sitz im Leben* Principle

I have already cited Noth's comments[129] that "the law [in Exod. 20. 21 - 23] itself is of course old, as it presupposes very simple conditions." He then adds, "We must therefore suppose this ordinance to originate perhaps from communities of nomadic herdsmen." We do not have to agree with all of Noth's speculations and conclusions regarding this law, but it seems obvious that nomadic conditions are evident at least in the first command to make an earthen altar. Its very nature implies a temporary cultic arrangement, which would be abandoned due to the constant migration of the nomadic worshippers, or fall into decay as a result of wind and rain. The explicit divine promise, to appear and bless the worshippers wherever they might invoke Him, constitutes further corroboration of the prevailing social conditions during the period of the conception of this custom, when a sacrificial locus would be expected at each station of the migration.

This type of custom is also reflected in the patriarchal narratives. W. Robertson Smith writes in The Religion of the Semites[130] that pilgrimage to distant shrines was a prominent feature of later Semitic heathenism, not its early period. J. Henninger writes[131] that pilgrimage constitutes a sedentary influence on the nomadic cult. We observe in the biblical narratives of the Patriarchs that they erected some sort of worship artifact whenever they reached some critical point in their migrations, and/or had a vision of an encounter with the Deity. These occurrences coincide perfectly with our verse, stressing the importance of the divine invocation, rather than the holiness of a particular place. For example, we read concerning Abraham: ויבן שם מזבח לה׳ הנראה אליו "There he [Abraham] built an altar to the Lord which appeared to him [Gen. 12: 7]; Abraham's naming of the place at which he built the altar to sacrifice Isaac: ה׳ יראה אשר יאמר היום בהר ה׳ יראה "God will see, as will be said today He will be seen on the mountain of God [Gen. 22: 14]";[132] concerning Isaac, after he experienced a theophany: ויבן שם מזבח ויקרא בשם ה׳ "And he [Isaac] built there an altar and called the name of God [Gen. 26: 25]"; concerning Jacob: ויבן שם מזבח...כי שם

---

[129] p. 176.

[130] W. Robertson Smith, *The Religion of the Semites* (N. Y., 1972), p. 80.

[131] J. Henninger, "La Religion Bédouine Préislamique," *Arabia Sacra,* Orbis Biblicus et Orientalis 40 (1981), p. 28.

[132] I do not need to elaborate on the interpretation of this somewhat obscure verse. It suffices for my thesis to establish the connection of theophany and altar, or a similar sign on such occurrences.

נגלו אליו האלהים "And he [Jacob] built there an altar…since there God appeared to him [Gen. 35: 7]." In some instances the Patriarchs built an altar, and in other occurrences they performed some other act of worship - planting a tree: ויטע אשל בבאר שבע ויקרא שם בשם ה' "And he [Abraham] planted a tamarisk tree in Beer Sheba, and called upon the name of the Lord [Gen. 21: 33]"; or setting up a pillar: וישם אתה מצבה ויצק שמן על ראשה "And he set it [the stone] as a pillar and poured oil on top of it [Gen. 28: 18]."

It is remarkable that in all of these archaic[133] traditions of the Patriarchs and their manner of worship, there is no mention of sacrifices being offered. This fact fits well with the obscure character of verse 21 with its vague command: וזבחת עליו…את צאנך ואת בקרך "You should slaughter on it your sheep and cattle," particularly if we eliminate the odd את עלתיך ואת שלמיך, as suggested earlier in the study.[134] I have also stressed the peculiar expression וזבחת עליו, which implies the slaughtering, not the burning or the presentation of the offering, on this earthen altar. K. Galling[135] declares that the whole- burnt offering is a late institution, unknown in the early history of the Orient. The burning of the offering displays a later sophistication in the sacrificial system; a worshipper, far away from the location of his deity, burnt the offering and created a smoke rising up to heaven, to be united in this symbolic way with his deity.[136] The term זבח does not connote the complete performance of an offering either in the biblical patriarchal narratives or in the neighbouring Ugaritic cultic texts, which are considered relevant for comparison with ancient Israelite custom. We encounter in Gen. 31: 54: ויזבח יעקב זבח בהר ויקרא לאחיו לאכל לחם "And Jacob slaughtered a repast in the hill country and invited his relatives to a meal." J. M. de

---

[133] Whether we attribute the redaction of these stories to E or J, it is obvious that the stories themselves originate in archaic oral transmissions, and enlighten us about circumstances in that early period.

[134] Cf. L. Schwienhorst - Schönberger, *Das Bundesbuch*, BZAW 188 (Berlin, 1990), p. 412, who declares that the phrase את עלתיך ואת שלמיך is the work of a deuteronomic redactor attempting to adapt the text of the Book of the Covenant to the deuteronomic narrative.

[135] K. Galling, *Der Altar in den Kulturen des Alten Orientes* (Berlin, 1925), p. 13.

[136] Although Galling's theory is based on speculation, it seems to me that his hypothesis has a reasonable basis. In a number of Chinese temples dedicated to the Lady of Mercy, the goddess Guanyin, one or more furnaces are placed at the entrance, and the worshippers burn papers in them on which they write their names and their specific supplications; in certain cases paper money is also burned as a token of offering to the goddess. The petitions and offerings through their rising smoke thus reach their destination, the goddess. See also section 9.2.1, in which I present another rationalization for the burning of sacrifices instead of the offering of food in monotheistic doctrine.

Tarragon[137] writes: "*dbh*, ce mot est riche de sens. Il peut désigner un repas sacrificiel qui n'est pas à proprement parler un sacrifice fait sur l'autel." ("*dbh* [similar to the Hebrew זבח] is a term with many nuances. It may designate a sacrificial meal, which is not really a sacrifice offered on the altar.") Such an indeterminate sense of the term זבח harmonizes perfectly with the general character of our verse, Exodus 20: 21, obviously without the interjected את עלתיך ואת ושלמיך. W. Zwickel[138] asserts that large altars for the burning of animal sacrifices such as the עולה cannot be verified archeologically in the Middle Bronze Age.

The pre-Islamic cult practices of the nomadic Bedouins are recognized by scholars as relevant for comparison with early Israelite custom.[139] Indications of nomadic influence are evident in the biblical narratives, and it is not necessary to substantiate them further in this study. An investigation of certain pre-Islamic cult practices may therefore assist us in correctly interpreting our pericope in Exodus 20. Henninger states:[140] " Il semble que le sacrifice n'était pas attaché à un endroit fixe." ("It seems that the sacrificial performance was not attached to a fixed location.") Referring to the act itself, he writes: "Le sang coulait dans la fosse qui se trouvait devant la pierre sacrée." ("The blood [of the sacrificed animal] trickled into the ditch in front of the holy stone.") One may observe an almost exact equivalence between the pre-Islamic custom and the rules in Exod. 20: 21: the insignificance of an established holy place for the performance of sacrificial worship, or even the absence of such places during the Israelite nomadic period, and the building of an earthen altar, which would allow the blood to run down and be absorbed by the earth.[141] Although the purpose of absorbing the blood is not

---

[137] J. M. de Tarragon, *Le Culte à Ugarit* (Paris, 1980), p. 56.

[138] W. Zwickel, *Der Tempelkult in Kanaan und Israel, Studien zur Kultgeschichte Palästinas von der Mittelbronzezeit bis zum Untergang Judas*, Forschungen zum Alten Testament 10 (Tübingen, 1994), p. 202.

[139] J. Morgenstern, *The Ark, the Ephod and the Tent of Meeting* (Cincinnati, 1945), writes in his Introduction p. 4 that there is a "basis of similarity of pre-Canaanite Israelite tribes with pre-Islamic and Bedouin beliefs - close relationship - in fact a relative identity."

[140] "Le Sacrifice chez les Arabes," *Arabia Sacra*, p. 197.

[141] We find a biblical passage which may possibly hint at such a purpose for the early altar, that is, the absorption of the blood by the surrounding earth around it as a symbol of offering to the Deity. This is the somewhat unclear text in I Sam. 14: 32 -34, which describes the people, being hungry and tired, slaughtering and consuming the meat of the plundered animals after their victory over the Philistines; in so doing they transgressed some known custom and ate the meat על הדם. The LXX translates this peculiar expression "on the blood," as σὺν τῷ αἵματι "together with the blood", as do the KJV and NIV. But the question is not solved by this translation, since the slaughtering at the large stone would not resolve the issue of eating "with the blood"; there is no indication in

explicitly stated in our pericope, we find other biblical citations which indicate such a custom. We read in Lev. 17: 13: ושפך את דמו וכסהו בעפר "drain the blood and cover it with earth" and in Deut. 12: 16: רק הדם לא תאכלו על הארץ תשפכנו כמים "But you must not eat the blood; pour it out on the ground like water." There is perhaps another indication in the record of the altar built by Elijah on Mount Carmel, in I Kings 18: 32: ויבנה את האבנים מזבח בשם ה' ויעש תעלה...סביב למזבח "With the stones he built an altar in the name of the Lord, and he dug a trench around it." It is possible that Elijah dug the trench so as to increase the amount of water to be consumed and so heighten the impact of the miracle; but it is certainly plausible that the digging of a ditch into which the blood was to run was the usual manner of preparing a place of sacrifice. Scripture tells us only of the

---

Scripture that the people stopped eating "with" the blood at the stone. Moreover, Saul's command should have been: "Stop eating the blood!" rather than: "Roll a stone!" Modern scholars as well as talmudic and later traditional commentators were aware of the problem, and proposed different solutions, according to their respective viewpoints. Stäuble writes in *I Samuel*, p. 272 that the sin was not a transgression of the command in Gen. 9: 4 and Deut. 12: 23 not to eat blood, but rather the people's failure to offer the Deity's share, that is the blood. The process of slaughtering on the stone so that the blood would run down into the earth would fulfil this precept. H. W. Hertzberg writes similarly in his *I & II Samuel, A Commentary* (Philadelphia, pp. 115-116): "It is not that the men had eaten the flesh 'with' its blood - that would have to be *b* and not *al*, cf. Gen. 9: 4 but that they prepared the meal 'on' the blood. The blood did not go, as we are to see later, to the place that belonged to Yahwe." The Talmud is aware that על הדם does not mean "with the blood," since in Lev. 19: 26 this expression לא תאכלו על הדם occurs together with the prohibition against practising divination and sorcery. In fact, there the LXX translates על הדם as ἐπὶ τῶν ὀρέων, "on the hills." From the context of the following verses, it is also obvious that the purpose of the interdictions in that pericope is to avoid idolatrous and alien practices, and not to prohibit the eating of blood, which is a ban of a different nature: כי הדם הוא הנפש "because the blood is the life [Deut. 12: 23]." There are a number of midrashim which attempt to explain the verse in Lev. 19: 26, and the expression על הדם. In Sifra קדשים יט פ"ו and in B. T. Sanhedrin 63a we read: לא תאכלו על הדם - לא תאכלו בשר ועדיין דם במזרק "Do not eat the flesh when there is still blood in the sprinkler [before all the blood was sprinkled on the altar]." Rashi in his commentary to Samuel follows these midrashim, but other traditional commentators, such as Radak and Ralbag, interpret this verse according to its plain meaning: do not act like the idolaters, whose custom is to eat the flesh sitting in the blood of the slaughtered sacrifices. The traditional commentators also interpret the transgression in Samuel in a similar way to the command in Leviticus. Only Radak adds another point: the blood did not drain out properly from the flesh, and by slaughtering the animal on a stone, this procedure was improved. Thus we see that the traditional sources also do not explain the sin in Samuel as "eating with the blood," though they were bound to interpret Samuel in harmony with other biblical precepts. I propose that the verse may be explained by the existence of an archaic custom with respect to the stone altar and its purpose was the absorption of the blood in the surrounding ditch; this routine was ignored by the people after the travail of battle.

large size of the ditch and stresses the greatness of the miracle. In the early writings there is no mention of a sprinkling of the blood on the altar, and consequently all the blood had to be covered with earth; the most practical way to accomplish this sacred task was to have a ditch into which the blood flowed and was absorbed, exactly as the pre-Islamic nomads did. Zwickel [142] reports, based on archeological findings of the Late Bronze Age, that in Hazor the animals were slaughtered on basalt panels and the blood was collected, and most probably discharged in some place. The drainage of the blood to the land symbolized the restitution of the blood, the life element of the animal,[143] to the Deity. We observe the same idea even at a later stage, in the Israelite cult; for certain sacrifices, all the blood[144] was sprinkled on the altar,[145] while for others, some of the blood was smeared on its corners, but the remaining blood had to be duly discharged onto the altar's foundation:[146] "ואת כל דם הפר ישפך אל יסוד מזבח העלה "And all the [remaining] blood he shall pour out at the base of the altar [Lev. 4: 7]."

As we have seen, the phrase in our verse וזבחת עליו should be interpreted literally as "on the altar," and such a procedure would also correspond to the pre-Islamic custom of letting the blood of the sacrifice run into the ditch in front of the holy stone. There is no mention in our pericope of priests performing the offering celebrations; many scholars stress the point that these

---

[142] W. Zwickel, *Der Tempelkult in Kanaan und Israel*, p. 201.

[143] As it is written: כי הדם הוא הנפש "because the blood is the life [Deut. 12: 23]" and referring to the creation of life by the Deity's breath: ויפח באפיו נשמת חיים ויהי האדם לנפש חיה "...and breathed into his nostrils the breath of life, and the man became a living being [Gen. 2: 7]." The נפש is the divine element in creation and is represented in the blood.

[144] This rule is according to the scriptural text, but Maimonides interprets certain talmudic rhetoric in B. T. Zebahim 52a to require that the blood remaining after the sprinkling was to be poured onto the altar's foundation. He writes in *Hilkhot Ma'aseh HaQorbanot* 5: 6: העולה והאשם והשלמים...ושירי הדם נשפכין על היסוד הדרומי "The *Olah* and the *Asham* and the *Shelamim*... the remaining blood is poured out on the southern foundation."

[145] This rule was applicable to the holocaust and the peace offering. K. Elliger, *Leviticus* (Tübingen, 1966), p. 35 speculates that the origin of this custom is rooted in the idea that the altar is the site of the presence of the Deity. Cf. R. Rendtorff, *Studien zur Geschichte des Opfers im Alten Israel* (Neukirchen, 1967), pp. 97ff. regarding the origin of the blood sprinkling, under the heading "Die Herkunft des Blutsprengens."

[146] This was the rule for the later sin offering. The issue of the blood ritual for the אשם sacrifice is complex, and quite confused in the scriptural text; fortunately, it is not relevant to our study. According to rabbinic opinion, also shared by Rendtorff and Elliger, the blood of the *Asham* was sprinkled on the altar's side walls, similar to the blood of the *Olah* and *Shelamim*.

rules are directed toward the people, and not to a special privileged class. Such a tradition is contrary to the evidence from Egypt and Mesopotamia. There the formal officiants, be they kings or priests, are in the forefront. On the other hand, with respect to the pre-Islamic Bedouin culture, G. Ryckmans states:[147] "Le sacrificateur paraît avoir été le dédicant lui même."[148] ("It seems that the officiant was the same as the offerer.") As in ancient Israel, the priests were not the sacrificers, but merely the guardians of the sanctuaries.[149] The slaughtering of the animal, an act of primordial significance in the sacrificial cult, remained the prerogative of the lay offerer even in the later period of the established Israelite cult. Rendtorff perceives in Lev. 1, in the first law of the holocaust sacrifice, traces of a transition from private offerers to priests in the various stages of the sacrifice. The offerer is described in the singular יקריבנו, יקריב, וסמך, ושחט, והפשיט, ונתח, ירחץ, and the priests are described in plural, והקריבו, וזרקו, ונתנו, וערכו.[150] But the slaughtering remained the task of the offerer, described in the singular even in the late P stratum of the Pentateuch. The Talmud also confirms that the slaughtering was performed only by the offerer, not by the priest.[151]

---

[147] "Das Opfer in der Altsüdarabischen Hochkulturen," *Arabia Sacra*, p. 22, n. 69.

[148] Rolf Rendtorff offers an almost identical statement in *Studien zur Geschichte des Opfers im Alten Israel*, p. 111: "Allerdings wissen die älteren Texte nichts von einer Trennung der Funktionen des Opfernden und des Priesters. Vom Priester ist überhaupt fast nie die Rede; vielmehr zeigen die Texte z.T. eindeutig, dass der ganze Opfervorgang vom Opfernden selbst vollzogen wird." ("Certainly the older texts do not know of a division of functions between the offerer and the priest. There is almost no mention of the priest; rather some texts show unequivocally that the entire offering procedure was performed by the offerer himself.")

[149] See J. Henninger, "Esquisse de la Religion bédouine préislamique," *Arabia Sacra*, p. 28: "Les prêtres mentionés dans les sources arabes n'étaient pas des sacrificateurs, mais plutôt des gardiens des sanctuaires, chaque homme étant autorisé á immoler sa propre victime." ("The priests mentioned in the Arab sources were not the [formal] sacrificers, but merely the guardians of the sanctuaries; each person was authorized to slaughter his own victim.") See also P. Heger, *Incense Cult*, p. 203, n. 46.

[150] K. Elliger, *Leviticus*, pp. 27ff extensively analyzes Rendtorff's literary analysis of this pericope and the issue of its period of redaction, as both issues relate to the demarcation between the offerer and the priest and their sacrificial performances.

[151] We read in Mishnah Zebahim 3: 1: כל הפסולין ששחטו שחיטתן כשרה שהשחיטה בזרים ובנשים ובעבדים ובטמאים ואפילו בקדשי קדשים "Slaughter by all those who are not fit to offer sacrifices, is [still] fit [for the offering], because slaughtering is allowed to be done by laics, women, slaves and the non-pure, even with respect to the most holy sacrifices." It is interesting that the Gemara explains this authorization by deducing it from a critical examination of the text in the same manner as Rendtorff, cited above. We read in B.T. Zebahim 32b: יכול אף בשחיטה ת״ל ושחט את בן הבקר לפני ה׳ והקריבו וכו׳ מקבלה ואילך מצות כהונה "Does it mean that the slaughtering [must also be performed by a priest]? Scripture teaches us [otherwise]: 'He is to slaughter

There are many rules in common between the early Israelites and the pre-Islamic Bedouin nomads.[152] I would like to mention here one additional similarity between the two cultures to corroborate my postulate, and that is the prohibition against breaking the bones of the sacrifice. The bones of the Passover lamb, the archaic communal meal, must not be broken, as it is written: ועצם לא תשברו בו "Do not break any of the bones [Exod. 12: 46]." Similarly, Henninger attests[153] a prohibition against breaking the bones of the sacrificial victim in the nomadic culture.

The final issue of relevance with respect to the early cult is the significance of stone. The veneration of stone is a universal phenomenon, evident in many cultures from the earliest times. The European menhirs, cromlechs, dolmens, cairns and other stone pillars are well known, as are other sacred stones spread over the planet among many primitive cultures.[154] As C. M. Edsman notes, "The symbolic meaning of sacred stones is not fixed....Interpretation is made difficult by the fact that many sacred stones come to us from religions and cultures for which there is little or no literary evidence.[155] I suggest that even where we have literary evidence, as in the

---

the young bull...[Lev. 1:5]' and then '[Aaron's sons the priests] shall bring the blood'; the commands from the receiving of the blood and onward are for the priests." The slaughtering is stated in singular and thus refers to the offerer, but the receiving of the blood is in plural, and thus refers to the priests.

[152] A. Lods, *Israel, Des Origines au Milieu du VIIIe Siècle*, Hebrew translation M. Halamish, ישראל קדמוניות העם והארץ (Tel Aviv, 1960), offers some interesting examples of common cultic customs. The shouting at the arrival of the ark in the camp, as recorded in Exod. 32: 17-18, I Sam. 4: 5 and other occurrences, is associated with the term הלל and הללויה, from the root ילל "to howl"; this is compared to the cries of pre-Islamic peoples called תחליל, from the same root, and its modified utterance לבייק "at your service," in the Islamic cult. Lods also traces the origin of the Hebrew חג, "the feast" from the ancient custom of dancing around the altar, and the associated terms חוג and חגג "to go round." The Arabic חג' for the pilgrimage to Mecca has the same origin and meaning, and signifies the circumambulation of the Kaaba. Lods mentions additional similarities between the pre-Islamic and Israelite cults, such as the interdiction against eating the flesh of an atonement sacrifice, similar to the Israelite sin offering which only the priest may eat; the custom of sprinkling blood on the door frames; the sprinkling of blood on the people at the occasion of making a covenant, similar to the blood sprinkled on the people by Moses after reading the Book of the Covenant: ויאמר הנה דם הברית "This is the blood of the covenant [Exod. 24: 6 - 8]."

[153] "Zum Verbot des Knochen-zerbrechens bei den Semiten," in *Studi Orientalistici in Onore di Giorgio Levi della Vida*, I, (Roma, 1956), pp. 448-458.

[154] See *The Encylopedia of Religion*, ed. Mircea Eliade (London, 1987), s.v. "Stones" by C. M. Edsman, where sacred stones are described in Madagascar, Lapland and among the American Indians.

[155] p. 50.

Israelite, Greek and Arab cultures, it is difficult if not impossible to establish the exact theology behind the reverence for stone. Theologies change continually, faster than the customs symbolizing them; therefore, we do not know their primeval origin. Among the extensive Israelite documentation, there are a number of quotations concerning stone and its various usages, out of which we may sometimes deduce the underlying theology; different conclusions may, of course, be reached, in part an unavoidable result of the changes in theology and cultic practice. There is also literary evidence of sacred stones in ancient Greece,[156] but it is more appropriate to compare the customs of the pre-Islamic Bedouins.[157] Even philologically, the pre-Islamic sacred stone pillar called a 'nsab is identical to the Hebrew מצבה.[158]

---

[156] In Greek mythology we find the λίθοι ἔμψυχοι βαιτύλοι "the animated stones," the Ἐρεμαιος λίθος "the heap of stones for the worship of Hermes," called מרקוליס in the talmudic literature, and the ὀμφαλὸς τῆς γῆς "the navel (center) of the world," similar to the Israelite אבן השתייה at the Temple Mount.

[157] In *Handbuch der Altarabischen Altertumskunde*, p. 241, we read: "Israel...hat - wie kein anderes nordsemitisches Volk - viele Elemente aus der altarabischen und altsemitischen Religion treu bewahrt." ("Israel...has, as no other north-Semitic people, faithfully preserved many elements of the ancient Arabic and Semitic religion.") One of the most significant characteristics is the lack of figurative representations of the Deity in both the Israelite and ancient Arabic cult. We read on p. 243: "Den altarabischen bildlosen Kult finden wir auch bei den Hebräern." De Lacy O' Leary, in *Arabia before Muhammad*, (London, 1927), p. 195 draws our attention to two ancient Arabian gods, whose names appear in Isa. 65: 11. Although this chapter is of a relatively late origin, I think it is still interesting to quote it. We read there: הערכים לגד שלחן והממלאים למני ממסך. The NIV translation is "who spread a table for (Gadd) Fortune and fill bowls of mixed wine for (Mani) Destiny." However, O' Leary states that the Arabs had a sanctuary in Hudhail for an impersonal power Manâ, and the deity Gadd appears in a Yemeni inscription. It is interesting to note the different interpretations of Rashi, the western European, who did not know Arabic, and Radak, who was knowledgeable in this language and culture. Rashi quotes a talmudic proverb to identify Gadd as the name of an idol, but has a problem with the term Mani; he speculates that its root is מנה "to count". Radak, on the other hand, identifies both terms as star - idols, and Gadd as the Arabic name for Jupiter. The Targum translates both terms with generic denominations for idols, טעון and דחלתהון; the LXX translates the term Gadd as δαίμων "god- spirit" and Mani as τύχη, "the goddess of fortune, Fortuna." Thomas Stäubli in *Das Image der Nomaden* (Göttingen, 1991), pp. 222 ff. compares the אהל מועד, the Tent of Meeting (corresponding to the tent with the oracle in Exod. 33: 7: ומשה יקח את האהל ונטה לו מחוץ למחנה...וקרא לו אהל מועד "Moses used to take the tent and pitch it outside the camp...calling it the Tent of Meeting") with the Arab *qubba*, the portable sanctuary. The latter is covered during transit by a red leather tent, similar to the ark: כסוי ערת אילם מאדמים ומכסה ערת תחשים (Num. 4: 6): and the Tabernacle: עור תחש (Exod. 26: 14). The affinity between the Midianites and the Israelites is well-known; Moses' theophany occurred in Midian during his stay with Jethro, the priest of Midian (Exod. chap. 3), and Jethro, whose family joined the Israelites (Jud. 1: 16), instructed

them on cultic and legal matters (Exod. 18: 12 - 23). These events and the interconnection with Midianite customs prevailed in the memory of the people, and we find the Arab *qubba* in Scripture, as a Midianite tent, set in opposition to the Israelite "Tent of Meeting." We read in Num. 25: 6: והמה בכים פתח אהל מועד "They [Moses and his loyal followers] were weeping at the entrance of the 'Tent of Meeting,'" and then we read that Phinehas went into the קבה "qubba", and killed the sinners (v. 8): Zimri, son of Salu, the leader of a Simeonite family, and the Midianite woman Kozbi, the daughter of Zur, a Midianite leader (vv. 14 - 15). The status and genealogy of the Israelite man and the Midianite woman demonstrate the strong connections among the highest ranks in both societies in cultic matters, and probably also in general cultural issues, a fact which Scripture does not find it necessary to state. This narrative reveals the later intent to alienate Israel from the ancient idolatrous Midianite customs, and to justify the High Priesthood for Phinehas' descendants, as a reward for his bravery. Stäubli also draws our attention to the red leather cover of the Tent (Exod. 26: 14), ועשית מכסה לאהל ערת אילם מאדמים, similar to the red leather cover of the *qubba*. The term קבה in Num. 25: 8, ויבא אחר איש ישראל אל הקבה "he followed the Israelite into the tent," has a phonetic similarity to the term קבתה in the following section of the verse: אל קבתה "her belly." There is another occurrence of the term קבה "belly" in Scripture, where its meaning is obvious: הזרע והלחיים והקבה "the shoulder and the jowls and the maw [Deut. 18: 3]," and such a translation is appropriate in the context for the expression קבתה. On the other hand, the term קבה "tent" does not occur elsewhere. Onkelos translates the first קבה in Num. 25:8 as קובתא, "arched room - store room" (Jastrow), a term unique in his writings, but which appears in other Targumim. The LXX translates the first קבה, oddly and inappropriately, as κάμινος "oven, furnace, kiln" (Liddell and Scott), and the second as μήτρα "womb", suitable to the context. Rashi translates the first correctly as "tent", probably deducing the meaning from the context, and the second as "belly"; Ibn Ezra, who knew Arabic, adds that in that language a similar term means tent, without specifically mentioning the *qubba*. Remarkably, he adds another explanation: the stomach is not unlike a tent; I can only assume that he attempted to dissociate the Arab cultic element from the biblical text.

This portable Israelite tent, comparable to the *qubba*, must have been the tent which Solomon brought into the Temple. We read in I Kings 8: 4: ויעלו את ארון ה' ואת אהל מועד "And they brought up the ark and the Tent of Meeting"; it could not have been the tent described in Exod. 26, because of its size. The wooden frames alone were thirty cubits long (20 x 1,5 each) and nine cubits wide (6 x 1, 5 each), and with the coverings it was much larger. Solomon's Temple was only sixty cubits long and twenty cubits wide (I Kings 6: 2); the Debir was twenty cubits wide, so that the *Heikhal*, the main hall, was only forty cubits long (I Kings 6: 16 - 17). A structure of thirty cubits would leave no room for the other implements in the hall. However, Scripture clearly records that the אהל מועד was brought into the Temple, in I Kings 8: 4 above and in II Chr. 5: 5: ויעלו את הארון ואת אהל מועד. See I. Knohl, "Two Aspects of the Tent of Meeting," in *Tehillah le-Moshe* (Winona Lake, 1997), pp. 73-9, who declares that two concepts of the Tent of Meeting are preserved in the Torah itself. The Talmud and the traditional commentators were aware of the difficulty in assuming the verses apply to the Tent of Meeting, and actually contradict them. We find in Tosefta Sotah (Liebermann) 13: 1 משנבנה בית ראשון נגנז אהל מועד "After the building of the First Temple, the Tent of Meeting was hidden." Radak, in his commentary to II Chr. 5: 5 attempts to introduce

The importance of stone in the pre-Islamic nomad cult is well-known, and need not be corroborated by text citation. The Kaaba, the ancient holy stone whose status probably dates to the stone age and which was retrojected in the traditional cult to the period of Abraham, resisted the enormous theological changes in Arab culture; its veneration subsisted not only in folkloric tales but also within the formal and official Muslim faith. It has remained an important vestige of this ancient religion, and is venerated even to this day.[159] The Muslim ritual of throwing stones at the Mecca pilgrimage, the Radjm at Mina, "one of the pre-Islamic rites preserved by Muhammad,"[160] may also be in some way connected to the ancient adoration of stone, or its numinous power.[161] As described in the Lexicon, "The stones have to be collected of

---

ויעלו את הארון ואת אהל מועד :order into this verse, and explains ויעלו את הארון ואת אהל מועד - פי' את הארון
מציון ואת אהל מועד מגבעון שהיה שם וכן כתוב במלכים אז יקהל שלמה
להעלות את ארון ברית ה' מעיר דוד היא ציון ואת אהל מועד גנזו באוצרות בית
אלהים עם הקדשים אבל הארון הכניסו אל מקומו אל דביר הבית..." that is, the
ark [was brought] from Zion, and the Tent of Meeting from Gibeon, as it says in I Kings
8: 1 'Solomon assembled...to bring up the ark of the Lord's covenant from Zion,' and the
Tent of Meeting they hid among the treasures of the House of God with the holy things,
and the ark they put in its place, in the Debir of the House." J. Morgenstern, in *The Ark,
The Ephod and Tent of Meeting*, p. 2, compares the ark with the Bedouin *mahmal* and
otfe.

[158] We read in *Die Araber in der Alten Welt*, ed. F. Altheim and R. Stiehl, I. Band (Berlin,
1964), p. 363:" Kultgegenstand bildeten vielmehr natürliche, mehr oder weniger
bearbeitete Steine, die entweder den Gott selbst darstellten oder als seine Wohnung."
("The cult element was constituted mainly by natural stones, or stones which were more
or less dressed, which represented the deity itself, or its dwelling.") De Lacy O'Leary
writes in *Arabia before Muhammad*, p. 196: "This upright stone with cup hollows was the
earlier type of altar.... Behind the monolith altar was undoubtedly the monolith deity, the
fetish spirit dwelling in the stone, to which Clement of Alexandria refers when he says
that 'the Arabs worship a stone.'" The similarity to the pillars erected by the Patriarchs is
remarkable.

[159] It is interesting to note that in Hindu mythology there is also a belief that the goddess Kali
was born from a black stone, fallen from heaven.

[160] *The Encyclopedia of Islam*, New Edition (Leiden, 1965), s.v. *Radjm* by M. Gaudefroy -
Demombynes (T. Fahd).

[161] The Mishnah tells us in Sanhedrin 7: 6 of another manner of worship related to stone:
"הזורק אבן למרקוליס זו היא עבדתו "Throwing a stone on Mercurius, is its worship."
The Encyclopedia of Islam, New Edition, s.v. *Radjm* by M. Gaudefroy-Demombynes (T.
Fahd), outlines the various speculations explaining the lapidation at Mina and concludes:
"Some exegetes have seen quite clearly that they represent ancient rites"; not surprisingly,
there is no clear indication of ancient rites and beliefs. Even if we assume that
stone-throwing is a means of driving away evil, a theory which would in any event be
inconsistent with the adoration of the stone pillars and the Kaaba, this would not
contradict my theory, to be discussed below, regarding execution by lapidation. The stone,
with its numinous or magic power, was chosen to chase away evil.

the proper size and not broken from a rock. Stones collected but not used should be buried; they have assumed a sacred character, which makes them dangerous." The affinity with the Israelite approach to stone, as expressed in the altar laws, is remarkable, as I shall elaborate. The significance of stone in the early Israelite cult, together with the relevant customs, disappeared entirely from the later established and organized cult.

Based on this overview, we may draw the following general conclusions:

a) Stone had great significance in the nomadic cult.

b) An ingrained custom subsists for a much longer period than the theology or aetiological mythology behind it; we may sometimes still find traces of the earlier belief or concept, but often the earlier ideas are entirely forgotten, or intentionally erased from memory, through an efficient and persuasive substitution of a new and contrasting theology or mythology.

c) The change in theology or mythology does in some instances invalidate the previous custom.

On the other hand, we must acknowledge that such changes and shifts in opinions and mythologies, as well as in custom, do not occur abruptly, but are the result of a long process of slow development. Even when the ruling power is able to force a change in custom, it cannot immediately succeed in eradicating the customs and beliefs of the masses. During some period, whether longer or shorter, both the old and the new customs and beliefs subsist together, even when they are entirely inconsistent, and continue to influence each other until a full or partial metamorphosis is accomplished. It is the task of the researcher to attempt to identify and individuate the various elements of particular customs or opinions, and possibly establish the chronology of the developmental stages; this we shall do in the next chapter.

2. Comparison and Contrast between the Two Pericopes with respect to their Mythological Vision and Historical Setting

We may now approach the verses Exod. 20: 22 and 23 and Deut. 27: 2 - 8, the rules of the stone altar, and examine the status of the element "stone" in both Israelite and pre-Islamic nomadic culture. This investigation should assist us in establishing those characteristics of the two pericopes in Exod. 20 and Deut. 27 which are shared, and those which are divergent.

2.1 The Significance of Stone in the Israelite Cult

2.1.1 Early Stone Pillars

The hallowed status of stone in the Israelite cult is found throughout Israelite history, and is adequately documented in its writings. We start with Jacob setting up a stone for a pillar and pouring oil on it, as a sign of the house of God: ויקח את האבן...וישם אתה מצבה "[Jacob] took the stone...and set it up as a pillar [Gen. 28: 18]"; he again set up a pillar as a symbol of the covenant with Laban, with the Deity as the patron and guarantor of the treaty: ויקח יעקב אבן וירימה מצבה "So Jacob took a stone and set it up as a pillar [Gen. 31: 45]"; and he set up a pillar and poured oil on it to mark his encounter with God: במקום אשר דבר אתו מצבת אבן "...a stone pillar at the place where God had talked with him [Gen. 35: 14]." In Gen. 33: 20 the unique and odd term נצב is used to describe the building of an altar: ויצב שם מזבח "He set up there an altar." One may speculate that the artifact here was actually a pillar, as the term נצב is the usual verb used for the erection of a מצבה "pillar"; for the construction of altars, the appropriate terms used in the Pentateuch are עשה and בנה.[1] Moreover, we find in the patriarchal narratives that Jacob, in contrast to the other Patriarchs, erected many מצבות; on only one occasion, in Beth El, is it recorded that Jacob built an altar (Gen. 35: 1, 3 and 7), possibly as an aetiological justification for the importance of the Beth

---

[1] A comparative list of the various biblical terms utilized to describe the construction of altars appears in W. Zwickel, "Die Altarbaunotizen im Alten Testament", *Biblica* 73-4 (1992), pp. 533 - 46.

El sanctuary. One may suspect therefore that in Gen. 33: 20 the term מצבה was at some occasion, intentionally or not, replaced with the term מזבח, but the verb ויצב, implying the erection of a pillar, remained.[2]

I would speculate that the stone pillar continued to be considered as a legitimate[3] worship site until a late period, at least to the time of Isaiah. We read in Isa. 19: 19: ביום ההוא יהיה מזבח לה׳ בתוך ארץ מצרים ומצבה אצל גבולה לה׳ "In that day there will be an altar to the Lord in the heart of Egypt and a pillar[4] to the Lord at its border." The numerous condemnations

---

[2] Cf. Claus Westermann, *Genesis*, Biblischer Kommentar Altes Testament, Band I/2 (Neukirchen, 1981), p. 645.

[3] The term מצבה occurs once in Exod. 24: 4, in connection with a legitimate act performed by Moses; suffixed forms occur in Exod. 23: 24 and 34: 13, מצבותיהם and מצבותם, respectively, where it is evident that they refer to idolatrous pillars. In Lev. 26: 1, we read לא תעשו לכם אלילם ופסל ומצבה לא תקימו לכם ואבן משכית לא תתנו בארצכם להשתחות עליה כי אני ה׳ אלהיכם "Do not make idols or set up an image or a sacred stone for yourselves, and do not place a carved stone in your land to bow down before it, because I am the Lord your God." The term מצבה here is strongly associated with idolatrous worship, and the end of the verse offers us the rationale: Because I am your God, and therefore you must not worship others. It is evident that in this verse too only the מצבה for idolatrous worship is prohibited. Ralbag in his commentary to I Kings 14: 23 states that the מצבה prohibited in Deut. 16: 22 also refers to pillars for the worship of God; likely he felt compelled to interpret the passage in this way since the pericope also criticizes the במות, and according to the traditional opinion these were prohibited after the building of the Temple. Ralbag ignores the particular association of the מצבה with the idolatrous אשרה in both this pericope and Deut., as well as the concluding v. 24 in I Kings 14, ככל התועבת הגוים "the detestable practice of the nations," which defines the alien idolatrous character of the antecedent deeds. In Ralbag's commentary to II Kings 18: 4, he also asserts that the מצבות destroyed by Hezekiah were idolatrous. We see that the מצבה in itself was a legitimate cultic element for a long period before the ban of Josiah. See further the next two notes.

[4] The KJV correctly translates "pillar", but the NIV interprets this as "monument" precisely to avoid implying that the pillar was still legitimate in Isaiah's period. The Targum makes no distinction between the legitimate מצבה in Isa., and illicit pillars, as in Jer. 43: 13, or in II Kings 23: 14; both types are translated as קמא. The LXX too makes no distinction and translates both types of מצבה as στήλη. The traditional commentators Rashi and Radak avoid the issue of whether the מצבה was a legitimate cultic element. Only מצודת דוד, it seems, was concerned about this issue, and adds as an explanation that מצבה indicates an altar made of one stone. There is no doubt that in Isa. one must understand from the context that the pillar is considered a legitimate place of worship. H. Wildberger, in *Jesaia*, Biblischer Kommentar Altes Testament (Neukirchen, 1974), pp. 736 ff. discusses Isa. 19: 19 at length. He is not convinced that the prophet looks to the future, and dates the verse to a later period when such an event might actually have occurred, that is, during Israelite cultic celebrations in Egypt. But such a proposition

of the מצבות in Scripture are aimed at the pillars set up for idols, or at places where idols were worshipped, but do not refer to pillars for the worship of the God of Israel.[5] The ban against מצבות occurs three times in Deut. In 7: 5 and

---

would evidently be in flagrant contradiction to the deuteronomic ban against sacrificial celebrations outside the Temple in Jerusalem, and the objection to the מצבות. After various deliberations, Wildberger proposes to date this pericope to the end of the Persian domination of Judah, and to solve the conflict with the deuteronomic regulations he proposes that this ban had not yet attained broad acceptance among all Jews, or at least those in the Egyptian diaspora. I do not think that we need postpone the dating of Isaiah's prophecy in order to avoid any foresight in his poetic imagination, and at the same time to imply that the prophet, or a later editor, as Wildberger supposes, would predict a cultic performance against the deuteronomic ban. At any rate, according to Wildberger's proposition, the legitimacy of the מצבה continued even later than I have proposed. Two homilies in B. T. Menahoth 109b connect the fulfillment of this righteous prophecy to two different events. The Rabbis, unlike Wildberger, had no hesitation in considering Isaiah's prophecy as an anachronistic discourse. One homily relates it to Onias, the priest who built a temple to the God of Israel in Egypt and converted Egyptian idolaters to the worship of the God of Israel, and another homily relates it to Hezekiah. It is told that after Sennacherib's retreat from the siege of Jerusalem, Hezekiah freed many Egyptian prisoners who came with Sennacherib and converted them to the faith of the God of Israel. They then returned to Egypt and worshipped God; Isaiah's prophecy refers to these converted Egyptians. At any rate, it is obvious that the Talmud considered these pillars legitimate.

[5]   In Hosea 3: 4 we find a doubtful occurrence of the term מצבה. We read there כי ימים רבים ישבו בני ישראל אין מלך ואין שר ואין זבח ואין מצבה ואין אפוד ותרפים "For the Israelites will live many days without king or prince, without sacrifice or sacred stones, without Ephod or idol." This is the NIV translation, based, in my opinion, upon the generally negative attitude towards מצבה in Scripture, and especially the disapproval of תרפים. The prophet refers to a period when the Israelites will be lacking anything of worth, such as kings, princes, sacrifices and an Ephod; from the context, one must deduce that the remaining two entities, the מצבה and the תרפים, are also meritorious items. However, the traditional commentators Rashi, Ibn Ezra and Radak had great difficulty considering the items in this light. Ibn Ezra quotes Rabbi Jephet, who, it seems, interprets the verse as addressed to Israel, and rejects his assumption. Ibn Ezra confirms that he might have considered the מצבה in a positive light, and as an evil element only when used for idolatrous worship, but he could not conceive such an interpretation concerning the תרפים; these are always illicit, in his opinion. All the commentators perform literary acrobatics, and interpret the verses as divided between worthy and unworthy items, and between Judah and Israel, according to Rashi, or between Judah and the idolatrous peoples, according to Ibn Ezra and Radak. Their interpretation of the verse would be as follows: No king, prince and sacrifice for Judah, and no pillar for Israel or idolaters; no Ephod for Judah and no idols for the others. Thus the commentators feel bound to consider תרפים, and possibly the מצבה, as evil elements. However, we see that Ibn Ezra does consider מצבה in a positive light, as is clear from Isa. 19: 19, and my thesis of the continuous reverence for the pillar is thus corroborated.
Further to the issue of this apparently ambiguous verse, I would like to discuss the term תרפים, and demonstrate that this element need not be automatically considered as illicit;

one need not tear the verse into shreds in order to achieve a logical interpretation. If we concede that the numerous denunciations in Scripture of pillars refer exclusively to those for idolatrous worship, we may assume that the same distinction applies to the תרפים; that is, there are licit and illicit ones. It is therefore interesting to examine how the early translators interpreted the various instances of תרפים in Scripture. Laban's תרפים are considered evil, and are interpreted by Onkelos as צלמניא, and by the LXX as eijvdwla "idols". Elsewhere the Targum differs from the LXX, and each uses distinct interpretations according to its assessment of the context. In I Sam. 19: 13 - 16, Michal's rescue of David, in II Kings 23: 24, the תרפים which Josiah destroyed, and in Zech. 10: 2 and Ezek. 21: 26, where the evil of the תרפים seems evident, the Targum translates צלמניא; in Jud. 18: 17, Micah's image, it uses the term דמאין "figure", from the root דמי "to imagine"; but in our verse in Hosea 3: 4, the Targum translates מחוי "announcer - teller" (Jastrow) from the root חוי "to show - tell", certainly not an element with an evil connotation. We see that the Targum interpreted the verse in Hosea so as to include מצבה and תרפים as worthy items. In I Sam. 15: 23, the Targum does not translate the text literally, and has no explicit translation of the term תרפים. The contextual interpretations of the LXX differ from those of the Targum. In Jud. 18: 17 and in I Sam. 15: 23, we can assume that the LXX translator did not wish to take a firm attitude, and therefore translated with the impartial θερασιν. On the other hand, he used the same term for the תרפים in II Kings 23: 24, where the evil association is obvious. In I Sam. 19: 13 - 16, probably wishing to avoid attributing evil to Michal, David's wife, the LXX translates with the vague κενοτάφια "monument". The same consideration was probably the reason for the neutral term ἀποφθεγγόμενοι in Zech. 10: 2. In Ezek. 21: 26, where the evil aspect is obvious, we find the clearly execrable term γλυπτοîς. In Hosea, the LXX translates תרפים as δήλων, "clairvoyants - prophets", comparable to הרואה "the seer" (I Sam. 9: 11); that is, they have a meritorious aspect, in tandem with the antecedent component of the pair, אפוד, translated as iJerateiva "priesthood". In Hosea 10: 1, we read כרב לפריו הרבה למזבחות כטוב לארצו הטיבו מצבות "As his fruit increased, he built more altars; as his land prospered he adorned his sacred stones." The traditional commentators such as Rashi and Radak assume, according to their understanding of the subsequent verses and on the basis of the Targum's interpretation, that the altars and pillars were dedicated to the idols. Ibn Ezra, on the other hand, does not take any position and simply quotes in his commentary הרבו למזבחות "they expanded the altars." without elucidating whether the altars were dedicated to idols, or to the God of Israel. I do not see any need to interpret the altars and pillars of this verse as idolatrous, and, in fact, the LXX interprets מזבחות as θυσιαστήρια, the usual expression for legitimate altars. Further, if we assume that the terms מצבה and תרפים in Hosea 3: 4 refer to legitimate cultic elements, we must assume that the same applies to the term מצבות in 10: 1. Hosea, like other prophets of his time, criticized the inordinate significance bestowed by the people upon the legitimate sacrificial cult, and their assumption that ritual celebrations would atone for their evil social behaviour.

Modern scholars have amply discussed the exegesis of the above verses in Hosea. See H. W. Wolf, *Dodekapropheton 1, Hosea*, Biblischer Kommentar Altes Testament, 3. verbesserte Auflage (Neukirchen, 1976); J. L. Mays, *Hosea, A Commentary* (London, 1969); H. D. Beeby, *Grace Abounding, A Commentary on the Book of Hosea*, International Theological Commentary (Edinburgh, 1946); W. Rudolph, *Hosea*, Kommentar zum Alten Testament (Gütersloh, 1966); A. Weiser, *Das Buch der Zwölf*

Kleinen Propheten, I, Das Alte Testament Deutsch, 5. verbesserte Auflage (Göttingen, 1967). Without analyzing in depth the exegesis of each of these scholars, I note that they are mainly concerned with the three areas in which Israel will be deprived: the political, the cultic and knowledge of the future. Some of the scholars perceive Hosea's criticism of these elements within the framework of the general prophetic censure of the sacrificial cult and the evil behaviour of the ruling classes. Some scholars add another factor, and speculate that Hosea objects to the fact that the Israelites took over these institutions from the Canaanites. They do not elaborate on the specific issue of the legitimacy of the cultic elements such as pillars and *teraphim* when utilized for the worship of the God of Israel. Some scholars add that the pillars might have been prohibited later in the deuteronomic codex based on Hosea's criticism. W. Zwickel, in "Die Altarbaunotizen im Alten Testament", pp. 533-46, asserts that in his prophecy in 10: 1 Hosea criticizes the change in the underlying underlying ideology of the altar builders; while previously the altar was a sign of extreme gratitude to the Deity, it now represented a desire to acquire *coram publico*, that is, to demonstrate one's piety in public. In *Der Tempelkult in Kanaan und Israel*, p. 315, Zwickel asserts, without any justification, that in Hosea the *Masseben* are clearly considered legitimate.

Additional support for my thesis is found in other sources. The Ephod is unquestionably a legitimate cult element, required to be borne by Aaron (Exod. 28: 6 - 12), and used by David ויאמר אל אביתר הגישה האפוד "He [David] said to Abiathar, Bring the Ephod [I Sam. 23: 9]"; however, it too is considered abominable when used for illicit worship. We read in Jud. 8: 27: ויעש אתו גדעון לאפוד ויצג אתו...ויזנו כל ישראל אחריו "Gideon made it [the gold] into an Ephod, which he placed....All Israel prostituted themselves 'afterwards'." The term אחריו can be interpreted in two ways: after Gideon, that is, after his death, as Rashi understands it, or after the Ephod, that is, to worship it, as Ralbag and Ramban apprehend it. It seems to me that Radak also interprets the term אחריו as after the Ephod, but adds his opinion that the event occurred after Gideon's death. Ramban, in his commentary to Gen. 31: 19, explains that the people used to approach the original Ephod made by Moses to ascertain God's will, but then made a counterfeit copy and followed its misleading answers; this was the sin involved in Gideon's Ephod. Ralbag in his comments on our verse states that the people erred and considered the Ephod as an idol, and at Jud. 10: 4 he explains the reason for this error: Gideon set up the Ephod in his home town, instead of in Shilo, where the official sanctuary stood; there it would not have been subject to error. As the Ephod could be considered to have both legitimate and illegitimate uses, so we must perceive the legality of the מצבה.

On the basis of the scriptural text, we must conclude that at least until the time of Hezekiah, Canaanite elements of worship were legitimate in Israel. Scripture tells us of many pious kings who followed God's commands before Hezekiah, but it was only he who וכתת נחש נחשת אשר עשה משה "broke into pieces the bronze snake Moses had made [II Kings 18: 4]"; such items were legitimate before his period. There is an interesting homily in Tosefta Abodah Zarah (Zuckermandel) 3: 19: וכי עבודה זרה היה "Was it והלא משה רבינו עשאו מלמד שטעו ישראל אחריו עד שבא חזקיה וגנזו [the bronze snake] idolatrous? [It could not be so] because our teacher Moses made it; we can deduce that [later] the Israelites erred [and considered it an idol] until Hezekiah came and hid it." It is interesting to observe the difference between the scriptural text, which uses the term כתת "crush" to portray the destruction of the bronze snake, and the reverence implied by the term גנז "to hide", reserved for an artifact made by Moses.

12: 3, it is clear from the pronominal suffix on the word מצבתם, "their altars", that the term refers to the idol's altars. In Deut. 16: 22 there is the indefinite ומצבה, but it seems to me that from the context it is evident that this refers to an idolatrous cultic element. The ban against erecting a מצבה is closely correlated with the prohibition against planting an אשרה, a cultic element which was never considered legitimate within Israelite custom. In contrast to מצבות, which were erected by Jacob (Gen. chaps. 28, 31 and 35) and Moses (Exod. 24: 4),[6] there is no record of a legitimate אשרה ever having been planted by biblical personalities.[7] It is evident from the text that the intent of Deut. 16: 21 and 22 was specifically to oppose the syncretism of planting an alien and idolatrous אשרה beside the altar of the Lord, and we must similarly interpret the erection of an idolatrous מצבה. The odd addition of אשר שנא ה' אלהיך in Deut. 16: 22 corroborates my interpretation that Scripture is specific about which pillars one must not erect: those which the Lord your God hates, namely those erected for the idols. There is support for this interpretation from the only other occurrence of such an expression in Deut. 12: 31: כל תועבת ה' אשר שנא "all kinds of detestable things the Lord hates"; here the phrase undoubtedly refers to idolatrous worship.[8]

We conclude that even according to the Talmud and the traditional commentators, such items as the מצבה were considered legitimate cult objects when utilized for the proper worship of the God of Israel, and the מצבה remained so at least until the period of Isaiah and Hosea, who did not criticize its presence.

[6] Joshua also erected pillars (Jos. 4: 5-9 and 5: 20), but the term מצבה is not utilized to portray these deeds.

[7] Abraham planted an אשל Gen. 21: 33), and built an altar at אלני ממרא (Gen. 13: 18); Jacob buried the foreign gods under the אלה (Gen. 35: 4), and buried Deborah under the אלון. These are probably all holy trees, but we have no mention of a legitimate אשרה.

[8] An interesting Midrash also connects and compares Deut. 12: 3 and 16: 22. We read in Midrash Tannaim to Deut 16: 21: ולא תקים לך מצ' ... שומע אני אף לא על קבר אביו ואמו ת"ל אשר שנא ה' אלה' נאמר כאן שנא ונאמר להלן (יב לא) שנא מה להלן בע"ז הכת' מדבר אף כאן בע"ז הכת' מדבר "Do not set up a מצבה...could I interpret [the ban to include] even a monument for one's parents? [No] It is written 'which the Lord your God hates.' Here it says 'hates' and there [Deut. 12: 31] it says 'hates'; as there Scripture refers to idolatrous worship, here too Scripture refers to idolatrous worship." Rashi interprets the ban to include even a pillar for the legitimate worship of God, and explains the reason: מזבח אבנים ומזבח אדמה צוה לעשות ואת זו שנא כי חק היתה לכנענים ואף על פי שהיתה אהובה לו בימי האבות עכשיו שנאה מאחר שעשאוה אלו חק לעבודה זרה "[God] commanded the building of an altar of stones and of earth, and hated this [the pillar], since it was a Canaanite custom. And although it [the מצבה] was agreeable to God at the period of the Patriarchs, He hates it now, because they [the Canaanites] built it as a practice in idolatrous worship." The Ramban, though his own solution is unsatisfactory, rightfully challenges Rashi's

T. Stäubli[9] speculates that the ark contained two מצבות - pillars in a box, similar to the Arab *qubba*, the portable sanctuary. Such an assumption would be appropriate given the nomadic character of the early Israelites, as expressed in the biblical desert narratives. There is possibly a recollection here of the two sacred pillars in the Debir, which were later changed into stone tablets inscribed with God's commands, as the desert epos was rewritten for aetiological purposes.[10] The existence of such pillars would also correspond to the scriptural record that Josiah "smashed the sacred stones" ושבר את המצבות (II Kings 23: 14).[11] Further, there is the talmudic dictum that the ark was hidden by Josiah. It is logical that Josiah would have had to destroy the legitimate pillars dedicated to the worship of the God of Israel, in order to centralize the cult in Jerusalem, just as he had the altars destroyed. At the same time, the ark disappeared, as we may learn from Jeremiah, a prophet in the period of Josiah (1: 2): בימים ההמה...לא יאמרו עוד ארון ברית ה' "In those days... men will no longer say 'The ark of the Covenant of the Lord' [v. 3: 16]." We read in the Talmud[12] ומי גנזו יאשיהו גנזו "Who hid [the ark]? Josiah hid it." The fact that the Talmud attributes the disappearance of the ark to Josiah is remarkable and must be considered as a record based on some reminiscence. The Rabbis did not attribute this act to Jeremiah, although the above verse hints at such a possibility; in fact, in II Macc. 2: 4 it

---

explanation. If the מצבה was banned because the Canaanites adopted it as an element of idolatrous worship, the same repudiation would be expected concerning the altar, which was also used by them for the same purpose. We thus see the difficulty in interpreting this verse as a ban against pillars dedicated to legitimate worship.

[9] Stäubli writes in *Das Image der Nomaden im Alten Israel und in der Ikonographie Seiner Sesshaften Nachbarn*, Orbis Biblicus et Orientalis 107(Göttingen, 1991), p. 224: "Das die beiden Gesetztafeln ursprünglich zwei Bethyle ware, is wahrscheinlich." J. Morgenstern had already written similarly in his book The Ark, The Ephod and Tent of Meeting (Cincinnati, 1945), p. 3: "The two former sacred stones or bethyls of the ark came rather speedily to be reinterpreted as two stones still sacred, but sacred now only because of a newly arisen tradition, viz., that upon them were written the ten 'words' of divine revelation." See also p. 78.

[10] The philological affinity between the term חקק "engrave" and the term חוק "statute" demonstrates that in ancient days the statutes were engraved on stone tablets, like the "Twelve Tables" in Rome. These circumstances may have facilitated the shift from pillars as sacred artifacts to stone tablets with engraved statutes, like the Ten Commandments.

[11] It is true that in II Kings 18: 4 the same phrase appears in the record of Hezekiah's deeds, but the issue of who started the reform of the centralization of the cult is a matter of discussion. The mainstream opinion is that the reform is to be attributed to Josiah, but it is possible that Hezekiah started the reform but was unable to complete it; it is, for instance, plausible that he started the destruction of the illicit pillars, and Josiah obliterated the pillars of the ark dedicated to the legitimate God.

[12] In Tosefta Sotah (Lieberman) 13: 1; B. T. Yoma 52b; B. T. Keritoth 5b; Y. T. Sheqalim 6: 1, 49c.

is written that Jeremiah hid the ark in a cave. The Rabbis must have had a valid reason for ignoring such evidence and attributing to Josiah the concealment of the ark with the stone tablets/pillars. It seems certain from Scripture that the golden ark with the tablets was not carried away by the Babylonians,[13] while it is logical that Josiah the reformer was behind the disappearance of every locus and symbol of worship outside the Temple; the destruction of all pillars outside the Temple provoked the disappearance of those inside the Temple. In conclusion, we may assert that the מצבה was a legitimate artifact of worship at least until the period of Josiah, when it was discarded as a result of the cult centralization, and not as an alien custom. Archeological evidence confirms the existence of מצבות in Strata XI and X at Arad and in Lachish,[14] that is, at least until the middle of the 8th century;[15] there is no evidence, at least in the archeological research published to date, for מצבות after this date. This lack of evidence does not conclusively prove that they were destroyed at this stage. On the other hand, it is possible that Hezekiah, who successfully accomplished a certain degree of cult reform, eliminated the said pillars in Beer Sheba.

2.1.2 Stone Tablets

The two tablets of the Law were of stone: (Exod. 24: 12; 31: 18; 34: 1; Deut. 4: 13). We must consider here two extraordinary and significant peculiarities:

---

[13] In the above cited Tosefta Sotah, other opinions are also mentioned. We read there: ר' "ליעזר אומ' ארון גלה לבבל ר' יהודה בן לקיש אומ' ארון נגנז במקומו Rabbi Liezer says: The ark was taken to Babylonia; Rabbi Judah ben Laqish says: The ark was hidden on its site [underneath the floor]." A Midrash in Mishnah Sheqalim 6: 1 - 2 states: והיכן היתה יתרה כנגד דיר העצים שכן מסורת בידם מאבותיהם ששם הארון נגנז מעשה בכהן אחד שהיה מתעסק וראה הרצפה שהיא משונה מחברותיה בא ואמר לחברו ולא הספיק לגמור את הדבר עד שיצתה נשמתו וידעו ביחוד ששם הארון נגנז "And where was the added [prostration]? At the storage room of the wood, because they had a tradition that the ark was hidden there. It happened that a priest working there observed that the floorboard was strange, and he recounted it to his friend; he did not finish his conversation and fell down dead. So they knew that the ark was hidden there."

[14] Zwickel, *Der Tempelkult in Kanaan und Israel*, p. 283.

[15] This dating is according to V. Fritz, *Tempel und Zelt, Studien zum Tempelbau in Israel und zu dem Zeltheiligtum der Priesterschrift*, WMANT 47 (Neukirchen, 1977), p. 45 n. 14, quoted by Zwickel, p. 271 n. 180. In the same note, Zwickel quotes Y. Aharoni, "Excavations at Tel Arad. Preliminary Report on the Second Season, 1963," *IEJ* 17 (1967), p. 248, who affirms that the מצבה stele found in Arad is from Stratum X, hence from a later date.

a) The exceptional writing on stone by the Deity, while other important and sacred words of God were written in books.[16]

b) For the second set of tablets, God commanded Moses: פסל לך שני לחת אבנים כראשונים "Chisel out two stone tablets like the first ones [Exod. 34: 1]," but there is no such command for the first set of tablets. We must thus understand from Scripture that the first set of tablets was given to Moses by the Deity Himself. We read in Exod. 24: 12 עלה אלי ההרה והיה שם ואתנה לך את לחת האבן "Come up to me on the mountain and stay there, and I will give you the tablets of stone." Whether we consider the everlasting stone as a symbol of God's eternal existence,[17] as incorporating the Deity,[18] or as the seat of the Deity,[19] we have here a unique connection between God and the stone tablets.[20]

---

[16] For instance, כתב זאת זכרון בספר "Write this on a scroll to be remembered [Exod. 17: 14]"; Exod. 24: 4 records only that "Moses wrote all the words of God" ויכתב משה את כל דברי ה', with no specific indication of the material on which he wrote, but in the following verse 7, the exact details are given: ויקח ספר הברית ויקרא "Then he took the book of the covenant and read it"; על כן יאמר בספר מלחמות ה "Therefore it is said in the Book of the Wars of the Lord [Num. 21: 14]"; את כל דברי התורה הזאת הכתבים בספר הזה "All the words of this law which are written in this book [Deut. 28: 58]"; ככל אלות הברית הכתובה בספר התורה הזה "All the curses written in this book [Deut. 29: 20]." There are, in fact, many other occurrences of ספר in Deut., and evidence that the book was to be kept together with the stone tablets, to serve equally as a witness to the Covenant: לקח את ספר התורה הזה ושמתם אתו מצד ארון ברית ה' אלהיכם והיה שם בך לעד "Take this Book of the Law and place it beside the Ark of the Covenant of the Lord your God. There it will remain as a witness to you [Deut. 31: 26]." (It is interesting to note that in B. T. Baba Bathra 14a-b we find a debate between two renowned Tannaim, Rabbi Meir and Rabbi Judah, with respect to where the scroll of the Torah was kept: inside the ark, or on a shelf protruding from the Ark.) Finally, the Shekhem Covenant, the parallel to the Sinai Covenant, was written by Joshua in a book: ויכתב יהושע את הדברים האלה בספר תורת אלהים "And Joshua recorded these things in the Book of the Law of God [Josh. 24: 26]."

[17] Arabia Sacra, pp. 16-17.

[18] Henninger cites R. Dussaud in "La Religion Bédouine Préislamique," p. 20:" Il faut se persuader que ce n'est pas à la pierre elle même que va l'adoration du fidèle, mais à la divinité q'elle incorpore." ("One must convince oneself that it is not the stone itself to which the veneration of the devotee is directed, but the divinity it incorporates.")

[19] W. R. Smith, *The Religion of the Semites*, pp. 189ff writes that the heathen Semite regarded the stone or cairn, which he had himself erected, as the dwelling place of a deity, a 'Beth El'. Cf. Gen. 28: 18 - 19: ויקח את האבן...וישם אתה מצבה...ויקרא את שם המקום ההוא בית אל "He took the stone...and set it up as a pillar...he called the place Beth El."

[20] This may have been the reason for a remarkable declaration in B. T. Baba Bathra 14a-b: אין בארון רק שני לחות אבנים [The verse"] לרבות שברי לוחות שמונחים בארון

2.1.3 Stoning as an Execution Method

One may also perceive the importance of stone in Arab and Israelite traditions in the fact of judicial execution by stoning. This method of execution is still applied today in certain Islamic states, who employ stoning for the sin of adultery, in accordance with the Muslim law.[21] This type of judicial execution is found in many instances in Scripture.[22] The Talmud

---

'There was nothing in the ark, only (that is, two negatives, and according to the talmudic interpretation rules, two negatives add up to a positive) two tablets (I Kings 8: 9)'] is there to include the broken pieces of the [first] tablets which were kept in the Ark."

[21] The stoning inflicted for adultery is not founded upon the Quran, but upon tradition, which relates it to oral instructions of the Prophet (Mishkat, book XV, chap. 1).

[22] Judicial stoning for transgressions is found in: Lev. 20: 2, Deut. 13: 11 and Deut. 17: 5 for idolatry; Lev. 24: 14, 16 and 23 for blasphemy; Deut. 21: 21 for the rebellious son; Deut. 22: 21 and 24 for adultery; Num 15: 35 - 6 for the desecration of the Sabbath; Jos. 7: 25 with respect to Akhan, who took items under the ban. This case requires some analysis. Akhan and his family were stoned and then burned. It seems that the death penalty was carried out by the stoning, and the burning served to destroy all the items. We observe that Scripture says: וירגמו אתו כל ישראל אבן וישרפו אתם באש ויסקלו אתם באבנים. ויקימו עליו גל אבנים גדול "Then all Israel stoned him and they burned them and stoned them with stones, and they heaped over him a large pile of rocks." This is the literal translation of the verse, but it seems that the translators and commentators had problems with the logic. The LXX does not mention burning and translates: καὶ ἐλιθοβόλεσαν αὐτὸν λίθοις πᾶς Ισραηλ καὶ ἐπέστησαν αὐτῷ σωρὸν λίθων μέγαν "and they pelted him with stones, and put on it a heap of large stones." The Targum has ורגמו יתיה כל ישראל באבניא ואוקידו יתהון בנורא בתר דרגימו יתהון באבניא ואקימו עלוהי דגור אבנין "And all of Israel pelted him with stones and burned them with fire after they pelted them with stones. And they put on him a heap of stones." This interpretation reverses the order of the Hebrew verse. The KJV and NIV interpret the verse in a manner similar to the Targum, namely: "...and burned them with fire after they had stoned them." It seems to me that in this case the Talmud has interpreted the verse in the most logical manner. In B. T. Sanhedrin 44a we read: וישרפו אתם באש ויסקלו אתם באבנים בתרתי אמר רבינא הראוי לשריפה לשריפה הראוי לסקילה לסקילה "'And they burned them with fire and pelted them with stones [Josh. 7: 25].' With two [punishments]? Said Ravina: What is suitable for burning, they burned, and what is suitable for pelting, they pelted with stones." I have stressed above the pronouns him and them; they stoned him, burned the other substances, and stoned them, his family and his animals. Then they made on top of him a great heap of stones as a symbol and admonition for the future. It may be that the stones were piled only on Akhan's body, and therefore this phrase is in singular; however, even if the stones covered all his family, the singular pronoun is appropriate, since Akhan was at the root of the trouble and the loss of life at the attack on Ai. There still remains a problem of consistency with verse 15: והיה הנלכד בחרם ישרף באש אתו ואת כל אשר לו "He who is caught with the banned things shall be destroyed by fire, along with all that belongs to him"; it seems that Akhan's punishment should have been by burning, not stoning. Rashi separates the phrase according to the intonation signs, to read: "That [property] under the ban which is caught

pronounces four methods of execution,[23] but in Scripture there are only two instances in which execution by burning is decreed,[24] both in the P stratum of the Pentateuch,[25] as well as the story of Tamar,[26] whom Judah ordered to be

---

[by the lot] should be burnt, and he and his animals should be pelted," so as to be consistent with the later narrative. Items under the חרם within the context of the story are equivalent to things devoted to God, like items later donated or promised to the Temple or to the priests. All the material contents of Jericho were devoted to the Lord: חרם היא וכל אשר בה לה׳ "[The city] and all that is in it are to be devoted to the Lord [Jos. 6:17]," therefore what Akhan took unlawfully must be burned. Perhaps we should read אתו "with him" instead of the אותו "him" of the Masoretic vocalization; this would imply that the purpose of this verse is not to order the manner in which the man should be punished, but to inform us that the "devoted things" are not to be returned to God, like other devoted items, but must be burned. Midrash Tanhuma (Ed. Buber), *Parshah* Massei offers an interesting solution, similar to the one I have proposed, to this apparent double punishment. Akhan took the things on Sabbath; thus he desecrated the Sabbath and had to be executed by stoning, as the law requires; the objects, however, had to be burned in accordance with verse 15.

Continuing with occurrences of stoning in the Bible, we read in I Kings 21: 10, 13 - 15 that Naboth was stoned for cursing God and king. The goring ox must also be stoned, as we read in Exod. 21: 28, 29 and 32. Ezekiel's metaphorical reference to stoning demonstrates that adulterous women were pelted with stones (Ezek. 16: 40 and 23: 47). There is also the use of stoning in lynchings, or non-judicial killings: Exod. 8: 22, 17: 4, 19: 13; Num. 14: 10; I Sam. 30: 6; I Kings 12: 18; II Kings 24: 21 and II Chr. 10: 18.

[23] We read in Mishnah Sanhedrin 7: 1 ארבע מיתות נמסרו לבית דין סקילה שריפה הרג וחנק "Four types of executions are administered by the court: stoning, burning, killing with the sword and strangling."

[24] There is one exception, and that is the case of an entire town which goes astray and practises idolatry (Deut. 13: 16); all the people must be killed by sword and all the contents burned. It may be that for practical reasons it would be impossible to stone the entire population of a town; or, as suggested *in Encyclopaedia Biblica*, Vol. 4, s.v. מיתות בית דין, pp. 946 ff., the town had first to be captured in battle, and therefore the people were killed by the sword. Two other instances of killing by sword, that of the priests of Nob by Doeg (I Sam 22: 19) and that of Uriah by king Jehoiakim (Jer. 26: 23), were both unlawful, and not judicially approved.

[25] We read in Lev. 21: 9: ובת איש כהן כי תחל לזנת את אביה היא מחללת באש תשרף "If a priest's daughter defiles herself by becoming a prostitute, she disgraces her father; she must be burned in the fire." This is the simple interpretation of the verse, and demonstrates that the priests instituted special regulations to preserve the genealogical purity and prominent reputation of their clan. The LXX translates לזנת as ἐκπορνεῦσαι, using the same term as used in v. 7 for אשה זנה וחללה לא יקחו, γυναῖκα πόρνην, which unmistakably refers to a prostitute. When a priest's daughter became a prostitute, she was liable to death, contrary to a lay person's daughter; though there is a general command against prostitution: אל תחלל את בתך להזנותה "Do not degrade your daughter by making her a prostitute [Lev. 19: 29]," there is no death penalty prescribed for either the father or the daughter. Moreover, in this case it is only the daughter who is degraded, but in the case of the priest's daughter, the priest, and with him the priesthood,

are also degraded. Since the sin of the priest's daughter is not as abominable as adultery, it is natural that she be condemned to a more lenient death than stoning, and that is burning. It is also possible that the priests, the authors of this rule, considered death by fire as particularly appropriate to their clan; this was the punishment of Nadab and Abihu for their particular ritual sin, so it was also appropriate for all the priestly clan as castigation for sin. They might also have attempted to reserve for members of their aristocratic clan a death less debasing then stoning. The Hammurapi codex contains different punishments for the different social classes, as did the Roman law. Both Noth, in his commentary to *Leviticus*, p. 156, and Elliger, in his *Leviticus*, pp. 280ff., affirm that verse 21: 9, proclaiming the distinct execution method for the priest's daughter, stands "in isolation, both in form and content" from the entire pericope. Its literary style is casuistic, in contrast to the apodictic style of verses 1 - 8. Noth speculates that the loose subject-relationship with v. 7, which mentions אשה זנה, may have been the reason for the insertion of v. 9 concerning the priest's daughter who תחל לזנת.

The Talmud, on the other hand, could not perceive that the death penalty was meted out to an unmarried prostitute simply because she was a priest's daughter, and therefore we read in Sifra on this verse, and in B. T. Sanhedrin 50b: יכול אפילו פנויה נאמר כאן אביה ונאמר להלן אביה מה להלן זנות עם זיקת הבעל אף כאן זנות עם זיקת הבעל יכול אפילו פנויה נאמר כאן אביה ונאמר להלן אביה מה להלן זנות עם זיקת הבעל אף כאן זנות עם זיקת הבעל "Is it possible that an unmarried [prostitute daughter of a priest must be burned]? [No!] It is said here 'her father' and it is said later 'her father' [Deut. 22: 21, the stoning of the adulterous woman]; just as there it refers to the fornication [of a woman] with respect to a husband, here too [it refers] to the fornication of [a woman] with respect to a husband." However, based on this interpretation Rabbi Simeon considers execution by burning to be harsher than stoning, and this is why the priest's daughter should be killed by fire. Affirming the possibility of different punishments for the same transgression, he argues that a priest's daughter should be executed with a more brutal and painful punishment, since her sin is greater: she defiled the priestly class. The orthodox modern scholar D. Hoffmann, *Leviticus*, pp. 89ff., has his comments conform to the talmudic interpretation, but must admit that the simple and plain meaning of the text is contrary to such an interpretation. He also notes that both Philo and Josephus interpret the verse according to its plain and simple message.

Execution by fire is also prescribed for a man who marries a woman and her mother (Lev. 20: 14), a rule which seems to be an extension of the purity codex in the P stratum of the Pentateuch. This illicit sexual intercourse does not seem to fall within the concept of incest; it is strange that they should be burned, whereas the punishment for 'real' incest, such as with a sister, is simply "being cut off" (Lev. 20: 17). Here too, Noth draws our attention to the odd form of the address in plural at the end of this verse (ולא תהיה זמה בתוככם "so that no wickedness will be among you"): "This would indicate that the verse did not belong to the basic form of the list of offences worthy of death" (p. 150). D. Hoffmann also observes in Leviticus, p. 71 that this verse is not in its correct place and should have been attached to the other types of incestuous intercourse. Verse 13 on homosexual intercourse divides, as it now stands, between the types of incestuous intercourse and the types of 'unnatural' sexual relations, such as those with an animal in v. 15. Hoffmann cites the talmudic range of execution methods to solve the oddity, declaring that the sequence of the verses follows the manner of execution; all the transgressions up to and including homosexual intercourse in v. 14 are punished by stoning, whereas the relations with a woman and her mother are punished by burning. Hoffmann's explanation does not hold, since the following verses 15 and 16 also deal with unnatural relations and are punished by stoning according to Mishnah Sanhedrin 7: 4. Thus it is verse 14, which decrees punishment by burning, which divides between the types of unnatural relations punishable by stoning in the antecedent verse 13 and the following verses 15 and 16; therefore, one must assume that v. 14 consists of a later interjection. I would speculate that the general codex of punishments was influenced by the Hammurapi Code, where most of the death sentences do not specify the method of execution. The same sort of a generic, non-specific death sentence, מות יומת, is encountered in the ancient Book of the Covenant in Exod. 21. Even in Exod. 21: 29, where stoning is decreed for the goring ox, the execution method for the owner is not specified. This lack of precise specifications may be due to a lax communal organization at that stage, when many rules of an established society were missing; on the other hand, it seems plausible that stoning was the common method of execution, and therefore it was not necessary to specify it. It was only an innovation, such as the stoning of the goring ox, which had to be explicitly emphasized. We may deduce such a postulate from two instances in Exodus, which refer to lynching by stoning as a method of killing. We read in Exod. 8: 22 (v. 26 in KJV): הן נזבח את תועבת מצרים לעיניהם ולא יסקלנו "And if we offer sacrifices that are detestable in their eyes, will they not stone us?" This method of killing was not used officially in Egypt (see *Lexicon der Ägyptologie*, ed. W. Helck und W. Westendorf [Wiesbaden, 1985], Band VI, s.v. "Todesstrafe"), hence it demonstrates an Israelite method of execution. The same conclusion can be drawn from the other occurrences of stoning, in Exod. 17: 4: עוד מעט וסקלני "They are almost ready to stone me," and in Num. 14: 10: ויאמרו כל העדה לרגום אתם באבנים "But the whole assembly talked about stoning them." We must come to the conclusion that stoning was the common method of execution in ancient Israel, and as we have seen, the two exceptional cases of execution by burning were later additions, as literary analysis confirms. We must also consider that in two cases in which the execution method was specifically decreed by God, for the blasphemer in Lev. 24: 14 and the wood-gatherer on Sabbath in Num 15: 35, stoning was proclaimed.

Two terms are utilized for stoning: סקל and רגם. I could not find any reason for this oddity. Only סקל appears in Exodus, while only רגם appears in Leviticus and Numbers, but in Deuteronomy both terms are utilized. Onkelos translates both terms with the verb רגם ; the LXX also does not distinguish between them and translates all occurrences with λιθοβολέω. It seems that there is no practical difference between the two terms; it is possible that some verses are from an earlier source than others, or both expressions were in use concurrently, and no importance should be granted to this variation. The Mishnah declares that stoning was performed in two phases, by tossing the convicted person down from a high point and then throwing stones on him. We read in Sanhedrin 6: 4: בית הסקילה היה גבוה שתי קומות אחד מן העדים דוחפו על מתניו... אם מת בה יצא ואם לאו השני נוטל את האבן ונותנה על לבו. "The House of the Stoning was two stories high. One of the witnesses pushed him [down] on his hips... if he dies [from this plunge] the sentence is carried out, and if not, the second [witness] takes the stone and drops it on his heart." B.T. Sanhedrin 45a derives this two-stage method from an expression in Exod. 19: 13, in the admonition against touching Mount Sinai during the revelation; we read there that the transgressor סקל יסקל או ירה יירה "shall be stoned or shot [with arrows]." The Talmud compares this to stoning and says: מניין שבדחייה "From תלמוד לומר ירה ומנין שבסקילה תלמוד לומר סקל יסקל או ירה יירה where do we know [that execution by stoning is performed by] plunging [him down]? Because it is written 'shall be shot [with arrows].' From where do we know that he should be stoned? Because it is written 'he shall be stoned or shot [with arrows].'" The Talmud makes no distinction between the terms סקל and רגם.

²⁶ It is not clear why Tamar should have been burned, or executed at all, being at that time a widow in waiting for the levirate. It is possible that for just that reason a special punishment was imposed rather than the usual stoning, perhaps based on custom. (Without discussing the historical authenticity of this story, I shall simply note that not only the punishment but the entire procedure does not comply with the levirate law in Deut 25: 5 - 10. According to that law, only a brother has the obligation to marry the childless widow, and only he can set her free by his public reluctance to do so. Her husband's father cannot discharge her from her obligation, and Tamar in our case should have suffered the same punishment for intercourse with Judah as for intercourse with a stranger.) The traditional commentators came up with several explanations to justify this severe punishment, so as to avoid inconsistency with the later Israelite law which does not dictate the death penalty; in their opinion the later law was already practised by the Patriarchs. Rashi says that Tamar was the daughter of Shem, who was a priest, and therefore the strict rule regarding prostitution of a priest's daughter in Lev. 21: 9 required her execution by fire. But Rashbam correctly objects that this punishment refers only to a betrothed or married woman, according to the talmudic law, not to one awaiting the levirate. He comes up with two solutions: one, that Judah was a prince and her behaviour was a *lesi majesta*, thus rendering her liable for death; and two, possibly in Judah's period adulterous wives were handed over to their husbands, who personally decided their punishment, as was the custom in Spain in Rashbam's period. (We may note that the Hammurapi Codex section 129, dating from approximately 1800 B.C.E., also allows the husband a certain discretion in deciding the fate of his adulterous wife.) Gunkel writes in his conclusion to the Tamar story in *Genesis*, 7. Auflage (Göttingen, 1966), p. 420 that even this late recension of the tale in Scripture bears the character of its very ancient origin. On the other hand, he speculates on p. 417 that death by burning for adultery is similar to the method of executing a priest's daughter accused of prostitution, as practised in Egypt, and was later replaced by stoning, as appears in Deut. 22: 23. With all respect, I suggest that Gunkel has confused prostitution and adultery, and does not offer a reasonable explanation for this method of punishment in the case of Tamar. The first question is whether a woman waiting for the levirate is considered pledged to a man, so as to fall within the circumstances in Deut. 22: 23ff., and is therefore liable to death by stoning, or, whether, according to rabbinic interpretation, a woman of such status is not liable to death for sexual intercourse. A second possibility is plausible, that her sin was prostitution, as Rashi suggests. C. Westermann, *Genesis*, Biblischer Kommentar Altes Testament, Band I/3 (Neukirchen, 1982), pp. 39 ff., offers an extensive exegesis of the Tamar saga. Westermann traces this saga from an oral transmission created during a period of mixed Israelite and Canaanite society, when intermarriage was a commonly admitted practice. Judah married a Canaanite woman, his friend Hira was probably a Canaanite, and likely Tamar, the woman he chose for his son, was also a Canaanite. Westermann also draws attention to the term קדשה "hierodule" utilized by Hira, which demonstrates the Canaanite esteem for the holy prostitute. I would add here that Judah himself only erroneously imagines Tamar to be a prostitute; the text says ויחשבה לזונה "he thought she was a prostitute," but Hira refers exclusively to a קדשה, a hierodule. The Canaanite influence on the story is evident, and therefore we may assume that death by burning was the common penalty for adultery in the Canaanite society whose way of life is portrayed in the story; it therefore does not bear witness that such a method was practised by the nomadic Israelite tribes which penetrated into Canaan.

burnt.[27] Abimelekh killed his seventy brothers on one stone: שבעים איש על אבן אחת (Jud. 9: 5); it is possible that this tale also had a mythological

---

I do not concur with Westermann's suggestion that the prior method of burning was later replaced by a milder method of stoning. Death by stoning, with all the humiliation attached to it, seems to be a harsher punishment than burning, as the rabbinic majority maintains in Mishnah Sanhedrin 7: 1, cited above. Only for stoning does Scripture decree an execution in public and by the public; we read in Lev. 20: 2: עם הארץ ירגמהו באבן "The people of the community are to stone him," in Lev. 24: 16: רגום ירגמו בו כל "The entire assembly must stone him," in Num. 15: 35: רגום אתו באבנים כל העדה "The whole assembly must stone him," in Deut. 13: 10-11 (9-10 in KJV): ידך תהיה בו בראשונה להמיתו ויד כל העם באחרונה. וסקלתו באבנים "Your hand must be first in putting him to death, and then the hands of all the people. Stone him to death," in Deut. 17: 5 – 7: יד העדים תהיה בו בראשנה להמיתו... וסקלתם באבנים "and stone them....The hands of the witnesses must be the first in putting him to death, and then the hands of all the people," in Deut. 21: 21: ורגמהו כל ... ויד כל העם באחרונה "Then all the men of his town shall stone him," and in Deut. 22: 21: וסקלוה אנשי עירו "the men of her town shall stone her." In Deut. 22: 24, the command to stone אנשי עירה the pledged maiden is addressed in plural: וסקלתם אתם "and stone them," and takes place in public: אל שער העיר "at the gate of that town." Furthermore, the body of the person stoned was then hanged for the entire day, an act of additional degradation. The decree to hang the executed person appears in Deut. 21: 22 right after the command to stone the rebellious son, and its plain interpretation is that it applies to all executed persons. We read there: וכי יהיה באיש חטא משפט מות והומת ותלית אתו על עץ "If a man guilty of a capital offence is put to death, his body should be hanged on a tree." Rabbi Eliezer consequently rules in Mishnah Sanhedrin 6: 4: כל הנסקלין נתלין "All those executed by stoning are hanged," but the other Sages maintain, based on complex rules of interpretation discussed in B. T. Sanhedrin 45b, that only idolaters and blasphemers must be hanged. Both sides do agree that the plain meaning of verse 22 demands the hanging of all those who are stoned. Rabbinic opinion sought to increase even further the disgrace of the convicted person, and ordered that he be stripped of his clothes before execution; we read in Mishnah Sanhedrin 6: 3: היה רחוק מבית הסקילה ארבע אמות מפשיטין אותו את בגדיו "At four cubits from the stoning site, he [the convicted] was stripped of his clothes." Though I have no objective criteria by which to judge which execution method is harsher, I suggest that the logical conclusion to be drawn from the above citations, particularly the opinion of the majority of Rabbis in Mishnah Sanhedrin 7: 1 who considered stoning to be the harshest method, would negate Westermann's assumption that burning was replaced by the milder stoning. I may also refer to the many occurrences in Scripture of lynching by stoning, a fact which suggests that stoning was the common method of execution, as it continues to be today in those Arab societies based on a nomadic culture.

[27] The threat by the men of Ephraim to burn Jephthah (Jud. 12: 1) for failing to call them to participate in the battle with the Ammonites was a proposed lynching, not a legal execution after a judicial process. Nor does the threat by the people of Timnah to burn Samson's wife and family (Jud. 14: 15) offer evidence contrary to my postulate of the prevalence of stoning in the Bible; this too was a proposed lynching, and the threat was made by Philistines, non - Semites.

basis.[28] In the following verse 6, we read that Abimelekh was king עם אלון מצב אשר בשכם "beside the great tree [the holy terebinth] at the pillar[29] in Shekhem."[30] We observe that even at the end of the Second Temple period, stoning was still the common Israelite method of execution for adulterous women, although the Romans had introduced their system of crucifixion. We read in John 8: 7 Jesus' proclamation concerning the adulterous woman: "If any one of you is without sin, let him be the first to throw a stone at her."[31]

It is possible that an ancient mythological belief was at the basis of execution by stoning.[32] Stone, a natural element associated with the eternal

---

[28] This scriptural narrative of multiple killings on one stone was likely the basis for certain talmudic homilies on the same subject. We read in B. T. Gittin 57b: סח לי זקן אחד מאנשי ירושלים בבקעה זו הרג נבוזראדן רב טבחים מאתים ואחת עשרה רבוא ובירושלים הרג תשעים וארבע רבוא על אבן אחת "An old Jerusalemite man told me that in that valley, the great executioner Nebuzaradan killed two million and one hundred and ten thousand, and in Jerusalem he killed nine hundred and forty thousand on one stone." W. Robertson Smith, *The Religion of the Semites* (New York: Paperback edition, 1972), p. 212, n. 2, also quotes a remarkable citation from Pliny, H. N. XXXVII: 161, similar to our text, about "an ordeal at the temple of Melcarth at Tyre by sitting on a stone seat."

[29] This is the NIV translation; the KJV interprets the term מצב similarly, translating "the plain of the pillar." J.A. Soggin, *Judges, A Commentary*, The Old Testament Library, trans. J. Bowden (Philadelphia, 1981), translates "by the oak of the pillar." Jonathan translates מישר קמתא and the traditional commentators follow, referring to pillars in the plain. The LXX, on the other hand, takes מצב as a verbal form and translates "the acorn standing in Shekhem."

[30] It is interesting to note that the Scots still revere today the stone on which their ancient kings were crowned. It has been stolen several times from Westminster Abbey, and recently returned to Edinburgh as a hallowed national treasure.

[31] I do not intend to discuss the complex issue of whether the Jews had the right to pronounce and carry out the death penalty during this period of Roman rule. Even if we assume that the Jews did not have this privilege, Jesus' utterance can be taken as a metaphorical use of an accepted procedure.

[32] There is a remarkable homily in Agadath Bereshith (Buber), בראשית א ט, פרק כו which suggests that stoning was both a primeval custom and a continuing method of execution: קין הרג את הבל אחיו באבן שנאמר ויקם קין אל הבל אחיו ויהרגהו והאיך הרגו אלא שנטל אבן והיה מכה בו בכל איבריו פצעים פצעים עד שמת... ואף קין נהרג באבן.. כך אבימלך זה הרג לאחיו באבן שנאמר ויהרג וגו' אבימלך על אבן אחת ונהרג גם הוא באבן שנאמר ותשלך אשה אחת פלח רכב על ראש אבימלך ותרץ את גולגלתו "Cain killed his brother with a stone, as it is written 'Cain attacked his brother and killed him [Gen. 4: 8],' and how did he kill him? He took a stone and hit all his limbs, injuring him until he died....And Cain too was killed by a stone [punishment similar to the crime];... and so Abimelekh, who killed his brothers with a stone, as it is written 'killed on one stone [Jud. 9: 5],' was also killed with a stone, as it is

power of the divine,[33] or the seat of the Deity, might have symbolized divine participation in the killing of the guilty,[34] just as the divine dwelling provides a safe-haven and rescues the innocent. The significance of pelting the convicted person with stones is emphasized by the distinct scriptural wording. In all instances in which the death penalty of a person is commanded, the material, אבן or אבנים, is added to the verb סקל[35] or רגם.[36]

---

written 'a woman dropped an upper millstone on his head and cracked his skull [Jud. 9: 53].'"

[33] It is certainly possible that execution by stoning in a nomadic society was instituted in order to enable the entire community to physically take part in its performance, or from some other anthropological motive. However, this does not prevent us from speculating on the precise reasons behind this particular execution method in the Arab and Israelite societies, or from positing a number of coexisting reasons. We read in *Enciclopedia delle Religioni*, chief editor A. M. di Nola (Roma, 1970), s.v. "Pietre", p. 1619 that for stone, as for other religious symbols, new significance may be added to previous mythological values; there is an ongoing process in which new "religious" experiences are added, as in a chain reaction, and create new mythological elements. We read further that the Bethyls in the Canaanite-Palestinian and Hebrew area represent the divine energy (p. 1624).

[34] The passage in Jos. 10:11 may also imply a divine slaying by stones. We read there: 'וה השליך עליהם אבנים גדלות מן השמים "The Lord hurled large stones on them from the sky." While it is true that in the second part of the verse these stones are called אבני הברד "hailstones", the text is remarkably different from other biblical narratives on hailstorms. The association of אבן "stone" with ברד "hail" appears only in this verse and in Isa. 30: 30, a verse which also stresses the might of God who chastises those whom He hates. We read there: והשמיע ה' את הוד קולו ונחת זרועו יראה בזעף אף ולהב אש אוכלה נפץ וזרם ואבן ברד "The Lord will cause men to hear his majestic voice and will make them see his arm coming down with raging anger and consuming fire, with cloudburst, thunderstorm and hailstone." We also notice that the hailstorm, as in other biblical instances, is associated with rain or thunderstorms, whereas in Jos. there is no mention of rain. One has the impression in Jos. that the hailstones were "hurled", as the term השליך indicates, in contrast to the hail in Egypt, where the phrase וימטר ה' ברד "and God has rained down hail [Exod. 9: 23]," is utilized. Although Exod. 9: 25 records ויך הברד... מאדם ועד בהמה "And the hail struck...both men and animals," it seems that the people were only hurt, not killed as in Jos. 10. We read in Ps. 78: 47 - 48 a description of the plagues of Egypt: יהרג בברד גפנם...ויסגר לברד בעירם ומקניהם לרשפים "He destroyed their vines with hail....He gave over their cattle to hail, their livestock to bolts of lightning." Similarly, we read in Ps. 105:32 – 33: נתן גשמיהם ברד אש להבות בארצם ויך גפנם ותאנתם וישבר עץ גבולם "He turned their rain into hail with lightning throughout their land. He struck down their vines and fig trees and shattered the trees of their country." In Egypt the hailstorm is associated with rain, and killed only the cattle and damaged the plants, but in Jos. the "stones", not associated with rain, killed more enemies than those killed by the sword; the divine might was thus manifested by the hurling of deadly stones.

[35] It is remarkable that the root סקל, which denotes in Hebrew execution by stoning, does not exist in Akkadian, and there is no evidence of this type of execution in the

These verbs in themselves suffice to express the act of pelting; in the penalty specified for the goring ox, for instance, only the term סקל is used[37] without the addition of the detail "with stones." Further, the association of סקל with אבנים occurs exclusively for judicial executions, whereas in references to lynching, only the term סקל appears.[38] It is therefore obvious that the term סקל would have been sufficient to describe an execution by pelting, and the addition of אבן in all instances of legal execution emphasizes the specific requirement of stone as the killing instrument, and its metaphysical significance. Other methods of killing were certainly known to the early Israelites, but they chose stoning as the principal method of legal execution. It is beyond the scope of this essay to extend the examination of anthropological issues, and thus I shall simply quote several similar examples. Robertson Smith[39] writes: "The slaying [of an animal, by the Arabs] involves a great responsibility, and must be justified by divine permission. The slaughterer is striking the victim in the name of his god." Robertson equates this attitude to the divine permission to kill living creatures for human sustenance as expressed in Gen. 9: 3: כל רמש אשר הוא חי לכם יהיה לאכלה "Everything that lives and moves will be food for you." He emphasizes[40] "the similarity between the ritual of sacrifice and the

---

Mesopotamian culture. It does, however, appear in Ugarit. *See Theologisches Wörterbuch zum Alten Testament*, s.v. סקל

[36] Lev. 20: 2; 20: 27; 24: 23 (the term אבן does not appear in the antecedent verses 14 and 16, but it is emphasized at the performance of the act itself in v. 23, where אבן appears clearly as the medium of execution); Num. 15: 35 - 36; Deut. 13: 11; 17: 5; 21: 21; 22: 21; 22: 24.

[37] Exod. 21: 28, 29, 32.

[38] Exod. 8: 22; 17: 4. There is only one exception to the rule in Num. 14: 10, the proposed lynching of the spies, where the term אבנים is added to the verb רגם. Although one would assume that the term רגם suffices without the addition of the material, as with the term סקל, I do not think that this exception negates the rule. The fact that here the medium, "stones", is explicitly named does not negate the proposition that the specific addition of "stones" in all occurrences of legal execution confirms its absolute significance in such executions.

[39] W. Robertson Smith, *The Religion of the Semites*, pp. 417ff.

[40] Ibid., p. 284. He also writes on pp. 418-9: "These coincidences between the ritual of sacrifice and of execution are not accidental; in each case they had their origin in the scruple against shedding kindred blood." W. W. Hallo, "The Origins of the Sacrificial Cult," in *Ancient Israelite Religion, Essays in Honor of F. M. Cross*, ed. P. D. Miller Jr., P. D. Hanson, S. D. McBride (Philadelphia, 1965), pp. 3-13, speculates on the feeling of guilt at the slaughter of a familiar domestic animal: "Myth and ritual, thus combined, invested what otherwise might have constituted essentially 'profane slaughter' with the aura of sanctity, literally 'making it holy'"(pp. 3-4). Also relevant to our investigation is

execution of a tribesman" in Arab society. The American Indian asked the forgiveness of the animal before killing it, because of a feeling that he was transgressing the law of nature, which guarantees life to all its elements.[41] In the Middle Ages, the courts invoked higher powers to establish the truth at the trial of an accused. His head was kept under water, and whether he survived or not served as evidence of innocence or guilt. The Bedouins today still use a hot iron to touch the tongue of an accused; if it is burned, he is considered guilty. We may deduce from the above practices that divine powers are being approached for guidance, and to sanction man's decision to convict and kill another human being. Execution by stoning in the ancient Semitic world may have fulfilled the same purpose.

2.1.4 The Significance of the Term צור

2.1.4.1 The Association of צור with Deity

The association of stone with numinous qualities in the ancient Semitic creed is especially apparent in the use of the term צור , a term meaning "rock", but which is also applied to the Deity. It is not within the scope of our study to examine the anthropological development of this belief; but we may substantiate its presence in biblical language in the use of צור as both a representation of the Deity and as a sacrificial locus. The term צור as a metaphorical denomination of the Deity is widespread in all sections of the Bible and needs no extensive substantiation.[42] In addition, the many theophoric names such as צוריאל, צורישדי, פדהצור, אליצור are evidence of the use of צור as one of the Deity's name. Scholars have observed the association of the Deity with the term צור since the earliest period of biblical research.[43] The Talmud also asserts that צור is the Deity's name. We read in B. T. Berakhot 5b: ואין צור אלא הקדוש ברוך הוא שנאמר צור ילדך תשי

---

the interesting fact that the Arabs pronounce the sacred utterance *bismala* "in the name of Allah" at the slaughter of an animal, as they do before other meaningful deeds.

[41] See John H. Bodley, *Anthropology and Contemporary Human Problems*, 2nd ed. (Palo Alto, Ca., 1976), p. 56, where we read: "Indeed, tribals generally consider themselves to be part of nature in the sense that they may... conduct rituals...and offer ritual apologies when animals must be killed."

[42] See *Theologisches Wörterbuch zum Alten Testament*, ed. G.J. Botterweck (Stuttgart, 1973), s.v. צור, section 5.

[43] See A. Wiegand, "Der Gottesname צור und seine Deutung in dem Sinne Bildner oder Schöpfer in der alten jüdischen Litteratur," *ZAW* 1 (1881), pp. 85 - 96, and the many studies published on this issue since.

"The Rock is only 'the blessed be He' [God], as it is said, 'Of the Rock who gave you birth you are unmindful [Deut. 32: 18].'"

The term צור "rock" as the seat of the Deity, the appropriate site of a theophany, and consequently as a place for offering sacrifices, is also evident.[44] In Jud. 13: 19 - 20, we also have evidence of the equation between the term צור "rock" and the term מזבח "altar", an equation which lies at the core of my thesis. We read there: ויקח מנוח את גדי העזים ואת המנחה ויעל על הצור לה' "Then Manoah took a young goat, together with the grain offering, and raised it upon the rock to the Lord," and then we read ויהי בעלות הלהב מעל המזבח "As the flame blazed up from the altar." Rock's significance is further evidenced in the hanging of Saul's descendants by the Gibeonites. We read in II Sam 21: 9 ויקיעם בהר לפני ה' "And they hanged[45]

---

[44] See *Theologisches Wörterbuch zum Alten Testament*, s.v. צור, section 4.

[45] The Targum translates וצלובינון "and they crucified them." The KJV translates "hanged" and the NIV "exposed". The LXX translates ἐξηλίασαν from the verb ἐξηλιάζω "to expose to the sun." The term נקע or יקע, if both forms are of the same philological root, is peculiar insofar as it has entirely different meanings in Qal and Hiph'il; or, perhaps each form has a different origin, and this would account for the different meanings. In Qal, it usually means "to move or turn away," as in Ezek. 23: 17, 18 and 22, and Jer. 6: 8; in the latter it appears with the subject נפש and is interpreted as "alienated" by the KJV, "turn away" by the NIV, and ἀποστῇ "stand away" (Liddell and Scott) by the LXX, all quite similar in meaning. The Targum translates the term in some instances with קצה and in others with רחק, both of which, when attached to נפש, have the meaning of "separate, to move away." In Gen. 32: 26, the expression ותקע כף ירך יעקב is translated by Onkelos with זע "it moved," but the LXX interprets ἐνάρκησεν "it grew stiff." In Num. 25: 4 the expression והוקע, identical in grammatical form to our term in II Sam., has a great variety of translations-interpretations. The KJV translates "hang them," the NIV interprets "kill them and expose them," Onkelos interprets it as וקטול "and kill," whereas the LXX interprets it as παραδειγμάτισον "make an example," in contrast to ἐξηλίασαν in II Sam. This seemingly odd interpretation of the LXX is probably due to the unclear or even contradictory narrative in Scripture. In Num. 25: 4, God commanded Moses to "hang them" (according to the talmudic exegesis, as I shall cite in the next footnote), but we have no record that any Israelites were actually killed or hanged. The concluding verse 9 declares: ויהיו המתים במגפה ארבעה ועשרים אלף "those who died in the plague numbered twenty-four thousand." It seems therefore that although we read in v. 5 that Moses conveyed God's command to the judges, it was not fulfilled. The Rabbis and the traditional commentators were aware of this equivocal pericope, and we find a fascinating homily in Y. T. Sanhedrin 10: 2, 28d, declaring that in the desert there were seventy-eight thousand and six hundred judges and officials, to whom Moses' command was addressed. This aggregate total is reached by dividing six hundred thousand, the number of men who departed from Egypt (Exod. 12: 37), by the number of officials over the thousands, hundreds, fifties and tens proposed by Jethro (Exod. 18: 21). Each one of them had to kill two sinners according to the command הרגו איש אנשיו "Each of you must put to death those of your men [Num. 25: 5]," that is two, since אנשיו is written in plural; hence one

them on the mountain before the Lord.'"[46] The term "on the mountain" is not defined, but the addition "before the Lord" unequivocally indicates a holy place;[47] the execution, which was to be an atonement for Saul's sin with the intent of conciliating the Deity and inducing the end of the famine, had to be carried out in God's presence, and thus those executed were exposed "before the Lord." The following verse indicates the precise place: ותטהו לה אל הצור "and spread it out by herself on a rock." The hanging took place on a rock before the Lord,[48] and the mother of the victims covered their bodies

---

hundred and fifty-seven thousand two hundred were killed. Rashi recites this explanation in his commentary in Num. 25, but the Ramban perceives the absurdity of such an exegesis that more than a quarter of those who left Egypt were killed at this event. He suggests therefore that the judges and officials did not start their action in time before Phinehas' vigilante act, which placated God's anger and terminated the plague. After Phinehas' courageous deed, there was no need for further action. But Ramban can plainly not dismiss the talmudic homily, speculating that there actually were such great numbers of sinners; but they were not killed, as a result of Phinehas' heroic action, which put an end to every kind of chastisement. It is therefore no wonder that the LXX utilized the vague παραδειγμάτισον "make an example."

[46] In view of the decree in Deut. 21: 22 that the one condemned to death had to be hanged after his execution, it is possible that here too the hanging was performed after the execution by the usual method, and therefore did not have to be mentioned; the main emphasis of the story is the men's exposure "before the Lord," and their mother's behaviour in protecting their exposed bodies. In fact, in his commentary to Num. 25: 4 where we find the same term in Hiph'il, והוקע, Rashi interprets it as "to hang them," and supports his view quoting our verse II Sam. 21: 6; he adds that idolatry, the sin in Num., demands the death penalty by stoning, and hanging afterwards. We observe that Rashi too considered that the hanging was performed after the stoning. His opinion originates from a talmudic interpretation in B. T. Sanhedrin 34b, where we read אמר רב חסדא מניין להוקעה שהיא תלייה דכתיב והוקענום לה' "Said Rav Hisda: How do we know that הוקעה means hanging? It is written in II Sam. 21: 6: 'exposed before the Lord.'" On the other hand, it is also possible that since they were handed over to the Gibeonites they were executed by impaling, a method common in Egypt and other surrounding cultures, as we learn from frequent mentions in Herodotus.

[47] The MT text does not indicate exactly where the executed persons were to be exposed, but another reading of II Sam. 21: 6 preferred by scholars (see Hertzberg, I & II Samuel, p. 380) indicates "Gibeon, on the mountain of the Lord" as the site of the exposure. If the latter reading is correct, one may postulate that the rock in Gibeon, האבן הגדולה of II Sam. 20: 8, and the צור in II Sam. 21: 10, were the primary elements of this most important sanctuary of that period; this was the reason for the Gibeonite demand to expose the bodies of the executed persons on the "mountain before the Lord."

[48] It is obvious that the traditional commentators could not consent to the idea that the execution was performed in the presence of the Deity, dwelling in the rock. Rashi and Radak explain in their commentaries to II Sam. 21: 6 that the Gibeonites' request to hang the men "before the Lord," actually meant "to make known God's legal decision." Another commentator explains: "It was according to God's decision." On the other hand, we find an interesting Midrash which would confirm my assumption that the execution of Saul's

against predators. Yet another explicit linkage of rock with the Deity is found in Exod. 17: 6: הנני עמד לפניך שם על הצור בחרב והכית בצור ויצאו ממנו מים "I will stand there before you by the rock at Horeb. Strike the rock and water will come out of it."[49]

From the numerous citations from the early writings, appropriate for comparison with our pericopes in Exodus and Deuteronomy, we thus observe the continuous significance of stone and rock in theological thought and its cultic applications. "Rock" symbolized the presence of the Deity, or was His dwelling place; this may have been the reason for the prohibition against wielding a sword on the stone, or breaking it, especially when it was dedicated as an altar.[50] This may also be the reason for the apparent oddity, discussed above, of the phrase כי חרבך הנפת עליה ותחללה "for you will defile it if you use a sword on it" in Exod. 20: 22, expressed in singular, following the first part of the phrase which appears in plural; this oddity emphasizes the sanctity of the "stone", as an element that is violated by wielding the sword upon it.

---

descendants was intentionally performed "before the Lord" to placate His ire, and achieve His pardon and succour. We read in II Kings 3: 27: ויעלהו עלה על החמה ויהי קצף גדול על ישראל "...[the king of Moab] offered [his firstborn son] as a sacrifice on the city wall. The fury against Israel was great." We read in Pesiqta d'Rab Kahana (Mandelbaum) *Parshah* 2, that the king of Moab asked his astrologers the reason for the Israelites' victory, and they told him that it was due to their ancestor Abraham, who offered his firstborn. He, therefore, offered his son on the wall. This Midrash maintains that he offered his son to the sun-god, because the term החמה is written without a ו, which reads as "the sun", but cannot explain why this idolatrous act would provoke fury against Israel. In B. T. Sanhedrin 39b, a sage declares that the king of Moab offered his son to the God of Israel, and this incited the fury against Israel. We observe that the king of Moab offered his son high up on the wall, in all likelihood to be noticed by the God of Israel, according to this Midrash. Cf. M. Rehm, *Das Zweite Buch der Könige*, who quotes a number of scholarly speculations on the reasons for God's anger.

[49] The parallel narrative appears in Num. 20: 7 - 13, but there the term צור is replaced by the term סלע; the story in the P stratum is obviously a repetition of the J narrative, with an aetiological purpose (see M. Noth, *Numbers*, pp. 144ff). I may add here additional support for Noth's assertion. In Exod. 17 the term הצור with the definite article is justified, since it refers to the known rock בחרב "at Horeb"; in Num. 20: 8, however, ודברתם אל הסלע "speak to the rock" would be incorrect, since the relevant rock is not specified. The editor of Num. 20 had to omit any reference to the rock at Horeb, since according to the context the Israelites were already at Kadesh. Further, the term סלע, a synonym of צור, also refers metaphorically in some instances to the Deity, as in II Sam. 22: 2; Ps. 18: 3, 31: 4, and 71: 3: ה' סלעי ומצדתי "The Lord is my rock and my fortress."

[50] H. W. Hertzberg, in *Die Bücher Josua, Richter, Ruth*, 3. Auflage (Göttingen, 1965), p. 61, suggests: "Das Behauen würde die Gottheit aus ihrem Wohnsitz verscheuchen." ("The hewing of the stones may chase away the Deity from his dwelling [in the stone].")

2.1.4.2 The Association of צור with Circumcision

Another unusual biblical narrative may also be related to the numinous significance of rock. We read in Exod. 4: 25: ותקח צפרה צר ותכרת את ערלת בנה ותגע לרגליו ותאמר כי חתן דמים אתה לי "But Zipporah took a flint knife, cut off her son's foreskin and touched [Moses'] feet with it: 'Surely you are a bridegroom of blood to me' she said." This pericope presents "one of the most obscure passages in the Book of Exodus," as Hyatt asserts, from both literary and exegetical aspects. It is unclear from the text who wanted to do the killing - the Deity Himself, or an angel or demon. Onkelos interprets מלאכא דה', "an angel of God," as does the LXX, with ἄγγελος κυρίου. The ambiguous text does not tell us the reason for God's will to kill, nor who was the intended victim: Moses, or the son who was circumcised; as it seems, this deed effected salvation. It is unclear whose feet Zipporah touched. There are also certain grammatical problems; for example, the expression ותגע לרגליו, in which the verb appears in Hiph'il, instead of Qal, as the context would require, and the use of the preposition ל, instead of the correct ברגליו.The explanation of the text is difficult. Both the Samaritan Pentateuch[51] and the LXX[52] already show certain more or less significant aberrations in the text, but are hardly more elucidating. The Talmud[53] and modern scholars[54] propose different solutions to explain this mythical text, heavily charged with mystery from beginning to end.

I have presented the background of this passage, but our interest is to be focused on the stone/flint, the implement of this mysterious salvation deed. The command for circumcision and records of its performance appear often in Scripture, but only in one other instance does stone occur as the instrument; there is no other citation which implies that such an implement is

---

[51] For example וירף ממנה "He let _her_ alone," instead of the MT text ממנו, "him".

[52] To avoid the enigmatic expressions חתן דמים and למולת, the LXX uses entirely different wording; it seems that the translator did not have before him another manuscript, but merely attempted to bring the cryptic text "down to earth." We read there in v. 25: ἔστη τὸ αἷμα τῆς περιτομῆς τοῦ παιδίου μου "This is the blood of the circumcision of my little child," and the same text is repeated in v. 26. It is interesting to note here the suggestion of a modern scholar, H.F. Richter, "Geschlechtlichkeit, Ehe und Familie im Alten Testament und seiner Umwelt", _BET_ 10 (1978) I25ff.; II, 20ff., that like the Samaritan Pentateuch, which reads וירף ממנה in feminine (see previous footnote), מולת is the plural feminine form of the person who performs the circumcision; this would demonstrate that the mystical element of the circumcision was reserved to women.

[53] See Y. T. Nedarim 3: 9, 38b.

[54] See Werner H. Schmidt, _Exodus_, Biblischer Kommentar Altes Testament II3 (Neukirchen, 1974), and C. Houtman, _Exodus, Historical Commentary on the Old Testament_, Vol. I (Kampen, 1993), both with extensive bibliographies on this subject.

required, or preferred. Gen. chap. 17 is entirely dedicated to the eternal Covenant with Abraham and his offspring, the pertinent change of his name, and the circumcision as the sign of the Covenant. There are precise indications regarding the implementation of the circumcision: to whom it applies, when it must be performed, and the sanctions for breaking the covenant by failing to fulfill this precept. One would expect here some indication of the preferred implement, if there were such a requirement, or even a predilection.[55] It is therefore odd that we read in Jos. 5: 2: בעת ההיא אמר ה' אל יהושע עשה לך חרבות צרים ושוב מל את בני ישראל שנית "At that time the Lord said to Joshua, 'Make flint knives and circumcise the Israelites again.'" Here the Lord explicitly commands Joshua to perform the circumcision with a stone implement, although one must acknowledge that metal knives, at least of bronze, were already in use in that period,[56] and in fact the term חרב appears often in Joshua.

The first question in Jos. 5:2 is the interpretation of the term חרבות צרים. The term צור, as we have seen in the instances cited above, must be interpreted as a rock, or metaphorically as a name of the Deity. In Exod. 4: 25, the term צר appears unaccompanied and must therefore be considered as a noun. Onkelos translates it as טינרא "stone", and the LXX similarly as ψῆφον. On the other hand, in Jos. 5: 2 we have the expression חרבות צרים and therefore the question arises whether the phrase is in construct form, whose interpretation would be "swords/knives of rock," or whether צרים is an adjective modifying the noun חרבות and its interpretation in the context would have to be "sharp knives." The Targum chose the second way, and interpreted this phrase as איזמלין חריפין "sharp cutting tools." Grammatical considerations, however, contradict such an interpretation. If the term חרבות is in absolute status, the vocalization of the ר should have been with a *qametz*; the actual *shewa* under the ר conforms with a construct status.

---

[55] Herodotus, *The Histories*, III: 8 writes on the method of pledging by the Arabs. A third person cuts the palms of the hands of the two involved people with a sharp stone, takes a tuft of wool and dips it into the blood, and smears the blood on seven stones which lie between them. We observe the significance of the stone both with respect to the cutting of the palms to obtain the blood for the covenant, as in circumcision (compare זאת בריתי אשר תשמרו ביני וביניכם...המול לכם כל זכר "This is my covenant with you and your descendants....Every male among you shall be circumcised [Gen. 17: 10]"), and as a witness to the pact, similar to Jacob's pact with Laban: ויאמר לבן הגל הזה עד ביני "Laban said: This heap is a witness between me and ובינך היום על כן קרא שמו גלעד you today; this is why it is called Galeed [Gen. 31: 48]."

[56] The ancient Code of Hammurapi, sections 215 and 218, discusses the penalties to be applied in the case of a "negligent" surgeon who operates with a bronze knife: Ch. Edwards, *The Hammurabi Code and the Sinaitic Legislation* (London, 1921), pp. 39-40.

Moreover, as an adjective, the attribute צרים must be in the same feminine gender as the noun חרבות.[57] The traditional commentators such as Rashi, Radak and Ralbag follow the Targum's interpretation and explain the term as "sharp knives." They quote as a similar paradigm the term צור חרבו in Ps. 89: 44, which seems to be a feeble help to their thesis; Rashi and Ibn Ezra translate צור חרבו in Ps. as "the sharpness of his sword," but support their interpretation by quoting our verse, Jos. 5: 2. The Targum translates Ps. with סיפיה "sword", ignoring the term צור, as does the LXX, which translates (88: 44) βοήθειαν τῆς ῥομφαίας αὐτου ̂"the aid of his sword." Only Radak, who considers the expression to be in construct status, offers another solution, possibly because of the above-mentioned grammatical problems; he suggests reading the combination as if it were "knives which have sharpness." The LXX, however, translates in Jos. 5: 2: μαχαίρας πετρίνας ἐκ πέτρας ἀκροτόμου "swords/knives of rock from sharp-cut rock." In conclusion, we must accept that flints were the implement required to perform this odd circumcision.

The real inconsistencies start with the narrative itself. In verse 2, we read ושוב מל את בני ישראל שנית "and 'again' circumcise the Israelites a 'second time.'"[58] It appears clearly from this verse that they have already been circumcised once, and here Joshua was commanded to perform circumcision again, a second time. But from verse 5, וכל העם הילדים במדבר בדרך בצאתם ממצרים לא מלו "and all the people born in the desert during the journey from Egypt had not been circumcised," one must assume that these people were actually circumcised by Joshua for the first time, not the second. The LXX has entirely changed verse 2, and has: καὶ καθίσας περίτεμε τοὺς υἱοὺς Ισραηλ "and sitting circumcise the sons of Israel." The LXX[59] has read ושב from the verb ישב "to sit", instead of ושוב, the adverb "again", but has ignored the fact that the MT text has the term שנית at the end of the verse, which would confirm that the circumcision was to be performed a second time. The odd name גבעת הערלות, the "Hill of the Foreskins" has also provoked various speculations, since "it seems unlikely to suppose that the people could have believed the hill to have been formed by the piling up of discarded foreskins in the course of the centuries," as A. Soggin[60] writes.

---

[57] See H. G. von Mutius, *Der Josua-Kommentar des Tanchum Ben Josef ha-Jeruschalmi* (Hildesheim, 1983), p. 30.

[58] In order to demonstrate the problems of this pericope, I have translated this phrase literally.

[59] The LXX has a completely different text for the entire pericope, which is somewhat more understandable, but retains the concept of knives of sharp rock, as we have seen.

[60] A. Soggin, *Joshua, A Commentary*, translated by R. A. Wilson (Philadelphia, 1972), p. 69.

An aetiological explanation for this particular name is suggested by Soggin and John Gray.[61] Soggin quotes Dhorme's proposition that the place near the Gilgal sanctuary "may have been marked by the presence on the ground of a large number of dressed flints,"[62] a suggestion which relates the story to an ancient myth. It is interesting to note Hertzberg's hypothesis, quoted by Soggin, that the performance of the circumcision with a flint knife, as late as in the Bronze Age, might be compared to the custom of setting up altars of undressed stones, as appears in Exod. 20: 22. Hertzberg considers the "preference for materials in the raw state" to be the common factor between the Law of the Altar and the circumcision with a flint knife. I regard his proposition as a support to my thesis, although I perceive a different symbolism underlying the pericopes: the ancient reverence for stone because of its numinous qualities, which assumed different patterns in its developmental stages.

It is not within the scope of this study to solve these problems, which have been much deliberated by scholars; I am only interested in examining whether the stories of the circumcisions by Joshua and Zipporah can support my thesis. Marten H. Woudstra[63] connects the two stories "as another parallel between the lives of Joshua and of Moses," and I also suggest a common pattern in these enigmatic texts, insofar as they are the only occurrences of circumcision with flints. A Midrash in Pirqei de Rabbi Eliezer, *Pereq* 28 ד"ה הנס השמיני explains that it would be impossible to assume that the Israelites were not all circumcised in the desert, but the ceremony was not performed correctly, שלא כתקנם. Such a proposition would explain the scriptural term שנית, that the circumcision had to be performed "a second time." This supposition led me to hypothesize a similar conjecture. At special occurrences, when the aid of magical or mysterious[64] deeds was necessary to avoid unusual dangers, the use of the archaic flint knives for the circumcision celebration was considered propitious, whether the circumcision was performed for the first time, or as a second symbolic blood letting. Such an occasion is explicitly described in Exodus at the Zipporah narrative, and might be implicitly understood from the concluding v. 9 of the Joshua narrative, היום גלותי את חרפת מצרים מעליכם "Today I have rolled away the reproach of Egypt from you." This statement apparently has no connection to the circumcision. However, Radak explains that the Egyptians were not circumcised and that was considered shameful, as Jacob's sons said

---

[61] John Gray, ed., *Joshua Judges and Ruth,* The Century Bible (London, 1967), pp. 69 ff.

[62] Ibid., p. 70.

[63] Marten H. Woudstra, *The Book of Joshua* (Grand Rapids, Michigan, 1981), p. 99.

[64] It is not my intention to discuss here the issue of magical versus mystical; I have therefore mentioned both terms.

to Hamor in Gen. 34: 14: לאיש אשר לו ערלה כי חרפה ה]י[א לנו "[We
cannot give our sister] to a man who is not circumcised. That would be a
dishonour to us." But we know that the Egyptians did circumcise their males,
and hence this suggestion does not resolve the meaning of חרפת מצרים.
Rashi suggests that the Egyptians had foretold a bad omen, involving blood,
for the Israelites, but did not fathom that it was the blood of the circumcision
which was foreseen; the meaning of this verse was then that the bad omen
was rescinded by the circumcision.[65] That the Joshua narrative is a special
occurrence, not just a regular circumcision, is also corroborated by the total
absence of the mention of the covenant ברית, the rationalization behind
circumcision.[66] The scholars quoted above assert the antiquity of the texts, or
of the stories, but it seems unreasonable to assume that the people of Israel
would retain so late in their history an idea that circumcision was still
generally performed with flint knives. On the other hand, it is plausible that
they might retain mythological recollections of such a custom at specific
times, when its ancient and mysterious power would be instrumental in
challenging and resisting supernatural forces.

Hertzberg[67] offers an interesting solution to the circumcision at the Gilgal
sanctuary: it was to prepare the people for the entrance into the holy land, a
cultic deed. This corporeal association of the Israelites with the sanctuary is
compared to the bodily contact of the prophet with the divine realm, at his
ordination for his preaching office, as in Isa. 6: 6 - 8 and Jer. 1: 9.[68] Hertzberg
considers the circumcision at the sanctuary as a symbolic encounter with the
divine, a proposition not entirely comparable to the pattern he notes in Isaiah
and Jeremiah. On the other hand, if we accept my suggestion of the numinous
attribute of stone, the circumcision with flint would constitute a direct
corporeal contact, and is thus identical to the situations in Isaiah and
Jeremiah.

We must consider that the circumcision of the sexual organ is intrinsically
a mythical custom,[69] dating back to prehistoric times and performed in

---

[65] W. H. Hertzberg, *Die Bücher Josua, Richter, Ruth*, p. 33, suggests interpreting חרפת
מצרים as "the mockery of the Egyptians" because the Israelites were not circumcised;
but both Hertzberg and Soggin, who quotes the above proposition, admit that this does not
offer a satisfactory solution.

[66] This absence of mention of the Covenant was observed by Soggin, p. 70.

[67] p. 32.

[68] We read in Isa. 6: 7: ויגע על פי ויאמר הנה נגע זה על שפתיך "He touched my mouth
[with the live coal] and said: 'See this has touched your lips.'" In Jer. 1: 9, we read: וישלח
ה' את ידו ויגע על פי "Then the Lord reached out His hand and touched my mouth."

[69] There is evidently a relationship between myth and ritual. Scholars debate whether rituals
develop as enactments of myths, or myths develop to justify rituals. Without arguing for

various forms by many primitive societies to this day. The phallus has a distinct status in the ancient patriarchal narratives. Abraham told his servant: שים נא ידך תחת ירכי ואשביעך בה' "Put your hand under my thigh and I shall make you swear by the Lord [Gen. 24: 2-3]."[70] The term ירך is a euphemistic expression for the phallus, as is clear from the terms יצאי ירכו "which came out of his loins [Gen. 46: 26]" and יצאי ירך יעקב "that came out of the loins of Jacob [Exod. 1: 5]." We may therefore consider that the other biblical narrative in which Jacob's "loins" are mentioned, Gen. 32: 26, which is again heavily mystical, also refers to his sexual organ. We find in Genesis Rabbah (Vilna) *Parshah* 77 an interesting homily on this narrative: ויגע בכף ירכו נגע בצדיקים ובצדיקות בנביאים ובנביאות שהן עתידין לעמוד ממנו "[The verse says]: 'He touched the hollow of his thigh.'[71] [This means] he touched the righteous men and women, the prophets and the prophetesses, who would be engendered from him in future." We have here a third enigmatic narrative connected with a supernatural force and in which the male sexual organ has a pivotal status. While there is no flint or circumcision in Jacob's story, it serves as support to my thesis of a pattern of mystical significance in the three narratives, and in two of them the flint knife has a distinct importance.

2.1.5 Stone and the Sacrificial Cult

We come now to our complex and aggregated pericope in Deut. 27: 2- 8 with a number of rules referring to various issues, such as the fulfillment of the Covenant, cult performances on an altar and the inscribing of the Law for posterity, all related to stone. אבנים גדלות, large stones, are to be set up at the Jordan crossing, other stones are to be set up at Mount Ebal, אבנים

---

one theory or another, I will simply note here my agreement that the two are intricately interrelated and have important functional connections with the social and psychological life of a people. See Clyde Kluckhohn, "Myths and Rituals. A General Theory," in *Reader in Comparative Religion, An Anthropological Approach*, ed. W.A. Lessa and E.Z. Vog (N.Y., 1979), pp. 66-77.

[70] We may note that the custom of the Arabs to swear by Allah's phallus continued until recent times. See *Handbuch der Altarabischen Altertumskunde*, in Verbindung mit Fr. Hommel und Nik. Rhodokanakis, ed. D. Nielsen, I. Band, *Die Altarabische Kultur*, (Kopenhagen, 1927), p. 224.

[71] The translation of this term is a complex issue. I have used the KJV translation in the text; the NIV reads "the socket of Jacob's hip." Onkelos translates בפתי ירכו, which could mean "the widening of his thigh, or hip" (Jastrow); the LXX translates τοῦ πλάτους τοῦ μηροῦ αὐτου, "the breadth of his thigh," and Jastrow translated accordingly. But the same term μῆρος is utilized by the LXX to translate the expression יצאי ירכו in Gen. 46: 26, which unmistakably refers to Jacob's sexual organ.

שלמות "whole/perfect" stones are to be used for the building of an altar, and finally there are the stones upon which the Law is to be written. The importance of stone in the entire social and cultural life of the Israelites cannot be underestimated. After the Jordan crossing, we find in Joshua chap. 4 that twelve stones were taken from the Jordan, from under the feet of the ark bearers, that another twelve stones were set up in the Jordan, and that there was a monument of twelve stones at Gilgal.[72] In Joshua chap. 8 we find the fulfillment of the command in Deut. 27: 2 - 8, that is, the writing of the Law on stones and the erection of an altar on Mount Ebal. In Joshua 24: 26 - 27 a great stone, אבן גדולה, was set up under the oak, in the sanctuary of the Lord תחת האלה אשר במקדש ה׳, to serve as witness to the Covenant between God and Israel: האבן הזאת תהיה בנו לעדה.

We have clear indications of the association of stone with the sacrificial cult in the earlier biblical writings, and historical evidence of the importance of certain stones, each of which kept its specific name in remembrance of some significant event. We do not know precisely what these events were, but we may speculate that miracles occurred, or were said to have occurred, at the sites of these megaliths. Certain narratives describe the Deity's dwelling at or appearance on these stones, from which derived their name, holiness and veneration. In I Sam. 4: 1 we read: ויחנו על האבן העזר "They [Israelites] camped at Eben Haezer," with no indication of the name's origin; but in I Sam. 7: 12 we read: ויקרא את שמה אבן העזר ויאמר עד הנה עזרנו ה׳ "He [Samuel] named [the stone] Eben Haezer, saying, Thus far has the Lord helped us." We need not dwell here on the apparent anachronism;[73] it suffices to demonstrate a link between the stone and a theophany.

The ark was returned by the Philistines on a cart pulled by cows, who kept to a straight road, turning neither right nor left; in the same miraculous way they stopped at a large rock ושם אבן גדולה (I Sam. 6: 14). At this holy rock the cows were offered as holocausts. This rock remained a holy place for a long period, as we read in v. 18: עד היום הזה "[a witness] to this day."[74]

---

[72] I have cited several midrashim concerning the number of stone piles set up by Joshua; the text is somewhat confusing, and the Rabbis attempted to find order in it.

[73] The name Eben Haezer occurs in I Sam. 4: 1, and the Israelites who camped there were severely defeated. Samuel's naming of the place Eben Haezer as a sign of the Israelites' victory occurred later, as narrated in I Sam. 7: 12. It follows therefore that Samuel's naming of the stone Eben Haezer is an aetiological justification for a name to be traced back to some other long forgotten event; at any rate, the name itself witnesses some miraculous occurrence. Such episodes were considered acts of divine intervention, and thus evidence of a divine appearance.

[74] Although the MT has אבל הגדולה, the LXX corrects to λίθου τοῦ μεγάλου, "the great stone," as does the Targum, where we find אבנא רבתא. Rashi too states: אבל הגדולה

היא האבן הגדולה האמורה למעלה שהלמ״ד באה במקום נו״ן" - "It is the large stone mentioned above" and adds the reasonable philological explanation that "ל and נ are interchangeable." S. R. Driver has also corrected the MT reading to אבן in his *Notes on the Hebrew Text and the Topography of the Books of Samuel* (Oxford, 1913), p. 57. From the context it is evident that we must read here האבן הגדולה instead of אבל הגדולה, since in v. 15 we read explicitly וישימו אל האבן הגדולה "and placed them on the large rock." The prepositions אל and על are often interchanged in Scripture; the Targum interpreted here על אבנא "on the stone" as does the LXX, translating ἐπὶ τοῦ λίθου. In other occurrences of the term אבל, such as אבל בית מעכה or אבל השטים, it is evident that the term is used in its meaning of "plain". It seems that because certain localities contained the term אבל, "The plain of ...," the error occurred here in the MT, and was legitimately corrected. H. W. Hertzberg, *I & II Samuel, A Commentary* (Philadelphia, 1964), p. 60, suggests that v. 15 would demonstrate a later deuteronomic influence, namely that "the great stone was only the resting place of the ark," and adds "This verse is meant to be understood as implying that the sacrifice took place elsewhere." I do not think that the text requires such an interpretation. Hertzberg mentions the issue of the Levites, who took down the ark, and I assume that this was his main reason for supposing a later influence. I would argue that Levites were a guild of knowledgeable clerics, who were dispersed all over the land, and it was only natural that they were on the spot to take down the ark from the cart and place it at the sacred locus, at the great rock. The Levites were not considered a tribe descended from a common forefather Levi, and no genealogical requirements were necessary for their participation in cultic activity. We read in Jud. 17: 7: נער...ממשפחת יהודה והוא לוי "A young man ...from the clan of Judah, who was a Levite." And in v. 9 the Levite vividly portrays his way of life as a cleric: לוי אנכי מבית לחם יהודה ואנכי הולך לגור באשר אמצא "I am a Levite from Bethlehem in Judah, and I am looking for a place to stay." For a general survey of the concepts of לוי and כהן at this early stage of the cult development, see P. Heger, *Incense*, pp. 259 ff. and relevant notes. A deuteronomic influence, as Hertzberg suggests, would have also corrected the idea, clearly stated in v.15, that lay people, not Levites or priests, offered the sacrifices: ואנשי בית שמש העלו עלות ויזבחו זבחים "The people of Beth Shemesh offered burnt offerings and made sacrifices to the Lord." The other possible reason for Hertzberg's interpretation is the apparent division in this verse between the phrase וישמו אל האבן הגדולה "and placed them [the ark and the chest with the gold objects] on the large rock," and the following phrase ואנשי בית שמש העלו עלות "and the people of Beth Shemesh offered holocausts," a literary structure which may imply that the offerings were performed at a place other than the stone. Hertzberg speculates that the verse distinguishes and divides the two elements, the resting place of the ark on the great stone, and the sacrifice of the whole-burnt offerings "on the legitimate altar," all according to the deuteronomic tradition. I do not see any reason to split the verse in this manner, and to imply a motive that was not intended. According to my thesis, the slaughtering was made on a simple earthen altar, near the stone, the Deity's dwelling; the ark was placed on the stone, and the offerings were made at the stone. This narrative thus confirms the numinous character of the stone, and the simple altars at the "sacred large stone."

There is no censure of the sacrificial celebration by the people at the great stone, which one would expect according to the deuteronomic code. The people were punished because they "looked" into the ark where the invisible God dwelled, an ancient Israelite belief, as

When the people sinned through improper handling of the blood of the slaughtered animals, Saul moved swiftly to rectify their misdeed, בגדתם, and to atone for the treason; he ordered a large stone to be rolled toward him, גלו אלי היום אבן גדולה (I Sam. 14: 33) and had the slaughter take place there, according to the correct cultic custom.[75]

---

we read in v. 19: 'ויך באנשי בית שמש כי ראו בארון ה "[God] struck down some of the men of Beth Shemesh, because they had looked into the ark of the Lord." S. R. Driver (p. 58) discusses the odd expression ראו בארון, which "does not mean to look into"; this oddity, and the fact that the LXX has a different text at the beginning of the verse, suggest to him that there must be some error in this verse. Hertzberg also discusses this issue, and attempts to see here an anachronism in the prohibition against laics seeing the ark. It seems to me that it was not the viewing of the ark which was prohibited in that period, but merely the handling of the ark by people not specifically dedicated or consecrated to that purpose, or the looking into the inside of the ark, the seat of the unseen Deity. It is obvious from the text that the people saw the approaching ark וישמחו לראות "and rejoiced at the sight [v.13]." There is no reproach here against their seeing and rejoicing, and there is no censure in the following verses 7: 1 - 2 where it is told that the men of Kiriath Jearim came and took the ark and kept it there. They too were not Levites, but they dedicated and consecrated one person to guard the ark: ואת בנו קדשו לשמר את ארון ה' "and consecrated [Eleazar] his son to guard the ark of the Lord." In II Sam. 6: 2 - 17, David and the people brought the ark to the City of David, and only Uzzah was struck down, because וישלח עזה אל ארון האלהים ויאחז בו "Uzzah reached out and took hold of the ark of God [v. 6]." The traditional translators and commentators were, it seems, also perplexed by this phrase כי ראו בארון; their focus was not the grammatical issue mentioned by Driver, that the phrase should have been written אל תוך הארון, but rather the substance of the sin. The Targum interprets דחדיאו ודחזו ית ארונא דה' "they enjoyed seeing the ark of the Lord," an association with the improper behaviour mentioned in Exod. 24: 11: ויחזו את אלהים ויאכלו וישתו "they saw God and they ate and drank." In B. T. Sotah 35a two Rabbis discuss this issue: רבי אבהו ורבי אלעזר חד אמר קוצרין ומשתחוים היו וחד אמר מילי נמי אמור מאן אמריך דאימרית ומאן אתא עלך דאיפייסית "Rabbi Abahu and Rabbi Eleazar: One said they were reaping and bowing [at the same time, that is, they did not address the proper reverence to the ark, and did not stop their work], the other said they also criticized [God's course of action, and said]: Who enraged you [so that you let yourself be taken in bondage] and who conciliated you so that you became conciliated [and returned]." In Numbers Rabbah *Parshah* 5 ד"ה ט, אהרן ובניו, we read an additional explanation: ר' לוי אמר נכפפה היריעה שעל הארון וראו בו "Rabbi Levi said, The cover of hides [Num. 4: 6] was bent [during transport], and so they looked at the ark." Midrash Tanhuma פרשת ויקהל סימן ז ד"ה ויעש בצלאל (ז) adds that the ark was uncovered by the blowing wind. The commentator Radak, on the other hand, prefers the simple and straightforward interpretation, and says שפתחו אותו וראו מה שבתוכו לפיכך אמר בארון ולא אמר ארון "They opened it [the ark] and saw what was inside, and therefore it is written in the ark, not just 'the ark.'"

[75]   See chap. 1 n. 141 for an extensive explanation of the nature of the transgression.

The decisive duel between Joab and Amasa took place in Gibeon, at האבן הגדולה "the large stone" (II Sam. 20: 8).[76] There is no indication here of the sacred significance of this stone, but we know from other sources[77] that located in Gibeon was the Great *Bamah*, where Solomon offered a thousand burnt offerings and experienced his most important theophany (I Kings 3: 4). It is plausible to assume that this "large stone" was an important element of, or perhaps the primary reason for, the location the Great *Bamah* at this site.

At the miraculous offering by Elijah at Carmel, he repaired the altar with twelve stones (I Kings 18: 31 - 32), שתים עשרה אבנים כמספר שבטי בני יעקב "one for each of the tribes descended from Jacob." We observe once more the significance of the stones, which here symbolized the unity of the people and were incorporated into the altar.

There are other instances of stones with particular names, a fact that demonstrates their significance, but we do not know the stories and events behind them - for example, אבן האזל [78]in I Sam. 20: 19 and אבן הזחלת in I Kings 1: 9. With respect to the latter, though we do not know the reason for the name,[79] we do know that the stone was unquestionably a dedicated site

---

[76] The expression there הם עם האבן הגדולה "While they were with the great rock" is somewhat odd, and the traditional commentators explain that it should be interpreted as "at the great rock." This may be so, given that prepositions may have a wide range of meaning; but there may also be a more subtle intention: they came to be with the sacred stone to experience a communion with the divine, or to pray for the success of their forthcoming battle.

[77] We do not have earlier evidence of the significance of this sacred place, but we may assume that it served as an ancient sanctuary long before Solomon's period; a location at which the most important *bamah* was established, and hecatombs of sacrifices were performed, must have been of ancient origin. There is an explicit statement in the Talmud that Gibeon was already a sacred place and the Tabernacle was situated there prior to the story of the duel in II Sam. 20: 8. We read in B. T. Zebahim 118b: ימי אהל מועד שבנוב וגבעון חמישים ושבע...כשמת עלי הכהן חרבה שילה ובאו לנוב כשמת שמואל הרמתי חרבה נוב ובאו לגבעון "The period that the Tabernacle existed in Nob and Gibeon was fifty-seven [years]....When Eli the priest died, [the tabernacle of] Shilo was destroyed and they went to Nob; when Samuel of Rama died, Nob was destroyed and they came to Gibeon." According to this Midrash, the Tabernacle was transferred to Gibeon at Samuel's death, an event announced in I Sam. 25: 1, at a time when David was still subject to Saul's pursuit.

[78] The Targum translates אבן אתא; following this the traditional commentators interpret it as a signpost at the cross-roads. The LXX has παρὰ τὸ εργαβ ἐκεῖνο.

[79] The Targum translates אבן סכותא "lookout stone". Rashi proposes another explanation, namely that it was a smooth stone which could be moved (זחל = crawl). Radak imagines water flowing around the stone. Interestingly, Ralbag admits, "We do not know the reason for that name" and ponders the possibility that it was moved, as in Rashi's proposal. The LXX simply has the name Ζωελεθ without any explanation.

where ceremonial sacrifices were habitually performed: ויזבח אדניהו צאן ובקר ומריא עם אבן הזחלת "Adonijah then sacrificed sheep, cattle and fattened calves at the Stone of the Zoheleth."

Even in much later times, when the theology behind the numinous attributes of stone was long forgotten, and we hear no more of bans on cut stones or on using iron in the Temple (as I shall illustrate in section 2.2.1 and 2.2.2), the stone preserved its momentous status in the parlance relevant to the Temple. We find in Zech. 3: 9 the prophet's promise that the Temple will be built with great care and attentiveness; stone is prominent in his symbolic portrayal: כי הנה האבן אשר נתתי לפני יהושע על אבן אחת שבעה עינים "See the stone I have set in front of Joshua. There are seven eyes on that one stone."

The אבן משכית in the later Lev. 26: 1 and משכיתם in Num. 33: 52, which are denounced as idolatrous elements, demonstrate that cultic stones were in use in Israel. Onkelos, it seems, did not know the specific purpose of this cultic stone, and translates in Lev. אבן סגידא "a stone for worship", and in Num. בית סגדתהון "their house of worship." The LXX, on the other hand, identifies these terms as oracle or protector stones; in Lev. the translation is λίθον σκοπὸν and in Num. τὰς σκοπιὰς αὐτῶν.

Later evidence is found in Mishnah Ta'anith 3: 9: אמר להן צאו וראו אם נמחית אבן הטועים "He said to them 'Go out and see if the Stone of the 'Claimants' [the conventional translation] disappeared [under the flood water].'" It seems from the Y.T's explanation of its peculiar name and purpose that this stone was extraordinarily tall and associated with lost items.[80] The talmudic explanation has charm, and perhaps during the period of Honi Hama'agel this stone was indeed employed for the stated purpose, but I suspect that there is another, philologically more appropriate explanation for this name. Onkelos, whose work dates from this period, uses various grammatical forms of טעה to translate אל נכר, אלהים אחרים and similar terms denoting idols and alien gods. He also uses טעה in Deut. 13: 14 (13 in KJV) for the translation of the term דחי, translating וידיחו את ישבי עירם as ואטעיו ית יתבי קרתהון "they have led the people of their town astray." The verb טעה "to err," "to be mistaken," "to lead astray" in Hiph'il,

---

[80] We read at Y.T. Ta'anith 3: 9, (66d): מה עיסקה דהדא אבן הטועים אלא כל מאן דהוה מובד מילה הוה נסב לה מן תמן וכל מאן דהוה משכח מילה הוה מייבל לה לתמן אמר להן כשם שאי איפשר לאבן הזאת להימחות מן העולם כך אי אפשר להתפלל על הגשמים שילכו להם "What was the purpose of this stone? Everyone who lost something retrieved it from there, and everyone who found something brought it there. Said [Honi Hama'agel] to them: As it is impossible for this stone to be flooded over [as this would require a deluge, which would be contrary to God's covenant], so one cannot pray to stop rain."

or as the noun "error", "mistake", is not identical to the verb אבד "to lose" and its noun "something lost." Thus the talmudic interpretation relating the name טועים to "lost things" is incorrect; my interpretation of טועים as "errant ones" is philologically correct.

This Stone of the Errant Ones, I suggest, was once used by the people to offer sacrifices to idols, and when this habit changed, this appropriate name was devised. It is probable that with the passing of time, the original meaning of the name fell into oblivion, as with other aetiological explanations of biblical names, and a new meaning came into being. Such a postulate, which I assume to be highly probable, would confirm the importance of stone, and particularly the large stone, in the early sacrificial cult.

Further late evidence is the continuing importance, even to this day, of the Jewish אבן השתייה, the rock upon which the world was founded,[81] and upon which the Arab Dome of the Rock was later built. The theologies behind the original belief in the holiness of this rock vanished long ago, but belief in its sanctity subsisted.

2.2 The Historical Setting

2.2.1 The Use of Iron

In Exod. 20, the term חרב "sword" represents a homicidal implement that defiles the numinous attribute of the altar, with no indication of the material of which it is made. In Deut., the material ברזל "iron" is indicated as the material which one is not allowed to wield upon the stones. In addition to the differences in the motive for the restrictions, discussed above, I suggest that one should also treat this distinction as significant. The Exod. pericope obviously dates from an early period, as is evident from the command to build an earthen altar. Its origin is probably in the Late Bronze Age; iron was not yet in use, and therefore the term "sword" is used to represent the concept

---

[81] We read in Y. T. Yoma 5: 3, 42a: משניטל הארון אבן היתה שם מימות הנביאים הראשונים ושתייה היתה נקראת גבוה מן הארץ שלשה אצבעות "After the ark was taken away, there was a stone there [in the Holy of Holies] from the time of the first prophets, and it was called 'Eben Hashtiyah', three fingers high from the ground." We observe that the tradition attributes an ancient origin to this holy stone. In Y. T. Yoma 8: 3, 45a, we read the rationalization of the name: למה נקרא שמה אבן שתייה שממנה הושתת העולם "Why is it called 'Eben Hashtiyah'? Because from it the world was founded [from the root shatah]."

of a killing tool. In the later Deuteronomy,[82] iron was already used in the production of tools, and therefore the term "iron" appears, used as a generic denomination of cutting and splitting tools.

Support for this postulate that a division between the Bronze and Iron ages[83] is evident in the text may be deduced from the comparison and contrast of a number of other pericopes. In the account of the building of Solomon's Temple and his palace in I Kings 5: 31 - 7: 51, a wealth of materials is described, including gold and bronze, but there is no mention of iron. In the parallel narrative in II Chr. 2: 2 - 4: 22, iron is mentioned in 2: 6 (v. 7 in KJV): איש חכם לעשות בזהב ובכסף ובנחשת ובברזל ובארגון "a man skilled to work in gold and silver, bronze and iron and in purple," and in v. 13. In I Chr. chaps. 22 and 29, there is a long list of materials prepared by David for the building of the Temple, an account which has no parallel in Kings, and in this list ברזל "iron" is prominent. There are six occurrences of "iron" in these two chapters, with an indication of its purpose (22: 3) and its significant quantity: וברזל מאה אלף ככרים "and a hundred thousand talents of iron [29: 7]." A further example of this addition of iron in the late book of Chronicles is found in II Chr. 24: 12, the repair of the Temple performed by Joash: וגם לחרשי ברזל ונחשת לחזק את בית ה' "...and also workers in iron and bronze to repair the Temple." In the parallel pericope in II Kings 12: 13, iron is not mentioned.[84] Thus iron appears in the later writings, and is absent in the earlier ones.[85]

---

[82] In fact, the term ברזל "iron" occurs exclusively in the Pentateuch in Deuteronomy and in the P stratum, with the one exception of Gen. 4: 22: תובל קין לטש כל חרש נחשת וברזל "Tubal-Cain, who forged all kind of tools, out of bronze and iron."

[83] I do not intend to enter into a discussion of the exact date when the Iron Age started and the dating of iron objects found in Israel. It suffices for our purpose to demonstrate that in David's period arms of bronze were still in use even by the Philistines, who were skilled blacksmiths. We read in II Sam. 21: 16: ומשקל קינו שלש מאות משקל נחשת "...whose [the Philistine's] bronze spearhead weighed three hundred sheqels." Although we read in I Sam. 17: 7 that Goliath's spear shaft had an iron point weighing six hundred sheqels, ולהבת חניתו שש מאות שקלים ברזל, we observe that the remainder of his equipment - the helmet, armour, greaves and javelin - were made of bronze. Iron was probably still scarce and its application restricted. Moreover, the Israelites had no skill in the treatment of metals, as we read in I Sam. 13: 19: וחרש לא ימצא בכל ארץ ישראל "Not a blacksmith could be found in the whole land of Israel."

[84] In the pericope II Chr. 34: 10 - 11 that records the repairs performed by Josiah, there is no mention of iron. This pericope is quite short and is almost identical in its text and style to the parallel record in II Kings. 22: 4 – 7; this similarity will be discussed further in chap. 8.

[85] It is interesting to note that in the Temple Scroll of the Second Temple period, iron is mentioned as one of the materials utilized for the building of the Temple. We read in

In Ezekiel, we find a plethora of rules on the building of the Temple and its furnishings, but there is no mention of any ban on using iron tools or iron as building material. The exact and complex structure and size of the holocaust altar is described in 43: 13 - 17, with no mention of its material or any limitations in the manner of its building. On the contrary, Ezekiel specifies that four tables for the holocaust should be of dressed stones וארבעה שלחנות לעולה אבני גזית (40: 42). If there were an interdiction against using dressed stones on which iron tools were wielded for the altar, as the pericope in Deut. 27 was interpreted, the same interdiction should apply to the tables for the holocaust.[86] Moreover, Ezekiel describes the wooden table-altar in 41: 22: המזבח עץ...זה השלחן אשר לפני ה׳ "There was a wooden altar... that is the table that is before the Lord," and it seems impossible to construct a wooden table with exact measurements without using metal tools. The Talmud describes a method of building a stone altar with exact dimensions without using metal tools,[87] but I cannot envisage how

---

Column III, line 7: נחו[שת וברזל ואבני גזית "bronze and iron and dressed stones." I shall not discuss the dating of the Temple Scroll and its interrelation with Chronicles; on this issue see D. Swanson, *The Temple Scroll and the Bible, The Methodology of 11QT* (Leiden, 1995), pp. 237ff. For our purpose it suffices to demonstrate that the mention of the term "iron" in Deut. 27, in contrast to "sword" in Exod. 20, confirms the former's much later origin.

[86] In *The Temple Scroll* (English version, 1983), Vol. I, p. 240, Yadin restores the missing words in Col. XII: 11 as אבנים שלמות, linking it to the command in Deut. 27. His conjecture is founded solely on a lacuna which may be of a size to allow this phrase; he thus carefully underscores "may be", because there is nothing left on this line on which to base any speculation. In light of my interpretation and deduction from the text of Ezekiel, whose model of the holocaust altar is similar to that described in the Scroll, as Yadin himself affirms, I cannot conceive of such a rule. There is no hint of any limitation regarding the type and quality of the stones in Ezekiel, and on the other hand, there are no dimensions or any rules regarding the altar's structure in Deut. 27, in contrast to Ezekiel's punctilious instructions. The lacuna in the Scroll could be filled in with the phrase אבנים גדולות "large stones"; this requirement may still have been in force in this period for aesthetic reasons, and such stones were, as we know, used for the building of the Temple and its surrounding walls by Herod.

[87] We read in B. T. Zebahim 54a תא שמע, דתני לוי כיצד בונין את המזבח מביאין מלבן שהוא שלשים ושתים על שלשים ושתים אמה וגובהו אמה ומביא חלוקי אבנים מפולמות בין גדולות בין קטנות ומביא סיד וקוניא וזפת וממחה ושופך וזה הוא מקום יסוד וחוזר ומביא מלבן שהוא שלשים אמה על שלשים אמה וגובהו חמש אמות ומביא חלוקי אבנים כו׳ "Come and hear, as Levi taught: How does one build the altar? One takes a square form thirty-two cubits by thirty-two cubits, and one cubit high, and one brings smooth stones [in their natural form, uncut and undressed], either large or small, and one brings lime and plaster and pitch and mashes it together and pours it [into the form] and that is the foundation [of the altar]. And he then brings a square form thirty cubits by thirty cubits and five cubits high, and brings smooth stones etc."; the process is then repeated to reach the top. Thus, with the help of lime and plaster, one can

a wooden construction of a specific size and form could be fashioned without the employment of such implements. Even if we might assume that primitive man had been able to achieve such an objective, the Israelites of the Persian period[88] would likely have forgotten this archaic skill. Such work would moreover still be in defiance of the law expressed in Exod. 20, which considers the wielding of a homicidal instrument to be a defilement of the altar; since Scripture does not specify the type of instrument, an implement made of sharpened stone would effect the same defilement as a metal sword. This consideration should also serve as evidence of the division in essence and in time of the two pericopes of our study. Similar considerations apply with respect to the law of the bronze-covered wooden altar in Exod. 27: 1 - 8;[89] this altar could not have been constructed as ordered, if the restriction on the use of homicidal implements still prevailed. We must conclude that at a certain juncture in history the restriction against using homicidal-type implements for the construction of sacred loci was obsolete and disregarded.

I do not think there is sufficient convincing evidence to state whether the pericope in Exod. 20 originates in its totality from one period, or whether verse 21, the command to build an earthen altar, derives from a primeval period when such altars were in common use, and verses 22 - 23, which allow for stone altars, were a later addition.[90] Both parts of the pericope

---

build an altar of undressed stones of exact dimensions. *The Interpreters Dictionary of the Bible* (New York, 1962), s.v. "altar" by K. Galling, asserts that an altar with exact dimensions could not possibly be built of unhewn stones. The author of the study declares, therefore, that "this prohibition did not prevail permanently." This statement corroborates my thesis of a change in the Law of the Altar, although my assumption is not deduced primarily from practical considerations, but from a change in the underlying theology.

[88] 6th century B.C.E., the period of Ezekiel.

[89] Even if we consider the traditional biblical statement that the Tabernacle and its furnishings were actually erected in the desert before the settlement in Canaan, that is, in the Late Bronze Age (1200 - 1400 B.C.E.), this specific skill would have been forgotten. It would certainly be impossible to construct such an altar without metal tools in the post-exilic period, when scholars assume that the chapters on the Tabernacle were compiled.

[90] Cf. Y. Sakowitz, ספר הברית מבאר את ספר הברית - תופעת הבומרנג in *Texts, Temples and Traditions, A Tribute to Menahmen Haran*, ed. M. V. Fox et alii (Winona Lake, 1996), pp. 59 – 64, who writes on pp. 60 ff. that the law of the stone altar in Exod. in the Book of the Covenant was "boomeranged" there from Deuteronomy 27: 5. While I admit that such retrojections from later sources were often inserted into older sources, I do not think that it is plausible to assume such a shift in our case. Such retrojections are usually almost identical in their choice of expressions and style, and neither is noticeable. Yet here we have חרב in one place and ברזל in the other, and מזבח אבנים and גזית in Exod. are replaced by מזבח and שלמות אבנים in Deut. Moreover, if vv. 22 - 23 in Exod. were copied from Deut., we must ask the question whence came the two concepts

reveal features of a nomadic culture.[91] The nomad offers protection to a guest in his dwelling,[92] including his enemy; that is, he prohibits the use of a sword against his guest. It is natural that the same sensitivity to the use of a homicidal implement should be granted to the altar, the Deity's dwelling, where a fugitive turns for safe shelter.[93] I suspect that this equation is the basis for the biblical custom of offering safety to one clinging to the altar.[94] The talmudic explanation for the prohibition against using the sword in the process of the altar's construction, because "the altar was created to prolong the life of man, and iron was created to diminish it," harmonizes perfectly with this conjecture.[95]

ותחללה and the prohibition against climbing up the altar in Exod., as they do not exist in Deut. The particular cult expression חלל as "profane" is unknown to the deuteronomic editor; the term חלל in Deut. has the notion of "start-begin-initiate." For instance, חללו in Deut. 20: 6 and תחללנו in 28: 30 both indicate the first gathering of grapes from newly planted vineyards, while other instances have the generic meaning "start", as for example תחל לספר "start counting" in Deut. 16: 9. See further on the meaning of חלל section 1.2.3.3.

[91] J. Henninger, *Arabia Sacra*, p. 235 ff. compares the altars of South Arabia with those of North Arabia. Whereas the first, originating from a settled society, are of an elaborate character, those from the northern nomadic tribes are not real altars but simply heaps of rough stones.

[92] The high priority bestowed upon the protection of a guest in one's dwelling in the early Israelite period is evident from two biblical narratives. Lot offered his own virgin daughters to the wicked men instead of delivering his guests to them, saying: כי על כן באו בצל קרתי "...for they have come under the protection of my roof [Gen. 19: 8]." Similarly, the old man who granted shelter to the Levite and his concubine offered his own virgin daughter to the evil people of Gibeah, declaring: אל תרעו נא אחרי אשר בא האיש הזה אל ביתי אל תעשו את הנבלה הזאת "Don't be so vile. Since this man is my guest, don't do this disgraceful thing [Jud. 19: 23]." It is remarkable that "the disgraceful thing" is not their desire for illicit sex, as he offers them his virgin daughter, but the violation of the sacred custom of granting shelter. I do not intend to authenticate these narratives, particularly the former, but they do verify the strict importance of this custom in the public mind.

[93] J. Gray writes in *I & II Kings*, p. 96: "The fugitive from vengeance...,was regarded as *ger 'elohim*, the protected sojourner with God"; cf. Arabic *jar Allah*, who has similar rights. The nomadic custom is identical as between Arabs and the ancient Israelites in this respect as well.

[94] Cf. C. Houtman, "Der Altar als Asylstätte im Alten Testament," *Revue Biblique* 103-3 (1996), pp. 343 -366. On p. 345, n. 7, he writes: "Natürlich ist das Gastrecht und das Asylrecht miteinander verwandt." ("The right of shelter [as a guest] and the right of asylum are certainly linked together.")

[95] It is interesting to note that the Sages demonstrate a "modern" comparative approach to the analysis of scriptural decrees, whereas the later traditional commentators are hesitant to adopt any explanation that might be considered comparable to the pre-Islamic custom.

We observe another common pattern between this pericope and the Book
of the Covenant, of which it seems to be an integral element according to
most scholars. The term מזבח appears often in the Pentateuch, but the
expression מזבחי , by which God refers to "<u>My</u> altar", appears only in in the
Book of the Covenant, in Exod. 20: 23 and in Exod. 21: 14, מעם מזבחי.[96]
The unusual utterance תעשה לי in vv. 21 and 22 of our pericope, in which
the Deity similarly commands the making of an altar "for Me", is perhaps[97]
another indication of a common ancient origin of these verses, which share
an anthropomorphic aspect.[98] One cannot exclude, therefore, the possibility
that all three verses of our pericope originate from the same nomadic period,
when there would have been sporadic building of stone altars either during a
longer stay at some oasis, or at a location where stones were readily
available, and their numinous quality was preferred for the sacrificial cult. On
the other hand, it is possible that v. 21 with its command for the building of
an earthen altar originates from an ancient period of wandering in the desert,
and vv. 22 - 23, permitting the construction of a stone altar, reflect a later
period, after the settlement in Canaan. As discussed above, older observances

---

We may assume that the Sages were aware that their rationale contained elements which
were similar to foreign custom and doctrine, but did not consider this fact as negating
their beliefs. Rashbam and Ibn Ezra, as we have seen in chap. 1 n. 78, seem to disagree
with the talmudic rationale for the prohibition against using a homicidal implement for the
building of the altar, and pursue other reasons. This disagreement is in itself odd, and
suggests a reluctance to incorporate hints of foreign influence or similarity. Rashbam's
opinion, in fact, emphasizes that the prohibition on using dressed stones was instituted to
counteract an alien custom.

[96] We may note that the asylum privilege of the altar, to which this phrase refers, is itself an
archaic custom, which was not operative in the later deuteronomic period. Hence, the
antiquity of this verse with the anthropomorphic language is again corroborated from this
pericope.

[97] I am suggesting this postulate with some reserve, because we find the same expression
מזבחי six more times in Scripture: in I Sam. 2: 28 and 33; in Isa. 56: 7 and 60: 7; and in
Mal. 1: 7 and 10. On the other hand, we must distinguish between these six occurrences,
where the prophet utters the phrase in the name of God, and our case in Exod. where it is
the Deity Himself who pronounces it: Exod 20: 21 - 23 follows the antecedent phrase (v.
20) ויאמר ה' אל משה כה תאמר אל בני ישראל "The Lord said to Moses: Tell the
Israelites this." The other occurrence of מזבחי in 21: 14 follows the antecedent in v. 1:
ואלה המשפטים אשר תשים לפניהם "These are the laws you are to set before them."
The expression תעשה לי "make for me" appears exclusively in our pericope in Exod.
20: 21 - 23.

[98] In fact, Onkelos interprets תעשה לי as תעביד קדמי "make it before me," in the same
manner as he interpreted the anthropomorphic phrase ריח ניחח לה' as דמתקבל ברעוה
קדם ה' "which is well-received before God." Onkelos considered this expression too to
be anthropomorphic, hence of ancient origin, not in the deuteronomic style; the later altar
law in Deut. 27: 5 - 6 has מזבח לה' אלהיך.

continue to subsist together with new ones for shorter or longer periods, and one might assume that this was the case with the earthen and stone altars in the early period of settlement, until the ultimate disappearance of the first type. In any event, the nomadic creed that a "sword" must not have any interaction with the altar, the Deity's dwelling, persisted for a longer period, as witnessed in vv. 22 - 23. One must admit that v. 23, prohibiting the climbing up or standing on the altar for reasons of piety, seems to support the first hypothesis; it portrays an extremely primitive way of life, when men covered themselves with only a piece of cloth, without any undergarment or trousers.

2.2.2 Effects of Cultural Change

The conditions which we perceive in Deut. 27 indicate an origin in a later period, after the settlement in Canaan. The earthen altar, characteristic of a nomadic society, has totally disappeared, being inappropriate for a settled, permanent community, and has been replaced by the type of stone altar used by the earlier settlers, the Canaanites. The nomadic sensitivity to the conflict between "sword" and "shelter" in both the human and the divine dwelling[99] had also lost its purpose and its philosophical justification. This concept fell into oblivion, but the attribution of a holy quality to stone, and its various expressions, obviously persisted into the monarchic period. These circumstances are evident in the rules of Deut. 27: 5 - 6 with respect to the handling of the stones for the construction of the altar.[100] The stone, or the altar,[101] is not defiled by connection with the sword,[102] but the sacredness of

---

[99] The concept of the altar as safe haven was replaced by the concept of the cities of refuge in the later P stratum.

[100] M. Weinfeld writes in מיהושע ועד יאשיהו (Jerusalem, 1992), pp. 177ff., that in Deuteronomy we encounter ancient laws from earlier sources which were adapted to the new objectives of the centralization of the cult. In the same manner we must assume that shifts in the way of life in Israel, and in the underlying theology, are also evident in other issues including the changes in the Law of the Altar. We perceive these changes in the alterations in the text and the rules in the deuteronomic pericope, when compared to the pericope in Exodus. Weinfeld also suggests, significantly, that the book discovered in Josiah's period is not the same as that which we have before us today; the former underwent yet further changes. We must therefore conclude that up to a certain point in time, constant changes and additions were made in the different biblical books, according to various ideological shifts, and hence an entire narrative, phrase or rule in a book considered to be of an earlier origin may actually be of a later date.

[101] I refer to my examination of the subject of the verb ותחללה and the pronoun עליה in section 1.2.2.1.

stone demands its inviolability as אבנים שלמות "whole-perfect stones." The stones for the altar may be smoothed, but not cut into pieces by wielding a hatchet or a pickax on them to break them into the sizes needed for construction. The stones are to remain entire, as brought up from the quarry. From the photos of the archeological findings, we observe that the מצבות "stone pillars" were slightly smoothed stone blocks, rounded on top, but with varying dimensions; most likely they were kept "complete" and unbroken, as they were found in nature.

It is reasonable to assume that after Josiah's period and the final disappearance of the מצבות, stone pillars, from the Israelite cult, particularly from the Debir, the inner sanctuary of the Temple, the notion of the sacredness of the stone ceased. But the custom of building the altar of complete and unbroken stones remained for some time; this custom was the motive for the rules in Deut. 27: 5 - 6. The old theology was no longer relevant, and might have been forgotten, but the custom subsisted.[103] There is ample proof from biblical sources of this process, according to which the custom prevails subsequent to a change in the theology; in some instances we

---

[102] God commanded Moses: פסל לך שני לחת אבנים "Chisel out two stone tablets [Exod. 34: 1]." If the prohibition on using hewn stones for the altar was still in force at the time of the writing of this verse, it would be reasonable to suppose that the same limitation would apply to the two sacred stone tablets with divine writing upon them - והמכתב מכתב אלהים הוא חרות על הלחת "The writing was the writing of God, engraved on the tablets [Exod. 32: 16]."

[103] It is also possible that the custom too was ignored for some time and was renewed much later, when more significance was bestowed upon the exact performance of the scriptural commands without questioning their rationale. One is tempted to speculate in this direction, since in Ezekiel we find no mention of a command to use complete stones or a prohibition against using iron tools for the construction of the altar, although exact and extremely complex instructions are set out by this prophet. Given these unique and most detailed ordinances in Scripture for the building of the altar, the absence of any rule based on the deuteronomic provision cannot be considered an oversight, nor as evidence ex silentio that such regulations were not in force at Ezekiel's period. On the other hand, we find a notion of such a custom in I Macc. 4: 47: καὶ ἐλαβον λίθους ὁλοκλήρους κατὰ τὸν νόμον καὶ ᾠκοδόμησαν θυσιαστήριον "and they took entire/perfect [the same term as the LXX uses in its translation of Deut. 27: 6] stones, according to the law and built an altar," whereas Josephus records in *Against Apion* I: 198 that the stones of the altar were ἀτμητων "uncut". The editor of Macc. offers us only the vague explanation "according to the law," with no specifics, in contrast to Jos. 8: 31, where we read: ככתוב בספר תורת משה מזבח אבנים שלמות אשר לא הניף עליה ברזל "...according to what is written in the Book of the Law of Moses - an altar of whole-perfect stones, on which no iron tool has been wielded." One has the impression that in this period the rationale behind the prohibition against using iron tools on the altar stones was alien to the existing theology and general philosophy, and therefore it was not mentioned; but the custom was kept, because of a desire to comply strictly with the biblical commands and ordinances.

find both new and old aetiologies,[104] but in other instances the custom subsists notwithstanding that the reason is entirely forgotten.[105]

---

[104] For example, in the aetiologies of the holy days. There are in Scripture two intermingled explanations behind the Feast of Unleavened Bread and the Passover: the archaic, agricultural Spring festival, and the memory of the deliverance from Egypt (Deut. 16: 1 and others). In Lev. 23: 34 - 43, we encounter an amalgamation of two originally disparate reasons for the Feast of Tabernacles. In v. 39 we read: באספכם את תבואת הארץ תחגו את חג ה' "After you have gathered the crops of the land, celebrate the festival of the Lord," and in vv. 42 – 43: we read בסכות...כי בסכות תשבו שבעת ימים הושבתי את בני ישראל בהוציאי אותם מארץ מצרים "Live in booths for seven days...that I had the Israelites live in booths when I brought them out of Egypt." The agricultural feast at the end of the harvest season, the only reason mentioned in the early Book of the Covenant (Exod. 23: 16) and in Exod. 34: 22, was replaced by a new aetiology, the exodus from Egypt. Even the name חג האסיף "the Feast of the Ingathering" as it is called in Exodus, was changed into חג הסכות, to emphasize its historical origin in the deliverance from Egypt. Regarding the Feast of Weeks the various changes are more interesting. The agricultural character of this Feast is radically evident in all biblical citations. It is the only feast with no fixed date, because it is the feast of the wheat harvest, and could not be fixed on a particular day, since the harvest is conditional on seasonal factors. The feast is called חג הקציר the "Feast of the Harvest" in Exod. 23: 16 and 34: 22. In Lev. 23: 16 - 21 there is no name for this feast, but the agricultural character is clearly evident. In Num. 28: 26 it is called יום הביכורים, the "Day of the First Fruits," but even in Deut. 16: 10, where it is called חג שבעות "Feast of Weeks," because the date is fixed seven weeks after the start of the harvest, its agricultural basis is amply elucidated in the following text. Only at the end of the pericope, an interjected verse which has no relation to the antecedent context mentions the exodus from Egypt as a general rationale for the keeping of all the aforesaid laws. It seems that due to the lack of any explicit historical justification for this feast in Scripture, another reason was introduced in the post-biblical period: it became a remembrance of the giving of the Torah. A specific calendar day could then be fixed. The first connection of this feast to a theological reason other than its scriptural agricultural character is found in the Book of Jubilees, in the Preamble and in 1: 1, where it is described as the day of the receipt of the two tablets by Moses, and in 6: 17, where it is described as the day of the renewal of the Covenant with Noah. The date is the fifteenth day of the third month, because the sect from which this Book originated had a different calendar and this was the date of the Feast of Weeks. In rabbinic Judaism the date of the feast is the sixth day of the third month, and we read in B. T. Sabbath 86b: תנו רבנן בששי בחדש ניתנו עשרת הדברות לישראל "The Rabbis taught: On the sixth [of the third month] were the Ten Commandments given to Israel." In the liturgy, only the later justification is mentioned regarding the Feast of Weeks, and the agricultural basis, so emphasized in Scripture, is entirely ignored. In reminiscence of its agricultural character there remained a custom in some synagogues to adorn the building with green plants.

[105] For example, the Red Heifer in Num. 19: 2 - 13. Whatever we may speculate concerning the archaic nature of this command, it is obvious that the underlying justification of this odd custom was already unknown at the period of its redaction. But the custom persevered notwithstanding its aetiological deficiency.

We encounter an interesting prophecy in Isaiah that portrays the breaking up of a pagan altar's stones as its ultimate destruction, and the climax of Israel's repulsion of idolatrous worship. We read in Isa. 27: 9: בשומו כל אבני מזבח כאבני גר מנפצות "When he makes all the altar stones like chalk stones crushed into pieces." By the specific deed of crushing the stones, Israel demonstrates its utmost contempt for this altar, in contrast to the reverence bestowed upon the stones of God's altar, which are not to be split. Such a symbolic violation of the enemy is a well-known custom even in contemporary primitive societies.

The fact that there is no restriction against using גזית "hewn stones" in Deut. may indicate that even hewn stones could be used, in whatever size and shape they were taken from the quarry; even these stones might have been considered שלמות "whole-perfect", and only further splitting was prohibited. But this fact may also demonstrate different stages in the development of this concept of the inviolability of stone, a concept ultimately deriving from the significance of stone in early Israelite mythology. In the first stage, only found stones could be used, in their natural size; a later stage permitted the utilization of hewn stones, as long as they remained undivided; and in the last stage this restriction disappeared entirely, together with the prohibition against using iron tools.[106] Similarly, the change in the standard of living and the consequently more refined garments worn by the people, including some type of trousers, made obsolete the prohibition against climbing up on the altar. In Deut. this restriction no longer appears; dissociating the pericopes in Exod. and Deut. both textually and chronologically, as I suggest,[107] resolves this inconsistency. Further, as customs changed the earthen altar disappeared.

We must also observe the unmistakable differences in the text between Exod. and Deut. Whereas we find the peculiar utterances מזבחי "my altar", and תעשה לי "make for me" in Exodus, as mentioned above, the text in Deuteronomy, which is already sensitive to anthropomorphic expressions of all kinds,[108] reads ובנית שם מזבח לה׳ אלהיך "Build an altar to the Lord

---

[106] For example, from the absence in Ezekiel of any limitations with respect to the building of the altar, and the huge quantities of iron used in the Temple building, according to Chronicles.

[107] C.f. M. Noth' *Exodus*, p. 177, who notes the apparent incompatibility of the prohibition against exposing one's nakedness on the altar with the command to make linen undergarments for the priests (Exod. 28: 42); Osumi, p. 161, who discusses the conflict between the prohibition against climbing on steps up to the altar, and the step altars of Ahaz and Ezekiel.

[108] For example the expression לשכן שמו "to cause His name to dwell" in Deut. 12: 11, in contrast to the anthropomorphic ושכנתי בתוכם "I will dwell among them" in Exodus 25: 8. I have elaborated on this issue in chap. 3 n. 1. R. P. Merendino, *Das*

your God." An additional remarkable feature of the early Book of the Covenant, in relation to the altar, is the right of asylum. In Exod. 21: 14, we find the identical expression מעם מזבחי "from **my** altar" with respect to this specific privilege. In the later Deuteronomy, where this expression is avoided, we no longer have any mention of the altar's association with asylum.[109]

Yet another distinction between the two laws may be attributed to a change in lifestyle. In the nomadic period, the Exodus rule stresses the triviality of the location, expressly declaring that every place is appropriate for the Deity's worship and no specific site is preferred to another. We must suppose that this is the purpose for the explicit declaration בכל המקום "in every place," a phrase which would otherwise be superfluous; it serves as a solemn proclamation of this concept. In Deut. on the other hand we find the altar is to be associated with a particular holy site, and this rule indicates a stable and settled society with permanently established sanctuaries. The shift in circumstances and theology is perceivable in both the laws of the altar and in the narratives concerning the altar.

2.2.3 Simplicity - A Common Feature of Both Pericopes

Though our analysis and textual investigation lead to the conclusion that the two pericopes of our study originated in different periods and circumstances, there is one feature that is shared by the two pericopes: the utmost simplicity of the altar, and the lack of any particular rules regarding its size. It is remarkable that in both the pre-monarchic and monarchic periods, we find the same approach to the building of the altar, with no precision as to size or material. One has the impression that no importance whatsoever was accorded to aesthetic considerations regarding the form and aspect of the altar; stark simplicity seems to have been the order of the day.[110] This attitude is evident not only in the accounts of spontaneous sacrificial offerings by individuals, but also in the records of altar-building by important personalities and kings.

Deuteronomische Gesetz (Bonn, 1969), writes on p. 392 that the concept of God's name is appropriate for a developed and matured theology.

[109] The abolition of the altar as a safe-haven may also have been due to other reasons, and I shall revert to this issue in chap. 6 nn. 51 and 67; but one cannot exclude as one of the reasons for its disappearance in Deut. a change in theology with respect to the altar as the Deity's dwelling.

[110] We may again compare this attitude to those of the pre-Islamic nomads. The ritual was spontaneous, with no fixed rules regarding the size and form of the altar, or the type of sacrifices.

I shall recapitulate these accounts according to the order of the MT canon, without consideration of actual chronological order, still a contested issue among scholars. Noah's building of the altar is described merely as ויבן נח מזבח "Then Noah built an altar [Gen. 8: 20]," with no particulars as to material, size or form. The same general expression, ויבן מזבח, describes the many altars built by Abraham (Gen. 12: 7; 12: 8; 13: 18; 22: 9). This lack of particulars regarding the appearance of the altar is especially remarkable in the last citation, where so many apparently insignificant or trivial details are included, as for example the splitting of the wood; yet nothing concerning the building of the altar is recorded. Scripture tells of only one altar built by Isaac (Gen. 26: 25), again with no details. Jacob set up pillars as a rule, and these were of stone; his "specialization" in the erection of pillars influenced the scriptural language,[111] and with respect to one of the two occurrences in which Jacob built an altar, we encounter the unique expression ויצב שם מזבח "He set up an altar [Gen. 33: 20]," instead of the usual ויבן. Both in this verse and the other record of an altar built by Jacob (Gen. 35: 7), no particulars of the altar appear. Moses built two altars,[112] as narrated in Exod. 17: 16 and 24: 4, again with no indication of their nature. The two and one-half tribes built an altar on the east side of the Jordan, as recorded in Jos. chapter 22, also with no specifics concerning its appearance.[113] In the Apocrypha, for example in *Jubilees*, in which many anachronistic details of the sacrifices of the Patriarchs are added to the biblical narratives,[114] we

---

[111] Cf. W. Zwickel, "Die Altarbaunotizen im Alten Testament," p. 541.

[112] I obviously do not include here the bronze altar - "made", rather than "built" - as recorded in the P stratum of the Pentateuch.

[113] I shall come back to the issue of this altar. There is a hint here as to its form, in the phrase ראו את תבנית המזבח "Look at the replica of the altar," but we do not know which type of altar was contemplated.

[114] For instance, in Jubilees 6: 1 - 3, Noah's offerings after the deluge; in 7: 3, Noah's first wine-making; in 13: 5, Abraham's burnt offering, in contrast to the parallel pericope in Gen. 12: 8, where such an offering is absent, and merely the building of an altar is mentioned; in 14: 11, the building of an altar at the site of the "Pieces of the Covenant Offering" with Abraham, in opposition to Gen. 15: 9 - 21; detailed lists of various offerings at the institution of the Feast of the First Fruits in 15: 2, and the institution of the Feast of Tabernacles in 16: 20 – 24, as well as the building of an altar in Beer Sheba, again with no details on material, form or size. In Gen. 21: 33, it is recorded that Abraham planted a tree in Beer Sheba. In Jubilees 18: 8 we find the building of the altar for the commanded offering of Isaac, with no details on the altar, although many particulars such as the wood, the knife and the fire are described; this report matches the Gen. 22 pericope exactly. The material of which Abraham built the altar remains a puzzle, since he brought with him all the other requisites for the sacrifice. In Jubilees chap. 21, Abraham transmits to Isaac a detailed list of rules for the celebration of sacrifices, including the requirement for particular types of wood for their burning, but no regulations seem to be required for

encounter no rules or specifications concerning the building of altars; we are merely told that the altars were built. The writers set out in great detail the particular number of offerings for the various festive occasions, the type of animals, the kind of auxiliary offerings (such as the meal sacrifice, the oil, the libation, the incense and the salt additive), and the specific woods for the burning; a complete sacrificial canon is recorded, yet there is no word about the type of the altar.

I have already cited various instances in Judges and Samuel in which sacrifices were offered on ordinary stones and rocks; however, these books also record the building of altars. Gideon built two altars (Jud. 6: 24 and 6: 26), and although we encounter exact particulars with respect to the location, and the wood to be used, there is no description of the altar itself. In Jud. 21: 4, at the grand gathering at Mizpah, we are told the purpose of the altar which was built especially for the occasion, but are left in the dark concerning the particulars of its construction. Samuel built an altar close to his home (I Sam. 7: 17), and Saul built an altar (I Sam. 14: 35) after his victory over the Philistines, but only the laconic ויבן מזבח records the building in each case. In II Sam chap. 24, Scripture lists a great many circumstantial details concerning the altar built by David: the specifically chosen place, the negotiations over price, the final price, the yoke used for the burning wood, and the type of offerings sacrificed; it is only information on the type of the altar which is missing. The records of altars built by Solomon (I Kings 9: 25), Jeroboam (I Kings 12: 33) and Ahab (I Kings 16: 32) offer no details on their appearance. The latter two, we are informed, were illicit altars, and their construction is expressed with the specific terms עשה and ויקם instead of the usual ויבן, probably to emphasize the difference between them and legitimate altars; yet there is no hint of a different outer appearance. Only regarding the altar repaired by Elijah (I Kings 18: 30 - 32) do we learn that it was built with twelve stones. It seems, however, that this specific information had the

the building of the altar. In Jubilees 24: 23, we read that Isaac built an altar in Beer Sheba and brought an offering, as in Gen. 26: 25, in which it is recorded that he built an altar and called on the name of the Lord. In Jubilees 31: 3, we encounter Jacob's building of the altar in Beth El, similar to the narrative in Gen. 35: 7. In Jubilees 32: 4 - 8, the installation of Levi into the priesthood, an extended schedule of the sacrificial canon is recorded, without any specific requirement for the altar's structure. In 43: 1 we learn that Jacob offered sacrifices in Beer Sheba, similar to the report in Gen. 46: 1; there is no record that he built an altar there, since Isaac had already done so, according to Gen. 26: 25. Gen. 46: 1 emphasizes that Jacob offered sacrifices to the God of his father Isaac, an odd and uncommon statement. We may note that Jubilees follows the pattern in Genesis concerning the altars built by the Patriarchs, merely adding particular data about the number, character and type of offerings missing in Genesis, with one exception. The event recorded in Gen. 33:20, ויצב שם מזבח "He set up an altar," using the verb ויצב instead of the habitual ויבן, is missing in Jubilees, an absence which serves to highlight this unconventional association of the term נצב - usually reserved for a מצבה - with a מזבח.

distinct purpose of symbolizing the unity and the amphictyonic tradition of Israel; the mention of the altar's building material was merely incidental.

2.2.4 Initiation of Elegant Altars

It seems that the first hint of any significance granted to the aesthetics of the altar is found in the passage concerning the altar copied by Ahaz from an alien culture, in Damascus: וישלח המלך אחז אל אוריה הכהן את דמות המזבח ואת תבניתו לכל מעשהו "The King sent to Uriah the priest a sketch of the altar, with detailed plans for its construction [II Kings 16: 10]." Until this time, there were no rules concerning the technical details for building public altars in Israel, and certainly none for the private, mainly spontaneous altars built by individuals. The nomadic tradition of the simple altar subsisted until that time, and probably continued, at least with respect to private altars, until Josiah's reform. One must note, however, that even this significant step of copying the form of an alien altar constituted only a shift in fashion, but not a radical shift in the overall attitude toward the altar. The narrator tells us, as I understand the passage, that the king was impressed by the altar observed in Damascus, which was certainly more imposing than the simple Israelite altars, and his self-esteem as a king prompted him to have a similar sumptuous structure in his main Temple, where he offered his royal sacrifices. But there was still no precise size prescribed for the altar.

We do not know whether the command of Ahaz in II Kings 16: 15 to Uriah the priest regarding the daily sacrifices is authentic and indicates a new-fashioned order of offerings, or whether Ahaz is referring to a previously established cult canon, which seems a remote possibility. A later retrojection of the list of offerings is also a possibility that should not be excluded, since this is the first appearance of an established daily order of sacrifices in Scripture.[115] One may also hypothesize that Ahaz was prompted

---

[115] The editor of Chr. was aware of this "grave" lacuna, and we perceive a systematic attempt to rectify it. In the narrative of the transfer of the ark to Zion in I Chr. 16: 40, we read: להעלות עלות לה׳ על מזבח העלה תמיד לבקר ולערב ולכל הכתוב בתורת ה׳ אשר צוה על ישראל "To present burnt offerings to the Lord on the altar of burnt offering regularly, morning and evening, in accordance with everything written in the Law of the Lord, which he had given Israel." In the parallel narrative in II Sam. chap. 6, such an arrangement is obviously not mentioned. In the Sam. and King narratives, the offerings of both David and Solomon are spontaneous, and performed at special occasions. Nor do we find any specific motive for these offerings, but simply: ולכל הכתוב בתורת ה׳ אשר צוה על ישראל "in accordance with everything written in the Law of the Lord, which he had given Israel." We may infer that there was not yet an established canon of daily offerings. In I Chr. 23: 31, we again find David's "testament" in which he instructs the priests and Levites: ולכל העלות עלות לה׳ לשבתות לחדשים

by his new awareness of an entirely different attitude to the sacrificial system, that is, a sumptuous altar and the pomp of an established canon of daily celebrations. However, though Ahaz might have wanted to copy the impressive system, we still cannot deduce from the text any precise dimensions for the altar. Such regulations would imply a fundamental change in the underlying theology, and demonstrate that a cultic significance was attached to the specific dimensions and materials, an attitude which we perceive in the later writings: such a shift in attitude is encountered for the first time in Ezekiel 43: 13 - 17 and in the P stratum of the Pentateuch. I must assert, therefore, my hesitation concerning the credibility of data which have been extrapolated by archeologists from altar dimensions which are equal or similar to those cited in the Bible[116] regarding the bronze altar. There are no

---

ולמעדים במספר כמשפט עליהם תמיד לפני ה' "and whenever burnt offerings were presented to the Lord on Sabbaths and on New Moon festivals and at appointed feasts. They were to serve before the Lord regularly in the proper number and in the way prescribed for them." There is no parallel to this pericope in Sam. or Kings, and it is in Chr., along with the P stratum of the Pentateuch and the other later books of the Bible, that we learn of regular specific offerings for the holy days, in a prescribed number. An additional attempt to confirm the ancient origin of the daily offering celebrations which appear in the P stratum of the Pentateuch is found in II Chr. 13: 11, at the occasion of a (doubtful) confrontation between Abijah, king of Judah and Jeroboam, king of Israel. Abijah declares that in his kingdom: ומקטירים לה' עלות בבקר בבקר ובערב בערב וקטרת סמים ומערכת לחם על השלחן הטהור ומנורת הזהב ונרותיה לבער בערב בערב "Every morning and evening they present burnt offerings and fragrant incense to the Lord. They set out the bread on the ceremonially clean table and light the lamps on the gold lampstand every evening." This verse represents an accurate restatement of the relevant commands in Exodus and Leviticus, but is not found in Sam. and Kings, and it is obvious that this verbal altercation is not mentioned in the parallel story of the war between Abijah (אבים in MT) and Jeroboam, in I Kings 15: 7. These multiple attempts by the Chr. editor(s) to authenticate the early origin of the canon of sacrifices as it is found in the P stratum demonstrate the sensitivity to the lack of any such evidence in the earlier writings, and consequently strengthen our perception in the opposite direction. W. Zwickel also asserts in "Die Kultreform des Ahas (2 Könige 16,10-18)," *SJOT* 7,2 (1993), pp. 250 - 262, that the verses with the lists of sacrifices are of a later post-exilic origin, interjected into the older text of verses 10, 11, 15a and 16 of II Kings 16, which represent the original Court Annals.

[116] See Aharoni, "Preliminary Report of the Fifth and Sixth Season. 1973-74 Excavation at Tel Beersheba," *Tel Aviv* 2 (1975), pp. 54 - 156, who writes on p. 155: "We may conclude that the altar's height was about 157 cm., measuring the top of the horns. This is the measurement of exactly three royal cubits, similar to the height of the altars at Arad, the Tabernacle (Exod. 27: 1) and probably the original altar of the Solomonic temple (Chr. 6: 13)." Apart from the fact that Yadin, in his essay "Beer Sheba: The High Place Destroyed by King Josiah," *BASOR* 222 (1976), pp. 5- 17, refutes Aharoni's identification of the altar (pp. 11ff.), Aharoni has also misinterpreted II Chr. 6: 13, which describes a כיור נחשת, a bronze "scaffold" (KJV) or "platform" (NIV). The LXX translates כיור as it is commonly understood, βάσιν χαλκῆν "a bronze basin/laver." None of the traditional

dimensions in Scripture for the stone altars before Ezekiel, and his measurements do not correspond to those of the Second Temple altar.

There is further evidence that before the reign of Ahaz there were no fixed rules concerning the form, character and dimensions of the altar, in the account of the building of Solomon's Temple in I Kings 6: 2 - 7: 51. We observe the minute discussions of the dimensions, ornamental style and opulence of the building and all the furnishings, with the striking exception of the holocaust altar; there is no mention at all of the construction of this altar.[117] One must assume that this peculiar absence is due to the fact that the

---

commentators, such as Rashi, Radak and Mezudath David, had anything to say about this term, and it seems that they saw no difficulty in interpreting it simply as a laver. Aharoni's identification of "basin" in Chronicles with the "original" Solomonic altar may have been influenced by the confusion initiated by Johannes de Groot, *Die Altäre des Salomonischen Tempelhofes* (Stuttgart, 1924). On p. 6, de Groot interprets כיור as "ein Gerät", the generic "implement", and is amazed that it has the same dimensions as the bronze altar in Exod. 27: 1. He then connects it to II Chr. 7: 7, where it is said that "the bronze altar Solomon had made could not hold the burnt offerings," and deduces that there were two altars. Both K. Galling in *Die Religion in Geschichte und Gegenwart, Handwörterbuch für Theologie und Wissenschaft* (Tübingen, 1957), s.v. "Altar. II. In Israel," and A. Reichert in *Biblischer Reallexicon*, s.v. "Altar", refute de Groot's postulate of two Solomonic altars. I shall revert to this issue in section 7.2.2, but I would like to draw attention to the fact that in Kings there is no mention that Solomon made a bronze altar, and the parallel verse in I Kings 8: 64 records only "the bronze altar before the Lord" with no indication of who made it. Aharoni's statement that the stone altar in Beer Sheba had the same dimensions as the biblical bronze altar has no foundation, and does not serve as evidence to identify the structure as an altar. Zeev Herzog et al., "The Israelite Fortress at Arad," *BASOR* 254 (1984), pp. 1-34, also compare the size of the stone altar in Arad to the dimensions of the bronze altar indicated in Exod. 27: 1. They write on p. 11: "As in the Tabernacle (Exod. 27: 1), the altar measured 'five cubits long and five cubits broad.'" Beth Alpert Nakhai, "What's a Bamah? How Sacred Space Functioned in Ancient Israel," *BAR* 20/3 (May/June 1994), pp. 18-29, 77-8, also states that the dimensions of the Arad altar "match those given in Exod. 27: 1 for the altar in the Israelite desert tabernacle." I wish to draw the attention of the reader to the fact that in the Law of the Altar in Exod. 20, the command to build altars refers to both earthen altars and unhewn stone altars of the type found in Arad, with no indication of the desired size. The altar in Arad may have been of similar dimensions to the one in Beer Sheba, but no dimensions are indicated in Scripture for a stone altar. The comparison is therefore between apples and oranges. It is also a fundamental question whether the bronze altar described in Exod. 27: 1 (the Tabernacle altar in Aharoni's statement) ever actually existed, and I shall revert to this question in chap. 7.

[117] The brief reference to an altar built by Solomon in I Kings 9: 25 is only an incidental part of the recitation of Solomon's deeds and accomplishments. The construction of the altar is not mentioned in the long list detailing the preparation of the Temple furnishings. There is no indication that the מזבח הנחשת לפני ה' in I Kings 8: 64 was built by Solomon, and this is a matter of discussion among scholars. J. Gray, *I & II Kings*, Old Testament Library (London, 1970), p. 233 raises a number of questions on the authenticity of this verse. M. Noth, in *Könige*, Biblischer Kommentar Altes Testament, IX/1 (Neukirchen, 1968), p. 191, critically analyzes this verse and stresses its numerous oddities. He declares

altar was constructed in the traditional simple style; thus there was nothing to record. I refer again to my argument that the offering of sacrifices on the grounds of the Temple (I Kings 8: 64) would only have been permitted in a socio-religious environment in which the usual habit required a simple unpretentious altar.

As far as the situation after Ahaz, it is possible that the same form of his altar was maintained; but it is at least plausible that after this altar fell into disrepair, the old simple form was restored. We must assume that any altar, and specifically Ahaz' complex altar,[118] had to be repaired frequently, yet we never learn of such repairs. In II Kings 12: 5 - 15 we encounter a detailed report on the repairs which Joash ordered for בית ה' "the house of the Lord." Scripture tells us exactly what was repaired in the house of the Lord: ולגדרים ולחצבי האבן ולקנות עצים ואבני מחצב לחזק את בדק בית ה' ולכל אשר יצא על הבית לחזקה "...[they gave money to] the masons and stone cutters. They purchased timber and dressed stones for the repair of the house of the Lord, and met all the other expenses of restoring the house [v. 13]." It is remarkable that there is no mention of any repair to the altar. There is a similar record of repairs in II Kings 22: 4 - 7,[119] performed by king Josiah, but again there is no mention of repairs to the altar. If the altar were of complex construction, demanding great care to maintain its appearance and

---

that there obviously must have been an altar in front of the Temple, of whatever form and material, but stresses the odd fact that that it is here for the first time that a bronze altar is mentioned. He also doubts, based on practical considerations, the authenticity of the statement regarding the great number of sacrifices offered. One may deduce from his conjectures that in his judgment this verse, or part of it, was a later interjection. I shall refer to this verse in my examination of the topic of the bronze altar. Regarding the golden altar and the table mentioned in I Kings 7: 48, see Appendix I.

[118] We have no indication of the type of altar Ahaz copied in Damascus; see K. D. Fricke, *Das Zweite Buch von den Königen*, Die Botschaft des Alten Testaments, 12/II (Stuttgart, 1972), p. 214. One may assume that it was a step-altar, similar to the ziggurat. See Osumi, p. 161, who implies this possibility in his discussion concerning the Ahaz altar. J. de Groot, in his booklet *Die Altäre des Salomonischen Tempelhofes* (Stuttgart, 1924), shows as design No. 1 a step-altar with the title "Der grosse Ahas-altar (Ez. 43)"; he thus asserts explicitly that Ahaz built a step-altar. However, De Groot's assertion of two altars in the court of Solomon's Temple is generally rejected; I shall refer later to this issue in section 7.2.2.

[119] I do not exclude the possibility that in reality there was only one tradition, which related that repairs were made to the Temple by a pious king. The texts in II Kings 12 and II Kings 22 are quite similar, almost identical, and the resemblance of the names of the two kings, יהואש (שׁ יואש in Chr.) and יאשׁידהו, make such a speculation quite plausible. I shall return to this issue in chap. 8. On the question of which pericope contained the original version of the narrative and influenced the other, see e.g. W. Dietrich, "Josia und das Gesetzbuch," *VT* 27 (1977), pp. 18-22; H. D. Hoffmann, *Reform und Reformen* (Zürich, 1980), pp. 192-197; H. Spieckermann, *Juda unter Assur in der Sargonidenzeit* (Göttingen, 1982), pp. 179-183.

its prescribed form and dimensions, one would expect to learn of repairs to this significant cult item. One may deduce from this lack of reference to repairs that after the period of Ahaz, the old type of altar was rebuilt.

We must also consider that in Deut., formulated in the period of Josiah, it is the construction of a simple altar that is prescribed; there are no specific designs, no dimensions, nor any other indications of a complex artifact. It is possible that there was opposition to the altar built to Ahaz' personal taste, and it was intentionally destroyed or allowed to decay; there was no great investment in its repair, and no special materials or skilled workers worthy of recording. A talmudic narrative may possibly hint at the preference for simplicity, or at least at the lack of elegance and refinement of the holocaust altar, even during the late period of the Second Temple. In Y. T. Yoma 1: 5, 39a we read that the altar was damaged after an improper ritual performance by a Sadducee High Priest:

נפגמה קרן המזבח ונתנו עליו גוש של מלח שלא יהא נראה כפגום שכל
מזבח שאין לו קרן וסובב ויסוד פסול הוא

The "corner/ horn" of the altar was damaged, and they placed upon it a block of salt, so that it would not look damaged, since an altar that has no horn and gangway is unfit [for celebration].

We observe that the absence of the horn was crucial to the altar's suitability, but its appearance was apparently irrelevant, as we must assume that a salt block would not restore or enhance the altar's aesthetic qualities. A similar story is narrated in B. T. Sukkah 48b, where the enraged people threw *etrogim* at the altar,[120] damaging its horn. There we read that בול של מלח, "a handful of salt," as Rashi explains, was placed upon the altar, and that too was enough for the altar to be considered complete.

2.2.5 Van Seters' Postulate

I believe I have adequately substantiated my postulate, and do not consider it necessary to examine all contrary theories. Nevertheless, I would like to consider the study of J. Van Seters concerning the altar law of Exodus 20: 22 - 23,[121] which posits the late origin of these verses and discusses the exilic

---

[120] Josephus relates in *Ant.* XIII: 372 that Alexander [Janneus] was pelted with *etrogim*, at the celebration of the Sukkoth festival, but does not record any damage to the altar; he merely records that Alexander placed a wooden barrier about the altar, blocking the people's way to him, thus avoiding a similar disturbance in future. Nonetheless, we may perceive a similarity between the different narratives and the common record of a construction or repair at the altar, and hence may assume a "kernel of truth" in the story.

[121] J. Van Seters, "Cultic Laws in the Covenant Code (Exod. 20, 22 - 23 - 33) and their Relationship to Deuteronomy and the Holiness Code," in *Studies in the Book of Exodus,*

conditions which were at the root of this particular altar law. Van Seters
asserts that the text of the law, "an altar of earth you may make...but if you
make an altar of stones...," does not indicate that the law applies to different
altars; it is preferable, in his opinion, to interpret it as "having reference to a
single altar." Following this assumption, Van Seters is compelled to emend
the term אזכיר in v. 21b to read תזכיר, in second person singular, and to
interpret the second part of the verse as entirely disconnected from its
introductory part and from its main subject, that is, the building of an altar
and the offering of sacrifices upon it. In his understanding, "it is better to
interpret v. 24b [=21b] as an alternative to the sacrificial cult." Van Seters
admits that "verses 25- 26 [=22-23] present an alternative to the earthen altar
of v. 24 [=21]." Consequently, 21a would refer to an altar for offering
sacrifices, 21b to a period when there were no altars and the invocation of
God was a substitute for the sacrificial cult, and vv. 22-23 regress to a
sacrificial cult, linked to 21a, and indicate an alternative to the earthen altar. I
can only say that this interpretation is similar to the tentative acrobatic
exercises which occur in rabbinic literature, and which are criticized there
with the aphorism סכינא חריפא מפסקי קראי "A sharp knife cuts the verses"
(for instance, B. T. Baba Bathra 111b).

There is also no logic in assuming that at a late date, much after the
portrayal of the desert tabernacle and its furnishings, including the altar, with
so many exact and intricate details,[122] a law was promulgated in which there
are no rules regarding the form and dimensions of the altar. Van Seters
wonders: "What is the point of a law that prescribes the building of an altar in
a particular manner?" I, however, consider that the text, in its style and
certainly in its spirit, indicates the opposite, that is, an emphasis on a simple,
unsophisticated form and the lack of any particular requirements regarding
material or location. The message in these verses stands in contrast to the
antecedent v. 20: "Do not make for yourselves gods of silver or gods of
gold." As some of the traditional commentators, such as Ramban and
Seforno, have asserted, Israel's deity does not need gold and silver artifacts or
temples; simple earthen altars suffice, and He will come to bless those who
invoke him in every place. To assume, as Van Seters suggests, that the scope
of these verses is "a law that prescribes the building of an altar in a particular

---

Redaction-Reception-Interpretation,   Bibliotheca   Ephemeridium   Theologicarum
Lovaniensium, CXXVI, ed. M. Vervenne (Leuven, 1966), pp. 319 - 346.

[122] Van Seters does not assert that this altar law in Exodus was written after the P stratum; he
merely emphasizes its post-deuteronomic origin, but we must assume, according to his
thesis, that it relates to a post-P period. I have claimed that the expression את עלתיך
ואת שלמיך, implying an established code of sacrifices, consists of a later P-minded
interjection, but Van Seters considers that this is an intrinsic part of the original narrative,
and therefore one must assume that v. 21 with its command to offer particular sacrifices is
grounded in a post-P era.

manner" seems to me incompatible with their language and spirit. God's command does not constitute a particular rule on how to build an altar; it conveys quite the opposite message, that there are no specific rules on how to perform sacrifices or construct the altar. The fact that there was no elaborate altar in Solomon's Temple, a fact that Van Seters emphasizes, demonstrates that the archaic nomadic custom of setting up a simple altar and sacrificing on the ground was maintained regarding the later altar, in contrast to the other new and sophisticated furnishings, likely influenced by the refined sanctuaries of the surrounding cultures.[123] This fact does not indicate, as Van Seters suggests, the lack of a "royal edict regulating altar construction"; such rules were not required, since everyone could set up a sacrificial locus, as appropriate or feasible according to local conditions: on a pile of earth, or on a stone.

The traditions of the archaic period, related to the Sinai epos, corroborate this philosophy. We read in Exod. 24: 4: ויבן מזבח תחת ההר "He [Moses] built an altar at the foot of the mountain," with no indication of the exact place,[124] form, dimension or substance. In Exod. 18: 12, there is no record at all that an altar was built. We read there: ויקח יתרו חתן משה עלה וזבחים לאלהים ויבא אהרן וכל זקני ישראל לאכל לחם עם חתן משה לפני האלהים "Then Jethro, Moses' father-in-law, brought a burnt offering and other sacrifices to God, and Aaron came with all the elders of Israel to eat bread with Moses' father-in-law in the presence of God." The antiquity of this narrative is obvious from the record of the communal meal,[125] and we observe that nothing is mentioned about the altar. This may be compared

---

[123] Cf. V. Hurowitz, *I Have Built You an Exalted House* (Sheffield, 1992).

[124] The rabbinic tradition is sensitive to the problem of the holiness of any place outside Jerusalem, and we read in Midrash Zuta to Canticles, *Parshah* 6: שהיו ישראל סבורים [שהר] סיני קדושת עולם ולא היה אלא קדושת שעה "The Israelites thought that Mount Sinai was consecrated as a holy place for eternity, but it was consecrated only temporarily."

[125] The Talmud was obviously aware of this sensitive expression "to eat in the presence of God," and interpreted it as follows in B. T. Berakhoth 64a: כל הנהנה מסעודה שתלמיד חכם שרוי בתוכה כאילו נהנה מזיו שכינה שנאמר (שמות י"ח) ויבא אהרן וכל זקני ישראל לאכל לחם עם חתן משה לפני האלהים. וכי לפני אלהים אכלו והלא לפני משה אכלו אלא לומר לך כל הנהנה מסעודה שתלמיד חכם שרוי בתוכה כאילו נהנה מזיו שכינה "Whoever enjoys a banquet in which a Sage takes part, it is comparable to enjoying the presence of God, since it is written in Exod. 18: 12 '...to eat bread...in the presence of God.' But they did not eat in the presence of God, only in the presence of Moses! Thus Scripture teaches us that whoever enjoys a banquet in which a Sage takes part, it is comparable to enjoying the presence of God."

with the offerings brought by David on the occasion of the Ark's transfer (II Sam. 6: 13), previously discussed.

The rules of the altar in Deut. 27: 4 – 8 already indicate a "particular" manner of construction: אבנים גדלות, אבנים שלמות, and a set of rules for this special cult occasion. The terminology of the established celebrations is also correct, namely והעלית עליו עלות and וזבחת שלמים ואכלת שם, which indicates an established, well-defined cult, in contrast to the non-specific וזבחת עליו את צאנך ואת בקרך in Exod.; as I have demonstrated, the phrase את עלתיך ואת שלמיך in Exod. 20: 21 is a later interjection into the archaic text.in comparison to our earlier law in Exod. 20. In chap. 3 we shall compare these rules with the details regarding the construction of Solomon's Temple.

3. The Correlation Between Deut. 27: 5 - 6 and I Kings 5: 31- 32; 6: 7 and 7: 9 - 11

3.1 The Use of Stone in Solomon's Temple

Having dissociated Deut. 27: 5 - 6 from Exod. 20: 22 - 23, we may now approach the correlation between the pericopes in Deut. and Kings, which are related in both style and period, and examine their shared features. First, let us summarize the conclusions derived from our critical analysis of the pericope in Deut. 27: this law of the altar still endorses the sanctity of stone and requires its inviolability by a prohibition against splitting the stone into fragments. It is possible that in addition to the pious reverence bestowed upon the stones, a more secular aesthetic attitude developed alongside it and coexisted with it for a certain period. A large stone came to be considered a symbol of abundance and lavishness; the exclusive use of particularly large stones for the building of the Temple was a mark of the wealth of its builder, the king, and a gesture of highest adoration to the Deity, whose dwelling he built. Solomon started his consecration speech with the assertion: בנה בניתי בית זבל לך מכון לשבתך עולמים "I have indeed built a magnificent Temple for you, a place for you to dwell for ever[1] [I Kings 8: 13]."

From a careful reading of the text in I Kings, we may speculate that it was the luxury associated with large stones which accounts for their use by Solomon. Or it may have been the biblical editor's intention to portray the opulence of the Temple, and to emphasize Solomon's piety in employing the most expensive materials for its construction, as well as to aggrandize Solomon's reputation and the high esteem he enjoyed among the surrounding

---

[1]   We may note the apparent intermixture of the notion of the Temple as the Deity's dwelling, as stated in this opening verse, and the perception that the house was built for the Name of the Lord, as found in the same pericope in verses 16, 17, 18, 19, 20, 29, 43, 44, 48. There are also the many occurrences of the expression ושמעת השמים "Let heaven hear," the simple translation, or "Hear from heaven," which the Targum translates as ואת תקבל מאתר בית שכינתך מן שמיא "Hear from heaven, the place of your dwelling." The LXX has καὶ εἰσακούσει ἐκ τοῦ οὐρανοῦ "hearken from heaven," as does the NIV; the KJV translates "Then hear thou in heaven." Such expressions are intentionally different from the crude notion of the Temple as God's dwelling. We must recognize how different and opposing theological conceptions exist together; they occur together in the same scriptural texts, and exist together in life. This fact must be borne in mind when we come to adjudicate on the authenticity of particular scriptural texts, and their relevance for the verification of historical circumstances.

kingdoms. The ancient reverence for stone and the ban against splitting it may also have served as motivation for the exclusive use of large stones, yet these reasons are not explicit in the passages delineating the Temple's construction.

On the other hand, we cannot perceive any relation between the rule in Exod. 20 and the building of Solomon's Temple. Whatever we presume was the philosophy behind the ban against using a "sword" to shape the stones of the altar, we must apply the same philosophy to the Temple, the dwelling of the Deity and the site of worship. Yet the text clearly records the use of שמנים אלף חצב בהר "eighty thousand stone hewers in the mountain," who must have used some type of metal implements,[2] and specifically states that Solomon used אבני גזית for the foundations, a type explicitly prohibited in Exod. 20. Moreover, he used timber in various sizes, and these must have been cut with metal implements, to comply exactly with the required dimensions.

The text stresses the excellence of the stones and their high valuation. We read their attributes: אבנים גדלות אבנים יקרות ליסד הבית אבני גזית "Great stones, costly stones to provide a foundation of dressed stones [5: 31 in MT, 5: 17 in KJV, 6: 1a in LXX[3]]"; והבית בהבנתו אבן שלמה מסע נבנה "In building the Temple [exclusively] of whole-perfect as carried stone it was built [I Kings 6: 7]"; כל אלה אבנים יקרת כמדות גזית מגררות במגרה מבית ומחוץ...אבנים יקרות אבנים גדלות אבני עשר אמות ואבני שמנה אמות ומלמעלה אבנים יקרות כמדות גזית "All costly stones, in the dimension of hewn/ squared stone, leveled with a plane,[4] in and outside... costly stones, large stones, stones of ten cubits and stones of eight cubits, and above costly stones in the dimension of hewn/ squared stones [I Kings 7: 9

---

[2] There would be no difference even if a stone cutting implement were used for the hewing of the stones or for the cutting of the timber. In contrast to Deut. 27, where "iron" is mentioned, the ban in Exod. refers to a "sword", that is a killing instrument of no specific material. It might have been of stone in the stone age, when such implements were used for killing and for other tasks, and similarly of bronze or iron in later periods.

[3] We read there λίθους μεγάλους τιμίους "great costly/ prized stones [Liddell and Scott]."

[4] The term מגרה is usually a saw, as the Targum translates here ממסרן במסרין "saws with saws," but may also be a plane, as Jastrow translates, quoting evidence from rabbinic sources. It seems to me that a special plane for scraping and smoothing stone is more appropriate here than a saw, which is ill-suited to scrape stone. The LXX ignores the term מגררות במגרה and translates only the expression כמדות גזית as κεκοκλαμμένα ἐκ διαστήματος, literally "chiselled in intervals," probably meaning the stones were cut in exact dimensions. We shall see later (n. 16) that the Mishnah also declares that the אבני גזית had specific and well-known dimensions.

-11, 46 - 48 in LXX]."[5] The many repetitions of the preeminence of the stones, their costliness, their elaborate surface and their enormous dimensions, emphasize Solomon's intent to use only the best and most precious stones for the Temple. The style used to describe the stones echoes the extensive and detailed accounts of the other sumptuous furnishings made by Solomon; the aim in both cases is to impress the reader with the marvelous elements of the Temple, and the king's piety.

There is no indication, even implicitly, that it was a legal restriction or prohibition that constrained Solomon to use these types of stones, rather than others. Yet the occurrence in Kings (e.g I Kings 6: 7) of the terms אבן שלמה and כלי ברזל, which appear in a different context in the Altar Law in Deut. 27, has led to the consideration that the relevant pericopes in both books derive from the same tradition, and that the later passages are an extension of the earlier. One understands the rabbinic stance in amalgamating all three pericopes referring to the use of stones for cultic purposes, that is, Exod. 20: 22 - 23, Deut. 27: 5 - 6 and the above-cited narratives in I Kings; this attitude fits well within their tendency to harmonize discordant passages, without being excessively concerned with the occasional illogical consequences reached as a result. Citations of certain talmudic homilies concerning the verses of our study will attest to this tendency. However, we may note that modern scholars are also not entirely immune to such tendencies.

3.2 A Rabbinic Solution

I have noted above the discussion in B. T. Sotah 48b,[6] which attempts to resolve the apparent conflict between the statement אבן שלמה מסע נבנה in

---

[5] Although these verses refer to the stones used for the building of Solomon's palace, we must assume that the discussion regarding these stones in I Kings 7: 9 - 11, in which they are described with the expression אבנים גדלות...אבנים יקרות כמדות גזית, is also valid in I Kings 5: 31 for the description of the stones of the Temple, in which a similar expression, including the term אבני גזית, also appears. In the Temple Scroll, Column III, Line 7, we read ואבני גזית לבן, correctly restored by Yadin, *The Temple Scroll* (English version, Jerusalem, 1983), p. 6, as לבנות "to build" the Temple, the subject of this Column. In I Chr. 22: 2, it is explicitly stated אבני גזית לבנות בית האלהים "dressed stones for building the house of God," with no qualification such as "for the foundation," as in I Kings 5: 31. In section 3.2 I refer to a discussion in which certain Rabbis also considered an interrelation between the description of the stones for the Temple and those for Solomon's palace.

[6] See chap. 1 n. 67.

I Kings 6: 7 , which according to the rabbinic understanding means that the stones were left unworked as brought in from the quarry, and the remark אבנים יקרת...מגררות במגרה "costly stones...sawn with a saw [I Kings 7: 9]," which suggests that the stones were cut. Rabbi Nehemiah says that the stones were dressed in the quarry, before being brought to the Temple site. According to this opinion, the stones were sawn outside as stated in 7: 9, and were then brought to the Temple site without further modification; this is the meaning of אבן שלמה מסע in 6: 7. We must assume that whatever was the reason behind such special treatment, it refers exclusively to the stones. However, there is no logical reason for such a distinction concerning where the stones were dressed.[7] We observe that there was no such restriction applied to other materials employed for the building of the Temple. We read in I Kings 7: 12: וטור כרתות ארזים "and one course of cedar beams"; and in chapter 6 we learn that wood of all types and applications was used in the building of the Temple and its furnishings. The wood was obviously cut to measure, in order to fit as panels and boards, and there is no hint that it was cut outside the building site.

We must therefore search for the particular motive for this special handling of the stones, that is, that they be cut exclusively outside the building site; neither the speculations of the traditional sources nor the scholarly assumptions discussed below offer a logical reason for a distinction between cutting the stones at the quarry and trimming them on the building site. We must also seek an explanation which is separate from the rationalizations in both altar laws in Exod. and in Deut. If we connect the

---

[7]   Cf. V. Hurowitz, *I Have Built You an Exalted House*, JSOT/ASOR Monograph Series 5, Supplement Series 115 (Liverpool, 1992), pp. 216-7, who suggests the possibility that the statues for Sennacherib's Temple "were actually sculpted in the quarries and brought to Nineveh in their complete state," so that "it is possible that the biblical verse (of I Kings 6: 7) means to state nothing more than the fact that the building stone was dressed in the quarry, and there was no need to do anything more to it at the building site." I do not dispute that such a direct influence from Mesopotamian custom might have been the cause of Solomon's course of action, but it would be questionable why the deuteronomic editor of Kings would record such an act, based on an alien custom. Moreover, we have no direct evidence of such a custom, and Hurowitz himself is extremely cautious in his proposition. From the Assyrian inscriptions we do not know whether there was a cultic rationale for this custom, or whether this was simply the way of telling the story, with the emphasis on the colossal statues dragged to the temple for the honour of the gods, and not on the fact that ready-made statues were brought into the temple. It is also possible that the statues were created in the quarries because the gods Assur and Ishtar showed the king the marble quarries from which the statues should be made; hence the quarries might have been endowed with a special numinous character. At any rate, the imitation of an Assyrian custom would also contradict the idea that Solomon's course of action concerning the stones for the Temple was a consequence of the Scriptural command לא תניף עליהם ברזל in Deut. 27: 5, a fundamental proposition of my thesis.

narrative in Kings to these altar laws, although Kings refers not to the altar but to the Temple,[8] we must start by assuming a common philosophy; yet the existence of a common principle would not be consistent with the distinction between allowing the splitting of the stones in the quarry and prohibiting such an act at the building site.

In the above-cited B. T. Sotah, Rabbi attempts a logical solution and suggests that 6: 7, which describes the carrying of the stones from the quarry without further cutting, refers to the stones for the Temple, whereas 7: 9, which states that the stones were sawn, refers to the stones for Solomon's palace. It seems that Rabbi perceived the difficulty with Rabbi Nehemiah's suggestion, and proffered a rational explanation which would also fit with the text. This would have been a perfect solution but for the statement in I Kings 5: 31 - 32 (5: 17 in KJV, 6: 1a in LXX) relating to the building of the Temple: אבנים גדלות אבנים יקרות ליסד הבית אבני גזית. ויפסלו...ויכינו הבית לבנות והאבנים העצים "Great stones, costly stones to provide a foundation of dressed stones for the Temple...and cut and prepared the timber and stone for the building of the Temple." We see that אבני גזית, cut dressed stones, were also used for the building of the Temple,[9] not just for Solomon's palace. This fact stands clearly in opposition to the precept in Exod. 20; it does not, however, contravene the ordinance of Deut. 27. In summary, Rabbi Nehemiah's opinion is illogical, and Rabbi's explanation is untenable because

---

[8]   The Rabbis also understood that the prohibition in Exod. 20 against building with cut stones refers exclusively to the altar. We read in the Mekhilta of Rabbi Ishmael, Jethro, *Parshah* 11: לא תבנה אתהן גזית בו אי אתה בונה גזית אבל אתה בונה בהיכל גזית ובקדש הקדשים "[It is written] 'Do not build it with dressed stones.' The altar you do not build with dressed stones, but you build the Great Hall and the Holy of Holies with dressed stones." It is because of the passage in I Kings 6: 7, כל והגרזן ומקבות בהבנתו בבית נשמע לא ברזל כלי "...and no hammer, chisel or any other iron tool was heard at the Temple site while it was being built," that the Midrash observes the similarity to the altar law and attempts to harmonize the two passages, declaring: בבית נשמע בחוץ אבל נשמע אינו "In the [building site of the] House, you do not hear [the noise of the hammer and ax], but you hear [it] outside." We observe that even the Rabbis must connect the Kings narrative with the Exodus pericope on the basis of the term גזית, in order to prohibit the use of iron tools; the Deut. pericope, which uses the term אבנים שלמות, would not justify such a restriction.

[9]   Ramban was aware of this difficulty and attempts to explain in his commentary to Exod. 20: 21 that Rabbi interprets verse I Kings 5: 31 as follows: כלומר שהסיעו גם אבני גזית והם לביתו "That is, they also carried dressed stones, but these were for his palace." I do not think the text in verses 31 and 32 supports such a deviation from the simple and clear meaning. It is possible that Rabbi Nehemiah proposed his solution of a distinction between cutting the stones at the quarry and cutting them at the building site precisely because he was aware of verses 5: 31-32, although they are not mentioned in the rhetoric.

he did not consider verses 5: 31 - 32. I would only add here that from the accounts in II Kings 12: 13[10] and II Kings 22: 6 we may deduce that cut stones were used for the repairs of the Temple. These passages do not specify whether the stones were cut at the quarry or at the site, but we note that cut stones were used, and we may infer, at least *ex silentio*, that where they were cut was no issue at all.

3.3 Scholarly Opinions

I noted in the first part of our study a number of scholars who made a connection between the pericopes in Exod. 20 and Deut. 27; it is possible that they would also have extended the connection to the Kings narratives, based on the use of the term אבן שלמה in both sources. For instance, Olyan [11] considers the difficulties in harmonizing the apparently contradictory verses in I Kings 5: 31; 6: 7; 7: 9 - 11 with Deut. 27: 5 - 6 and Exod. 20: 25 [=22]. He perceives a conflict between אבן שלמה (I Kings 6: 7), which according to his understanding means "unfinished stone", and אבני גזית "finished stones" used for the foundation of the Temple (I Kings 5: 31).[12] Olyan sees a

---

[10] ולגדרים ולחצבי האבן ולקנות עצים ואבני מחצב לחזק את בדק בית ה' "The masons and stonecutters; they purchase timber and dressed stone for the repair of the Temple of the Lord [v. 12 in KJV]." We must thus acknowledge that cut stones were used for the repair of the Temple, contrary to Ramban's attempt, cited in the previous footnote, to interpret 5: 31 - 32 as referring to Solomon's palace. II Kings 22: 6 is similar: לחרשים ולבנים ולגדרים ולקנות עצים ואבני מחצב "...the carpenters, the builders and the masons. Also have them purchase timber and dressed stone...."

[11] p. 165.

[12] Although Olyan does not declare so explicitly, it seems that he distinguishes between the stones used for the foundations and those used for other buildings. However, it appears that he overlooked 5: 32, which starts with the term ויפסלו "they carved" and ends with the phrase לבנות הבית "to build the Temple." Here it is clear that the hewn stones are for the entire Temple, not only for the foundation; there is also no reason for the stones of the foundation to be subject to different rules than those for the walls, especially when, according to Olyan's view, they are profaned by the cutting with an iron implement, as an extension of the law in Exod. 20. Olyan also quotes (Note 18) I Chr. 22: 2, from which it results that David prepared גזית, hewn stones, for the building of the Temple, and concludes, following D. Vanderhooft, that the building of the Temple with such stones may be implied from I Kings 5: 32. I do not contradict this postulate, but I do not consider it appropriate to compare quotations of Kings and Chr. The latter derive from a later period, and considerable differences are evident in the two narratives. I note here another oversight by D. Vanderhooft, although it is not directly connected to our study. Since I Kings 6: 18 declares that cedar covered the walls so that "no stone was seen" in the Temple, he asserts that "It is unlikely that ashlar was used below the wood; precisely

connection between I Kings 6: 7 and Deut. 27: 5 - 6, but then adds "But that law, and the similar one in Exod. 20: 22 (25 in KJV) concern not the Temple building but the altar... what we seem to have in I Kings 6: 7 is an extension of the altar law of Deut. 27: 5 - 6 to cover the Temple building as well."

Olyan does not make an explicit connection between Exod. 20: 22 and I Kings 6: 7, but this would follow logically: if A is similar to B, and B is similar to C, then A is similar to C. And it is this equation which seems to have brought M. Noth to interpret the Kings passages concerning the stones in the way he has done. He writes in his commentary[13] to I Kings 6: 7: "Er soll aus Bruchstein bestehen, wie sie aus dem Steinbruch kommen" ("The [building] should consist of hewn stones, as they arrive from the quarry"). Noth interprets מסע as "(Steine) brechen, entweder den Ort (der Steinbruch) oder die Handlung (das Steinbrechen)" ("a (stone)breaking, either the location (the quarry), or the activity (hewing)"). He then writes: "Die ausschliessliche Verwendung von Bruchsteinen - im Unterschied von Quadersteinen, wie sie nach 6: 36, 7: 9, 11 - 12 für die Umfassungsmauern und Palastbauten vorgesehen werden - geschah um der Intaktheit des heiligen Tempel - 'Hauses' willen (vgl. Exod. 20: 25)" ("The exclusive use of rough /untrimmed stones - in contrast to dressed stones...as intended for the surrounding walls and palace buildings - occurred for the sake of the integrity of the Temple - House (Cf. Exod. 20: 25; 22 in the MT)").

We observe that Noth establishes a connection between the Kings narrative and the Law of the Altar in Exod. 20. In view of his postulate it would follow that for the building of the Temple only hewn, but untrimmed, stones were used (I Kings 6: 7), in conformity with the extension of the law of Exod. 20 to the Temple;[14] for the other buildings, cut stones were used (6: 36 , 7: 9, 11 - 12), since the decree to use whole stones applied only to the Temple. Noth's ideas, in my opinion, lead to two difficulties:

a) If Noth acknowledges the extension of Exod. 20 to the Temple, only stones in their natural state, untouched by metal tools, should be used; this would exclude *Bruchsteine*, stones from the quarry, as he suggests, which are hewn from the rock and are worked with human tools.[15] We have seen that

---

the opposite seems likely." Yet he did not consider that it was the exterior of the walls which would be seen by the masses from far away and not be covered with wood. This consideration would be a sufficient, if not crucial, reason to build the walls with smoothly dressed stones.

[13] pp. 115-116.

[14] Noth does not say this specifically, but one must conclude this from his proposition; he speaks of whole stones in their original integrity, a notion that would imply stones unworked with tools.

[15] In his commentary to Exod. 20, Noth writes (p. 176): "But the stones must remain unworked, as working with human tools would do away with their original condition and integrity and hence their requisite holiness."

the Rabbis interpreted the Exodus law as requiring the altar stones to be dug out from under the ground, and not hewn by iron tools. We read in Mishnah Midoth 3: 4: "One digs below the untouched soil and one brings up from there whole stones on which no iron was wielded since iron defiles by contact."

b) Noth comes into conflict with the content of I Kings 5: 31 - 32 (17-18 in KJV), in which it is recorded that dressed stones, גזית, were used for the building of the Temple's foundations. He does not refer to this problem in the passages quoted above, but in his commentary to I Kings 5: 31-32, he suggests that these verses are a later interpolation, duplicating or influenced by I Kings 7: 10 - 11, which contain similar terms. He reaches this conclusion based on textual difficulties in verses 5: 31 – 32; but I suggest that the use of common terms is not a sufficient criterion on which to declare these verses a later interpolation, copied from other verses.

3.4 Conclusion

I propose that the passages in Kings are possibly connected to the Law of the Altar in Deut. 27: 5 - 6. It is the theological reverence for stone which may be the common principle underlying these pericopes, rather than an extension from the altar to the Temple. The decrees in Exod. 20 and Deut. 27 refer exclusively to the altar, not to the Temple. But as argued above, the text in I Kings does not constrain us to assume such an extension of the altar laws; aesthetic considerations would also explain why the text emphasizes the type and quality of the stones.

In I Kings 5: 31, we read ויסעו אבנים גדלות אבנים יקרות ליסד הבית אבני גזית. There is no conjunctive ו "and" between the first part of the sentence and the last two words; hence we do not know whether these words impart additional information about the large, costly stones, or whether one should understand them as if joined with a conjunctive "and". If the first interpretation is correct, Scripture is stressing that even these large stones were dressed, אבני גזית[16] if the second interpretation is correct, as accepted

---

[16] The term אבני גזית occurs only once in the Pentateuch, in Exod. 20: 22; in the rest of the Bible it occurs in the I Kings narrative, in its I Chr. parallel, the subject of our study, and in four other places. We have no indication of its precise meaning, but the root גזז "to shear or clip" is applied to shearing sheep and the shaving of a man's hair, as in: ויגז את ראשו "and shaved his head [Job 1: 20]"; thus we may assume that אבני גזית indicate planed, smooth stones. From the Mishnah, we have an indication of the thickness of these stones, but not of their length, and it seems that the standard measure for this type of stone was expressed only in terms of thickness, not length; the length could vary. In

by the traditional commentators,[17] Scripture is relating that large untrimmed[18] stones were used for the Temple's foundation, and trimmed stones for the walls upon the foundation. It is difficult to decide which is the correct interpretation, as there are valid arguments supporting both cases. If the foundations were all hidden under the ground, there would be no reason to dress the large stones for them, and one could assume that only the upper stones were dressed; this would support the second reading. On the other hand, it would bring up the question of why אבנים גדלות אבנים יקרות "large stones, costly stones" were used for the foundations, as recorded in 5: 31 and 7: 10. The traditional commentator Metzudath David was aware of this problem, and considered both ways of reading the verse in question; he suggests, as an explanation for the first reading, that Scripture wished to emphasize Solomon's piety, in that he used costly and dressed stones even for the foundations although they were hidden.

I Kings 7: 9 - 12 indicates a distinction between large stones for the foundations and smaller stones: the latter are described in verse 9 as כל אלה אבנים יקרת כמדות גזית מגררות במגרה, "costly stones in the 'standard size' of the regular dressed stones leveled with a plane," and in verse 11 as כמדות גזית "in the size of dressed stones."

This is a new concept, that of stones in the specific size of "dressed stones." From the Mishnah, we know that these dressed stones, אבני גזית, had a standard width, but here one must assume that at the time of the writer of I Kings, or of these verses, there was also a standard length for dressed stones. The measure of ten and eight cubits for the large foundation stones is evidently their length, and therefore it is likely the standard size of the dressed stones must also refer to their length. At any rate, we see that dressed

---

Mishnah Baba Bathra 1: 1 we read of the necessary width of land which must be ceded by each of two neighbours who wish to build a fence between their fields: בגויל זה נותן שלשה טפחים וזה נותן שלשה טפחים בגזית זה נותן טפחיים ומחצה וזה נותן טפחיים ומחצה "For a fence of undressed stones, one yields three handbreadths and the other one three handbreadths, for [a fence of] dressed stones, one yields two and one-half handbreadths and the other one two and one-half handbreadths." We observe that the גזית, the dressed stone, had a standard width of five handbreadths, because it was smoothly planed.

[17] Radak compares this verse to the use of שמש ירח in Hab. 3: 11, which means "sun and moon" although there is no conjunctive"ו", thus giving "The large stones for the foundations, and the smaller dressed stones for the walls." This interpretation corresponds to the talmudic assertion that the stones for the Temple were dressed, but at the quarry, not at the building site. The Targum does not add the conjunctive "ו" in its translation, but the LXX adds καὶ in its text.

[18] This is not explicitly declared, but if we read the elements of the verse separately, we may deduce that trimmed stones were used only for the upper walls, not for the foundations.

stones were used for the Temple building, for both the foundations and the walls, or perhaps only for the walls.

From the phrase in 7: 9, כל אלה אבנים יקרת כמדות גזית "costly stones in the size of dressed stones," we would not know whether these stones were dressed, or were only in the size of dressed stones; we might simply assume that they were costly stones of superior quality, and they were large. Therefore, their description follows: מגררות במגרה מבית ומחוץ "leveled with a plane, inside and outside." As in other instances, Scripture indicates Solomon's largesse by stressing that the stones were smoothed on both sides, although the inside walls were hidden behind cedar boards. We thus observe three criteria by which the superior merit of the stones is judged: their premium quality אבנים יקרות, their large size אבנים גדלות, and their smoothness on both sides מגררות במגרה מבית ומחוץ.

In order to preserve the desired attribute of largeness, or for reasons having to do with the ancient reverence attached to stone for its numinous quality, the stones had to remain intact, and could not be split in order to facilitate their incorporation into the walls. Scripture therefore records that Solomon took the additional precaution of building the walls exclusively with large stones; no stone was smaller than the standard size of "dressed stone", although this would require great skill and care. This exceptional achievement is alluded to in I Kings 6: 7: אבן שלמה מסע נבנה ומקבות והגרזן כל כלי ברזל לא נשמע בבית בהבנתו "[The Temple] was built of whole-perfect stones in the sizes they were brought in from the quarry, and no hammer or ax, nor any other iron tool for splitting was heard at the Temple site when it was being built." The emphasis in this verse is on the fact that only large stones were used, and they were not split into smaller fragments to accommodate the builders. The builders thus had to use their greatest care and skill to build the walls exclusively with large stones.

Thus we may conclude that the Law of the Altar was not extended to the Temple building, and if there was a connection between the altar and the Temple, this was solely due to the reverence accorded to stone, as a result of which the splitting of the stone would constitute a violation. Smoothing and leveling the stones, on the other hand, a procedure that enhanced their appearance, was not regarded as an abuse. It also did not impinge on their integrity; they remained שלמה "whole-perfect."[19] Thus there is a logical explanation for the two apparently conflicting verses in Kings.

---

[19] We do not know the precise operation of the מגרה that leveled the stones, as mentioned in I Kings 7: 9. We may surmise that it was not a procedure in which an iron implement such as a chisel was hit with a hammer upon stone, but rather the stones were dragged under a device that smoothed them, similar to modern electrical saws that cut marble. The verb גרר "to drag" is in Pu'al here, מגררות, which implies that the stones were

A supporting citation is found in B. T. Baba Qama 119b: מה שהחרש
מוציא במעצד והנפסק במגירה הרי אלו של בעל הבית והיוצא מתחת
מקדח ומתחת רהיטני והנגרר במגירה הרי אלו שלו "[The shreds] that the
carpenter takes off [working] with the adze and cuts off with the saw, belong
to the owner [of the timber, who gave it to the carpenter to produce some
object for him], [but] what comes out from [working] with the drill and the
chisel and from dragging [through] the saw, belongs to the carpenter." We
observe first the difference between sawing off pieces with a saw, in order to
level the wood, and dragging the wood under a saw. In our case, we note the
precise statement in I Kings 7: 9 that the leveling of the stones was
accomplished specifically by the second method. Second, whereas the pieces
of wood cut off with a saw are considered a part of the material and belong to
the owner, the shreds shaved off by dragging the wood through the saw are
not considered as part of the wood block, and belong to the carpenter. In a
similar way, we may conclude that the procedure of dragging the stone slab
through the cutting device did not infringe on the wholeness / integrity of the
stone.[20]

Our passages, therefore, refer to "dressed stones," more luxurious and
impressive than rough unworked stones, and so the First Temple was built.

---

dragged through this device. This procedure is entirely different from the wielding of an
iron tool expressed in Deut. 27: לא תניף עליהם ברזל, or in Exod. 20: כי חרבך הנפת

[20] Although the talmudic citation seems to perfectly support my thesis, I must, for the sake
of intellectual integrity, present its problematic aspect. It is possible that the Talmud's
criterion for deciding what belongs to the owner and what to the carpenter is not based on
whether a piece is considered part of the wood block, but is based on the value of the
piece, and whether the owner agrees beforehand to give up the shreds. The piece of wood
which was cut off might have more value and the owner would wish to retain it, whereas
the shreds from the drilling or levelling are not of great value, and the owner tacitly
agrees beforehand to relinquish them to the worker. This idea that the owner might have
different attitudes to different types of waste appears in a later discussion in the Talmud.
Regardless, however, of the underlying principle, this quotation substantiates the
different procedures for smoothing stones.

4. Archeological Evidence

4.1 Excavations of Israelite Stone Altars

It is little wonder that archeologists have granted much attention to the discovery of stone altars in Israel, and have attempted to utilize biblical texts to assist them in their identification. Of course, there is no chance of finding the archaic earthen altars, which could not withstand the rigours of time, nor were bronze altars found in Israel. On the other hand, stone constructions of various types were identified as altars. One must also take into consideration that the precise identification of altars is beset with many difficult hurdles: the exact date of construction, or destruction, whether the structure is a *bamah* or an altar, and, if identified with certainty as an Israelite worship site, whether it was constructed in strict adherence to the existing regulations, or whether there is a possibly that the law was not followed closely in that particular location. Remnants of alien altars may also confuse the situation.

The archeologists, as we shall see, have compared their findings with scriptural regulations, and attempted to draw conclusions based on the conformity of the structure with those regulations, without taking into account the possibility that one or more of the above factors might be influencing their interpretation. The fact that an altar was built with dressed stones does not positively identify it as an alien altar, or a *bamah*, even if the use of such stones for the altar had always been prohibited, a situation which I disputed above; it should also be taken into account that the altar might have been constructed in violation of the law. The prophets offer us ample evidence of failure to adhere to the law in matters of the utmost importance, such as idolatrous worship. Why is it necessary to assume that a structure built with dressed stones could not have been an altar, but must have been something else? The law of Exod. 20 may have been superseded by the later law of Deut. 27. In my opinion the later text does not prohibit the use of such stones; or perhaps the prohibition in Exod. 20 might have been disregarded altogether by the builders.

It is also possible that the laws of the altar, which, as we have seen, had theological underpinnings - however we interpret them - were observed in some places in conformity with the old law, and in others according to the new law. And both may have been considered legitimate, since we perceive differing philosophical attitudes from various prophets on the same issue. J.

Knohl,[1] for example, demonstrates entirely divergent viewpoints between the deuteronomic editor and Micah on the one hand, and Isaiah and Zephaniah on the other, concerning the Israelite perspective regarding the idolatrous worship of the gentiles. Whereas Micah and Deuteronomy approve such worship for the gentiles, Isaiah and Zephaniah promulgate one universal God, and criticize the behaviour of the gentiles. We must consider that Isaiah was active prior to Deuteronomy, if we assume that the latter originated in the time of Josiah. Micah and Isaiah were contemporaries, and Zephaniah preached in Josiah's period. We not only observe different philosophies on such a crucial issue, but must also consider that Isaiah's opinion was not accepted by all, and opposing theories existed together, at least in the time of Josiah.

4.2. Beer Sheba: Yadin versus Aharoni

Contrasting opinions and customs concerning the use of dressed stones for the altar could certainly have coexisted over a period of a hundred years; it is this amount of time on which Aharoni and Yadin are in disagreement

---

[1] J. Knohl, יחס המקרא לאלילות של הנוכרים *Tarbiz* 64/I (1995), pp. 5-12, interprets the passages in Deut. 4: 19, וראית את השמש ואת הירח...ועבדתם אשר חלק ה' אלהיך אתם לכל העמים "and see the sun, the moon...and worshipping things the Lord your God has apportioned to all the nations"; Deut. 29: 25, ויעבדו אלהים אחרים...אשר לא ידעום ולא חלק להם "and worshipped other gods...they did not know, he had not given them"; and Deut. 32: 9, כי חלק ה' עמו "For the Lord's portion is his people," to imply that while the Israelites are God's portion, the other peoples have their gods, which God has apportioned to them (the sun, the moon), just as He has apportioned the Israelites for Himself. The same opinion is found in Micah 4: 5: כי כל העמים ילכו איש בשם אלהיו ואנחנו נלך בשם ה' אלהינו לעולם ועד "All the nations may walk in the name of their gods, we will walk in the name of the Lord our God for ever and ever." A different attitude, the extinction of the foreign gods and the predominance of one single God, is observed in Isaiah 2: 17-18: ונשגב ה' לבדו ביום ההוא. והאלילים כליל יחלף "The Lord alone will be exalted in that day. And the idols will totally disappear"; in Isa. 44: 6: אני ראשון ואני אחרון ומבלעדי אין אלהים "I am the first and I am the last, apart from me there is no God"; and in Zephaniah 3: 9: כי אז אהפך אל עמים שפה ברורה לקרא כלם בשם ה' "Then will I purify the lips of the peoples, that all of them may call on the name of the Lord." We thus observe two opposing doctrines: a particular God of the Israelites in a pantheon of gods, versus the monotheistic ideology of the One, single, universal God of all the world and for all humankind.

regarding the findings at Beer Sheba.[2] The reliability of archeological statements in this particular field is at the least questionable, and it is little wonder that the propositions of one archeological scholar are zealously attacked by another of his peers. I shall quote several examples of completely contrasting identifications of altars among well-known archeologists, and I shall add my reservations concerning their interpretations of the scriptural texts on which they rely to arrive at their conclusions.

The most notorious confrontation relates to the excavations at Tel Beer Sheba by Aharoni, and Yadin's disputing of Aharoni's identification and conclusions regarding a certain altar-like structure. Aharoni[3] reaches his conclusion that this structure was an altar based on the width of the bronze altar as stated in Exod. 27: 1, and on the finding of three intact corner stones in the shape of horns. He also compares the probable size of the structure to the dimensions of the כיור mentioned in II Chr. 6: 13. As already noted, the biblical altar dimensions refer to a bronze altar, not to a stone altar. Moreover, Aharoni deduces from the size of the כיור in II Chr. 6: 13 that it was "probably the original altar of the Solomonic Temple," but ignores two important facts: 1) there is no mention in Kings of an altar built by Solomon, and 2) the Chronicles' compiler or editor, aware of this odd flaw, which did not correspond to the reality in his period, indicates a bronze altar built by Solomon of a much larger dimension: "twenty cubits long, twenty cubits wide, and ten cubits high [II Chr. 4: 1]." Hence, if Aharoni acknowledges the record of Chronicles as evidence for the Solomonic Temple, an approach which I would not suggest, he should have considered as evidence the clear record of its size in II Chr. 4: 1, and not the obscure mention of a כיור, "laver", in II Chr. 6: 13. On the other hand, Aharoni is amazed at the use of "well-smoothed ashlar" stones for the altar, in apparent contradiction to his interpretation of Jos. 8: 31 that the altar should be built "of unhewn stones." In fact, in both Jos. and Deut. 27 the text speaks of אבנים שלמות, whole stones, without prohibiting the use of גזית, as in Exod. 20. I shall discuss the issue of the horns in chap. 6, but I mention here that stone horns must have been made using metal tools; hence, wherever one finds stone altar horns (and many were found both of large altars and of small incense altars), the command of Exod. 20: 22 against defiling the stones with a sword was not in effect. Aharoni assumes that "this ancient tradition was evidently

[2]   H. Niehr, "Die Reform des Joschija," in *Jeremia und die Deuteronomistische Bewegung*, B. B. B. Band 98, ed. W. Gross (Weinheim, 1995), cites on p. 35 recent scholarly opinion that questions the reliability of previous archeological assumptions with respect to the altars of Arad and Beer Sheba, and their relevance to the issue of Josiah's reform.

[3]   Y. Aharoni, "Preliminary Report of the Fifth and Sixth Season 1973-74, Excavation at Tel Beersheba," *Tel Aviv* 2 (1975), pp. 54 – 156, p. 155.

disregarded at Beer Sheba," but does not refer to the biblical pericope in Deut. 27, which might indicate an official change of theology and custom regarding the regulations for the building of an altar. I must also draw attention to the confusion which results from the linkage of the laws of the stone altar in Exod. 20: 22 - 23 and Deut. 27: 5 - 6 with the command to build the bronze altar in Exod. 27: 1 - 8. The requirement for horns does not apply to the stone altar, but only to the bronze altar and the golden incense altar. In fact, we encounter no mention in Scripture of the making of horns in the numerous records of altar constructions.[4] Aharoni deduces from the identification of this altar in Beer Sheba: "The discovery of the demolished horned altar of burnt offering constitutes the first clear evidence of the existence of a Temple at Beer Sheba during the period of the monarchy." On one of the stones, Aharoni detected "a deeply engraved decoration of a twisting serpent,"[5] which he relates to the bronze serpent kept "until the days of Hezekiah [II Kings 18: 4]." Although he does not declare so explicitly, it seems that it was from this emblem of the serpent that Aharoni deduced that "the dismantling of the altar took place in the reign of Hezekiah (II Kings 18: 4 and 22)."

4.3 The Interpretation of מגבע עד באר שבע

Y. Yadin, in his study "Beer Sheba: The High Place Destroyed by King Josiah,"[6] rejects Aharoni's assertion and contends that the structure in Beer Sheba is a high place, destroyed by Josiah, not by Hezekiah. At the start of his study, Yadin establishes his theory on the basis of the phrase in II Kings 23: 8, where we read ויטמא את הבמות...מגבע עד באר שבע "and [Josiah] desecrated the high places from Geba to Beer Sheba." This verse is taken by Yadin as evidence for the existence of a *bamah* in Beer Sheba and its destruction by Josiah,[7] and not as describing the specific character of the

---

[4] Only Ezekiel requires horns on the stone altar, in 43: 15. I shall discuss this issue in section 6.3, as well as the mentions of "horns" in I Kings chaps. 1 and 2.

[5] It is noteworthy that Rashbam explains the prohibition in Exod. 20: 22 against iron tools for the dressing of the stones as designed to minimize the risk of engraving on the stones, an idolatrous practice, as we find in Isaiah 44: 12: חרש ברזל מעצד ופעל בפחם ובמקבות יצרדהו "The blacksmith takes a tool and works in the coals, he shapes [an idol] with hammers."

[6] *BASOR* 222 (1976), pp. 5-17.

[7] He writes on p. 8: "At the time I had no explanation for it [the building], nor did I see in it the *bamah*. What redirected my attention to this building was my rereading of II Kings 23: 8, the verse describing Josiah's action in respect to the *bamah* in Beer Sheba."

structure. Yadin's interpretation of this verse, however,, is somewhat convoluted. I do not deny that there might have been a *bamah* in Beer Sheba in the period of Josiah,[8] but I contend that this verse does not serve as evidence for this fact.

---

[8] We find in Amos 5: 5: אל תדרשו בית אל והגלגל לא תבאו ובאר שבע לא תעברו "Do not seek Beth El, do not go to Gilgal, do not journey to Beer Sheba," and in 8: 14: ואמרו חי אלהיך דן וחי דרך באר שבע "As surely as your god lives, O Dan, and as surely as the 'way' to Beer Sheba lives," and in both cases it is evident that the phrase refers to sanctuaries. On the other hand, both verses present some difficulties. Amos was a prophet of the northern kingdom, and Beer Sheba was at the southern tip of Judah. The odd expression דרך באר שבע "the way of Beer Sheba" is unclear. S.M. Paul in his commentary to Amos, מקרא לישראל, פירוש מדעי לתורה, ed. M. Greenberg and S. Ahituv (Jerusalem, 1994), alleges that verse 5: 5 demonstrates that people from the north travelled to the sanctuary of Beer Sheba. On the other hand, he does not have a logical explanation for the expression דרך in 8: 14. It is also doubtful whether numerous pilgrims went from the northern kingdom to a distant sanctuary such as Beer Sheba, so as to induce the prophet to denounce it and associate a visit there with visits to the venerable and official sanctuaries of Dan and Beth El. H. P. Chajes, in his commentary to Amos, *Biblia Hebraica, Prophetae, Liber duodecim prophetarum*, ed. A. Kahana (Kiev, 1906, reprint Jerusalem 1969), suggests that there was also a locality called Beer Sheba in Galilee, and he supports his statement with a citation from Josephus' *War* II: 20: 6, where one must conclude that Beer Sheba was in Galilee. Such a presumption would provide a logical reason for Amos' incorporation of Beer Sheba among the northern sanctuaries. There may be confirmation of the existence of a Beer Sheba in Galilee from I Kings 19: 3: וילך אל נפשו ויבא באר שבע אשר ליהודה "And he [Elijah] ran for his life and came to Beer Sheba in Judah." The fact that the editor emphasizes "Beer Sheba [which is] in Judah" suggests that there was another locality of the same name in the northern kingdom. The LXX could not accept, it seems, that Amos referred to a sanctuary in the southern tip of Judah, and interprets the Hebrew באר שבע in 5: 5 as φρέαρ τοῦ ὅρκου "the well of the oath." In 8: 14, on the other hand, the LXX ignores the term דרך in the MT, or had another text, and translates "and your god Beer Sheba," parallel to the first part of the verse, "your god Dan." The traditional commentators also perceived the difficulties and attempted to find solutions, each in his own way. Rashi does not resolve the geographical difficulties of his exposition, but offers a reasonable explanation for the inclusion of Beer Sheba in Amos' prophecy and for the term דרך, and a logical motive for the absence of Beer Sheba in the impending punishment. He explains in Amos 5: 5 that there was no idol in Beer Sheba and for that reason Beer Sheba would not be punished like Beth El and Dan. He refers to verse 8: 14 and explains the term דרך "the way" as a crossing point of the people on the way to the idolatrous sanctuaries of Beth El and Gilgal; before reaching this point, they could go to the legitimate sanctuary in Jerusalem, but once having crossed it, they were on their way to the idolatrous sanctuaries. Radak suggests that the people of Judah went from the extremity of their land to the idolatrous sanctuaries in the north, and the prophet mentions Beer Sheba to demonstrate that all the people went to the northern sanctuaries, as in the expression "from Dan to Beer Sheba," which indicates the entire land.

The verse מגבע עד באר שבע "from Geba to Beer Sheba" in this verse is simply an idiom to express the magnitude of the entire kingdom, or country.[9] It is a parallel to the well-known expression מדן ועד באר שבע "from Dan to Beer Sheba," which appears seven times in Scripture,[10] and twice in

---

[9] H. Niehr, "Die Reform des Joschija," also did not correctly interpret the expression מגבע עד באר שבע. He claims (p. 48) that this phrase, in his opinion an element of the original primary text, does not indicate that all the sanctuaries between Geba and Beer Sheba were desecrated; on this basis, he questions whether Josiah actually effected the eradication of the *bamoth*, as the later edited text wishes us to comprehend

[10] In I Sam. 3: 20: וידע כל ישראל מדן ועד באר שבע כי נאמן שמואל לנביא "And all Israel from Dan to Beer Sheba recognized that Samuel was attested as a prophet of the Lord."
ולהקים את כסא דוד על ישראל ועל יהודה מדן ועד באר שבע In II Sam. 3: 10: "...and establish David's throne over Israel and Judah, from Dan to Beer Sheba." It is odd that H. W. Hertzberg, in his *I & II Samuel, A Commentary*, The Old Testament Library, transl. J.S. Bowden (Philadelphia, second revised edition 1960), adds in his comments to both the above verses a reference to the sanctuaries from the northernmost to the most southerly. I do not see any reason from the context to justify such a supplementary interpretation. There is no mention of any sanctuary in reference to Samuel's recognition as a prophet, and In II Sam. 3: 10 it is clearly evident that the expression "from Dan to Beer Sheba" is intended to emphasize David's reign over all the people, both Judah and Israel, as the verse explains in detail. For the next occurrences of "from Dan to Beer Sheba" in II Sam 17: 11 and 24: 2, Hertzberg makes no reference to the sanctuaries. Further, in his comments on this expression in II Sam. 24: 15, he explicitly perceives the phrase to refer to the geographical area, and writes: "'From Dan to Beer Sheba' is meant to point to the area which was the scene of the king's sinful action."
In II Sam. 17: 11: יאסף עליך כל ישראל מדן ועד באר שבע "Let all Israel, from Dan to Beer Sheba, be gathered to you"; in II Sam. 24: 2: שוט נא בכל שבטי ישראל מדן ועד באר שבע "Go throughout the tribes of Israel from Dan to Beer Sheba"; and in 24: 15: וימת מן העם מדן ועד באר שבע שבעים אלף איש "And seventy thousand of the people from Dan to Beer Sheba died."
In Jud. 20: 1: ותקהל העדה כאיש אחד למדן ועד באר שבע "Then all the Israelites from Dan to Beer Sheba came out as one man." J. A. Soggin comments here in *Judges, A Commentary*, The Old Testament Library, transl. J. Bowden (Philadelphia, 1981): "Dan...Beer Sheba are the extreme northern and southern points of ancient Israelite Palestine from the time of David onwards."
In I Kings 5: 5 (v. 25 in KJV): וישב יהודה וישראל לבטח איש תחת גפנו ותחת תאנתו מדן ועד באר שבע "Judah and Israel, from Dan to Beer Sheba, lived in safety, each man under his own vine and fig tree."
In I Chr. 21: 2: לכו ספרו את ישראל מבאר שבע ועד דן "Go and count the Israelites from Beer Sheba to Dan." The parallel verse in II Sam. 24: 2 has the expression מדן ועד באר שבע.
In II Chr. 30: 5: להעביר קול בכל ישראל מבאר שבע ועד דן "...to send a proclamation throughout Israel from Beer Sheba to Dan." There is no parallel to this pericope in II Kings. The reverse order, "from Beer Sheba to Dan," is entirely justified

reversed form מבאר שבע ועד דן "From Beer Sheba to Dan." In none of the examples does the phrase attest that there was something specific in Dan or Beer Sheba; it simply denotes the *oikoumene*, the land permanently settled by the Israelites. It does not encompass the territories which were sporadically captured and temporarily held by certain Israelite kings, such as the southern part of the Negeb, or the northern lands, including Damascus and Hamath. The southern Negeb and the port of Etzion Gaber were under transitory Israelite control: in the time of Solomon (I Kings 9: 26 and II Chr. 8: 17), and in the period of Jehoshaphat, who had ships there and probably controlled it militarily and politically (I Kings 22: 49-50). Amaziah defeated the Edomites in the south (II Kings 14: 7), but Judah was chased from Eilath, as we read in II Kings 16: 6: וינשל את היהודים מאילות "He drove out the men of Judah from Eilath." In the north, Damascus was defeated by David, and he put garrisons in their kingdom (II Sam. 8: 6), but though it seems that these territories were later conquered again by the Israelites (II Kings 14: 28), they were not considered part of the heartland of Israel, which remained מדן ועד באר שבע.

Even in Solomon's reign, concerning which we read in I Kings 5: 1(4: 21 in KJV): ושלמה היה מושל בכל הממלכות מן הנהר ארץ פלשתים ועד גבול מצרים "And Solomon ruled over all the kingdoms, from the River to the land of the Philistines, as far as the border of Egypt," we still encounter in verse 5 (v. 4: 25 in KJV): וישב יהודה וישראל לבטח איש תחת גפנו ותחת תאנתו מדן ועד באר שבע "Judah and Israel, from Dan to Beer Sheba, lived in safety, each man under his own vine and fig tree." There were certainly Israelites living outside these borders, as we read in I Kings 8: 65: ויעש שלמה בעת ההוא את החג וכל ישראל עמו קהל גדול מלבוא חמת עד נחל מצרים "So Solomon observed the festival at that time, and all Israel with him - a vast assembly, people from Lebo Hamath to the Wadi of Egypt," but the firmly established idiom which implied the extent of the traditional heartland of Israel remained מדן ועד באר שבע. The two reversed expressions in Chr. derive from the Second Temple period, when the North was not a part of the Israelite domain, and the people looked at the holy land of the previous era from their perspective, from the South. This fact demonstrates beyond any doubt that these expressions, "from Dan to Beer Sheba" or "from Beer Sheba to Dan," imply an imaginary political-geographic entity as perceived by the people, within the frame of

in this case, since the proclamation came from the south, from the king of Judah, and was also addressed to the people of the north, up to the border at Dan. From all the above citations, it is clear that this expression "from Dan to Beer Sheba" is an idiom, which represents the extent of the heartland of Israel, and its unity under Davidic rule.

the two extreme border points. The only significance of the border points was as a delimitation of the realm. Just as in I Kings 5: 5 the phrase does not imply that every man in Beer Sheba had a vineyard - there were likely no vineyards in Beer Sheba, due its geographic limitations - the phrase מדן ועד באר שבע in II Kings 23: 8, regarding the *bamoth* desecrated by Josiah, is also not to be taken literally; the narrative records only that Josiah performed these acts throughout the country, and in his period the country extended only from Geba in the North to Beer Sheba to the South.

Geba was the northern border of Benjamin, as we learn from I Kings 15: 17 -22. In v. 17 we read: ויעל בעשא מלך ישראל על יהודה ויבן את הרמה לבלתי תת יצא ובא לאסא מלך יהודה "Baasha king of Israel went up against Judah and fortified Ramah to prevent anyone from leaving or entering the territory of Asa king of Judah." Obviously, Baasha carried out a blockade against the kingdom of Judah, at its border. But when this blockade was terminated and Baasha was forced to retire thanks to Ben Hadad's military intervention, we read in v. 22: וישאו את אבני הרמה ואת עציה אשר בנה בעשה ויבן בם המלך אסא את גבע בנימן ואת המצפה "And they carried away from Ramah the stones and timber Baasha had been using there. With them king Asa built up Geba in Benjamin and also Mizpah." Geba came to be the northern border point, as we observe from this narrative, and we infer from the name מצפה "watchtower"[11] that this was the border town between Judah and Israel.[12]

Scholars argue about the structure of the pericope in II Kings 23, which seems to be an amalgamation of a variety of actions with no apparent

---

[11] The LXX translates מצפה as σκοπιάν "a watchtower - a look-out place" (Liddell and Scott); Jonathan translates מצפיא, in plural, which demonstrates that in his opinion, Scripture records that Asa built "watchtowers", as is common at the border.

[12] As discussed in the text, the expression מלבוא חמת עד נחל מצרים (I Kings 8: 65) represented the borders in Solomon's period, but this situation prevailed only for a short period. King Jeroboam, son of Joash, conquered the northern territory again, as we read in II Kings 14: 25: הוא השיב את גבול ישראל מלבוא חמת עד ים הערבה "He restored the boundaries of Israel from Lebo Hamath to the Sea of the Arabah." Amos, in his castigation of Jeroboam, specified the entire country under his control: כי הנני מקים עליכם ...גוי ולחצו אתכם מלבוא חמת עד נחל הערבה "I will stir up a nation against you...that will oppress you all the way from Lebo Hamath to the Sea of the Arabah [Amos 6: 14]," the same expression as in II Kings 14: 25. Although Ezekiel fantasized on the return to such an expanded territory, as we read וזה הגבול לפאת צפונה...חמת ברותה סברים אשר בין גבול דמשק ובין גבול חמת "On the north side...Hamath, Berothah and Sibraim, which lies on the border between Damascus and Hamath [Ezek. 47: 15-16]," the realities were different.

order.[13] Among the many explanations for this strange sequence,[14] one view proposes that our phrase in v. 8, "from Geba to Beer Sheba," is related to the

---

[13] Vv. 4 -7 contain a mixture of actions concerning the artifacts for the idols in the Temple, the clerics of the high places throughout the country, the Ashera, and then the buildings for the male prostitutes and the Ashera's artifacts. V. 8 records the issue of the clerics of the high places, the profanation of the high places and the destruction of a specific high place, whose location is either Jerusalem or Beer Sheba, as Yadin suggests. Vv. 10- 13 record the profanation of the *Tofeth*, the eradication of special horses and chariots dedicated to the sun, demolition of altars built on roofs and in the Temple's courtyard, with no indication as to whether they were initially built for God or for idols (we learn only from II Kings 21: 5 that they were consecrated to idols), and the profanation of high places built by Solomon. V. 14 records the breaking of stone pillars and cutting down of sacred plants. V. 15 starts another pericope detailing the actions undertaken by Josiah in the territory of the previous northern kingdom; these differ from the acts performed in Judah to eradicate both the idolatrous and the legitimate places of worship.

[14] See K. D. Fricke, *Das Zweite Buch von den Königen* (Stuttgart, 1972), pp. 322 ff., who suggests that contrary to the presentation of the text which seems to imply a simultaneous range of actions, one must deduce from the illogical sequence that they were performed in different stages, and the text reflects this in its odd composition. M. Rehm, in *Das Zweite Buch der Könige* (Eichstatt, 1979), pp. 215ff., also discusses this issue and quotes other scholars who propose to change the sequence of the verses, or suggest that the reforms were made in three separate stages, each with a distinct objective. He does not offer any explanation for the apparent division of v. 8, whose part b, the demolition of the "idolatrous" high places at the gates, would be included in the first stage, whereas 8a, the assembly of the priests and the desecration of the regular high places, would be included in stage two. The issue seems even more intricate if we consider the many expressions of destruction and desecration utilized in this pericope, such as: שרף "burn", נתץ "demolish", שבת "bring to an end," טמא "defile", שבר "break" and גדע "cut off". In addition to these distinct actions, we encounter supplementary acts, such as taking the ashes of the artifacts to Beth El (v. 4), grinding the *Asherah* to powder and scattering the dust over graves (v. 6), throwing the rubble into the Kidron valley (v. 12), and covering the sites of the pillars and sacred trees with human bones (v. 14). In Beth El and Samaria there are further types of desecration: crushing the burned altar to powder (v. 15), burning human bones on the altar, probably for a stronger type of defilement (v. 16), and slaughtering the priests upon the altars (v. 20). I suggest that the different acts of destruction and defilement recorded in the pericope are not a haphazard array of deeds, but that each corresponds to a specific type of illegitimate worship or artifact. We do not know the precise attitude of the reformers to each cultic misdemeanour and at the same time the possible opposition and resistance of the priests and the people to the harsh measures carried out by Josiah and his Jerusalemite priestly team. We might have a hint of such opposition, for example, concerning the priests of the high places. In v. 4, Hilkiah the High Priest and his team removed the artifacts of the idols from the Temple, probably without opposition, and then did away (it is unclear in what way) with the priests. On the other hand, it seems that Josiah had to lead the priests away from their high places in the towns of Judah and bring them to Jerusalem, before defiling their places of worship. I assume that Josiah was concerned that he would be unable to desecrate the high places if the priests were on location and had the opportunity to mobilize the masses into opposing such a defilement of the sacred places. We also do not know the magnitude of the act expressed

cult centralization process. According to the deuteronomic rule, the cult in the sanctuaries throughout the land "from Geba to Beer Sheba" had to be eradicated, and that is the message of verse 8a.[15] At any rate, Josiah did not demolish the *bamoth*, he merely defiled them, except for the specific במות השערים mentioned in II Kings 23: 8b. The exact meaning of this phrase is

---

by the term טמא and its implication in the minds of the people; similarly, we do not know the precise meaning of the term שבת referring to the procedure against the כמרים and the horses. We may understand the reason for not demolishing the previously legitimate high places and only defiling them to make them inappropriate for cult use, but it remains perplexing why the high places built by Solomon, unquestionably for the worship of idols, were not destroyed. We must therefore assume that for various reasons Josiah perpetrated distinct acts of degradation for each type of illicit worship. Following this thesis, we find a logical order in the narrative of this pericope. Verses 4 - 7 refer to the worship of Baal, *Asherah*, the starry hosts and their priests כמרים. Verses 8 - 9 refer to the previously legitimate high places and their distinct priests כהנים. An exception was made for the high places at the gates, or for the demons, which were demolished, not only defiled; this verse remains unclear no matter which way we consider this pericope. We then have the report of special idolatrous places, the *Tofeth* (v. 10), the horses and chariots (v. 11), the altars on the roof (v. 12), Solomon's high places (v. 13) and the pillars and the sacred trees in v. 14, each a distinct class of illegitimate worship with its clerics, and each with its specific type of destruction or defilement. The pericope is thus perfectly logical. Although we do not know the precise meaning of the term והשבית in v. 5, we observe a different treatment of the כמרים in this verse and the כהנים in v. 9, each group according to its association with a particular cult.
K. Koch, "Gefüge und Herkunft des Berichtes über die Kultreform des Königes Josia," *Alttestamentlicher Glaube und Biblische Theologie, Festschrift für H. D. Preuss* (Stuttgart, 1992), pp. 80-92, proposes a method for the literary analysis of these verses so as to identify their various sources, based on grammatical distinction, namely the different modes of conjugation of the verbs. He suggests that the apparently odd order of the narrative is based on a rationale of "cultic geography", that is, the elimination first of the idolatrous elements in the Temple, then those in the vicinity of the Temple, then the solar idolatry, and last the cleansing of the rest of the country, including Beth El. This proposition would be a reasonable solution but for the fact that it does not correspond with the order in the text. We already encounter in v. 5, in the midst of the cleansing of the Temple, the discharge of the pagan priests, the כמרים , and in v. 8 the degradation of the provincial priests of the high places, before the profanation of the idolatrous sites in Jerusalem in the vicinity of the Temple.

[15] M. Weinfeld, in his book מיהושע עד יאשיהו (Jerusalem, 1992), p. 169 also considers the interpretation of the term מגבע עד באר שבע in II Kings 23: 8 to imply the centralization of the cult in all of Judah. He concurs with the splitting of verse 8, of which part *a* refers to the centralization process and part *b* to the cleansing of the cult in Jerusalem and its vicinity. Thus in his opinion the demolition of the *bamoth* at the gate refers to Jerusalem, not to Beer Sheba.

unclear and much debated;[16] some scholars suggest reading it *ha-seirim*,[17] "the demons," not *ha-shearim*, "the gates."

Yadin argues against identifying this verse with a *bamah* in Jerusalem based on the following: a) no governor named Joshua is known, b) no such gate is mentioned in any other source, c) it is unlikely that a *bamah* was situated inside the city of Jerusalem, and d) such a *bamah* would have been well-known, and hence there would have been no need to describe its exact location. The text, therefore, must refer to *bamoth* in Beer Sheba. Yet it is odd that it was only in Beer Sheba that the specific *bamoth* of the gates were treated differently then the other *bamoth* - they were demolished, in contrast to all the others which were only defiled.[18] Given also that there was more than one, as we read ונתץ את במות השערים, in plural, and given the unusual term השערים, however we read it, they must have been of a special kind to be mentioned separately and to be demolished. Further, we must also assume that Solomon's *bamoth* were well known - they existed for such a long period - and Scripture nevertheless indicates their exact location. Joshua's gate was only one gate among many in the city gate complex, and therefore it may not have been mentioned on any other occasion. Regarding point c) of Yadin's postulate, one must consider that the *bamoth* were not in the city, but at the gate, and it is certainly unclear whether they were inside or outside. The expression אשר על שמאול איש בשער העיר "...which is on the left of the city gate" suggests that they were at the left side of a man entering the city, hence on the outside. Jonathan translates במיעליה תרע קרתא "at the coming up to the gate of the city," and Radak also explains it in this way. As argued above, 8b refers to the eradication of a particular type of illegitimate worship at *bamoth*, and both logic and literary examination of the pericope suggest that the *bamoth* and the other special idolatrous sites enumerated in the pericope were in Jerusalem, and not in Beer Sheba.

---

[16] The LXX translates the term במות השערים as τὸν οἶκον τῶν πυλῶν, "the place of the gates"; either the translators avoided the term במות, or they had another *Vorlage*. Thus the LXX offers no clarification of this odd verse.

[17] See Fricke, p. 322 ff., who also refers to W. Eichrodt, *Theologie des Alten Testaments*, Teil 2, 2. Aufl. p. 120, and to Lev. 17: 7: ולא יזבחו עוד את זבחיהם לשעירם "They must no longer offer any of their sacrifices to the goat idols [the NIV's translation of this term]."

[18] The traditional commentator Radak was aware of this difficulty, and proposed the reading ונתץ את במות השערים ואשר פתח שער יהושע "and he demolished the *bamoth* of the gates, and [the *bamah*] at Joshua's gate." He thus interpreted the verse: he demolished all the *bamoth* at the gates including the one at Joshua's gate, which is mentioned separately because it was larger [or more important] than the others. But the question still remains as to why Josiah demolished the *bamoth* of the gates and not the others, which he merely defiled.

Both scholars, Yadin and Aharoni, agree that dressed ashlar stones were used for the construction of the altar at Beer Sheba, and the upper stones were horned. Their argument concerns whether the structure was an illicit *bamah*, with an adjacent altar, as Yadin asserts, or a legitimate temple with an altar. Yadin contends that the use of dressed stones demonstrates that it was an altar not built according to Jewish law, whereas Aharoni suggests that the law against using unhewn stones was disregarded in Beer Sheba, or alternatively the stones were cut with tools of metal other than iron. They both establish their theories based on the Exod. pericope,[19] without considering that the deuteronomic pericope does not prohibit the use of גזית "hewn stones". Moreover, the *bamoth* were legitimate places of worship and sacrificial slaughter[20] before Joshia's reform, and one must therefore assume that if in that period hewn stones were not used for the altar, they were not used at the *bamoth*. We need only cite the great *bamah* of Gibeon, Solomon's official sacrificial locus, clearly sanctioned by the deuteronomic editor of Kings.[21] The altar law in Deut., as I have argued, should be

---

[19] Aharoni mentions the Exodus pericope, but also mentions iron, which appears only in the Deut. pericope.

[20] Yadin identifies the altar with horns at another site of the compound.

[21] We encounter the same favourable attitude toward the *bamah* in I Sam. 9: 12 ff., and in I Kings 3: 2: רק העם מזבחים בבמות כי לא נבנה בית לשם ה' עד הימים ההם "The people, however, were still sacrificing at the high places, because a Temple had not yet been built for the Name of the Lord," as well as many instances of the stereotypical phrase in Kings רק הבמות לא סרו "The high places were, however, not removed." These confirm that the *bamoth* were not as Yadin asserts: "The builders of the *bamoth* obviously were not guided by these prohibitions and followed the practice of the pagan world to some of whose deities, in fact, the cult was dedicated." We also observe the distinct manner of debasement applied by Josiah against the legitimate *bamoth* and their clerics, in contrast to the devastation wrought upon the illegitimate, idolatrous *bamoth*. There is a somewhat odd verse in Ezek. 20: 29: ואמר אלהם מה הבמה אשר אתם הבאים שם ויקרא שמה במה עד היום הזה. The NIV translates this literally: "Then I said to them: What is this high place you go to? (It is called *bamah* to this day)." Although it is clear from the context that the censure refers to idolatrous *bamoth*, the traditional commentators have problems with its interpretation. Rashi interprets only the second part of the verse, claiming that it is a degrading expression, namely, "What is its significance?" It seems to me that Rashi suggests reading (or interpreting) *ba-meh* "what" instead of *bamah*, as the MT vocalization reads. Radak attempts to interpret the entire verse and writes that the prophet denounces two evils, the building of *bamoth* for God's worship in many places, contrary to the command to sacrifice in only one place, and also the sacrifices to idols on some of the *bamoth*. Thus he formulates the accusation as follows: "Why have you built high places, when I commanded you to build a low earthen altar? You have copied the custom of the gentiles to build high places." I do not agree with Radak's interpretation, since it is clearly in opposition to Ezekiel's description of the altar in chap. 43 as ten cubits high; however, the interpretation does support my thesis in section 1.3 that the law of the altar

considered distinct from the law in Exodus, and thus the assertions of Yadin and Aharoni, based exclusively on the altar law of Exod., must be called into question. Rather, the dressed stones found at the Beer Sheba sanctuary confirm my thesis that according to the deuteronomic law the use of dressed stones was no longer prohibited. A similar argument applies to the altar steps. Yadin assumed "...this element too was constructed in contradiction to the Mosaic prohibition which follows that concerning the hewn stones"; again, he did not consider that the deuteronomic law does not prohibit the construction of steps to the altar.[22]

4.4 Further Archeological Dissension

I shall now summarize two additional disputes which confirm my postulate that one should not accept archeological conclusions without a critical examination of all the relevant texts. Adam Zertal published an extended essay entitled "Has Joshua's Altar Been Found on Mt. Ebal?"[23] Although Zertal puts an interrogation mark at the end of the title, and finishes his essay with the intellectually responsible remark "As scientists, we must say that the case has not yet been proven," he does not seem to have doubts about the identification of the altar in the course of his article. He writes on p. 35: "Suddenly it all became clear: the filling and the structure were

---

in Exod. 20 requires a simple low altar, which one does not have to climb. The Talmud too considered the *bamoth* legitimate places of worship in the periods when there was no official central sanctuary. We read in B.T. Zebahim 112b: באו לגלגל הותרו הבמות...באו לשילה נאסרו הבמות...באו לנב ולגבעון הותרו הבמות...באו לירושלים נאסרו הבמות "When they came to Gilgal, the *bamoth* were permitted...when they came to Shilo the *bamoth* were prohibited...when they came to Nob and Gibeon, the *bamoth* were permitted...when they came to Jerusalem the *bamoth* were prohibited." The LXX has different translations for the term במה, such as βαμα, ὑψηλός and the unusual Αβαμα in the above verse in Ezekiel. It seems that this variety does not indicate legitimate or illegitimate *bamoth*, but merely reflects the choice of the translator; the translator of Sam. uses the term βαμα, and the translator of Kings uses the term ὑψηλός, for both types of altars indiscriminately. Cf. M. Weinfeld, p. 173, who interprets the verse in Ezek. differently. In his opinion, the prophet compares the worship at the *bamoth*, even to God, with the idolatrous *bamoth*.

[22] Strangely enough, Yadin is aware of contradictions to the Exod. law, as he notes: "Ezekiel's altar must have had some stairs." But he apparently could not envisage a separation between the two laws, or a process of development in the altar-building rules, as in many other cult practices.

[23] *BAR* (Jan./Feb. 1985), pp. 26-43.

together one complete unit - an altar!"[24] He then writes on p. 38: "But the most striking feature of the site is the central structure, which, it seems, must now be interpreted as an altar," and further on p. 39 that in "this case, where biblical tradition and concrete archeological evidence coincide, [it] cannot be ignored." It is not within the scope of this study to contradict Zertal's statements on the basis of archeological concepts - this has been adequately handled by archeologists - [25] I wish merely to critically scrutinize the biblical evidence cited in support of his thesis.

Zertal identifies the filling of the structure as a characteristic typical of the Israelite altar; this is based on the *Biblical Encyclopedia*, which asserts that the Tabernacle altar "was filled with earth and stones to its full height." The Encyclopedia interprets in this way the expression נבוב לחת "hollow with boards" or "hollow of boards" in Exod. 27: 8, and I can only wonder how the term "hollow" is interpreted to mean "filled". Onkelos and all the traditional commentators translate נבוב as חלול "hollow", which is the antonym of "filled". Haran, the author of this section of the *Encyclopedia*, apparently tried to avoid a practical difficulty raised by this biblical description, and therefore, based on certain talmudic dicta which I shall explain below, he concluded that the altar was filled with "earth and stones."

According to the biblical text, the inside of the altar was hollow and consisted of wooden boards, with a grate on top where the sacrifices were burnt. The obvious question arises as to how the wood could resist the heat of the coals and fire on the grate.[26] To answer this enigma, Haran uses rabbinic homilies, which originated, not for the purposes of solving this mystery - practical problems were not their concern[27] - but to explain the obvious contradiction between the three types of altars commanded in Scripture: earth, stone and bronze. We read in B. T. Zebahim 62b: רבי נתן

---

[24] I shall revert to the issue of the filling below.

[25] See H. Shanks, "Two Early Israelite Cult Sites Now Questioned," *BAR* 14/1 (Jan/Feb. 1988), pp. 48-52, where we read statements such as "A bitter dispute has arisen about the Mt. Ebal site. Is it really a cult site or is it nothing more than an old farmhouse?" A. Kempinski in his article "Joshua's Altar - An Iron Age Watchtower," *BAR* 12/1 (Jan./Feb. 1986), pp. 43-9 objects to Zertal's identification of the site as cultic, but M. Coogan, who states that the Mt. Ebal site "probably is a cultic site," as quoted by Shanks, questions whether it can be identified as an Israelite site and concludes that it may have been "a local Canaanite shrine, which was also (or later) used by Israelites, or at least that it was 'Israelitized.'"

[26] Cf. M. Noth, *Exodus, A Commentary*, The Old Testament Library, transl. from German by J. S. Bowden (London, 1965), p. 215: "No question is asked as to whether such a construction could withstand the heat when animal sacrifices were being burnt."

[27] Some traditional commentators seem to have been conscious of this problem; Rashbam and Seforno add to their commentary on the hollow altar that when the Israelites camped, they filled the altar with earth and sacrificed upon it.

"Rabbi Nathan אומר מזבח של שילה של נחושת היה חלול ומלא אבנים
says the altar of Shilo was [made] of bronze, was hollow and filled with
stones." This dictum appears at the end of a rhetorical debate on the
following homily: מה תלמוד לומר אבנים אבנים אבנים שלש פעמים אחד
עולמים ובית וגבעון נוב של ואחד שילה של "What do we learn from the
three repetitions of stones [in Exod. 20 and Deut. 27]? [That there were]
three stone altars: one in Shilo, one in Nob and Gibeon, and one in the
Temple." The apparent contradiction on the structure of the altar is thus
solved by Rabbi Nathan's dictum: the stones are the filling. In the
subsequent discussion it is asked: ומאי מזבח אדמה "What is meant by the
command to make an earthen altar [in Exod. 20: 21]," and there are two
answers: מעיקרא סבר מזבח אדמה שהוא אטום באדמה ולבסוף סבר
שהוא מחובר באדמה ...Originally one thought that [it meant] an altar
blocked with earth, and then one thought...[it meant] attached to the
ground," that is, on the earth, not on vaults. We observe that Haran took the
two rabbinic homilies and put them together in his statement that the altar
was filled with "earth and stones."

Zertal then attempts to substantiate his thesis by identifying a ledge three
feet below the top of the altar, and comparing this peculiarity to the כרכב
"ledge" of the bronze altar described in Exod. 27: 5. The exact meaning of
the term כרכב remains unclear, notwithstanding the common translation as
"ledge". Onkelos translates with סובבא "something which encircles," with
no precise indication of its nature. The LXX translates as ἐσχάρα "hearth,
fireplace", as the term מכבר is commonly translated as "grating". In the
Talmud, we find two different opinions; we read in B. T. Zebahim 62a:
איזהו כרכוב רבי אומר זה כיור רבי יוסי ברבי יהודה אומר זה הסובב
"What is the *Karkov*? Rabbi says: It is a drawing. Rabbi Jose b'Rabbi Judah
says: It is the encircling gangway [one cubit wide where the priests walked
around the altar]." It is clear that the סובב, the gangway, is not a protruding
ledge, as Zertal describes it, but an intruding rim, found in the mishnaic rule
which Zertal himself quotes.[28] Although Ezekiel's description of the altar

---

[28] We read in Mishnah Midoth 3: 1: המזבח היה שלשים ושתים על שלשים ושתים
עלה אמה וכנס אמה זה היסוד נמצא שלשים על שלשים עלה חמש וכנס אמה
"זה הסובב נמצא עשרים ושמנה על עשרים ושמנה ושמנה "The altar was 32 x 32 cubits;
up one cubit, it narrowed one cubit, this is the base, 30 x 30 cubits; up five [cubits], it
narrowed one cubit, and that is the gangway, 28 x 28 cubits." At any rate such a
"gangway", the סובב according to Rabbi Judah, could not be predicated for the bronze
altar; this altar maintained the same width and length throughout its entire height,
according to the Pentateuchal command, in contrast with Ezekiel's altar, where a
step-construction is distinctly prescribed. Cassuto perhaps envisaged such a protruding
structure for the bronze altar; see section 5.5.1.

does not correspond exactly to the mishnaic form and dimensions,[29] it reflects the same principle, that is, a step-like construction, narrowing at each elevation.

Noth[30] interprets the biblical כרכב as "a 'ledge', to be understood as a kind of ridge," not the protruding wide ledge of Zertal's altar; Sarna[31] explains, "It may have been purely decorative," similar to Rabbi's opinion. According to Mishnah Midoth 3: 1,[32] there was a red line in the middle of the altar of the Second Temple, to divide the altar in two parts; the blood of certain sacrifices had to be sprinkled on the upper part, and that of others on the lower part. The Sages[33] deduced this line in the middle of the altar precisely from our verse Exod. 27: 5: ונתתה אתה תחת כרכב המזבח מלמטה והיתה הרשת עד חצי המזבח "Put it under the ledge of the altar so that it is halfway up the altar." Moreover, either the line or the gangway surrounded all four sides and remained the same width,[34] in contrast to the ledge on Zertal's altar, which was found only on three sides and which widened "from about two feet until it reaches a width of 7,5 feet" (p. 38). At any rate, the כרכב, whatever it implied, is a characteristic of the Tabernacle's bronze altar, but is not mentioned in the altar laws concerning the stone altars, or in Ezek. 43 or the rabbinic description of the altar in Mishnah Midoth 3: 1.

---

[29] We read in Ezek. 43: 14: ומחיק הארץ עד העזרה התחתונה שתים אמות רחב האמה אמה אחת ומהעזרה הקטנה עד העזרה הגדולה ארבע אמות ורחב "From the gutter on the ground up to the lower edge it is two cubits high and a cubit wide, and from the smaller ledge up to the larger ledge it is four cubits high and a cubit wide." The talmudic term סובב "gangway" does not appear in Ezek., and the parallel elevations are different: four cubits in Ezek. against five cubits in the Mishnah.

[30] p. 216.

[31] *Exodus*, p. 173.

[32] חוט של סקרא חוגרו באמצע "A red line embraced [the altar] in its midpoint."

[33] We read in B. T. Zebahim 53a: חוט של סקרא חוגרו באמצע כדי להבדיל בין דמים העליונים לדמים התחתונים מנא הני מילי אמר רב אחא בר רב קטינא שנאמר והיתה הרשת עד חצי המזבח נתנה התורה מחיצה להבדיל בין דמים העליונים לדמים התחתונים "A red line embraced [the altar] in its midpoint in order to divide between the upper blood [to be sprinkled above the line] and the lower blood. From where do we know it? Said Rav Aha son of Rav Qatina: Because it is written 'and the grating should be halfway up the altar [Exod. 27: 5].' The Torah has provided a partition to divide between the upper and the lower blood. "

[34] From the above-cited Mishnah Midoth 3: 1 the סובב "gangway" was one cubit wide on all four sides, as we read there עלה חמש וכנס אמה זה הסובב "...up five [cubits], [the altar] narrowed one cubit, that is the 'gangway'." The surface of the altar decreases from 30 x 30 cubits square at the base to 28 x 28 cubits square at this level of the altar. Hence the gangway had the same width all around the altar.

We must recognize that the "biblical tradition" quoted by Zertal to prove his case is a mixed bag of evidence from various sources, at times not correctly interpreted, and often conflicting among themselves. The Rabbis attempted to harmonize all the relevant biblical texts: the three conflicting pentateuchal altar laws,[35] the contrasting reports on the bronze altar in Kings,[36] Ezekiel's vision of the holocaust altar and the mishnaic record of the Second Temple altar. [37]Their creed constrained them to devise all kinds of dialectic acrobatics to integrate the portrayals of altars of different periods, sizes and materials, and in consequence to impose technical descriptions of small bronze altars on large stone altars. But one must wonder that a modern scholar followed the same system.

The third example of archeological dissension relates to purely archeological criteria. I shall therefore abbreviate the discussion on this perspective of the archeological discipline. David Ussishkin reviews[38] Schumacher's earlier excavation of the shrine at Meggido, which he calls "the *massebot* Temple,"[39] and records in his summary on p. 163 the following finds: "Three limestone altars...two...are 55 cm. high and characterized by a thick protruding strip which surrounds them and by four horns. The third altar is 68 cm. high; its sides are differently carved, and it has slightly curved-up corners in lieu of the more sharply defined horns." He also notes "a round limestone altar or offering stand...its sides are smoothed, and their upper part is decorated with horizontal incised lines and a strip of zigzag decoration." Ussishkin also records the finds of offering tables, of which one "was 70 cm. long, 50 cm. wide and 20 cm. high; it contained an accurately-cut round depression." E. Stern [40] then questioned "the validity of the reconstruction method used by Ussishkin." Stern identifies the offering tables as "stone basins often found on the floors or beside the pillars of Iron Age houses...and their function in everyday activities is clear" (p. 104). Concerning the *massebot*, Stern writes "I believe that they are part of an industrial installation." Regarding the altars, Stern puts in question

---

[35] As amply discussed in chap. 1.

[36] There is no mention in Kings of a bronze altar made by Solomon, whereas we find in II Chr. 4: 1 that Solomon made a bronze altar with dimensions completely different from those commanded in Exod. 27: 1- 8. The Talmud attempted to reconcile the divergent dimensions, as well as other contrasting descriptions of the bronze altar. I shall revert to this issue in the examination of the bronze altar pericope.

[37] See previous footnote concerning these differences.

[38] D. Ussishkin, "Schumacher's Shrine in Building 338 at Meggido," *Israel Exploration Journal* 39 (1989), pp. 149 - 172.

[39] Ibid., p. 154, referring to "two large monolithic stelae, Schumacher's *massebot*" (p. 155).

[40] E. Stern, "Schumacher's Shrine in Building 338 at Meggido, A Rejoinder," *Israel Exploration Journal* 40 (1990), pp. 102 - 107.

Ussishkin's allegation that the site was a shrine. He writes: "The above leads to the conclusion that Building 338 was never a shrine but was rather one of the palaces of Israelite Meggido." I shall obviously not attempt to decide whose assumptions are historically correct. I merely note that according to Ussishkin's identification, the altars and the offering tables at Solomon's shrine were constructed of ashlars, that is, dressed stones, and the archaic custom of building altars exclusively from natural, unworked stones was already extinct.

4.5 Conclusion

One must concede that in addition to the methodological disagreements among archeologists concerning the identification of artifacts, they sometimes lack the determination or competence to explore the correct and minute analysis of the relevant texts.[41] The conscientious examination of the texts is an indispensable tool in the accurate identification of archeological findings, or could serve, at the least, to put a question mark on certain apparently categorical statements by archeologists. I may conclude, therefore, that the findings of altars from the monarchic period, constructed both of unworked and ashlar stones, support my thesis that the archaic custom of building primitive altars of unworked stones was no longer considered mandatory. Permanent shrines, built by the Israelites, or taken over from the previous inhabitants, were constructed of dressed stones, since the archaic nomadic theology which rejected the defilement of the Deity's dwelling by the use of a sword was no longer relevant. On the other hand, the old custom may have subsisted alongside the new, as often happens, and that would explain the findings of both types of altars from the same period. I wish to reiterate my thesis, corroborated by textual evidence, that until the reign of Ahaz there were no official rules on how to erect an altar; there was only a custom to build them in a simple fashion, and of low stature.

---

[41] I may add here a few brief quotations by M. Noth in this respect from his "Introduction" in *The History of Israel*, revised translation by P. R. Ackroyd (London 1960), pp. 46ff: "Historical synthesis is indispensable even in the interpretation and utilisation of archeological findings....One has to be very clear what the results of archeological work can prove and what they cannot prove....What knowledge of any real accuracy and historical substance of the Ancient Orient should we possess if we had all the material remains excepting the literary relics in the widest range of the word?"

5. The Bronze Altar: Exod. 27: 1-8

I have already noted that the command to build a bronze altar - in fact, a wooden altar overlaid with bronze - in Exod. 27: 1 - 8 contradicts the two laws regarding earthen or stone altars. I shall examine the character of this altar and its use, and pose the question of whether such an altar ever existed. Before approaching these issues, a critical examination of the biblical text is appropriate; some repetition is, regrettably, unavoidable.

5. 1 Exod. 27: 1

ועשית את המזבח[1] עצי שטים חמש אמות ארך וחמש אמות רחב רבוע
יהיה המזבח ושלש אמות קמתו

Build an altar of acacia wood, three cubits high; it is to be square,[2] five cubits long and five cubits wide.

The first verse indicates the dimensions of the altar, five cubits long and five cubits wide, and emphasizes its square form; it then adds the height, three cubits. This appears to be a clear and incontestable statement that the bronze altar was three cubits high, and five cubits square throughout its height, but nothing is impossible when the harmonization strategy has the upper hand. The Rabbis deemed it necessary to reconcile this law as well as the conflicting descriptions of the bronze altar in II Chr. 4: 1 and in Ezek. 43: 13- 17. Thus the apparently precise dimensions of our verse are grossly modified. The talmudic Sages and their commentators propose various

---

[1]   Wevers has emphasized in his *Notes on the Greek Text of Exodus*. Septuagint and Cognate Studies 30. (Atlanta, 1990), p. 431 the fact that the LXX has here the indefinite form θυσιαστήριον instead of the definite המזבח in MT. He adds "Since the building of an altar of incense is detailed in 30: 1-10 it seemed inappropriate to call this altar 'the altar.'" This may also indicate that the pericope with the command to build the incense altar originates from a later date than our pericope. The definite article is thus appropriate before the command to make the incense altar, since in the writer's mind it was definite that only one altar, the holocaust altar, was to be made. The LXX probably corrected this apparent imperfection, or, as in many occurrences, followed the Samaritan Bible (in which the incense altar appears in chap. 25), which has the indefinite מזבח. The Samaritan Targums also show the indefinite מדבחא, but Targum Neophyti follows the MT with the definite form ית מדבחא

[2]   This is the NIV translation commonly used in this study. The KJV correctly avoids translating יהיה as a modal, with "the altar shall be foursquare."

dimensions, which are also reflected in Maimonides' Codex as firm rules.[3]
One opinion states that the area was ten cubits square, instead of five, as

---

[3]   We read in B.T. Zebahim 59b: ר' יהודה לטעמיה דאמר מזבח שעשה משה גדול
היה דתניא חמש אמות ארך וחמש אמות רחב דברים ככתבן דברי ר' יוסי ר'
יהודה אומר נאמר כאן רבוע ונאמר להלן רבוע מה להלן מאמצעיתו היה
מודד אף כאן מאמצעיתו היה מודד והתם מנלן דכתיב והאריאל שתים
עשרה אמה לכל רוח או אינו אלא י"ב על י"ב כשהוא אומר אל ארבעת
רבעיו מלמד שמאמצע הוא מודד ור' יוסי כי גמר גזירה שוה בגובהה הוא
דגמיר דתניא ושלש אמות קמתו דברים ככתבן דברי רבי יהודה רבי יוסי
אומר נאמר כאן רבוע ונאמר להלן רבוע מה להלן גובהו פי שנים כארכו אף
כאן פי שנים כארכו "Rabbi Judah decides according to his opinion, as he said: The
altar made by Moses was big, as it was taught: 'Five cubits long and five cubits wide
[Exod. 27: 1],' the matter is exactly as written; these are the words of Rabbi Jose;
Rabbi Judah says: It is said here רבוע 'square' and it is said there [Ezek. 43: 16]
רבוע 'square'; as there [the intent is that] it be measured from the middle [of the
altar, hence it is really double the length], so here too it is measured from the middle.
[Hence in his opinion the bronze altar was ten cubits square]. [The Gemara asks] And
how do we know there [in Ezek. that it is measured from the middle]? It is written
[Ezek. 43:16] 'the *Ariel* is twelve cubits' from each aspect - perhaps it really implies
twelve by twelve? Since it is said: 'To its four quarters רבעיו,' it comes to teach us
that it is measured from the middle [of the altar, and thus there are four quarters]. And
Rabbi Jose [how does he interpret the identical term רבוע in both pericopes which
demonstrate a parallelism]? He interprets it as an analogy concerning its height, as we
learned: 'Three cubits high [Exod. 27: 1],' the matter is exactly as written, [are] the
words of Rabbi Judah, [but] Rabbi Jose says: It is said here רבוע 'square' and it is
said further [in Exod. 30: 2, at the incense altar] רבוע 'square', as there its height is
double its length [one cubit long and one cubit wide and two cubits high], here too [its
height is] double its length." Thus Rabbi Judah alleges that the bronze altar was ten
cubits square and three cubits high, and Rabbi Jose asserts that the altar was five
cubits square and ten cubits high.
In the course of the rhetoric it is asked how Rabbi Jose explains the explicit height of
three cubits in Scripture, and the answer is: משפת סובב ולמעלה "from the edge of
the 'gangway' upwards." Again, there is no such structure סובב either in Exodus or in
Ezekiel; it appears only in Mishnah Midoth 3: 1, and in B.T. Eirubin 4a as an
interpretation of Ezekiel's description of the altar, and its relationship to the rabbinic
nomenclature. We read there: וחיק האמה זה יסוד ואמה רחב זה סובב וגבולה
אל שפתה סביב אלו הקרנות "'Its gutter is a cubit deep [Ezek. 43: 13]' is [the
equivalent of] the foundation [the rabbinic name in Midoth], and 'a cubit wide' is the
gangway [the equivalent of the rabbinic term סובב], and 'the span around its edge'
refers to the horns /corners." It is remarkable that the rabbinic rhetoric does not quote
here the height of Solomon's bronze altar, which, according to II Chr. 4: 1, was ten
cubits high. It is possible that the Sages wanted to avoid defending the additional
discrepancy between the two bronze altars concerning their length and width; in both
passages the altars are of the same height, namely ten cubits, but quite different in
area: one is twenty cubits square and the other five cubits square. Such a difference

indicated in Scripture, and ten cubits high, instead of three; another opinion ruled that the hearth was only one cubit square. We observe the extent to which the enthusiasm for harmonization dominates, both in this case and in the attempt by the traditional commentators and certain scholars to harmonize the two altar laws in Exodus and Deuteronomy.

רבוע יהיה

...it is to be square

This additional characteristic seems superfluous; if Scripture states "five cubits long and five cubits wide" there is no need to add that it should be

---

would also pose an aesthetic problem concerning the relation between surface and height, an issue of which the rabbis were aware.

We observe how the harmonization method in the above talmudic passage leads to the conclusion that the bronze altar was ten cubits high but of differing widths, corresponding to Ezekiel's altar. A more explicit declaration in this respect is found in B. T. Zebahim 62a: מדת ארכו ומדת רחבו ומדת קומתו אין מעכבין א״ר מני ובלבד שלא יפחתנו ממזבח שעשה משה וכמה אמר רב יוסף אמה מחכו עליה חמש אמות ארך וחמש אמות רחב רבוע יהיה המזבח אמר ליה אביי דלמא מקום מערכה קאמר מר "The length, the width and the height [of the altar] are not absolute, said Rav Mani, but they must not be smaller than the altar made by Moses. And how [big was that]? Said Rav Joseph: One cubit. They smiled [at this declaration, since it is written] 'The altar should be a square five cubits long, and five cubits wide [Exod. 27: 1]'; Said to him Abaye: Maybe the hearth was intended [the upper part of the altar, which was only one cubit wide, because of the diminishing sizes of the upper levels]." This is the correct interpretation of this statement, and is corroborated by Rashi and Maimonides. We read Rashi's explanation on B. T. Zebahim 59b: שהרי מזבח של משה כתיב ביה ה׳ אמות אורך וה׳ אמות רוחב צא מהם מקום הקרנות אמה לכל צד ומקום הילוך רגלי הכהנים אמה לפנים מן הקרנות סביב המערכה נמצא מקום המערכה אמה על אמה הכי אמרינן לקמן בפירקין (זבחים דף סב) "Since for Moses' altar it is written five cubits long and five cubits wide, take off for the horns one cubit [according to Ezek. 43: 16 - 17, through extrapolation] on each side [hence three cubits remain], and the space for the priests to go around one cubit inward of the horns, the resulting size of the hearth is one cubit by one cubit, as we say further on in the chapter [Zebahim 62]." And Maimonides, based on the talmudic rhetoric and on the rabbinic maxim that Rabbi Jose's opinion supersedes that of Rabbi Judah, declares in Hilkhot Beit HaBehirah 2:5: מזבח שעשה משה ושעשה שלמה ושעשו בני הגולה ושעתיד להעשות כולן עשר אמות גובה כל אחד מהן חה זה הכתוב בתורה ושלש אמות קומתו מקום המערכה בלבד "The altar made by Moses, and which Solomon made, and the exile returnees made, and the one which will be made, are each ten cubits high; and what is written in the Torah 'and three cubits high' refers to the hearth [the upper part, including as in Rashi's explanation the horns and the space for the priests to go around]." In 2: 17, Maimonides repeats Rav Joseph's declaration that an altar must be at least three cubits high and one cubit square, and adds a remarkable statement at the end: כשיעור מקום המערכה של מזבח מדבר "like the dimensions of the altar in the desert."

square. In II Chr. 4: 1, at the description of Solomon's bronze altar, we read עשרים אמה ארכו ועשרים אמה רחבו ועשר אמות קומתו "twenty cubits its length and twenty cubits its width and ten cubits its height"; there is no addendum regarding its square form. In the Pentateuch, the same characteristic "square" is added to the incense altar (Exod. 30: 2) and the breastplate (Exod. 28: 16), where it also seems superfluous. To our regret, there is no other comparison in the Pentateuch[4] from which to determine whether this additional rule has some particular purpose. It seems that for aesthetic, traditional or practical reasons[5] there was an absolute requirement that the altar should be square with four pointed, not rounded, corners.[6] The command to add "horns" to the bronze altar, a rule entirely lacking with

---

[4]   The ark and the table are not square; the lampstand has no dimensions at all, an odd exception considering that it is one of the three significant furnishing of the Tabernacle. The Rabbis debated the absence of an indication of height for the atonement cover of the ark in B. T. Sukkah 5a: דתני רבי חנינא כל הכלים שעשה משה נתנה בהן תורה מדת ארכן ומדת רחבן ומדת קומתן כפרת מדת ארכה ומדת רחבה נתנה מדת קומתה לא נתנה "Rabbi Hanina taught: All the furnishings which Moses made, the Torah gave the dimensions for their length, width and height; for the *kaporeth*, its length and width are given, but not its height." The Talmud does not ask about the dimension of the lampstand, because we read in B. T. Menahoth 28b: אמר שמואל משמיה דסבא גובהה של מנורה שמנה עשר טפחים "Samuel said in the name of an old man: The height of the lampstand was eighteen handbreadths." Maimonides, in his commentary to Mishnah Menahoth 3: 7, writes that we know the lampstand's height by tradition. In biblical sources the feature "square" is added in some instances but not in others. It appears in Ezek. 43: 16 at the description of the altar, but not in v. 17; it appears in Ezek. 45: 2 in stating the dimensions (five hundred by five hundred) of the holy precinct, but not in 42: 20 regarding the dimensions of the wall surrounding it; it does not appear in the description of the area of the Temple (one hundred by one hundred) in Ezek. 41: 13-14; and it does not appear in the dimensions (twenty by twenty) of the Holy of Holies in Ezek. 41: 4, nor in the similar description of the Debir (twenty by twenty by twenty) in Solomon's Temple in I Kings 6: 20.

[5]   It is also possible that an altar with straight lines and corners was required to differentiate it from the archaic Assyrian round form of the altar, similar to the form of a bowl. The *Encyclopaedia Biblica* (Jerusalem 1962), s.v. מזבח contains a picture of a round Assyrian stone altar (p. 770). K. Galling, *Der Altar in den Kulturen des Alten Orientes* (Berlin, 1925), p. 50, explains the origin of the Assyrian round altars. The term *passuru* for altar originates from the term for "bowl"; this round utensil was placed on a tripod and represented the early form of a furnishing for the offering of food to mankind and the gods. The altars, like the tables, changed their forms and became square or oblong, but some altars subsisted in their conservative round form.

[6]   We read in B. T. Zebahim 62b: ואצטריך למכתב סביב ואצטריך למכתב רבוע דאי כתוב רחמנא סביב הוה אמינא דעגיל מעגל "And it had to be written 'around' and 'square', since if only 'around' were written, I would have said that it might be round."

respect to the earthen and stone altars, may possibly be the reason for the emphasis on the requirement for pointed corners.

5.2 Exod. 27: 2

ועשית קרנתיו על ארבע פנתיו ממנו תהיין קרנתיו וצפית אתו נחשת

Make its horns at each of the four corners, so that the horns and the altar are of one piece, and overlay the altar with bronze.

There are some odd translations of this verse. Onkelos follows the MT exactly, but Jonathan adds קרנוי זקיפין לעיל "its horns [to be] erected upwards," or "on the upper edge." Targum Neophyti, which usually follows Jonathan, also adds here מן משחת רומא "from the measure [length] of its height," a statement that would indicate Jonathan's לעיל is to be interpreted as "on the upper edge". This addition seems odd, or at least tautological, particularly as expressed by Neophyti, which reverses the order in Jonathan, and states מן משחת רומא מנה יהוויין קרנתה "from the measure [length] of its height from it should be its horn." Where else would the horns be, if not along its height?

Another oddity is the singular form of קרנתה "horn," without the pronominal suffix, in Onkelos and in Jonathan, though the relevant verb יהוויין is in plural. Yet more bizarre is the fact that although the Samaritan Bible follows the MT text[7] with קרנתיו, in plural with the pronominal suffixes,[8] both manuscripts of the Samaritan Targum have קרנתה, in singular, without the pronominal suffix, and like the Neophyti the verb יהן is in plural. The LXX, on the other hand, has the term κέρατα in plural, in both occurrences, but without any pronoun referring to the altar. Wevers[9] correctly comments that the plain meaning of the LXX text would be to overlay only the horns with bronze. The MT speaks of the horns in plural, but reverts to singular in the command to overlay with bronze, indicating that this refers to the altar; but the LXX, which has the two occurrences of κέρατα in plural, and then the pronoun αὐτα "them" referring to the overlaying, must be understood to mean that only the "horns" should be covered with bronze.[10] I

---

[7] Except that the word תהיין in the MT is written תהיינה in the Samaritan Bible.

[8] I cannot exclude the possibility that the Aramaic translators had another *Vorlage* with a different text.

[9] pp. 431-2.

[10] It is possible that the LXX editor actually understood this verse to indicate that only the horns should be covered with bronze. See chap. 7 n. 54 concerning the odd LXX record that the altar was covered with the bronze sheets made from the censers used by the rebellious Korah group.

do not have a logical explanation for these many oddities in the various translations, but the fact that they occur in all the sources indicates either different *Vorlagen*, or the uncertainty of the translators as to how to interpret this verse, particularly the phrase ממנו תהיין קרנתיו. The literary style of the first part of the verse is odd, and may have induced the LXX emendation to render the verse intelligible.

We must compare this phrase regarding the horns with the slightly different literary style regarding the horns of the incense altar. We read there (Exod. 30: 2) ואמתים קמתו ממנו קרנתיו[11] "and two cubits its height, from it [make] its horns." It seems odd that, in contrast to our pericope, there is no explicit command to make horns; it is only to be implicitly understood. Nor is their number indicated; we might assume two horns,[12] not four, from this verse alone, simply from the use of קרנות, if we assume that the term קרנות applies exclusively to horns, not to corners. There is nowhere in Scripture an indication that the golden or incense altar had four horns[13] and the term קרנות might represent the two animal horns found in nature as well as in biblical metaphors.[14] The metaphorical concept of four horns in Zech. 2: 1 (1:

---

[11]   Here too Jonathan adds מניה יהון קרנוי זקיפון "from it [from its height] [are] its projecting horns." This expression is not entirely identical to Jonathan's interpretation in Exod. 27: 2 regarding the horns of the bronze altar, but it demonstrates that Jonathan had some difficulties with the interpretation of these phrases concerning the horns.

[12]   This would be particularly true if we were to agree with the opinion of some scholars that the altar "horns" symbolize the holy bull's horns.

[13]   In the records of the construction of the altars, we encounter the same particular text for each altar. In Exod. 37: 25, with respect to the incense altar, there are no indications that it had four horns, and we read a similar expression to that in Exod. 30: 2: ממנו קרנתיו; but in Exod. 38: 2, concerning the bronze altar, we read: ויעש קרנתיו על ארבע פנתיו ממנו היו קרנתיו "And he made its four horns on its four corners, from it were its horns." There is no parallel in the LXX for these verses, since the record of the execution of the commands is much shorter: J. W. Wevers, "The Composition of Exodus 35 to 40," in *Text History of the Greek Exodus*. Mitteilung des Septuaginta Unternehmens XXI (Göttingen, 1992), pp. 117-146. The problem of the location of the incense altar pericope in Exod. 30 is well known, and we may speculate that it was inserted intentionally after the command to build the holocaust altar precisely for this reason, that is, to provide a textual reference for an altar having four "horns". The Samaritan Pentateuch, in which the incense altar pericope appears in Exod. 25 before the command of the bronze altar, leaves us without a clear ordinance concerning the "horns" and their number.

[14]   For example, וקרני ראם קרניו "his horns are the horns of a wild ox [Deut. 33: 17]"; ויעש לו צדקיה... קרני ברזל "And Zedekiah had made iron horns [I Kings 22: 11]"; ובקרניכם תנגחו "with your horns you will gore [Ezek. 34: 21]"; וכל קרני רשעים אגדע תרוממנה קרנות צדיק "I will cut off the horns of the wicked but the horns of the righteous will be lifted up [Ps. 75: 11 in MT, 10 in KJV]." In these and similar occurrences the metaphorical symbol of strength is either one horn or two. There are two instances in which four horns are implied. In Dan. 8: 2 - 7, a ram with two horns is

18 in KJV) is meant to convey the idea of totality, similar to the "four winds of heaven" כארבע רוחות השמים[15] (Zech. 2: 10; 2: 6 in KJV), or as we would now say, the "four corners of the world," indicating the entire world. We must therefore consider the metaphorical associations of the two definitions of the term קרן[16] and the particular hermeneutics of each with respect to the altar; I shall return to this issue in chap. 6.

5.3 Exod. 27: 3

ועשית סירתיו לדשנו ויעיו ומזרקתיו ומזלגתיו
Make its pots to remove the ashes, and its shovels, sprinkling bowls, meat forks...

The list of the altar's utensils appears in Exod. 38: 3 in the same order, but without the expression לדשנו as the intended purpose of the pots. In Num. 4: 14, the pots סירת do not appear at all, although at the end of the list we read כל כלי המזבח "all the utensils," exactly as in Exod. 38: 3, and similar to לכל כליו "all its utensils" in Exod. 27: 3. The issue of the סירת "pots" is therefore intriguing: why are they missing in the list of "all" the utensils enumerated in Num. 4: 14, and why is their purpose missing in Exod. 38: 3, the record of the preparation of the utensils, which is almost a repetition of the text in 27: 3? Yet another problem is the fact that we do not know the exact translation

---

described; in vv. 8 - 22, the metaphorical one-horned goat generates four horns, to symbolize the four diadochic kingdoms after Alexander's death. Similarly, there is an explicit motive for the four horns in Zech. 2: 1 (1: 18 in KJV), as explained in the following note.

[15] This is the motive for the reference to four horns in Zech. 2: 1; from the context one observes that the intent is to imply the totality of a site, up to its four corners. See A. Kahana, ספר תרי עשר, חגי וזכריה (Tel Aviv, 1930), who links the two metaphorical concepts, and writes in his commentary on verse 2: 1: הכוונה היא אלה אומות אשר "This is the intent בארבע רוחות השמים אשר נגחו בקרניהן את יהודה וירושלים [of the prophet]: The nations of the four corners of the world who gore with their horns Judah and Jerusalem." The prophet also uses the number four to portray four craftsmen, and to imply the wholeness of the world he utilizes the metaphor of the "four winds of heaven." The number four became a symbol of totality. The equating of "four corners" with "four horns" as a metaphorical symbol of "totality" will be discussed with respect to the altar.

[16] The term קרן in the meaning of "corner" does not appear in Scripture, but does appear in post-biblical talmudic literature, as for example יושבי קרנות "those sitting at street corners." I would speculate that the notion of "totality" associated with "the four winds of heaven" or "the four corners of the world" was behind the extension of the concept of קרן to mean "principal" or "capital" as well as "corner", which we encounter in the talmudic literature. An earlier use cannot be excluded, but cannot be substantiated from Scripture.

of יעים. Onkelos translates it as מגרפות, "rakes" in modern Hebrew, and in the talmudic literature implements with which to drag something. Rashi explains with respect to Exod. 27: 3: מגרפות שנוטל בהם הדשן והן כמין כסוי הקדרה של מתכת דק ולו בית יד "*Magrefoth*, to draw the ashes, and they are similar to an iron cover of a pot with a handle." Its use for raking the ashes on the altar is confirmed in Mishnah Tamid 2: 1: נטלו את המגרפות ואת הצינורות ועלו לראש המזבח "They [the priests] took the rakes and the shovels and climbed up the altar [to arrange the unburned pieces of flesh and the ashes upon it]." The term גרף, the root of מגרפה, appears twice in Scripture. In Jud. 5: 21, נחל קישון גרפם "the river Kishon swept them away," the meaning of the term גרף is evident,[17] and serves as the root for an implement that performs the task of "moving/dragging." If we conclude that the correct translation of יעים is מגרפה, as Onkelos and the traditional commentators assert,[18] there is an additional oddity in the word order of our

---

[17] The other occurrence in Scripture of the term גרף is in Joel 1: 17: עבשו פרדות תחת מגרפתיהם, but its meaning is disputed by the various traditional commentators. The LXX translates מגרפתיהם as φάτναις αὐτῶν "their mangers", a term which has nothing in common with the verb גרף.

[18] This translation is very doubtful; the term יעים appears in Scripture exclusively with respect to the altar utensils. We have no other scriptural reference to corroborate this translation. The commentators refer in their comments on Exod. 27: 3 to Onkelos' translation, and to the verb יעה in Isa. 28: 17 ויעה ברד מחסה כזב, whereas in their comments on the verse in Isa., they refer to our verse in Exodus to substantiate their translation; this is circular reasoning. Isa. 28: 17 is translated by the NIV as " hail will sweep away your refuge, the lie," but the LXX has a totally different exegesis of this verse: καὶ οἱ πεποιθότες μάτην ψεύδει "those who have trusted in vain in falsity", with nothing analogous to the term "sweeping" for the verb יעה. The real meaning of the term יעים therefore escapes our knowledge, and it seems we are in good company in this respect. The LXX, in its translation of verses Exod. 27: 3, 38: 23 (38: 3 in MT) and Num. 4: 14 does not translate the term יעים, and we do not know whether the translators had another text, or did not know how to translate this term and simply ignored it. This latter supposition is plausible in Num. 4: 14, in which the texts of the MT and the LXX correspond, and only the translation of היעים is missing. In Exod. 27: 3, the LXX certainly had another *Vorlage*, since its text is entirely different than the MT. Instead of the phrase ועשית סירותיו לדשנו ויעיו, we read καὶ ποιήσεις στεφανήν τῷ θυσιαστηρίῳ καὶ τὸν καλυπτῆρα αὐτοῦ "And make a brim to the altar and its cover." It follows with φιάλας, which corresponds with מזרקתיו , translated as "sprinkling bowls." Another inconsistency with the MT is the last item, ומחתתיו "its coal pans," expressed in plural, whereas the LXX uses the singular τὸ πυρεῖον αὐτοῦ. It is difficult to reconcile these two divergent texts. In Exod. 38: 23 (MT 38: 3) for the MT את הסירת ואת היעים...ואת המחתת the LXX has καὶ τὸ πυρεῖον αὐτοῦ καὶ τὴν βάσιν "and its firepan and its step." There is a different sequence of words, but only the translation of היעים is missing. The term הסירת is translated as βάσιν "a step" and

verse. Both the סירת and the יעים would refer to utensils for the removal of
the ashes, and their purpose לדשנו should therefore appear after יעיו, not
after סירתיו; the existing word order implies that only the סירת are utensils
for the removal of the ashes, but not the following term יעיו.

This apparently incorrect placement of the purpose of the utensils, לדשנו,
as well as the absence of the term in the other two verses listing the altar's
utensils, supports my supposition that the term was interjected into our verse
at a later date, with the objective of modifying the original meaning of the
two utensils: סירת and יעים. We have seen that the interpretation of the term
יעים is doubtful; the LXX on the Pentateuch,[19] an opus of unmixed origin,
does not translate this term.[20] The same uncertainty also applies to the term
סירת, which appears twice in the MT in Exod. 27: 3 and 38: 3,[21] but in the
LXX we read in 27: 3: καὶ ποιήσεις στεφανήν τῷ θυσιαστηρίῳ καὶ τὸν
καλυπτῆρα αὐτοῦ "And make a brim to the altar and its cover," and in 38:
23, corresponding to MT 38: 3, the plural term הסירת appears as τὴν βάσιν
" step", in singular.[22] Added to the ambiguous location of the term לדשנו in

---

המחתת "firepans", in plural in the MT, occurs again in singular in the LXX. This is an
issue I shall elaborate upon in the text.

[19] On the other hand, in other scriptural sources we encounter different translations of the
term יעים. In I Kings 7: 40, we read: ויעש חירום את הכירות ואת היעים ואת
המזרקות and in the corresponding v. 7: 26 in the LXX we read: καὶ ἐποίησεν Χιραμ
τοὺς λέβητας καὶ τὰς θερμάστρεις καὶ τὰς φιάλας "And Hiram made the basins in
which purifying water was handed to guests before meals [Liddell and Scott; the
translation could also be "kettles", a definition which would be appropriate for a reading
הסירות instead of הכירות, as appears in the following v. 45, a repetition of v. 40] and
the pans to warm up, and the sprinkling bowls." The beginning of the verse and its ending
are the same as in the MT, and therefore we must assume that the translation follows the
MT text. We observe that היעים is translated as cooking utensils, and not as a shovel or
a rake. The interpretation of היעים in I Kings 7: 45 appears again as θερμάστρεις, a
cooking utensil, in the corresponding verse 7: 31 in the LXX. The term היעים in II
Kings 25: 14 is translated in the LXX as τὰ ιαμιν, with no accent, which demonstrates
that the translator did not understand the term and merely repeated the Hebrew without
translating it into Greek; perhaps he had a *Vorlage* reading היעמים instead of היעים, that
is, with one letter different. The term היעים in Jer. 52: 18 is entirely ignored in the LXX.

[20] This is true if we do not assume that the καλυπτῆρα in Exod. 27:3, following the order
of words in the MT, would be the translation of יעים.

[21] The term סירת does not appear in Num. 4: 14 together with the other utensils of the
altar.

[22] The LXX interpretations of this term in other scriptural books vary. In I Kings 7: 26, the
term הכירות of the corresponding MT 7: 40 is translated as λέβητας (as indicated in n.
19 above, it is possible that the LXX translator had הסירות in his *Vorlage*, instead of
הכירות in the MT; Rashi on this verse says: הכירות הן הן סירות "The term כיור is

one verse, the radically different text in the LXX in all three verses suggests that different definitions than those advanced by the traditional translators and commentators should be conferred upon these terms.[23] I propose to

---

equal to סיר)"; in I Kings 7: 31 the LXX has λέβητας for the corresponding הסירות in MT 7: 45; in II Kings 25: 14 the MT הסירות is translated in the LXX as λέβητας in Jer. 52: 18 the term הסירת is not translated (the LXX text is entirely different than that of the MT, and I do not consider the first word of the verse, τὴν στεφάνην "a brim, crown", to correspond to the first word in the MT verse הסירת); in Jer. 52: 19, the translation of the MT הסירות, in the middle of the verse, is missing in the LXX. In Zech. 14: 20-21 the MT הסירות is translated as λέβητας in the LXX, but we must consider the great difference between these verses and the previous ones, cited above; in Zechariah the pots are not specifically utensils of the altar itself. The pots are used in the Temple in Jerusalem, in some connection with the offerings, but do not serve at the altar. The text intentionally makes this distinction, as we read: והיה הסירות בבית ה' כמזרקים לפני המזבח. והיה כל סיר בירושלם וביהודה קדש לה' צבאות ובאו כל הזבחים ולקחו מהם ובשלו בהם "and the cooking pots in the Lord's house will be like the sprinkling bowls in front of the altar. Every pot in Jerusalem and Judah will be holy to the Lord Almighty, and all who come to sacrifice will take some of the pots and cook in them." It is evident that these pots served for cooking the flesh of the sacrifices that were eaten by the offerers; the prophet compares them metaphorically in their holiness to the sprinkling bowls used at the altar. But again the סירות used in the Temple precinct are definitely cooking utensils, not shovels for the removal of ashes. Further corroboration of this point, from a period close to Zechariah, is encountered in II Chr. 35: 13: ויבשלו הפסח באש כמשפט והקדשים בשלו בסירות ובדודים "They roasted the Passover animals over the fire as prescribed [צלי אש 'roasted over the fire (Exod. 12: 8)'] and boiled the holy offerings in pots and cauldrons."

23   Onkelos translates the term סירת as פסכתר from the Greek ψυχθήρ " wine cooler", a large pot. The rabbinic literature uses this term, which represents a specific cooling vessel, to describe the pot used at the altar for the removal of the ashes from the altar, for covering scattered coals and unclean animals, and also for covering the coals on the bronze altar while it was in transit. We read in Mishnah Tamid 5: 5: ושלשה דברים היתה משמשת כופין אותה על גב גחלים ועל השרץ בשבת ומורידין בה את הדשן מעל גבי המזבח [The פסכתר] served three purposes: It was placed on the [scattered] coals and on a creeping animal on Sabbath [if found at the altar it could not be removed because of the prohibition to do so an a Sabbath], and one removed the ashes from the altar with it." We also read in Sifra צו פרשה א' פ"ב: אש תמיד, תמיד אף בשבת תמיד אף בטומאה לא תכבה אף במסעות מה עושים לה כופים עליה פסכתר דברי רבי יהודה ר' שמעון אומר אף בשבת ומסעות מדשנים אותה שנאמר ודשנו את המזבח ופרשו עליו בגד ארגמן "'A continuous fire' [must be kept burning on the altar] [Lev. 6: 6; 6: 13 in KJV] - 'continuous', even on Sabbath, 'continuous', even when unclean, 'it must not go out,' even when in motion; how do you achieve this? Rabbi Judah said: One puts a pot on it [the fire]; Rabbi Simeon said: Even on Sabbath and when in motion, one removes the ashes [and one does not cover the fire with a pot], since it is written: 'They are to remove the ashes from the [bronze] altar and spread a purple cloth over it [Num. 4: 13].'" Both opinions create a number of problems,

consider the term סיר, and possibly יעה,[24] as originally pots for cooking, not utensils for removing the ashes. The change of definition reflects a rabbinic attempt to modify the interpretation of the archaic eating utensils on the table, enumerated in Exod. 25: 29:[25] קערתיו וכפתיו וקשותיו ומנקיתיו "its plates and spoons and pitchers and bowls." These utensils are all superfluous and inappropriate on a table on which only showbread was exposed, as described in Scripture. The rabbinic literature attempted to modify the anthropomorphism suggested by these utensils, and proposed totally different definitions for them.[26] For the same reason in our case, an editor may have

---

ד"ה some of which have been taken up by Midrash Numbers Rabbah, *Parshah* 4: 17 מזבח הנחש. There is an inconsistency between the command in Lev. 6: 6 (6: 13 in KJV) to keep the fire going continuously on the altar: לא תכבה "it must not go out," and the command in Num. 4: 13 "They are to remove the ashes from the [bronze] altar and spread a purple cloth over it," when moving the altar; the plain interpretation of the latter implies an extinguishing of the fire, in contradiction to the prohibition against such extinguishing. This prohibition also creates a practical problem: how can one cover a burning fire, or even live coals, with a cloth? The omission of the סירת in Num. 4: 14 among the utensils of the altar is also intriguing. Numbers Rabbah attempts a solution to this problem that would accord with the opinions of both Rabbi Judah and Rabbi Simeon. The Midrash suggests that according to Rabbi Judah's proposition, the ashes are removed from the altar to comply with the relevant command, and then fire is again placed on the altar, covered by the פסכתר "pot", and the purple cloth then spread over it. This procedure would solve the problem of the absence of the "pot" among the other utensils, since the pot would be under the purple cloth, whereas the other utensils would be placed upon this cloth and covered by the hides. It also obviously complies with the command to remove the ashes and at the same time not extinguish the fire on the altar. According to Rabbi Simeon's opinion, the missing "pot" would be included in the summary phrase ונתנו עליו את כל כליו "They are to place upon it all the utensils," and the removal of the ashes would not pose a practical problem during the moving of a clean altar covered by the purple cloth. Yet this does not solve the contradiction between the two commands; further, the fire upon the altar would be extinguished in transit, in transgression of the law which demands a continuous fire. I think it superfluous to comment on the acrobatic exercises applied to harmonize between two contrasting verses. On the other hand, we must appreciate that the Rabbis critically examined the biblical texts, and were well aware of the discrepancies; they attempted to reconcile them in a manner not conflicting with their credo, and we should appreciate their erudition and their creativity. Targum Jonathan translates סירת as דידיתא "cauldron, pot, boiler" (Jastrow). The Samaritan Targum translates with עיריו, which seems to me to be a vessel for pouring, from the same root as ותער כדה אל השקת "she emptied her jar into the trough [Gen. 24: 20]."

[24] It is interesting to note that the Samaritan Targum, in both MSS A and J, translates the term יעיו as דודיו, unequivocally to be understood as "pots, cauldrons, boilers," in contrast to the term מגרפות "rakes" used by the other Aramaic translators such as Onkelos and Neophyti, and the traditional commentators who followed them.

[25] And in Exod. 37: 16, Num. 4: 7 and I Chr. 28: 16-17.

[26] For an extensive discussion of this issue, see P. Heger, *Incense*, pp. 116ff.

tried to change the meaning of סירת by inserting the term לדשנו;[27] that is, to shift the common interpretation of סיר as a cooking pot[28] to an implement for the removal of ashes. W. Zwickel[29] states that in the archeological findings of the Late Bronze Age, cooking pots were almost always found in the temple courtyards. This demonstrates that the meat of the sacrificial meals, זבח, was cooked and consumed in the temple's precinct. Thus, we observe traces of old practices in the later P writings in this passage, as in many others. The interpretation of the term יעים followed the same process and was translated similarly as מגרפות, utensils for the removal of ashes.

The terms ומזרקתיו ומזלגתיו offer no difficulties. Onkelos and Neophyti translate ומזרקתיו as מזרקוהי, utilizing the same Hebrew term. The Samaritan Targum translates as ופנכיו, considered by Jastrow to derive from the Greek πίναχ a particular type of a plate; since this term was taken over from a foreign language, it is possible that the alien term acquired a different meaning in the new language. The LXX translates it as φίαλας "bowl." The term ומזלגתיו is translated by Onkelos as וציגורייתיה, originally "hooks - curved pins" (Jastrow), which could have developed by association into "fork". Jonathan, Neophyti and the Samaritan Targum translate it as משיליא in various orthographic forms, meaning utensils for lifting, from the root שלי, hence "forks". The LXX translates it as κρεάγρας "flesh-hooks." As with the סירת, the pots, there is the same idea of eating utensils with respect to their use at the altar. This term appears in Scripture, in addition to the various verses listing the altar's utensils, only in I Sam. 2: 13 and 14. There it is evident from the context that the forks were used by the priest's assistant to lift the desired piece of meat from the cauldron in which the offerer boiled it, and it was not a utensil used at the altar by the priests. This again raises the question of why these implements are enumerated here with the altar's accessories and carried upon the altar on its journeys. An archaic list of utensils must have been the basis of their presence in this list.

ומחתתיו
...its firepans...

The term ומחתתיו "its firepans" presents no philological problems. Onkelos, Jonathan, Neophyti and Samaritan MS J use the same term in their

---

[27] As may be expected, the LXX has no equivalent for the expression לדשנו.

[28] Cf. סיר הבשר "pot of meat [Exod. 16: 3]"; סיר הנזיד "pot of stew [II Kings 4: 39]"; שפת הסיר שפת "Put on the cooking pot, put it on [Ezek. 24: 3]," and many other occurrences in which the term סיר is unequivocally a cooking pot, and never a shovel-like implement to remove ashes.

[29] W. Zwickel, *Der Tempelkult in Kanaan und Israel*, pp. 200-201.

translation. The Samaritan MS A uses ומגמריו. Jastrow translates the term
מגמר as " spices put on coals, offered after dinner, perfume," and one
interpretation of the verb גמר is "to perfume clothes." It is interesting to note
the associative process by which a "firepan" was derived from the root גמר,
based on the perfuming performed at the end of a meal on this particular
utensil.

On the other hand, the association by this Samaritan Targum of the מחתה
"firepan" with incense leads us to examine the use of these bronze pans. In
the Pentateuch, the "firepans" in the narratives concerning Nadab and Abihu
and Korah's group[30] are all associated with the incense celebration; they are
unequivocally "censers", and are not accessories to the ceremonial of the
bronze altar. Solomon made only golden "firepans," as we read in I Kings 7:
50: והמחתות זהב טהור. The translation "censers" by the KJV and NIV[31] is
not supported by the evidence, since these utensils appear in a concluding
summary of the various items made by Solomon, following the lampstands,
which had golden מחתת, as we read in Exod. 25: 38: ומלקחיה ומחתתיה
זהב טהור "its wick trimmers and 'pans'[32] of pure gold." In the parallel verse
to I Kings 7: 50 in II Chr. 4: 22, the מחתות are also of gold. In the list of
utensils looted by the Babylonians, in II Kings 25: 15 and Jer. 52: 19, we
read "ואת המחתות ואת המזרקות אשר זהב זהב ואשר כסף כסף "the
censers and sprinkling bowls, all that were made of pure gold or silver." In
the list of bronze utensils in the previous verse II Kings 25: 14, מחתות are
absent.

Even in the rabbinic literature, all the uses of the "firepans" associated
with the incense celebration[33] are of gold and silver, with one exception: for

---

[30] Scripture in Lev. 10: 1 does not inform us concerning the material of which the מחתות
"censers" of Nadab and Abihu were made, but the מחתות "censers" of Korah's group
are all made of bronze, as clearly appears in the closing phrase of the event in Num. 17: 4
(Num. 16: 39 in KJV): את מחתות הנחשת אשר הקריבו השרפים "the bronze
censers brought by those who had been burned up."

[31] The LXX translates it here as θυίσκαι, an unspecified utensil to burn either offerings or
incense.

[32] The translators had problems with this plain translation, since a "firepan" or "censer" was
considered appropriate for use as an accessory to the lampstand. Onkelos and Jonathan
followed the MT and translated with the same term. Rashi explains that they were small
containers in which the priest put the ashes of the burned wicks, when he cleaned the
lamps and put in new wicks. The LXX interpreted it as a totally different furnishing, τὰ
ὑποθέματα "appendage," and the KJV and NIV translate it as "plate" or "dish".

[33] See for example: Mishnah Yoma 4: 3 and the following mishnayot in which the incense
ceremony at the Day of Atonement is described; we read in 4: 4: בכל יום היה חותה
בשל כסף ומערה בתוך של זהב והיום חותה בשל זהב ובה היה מכניס "Every
day he used to rake [the coals on the altar and heap them] on a silver [firepan] and empty

the removal of the ashes from the holocaust altar, the use of a silver "firepan" is mentioned.[34] This removal of the ashes is commanded in Lev. 6: 3 - 4, and is the sole occasion in which the Rabbis prescribe the use of a "firepan" as an accessory for the holocaust altar; but one should bear in mind that Scripture itself does not indicate how this removal of ashes was to be performed and does not mention the מחתה as a utensil.

The LXX translation of ומחתתיו gives rise to some amazement. In our pericope this term appears in plural, and we must assume that all the other translators had a *Vorlage* in plural; but the LXX translates the term as πυρεῖον, in singular, although the other utensils appear in plural. The plural המחתת in MT Exod. 38: 3 similarly appears in LXX Exod. 38: 23 as πυρεῖον, in singular. Only in Num. 4: 14 does the LXX have τὰ πυρεῖα, in plural, following המחתת in the MT. On the other hand, in other occurrences in which firepans are mentioned in the Pentateuch,[35] the LXX follows the MT text exactly, and uses the singular and plural as required by the MT text. We must therefore assume that in these two occurrences in Exod. 27: 3 and 38: 23 the LXX translator had something in mind other than firepans, perhaps some essential element of the altar located on its top, where it came into contact with the fire, πῦρ, the root of πυρεῖον. The LXX text in both these verses describes both the structural elements of the altar and the utensils, in contrast to the MT text that indicates only the utensils.[36] We have seen that in Exod. 27: 3, the LXX records a rim στέφανος and a cover καλυπτῆρα for

---

them on a golden one, and today [on the Day of Atonement], he rakes them on a golden [firepan] and brings in it [the incense into the Holy of Holies]." In Mishnah Tamid 5: 5 the daily incense celebration is portrayed, and there we read מי שזכה במחתה נטל מחתת הכסף "The [priest] who won [by the lot] the right [to celebrate the incense ceremony] with the firepan took the silver firepan."

[34] The Talmud divides the removal of the ashes commanded in Lev. 6: 3 - 4 into two separate performances: a daily ceremonial removal of a small quantity, and a ceremonial in which all the ashes were removed from the altar and carried out of the Temple precinct, executed whenever necessary according to the accumulation. In Mishnah Tamid 1: 4, the daily ceremonial removal of the ashes is described: מי שזכה לתרום את המזבח...נטל מחתת הכסף ועלה לראש המזבח "The [priest] who won [by lot] the right to collect ashes from the altar...took the silver firepan and climbed upon the top of the altar."

[35] At the story of Nadab and Abihu, in Lev 10: 1; at the incense celebration in the Holy of Holies, in Lev. 16: 12; and at the Korah rebellion in Num. chaps. 16 -17.

[36] Noth, in *Exodus. A. Commentary*, p. 216, therefore assumes that this verse describing the utensils "interrupts the description of the altar and may be an addition." The LXX interpretation, as I suggest, combines auxiliary structural elements and accessories and hence does not appear as an interruption.

the altar together with its utensils, its bowls and forks.[37] The same principle is encountered in Exod. 38: 23; we have there the πυρεῖον and the step βάσις, together with the same utensils, the bowls and forks. In Num. 4: 14, Scripture emphasizes that the list includes את כל כליו אשר ישרתו עליו בהם "all the utensils used for ministering at the altar" and which are placed upon the altar; the LXX therefore translates the מחתת in plural as τὰ πυρεῖα.[38]

לכל כליו תעשה נחשת
Make all its utensils of bronze

The command to make the furnishings of bronze is essential, since the first mandate in v. 2 refers solely to the altar and does not imply that its furnishings too must be made of bronze. On the other hand, the preposition ל of לכל is irregular.[39] Rashi is aware of this, and explains לכל כליו כמו כל כליו, that is, it should be understood as if it were written כל כליו, without the ל. Onkelos follows the MT, but Jonathan and Neophyti correct the apparent fault, and write כל; the LXX too disregards the erroneous expression. This seemingly unimportant *erratum* must be added to the many previously recorded oddities in the text and its translations, and hints at probable tampering. Two causes for such tampering suggest themselves: the desire to detach the utensils from any anthropomorphic association, as discussed above, and the vague physical description. The latter induced attempts to understand the altar's structure according to different conceptions and beliefs, and resulted in appropriate changes in the text. The radical difference between the MT and the LXX wording, in this verse and in the following, as we shall see further, validates such an hypothesis. This conjecture should be considered in light of the entire problematic of the bronze altar, an issue which I shall discuss in chap. 7.

---

[37] Wevers has already stated in his *Notes on the Greek Text of Exodus*, p. 433, with reference to Exod. 27: 5: "Obviously Exod. has another kind of altar construction in mind than the one which would be implied from the plain interpretation of the MT text."

[38] While the καλυπτῆρα "cover" also appears in v. 14 together with the utensils, we must assume that the text is corrupt, because the καλυπτῆρα already appears in v. 13, which is different than the verse in the MT. In LXX v. 13 the καλυπτῆρα is placed upon the altar and covered with a purple cloth, but then in v. 14 all the altar's utensils, together with the καλυπτῆρα, are placed upon the purple cloth and covered with the hide covering. According to this text, we would have two "covers": one καλυπτῆρα under the purple cloth, and another over it, together with all the other utensils, and this would not make sense.

[39] For the possible nuances of ל see Joüon, *A Grammar of Biblical Hebrew*, Vol. II, pp. 487-8, 133d.

5.4 Exod. 27: 4

ועשית לו מכבר מעשה רשת נחשת
Make a grating for it, a bronze network

The NIV translates מכבר as "grating", but this is an interpretation, and has no philologically justified foundation. The term מכבר already has the notion of a web-like, perforated item,[40] like a sieve, as in כאשר ינוע בכברה "as [grain] is shaken in a sieve [Amos 9: 9]," and therefore the additional phrase מעשה רשת seems superfluous. In fact, the addendum מעשה רשת does not appear in other descriptions of the 'grate',[41] confirming its redundancy here. Onkelos translates סרדא עובד מצרתא, and again we must ask the same question, since סרדא itself indicates a plaited web; Onkelos translates קלעים, "the twisted curtains" in Exod. 27: 9,[42] as סרדי. Jonathan and Neophyti translate קנקל עובד מצדתא, and in this case too קנקל indicates a "perforated vessel, grating, network" (Jastrow), hence the additional description "a work of net"[43] is tautological. The different reading מצרתא in Onkelos does not solve the question of the duplicate description. The Samaritan Targum does not translate the term מכבר and uses the original Hebrew term.

The attribute נחשת is stylistically not correct; Onkelos and Jonathan add the preposition, and write דנחשא. Ibn Ezra explains that one should understand the phrase as if it were written מכבר נחשת כמעשה רשת "a bronze 'grating' made in the form of a net."

ועשית על הרשת ארבע טבעת נחשת על ארבע קצותיו
...and make a bronze ring at each of the four corners of the network

From the first part of this verse, we must assume that the מכבר "grating" is the main subject, and "in the form of a net" is its modifier. We would therefore expect that the rings should be made on the מכבר, the subject, and not on - as the preposition על implies - the רשת, its attribute. The meaning of the end of the phrase is yet more elusive, and we do not know the subject of

---

[40] The straightforward commentary of Ibn Ezra explains: מכבר, כמו כברה "...as if it were written כברה 'sieve'." Rashbam too explains the term מכבר as a sieve.

[41] It does not appear in Exod. 35: 16, 38: 30 and 39: 39, in which solely the term מכבר appears.

[42] Rashi explains there ותרגומו סרדין כתרגומו של מכבר המתורגם סרדא לפי שהן מנוקבים כסרדא "And its translation is 'nets', like the translation of מכבר which is translated [by Onkelos] as סרדא because they are perforated like a net."

[43] According to this version מצדתא has its root from the term צוד "to hunt"; a net was used for catching fish or animals.

the locative description "on its four corners." It is difficult to say definitely whether it concerns the רשת, since the suffix is masculine and רשת is feminine.[44] It may refer to the מכבר "the grating", or to the מזבח, the altar, the main subject of the verse; the former interpretation would be perfect from a syntactical point of view since the verse would then start with the command to make the מכבר for the altar, ועשית לו מכבר, followed with its description, in the form of a net, and then its auxiliaries, the four rings. However, the opening of the next verse with the feminine ונתת אתה refers to the רשת, and thus our question concerning the shift of the subject remains without solution. We must also ask the purpose of this net. The description of the מכבר and the purpose and location of the רשת seem also to have eluded the commentators. Their desire or absolute need, for reasons of faith, to harmonize the various biblical pericopes regarding bronze and stone altars in the Pentateuch and Ezekiel, tightens the mesh in which they find themselves, with no escape to a rational hypothesis.

5.4.1 The LXX Text

The LXX has an entirely different text, as it does for the following verses, and has a different conception of the structure of the altar than the MT text presents.[45] I do not wish to discuss the issue of whether the LXX editor had another *Vorlage*, or attempted to create an intelligent portrayal of the altar from the confused and unclear MT text; this is a dilemma beyond the scope of our examination. The LXX translates the term מכבר as ἐσχάραν "hearth, brazier"[46] and therefore the description ἔργῳ δικτυωτῷ, "with which the hearth should be made," is appropriate in the context. The attribute χαλκῆν "of bronze"[47] in the accusative correctly modifies its subject, the hearth. It is appropriate to note at this point that the LXX considered the problem created by the fact that the MT text does not indicate what was on the top of the altar, and attempted to solve this irregularity both from the point of view of practicality and in accordance with the text. An altar must have a top, and the incense altar does have one, as is apparent in Exod. 30: 3: וצפית אתו זהב טהור את גגו ואת קירתיו "Overlay the top and all the sides with pure gold."

---

[44] A suffixed pronoun may take the masculine instead of the feminine; see Joüon, *A Grammar of Biblical Hebrew*, Vol. II, p. 551, 149b.

[45] Cf. Wevers, *Notes on the Greek Text of Exodus*, p. 433.

[46] Wevers, ibid., states in note 2: "Later Revisers use κοσκίνωμα 'grating' which is a more exact equivalent for מכבר of MT."

[47] I am not discussing the issue of whether χαλκός should be translated as "copper" or "bronze"; it is of no interest in our investigation of textual problems.

The LXX has therefore translated with the same term ἐσχάραν both the term גגו of the incense altar and מכבר of the bronze altar. In the record of the altar's construction in Exod. 38: 24, corresponding to Exod. 38: 4 in the MT, the LXX has translated the term מכבר as παράθεμα, to emphasize its interpretation as a cover on the altar's top. The four rings are made τῆ ἐσχάρα "for the hearth," according to the LXX text, in contrast to the explicit MT command that they be made על הרשת "on the net."[48] We shall investigate this issue of the top of the altar in the examination of the following verse, in which the placement of the מכבר or the רשת is hinted at.

5.5 Exod. 27: 5

ונתת אתה תחת כרכב המזבח מלמטה[49]

Put it under the ledge of the altar

The term כרכב does not appear elsewhere in Scripture, and therefore was already a puzzle to the Sages.[50] We read in B. T. Zebahim 62a: ונתתה אותה תחת כרכוב המזבח מלמטה ותניא איזהו כרכוב רבי אומר זה כיור רבי יוסי ברבי יהודה אומר זה הסובב "'Put it under the 'ledge'[51] of the altar on its underside [Exod. 27: 5]' and we learned: What is this כרכוב? Rabbi says: It is a drawing.[52] Rabbi Jose son of Rabbi Judah says: It is the gangway [around

---

[48] Onkelos, Jonathan, the Samaritan Targum and Neophyti repeat the Hebrew על in their translations, which must be understood as "on". They make a clear distinction between ועשית לו "make for it" at the beginning of the verse, translated as ותעביד ליה, and על הרשת which they translate with על.

[49] The MT has the term כרכב without the "ו" but the rabbinic literature and the commentators write כרכוב with a "ו"; therefore, the term appears in my text in both forms.

[50] The Sages and most of the traditional commentators following them attempted to propose various explanations that we may or may not accept as plausible. We may remark that Ibn Ezra, the straightforward commentator, did not even try to derive a convincing description; he writes: ומלת כרכב. אין לו ריע במקום אחר "And the term כרכב has no analogue anywhere else [in Scripture]"; Ibn Ezra prefers to leave us in ignorance, rather than offer an unreasonable explanation.

[51] This is the NIV interpretation, as clarified in the Introduction n. 11, and I use it for want of a decisive interpretation.

[52] Rashi explains זה כיור - ציורים סביב למעלה מאמצע "Drawings around [the altar] above mid-height [to trace a line between the upper and lower halves of the altar, in order to distinguish between the blood of offerings to be sprinkled on the upper half, and that to be sprinkled upon the lower half]."

the altar]."[53] In the following rhetorical discussion, the Gemara quotes another Baraita: ת״ר איזהו כרכוב בין קרן לקרן מקום הילוך רגלי הכהנים אמה אטו הכהנים בין קרן לקרן הוו אזלי אלא אימא ומקום הילוך רגלי הכהנים אמה והכתיב תחת כרכובו מלמטה עד חציו אמר רב נחמן בר יצחק תרי הוו חד לנוי וחד לכהנים דלא נשתרקו "What is the כרכוב? A one cubit wide gangway between the 'horns' for the priests to walk [around the assemblage of offerings in the fire on the top of the altar]. Could it be that the priests walked between the 'horns' [the horns at the corners would have impeded their movement]? So we must say: And in addition one cubit for the priests to walk. But it is written [Exod. 38: 4] that the כרכוב was at the side of the altar.[54] Said Rabbi Nahman son of Isaac: There were two, one [engraved drawing] for decoration[55] [around the sides of the altar] and one [projecting rim][56] for the priests [at the altar's top where they walked], so that

---

[53] Note also the discussion of this dictum in the archeological examination above.

[54] Rashi explains: מכבר מעשה רשת נחשת שנתנוהו תחת כרכובו מלמטה עד חציו הקיפוהו למזבח מאמצעו ולמעלה לבוש כמין היקף של כברה והוא עשוי נקבים נקבים ככברה ורשת של דגים ומגיע למעלה עד מתחת לכרכוב אלמא בקיר מזבח סביב הוה דאי בראש המזבח היכי קרי למכבר הנתון סביב הקיר תחת כרכובו "The bronze net-like מכבר, which was placed under the כרכוב up to the midpoint [of the altar]; that is, the altar was adorned from its middle and upward with some type of net with holes as a sieve or a fishing net which reached up to the כרכוב; hence we must assume that the כרכוב was on the side walls of the altar, because if it were on its top, how could Scripture say that the net which was around the side walls was below the כרכוב."

[55] Rashi discusses in B. T. Zebahim 62a the statement of Rabbi that זה כיור - ציורים [The כרכוב] is a כיור - drawings around [the altar] above its" סביב למעלה מאמצעו middle." Rashi explains what type of drawings are meant: ציורים של פרחים וציצים וקלעים סביב למזבח כמו סיידו וכיירו "Drawings of flowers and blossoms and [ropelike] twistings around the altar, like [the meaning of] 'whitewashed and painted' [for the idol described in Mishnah Abodah Zarah 3: 7]." In the printed editions וכיידו appears with a "ד", but Maimonides and Rashi had MSS with וכיירו. From Maimonides' explanation, as translated from the Arabic by Kapah, it seems that the term כיור includes both painting and engraving, and one must assume from rabbinic rhetoric that the drawing on the walls of the altar was not painted, but engraved. Therefore, the term כרכוב could be understood as a drawing made by a superficial etching, or as a deep engraving which produced around it a projected elevation; see Rashi's second interpretation of כרכוב in n. 56.

[56] Rashi elucidates: ולמעלה בראש המזבח העמיקו סובב כמין חריץ עמוק דבר "And on the top of מועט להיות להם שפתו היקף מעקה קטן סביב שלא יחליקו the altar they dug around like a small ditch, so that its edge served them as a surrounding low railing to avoid their slipping [off the altar]."

they would not slip."[57] Accordingly, the כרכוב mentioned in Scripture is on the sides of the altar, because of the explicit scriptural text, and the above dispute between Rabbi and Rabbi Jose refers to this fact; Rabbi Jose, who asserts that the bronze altar was ten cubits high,[58] allows for the type of gangway, סובב, described in Mishnah Midoth 3: 1 with respect to the stone altar, and Rabbi maintains that the bronze altar was only three cubits high, and therefore the כרכוב is only an etched drawing one cubit high. Below this element was attached the net, which reached until the midpoint of the altar, and served to divide the walls into two halves for the purpose of distinguishing the blood to be sprinkled on the upper half from that to be sprinkled on the lower half.

והיתה הרשת עד חצי המזבח

...so that it is halfway up the altar.

Scripture leaves us in the dark about the purpose of the net itself and its placement at the midpoint of the altar. The Talmud[59] sees its purpose to divide the blood of the different offerings, and compares it to the red line traced for this purpose on the Second Temple altar. On the other hand, it is unclear why this division was accomplished with a net on the bronze altar, and not with a line as on the stone altar, or conversely why a net was not made for the stone altar. This solution is yet more perplexing given the usual rabbinic attempts to harmonize the various scriptural commands and apply their individual and distinct details to all the altars. As Scripture provides specific characteristics only for the bronze altar, one would expect that the

---

[57] Some versions have נשתרקו and others נשתרגו; there is no real difference between them, as both terms suggest "skip, leap, slide, glide."

[58] This dispute in B. T. Zebahim 59b is quoted in n. 2. The linkage between the dispute concerning the כרכוב and that concerning the height of the bronze altar is made by Rashi, although the names of the Tannaim do not correspond exactly. In the dispute about the כרכוב there appear רבי and רבי יוסי ברבי יהודה, whereas in the dispute about the altar's height in Zebahim 59b there appear רבי יוסי and רבי יהודה. Since רבי יוסי and רבי regularly dispute in the Talmud (see H. Albeck, מבוא למשנה [Tel Aviv, 1959], p. 232), and the name of רבי was יהודה, Rashi probably assumed that they were identical.

[59] We read in B. T. Zebahim 53a חוט של סקרא חוגרו באמצע כדי להבדיל בין דמים העליונים לדמים התחתונים מנא הני מילי אמר רב אחא בר רב קטינא שנאמר והיתה הרשת עד חצי המזבח התורה נתנה מחיצה להבדיל בין דמים העליונים לדמים התחתונים "A red line embraced the altar at its midpoint in order to divide between the upper blood [to be sprinkled above the line] and the lower blood. From where do we know this? Said Rav Aha son of Rav Katina: 'Because it is written 'And the grating should be halfway up the altar [Exod. 27: 5].' The Torah has provided a partition to divide between the upper and the lower blood. "

stone altars would be imbued with as many features of the scriptural bronze altar as possible.

5.5.1 Examination of M. D. Cassuto's Solution

In addition to the previously quoted theories of Haran, who attempts to rationalize the scriptural contradictions with the help of the rabbinic homilies, the modern but traditional scholar M. D. Cassuto[60] approaches the contradictions in the same fashion, and also offers an explanation for the purpose of the רשת. Cassuto asserts that the character of the bronze altar had to comply with two apparently contradictory commands:

a) that the altar should be of earth or stones;

b) that the altar should not be a temporary structure, built anew at every camp, but should be of a permanent nature, and at the same time portable.

The solution was, therefore, to make a hollow wooden structure, overlaid with bronze, which could easily be filled with earth and stones at each stop. This hollow frame had no top, in contrast to the incense altar.

Cassuto thus presumes to have answered the question raised by scholars concerning the inability of a wooden altar to withstand the fire; in his opinion, the fire was arranged on the earth and not on a bronze roof. The כרכוב was, according to his opinion, a horizontal projection encompassing all four sides of the altar, situated at about a third or quarter of the way down from the top, and had solely an ornamental purpose. Regarding the מכבר "net" Cassuto suggests a revolutionary idea; the walls themselves were pierced and had window-like holes, mainly in their lower part, to facilitate the aeration of the fire on the top. The net was attached to the lower half of the altar, and its purpose was to reinforce the fragile walls there because of the many holes. He interprets the Scriptural indication והיתה הרשת עד חצי המזבח to imply the lower part of the altar, in contrast to the talmudic interpretation which, as we have seen, understands that the net was attached to the upper part, from the כרכוב down to its midpoint. One must agree that Cassuto has attempted to offer answers to all the questions, but his imagination has created many new difficulties. It is possible that Cassuto was influenced in his conjectures by the model of the altar in Ezekiel and by the talmudic description of the Second Temple altar, which was larger at its base and narrower at the top.

I shall start with the literary problems. His image of the altar does not reflect the text; due to his intention to reconcile the different texts, he does not approach the text respectfully, and attempts to include in it notions alien

---

[60]   M. D. Cassuto, פירוש על ספר שמות (Jerusalem, 1952), pp. 253 ff.

to it. The critical scholars hold the text in esteem and attempt to understand precisely what it originally meant, or intended to express; Cassuto ventures to insert his personal ideas into the original text. There is no way to "read into" the text that the altar had window-like holes in its walls. He writes that the כרכוב was a horizontal projection, situated on the upper part of the altar, as the Talmud too understood it, according to the text; and it is obvious that the "net" had to be attached under this projection, hanging downward, so that it extended to the middle of the altar. In Cassuto's imagination, the "net" covered the lower half of the altar, and this is evidently contradicting the text.[61] The idea that the "net" served to reinforce the altar walls, and that the altar had to be filled and emptied each time, also has no basis in Scripture. The latter notion, discarded even by the Rabbis in their deliberations.[62] also

---

[61] It is remarkable that Keil & Delitzsch, pp. 186-7 offer the same solutions as Cassuto to the Exod. 27 pericope concerning the bronze altar. Cassuto understands that the net was placed on the lower part of the altar walls, likely reading the phrase in v. 5, ונתתה אתה תחת כרכב המזבח מלמטה והיתה הרשת עד חצי המזבח as "Place the net under the 'projecting bench' of the altar from beneath to reach half-way up." Consequently, the "projecting bench" must have been at the midpoint of the altar, so that the net, which started at the bottom of the altar, reaches the midpoint of the altar and is fixed under the "projecting bench." But Scripture declares that it is the "net" that should be half-way up the altar, not the כרכב, whatever this means. In both verses in which the arrangement of the altar is described, one must interpret that the term מלמטה refers to the altar's כרכב "ledge", where the net is to be fixed, and the term חצי refers to the altar. In Exod. 27: 5, it is evident that the net fixed under the "ledge" should "extend [downward] to the middle of the altar." The same syntactic and grammatical analysis is valid for the interpretation of Exod. 38: 4 in which the text is slightly differently worded, and this text also demonstrates that the "net" must be hung downward to extend to the middle of the altar. We read there ויעש למזבח מכבר מעשה רשת נחשת תחת כרכבו מלמטה עד חציו "And he made a 'grating' for the altar, a bronze network, under its [the altar's] 'ledge' to its [the altar's] middle." "Under" refers to the altar's "ledge" and "middle" refers to the altar. Cassuto and Keil & Delitzsch must twist the verse and read the preposition מלמטה as referring to the altar, and not attached to the antecedent "its ledge." It is obvious that Rashi clearly accepted the talmudic interpretation that the "net" should be on the upper half of the altar, not on its lower part, and reached half-way up it. We read in his commentary to B. T. Zebahim 62a: מכבר מעשה רשת נחשת שנתנוהו תחת כרכובו מלמטה עד חציו הקיפוהו למזבח מאמצעו ולמעלה לבוש כמין היקף של כברה והוא עשוי נקבים נקבים ככברה ורשת של דגים ומגיע למעלה עד מתחת לכרכוב "The network...was fixed under its 'ledge' from below up to its mid-point; they surrounded the altar from its [the altar's] mid-point and upward with an outfit like an encasing of a sieve, made with holes like a sieve, or a net for catching fish, so that it extends upward to under the ledge."

[62] We read in B. T. Zebahim 61b: מעיקרא סבור מזבח אדמה שהוא אטום באדמה "In the beginning it was thought [that the meaning of] an earthen altar is that it should be filled with earth, but in the end it was considered that drink is like food [a metaphorical

contradicts the clear text in Exod. 20: 21, in which an <u>altar</u> of earth, not a filling, is commanded.

We must also examine whether the type of altar imagined by Cassuto contradicts the consequences of other scriptural commands relating to the altar. Num. 4: 13-14 orders the following to be done before moving the altar (evidently here the bronze altar):.ודשנו את המזבח ופרשו עליו בגד ארגמן ונתנו עליו את כל כליו "They are to remove the ashes from the altar and spread a purple cloth over it. Then they are to place upon it all the utensils." A question then arises: Why would one need to remove the ashes from the earth filling which is going to be dumped out?[63] A further question is of a purely practical nature: How would all the utensils be kept on a piece of cloth spread over a hollow surface of five cubits square, without falling into the hole? We observe from the text that there were a great number of utensils to be placed on the bronze altar, and of such a weight as to draw down the purple cover. In contrast, the few utensils of the golden altar were wrapped in a blue cloth and carried on a pole rather than placed on its top. One may also wonder why Scripture would not mention here the emptying of the earth filling, similar to the other minute preparations required before the altar was moved. Cassuto asserts that the windows of the altar's walls served to aerate and enhance the fire from below. This could only be accomplished with a filling of stones, through which air could flow freely, but would be ineffective with an earthen filling. Cassuto is aware of this problem, and asserts that since Scripture refers to both earth and stones it intended a mixture of both, but he ignores the plain and evident meaning of the pericope in Exod. 20: build either an altar of earth or an altar of stones, but not a filling mixed from both elements. I am not commenting on the practical question of whether such a filling would allow the burning of fire upon the altar, a point doubted by scholars, since I have no way of effecting a systematic test on such a model.[64]

Cassuto has attempted to find a purpose for the מכבר, the "net-like structure," an insoluble riddle if it is not considered as a "grating" on the top of the altar. His solution is challenged by two further questions:

a) If the item had some cult significance, why was it not applied to the later altars? It obviously does not appear with Ezekiel's altar, or with the

---

expression which compares the solid offerings of flesh and flour to the liquid libations; and just as the solids have to be burned on the altar, so the libations must be 'consumed' by the altar itself, and not absorbed by the earth filling]; so what is meant by an earthen altar? That it is attached to the ground."

[63] I do not think that Scripture intends in this pericope that the ashes be carried out of the camp, as ordered in Lev. 6: 4. The passage deals merely with the preparation of the altar and all the other furnishings before departing.

[64] Cf. N. H. Gadegaard, "On the So-called Burnt Offering Altar in the Old Testament," *PEQ* 110 (1978), pp. 35-45.

Second Temple altar, as described in the Talmud and by Josephus. While the מכבר is specifically mentioned at every step of the bronze altar's construction, in Exod. 27: 4, 35: 16, 38: 4, 38: 5, 38: 30 and 39: 39, demonstrating its importance, it entirely disappears in any other reference to the holocaust altar, even where "bronze altars" are mentioned in Scripture.[65]

b) If a net structure surrounded the altar, the blood of the offerings was really sprinkled on the net, and not on the altar itself, a situation seemingly in contrast with the innumerable commands to sprinkle the blood on the altar. We observe that Scripture is specific about sprinkling the blood against the altar on all sides,[66] or sprinkling the blood of the sin offering on one wall of the altar,[67] or putting some of the blood on the horns of the altar,[68] and it is difficult to interpret these provisions to mean that the blood is to be sprinkled on the "net",[69] not on the altar.[70] It is also possible that Cassuto attempted to find a solution for another odd attribute of the מכבר. Its description as a "net" implies that it was of a soft and flexible nature.[71] On the other hand, Scripture orders the rings for carrying the altar to be attached to the "net", not to the altar's walls. A practical question would arise from such an arrangement, and that is how the weight of the entire altar could be sustained

---

[65] An analysis of these occurrences, with respect to their authenticity and "real" purpose, will be made in section 5.2.2.

[66] Lev. 1: 5: וזרקו את הדם על המזבח סביב "...and sprinkle the blood against the altar on all sides...."

[67] In Lev. 5: 9 there is a distinct term for this type of sprinkling: והזה מדם החטאת על קיר המזבח "...and is to sprinkle some of the blood of the sin offering against the side of the altar...."

[68] Lev. 4: 7: ונתן הכהן מן הדם על קרנת מזבח קטרת הסמים "The priest shall than put some of the blood on the horns of the altar of fragrant incense....". Here too there is a different term for this type of smearing of the blood on the horns.

[69] As noted above, the blood of some offerings had to be sprinkled on the upper half of the altar and the blood of others upon the lower half. We read in B. T. Zebahim 10b, in a Baraita: דתניא דמים התחתונים ניתנין מחוט הסיקרא ולמטה והעליונים מחוט הסיקרא ולמעלה "The lower blood was given [sprinkled] from the red line down, and the upper [blood] from the red line upward." As we have seen, the red line on the stone altar substituted for the כרכוב of the bronze altar. Thus, wherever the net was affixed, whether on the upper or lower half, some of the blood would be sprinkled on the net, instead of on the altar itself.

[70] Alternatively, if we consider the מכבר "net" as an integral part of the altar, the literary sequence of the pericope would be illogical. Vv. 1 and 2 describe the construction of the altar and the subsequent vv. illustrate its various utensils, starting in v. 3 with the pots and shovels. If the "net" were an integral part of the altar's construction, vv. 4 and 5 describing its characteristics and placement would be an illogical interjection in the list of separate accoutrements.

[71] We have seen (n. 61) that Rashi compares it to a net for catching fish, obviously a flexible item.

on the soft and weak net, at whose extremities the rings were attached. Cassuto might therefore have imagined the net to be a sturdy bronze enclosure, with a few holes for aeration, whose purpose would be to reinforce the inner perforated fragile wall. This conjecture would confer a purpose on the מכבר, but would reverse the scriptural text; the "net" would be inside, and the sturdy wall outside, in complete contrast to the text, which clearly asserts the opposite.

5.5.2 Proposed Solution Based on the LXX Text

One could continue with further imaginative speculations and rabbinic rhetoric, but the above citations suffice to demonstrate the enigmatic nature of the term כרכוב in particular, and of the entire description of the altar in general. The speculations of the Rabbis and the traditional commentators are even less close to reality, since they originate in, and at the same time are made futile by, their desire to adapt the scriptural characteristics of the bronze altar to the stone altars of Ezekiel and of the Second Temple. Onkelos, Jonathan and Neophyti translate כרכב as סובב, probably referring to the rabbinic dictum cited above: רבי יוסי ברבי יהודה אומר זה הסובב "Rabbi Jose son of Rabbi Judah says: [the כרכב] is the סובב, the gangway" on the altar of the Second Temple, created by its narrowing at the top. MS J of the Samaritan Targum uses the original Hebrew term כרכב; but MS A has כתי שקו "under its depression" which may be understood as a deep engraving creating a protruding elevation at its edge, similar to Rashi's explanation, or as the talmudic "gangway", similar to the *ziggurat*, created by the narrowing of the altar at every level.

In conclusion, we must assume that according to the rabbinic interpretation, the bronze altar had no "grating" on its top, since the מכבר "net" was attached under the כרכב of the altar; whatever this represents, it was on the altar's side walls, and not on its top. The latter interpretation was necessary to reconcile between this ambiguous MT text and the law requiring an earthen or stone altar in Exod. 20: 21 – 22. As previously noted,[72] there

---

[72] I repeat some of these dicta: B. T. Zebahim 62b: רבי נתן אומר מזבח של שילה של נחושת היה חלול ומלא אבנים "Rabbi Nathan says the altar of Shilo was [made] of bronze, was hollow and filled with stones." Mekhilta d'Rabbi Ishmael, Jethro, *Parshah* 11: איסי בן עקיבא אומר מזבח נחשת מלא אדמה תעשה לי "Issi son of Akiba says: [The meaning of מזבח אדמה is really] 'the bronze altar filled with earth you should make for me.'" Rashi, in his commentary on Exod. 20: 21, elucidates: דבר אחר שהיה ממלא את חלל מזבח הנחשת אדמה בשעת חנייתן "Another interpretation

are rabbinic dicta suggesting that the bronze altar was hollow and filled with earth and stones during each rest and emptied before each move, while another homily asserts that the altar must be attached to the ground.

The LXX, as we have seen, has an entirely different concept of the bronze altar.[73] We shall attempt to portray its imagined altar, analyze its relation to the MT text, and consider its feasibility. The bronze altar and its specific elements, which are problematic in the MT and in the LXX, appear with diverse names in Exod. 27: 3 -5, in 38: 22 - 24 (38: 2 - 4 in MT) and in 39: 9 (39: 39 in MT). It is obvious that the LXX's altar has a hearth on its top, but for some reason it is called by different names in the various pericopes describing the altar's elements; we must also compare certain terms used with the incense altar in Exod. 30: 3 - 4. The term מכבר is translated in 27: 4 as ἐσχάρα, but in 38: 24 and 39: 9 as παράθεμα. We ought therefore to assume that they are identical, and that the ἐσχάρα in 27: 4 is the same attachment to the altar as the παράθεμα in the other two pericopes. Further details corroborate this proposition: In 27: 4 and 5, the four rings are attached to the four ends of the ἐσχάρα, and in 38: 24 they are put to the four parts of the παράθεμα.[74] Both terms are described as being in the manner of a "network", and both must extend to the middle of the altar.

It seems to me that the translation by the LXX of πυρεῖον in singular for the MT מחתתיו in plural, as discussed above, is the key to the understanding of the LXX pericopes. I consider that the πυρεῖον in Exod. 27: 3 and 38: 23 and 24 represents the hearth, that is, the top part of the altar, on which the offerings were burned.[75] The ἐσχάρα and the παράθεμα, on the other hand, portray the appendage around the upper part of the altar, and are of a "netlike" nature. The text in 38: 24 is very clear and I shall quote the relevant part, together with a word by word translation: ἐποίησε θυσιαστηρίῳ

[we have seen that the Talmud also has another opinion on the meaning of this verse] is that he filled the hollowness of the bronze altar with earth when they camped."

[73] Cf. Wevers, p. 433.

[74] There are certain philological and stylistic differences between the texts in relation to the rings, but this fact should not necessitate a dissimilar interpretation. For example, in Exod. 27: 4 the rings for the ἐσχάρα are ἐπὶ τὰ τέσσαρα κλίτη, and in 38: 24 the rings are on the μερῶν τοῦ παραθέματος. The literary style of the command in 27: 5, καὶ ὑποθήσεις αὐτους, in which the pronoun refers to the rings, is different from the description of the work in 38: 24, where the pronoun αὐτῶ refers to the παράθεμα.

[75] I reiterate that πυρεῖον in singular cannot be understood here as a censer, or a firepan; there would have been more than one such item, as is apparent in the MT, similar to the other utensils described in plural both in the MT and the LXX. Except in specific occurrences in which one מחתה "firepan" is required, such as Lev. 16: 12 in which the High Priest enters with one pan into the Holy of Holies on the Day of Atonement, the term always appears in plural whenever it refers to accessories of the altar. See e.g. Num. 4: 14; I Kings 7: 50; II Kings 25: 15; Jer. 52: 19 and II Chr. 4: 22.

παράθεμα ἔργον δικτυωτὸν κάτωθεν τοῦ πυρείου ὑπὸ αὐτὸ ἕως τοῦ
ἡμίσους αὐτοῦ "He made an 'appendage' for the altar, a network, under the
hearth, beneath it, until the middle of it." The redundant κάτωθεν and ὑπὸ
αὐτὸ represent the Hebrew doublet תחת and מלמטה, which express the
same redundancy.

We may now deduce the correct interpretation of both pericopes, by
synthesizing the two and filling in the unclear or missing details in one from
the other. From Exod. 38: 22-24 in the LXX, it is clear that the net-like
appendage extended from just under the hearth, κάτωθεν τοῦ πυρείου, until
the middle of the altar, ἕως τοῦ ἡμίσους αὐτου;[76] it is not on the lower part
of the altar, as Cassuto has understood the MT text, though we might have
understood this position from the text in 27:5b: ἔσται δὲ ἡ ἐσχάρα ἕως τοῦ
ἡμίσους τοῦ θυσιαστηρίου. On the other hand, from 38: 24 we would not
know whether the rings at the extremities of the appendage should be
attached to the upper parts, which start just under the hearth, as we read
τέσσαρας δακτυλίους ἐκ τῶν τεσσάραν μερῶν, but in 27: 5 their
placement is precisely indicated as "under the appendage" καὶ ὑποθήσεις
αὐτους ὑπὸ τὴν ἐσχάραν τοῦ θυσιαστηρίου κάτωθεν. In 39: 9, the LXX
mentions only the παράθεμα as the most significant and noticeable
"appendage", a net-like item encasing all four sides of the altar; it does not
mention the πυρεῖον, the "hearth", an obvious element of the altar.

There remains one apparent difficulty, the translation of גגו, "the roof /
top" of the incense altar, as ἐσχάρα in Exod. 30: 3; this term, as we have
seen, is also used for the appendage of the bronze altar, along with the term
παράθεμα. I have no answer for this divergence; I can only draw attention to
all the cases in these pericopes in which different terms are utilized for the
same Hebrew expressions. The first example is this interchange of ἐσχάρα
and παράθεμα; another oddity we encounter is the translation of the Hebrew
term בדים, the "poles" for carrying the various furnishings. For this item,
which served the same purpose in Exod. and in Num. chap. 4, there are three
Greek terms: ἀναφορεῖς, φορεῖς and διωστῆρες; and for the בדים of the
incense altar[77] in Exod. 30: 4, the term σκυτάλαις occurs. Thus we
encounter in Exod. 30 the same oddity of unique translations for both the
poles and the hearth. According to scholarly opinion, the pericope Exod. 30:
1 - 10 regarding the incense altar consists of a later interjection; this may
offer a reasonable explanation for this solitary translation of גגו as ἐσχάρα,

---

[76] The pronoun αὐτου refers to the altar, as appears clearly in Exod. 27: 5 in the parallel
phrase τοῦ ἡμίσους τοῦ θυσιαστηρίου.

[77] Cf. Wevers, p. 621: "Exod uses διωστῆρες, rather than ἀναφορεῖς of A to designate the
staves. Actually except for 35: 11 where the ark's staves are called ἀναφορεῖς Exod B
uses only διωστῆρες, whereas Exod A uses (ἀνα)φορεῖς throughout, except for
σκυτάλαις at 30: 4."

meaning "hearth", in contrast to the other pericopes regarding the bronze altar, in which this expression is identical to παράθεμα, and represents the surrounding "appendage." In conclusion, it appears to me that the LXX, unencumbered by the need to harmonize diversified sources, attempted to present the most reasonable and practical projection of a nebulous description of an imaginary furnishing.

It is interesting to note here the Vulgate[78] translation of the above verses, which is *sui generis*; it is not identical to either the MT text or to the LXX translation.. The text reads as follows: *qous pones subter arulam altaris eritque craticula usque ad altaris medium*. We observe that the term כרכב המזבח is translated as "the rim of the altar." The LXX, as we have seen, has στεφανήν, "rim" in verse 3 instead of the סירת "pots" of the MT. The Vulgate translates the סירת in v. 3 appropriately as *lebetas* "kettles, cauldrons," but adds a " rim" in v. 5, as it considers that such a practical ornament should have been an element of the altar. In addition to this oddity, which I shall discuss in section 7.2.5, this translation demonstrates that the translator of the Vulgate, who followed the MT text here rather than the LXX text, understood that the כרכב "rim" was at the top of the altar similar to the rim of the ark and the table; the *craticula*, the "net-like structure," had to be put under the rim, hanging down *usque* "all the way" to the middle of the altar.

5.6 Exod. 27: 6

ועשית בדים למזבח
Make poles for the altar

The term בד has many interpretations, entirely different one from another, and it is remarkable that this term was chosen to describe the poles used with the tabernacle's furnishings, that is, the altars, the ark and the table. in addition to this occurrence in the Pentateuch, the term has this meaning only in I Kings 8: 7 and 8, and in II Chr. 5: 8 and 9, in relation to the poles of the ark. The closest use of the term in connection with something similar to poles is encountered in Hosea 11: 6,[79] in Ezek. 19: 14[80] and in a few occurrences in

---

[78] *Biblia Sacra iuxta latinem vulgatam versionem ad codicum fidem iussi Pii*, Deutsche Bibelgesellschaft, 3rd ed. (Stuttgart, 1983).

[79] וכלתה בדיו "consume his branches [KJV]." Radak also interprets: פי' בדיו ענפיו "...the interpretation of בדיו is 'its branches.'"

[80] ממטה בדיה "a rod of her branches [KJV]." The traditional commentator Metzudath David interprets בדים - הם הענפים הגסים "...the thick [or solid] branches."

Job.[81] In all these verses the term בד refers to branches, and it is odd that this term was chosen to describe poles, presumably straight and even, which are correctly called מוט in Num. 4: 10, 12 and 13: 23.[82] In the latter verse, the term מוט is certainly an accessory for the carrying of the Temple's furnishings. The LXX has for all these occurrences the terms φορεῖς or ἀναφορεῖς "poles", except in Exod. 30:5 where we find σκυτάλας "staff".[83] Onkelos too uses the same term אריחא in all the above occurrences, in singular and in plural, for both terms בדים and מוט.

Since the term בדים appears in I Kings in connection with the ark, we must assume that this was the reason for its being carried over into the Exodus narrative concerning similar square and oblong furnishings. But we must distinguish between the simple branch used to carry the ark, a vestige of the archaic nomadic period, and its presumed use with later furnishings. The ark, a sacred element, was kept by tradition in its original state with its customary simple carrying rods, and thus its appearance with the term בדים is appropriate in the Kings narrative. The old and cherished memory of nomadic days inspired the conservation and explicit exposure of the branch-poles of the ark, so eloquently described during the ark's transfer to Solomon's Temple:[84] ויהיו שם עד היום הזה "and they are still there to this day [I Kings 8: 8]." The significance of the "branches" may also be due to the holiness of certain trees, an ancient tradition of Israel.[85] For our

---

[81] יאכל בדי עורו "the strength (the bars) of his skin [Job 18: 13, KJV]"; that is, the ramifications (branches) of his skin. Ralbag interprets Job 18: 13 similarly: - בדי עורו ענפי עורו ובדיו "...the branches and ramifications of his skin," and Metzudath David explains for Job 41: 4: (והוא /יח /איוב/ לעיל) עורו בדי יאכל וכן אבריו - בדיו "בדיו" מושאל מבדי האילן implies here his limbs, similar to our verse Job 18: 13, and it is a metaphorical expression, adopted from the branches of a tree." In Isa. 16: 6 we find לא כן בדיו, whose interpretation is unclear; though there are a number of different explanations, none of the traditional interpreters or the LXX consider the meaning as branches or poles.

[82] In Num. 4: 10 and 13, ונתנו על המוט "...and put it on a carrying frame," and in 13: 23, וישאהו במוט בשנים "Two of them carried it on a pole between them...."

[83] This exception is most interesting and may substantiate the scholarly assessment of the late origin of this pericope regarding the construction of the golden incense altar. See Heger, *Incense Cult* for a full list of the scholarly opinions.

[84] We read there: ויארכו הבדים ויראו ראשי הבדים מן הקדש על פני הדביר "These poles were so long that their ends could be seen from the Holy Place [I Kings 8: 8]."

[85] This is a well-known fact and thus it is unnecessary to substantiate it here; I shall simply quote a few such occurrences in Scripture: Abraham planted a tamarisk tree in Beer Sheba (Gen. 21: 33); Jacob buried the foreign gods "under the oak at Shekhem" (Gen. 35: 4); the rock that served as witness to Joshua's covenant was erected "under the oak near the holy place of the Lord" (Jos. 24: 26); an angel revealed himself to Gideon under the oak (Jud. 6: 11- 19), where the sanctuary "'The Lord is Peace'...still stands" (v. 24); the

hypothesis, it does not matter whether tradition bestowed significance on the primitive form of the branch, or the type of the tree of which the poles were made; it suffices to establish the "hidden" motive for the use of the odd term בדים instead of מוט. There is no mention of poles for any of the other Temple furnishings; this is not surprising, as the tables made by Solomon did not need to be carried, the holocaust altar was of earth or more likely of stone, and the golden incense altar did not yet exist;[86] the only ancient holy element was the ark with its traditional attachments. But even in the Pentateuch we observe a distinction between the poles of the ark, which must not be removed,[87] and the poles of the other furnishings, for which this

---

people of Shekhem crowned Abimelekh at the "oak tree" (Jud. 9: 6); the man of God sat under "the oak tree" (I Kings 13: 14); the people sacrificed "under oak and poplar and terebinth" (Hos. 4: 13); and Isaiah proclaims (1: 29): "You will be ashamed because of the sacred oaks in which you have delighted."

[86] O. Kaiser writes in *Einleitung in das Alte Testament*, p. 98: "Der Archaismus zeigt sich darin, dass das Wüstenheiligtum, diese merkwürdige Mischung zwischen einem alten Zeltheiligtum und dem Jerusalemer Tempel, der vorausgesetzten Situation so angepasst wird, dass er als transportabel erscheint...Der Brandopferaltar wird zu einem hölzernen, mit Erzplatten überzogenen Gerüst. " (The archaism is evident in the fact that the desert sanctuary, this odd fusion of an archaic tent sanctuary and the Jerusalem Temple, was so adapted to the presumed circumstances as to appear to be a portable entity....The holocaust altar came to be a wooden, bronze-covered structure.")

[87] We read in Exod. 25: 15: בטבעת הארן יהיו הבדים לא יסרו ממנו "The poles are to remain in the rings of this ark; they are not to be removed." Rashi adds here לא יסרו ממנו - לעולם "'Not to be removed' - ever." The Rabbis asked in B. T. Yoma 72: כתיב בטבעת הארן יהיו הבדים לא יסרו ממנו וכתיב והובא את בדיו בטבעת הא כיצד מתפרקין ואין נשמטין "It is written [Exod. 25: 15] 'The poles are in the ring of the ark, they should not be removed,' and it is written [Exod. 27: 7] 'The poles are to be inserted'; [if we interpret the first to mean that the poles are fixed] how is this possible? [The answer is] they may move [in the rings], but could not be taken out [of the rings]." Rashi explains that they were thicker at their extremities, and inserted inside the rings by force; they could then not be removed or fall out during transit because of these thicker ends. But it is strange that only Tosafoth at B. T. Yoma 72a ask a much more difficult question, regarding the definite contradiction between the command in Exod. 25: 15 and the rule in Num. 4: 6, ושמו בדיו "and put the poles" in the ark preparatory to moving the camp and the Tabernacle; the latter implies that the poles were not permanently in the ark's rings but were only inserted before the move. This is seemingly an oversight of the redactor, writing according to his vision of the scene; he compared the ark to the other furnishings for which such a command does not appear, and concluded that as the poles were inserted in those furnishings before transit, so the same procedure would follow for the ark. It is obvious that the traditional commentators could not admit such a solution, and they attempted to reconcile the contradiction with two propositions, both of which were also challenged. The first solution is offered by Rabbi Jacob of Orleans, who suggested interpreting the phrase ושמו בדיו to mean that the poles were placed on the shoulders of the Levites who carried the ark. Although this seems an elegant escape from the inconsistency, it is challenged by Tosafoth, since it would contradict another

command does not appear. This peculiarity demonstrates the uniqueness of the ark's branch-poles, based on ancient tradition, versus the poles of the other "imaginary" furnishings.

5.7 Exod. 27: 7

והובא את בדיו

The poles are to be inserted

הובא is an impersonal הופעל form, in contrast to the direct form of all other commands concerning the construction of the furnishings in general and the insertion of the poles in particular. It represents the only exception in the entire pericope; further, in Exod. 38: 7 this action is expressed using the same הפעיל third person form found with the rest of the actions concerning the altar and the other furnishings. This expression הובא occurs only three other times in the Bible, and exclusively in connection with the מצרע, the leper to be brought to the priest, connoting an action against his will.[88] It is

---

scriptural requirement: it is only after the priests have duly executed their duty of covering the furnishings and their accessories that the Levites of the Kohath clan come into the picture and begin their task of carrying. This is evident in Num. 4: 15: וכלה אהרן ובניו לכסת את הקדש ואת כל כלי הקדש בנסע המחנה ואחרי כן יבאו בני קהת לשאת ולא יגעו אל הקדש ומתו "After Aaron and his sons have finished covering the holy furnishings and all the holy articles, and when the camp is ready to move, the Kohathites are to come to do the carrying. But they must not touch the holy things or they will die." Hence, the phrase ושמו בדיו in v. 6 could not refer to the Kohathites who were not yet allowed to approach the holy furnishings. The second proposition is far-fetched and quite fantastic, and Tosafoth thus end their discussion on a doubtful note, suggesting the matter requires further reflection. This solution requires the assumption of two sets of poles: one fixed, which was never removed, and another special set of poles for carrying, inserted whenever the ark was prepared for a move. An extended deliberation follows this proposition in an attempt to justify it, but as the Tosafoth themselves hesitate to accept it, I do not think it is necessary to record it here.

[88] One may deduce this from the context and the grammatical form הפעיל, which implies that the action is to be performed by someone else and hence against one's will. The Sages understood these verses similarly. The commentator to Ibn Ezra explains in his comments to Lev. 13: 2: והובא ברצונו ושלא ברצונו, כי הרואה בו אחד מסימנים אלו יכריחנו שיבא "'He should be brought' - willingly or against his will; one who observes in him one of these symptoms must compel him to go [to the priest]." This is probably based on a Midrash in Sifra, in Metzorah, Parshah 1, ד"ה תורת המצורע: והובא אל הכהן שלא ישהא "'He should be brought to the priest' - he should not delay his visit to the priest." The interpretation by the Rabbis of the term והובא as implying coercion may also be deduced from the discussion quoted above from B. T. Yoma 72a. The Talmud observes an apparent contradiction between the interdiction in

certainly odd to use this expression in our pericope. The translators use an active form rather than a passive. The LXX translates it as εἰσάξεις in second person, similar to the other verbs in the pericope. Onkelos too uses the Aramaic active אפעל and translates ויעיל.[89] The Samaritan Bible has the active form והבאת את הבדים "you should insert the poles," exactly like the other verbs in this and similar pericopes. The Samaritan Targum[90] evidently follows its original, with ותעל in MS J, and ותנדי in MS A, both in second person active. The Neophyti Targum[91] also has ותעל. The question now remains whether the LXX "has correctly interpreted" the MT, as Wevers states,[92] or the LXX translators had before them a *Vorlage* with Samaritan characteristics, as in many other instances in which the LXX follows the Samaritan text, particularly with regard to minor grammatical issues.

5.8 Exod. 27: 8

נבוב לחת תעשה אתו

Make the altar hollow, out of boards

The phrase נבוב לחת contains a participle נבוב in construct state, which generally shows a genitival relationship between the governing noun, adjective or participle and the governed element, as for example לנשברי לב "the brokenhearted" (Isa. 61: 1). Our phrase if taken as a genitival relationship would thus imply hollow boards, an impossible interpretation. From the context, one must interpret our phrase as "hollow, of boards." Both

---

Exod. 25: 15 against removing the poles of the ark, לא יסרו ממנו, and the command in Exod. 27: 7 to insert the poles, והובא את בדיו. The Tosafoth, also quoted above, wonder why the Rabbis quote the phrase והובא, which refers to the bronze altar, and did not base the question on the phrase והבאת את הבדים בטבעת in 25: 14, which refers to the ark; this question remains unanswered. I would suggest that the Rabbis used the term והובא in the passive הופעל because this form indicates a forceful action, and this interpretation is suitable for the Rabbis' solution that the poles were thicker at the extremities and to be inserted by force. They thus used this form intentionally to emphasize that force was involved, which could not be implied from the regular term והבאת, and applied this stratagem to make their point understandable.

[89] Franz Rosenthal, *A Grammar of Biblical Aramaic* (Wiesbaden, 1961), p. 69 quotes a form for our verb עלל. This is not the place to discuss whether Aramaic has a הופעל form that Onkelos could have used.

[90] A. Tal, ed. התרגום השומרוני לתורה (Tel Aviv, 1980 - 1982).

[91] A. Diez Macho, ed. *Neophyti, Targum Palestinense*, MS de la Biblioteca Vaticana (Madrid, 1971).

[92] p. 433.

terms in the construct state would refer not to each other, but to a third element, the altar, each one separately modifying the altar in an adjectival or adverbial relation.[93] The LXX has in fact translated the two terms in our verse separately, not in a genitival relation: κοῖλον σανιδωτόν "hollow, made of planks";[94] our other example of a construct state with a participle in Isa. 61: 1 is, in contrast, translated as συντετριμμένους τῇ καρδίᾳ in a clear genitival relation. Onkelos follows the MT text and translates חליל לוחין in construct state, with a *Shewa* under the ח.

According to above interpretation, one may concede that the command to construct the altar נבוב "hollow" is essential, although one might understand this implicitly from the text; such a directive does not appear with respect to the two other furnishings, the ark and the golden altar, although they too were hollow. On the other hand, there is a difference between these and the bronze altar. The ark was hollow but had a bottom. We may assume that the golden altar was also hollow,[95] not one solid block of wood, though this is not clearly stated as it is for the ark and the bronze altar; at any rate, it did have a roof גג (Exod. 30: 3). Only the bronze altar was entirely open on both sides, and this may be the reason for the specific command "make it hollow."[96] The term לחת "of boards" is altogether superfluous, and does not appear with respect to the construction of the ark, the other hollow, box-like furnishing, which must also have been made of boards rather than a solid wooden block.[97] And notwithstanding this apparent tautology, this phrase is repeated in Exod. 38: 7 at the record of the altar's construction; it must have been considered by the editor as a significant characteristic of the altar, or else he

---

[93] As Gesenius notes (128f) the construct situation need not always represent a genitival relation. See also 128a for examples of a wider construct structure, such as בתולת בת ציון (II Kings 19: 21), and 116k for examples of passive participles in construct relations.

[94] Wevers writes on this phrase, p. 434: "The construction of the altar is doubly characterized."

[95] It must have been hollow, and not a solid block of wood, in order that the two tablets could be placed in it. The text also supports the idea that it was hollow: "Overlay it with pure gold, *both inside and out* [Exod. 25: 11, emphasis added]."

[96] The net-like grating on the top does not change the structure and the form of the altar itself, which remained hollow. The net placed upon the altar was solely an accessory to it, as clearly implied in the text ועשית לו מכבר "make a grating for it," and did not affect the hollowness of its main framework.

[97] The term נבוב לחת is the opposite of an altar made of a solid wooden block. In his commentary to our verse Exod. 27: 8, Rashi relies on Onkelos' translation חליל לוחין and explains: "Boards of acacia wood on every side and hollow in the middle, and not one block of wood five cubits by five cubits like a type of anvil." We may also observe from Rashi's comment that the net-like grating on top of the hollow altar did not change its characteristic hollowness. Cf. Wevers, p. 434 on this issue.

failed to understand its purpose. This obscure phrase adds to the other oddities of this pericope.

5.9 Conclusion

The result of this thorough examination of the text must lead us to the conclusion that the description of the altar was not based on a real furnishing, but on some vague imagination. The numerous, often entirely contrasting attempts to portray the altar's structure by such a diversity of commentators, from the rabbinic Sages to modern scholars, confirm the difficulties of our pericope. The radically divergent text of the LXX, whose authors, I assume, attempted to create a plausible picture of an altar, validates such a proposition. It would be hard to presume that the LXX translators had such a different *Vorlage* before them; a number of facts substantiate the opposite. They added a rim to the altar, assuming that since the other furnishings - the ark (Exod. 25: 11), the table (25: 24) and the incense altar (30: 3) - each had a זר, it would only be natural that the bronze altar should also have some such ornament. The rim would also have had a practical use, to prevent the contents of the altar from falling over the top, similar to the rim of the table. The absence of a translation in the LXX for the singular term כרכב in the MT confirms that the translators had no idea what it represented, an incomprehension which appears to have been common,[98] and thus they ignored it, in order to present a plausible description. I therefore tend to assume that the LXX translators did not possess another Hebrew text, and their altered text is a result of an intellectual effort to make the altar appear real. Scripture itself is aware that the description of the bronze altar is intricate and obscure, and therefore adds at the end of the pericope כאשר הראה אתך בהר כן יעשו "It is to be made just as you were shown on the mountain."[99] A similar problem is encountered in the Vulgate translation,

---

[98] The debate in B. T. Zebahim 62a, starting ותניא איזהו כרכוב "And we learned in a Baraita: What is the כרכוב," demonstrates from the style of the question that the Sages did not know what the term represented. The divergent opinions of the Sages regarding its identification only strengthen this proposition; they attempted to imagine something from their perception of the stone altar, which they considered to have some similarity with Moses' bronze altar.

[99] This "exhibition on the mountain" appears as a general introduction to the command to build the Tabernacle and its furnishings in Exod. 25: 9: ככל אשר אני מראה אותך את תבנית המשכן ואת תבנית כל כליו וכן תעשו "Make this Tabernacle and all its furnishings exactly like the pattern I will show you," and in the concluding verse 26: 30, the command to erect the Tabernacle, where there is no mention of its furnishings:

והקמת את המשכן כמשפטו אשר הראית בהר "Set up the Tabernacle according to
the plan shown you on the mountain." In addition to these general indications of a
"model", there are two particular "exhibits", one for the lampstand, the most intricate
appliance, in 25: 40: וראה ועשה בתבניתם אשר אתה מראה בהר "See that you
make them according to the pattern shown you on the mountain," and one for the bronze
altar in 27: 8: כאשר הראה אתך בהר "It is to be made just as you were shown on the
mountain." This peculiarity confirms the impression that these two furnishings were the
most obscurely portrayed. In the command for the golden incense altar, such a "heavenly
model" was unnecessary, nor does such a model appear in the commands for the
construction of the ark and the table. I have interpreted the plural בתבניתם in v. 25: 40
as referring to the lampstand and its specific accessories since it follows the description
of the lampstand and seems to conclude this passage. Rashbam also interprets this verse
in this way and states: ממש הראו לו תבנית המנורה "He was shown a real model of
the lampstand." The Talmud opposes this interpretation in one homily, but in another
confirms that the making of the lampstand was the most intricate work and was shown to
Moses by God Himself. We read in B. T. Menahoth 29a: תניא רבי יוסי ברבי יהודה
אומר ארון של אש ושלחן של אש ומנורה של אש ירדו מן השמים וראה משה
ועשה כמותם שנאמר וראה ועשה בתבניתם אשר אתה מראה בהר "It was
taught in a baraita: R. Jose son of R. Judah says: An ark of fire, and a table of fire, and a
lampstand of fire descended from heaven, and Moses saw them and constructed [these
items] in their likeness, as it is said: 'See that you make them according to the pattern
shown you on the mountain [Exod. 25: 40].'" The ensuing rhetorical discussion questions
the difference between the lampstand and the other furnishings, concluding that it was
only the lampstand of all the furnishings that Moses did not understand: תנא דבי רבי
ישמעאל שלשה דברים היו קשין לו למשה עד שהראה לו הקב״ה באצבעו ואלו
הן מנורה וראש חדש ושרצים "It was taught at Rabbi Ishmael's college: Three
subjects were difficult for Moses to understand, until God showed them to him with His
finger, and these are: the lampstand, the new moon [how to recognize the form of the
new moon to enable the fixing of the new month] and the [identification of the] various
creeping animals [to discern which are prohibited and which are allowed to be
consumed]." It must also be noted that in the record of the construction of the Tabernacle
and its furnishings in chapters 36: 8 - 38: 31, there is no mention of the fact that they
were made according to the "model" shown to Moses, although all the details (with some
minor exceptions) are fully and seemingly unnecessarily repeated. It is yet more unusual
that the phrase כאשר [את כל אשר] צוה ה' את משה "As the Lord commanded
Moses" appears in this pericope only with respect to the making of the priestly garments
and particular sacramental auxiliaries, and the setting up of the Tabernacle and the
placement of its furnishings. There is no such endorsing attribute following the
construction of the main furnishings, such as the ark, the table, the lampstand and the two
altars. It is also interesting to note that in Ezekiel's description of the Temple and its
furnishings, he is shown how the Temple, its surrounding walls and its gates should be
built, and we read in Ezek. 40: 4: וידבר אלי האיש בן אדם ראה בעיניך ובאזניך
שמע ושים לבך לכל אשר אני מראה אותך כי למען הראותכה הבאתה הנה
הגד את כל אשר אתה ראה לבית ישראל "The man said to me: Son of man, look
with your eyes and hear with your ears and pay attention to everything I am going to
show you, for that is why you have been brought here. Tell the house of Israel
everything you see." In contrast, when Ezekiel describes the style and measurements of
the holocaust altar in 43: 13 - 17, he does not rely on a vision in which he was told or

which also translated the כרכב as a "rim" on the upper part of the altar. In
conclusion, one is tempted to hypothesize that the description of this bronze
altar was not a portrayal of a real furnishing, but drawn up on the basis of
ancient memories, or numerous historical records blended together; it thus
likely displays the diverse characteristics of such furnishings from several
periods. One should also not exclude the possibility that the records were
intentionally obscured in order to conceal popular memories of altars with
different uses in the past, so as to validate only the stone altar and its
utilization in that period. The description of the bronze altar was also
obviously driven by the necessity of portraying a portable altar for the
wanderings in the desert, and such a furnishing was non-existent; it had to be
invented. I shall revert to the examination of this issue in section 7.2.5.

---

shown how the altar should be realized. The antecedent v. 12 concludes the vision
regarding the Temple: הנה זאת תורת הבית "Such is the law of the Temple," and the
subsequent v. 18 starts with the commands concerning the offerings: ויאמר אלי בן
אדם כה אמר אדני ה' אלה חקות המזבח " He said to me: Son of man, that is what
the Sovereign Lord says: These will be the regulations for sacrificing." Rashi too restricts
the introductory verse of Ezekiel's vision in 40: 4: לכל אשר אני מראה אותך - ענין
הבנין "'Everything I am going to show you' - the issue of the building." See W.
Zimmerli, *Ezekiel 2, A Commentary on the Book of the Prophet Ezekiel, Chapters 25-48*
(Philadelphia, 1983), pp. 422ff., who elaborates upon the "self-contained" nature of this
pericope, "which is formulated stylistically without any reference to guidance or
measurement."

6. Excursus: ועשית קרנתיו על ארבע פנתיו "Make Its Horns at Each of The Four Corners [Exod. 27: 2]."

6.1 "Horns" in the Israelite Cult

The issue of the "horns", namely their origin, significance and purpose in the Israelite cult, has captured the attention of many scholars, and various hypotheses have been advanced to solve this puzzle. Hugo Gressmann,[1] and following him K. Galling,[2] postulated that the "horns" of the altars represent the *matzeboth*, "pillars", which were pushed out from their significant position in the center of the altar to the four corners to annul their prior pagan character. Both F. J. Stendebach[3] and H. Th. Obbink[4] dispute this theory in their essays. Stendebach[5] quotes other scholarly speculations, such as J. B. Pritchard's assumption that the raised projections or horns at the extremities of the small limestone incense altars found in Canaan had as their purpose to firmly hold the incense bowl. Stendebach does not exclude this possibility, but considers it a secondary motive. I may add that Pritchard's theory does not offer an explanation for the biblical command to make such projections/horns on the larger altar for whole-burnt sacrifices, or for the "horns" found on such an altar in Beer Sheba.[6] Stendebach prefers to endorse the theory of May and Engberg[7] that a relation existed between the "horns" of the altar and the bull motif prevalent in the religions of the Ancient Orient, without any further explanation. Obbink, on the other hand, pursues a tortuous path; he starts with the fact that in Babylonian mythology the gods wear a four-horned helmet, adding that "accordingly many gods are called

---

[1] Hugo Gressmann, *Die Ausgrabungen in Palästina und das Alte Testament*, Altorientalische Texte zum Alten Testament 133 (Tübingen, 1908), p. 28.

[2] Kurt Galling, *Der Altar in den Kulturen des Alten Orients* (Berlin, 1925), p. 59.

[3] F. J. Stendebach, "Altarformen im kanaanäisch-israelischen Raum," *Biblische Zeitschrift* 20 (1976), pp. 180 - 196.

[4] H. Th. Obbink, "The Horns of the Altar in the Semitic World, Especially in Jahwism," *JBL* 56 (1937), pp. 43 - 49.

[5] Pp. 190-2.

[6] See the discussion of the dispute between Aharoni and Yadin concerning this altar in section 4.2. Both agree that there was an altar with such projections/horns, and for our purpose it is of no significance whether the altar was in a temple court or at the site of a *bamah*.

[7] Stendebach refers to H. G. May and R. M. Engberg, *Material Remains of the Meggiddo Cult* (Chicago, 1935), p. 12.

'the horned ones', i.e., the divine...since the horns can represent the god himself, they are found on shrines in Babylonia and everywhere (?)...[and] on the top of altars." [8] He then states that "these horns are undoubtedly bull's horns." The next step of Obbink's trail is Dalman's contention in *Petra, 79*: "Altar and throne often are the very same. The altar itself is a bethel....Thus the altar was the symbol of the god; since the god was horned, therefore the altar too had to be horned." The mathematical analogy, that is, if *a* is similar to *b*, *b* is similar to *c*, and *c* is similar to *d*, then *a* equals *d*, does not seem particularly convincing in this case; Obbink himself acknowledges this at the end of his essay, declaring "I am aware that not all I have said is convincing." I shall comment on this and other scholarly postulates in sections 6.2.3 and 6.3.

I am tempted to add my voice to this large chorus of opinions, and hope to shed light on this obscure issue from a slightly different perspective. I shall start with a philological and semantic scrutiny of the term קרן and an analysis of the relevant biblical texts. I shall follow up with a critical examination of the quoted scholarly opinions, and shall investigate the impact of the archeological discoveries on our inquiry.

6.2 Semantic Range of קרן

It is evident that the original meaning of the term קרן in Hebrew, as well as in related languages, referred to the horns of particular animals that were familiar to humans;[9] the specific protrusions on their heads prompted the devising of a name for these peculiar outgrowths. The utilization of the empty horns as containers[10] and as musical instruments[11] led to the

---

[8]   Pp. 46-7.

[9]   Gen. 22: 13: והנה איל אחר נאחז בסבך בקרניו "There in a thicket he saw a ram caught by his horns."

[10]   We read in I Sam. 16: 1: מלא קרנך שמן "Fill your horn with oil." We may speculate that there was special significance bestowed on the "horn" container for the anointing of the king. At king Solomon's anointing by Zadok the priest (I Kings 1: 39), a "horn" container is also used for the anointing oil: ויקח צדוק הכהן את קרן השמן מן האהל וימשח את שלמה "Zadok the priest took the horn of oil from the sacred tent and anointed Solomon." On the other hand, Saul was anointed by Samuel with oil from an "ordinary" flask, as we read in I Sam. 10: 1: ויקח שמואל את פך השמן ויצק על ראשו "Then Samuel took a flask of oil and poured it on Saul's head." Jehu too was anointed by Elisha with oil from a flask, as we read in II Kings 9: 3: ולקחת פך השמן ויצקת על ראשו "Take the flask and pour the oil on his head." There are other terms in Scripture for oil containers, such as צפחת "jug" (I Kings 17: 12), אסוך "jar" (II Kings

metonymous use of the term קרן for these items. A further sophistication created the association of the term קרן with other matters with a similar visual appearance, that is, with protruding elements[12] or projecting corners. It is interesting to note that in English the term "corner" originates from the concept of "horn"; the Greek κέρας encompasses[2] a broad range of projections, such as the peak of a mountain, and extremities, such as the wing of an army[13] or the branch of a river (Liddell and Scott); and the Latin *cornus* expresses among other meanings the arms of a river, the extremity of a country, and the pointed end of any object (Cassel's Latin Dictionary). In Assyrian literature we similarly find the term *qarnu*, which describes, among

---

4: 2) as well as פך, but only David and Solomon were anointed with oil from a "horn" container, according to the explicit divine command. Y.T. Horayot 3: 2, 47c, explained this difference: אין מושחין מלכים אלא מן הקרן שאול ויהוא נמשחו מן הפך היתה מלכותן מלכות עוברת דוד ושלמה נמשחו מן הקרן היתה מלכותן מלכות קיימת "One anoints kings only from the horn. Saul and Jehu were anointed from the flask, and the dynasty of each was temporary; David and Solomon were anointed from the horn, and their dynasty was permanent." The traditional commentator Radak used similar reasoning in explaining I Sam. 10: 1 and II Kings 9: 3.

[11] We read in Jos. 6: 5: והיה במשך בקרן היובל "When they make a long blast on the ram's horn...."

[12] For example, כרם היה לידידי בקרן בן שמן "My loved one had a vineyard on a fertile hillside [Isa. 5: 1]." This NIV interpretation avoids giving the literal meaning of the term קרן, but the traditional commentators do attempt to render it. Rashi explains: "In the corners [of the site] on which grow 'fat' fruits such as the good oil." Radak follows the Targum and interprets "On a high hill and in a fertile soil, and the association is with horns which are the highest point of the [bull's] body." Both interpretations, "corner" and "highest point", allude to the form of an animal's horn. *The Theologisches Wörterbuch zum Alten Testament*, s.v. קרן accepts the interpretation "corner" in this specific verse, assuming that the farmer would have chosen a fertile corner of the hill for his vineyard rather than the barren peak of a mountain.

It is not within the scope of my study to categorize the nature of the verb קרן "radiate" in Exod. 34: 29, 30, 35 , קרן עור פניו, "his face was radiant," and the possibly related noun in Hab. 3: 4, ונגה כאור תהיה קרנים מידו לו, "His splendour was like the sunrise; rays flashed from his hand...," referring to rays of the sun or other light source. It is possible that the pattern of the sun's rays appearing between the clouds seemed to the people similar in their structure to the "horns" of an animal, and this induced them to describe the rays as קרנים. We encounter such an association in rabbinic literature, in Sifrei Zuta, *Pisqa* 27, ונתת ד"ה כ. שנאמר וראו בני ישראל את פני משה כי קרן עור פני משה מלמד שקרנים היו יוצאות מפני משה כקרנים שיוצאות מגלגל חמה שנא' ונגה כאור תהיה קרנים מידו לו "As it is said: 'And the Israelites saw that Moses' face was radiant [Exod. 34: 35],' we deduce from this that rays came out from Moses' face similar to the rays which appear from the sun, as it says 'His splendour was like the sunrise, rays flashed from his hand [Hab. 3: 4].'"

[13] It is interesting that Josephus uses the term κέρας extensively to describe the wings of an army.

other associations, the cusp of the moon and other celestial bodies, and protruding (horn-shaped) parts or decorations of objects (Chicago Assyrian Dictionary, s.v. *qarnu*).

Given that corners are the extremities of any object, the association of the horn, the extremity of the animal, with the concept of "corner" is not surprising. There is no doubt that in post-biblical literature the term קרן does include the meaning "corner", among others;[14] but in Scripture there is only the above-cited verse in Isa. in which the term קרן appears to allude specifically to "corner", as well as the many occurrences of this term which refer to the altar. The exact meaning in these occurrences does not seem to me to be as evident as many have assumed.

The term קרן in Scripture expresses figuratively the ideas of strength and might,[15] and in rabbinic literature it also signifies something persistent and permanent, such as the principal amount of a debt.[16] We note such extensions in other languages as well. In Assyrian, for instance, the term *qarnu* "horn" also expresses, by transference, the idea of power;[17] similarly the Latin term *cornu* signifies in poetic literature strength and courage.[18]

The great variety of metonymic and metaphoric associations of the term "horn" in Hebrew as well as in other languages must induce us to reflect on the precise meaning of the scriptural term קרנות in the descriptions of the altar. I suggest that in these cases we avoid any concrete or figurative association of the term with animal horns, and propose to consider the קרנות as referring exclusively to protruding projections of the altar.

As the first support for my postulate, I shall draw attention to the fact that we have in Scripture two distinct terms for the plural of קרן, namely the dual

---

[14] We read in Mishnah Tamid 4: 1: השוחט עומד במזרח ופניו למערב של שחר היה נשחט על קרן צפונית מערבית על טבעת שניה "The slaughterer [of the Tamid offering] stands in the east, his face turned to the west; [the Tamid] of the dawn was slaughtered on the north-west corner, on the second ring."

[15] For example: וקרני ראם קרניו "His horns are the horns of a wild ox [Deut. 33: 17]" and ביום ההוא אצמיח קרן לבית ישראל "On that day I will make a 'horn' [strength] grow for the house of Israel [Ezek. 29: 21]." In some occurrences animal horns serve as a symbol for strength, as in I Kings 22: 11: ויעש לו צדקיה בן כנענה קרני ברזל ויאמר כה אמר ה' באלה תנגח את ארם עד כלותם "Now Zedekiah son of Kena'anah had made iron horns and he declared: This is what the Lord says: 'With these you will gore the Arameans until they are destroyed.'"

[16] We read in Mishnah Baba Qama 9: 7: מצא אבידה וכחש בה ונשבע על שקר הרי זה משלם קרן וחומש "If he found a lost object and denied it and swore falsely, he pays the principal [value of the object] and a fifth of its value [as a fine]."

[17] *The Assyrian Dictionary*, s.v. "qarnu".

[18] *Cassel's New Latin English, English Latin Dictionary*, s.v. "cornu".

form קרנים for all occurrences associated in some concrete or figurative way with animal horns, and the regular plural form קרנות in other instances. I shall then examine the metaphorical nuances associated with these differences, and shall the review the issue of whether horn symbolism is prominent in Israelite mythology.

6.2.1 Distinction between קרנים and קרנות

In addition to the term קרנות utilized in the portrayal of the altar, there are only three other occurrences in Scripture in which the term is unequivocally not associated with horns. In Ezek. 27: 15: קרנות שן is used for elephant's tusks. Ezekiel was aware that these ivory objects were not horns but teeth, and therefore he used the plural. In Ps. 75: 11, we find תרוממנה קרנות צדיק "the strength of the righteous will be lifted up," used in the abstract to convey the idea of power.[19] The use of the term קרנות most similar to the expression utilized for the altar is found in Zech. 2: 1 - 2 (1: 18 - 19 in KJV): ואשא את עיני וארא והנה ארבע קרנות ואמר אל המלאך הדבר בי מה אלה ויאמר אלי אלה הקרנות אשר זרו את יהודה את ישראל וירושלם "Then I looked up - and there before me were four horns. I asked the angel who was speaking to me 'What are these?' He answered me 'These are the horns that scattered Judah, Israel and Jerusalem.'" It is evident that the four horns represent here the dispersion of the Israelites to the four corners of the world,[20] as is clearly indicated in the following v. 10 (2: 6 in KJV): כי כארבע רוחות השמים פרשתי אתכם "For I have scattered you to the four winds of heaven."[21] The statement is comparable to Isaiah's prophecy: ואסף

---

[19] There may be a metaphorical association with horns here, as in many other occurrences. It is possible that for poetic reasons Ezekiel utilized the term קרנות for the righteous, in contrast with the term קרני for the wicked.

[20] Rashi explains the phrase אלה הקרנות as אלה הבבליים אשר בארבע רוחות השמים "These are the Babylonians of the four corners of the world." Ibn Ezra interprets this phrase as מארבע פאות ירושלים "from the four sides of Jerusalem." The number four represents, as we observe, the four corners.

[21] Ezekiel used the same metaphor in 7: 2: כה אמר אדני ה' לאדמת ישראל קץ בא הקץ על ארבעת כנפות הארץ "This is what the Sovereign Lord says to the land of Israel: The end! The end has come upon the four corners of the land." H. Fox, שמחת בית השואבה, *Tarbiz* 55/2 (1986), pp. 173-216, draws attention to the fact that the rabbinic expressions כנפי השכינה and תחת כנפי הארץ, meaning "under the protection of the Holy Spirit," originate from the term כנפות הארץ; the latter connotes the infinite, the four directions of the universe, rather than wings (pp. 213-16).

נדחי ישראל ונפצות יהודה יקבץ מארבע כנפות הארץ "and gather the exiles of Israel; he will assemble the scattered people of Judah from the four quarters of the earth [Isa. 11: 12]." The four corners represent not only the outermost places of the world, but also the furthermost extremities of the universe, its corners, at a period when the universe was considerd to be a flat rectangular surface. Two horns symbolize power, but the number four indicates the four corners of the world, that is, its totality. [22] Zechariah uses this symbol in 6: 5: ויען המלאך ויאמר אלי אלה ארבע רחות השמים "The angel answered me 'These are the four winds of heaven.'" The term רחות השמים, translated as winds, actually represents the four cardinal points, as we read in I Chr. 9: 24: לארבע רוחות יהיו השערים מזרח ימה צפונה ונגבה "The gates were on the four sides: east, west, north and south."

Thus the term קרנות represents metaphorically the four corners, not horns, whereas the dual term קרנים is associated with horns, even in those occurrences in which there are more than two horns. [23] In Dan. 7: 7 we read וקרנין עשר לה "It had ten horns"; although an animal has only two horns and this is the reason for the dual form קרנים, the dual is employed even for the portrayal of ten horns. In the course of the development of the language, the dual term came to be associated with horns, whether used in a concrete or metaphorical sense, irrespective of the number, while the regular plural expressed other associations, such as extremities, projections and consequently corners. We observe a similar linguistic development for the term רגל "leg"; the dual רגלים with a *pathah* under the ל indicates "legs", whereas the plural רגלים with a *qamets* under the ג denotes "times" (Exod.

---

[22] We find a similar use of the number four to denote total dispersion in Jer. 49: 36: והבאתי אל עילם ארבע רוחות מארבע קצות השמים וזרתים לכל הרחות האלה "I will bring against Elam the four winds from the four quarters of the heavens; I will scatter them to the four winds." Total destruction is also symbolized through four types of devastation; we read in Jer. 15: 3: ופקדתי עליהם ארבע משפחות נאם ה' את החרב להרג ואת הכלבים לסחב ואת עוף השמים ואת בהמת הארץ לאכל ולהשחית "I will send four kinds of destroyers against them, declares the Lord, the sword to kill, the dogs to drag away and the birds of the air and the beast of the earth to devour and destroy," and in Ezek. 14: 21: ארבעת שפטי הרעים חרב ורעב וחיה רעה ודבר שלחתי אל ירושלם להכרית ממנה אדם ובהמה "My four dreadful judgments, sword and famine and wild beasts and plague, I sent against Jerusalem to kill its men and animals."

[23] In Dan. 7: 7 we read וקרנין עשר לה "It had ten horns"; although an animal has only two horns and this is the reason for the dual form קרנים, the dual is employed even for the portrayal of ten horns. For a discussion of the use of the dual for things that go in pairs and the use of the feminine plural when these nouns are used in a figurative sense, see Joüon, *A Grammar of Biblical Hebrew*, Vol. I, pp. 273-4, 91c and d.

23: 14; Num. 22: 28, 32 and 33). The same rule applies to the term יד: there is the dual form ידים for the concrete and metaphorical meanings associated with "hands",[24] and the plural form ידות with totally distinct meanings not directly associated with "hands",[25] similar to the English "army" derived from "arm".

6.2.2 Metaphorical Interpretation of ארבע קרנות

Thus the common root was separated into two distinct trends of meaning, the dual form expressing a different notion than the plural form. I postulate therefore that the four קרנות of the altar, expressed in the regular plural form, are not associated with the natural dual pattern of horns, and refer instead to projections on its four corners; these allude metaphorically to the four corners of the world,[26] the seat of the Deity, or to the totality of the altar, with respect

---

[24] For example תחזקנה ידיכם "Be strong [NIV translation] [II Sam. 2: 7]" and its antithesis וירפו ידיו "He lost courage [II Sam 4: 1]." A similar metaphorical use of this term is encountered in II Kings 15: 19: להיות ידיו אתו להחזיק הממלכה בידו "To gain his support and strengthen his own hold on the kingdom." There is thus a metaphorical use of both the singular and dual forms of the term ידים associated with hands.

[25] The term ידות "projections" (NIV) or "tenons" (KJV) is used for the boards of the Tabernacle (Exod. 26: 17ff.). Onkelos translates this as צירין, "hinge, pivot" according to M. Sokoloff, *A Dictionary of Jewish Palestinian Aramaic* (Ramat Gan, 1990). The LXX, probably unsure of the actual form, translates as ἀγκωνίσκους "small corners." The ידות in I Kings 7: 32 -36 are translated by Jonathan as אשדת , "support" (Jastrow), as "axles" and "support" (NIV), and as "axletrees" and "ledges" (KJV). In I Kings 10: 19 ידת is again translated as אשדת by Jonathan, and as "armrests" (NIV) and "stays-bands" (KJV). The LXX translates χεῖρες "arms". These occurrences may still have some distant association with "hand", but in the narrative of Joseph and his brothers in Gen. 43:34, the term חמש ידות must be interpreted as "shares" or "portions". It is translated as "five portions" (NIV), "five times" (KJV), חולקין "shares" (Jonathan) and πενταπλασίως "five-fold" (LXX). In Gen. 47: 24 the share of the Egyptian tenant-farmers, ארבע הידת, is similarly translated ארבע חולקין "parts" (Onkelos), τέσσαρα μέρη "four parts" (LXX), and as "four parts" (KJV); the NIV interprets it as "four-fifths". In II Sam. 19: 44 the term ידות is similarly translated as "shares"/"parts" and חולקין; but the LXX translates χεῖρες In Dan. 1: 20 we find עשר ידות translated as "ten times", and a δεκαπλασίως in the LXX. Despite the slight differences in the English translations, it is evident that in all these occurrences the context requires an interpretation of "parts" or "shares".

[26] Philo, in *Questions and Answers on Exodus*, transl. R. Marcus (Loeb Classical Library, 1953), Book II, p. 149 symbolically interprets the motif of the altar's horns as pointing toward the four sides of the world. In Mesopotamian mythology we find a similar

to the performance of certain celebrations requiring the entire surface. In both cases, the term expresses, like the four winds, a concept of totality. The specific command ועשית קרנתיו על ארבע פנתיו ממנו תהיין קרנתיו "Make a horn at each of the four corners,[27] so that the horns and the altar are of one piece," emphasizing that the "horns" are not to be placed in the middle of the altar's walls but strictly on its corners, supports the postulate that in Israelite doctrine the "horns" of the altar signified the Deity's seat dominating the entire universe, symbolized by the four corners of the world. For this reason they were placed at the corners, and required to be an intrinsic element of the altar. A similar idea is evoked by the altar of twelve stones built by Elijah (I Kings 18: 31) and the memorial built by Joshua at the crossing of the Jordan (Jos. 4: 20); these symbolized the twelve tribes, the entire people of Israel.

6.2.3 Horn Symbolism in Israelite Mythology

There is no suggestion in Israelite mythology that the "horned" Israelite altar is related to bull's horns as a divine motif, as suggested by Stendebach and Obbink. The bull motif may have had a theological function in the

---

concept of the god who marches over the four corners of the world, symbolizing his universal dominion. We read in "Laws from Mesopotamia and Asia Minor," in Pritchard, *ANET*, p. 164, vv. 62-3: "Who purified the cult of Eabzu; the one who strides through the four quarters of the world." W. F. Albright, "The Babylonian Temple-Tower and the Altar of Burnt-Offering," *JBL 39* (1920), pp. 137 - 142, states regarding the Israelite altar (p. 141): "The cosmic symbolism appears clearly in the four horns, or rather four mountains, if we may judge from the four 'horns' on an altar at Petra." See also Zimmerli, *Ezekiel 2*, transl. J. D. Martin (Philadelphia, 1983), who quotes the scholarly discussion concerning רבוע אל ארבעת רבעיו "a square with its four sides" in Ezek. 43: 16 and אל ארבעת רבעיה in v. 17, where one would expect the preposition על instead. It is possible that the entire expression אל ארבעת רבעיו, which seems superfluous, has a symbolic meaning, pointing to the four directions of the universe. Mishnah Midoth 3: 1 attempts to reconcile the dimensions of Ezekiel's altar with those of the Second Temple, and interprets the strange phrase in this light. We read there: נמצא עשרים וארבע על עשרים וארבע מקום המערכה "Hence the hearth is twenty-four [cubits] by twenty-four." However, in Ezek. 43: 16 it is indicated that the hearth was only twelve cubits square: והאראיל שתים עשרה ארך בשתים עשרה רחב רבוע. Therefore the Mishnah continues and asks: יכול שאינו אלא שתים עשרה על שתים עשרה כשהוא אומר אל ארבעת רביעיו מלמד שמן האמצע הוא מודד שתים עשרה אמה לכל רוח "Is it possible that that [the hearth of Ezekiel's altar] was only twelve [cubits] by twelve? Since it is written אל ארבעת רביעיו 'to its four sides' we learn from it that one measures from the centre [of the hearth], that is, twelve cubits in each direction."

[27] As already noted, this specific command is absent among the rules for building the incense altar in Exod. 30: 1 - 5.

narrative of the "golden calf,"[28] or in the description of the two golden calves made by Jeroboam[29] for his sanctuaries. We must therefore assume that such horns had no foundation in Israelite theology; historical narratives as well as various biblical rules attest to this proposition.

6.3 The Structure of the Altar "Horns"

We may start with a critical analysis of the command to add the קרנות in Exod. 27: 1 - 8. Scripture indicates the precise structural framework and dimensions of the altar, with all its intricate details, but avoids informing us of any particulars regarding the "horns", such as the height, width or overall appearance: whether they were pointed or flat, round or square, or pointing upwards or sideways.[30] Had theological significance been bestowed upon the "horns", such details would likely have been mentioned in the relevant command.

We have no information on the structure of the apparently complex altar built according to the design that Ahaz copied in Damascus,[31] and Ezekiel 43 contains data only on a theoretical altar. But according to the indicated measurements,[32] the "horns" were blocks one cubit square,[33] hence entirely

---

[28]   In Exod. 32.

[29]   In I Kings 12: 28 - 30.

[30]   Philo for example, in *Questions and Answers on Exodus*, assumes that the "horns" of the altar are inclined and face toward the four sides of the world. This assumption seems contradictory to Ezekiel's vision in 43: 15 that the "horns" pointed upward: ומהאראיל ולמעלה הקרנות ארבע "and four horns project upward from the hearth." W. Zimmerli, *Ezekiel 2*, also translated this phrase as "and from the hearth upwards (rose) the horns."

[31]   Cf. Zimmerli, p. 428.

[32]   We read in Ezek. 43: 17: והעזרה ארבע עשרה ארך בארבע עשרה רחב "The upper ledge also is square, fourteen cubits long and fourteen cubits wide," and on top of this ledge were placed the קרנות, "horns", leaving for the hearth a space of twelve square cubits, as we read in vv. 15-16: ומהאראיל ולמעלה הקרנות ארבע. והאראיל שתים עשרה ארך בשתים עשרה רחב רבוע "...and four horns project upward from the hearth. The altar hearth is square, twelve cubits long and twelve cubits wide." Hence, each "horn" is one cubit wide and therefore the upper hearth is two cubits smaller than the upper ledge on which the "horns" are placed. Mishnah Midoth 3: 1 confirms this dimension for the "horns": מקום הקרנות אמה מזה ואמה מזה "The surface of the 'horns' [takes up] one cubit from one side and one from the other side." B. T. Zebahim 54a, describing the method of building the altar of natural, unhewn stones, also declares that the "horns" were one cubit square; we read there: וחזר ומביא מלבן שהוא אמה על אמה "And he again brings a form one cubit by one cubit [for pouring the stones and

distinct from any comparison or association with animal horns.[34] The two other altar laws in Exod. 20: 22 - 23 and Deut. 27: 5 - 6 contain a number of complex rules regarding the building of the altar, yet there is no hint of "horns". Particularly significant is the lack of such "horns" in the rules of Exod. 20, a component of the ancient Book of the Covenant, where one would expect traces of primeval conceptions and customs, such as the bull's horns[35] or the "horned" deities proposed by some scholars. It also seems technically impossible to construct "horns" on the type of earthen altar commanded in Exod. 20: 21. Similarly it would be extremely difficult, if not impossible, to form "horns" of unworked natural stones. The Talmud, as we have seen, did devise such a system, but this was applicable only to projections of substantial width, and not to something similar to "horns."

---

other bonding materials for the construction of the 'horns'].'" There is no exact measure of their height in Ezek., only of the height of the altar up to the horns. Zimmerli, p. 427, writes: "And [the altar] rises to a height (excluding the horns) of ten cubits from its own base." But Maimonides, in Hilkhoth Beth HaBehirah 2: 8, declares: גובה כל קרן וקרן חמשה טפחים "Every 'horn' was five handbreadths high," that is, the regular cubit consisting of five handbreadths, whereas other elements of the altar were measured by the greater cubit אמה וטפח "one cubit and a handbreadth [Ezek. 43: 13]." Maimonides deduces this from various talmudic indications of the height of the altar and the width and height of its recesses.

It is interesting to note that although the MT does not indicate the height of the "horns", the LXX does do so by changing the text; it indicates the height of the horns as one cubit instead of the number of horns as four (as in the MT). See J.W. Wevers, *Ezekiel*, The Century Bible (1969), p. 314.

[33] According to Mishnah Midoth 3: 2 the square construction on the south-west corner of the altar, the קרן, had two built-in pipes which served to discharge the blood and the libations and convey these liquids to the sewer beneath. We read there: ובקרן מערבית דרומית היו שני נקבים כמין שני חוטמין דקין שהדמים הניתנין על יסוד מערבי ועל יסוד דרומי יורדין בהן "On the south-west 'horn' there were two holes like narrow nostrils, through which descended the blood that was poured over the western base and over the southern base." Hence, these "horns" must have been of a substantial thickness and standing straight upward.

[34] In the rabbinic literature there is a story confirming the plain, possibly uneven, form of the "horns." (Stories, we may note, habitually carry a greater sense of authenticity than other literature.) We read in Y. T. Yoma 1: 5, 39a: בו ביום נפגמה קרן המזבח ונתנו עליו גוש של מלח שלא יהא נראה כפגום שכל מזבח שאין לו קרן וסובב ויסוד פסול "On that day the 'horn'/ 'corner' of the altar was damaged, and they brought a block of salt and put it upon [the altar], so that it should not give the impression of being defective, because every altar which has no 'horn' or gallery [around the altar] or foundation is disqualified." A rudimentary block of salt is evidently not similar in appearance to a bull's horn.

[35] Moreover, if the altar's "horns" were to symbolize the bull deity, one would expect two horns, not four.

With respect to the many verses in Scripture concerning the building of altars or their use for offerings (a great number of which were quoted in section 2.2.3), we must conclude that these did not contain "horns". The Temple's courtyard dedicated by Solomon for offerings in lieu of an altar could have had no "horns", nor could the stones and rocks on which sacrifices were offered throughout the two books of Samuel. We may note again the many sacrifices offered by David during the transfer of the ark to the City of David (II Sam. 6:13-18); these offerings must have been celebrated on *ad hoc* mounds of earth or stones, without "horns." Regarding David's altar on Arauna's threshing floor (II Sam. 24: 18 -24), we must deduce from the narrative that David came to Arauna without any materials; he had to buy the oxen for the sacrifices and the sledges and yokes for the wood. Then we read that an altar was built, and the question arises: where did David get the material for it? The only possible answer is that he built an altar by gathering up a mound of earth or stones found at the site, for he brought no hewn stones with him. These simple materials were certainly not appropriate for the building of an altar with "horns," and we must therefore conclude that the "horns," even if they were an element of the altar in the pre-monarchic and early monarchic period, were unequivocally not a significant or an absolute requirement, even for the official cult celebrations.

In Ezra 6: 3 - 4 we find measurements and particulars concerning the construction of the Temple, but no information on the altar, its size or design. There is only the neutral statement in 3: 2: ויבנו את מזבח אלהי ישראל להעלות עליו עלות "And they built the altar for the God of Israel to sacrifice burnt offerings on it." In I Macc. 4: 47, a thorough report of the destruction of the old altar and the building of the new one, we do find mention of the scriptural command to use perfect stones, ὁλοκλήρους, but nothing about horns. These are proofs *ex silentio*, but may be conceived as valuable support when added to the above considerations.

It is remarkable that Josephus does not mention the "horns" in his narrative concerning the holocaust altar in *Ant*. III: 149, although he informs us of other specific characteristics of this altar. In *Ant*. VII: 361, on the other hand, concerning Adonijah who "took hold of the horns of the altar (I Kings 1: 50)," Josephus writes: τοῦ θυσιαστήριον κεράτων ἃ δὴ προεῖχεν ἑλλαβόμενος "[he] grasped the horns of the altar - that is, its projections."[36] In *Ant*. II: 23, Josephus describes the smearing of the blood of the sin offerings on the altar's corners, referring to the rules of such offerings in Lev. 4: 18, ומן הדם יתן על קרנת המזבח (and similar rules in vv. 7, 25, 30, 34); he states: οὐκ ὡς τὸ πρῶτον ἀλλὰ τῶν γωνιῶν τὰς ἐξοχάς "...not, however, as before [in which the blood was sprinkled on the altar], but only

---

[36] *Jewish Antiquities*, Loeb Classical Library, 10 vols, edited and translated by H. St. J. Thackeray, R. Marcus, and H. Feldman (London, 1926-1965).

the projecting corners." From this quotation we may observe that Josephus understood the "horns" as projections. In *War* V: 225, he describes the Second Temple altar using κερατο-ειδεῖς προανεχων ψωνίας "with horn-like projections at the corners"; this is rather vague, and we must consider that this description of the altar is somewhat obscure in general since its dimensions do not correspond to any other texts, even to Josephus' own description in *Against Apion* 198 in which he indicates quite different measurements.

6.3.1 The "Horns" on the Altar of Ahaz

On the basis of all the above, one might downplay the significance of the altar's "horns" in the commands for the construction of the Tabernacle's altars in Exod. 27 and 30, and consider these references in light of the scholarly opinion that all the rules for the desert Tabernacle are late retrojections with the purpose of attributing such cult customs to Moses. Since it is evident from the above citations that in the Second Temple period the altar had some sort of projecting elements at its corners, the P editors also included them with the desert "bronze" altar. I postulate, therefore, that the altar of Ahaz was the first Israelite altar to have "horns" or projections. We have no textual or convincing archeological evidence for this conjecture, but the above textual analysis, the specific description of the complex altar built by Ahaz as a copy of an alien altar,[37] and the fact that the "horns" are mentioned in Ezekiel's vision, seem to point to such a conclusion. From the text in II Kings 16: 10 -16, moreover, we must deduce that Ahaz effected a radical transformation of the cult in Jerusalem. He institutionalized the performance of the cult, and carried out the transition from the modest nomadic system of sporadic and spontaneous cult offerings on simple unadorned sites to a regulated system of daily sacrifices on an ornate and permanent altar. For the first time we read of a systematic routine of daily sacrifices in Jerusalem,[38] each with its specific dedication and auxiliary

---

[37] K. D. Fricke, *Das Zweite Buch von den Königen* (Stuttgart, 1972), p. 215, writes that we do not know whether the altar of Ahaz was a copy of a Damascus-type altar, or of an Assyrian altar. I do not think that for our purposes it is significant to deliberate on the much-debated issue of whether Ahaz built an alien type of altar under political pressure from the Assyrians, or to demonstrate his submission to the great power of Assyria and its gods, as Fricke asserts. Cf. W. Zwickel, "Die Kultreform des Ahas (2Kön 16,10-18)," *SJOT* 7,2 (1993), pp. 250- 262. See also H. Spieckermann's extended analysis of this issue in *Juda unter Assur in der Sargonidenzeit* (Göttingen, 1982), pp. 362 ff.

[38] We read in I Kings 18: 29 that Elijah waited to start his sacrifice on Mount Carmel עד לעלות המנחה, translated "until the time of the evening sacrifice"; this report demonstrates a daily afternoon offering of some animal or vegetal nature, but it is

offerings. The Israelites took over an alien altar design, probably among other cult celebrations,[39] but without the original mythological beliefs; during the process of acculturation they may have added their own aetiological rationales, as occurred with many other customs and rules.[40] The editor(s) of Chronicles, who attributed to Solomon the construction of a large bronze altar (II Chr. 4: 1), could not endorse the notion that such a large structure could have been easily moved, or that there was enough space in the inner court for two large altars. They might also have been uncomfortable with the idea of a special daily king's offering, as this was not specified in the P segments of the Pentateuch. For these reasons it is plausible that Chr. ignored the entire record of the new altar, and substituted a different outline of the deeds of Ahaz.[41]

6.4 Analysis of Biblical Citations of קרנות המזבח

We must now analyze the verses in Scripture which refer to the קרנות המזבח, other than those appearing in the P section of the Pentateuch. We find in Amos 3: 14 the phrase ונגדעו קרנות המזבח ונפלו לארץ "The horns of the altar will be cut off and fall to the ground"; this suggests the existence of "horns" on the northern altar of Beth El[42] shortly before the period of Ahaz.[43] One may assume that the Northern Kingdom had imitated, earlier

---

possible this refers to a practice in the Northern kingdom, not in Judah. See M. Rehm, *Das Erste Buch der Könige, Ein Kommentar* (Eichstatt, 1979), p. 180.

[39] As for example the "king's burnt offering," a sacrifice which was not incorporated in the later P segment of the Pentateuch, and is not mentioned in any other biblical source. It was common in the surrounding cultures to find the king as the head of the cult and a main performer of the celebrations.

[40] See chap. 2 nn. 104-105.

[41] Cf. Fricke, p. 216 and Ehud Ben Zvi, "A Gateway to the Chronicler's Teaching," *JSOT* 7,2 (1993), pp. 216 - 249, esp. pp. 228 ff.

[42] The first part of the verse refers to such altars: ופקדתי על מזבחות בית אל "I will destroy the altars of Bethel" (NIV), "I will also visit the altars of Bethel" (KJV). While "destroy" is a stretched interpretation of פקד, it is more suitable in the context than "visit". The term פקד has a great variety of meanings and must be considered according to the context; in our verse a punishing action is definitely appropriate. The LXX uses the term ἐδικέω " punish - avenge." A remarkable parallel is encountered in Jer. 51: 44: ופקדתי על בל בבבל והצאתי את בלעו מפיו ולא ינהרו אליו עוד גוים גם חומת בבל נפלה "I will punish Bel in Babylon and make him spew out what he has swallowed. The nations will no longer stream to him. And the wall of Babylon will fall."

[43] Amos was active in the period of Uzziah of Judah (784 - 746) and Jeroboam, son of Joash, of Israel (786- 746). Ahaz reigned from 742 to 727, hence somewhat later.

than the Judean kingdom, the elaborate form of the altars of neighbouring Damascus with projections on the extremities. Yet we must consider that the use of the term קרנות המזבח by Amos does not necessarily refer to such "horns", but may be a vivid expression of wreckage: the destruction of the corners indicates the total devastation of the altar,[44] just as the four corners of an entity represent its totality. The other two occurrences of קרנות with המזבח are encountered in Jer. 17: 1 and Ps. 118: 27. Jeremiah's utterance is metaphorical (as is the antecedent expression לוח לבם, "the tablets of their heart" on which the sin is engraved with an iron tool), and offers no indication of the literal meaning of קרנות. The idea that Jeremiah attempted to figuratively associate the "corners" with the foundation and totality of the altar seems to me more appropriate here than a literal interpretation as "horns". The phrase in Ps. 118: 27 originates from a late period, probably post-exilic, according to the context and the prominence of the house of Aaron in v. 3. At that period, the projections on the altar were an established pattern.

6.4.1 The "Horns" of the Altar in Connection with Asylum

Further references to קרנות המזבח are associated with the altar as a safe haven, in I Kings 1: 50 and 2: 28. In both occurrences, concerning Adonijah and Joab, the relevant expression concerning the conduct of the asylum-seeker is identical: ויחזק בקרנות המזבח "[He] took hold of the 'horns' of the altar," a translation in accordance with the plain definition of קרן. Here there is no contextual indication as to whether the term is "corners" or "horns." As shown above, however, the plural form קרנות would imply some kind of projection on the four corners and allude metaphorically to the four corners of the world, or to the altar's wholeness. Thus by touching or grasping the altar's corners or its projections, one is symbolically attached to it and enjoys its right of asylum. As discussed in section 2.2, the ancient custom of the altar as a safe haven is based on the nomadic right to shelter, transposed to the notion of the altar as the dwelling of the Deity. In order to

---

[44] The traditional commentator Radak interprets the term קרנים here as "corners", and writes: קרנות המזבח זכר הקרנות כי בנפול הקרנות יפול המזבח כי הקרנות מעמידות הבנין כמו פנות הבית ועוד זכר הקרנות כי עליהם היו מקריבים וזורקים הדם "The 'corners' are mentioned because when the corners cave in, the altar will collapse, since the corners support the structure, similar to the corners of the house. And the corners are also mentioned since the blood was offered and sprinkled upon them."

simulate the entering into a dwelling, one grasped the altar's corners, and this became the accepted convention.

C. Houtman [45] asks a practical question regarding the asylum procedure at the altar, or at a sanctuary: what happened after the asylum-seeker touched the altar, since he could not remain there forever? He proposes that the first respite between the blood avenger and the unintentional killer, created by the shelter provided by the sanctuary, allowed the parties to enter into negotiations for ransom or other method of compensation. I would postulate a different possibility. The primary text in the Book of the Covenant referring to the altar as a safe haven is very concise[46] and leaves open many questions, which are complemented by the later writings[47] in Num. 35 : 11 - 28 and Deut. 19: 1 - 13. This arrangement does not absolutely imply that all the procedural details in Deut. and Num. were of later origin; some may certainly be so, given also the abolition of the altar as a safe haven and the substitution of the cities of refuge,[48] but others were of ancient origin, and simply not described in the Book of the Covenant. The method of execution of the death penalty, and the system for determining the type of killing, are missing; there were undoubtedly established customs surrounding these issues and many others in the early period of settlement,[49] the probable period of origin of these primary laws of the Book of the Covenant. Thus we may consider at least some of the rules[50] of blood vengeance and asylum described in the later[51] Deut. and Num. as simply reflecting customs that had been established in the early period of the Book of the Covenant.

---

[45] C. Houtman, "Der Altar als Asylstätte im Alten Testament," *Revue Biblique* 103-3 (1996), pp. 343-66, on pp. 355-6.

[46] M. Noth, *Exodus*, p. 180 speculates that the casuistic protases in Exod. 13 and 14, making a distinction between unintentional killing and premeditated murder, are a secondary addition and "were perhaps inserted after the compilation of the Book of the Covenant."

[47] We read in B. T. Sotah 3a an interesting dictum: דתנא דבי רבי ישמעאל כל פרשה שנאמרה ונישנית לא נישנית אלא בשביל דבר שנתחדש בה "As it was said in the school of Rabbi Ishmael: Every reiterated pericope was restated solely to add something new."

[48] Cf. G. von Rad, *Deuteronomy, A Commentary*, The Old Testament Library, transl. D. Barton (Philadelphia, 1966), pp. 128-129.

[49] M. Noth, *Exodus*, p. 174 writes: "...even though some groups of judgements which have been incorporated in it may be still older."

[50] G. von Rad, *Deuteronomy, A Commentary*, p. 128, writes: "In Israel the practice was more general than the few legal ordinances enable us to recognize."

[51] The various procedures involved in the right of asylum, as described in three different passages, allow us to establish the sequence of its development, and consequently the succession of scriptural pericopes. The oldest source is in the Book of the Covenant, from a period when there were local altars to which one was able to run for refuge with ease.

From a close reading of the two pericopes in Deut. and Num., we must
come to the conclusion that even in that late period, and certainly in the
earlier epoch, the relative of the deceased had not only the right to blood
vengeance, but also a civic duty to kill the perpetrator of the crime. Society
expected him to abide by this primeval law of vengeance to restore the
honour of the family. Similar socially grounded constraints exist even today
in a number of Arab societies, in which a woman who has defamed the
honour of the family through "immoral" sexual behaviour must be killed by
her father or brothers to "save" the family's tarnished honour. In rural Sicily,
a father or a brother is expected to kill the man who defiled a daughter or
sister and does not marry her, and a man is expected to kill the lover of his
wife. We read in Deut. 19: 12 the procedure concerning the man who killed
intentionally and escaped to the cities of refuge: ולקחו אתו משם ונתנו אתו
ביד גאל הדם ומת "They should bring him back [from the city] and hand
him over to the blood avenger to die." In Num. 35: 19 and 21 Scripture is
more explicit, stating: גאל הדם הוא ימית את הרצח "The blood avenger
shall put the murderer to death."[52] If there is a relative, a blood avenger, it is
he, not society, who should kill the murderer. The law of refuge for the
unintentional killer who sought shelter at the sanctuary had two aspects: it
removed the obligation of the blood avenger to slay the killer, and obligated
society to ensure the killer's safety after his compliance with the correct
formalities, and an investigation into the *bona fides* of his assertion of
involuntary homicide. We must assume that this obligation of a relative to
avenge the blood of his kin was a common custom in the earliest period; he
could be released from this obligation only when the killer sought a safe
haven at the seat of the Deity, the altar. Grasping the corner of the altar was
considered equivalent to being in God's dwelling;[53] the killer could then
leave the sanctuary.

The deuteronomic pericope reflects changed conditions; there was only one central altar
in Jerusalem and a number of sites had to be provided, for practical reasons, to allow an
involuntary killer to seek refuge. In the P segment in Num., the cities of refuge are in the
possession of the Levites. The amnesty at the death of the High Priest seems to be a late
priestly innovation, replacing the role previously played by the king. See on this last topic
M. Noth, *Numbers, A Commentary*, The Old Testament Library, transl. J. D. Martin
(Philadelphia, 1968), p. 255.

[52] There is an interesting quotation in B. T. Sanhedrin 45b: דתניא גאל הדם הוא ימית
את הרצח מצוה בגואל הדם "We have learned: [It is written in Num. 35: 19] 'The
avenger of blood shall put the murderer to death'; it is a command that the blood avenger
[should do this]."

[53] A similar symbolic act might be behind the command גדלים תעשה לך על ארבע
כנפות כסותך "Make tassels on the four corners of your cloak that you wear [Deut. 22:
12]." A remarkable homily in Sifrei Num. *Pisqa* 166 s.v ויאמר states: ויאמר על כנפי
בגדיהם שומע אני אף בעלי שלש ובעלי חמש ובעלי שש ובעלי שבע ובעלי

6.4.2 Blood Rituals

Other rituals performed at the altar also demonstrate that its four corners symbolized its totality. At the purification of the altar during its consecration, when the entire altar should have been cleansed with the blood of the sin sacrifice,[54] the smearing of the blood on its "horns"/ "corners" was determined to be equivalent to an application over the entire surface. The consecration of the altar and of Aaron and his sons required the smearing of the blood with a finger, as we read in Exod. 29: 12;[55] Lev. 8: 15 and 9: 9. The same special purification had to be performed for the celebrations on the Day of Atonement, and at the offering of the sin sacrifices.[56] In these occurrences, the blood served to purify the altar from the uncleanness of all

שמנה במשמע ת״ל על ארבע כנפות כסותך יצאו בעלי שלש ובעלי חמש ובעלי שש ובעלי שבע ובעלי שמנה מן המשמע "And [God] said [to make tassels] on the corners of their garments [Num. 15: 38],' [and from that] I could understand [that this rule] also applies to garments with three, five, six, seven and eight corners, [therefore] it says 'On the four corners of your cloak [Deut. 22: 12]' to teach us that garments with three, five, six, seven and eight corners are excluded." The command to make the tassels is definitely explained in Scripture: וראיתם אתו וזכרתם את כל מצות ה' ועשיתם אתם "...to look at and so you will remember all the commands of the Lord, that you may obey them [Num. 15: 39]." The Israelite man must retain constant and total control over the lusting of his heart, eyes and total being, by looking at the tassels on the four corners of his sheltering, wrap-around cloak, a symbol of utmost totality. In Israelite culture, this totality is symbolized by the number four, and therefore only a four-cornered garment is appropriate for this requirement. Sifrei then quotes another homily on the above verse: שכל המקיים מצות ציצית מעלים עליו כאלו קיים כל המצות כולן "Everyone who performs the precept of the tassels is considered as having performed all the precepts [of the Torah]."

54 S. H. Hooke, *Babylonian and Assyrian Religion* (Oklahoma, 1963), p. 52 writes concerning such a cleansing procedure: "A *mashmashu*, or exorcist priest, together with a slaughtering priest, cut off the head of a sheep and with its carcass smeared the walls and door of the shrine, thus ceremonially wiping off any defilement on to the carcass of the sheep; then the head and carcass of the sheep were thrown into the river which carried them away together with the defilement they bore." The purification procedure in the Israelite cult had a different ideology behind it, but we observe that the cleansing in Babylonia required the smearing of the entire shrine. In Israel, the smearing on the four corners of the altar symbolized its totality.

55 The texts are similar, and I therefore quote only Lev. 8: 15, a reiteration of the Exod. 29: 12 pericope, in which the purification of the altar is explicitly stated: וישחט ויקח משה את הדם ויתן על קרנות המזבח סביב באצבעו ויחטא את המזבח ואת הדם יצק אל יסוד המזבח ויקדשהו לכפר עליו "Moses slaughtered the bull and took some of the blood, and with his finger he put it on all the horns of the altar to purify the altar."

56 Philo in *The Special Laws*, I: 231 explains the smearing of the blood on the four corners at the High Priest's sin offering as τετράγωνον γάρ ἐστι, "corresponding to its four sides."

the people on the day of Atonement,[57] or from the sins of each individual who transgressed the law;[58] sin profaned the altar, which thus had to be cleansed, and Scripture uses the terms כפר and חטא[59] on these occasions. This particular act of purification required the scrupulous and precise smearing of the altar with blood, rather than the random sprinkling of blood[60] performed at the עולה and שלמים. We must also consider that these cult celebrations are considered to be of late origin, after the institution of the sin-offering.[61] Hence these occurrences do not serve as evidence for the existence of altar "horns" in the First Temple period.

Further evidence that a blood celebration at the corners or some other significant element of an entity was considered a symbolic purification of the whole is encountered in Ezekiel. We read in 43: 20 concerning the altar: ולקחת מדמו ונתתה על ארבע קרנותיו ואל ארבע פנות העזרה ואל הגבול סביב וחטאת אותו וכפרתהו "You are to take some of its [the sin offering's]

---

[57] There are two verses concerning this specific performance, Exod. 30: 10 and Lev. 16: 18, the second of which I quote here: ויצא אל המזבח אשר לפני ה' וכפר עליו ולקח מדם הפר ומדם השעיר ונתן על קרנות המזבח סביב "Then he shall come out to the altar that is before the Lord and make atonement for it. He shall take some of the bull's blood and some of the goat's blood and put it on all the horns of the altar." Concerning the issue of whether both verses refer to the same altar, or Lev. 16: 18 concerns the holocaust altar and Exod. 30: 10 the incense altar, see Heger, *Incense*, p. 232, n. 140.

[58] Lev. 4: 7, 18, 25, 30 and 34. In all these occurrences the blood must be smeared on the "horns"/ "corners" of the altar, and the term כפר is used for the atonement procedure.

[59] It is not within the scope of this essay to delve into the meaning of the term כפר in other ancient Semitic languages. Cf. B. Levine, כיפורים, *Eretz Israel* 9 (1969), pp. 88-95.

[60] In all occurrences the smearing of the blood renders the blood sprinkling unnecessary, except at the celebration on the Day of Atonement; on that occasion a sprinkling is also required, as we read in Lev. 16: 19. K. Elliger, *Leviticus,* Handbuch zum Alten Testament, Erste Reihe 4 (Tübingen, 1966), p. 214, attempts to resolve this particular double act of cleansing, that is, both the smearing of blood on the horns and the sprinkling of blood on the altar. A homily in Sifra ד פרשה מות אחרי elaborates on the subsequent verse 20: וכלה מכפר את הקדש זה לפניי ולפנים את אהל מועד זה היכל המזבח זה המזבח "'When [Aaron] has finished making atonement for the Holy Place,' this refers to the Holy of Holies; 'the Tent of Meeting' refers to the *heikhal*; and 'the altar' refers to the altar." The traditional commentator Ramban states on this homily that each of the various sprinklings cited in the previous verses in Lev. refers to a separate purification. It is therefore implicit that the sprinkling on the altar, in addition to the smearing of its corners, concerns the purification of the Tent of Meeting. We shall see in the text that Ezekiel had another method of symbolically purifying the entire Temple, the successor to the Tent of Meeting. Scripture does not specify in Lev. 16: 19 where the blood has to be sprinkled, stating only עליו והזה "He shall sprinkle on it"; Rashi deduces from the term עליו "upon it" that it should be sprinkled on the top of the altar.

[61] See R. Rendtorff, *Studien zur Geschichte des Opfers im Alten Israel*, Wissenschaftliche Monographien zum Alten und Neuen Testament (Neukirchen, 1967), pp. 34ff. and 199.

blood and put it on the four horns of the altar and on the four corners of the upper ledge and all around the rim, and so purify the altar and make atonement for it." Ezekiel considered the hearth, the אריאל, as a separate holy entity,[62] and therefore the upper ledge had to be purified separately.[63] With respect to the גבול, the base or the foundation of the altar, the extremities were likely not visible, and therefore the purification had to be performed "all around" instead of on the corners. We may thus argue that the cleansing of the corners, whenever feasible, equaled the purification of the whole. Yet stronger support for this thesis may be deduced from the procedure for the purification of the Temple and its inner court described in Ezek. 45: 19 and 20: ולקח הכהן מדם החטאת ונתן אל מזוזת הבית ואל ארבע פנות העזרה למזבח ועל מזוזת שער החצר הפנימית. וכן תעשה בשבעה בחדש מאיש שגה ומפתי וכפרתם את הבית "The priest is to take some of the blood of the sin offering and put it on the doorposts of the Temple, on the four corners of the upper ledge of the altar and on the gateposts of the inner court. You are to do the same on the seventh day of the month for anyone who sins unintentionally or through ignorance; so you are to make atonement for the Temple." We observe here two significant concepts: first, that the sin of man affects the purity of the Temple, which must be cleansed by the blood of the sin sacrifice, and second, that the blood applied to significant elements or parts of the Temple, such as the doorposts, or the corners of the altar's ledge (not its "horns"/ "corners"), served to purify the entire Temple, its furnishings and its court. In both ancient times[64] and modern[65] a symbolic action is often performed to signify the legal and factual completion of a transaction. The grasping of the "horns, the four extremities" of the altar, symbolized the entrance into the Deity's dwelling for the purpose of shelter, and the blood rite on the altar's corners or the Temple's doorposts symbolized the purification of the entire structure.

---

[62] In the pentateuchal Laws of the Altar, there are no specific names for each of the altar's elements, as the altar is perceived as one entity; Ezekiel stresses the significance of its parts.

[63] Zimmerli, *Ezekiel 2, A Commentary*, p. 433, in his exegesis of this verse offers another solution for this triple purification process. He writes: "In this application of blood to the top, the middle and the foot of the altar one can easily recognize a certain analogy with the application of the blood of the 'ram of ordination' to the lobe of the right ear, the thumb of the right hand and the big toe of the right foot at the consecration of the Aaronites (Lev. 8: 22f)."

[64] For example, a servant who does not want to be freed after seven years has his ear pierced at the doorpost (Exod. 21: 6).

[65] For example, the transfer of the key of a house completes the transfer of ownership.

6.4.3 Four Corners as a Symbol of Totality

We may return to the issue of the shelter-seeking Adonijah and Joab, and interpret their actions and the reference to the "horns" in light of the above hypothesis. We may assume that there is no particular significance for the קרנות,[66] and that Scripture in Kings simply recorded a trivial detail, or that the term קרנות is a later interjection to harmonize the primary text with the post-exilic structure of the altar that had some kind of projections on its four corners, and with the pentateuchal P text. Let us proceed with the textual analysis of the relevant verses. We must first recollect the significant fact that in the early Book of the Covenant in Exod. 21: 14, there is no mention of touching "horns" or "corners" to attain a safe haven at the altar; we read there: מעם מזבחי תקחנו למות "Take him away from my altar and put him to death."[67] There were no "horns" at these early altars commanded in the Book of the Covenant. Nor was it technically possible to make such "horns"

---

[66] In fact, the Rabbis contend that Joab was mistaken in assuming that the "horns" offer refuge, since only the "top" of the altar bestows this privilege. We read in B. T. Makoth 12a: אמר רב יהודה אמר רב שתי טעיות טעה יואב באותה שעה דכתיב וינס יואב אל אהל ה׳ ויחזק בקרנות המזבח טעה שאינו קולט אלא גגו והוא תפס בקרנותיו טעה אינו קולט אלא מזבח בית עולמים והוא תפס מזבח של שילה אביי אומר בהא נמי מיטעא טעה טעה שאינו קולט אלא כהן ועבודה בידו והוא זר היה "Said Rav Judah in the name of Rav: Joab made two errors on that occasion, as it is written 'And Joab fled to the tent of the Lord and took hold of the horns of the altar [I Kings 2: 28]'; he erred because he took hold of the horns, but only the top [of the altar] offers refuge, and [his second] error was that only the altar of the Temple offers refuge, but he grasped the altar of Shilo. Abaye says: He erred also in this, that the altar offers refuge only to a priest and Joab was a layman." The following note elaborates upon Abaye's statement.

[67] The Rabbis had difficulty harmonizing this command with the prohibition against a layman touching the altar. They therefore interpreted this verse as referring to a priest, and we find two different interpretations. In B. T. Yoma 85a we read מעם מזבחי תקחנו למות מעם מזבחי ולא מעל מזבחי ואמר רבה בר בר חנה אמר רבי יוחנן לא שנו אלא להמית אבל להחיות אפילו מעל מזבחי "[Rabbi Akiba said: It is written]'Take him from [the side of] my altar' [before he started the sacrificial celebration], but not from on [top of] my altar [in the middle of the celebration]. And Rabbah bar bar Hana said in the name of Rabbi Johanan, that [this distinction] applies only [in the event of a priest who must go to court to testify against a murderer] to execute him, but [if the priest must testify in favour of an accused in order] to save him from a wrongful execution [then he may even interrupt his celebration] and [the priest] may be taken down from the top of the altar." A straightforward interpretation, but still referring to priests, is found in Mekhilta d'Rabbi Ishmael Mishpatim Parshah 4: מעם מזבחי תקחנו למות מגיד שמבטלים העבודה מידו ויוצא ליהרג "[It is written] 'Take him from my altar...,' to assert that one cancels the celebration at the altar [of a priest who committed a murder] and executes him."

on altars constructed of earth or stones in their natural form. The various *ad hoc* altars mentioned in the Bible,[68] including those which, from the context, certainly subsisted as local shrines, evidently had no "horns." Nor were horns an essential part of the procedure for attaining refuge, or for the slaughtering of offerings.

We must observe the phrasing used in both narratives to record the events occurring after the grasping of "the horns of the altar" by Adonijah and Joab. In I Kings 1: 50 we read that Adonijah took hold of the horns of the altar, ויחזק בקרנות המזבח. In v. 51, it is stated that Solomon was told that Adonijah אחז בקרנות המזבח, "[was] clinging to the horns of the altar,"[69] but in v. 53, at the conclusion of the affair, we read ויורדהו מעל המזבח "And they brought him down from the altar." We discover that Adonijah had climbed for shelter onto the top of the altar, from which he was taken down,[70] and the "horns" are entirely omitted; it was not the horns that offered shelter, but the top of the altar. The text in I Kings 2: 28 - 34 is yet more inconsistent. In v. 28 we read וינס יואב אל אהל ה׳ ויחזק בקרנות המזבח "And Joab fled to the tent of the Lord and took hold of the horns of the altar," but in v. 29 we read that Solomon was told כי נס יואב אל אהל ה׳ והנה אצל המזבח "Joab fled to the tent of the Lord and was beside the altar." From this text, we may deduce that it was the tent of the Lord that Joab believed would offer him shelter. He first grasped the horns, but this specific act seems not to have had significance in the granting of refuge, since it was not told to Solomon; rather, it was the fact that Joab was in the tent standing near the altar that seems to have been the appropriate formality to gain shelter.

The narrative offers no indication as to where Joab was ultimately killed by Benaiah: in the tent, on the altar, or outside the tent. In the latter case, we might assume that while Solomon did not grant Joab the immunity of the altar, he would not have allowed Benaiah to profane the sanctuary by killing a person inside it. Scripture states in Exod. 21: 14 מעם מזבחי תקחנו למות "Take him <u>away</u> from my altar and put him to death"; the altar does not offer shelter to the perpetrator of a premeditated murder, but he should not be executed there. The fact that in both the occurrences in Kings the "horns" of the altar appear in the first part of the narrative but disappear in the second,

---

[68] I have quoted the relevant citations in the latter part of section 1.3.

[69] The KJV translates more precisely: "He hath caught hold on the horns of the altar."

[70] M. Noth, *Könige*, Biblischer Kommentar, Altes Testament, IX/1 (Neukirchen, 1968), p. 29, assumes that the sanctuary was located on a site higher than the king's dwelling: "Das Heiligtum lag danach höher als der königliche Wohnsitz." However, the text specifically states that Joab was taken down from the altar, not from the tent; though the tent is mentioned at the Joab episode, it is not mentioned in the Adonijah narrative.

more significant, part of the action, seems to indicate that the term קרנות was a later interjection with a harmonizing intent, as suggested above.[71]

Before closing this argument on the Kings narrative, I would like to draw attention to the fact that we have here two unusual cases of shelter-seekers; these were not common murderers, but perpetrators of politically motivated executions. Both the behaviour of the hunted persons and that of the king who intended to dispose of them may, but need not necessarily, bear witness to the actual procedures for common people and unintentional killers.

6.5 Archeological Evidence

The archeological findings of altars in Israel confirm the thesis that the projections on the four corners of the altars had no similarity whatsoever to bull horns. According to Scripture there were altars of earth, natural stones, and also hewn but perfect stones, the latter confirmed by the altars at Beer Sheba[72] and certain other sites. It is obvious that we cannot expect to find identifiable altars made of earth;[73] stone altars of unhewn stones were found, for example in Tel Arad,[74] a site amply described by archeologists.[75] The

---

[71]   I may note that the LXX has a different text of I Kings 2: 28 ff.; the term "horns" appears in both v. 28 and v. 29, though it is missing in the MT version of the latter. It seems that the LXX editors attempted to amend their available text and improve both its style and substance. There is an interesting passage in this additional text: Solomon sends a messenger to ask Joab why he ran away to the "altar" θυσιαστήριον, but Joab answers that he fled "to the Lord" ἔφυγον πρὸς κύριον, not to the altar or the horns. The MT text in the Joab narrative stresses the sanctuary as the principal locus of refuge, but omits this in the Adonijah narrative. Noth, Könige, p. 28 quotes a Septuagint MS in which the same phrase, εἰς τὴν σκηνὴν τοῦ κυρίου "to the tent of the Lord," is added to emphasize that Adonijah, like Joab, fled to the authentic protector, the sanctuary.

[72]   For our purposes, it is of no significance whether the sanctuary in Beer Sheba was a temple, as Aharoni asserts, or a bamah, as Yadin maintains (see previous discussion concerning this issue, chap. 2 n. 116 and section 4.2). The rule to build altars with "horns" was decreed to ensure a legal status for a common custom, and we may assume that the pattern of the altars was the same for both temples and bamoth.

[73]   Cf. F. J. Stendebach, "Altarformen im Kanaanäisch-israelitischen Raum," Biblische Zeitschrift 20 (1976), pp. 180 - 196, regarding the speculation that certain remnants of mud-brick constructions might have been such altars (pp. 180-1).

[74]   In Stratum X, from the 9th century B.C.E. See Ze'ev Herzog et al., "The Israelite Fortress at Arad," BASOR 254 (1984), pp. 1-34, on p. 4.

[75]   Stendebach attempts to classify this altar as an earthen altar, since it is constructed of stones and mortar. Herzog, p. 11, states that the altar "was made of unworked stones laid in mud mortar. On top of it was placed a large flint slab with plastered channels." According to Stendebach, the slab was "glatt behauen," that is, smoothly trimmed; this description is confirmed by the photos. I must reiterate my previous observation that

absence of "horns" on the large altar at Tel Arad, presumably serving for burnt offerings,[76] cannot serve as incontrovertible evidence that there were no forms of projections on the corners of such altars.[77] I wish only to reiterate that such projections, if they existed, could not symbolize "horns", for technical reasons. There were also found in the presumed "Holy of Holies" at Tel Arad two well-finished stone altars.[78] Aharoni does not question why these altars were made of hewn stones, in contrast to the natural fieldstones of the big altar "in accordance with biblical law (Exod. 20: 25 etc.[KJV])." While Aharoni states that "on their concave surfaces were found the charred remains of some organic material, evidently the last burnt offerings," Herzog assumes that they were incense altars;[79] even in the latter case, the prohibition against using hewn stones would have applied to both altar types, if this limitation were still in force. Neither Aharoni nor Herzog states explicitly that these altars had no "horns", but from the pictures this is evident. Zwickel confirms this fact and describes the altars as "die beiden hörnerlosen Räucheraltäre," the two incense altars without horns. Hence we have at one site of the same period, Stratum X, an altar of unhewn stones,

---

archeology cannot always solve problems of textual uncertainties. Yadin attacked Aharoni's identification of the site in Beer Sheba as a temple, because the altar was made of hewn stones, in contrast to the Tel Arad altar, which was made of natural, unhewn stones. The existence of the smooth slab is in fact an obstacle to those who attempt to grant archeology a decisive voice in cult issues. I may quote here a passage from a seminal essay by the noted archeologist W. G. Dever, "Will the Real Israel Please Stand Up?" *BASOR* 297 (1995), pp. 61-80. He writes on pp. 72ff.: "No one would argue more forcefully than I that archeology cannot be used to 'prove the Bible.' Nevertheless, there are a number of points at which datable Iron Age archeological evidence and literary references in the Bible do 'converge' in such a way as to suggest contemporaneity - a fact that responsible historians cannot deny."

[76] Niels H. Gadegaard, "On the So-Called Burnt Offering Altar in the Old Testament," *PEQ* 110 (1978), pp. 35-45, asserts on p. 39 that the flint on top of the altar could not withstand the heat of a fire; after stating: "It is very improbable that the Tell Arad altar has ever been a burnt offering altar," he concludes positively: "There has never been a fire upon the altar at Tell Arad."

[77] Herzog, p. 11, writes: "It is impossible to determine whether or not there were horns at the corners of this altar, as on the ashlar altar at Beersheba; perhaps they were fashioned from clay or wood and thus not preserved." This statement has not been thought through. If Herzog assumes the altar was fashioned in accordance with the biblical rule in Exod. 27: 2, he should have noted that the second part of the verse specifically requires ממנו תהיין קרנתיו "so that the horns [and the altar] are of one piece," rather than an altar of stones with "horns" made of a different material such as clay or wood. He also did not question how wooden "horns" on top of an altar on which offerings were burned (on a metal rack, in Herzog's view) could withstand the fire.

[78] Y. Aharoni, "Arad: Its Description and Temple," *The Biblical Archeologist* 31 (1968), pp. 2-32, on p. 19 and p. 20, fig. 13.

[79] Ibid., p. 22.

most probably without horns, and two altars of hewn stones, certainly without horns. Herzog records that a "ceramic incense stand" was also found in this Stratum;[80] Aharoni states:[81] "Fragments of a smashed incense burner of clay were found." These clay incense burners, many of which were found at other sites, have no corners or horns, and thus we must conclude that the "horns" were of no significance in the cult practices at this site.

There is no question that altars with "horns" were found at Beer Sheba and other archeological sites. The cornerstones of the Beer Sheba altar are similar to the pointed forms of the elevated extremities of the small incense altars found in Meggido,[82] but they are far from revealing bull's horns. On this evidence, I would like to quote from an article by E. Stern[83] in which the author describes the four limestone incense altars found at Beer Sheba: "two of the altars are characteristic of the Late Iron Age, the third is of the Persian period, and the fourth belongs to the Hellenistic period." With respect to the two Iron Age altars, which have no horns,[84] he concludes that similar incense altars "were exceedingly common in Assyria at that time; they had already been introduced into Israel during the Late Iron Age....It now seems that they replaced the well-known 'four horned' type." According to this last statement, it would appear that there were "horned altars" in the Israelite cult at an early period, corresponding to the era of the Book of the Covenant, in which no "horns" are mentioned; these were replaced by altars without "horns" in the later period, when such altars clearly emerge in the writings of Ezekiel, in the P segment of the Pentateuch, and in the historical evidence attesting to the presence of horns on the altar of the Second Temple.

6.6 Conclusion

The idea of "horns" as suggestive of bull's horns is not substantiated either from the textual evidence or from the archeological findings. I suspect that if it were not for the occurrence of the term קרנות in the biblical texts with

---

[80] Ibid., p. 11.

[81] Ibid., p. 19.

[82] See the photographs of both the Beer Sheba and Meggido altars in Alpert Nakhai, *BAR* 20/3 (May/June 1994), pp. 18-29, 77-8, on p. 28.

[83] E. Stern, "Limestone Incense Altars," in *Beer Sheba I. Excavations at Tel Beer Sheba 1969-1971 Season*, ed. Y. Aharoni (Tel Aviv, 1973), pp. 52-53.

[84] With respect to the description of the first, he writes: "Its upper cavity has been hollowed in the shape of a square with rounded corners," and for the second, he states: "The cavity in its centre is square; the sides slant inwards." These descriptions would completely preclude the existence of a "horned" altar.

reference to the altar, the archeological findings would not have suggested an identification of the raised extremities as "horns", and scholars would not have required a theological explanation for them. I believe I have put into question the philological certitude of this identification. It is evident from the textual analysis that in the early Israelite period the form and structure of the altars were of no significance; the altars of the period either had no horns or other projections, or the projections, if they existed, had no theological basis. If "horns" had been part of some meaningful pattern, one may assume that they would have been installed on all altars, and there would have been some reference to them in the numerous biblical narratives on the construction of altars and offerings, outside the P segment of the Pentateuch.

One may also wonder at the lack of any justification for the "horns" of the altar, if they had theological or cult significance. Although Scripture contains a broad range of aetiological justifications for almost every imaginable name[85] or custom [86] in order to justify their theological import, it proffers no hint of an explanation for this supposedly "meaningful" element of the altar and the cult. I therefore conclude that the projections on the altar were simply a fashion, with no significant theological association other than a consideration that the four corners represented the whole, a common metaphor in Israelite thought. The sophistication apparently introduced into the Israelite cult by Ahaz in the late monarchic period (as it seems from II Kings 16) probably influenced the later custom of the blood ritual on the four stylized projections on the altar's extremities. If the Israelites copied this fashion from another culture, I suggest that they took over only the external appearance without any associated theological concepts.

The four corners might also have been a remnant of the former rim and molding, מסגרת and זר, of the table - altar. We observe from Exod. 25: 25 and 37: 12 that the table had these two useful accessories, while the small golden altar had only the molding;[87] the bronze altar in Exod. 27: 1 - 8 had neither the rim nor the decorative molding. I shall elaborate in section 7.2.3 on the linkage between the table and the altar, but we may note here the equivalence between these two items in Ezekiel 41: 22.[88] The table-altar described by Ezekiel has an odd characteristic, מקצעותיו; the exact

---

[85] For instance, the names of the tribes; the names of sanctuaries such as Beth El, whose construction was retrojected to Jacob.

[86] For instance, certain festival practices, such as the eating of unleavened bread or the use of tabernacles; the prohibition against eating the tendon of the hip, גיד הנשה.

[87] The ark also had a gold molding (Exod. 25: 11).

[88] We read there: המזבח עץ... זה השלחן אשר לפני ה' "There was a wooden altar...This is the table that is before the Lord."

interpretation of this term both here and in Exod. 26: 23ff is not clear.[89]
Ezekiel may refer to a rim or a molding, as the LXX translates מקצעותיו
there as κέρατα "horns", the term it uses for קרנתיו in Exod. 27: 2 with
respect to the bronze altar; in contrast, מקצעת in Exod. 26: 23ff. is translated
as γωνιῶν "corners" with respect to the frames of the Tabernacle. We should
not wonder at this interpretation, since, as I noted in section 5: 3 that the
LXX adds a surrounding molding, στέφανος to the bronze altar in the
translation of Exod. 27: 3, the same component as is provided for the table
and the golden altar. The rim or molding was necessary for the small
presentation table (the presumed model for the portable bronze altar, similar
to the Assyrian archetype[90]), in order to prevent the food set upon it from
falling off; this became superfluous when the table was replaced with the big
stone altar for burnt offerings. It would also create practical problems for the
priests, who now had the task of arranging the wood and the large animal
parts on the altar to ensure the proper burning of the offerings. In order to
maintain some remnant and semblance of the rim of the discarded table-altar,
four projections were constructed on the four corners.

---

[89] See M. Noth, *Exodus*, p. 212. This term, from the root קצע, appears in two forms, as a
verb "to scrape" in Lev. 14: 41, and as a noun. The noun can mean "a plane", but in some
occurrences it is clear that the term expresses "extremities"or "corners", as in Neh. 3: 20,
24 and 25, and in II Chr. 26: 9. In Exod. 26:23ff. the term is translated by Onkelos as
זוית "corner", also used by Jonathan in Ezek. 41: 22 and 46: 21. Rashi in Exod. 26 does
not translate the term, but one may understand from the context that he considered it to be
"corners". On the other hand, he is hard put to find a reasonable solution for the term in
Ezek. 41: 22 in the context and offers a very unclear explanation. In B. T. Menahoth 97a,
Rashi states that it means "square", since there is no width for the table-altar indicated by
Ezekiel. The KJV and NIV translate the term מקצעת in these occurrences in Exod. and
Ezek. as "corners", but the LXX has in Ezek. 46: 21 two terms: μέρη "parts" and κλίτος
"slope". The LXX has, as we observe, three different terms for each of the three
occurrences.

[90] K. Galling, *Der Altar in den Kulturen des Alten Orients* (Berlin, 1925), describes the
portable Assyrian tin altar as square with adornments on top (p. 45). According to
Galling, these altars were used in wartime, carried by the troops (p. 42).

7. The Bronze Altar - Real or Fictional?

Minute textual analysis of the bronze altar ordinance in Exod. 27 and comparison of this law with the two earlier[1] altar laws in Exod. 20 and Deut. 27 have provoked a great degree of skepticism concerning the reality of the bronze altar. Since the initiation of Bible criticism, the scholarly world has assumed that the description of the desert sanctuary represents a late retrojection with the purpose of attributing to Moses contemporary cult practice. I wish to focus my inquiry on the question of whether such an altar ever actually existed, and if so, its likely function. A great number of biblical narratives can be interpreted to suggest that such an altar never existed; on the other hand, there is specific mention of this altar in a number of occurrences.

7.1 Evidence Against the Existence of a Bronze Altar

I shall first proceed with an examination of the arguments against the existence of such an altar, and then discuss the bronze altar of Ahaz. Although we find in I Kings 7 a detailed description of various bronze objects, prepared by Solomon, including furnishings and even specific altar accessories such as sprinkling bowls, no bronze altar is mentioned among them. Nor do we find such an altar in the list of the bronze objects of the Temple seized by Nebuzaradan and carried away to Babylon (II Kings 25: 13 - 17), or in the parallel list of the looted bronze objects enumerated in Jer. 52: 17 - 23. This oddity has been observed by scholars,[2] but I wish to add several further observations.

---

[1]   The altar law in Exod. 20 in the Book of the Covenant is recognized as one of the earliest elements of the Pentateuch. It is not within the scope of this study to deliberate on the complex issue of the relative dating of the deuteronomic and priestly segments of the Bible, but it seems to me that from an examination of the altar laws one must concede that the bronze altar decree, like the entire section concerning the construction of the desert Tabernacle and its furnishings, is of a later date than the deuteronomic stone altar described in chap. 27.

[2]   See my explanation of this apparent oddity in section 7.2.4. It is doubtful whether this oddity may serve as effective evidence for the thesis that there was no such altar in the Temple.

7.1.1 What Was the Function of the Bronze Altar?

It is remarkable that the law of the bronze altar in Exod. 27: 1 - 8 states neither a purpose for this altar nor its name, מזבח העלה, the holocaust altar.[3] This is in contrast to the Tabernacle itself, whose purpose is stated as ועשו לי מקדש ושכנתי בתוכם "Have them make a sanctuary for me, and I will dwell among them [Exod. 25: 8]," and to all its other furnishings, whose purposes are indicated along with the commands to construct them: the ark (25: 16), the *kaporeth* (25: 21 - 2), the table (25: 30), the lamp (25: 37), the curtains (26: 13), the hides (26: 14), the frames of the Tabernacle and various accessories (26: 15 - 30), the dividing curtain (26: 33), and the entrance curtain (26: 36). Further, the precise use of the priestly garments is indicated (28: 2), as well as those of the Ephod (28: 12), the breastplate (28: 30), the bells (28: 35), the headpiece (28: 38), and undergarments (28: 43). The function of the incense altar is similarly indicated in 30: 7, as well as that of the laver in 30: 19 and the spices in 30: 26 - 28 and 30: 36. We note also that defined purposes are set out for the earthen and stone altars in Exod. 20: 21 (וזבחת עליו) and Deut. 27: 6 (והעלית עליו עלות), a fact that accentuates the mysterious absence of purpose for the bronze altar.

Another oddity is that the term מזבח הנחשת appears only twice in the Pentateuch, in the record of the quantities of materials used for the production of the various furnishings (Exod. 38: 30),[4] and in the list of the fixtures brought to Moses (Exod. 39: 39).[5] There is no mention of the term at all in Leviticus, though the altar's use as the site for burning sacrifices is described. The term reappears only in Kings, in the ambiguous passages regarding Solomon's dedication of the courtyard for the performance of sacrifices in I Kings 8: 64, and Ahaz' displacement of this altar in I Kings 16: 14 - 15. The term is mentioned once in Ezek. 9: 2; there is no indication here of its use, and it is the permanent altar, presumably of stone, which is intended for the burning of sacrifices, as described in chap. 43. The altar reappears again in Chronicles, and this use will now be examined.

---

[3] This term appears seven times in Exod., starting with the altar's anointing in 30: 28.

[4] The variations in the LXX text of these records is well known, and it is remarkable that in the LXX parallel in Exod. 39: 6 - 9, listing the bronze items, the term θυσιαστήριον τὸ χαλκοῦν does not appear. It does appear, however, in 38: 22 in the record of the production of these items, though it is missing in the parallel passage in the MT.

[5] In the parallel LXX text, Exod. 39: 13 - 23, the holocaust altar is entirely missing.

7.1.2 The Bronze Altar in Chronicles

The Chronicles editor(s) attempted to remedy this absence, recording in II Chr. 4: 1 a brief mention of the altar: ויעש מזבח נחשת עשרים אמה ארכו ועשרים אמה רחבו ועשר אמות קומתו "He made a bronze altar twenty cubits long, twenty cubits wide and ten cubits high." This attempted solution is unsuccessful; on the contrary, it provokes further controversy. First, it provides no technical details except the altar's dimensions. Did this altar, for instance, have characteristics similar to the "presumed" altar of Moses - hollow, with a grating on top, and a מכבר placed under its כרכב - or had it a solid top, similar to the golden incense altar? Where would the priests have stood? On a structure as high as ten cubits[6] they would have had to stand on the top, yet the heat conducted by the bronze metal would have been unbearable. How would the priests have climbed up the altar, considering the prohibition in Exod. 20: 23 against "going up on steps"? Had the altar "horns" and poles like the portable desert altar, or had these already been abolished? This last question leads to another: what was Solomon's motive (at least as assumed by the Chronicles editor) in building a bronze altar? If he were driven to carry out God's command in Exod. 27, the altar should have retained its original form and dimension; God's decree is eternal concerning the form and size of the altar, as in all other rules of the cult.[7] If the point was

---

[6] The altar of Moses was three cubits high, and one could imagine that the priests stood on the ground and from there managed to perform the celebrations on the altar's grating.

[7] This issue disturbed the Rabbis; we read in B. T. Sanhedrin 16b אמר רב שימי בר חייא אמר קרא ככל אשר אני מראה אותך את תבנית המשכן ואת תבנית כל כליו וכן תעשו לדורות הבאין "Said Rav Shimi son of Hiya: Scripture says [Exod. 25: 9] 'Make this Tabernacle and all its furnishings exactly like the pattern I will show you' - [the phrase וכן תעשו allows the interpretation] in the next generations." Rashi stresses explicitly in his commentary to Exod. 25: 9 וכן תעשו - לדורות אם יאבד אחד מן הכלים או כשתעשו לי כלי בית עולמים כגון שולחנות ומנורות וכיורות ומכונות שעשה שלמה כתבנית אלו תעשו אותם "'And so you shall make' - forever, if one of the furnishings is lost, or when you make furnishings for the Temple such as the tables, lampstands, basins and stands that Solomon made, you should make them like these models." It seems that Rashi is careful not to mention here the bronze altar, since he is aware that Solomon made a larger altar, as is recorded in II Chr. 4: 1; but the controversy still remains unsolved. The Rabbis were also aware that the altar in the Second Temple period was made of stone and not of bronze, as it ought to have been according to this command, and therefore we read another homily in Mekhilta d'Rabbi Ishmael, Jethro, *Parshah* 11, ד"ה ואם מזבח which attempts to reconcile this apparent contradiction: ומה ת"ל ואם מזבח אבנים אלא רצה לעשות של אבנים יעשה של לבנים יעשה "What does the phrase 'and [if you make] an altar of stones' [Exod. 20: 22] teach us? Its purpose is [to instruct us that] if he wishes to make a stone altar, or a brick altar, he may [do so]." There is thus permission to build the altar of different

that an altar of bronze, unlike one of earth or even of stone, would endure for a long period, one might posit that Solomon ought to have used the altar made by Moses in the desert, just as he retained the ark.[8]

It is remarkable that neither Kings nor Chr. indicates the dimensions of those Temple furnishings made by Solomon which have their parallel in Exod. as part of the Tabernacle's equipment; in stark contrast, there is a precise description, with much detail as to structure and dimension, of all the new furnishings created for the Temple.[9] We therefore have no evidence as to whether the tables and the other furnishings made by Solomon were of the same dimensions as those commanded in Exodus for the Tabernacle furnishings. There is, however, explicit evidence that the table of the Second Temple had the same dimensions as indicated in Exod. 25: 23 for the table of the Tabernacle. We read in the *Letter of Aristeas* 52 - 59 the deliberations concerning the size of the table to be built for the Temple and the king's hesitation to create a table bigger than that indicated in Scripture; the king did make some aesthetic modifications with respect to elements not indicated in Scripture,[10] but left the size unaltered: two cubits by one cubit and one and

---

    materials, as Scripture itself allows the building of altars of earth and stone, but we do not find any authorization to change its size.

[8] It is remarkable that Rashi asks the same question regarding the golden incense altar. Since the traditional commentators interpret ויצף מזבח ארז "He overlaid the altar of cedar" in I Kings 6: 20 as referring to the incense altar, Rashi asks הוא מזבח הקטרת ותמיה אני ושל משה למה נגנז "This is the incense altar, and I wonder why Moses' altar was hidden [disposed of]."

[9] The strict adherence to this method of avoiding any contradiction between the sizes of the two classes of furnishings is remarkable, and one is tempted to assume that the editing was performed carefully to reach this objective. For our purpose it is of no significance to postulate by whom and when this co-ordinated editorial effort was performed. The כיור "basin" whose dimensions, in contrast to the other furnishings, are not indicated in Exod. 30: 18, is amply described with exact dimensions in I Kings 7: 38 - 39. The כפרת "ark's cover", whose dimensions are indicated in Exod. 25: 17, was not fashioned by Solomon; the כרבים cherubim, which were made by Solomon, have specific dimensions indicated in I Kings 6: 24 - 28 but none in Exod. 25: 19- 20. The Rabbis were even more sensitive to this issue, and we encounter an interesting observation in Y. T. Sabbath, 1: 5, 2d: תנא רבי חנניה בר שמואל כל הכלים שהיו במקדש נתנה התורה מידת ארכו ורוחבו ונתנה שיעור קומתן חוץ מן הכפורת שנתנה התורה מידת אורכה ורחבה ולא נתנה שיעור' קומת' "Rabbi Hananiah son of Samuel taught: The Torah indicated the length, width and height of all the furnishings which were in the Temple, except the ark's cover for which the Torah indicated only its length and width and did not give us its height." Any indication of its height might have conflicted with the size of Solomon's cherubim which were ten cubits high (I Kings 6: 26).

[10] We read there: "Hence the correct measure must neither be deviated from nor surpassed. But as for the diversity in artistic ingenuity, he ordered that it be applied in lavish

one-half cubits high. We observe that it was axiomatic[11] that cult furnishings of the Temple were to be of the same dimensions as those made by Moses, and we must assume that the incense altar of the Second Temple had the dimensions indicated in Exod. 30: 2.[12] The altar for burnt sacrifices was, exceptionally and for indeterminate reasons, made of stone and not of bronze like Moses' altar. I shall revert to this perplexing exception, and simply note here the anomaly created by the above-cited interjection by Chronicles concerning a bronze altar: the verse purports to demonstrate adherence to the divine commands given to Moses concerning the cult procedure, and a continuity with the Tabernacle's furnishings, yet the change in the altar's size completely negates this attempt.[13]

In contrast to the narrative in II Kings 16, Chronicles is silent on the new altar of Ahaz and indicates no reason for the disappearance of the bronze altar and its replacement by a stone altar in the Second Temple period. A further problem is thus raised by the Chronicles text: if the Chronicles' editor(s) assumed that Solomon followed the rules of Exod. 27, copying

---

measure...And so they fashioned a table 'two cubits in length and a cubit and a half in height'": M. Hadas, trans., *Aristeas to Philocrates*, (New York, 1951).

[11] The rules for the sacrificial system do not appear to be valid only in the desert; on the contrary, one has the impression that these statutes are eternal. There is one exception concerning the supplementary offerings, the grain and libation, set out in Num. 15: 3-16 with the preamble in v. 2 כי תבאו אל ארץ מושבתיכם "After you enter the land." It seems that this contingency is due to the linkage with the following pericope in vv. 18-21 concerning the special tithes of *Terumah* and *Halah*; these are due only from the fruits of the settled farmland, as is specifically stressed in v. 19: והיה באכלכם מלחם הארץ "when you eat the food of the land."

[12] I base this contention on the scholarly postulate that this pericope represents a late interjection concerning this altar, which was constructed only in the Second Temple period; one must thus assume that its dimensions as indicated in Exod. 30: 1-5 are those of the actual model in use. See Heger, *Incense*, "Introduction".

[13] The Rabbis were well aware of this problem and as usual came up with a solution. We read in B. T. Zebahim 62a (quoted in full chap. 5 n. 2): אמר רבה בר בר חנה א״ר יוחנן שלשה נביאים עלו עמהם מן הגולה אחד שהעיד להם על המזבח ואחד שהעיד להם על מקום המזבח "Three prophets came up with them [the exiles] from the exile: one gave witness to them as to [the size of] the altar, one gave witness as to the place of the altar...." Rashi explains אחד העיד להם על המזבח שיש לו מקום להוסיף עד ששים אמה "'One gave witness as to the altar' - that one may add [to the size of the altar] up to sixty cubits." Following this prophetic permission the Rabbis taught: קרן וכבש ויסוד וריבוע מעכבין מדת ארכו ומדת רחבו ומדת קומתו אין מעכבין "The horn and the ramp and the foundation and the square form [of the altar] are absolutely required, but its length, width and height [commanded in the Torah] are not an absolute requirement." The dimensions may thus be changed, on condition that the altar is not smaller than the one made by Moses, as is subsequently elucidated by Rabbi Mani: ובלבד שלא יפחתנו ממזבח שעשה משה.

Moses' bronze altar, there is no historical explanation or theological justification for the building of a stone altar for the Second Temple. Yet another problem is the altar's identification as מזבח נחשת in the Chronicles verse. In the Pentateuchal command for the construction of the altar in Exod. 27: 1, we read ועשית את המזבח עצי שטים "Build an altar of acacia wood," and after further structural details we read in v. 2: וצפית אתו נחשת "and overlay the altar with bronze." Hence this is a wooden altar overlaid with bronze, and not a bronze altar. In Exod. 38: 1, the record of the altar's construction, its wooden structure is again stressed, and we read there ויעש את מזבח העלה עצי שטים "They built an altar of burnt offering of acacia wood." The laver, in contrast, was of bronze, as described in v. 8: ויעש את הכיור נחשת ואת כנו נחשת "They made the bronze basin and its bronze stand."[14] The usual description of this altar in the Pentateuch is the neutral מזבח העלה[15] with no indication of its material; in the rules of the sacrificial cult it is called simply מזבח.[16] We must therefore ask whether the term מזבח

---

[14] Another corroboration of the particular concern of Scripture to distinguish between the **wooden** altar overlaid with bronze and the **bronze** furnishing is encountered in Exod. 35: 16: את מזבח העלה ואת מכבר הנחשת "the altar of burnt offering and its bronze grating." On the other hand, we find two occurrences of the term מזבח הנחשת, in Exod. 38: 30 and 39: 39, but the authenticity of these two verses may be doubted; one must consider the possibility that this is a late interjection by an editor who may have intentionally used the term מזבח הנחשת in Exod. to conform with the name of this altar in II Chr. 4: 1. As is well known, the LXX text of Exod. chaps 38-39 deviates entirely from the MT text; the term מזבח הנחשת in MT 38: 30 may correspond to the LXX 39: 9 παράθεμα τὸ χαλκοῦν "an appendage of bronze," that is, the מכבר רשת נחשת מעשה (Exod. 27: 4) made entirely of bronze. It may also correspond to LXX 38: 22, in which the term θυσιαστήριον τὸ χαλκοῦν appears, but the latter verse is totally different from the MT text, and declares that this bronze altar was made from the censers of the men who took part in the Korah rebellion. This altar therefore has no relation to the מזבח עצי שטים commanded in Exod. 27: 1, and cannot serve as evidence for our purpose. The מזבח הנחשת in MT 39: 39 may correspond to LXX 39: 15, which has the generic θυσιαστήριον with no indication as to whether it refers to the burnt offering altar or to the incense altar. I would assume that the Greek term refers to the burnt offering altar, similar to the non-specific MT term המזבח that unequivocally describes this altar. See also J. W. Wevers, "The Composition of Exodus 35 to 40," in *Text History of the Greek Exodus,* Mittelung des Septuaginta Unternehmens XXI (Göttingen, 1992), pp. 117 - 146, and Heger, *Incense,* "Introduction", p. 10, regarding the authenticity of the text of these chapters with respect to the later interjection of the incense altar.

[15] Exod. 30: 28; 31: 9; 38: 1; 40: 6, 10 and 29, in addition to Exod. 35: 16 cited above.

[16] The one exception to this is found in chapter 4 of Lev. concerning the performance of the various sin offerings; these were introduced in a later period, and it was necessary to distinguish between blood celebrations on the burnt offering altar and offerings on the

נחשת used in II Chr. 4: 1, our verse, in 1: 5 - 6[17] concerning the altar in
Gibeon, and in 7: 7 regarding the inadequate size of the bronze altar,
corresponds to the מזבח עצי שטים of Exod. 27. 1 - 8.

7.1.3 Is the Bronze Altar in Chronicles Identical with that in Exodus?

In its pursuit to correct the apparent lack of any reference in Kings to an altar
made by Solomon and to harmonize this correction with Moses' altar of
Exod. 27: 1- 8, the Chr. editor (s) simply created more confusion. One such
problem is that the size of the "bronze" altar is completely inadequate to
accommodate the plethora of sacrifices offered by Solomon at the Temple's
consecration, as narrated in I Kings 8: 64 and II Chr. 7: 7. I Kings 3: 4 does
not specifically identify the altar on which Solomon offered a thousand burnt
offerings in Gibeon; we read there only על המזבח ההוא "on that altar." We
do not know how large this altar must have been to enable the burning of
such a great number of animals. I Kings 8: 64 similarly does not identify
which altar was inadequate to handle all the offerings at the Temple's
consecration, or set out its size; we read there כי מזבח הנחשת אשר לפני ה'
קטן מהכיל "because the bronze altar before the Lord was too small to hold
[the offerings]." There is therefore no basis on which to make a comparison
between the two altars or to assess the authenticity or logic of the statement
in I Kings 8: 64. Chr. on the other hand does specifically identify the altars,
and provides us with their dimensions as well as those of the bronze altar
made by Solomon, thus making possible a comparison between them.

II Chr. 1: 5 - 6 identifies the altar in Gibeon on which Solomon offered a
thousand burnt offerings as the one made by Bezalel, obviously to
demonstrate the continuity of the cult from its inception by Moses; we read in
v. 5: ומזבח הנחשת אשר עשה בצלאל בן אורי בן חור שם לפני משכן ה'
"The bronze altar that Bezalel son of Uri, the son of Hur, had made was in
Gibeon in front of the Tabernacle before the Lord." The dimensions of this
altar are well known from Exod. 27: 1: חמש אמות ארך וחמש אמות רחב

---

incense altar. Elsewhere the generic term מזבח is used in the rules for the burnt offerings
and peace offerings.
[17] In other occurrences Chr. uses the term מזבח העלה in I Chr. 6: 34; 16: 40; 21: 26, 29;
22: 1 and II Chr. 29: 18; מזבח ה' or מזבח לה' in I Chr. 21: 18, 22; II Chr. 6: 12; 8: 12;
15: 8; 29: 19, 21; 33: 16 and 35: 16; and מזבח in II Chr. 5: 12; 7: 9; 29: 27; and 32: 12
(Ravshaqeh's speech). In some instances the use in Chr. matches the term in the parallel
verse in Kings, but in many other instances Chr. emphasizes its own ideology, and has no
parallel in Kings. For example, neither David's prayer at the transfer of the ark to the
City of David (I Chr. chap. 16) or the Passover "sacrifice" in Hezekiah's period (II Chr.
chap. 29) has a parallel in Kings.

רבוע יהיה המזבח ושלש אמות קמתו "The altar is to be square, five cubits long and five cubits wide, and three cubits high." Its surface was twenty-five square cubits, on which Solomon offered a thousand burnt offerings consisting of entire sheep or oxen. Yet II Chr. 4: 1 informs us that Solomon made for the Temple a bronze altar[18] עשרים אמה ארכו ועשרים אמה רחבו "twenty cubits its length and twenty cubits its width"; this was a surface of four hundred square cubits, that is, sixteen times larger than Moses' altar in Gibeon, and this altar was inadequate for the offerings at the consecration. It is true that the number of offerings in II Chr. 7: 5 was much greater than sixteen times the offerings at Gibeon on Moses' altar (ויזבח המלך שלמה את זבח הבקר עשרים ושנים אלף וצאן מאה ועשרים אלף "Solomon offered a sacrifice of twenty-two thousand head of cattle and a hundred and twenty thousand sheep"); but we must consider that at Gibeon the entire bodies of a thousand animals had to be burned,[19] whereas on the Temple's altar only the fat of the peace offerings had to be consumed.[20] Fat is much less bulky than an entire carcass, and is melted and consumed more quickly than the time taken for flesh and bone to turn into ashes. The statement in II Chr. 7: 7 כי מזבח הנחשת אשר עשה שלמה לא יכול להכיל את העלה ואת המנחה ואת החלבים "Because the bronze altar Solomon had made could not hold the burnt offering, the grain offering, and the fat offerings" clearly distinguishes the burnt offering and the grain offering in singular, and the fat of the peace offerings in plural. The parallel quotation of this verse in I Kings 8: 64 makes the same distinction, את העלה ואת המנחה ואת חלבי השלמים; that is, the two permanent daily offerings are stated in singular[21] and the large number of peace offerings for the special occasion is stated in plural. The authenticity of the statement that the altar was inadequate, which appears with almost identical detail[22] and style in I Kings 8: 64 and II Chr. 7:

---

[18] II Chr. 7: 7: כי מזבח הנחשת אשר עשה שלמה "Because the bronze altar Solomon had made...."

[19] As we read in II Chr. 1: 6: ויעל עליו עלות אלף "he offered a thousand burnt offerings." The parallel narrative in I Kings 3: 4 concurs exactly: אלף עלות יעלה שלמה.

[20] II Chr. 7: 5, as we have seen, uses the specific terms ויזבח and זבח הבקר to denote the huge number of peace offerings, שלמים, in contrast to the term עלה used in II Chr. 1: 6 for the description of the thousand burnt offerings, עלות.

[21] It is doubtful whether the daily burnt offering and grain offering were already in practice in Solomon's period. One must bear in mind that at least this phrase concerning the daily offerings is of priestly origin, interjected later; it emphasizes the daily offerings, a priestly rule, and the increased amount of space necessary for the multitude of offerings. Cf. M. Rehm, *Das Erste Buch der Könige, Ein Kommentar* (Eichstatt, 1979). I shall revert to the issue of the origin of this entire verse; see nn. 23 and 24.

7, should therefore be doubted,[23] and we must reflect on the purpose of the editor in interpolating[24] it in both books. Solving this enigma should guide us

---

[22] As already emphasized, the origin of the altar is not specified in Kings, which simply states מזבח הנחשת אשר לפני ה' "before the Lord," whereas Chr. identifies it as the altar "Solomon had made" מזבח הנחשת אשר עשה שלמה.

[23] The Rabbis were aware of this dilemma, but since they also attempted to harmonize the size of the altar in Ezek. 43 with the altars in Kings, Chr. and Exod. 27: 1, they had a bigger problem to solve. We read in B. T. Zebahim 59b: והלא כבר נאמר אלף עולות יעלה שלמה על המזבח ההוא ואילו בבית עולמים הוא אומר ויזבח שלמה את זבח השלמים אשר זבח לה' בקר עשרים ושנים אלף וכשאתה מגיע לחשבון עולות ולמנין אמות זה גדול מזה "It is already written: 'Solomon offered [in Gibeon] one thousand burnt offerings on that altar' [I Kings 3: 4; although the homily quotes the verse in Kings, which does not identify the altar, it relies on the verse in II Chr. 1: 5 to establish its size], and [for the offerings] in the Temple it says: 'Solomon offered a sacrifice of twenty- two thousand head of cattle and a hundred and twenty thousand sheep' [I Kings 8: 63]. When you compare the number of burnt offerings and the size [the number of cubits], this one [in the Temple] is larger than the other [the one in Gibeon - that is, why was Solomon's altar not large enough to contain all the offerings, so that he had to consecrate the courtyard]." The Talmud does not go into the particulars of the mathematical equation, and so we do not know on what ratio it is based and whether it took into account the distinction between the surface required for burning the flesh and bones of the burnt offerings as opposed to the fat of the peace offerings. Rashi, whose explanation I shall quote, was apparently not concerned about this problem, but the traditional commentator Radak was aware of it and attempted to propose a solution; he suggested that in addition to the peace and grain offerings recorded in Scripture there were also burnt offerings which were not counted. He ignored the fact that in v. 64 the burnt offering and the grain offering are explicitly stated in singular, to demonstrate the distinction between this class of offerings and the peace offerings for the consecration, which are stated in plural. On the other hand, Radak's comment again confirms my postulate that the traditional commentators critically analyzed the biblical texts and were well aware of the inconsistencies and contradictions, but attempted to solve them within the dictates of their belief in the divine origin of the Torah, and hence its absolute infallibility. We may now return to Rashi, who took for granted that the hearth of Moses' altar was only one cubit square. This results from a discussion in B. T. Zebahim 62a following the declaration (see chap. 5 n. 2) that the size of the altar is not fixed, but should not be smaller than the one made by Moses: א"ר מני ובלבד שלא יפחתנו ממזבח שעשה משה וכמה אמר רב יוסף אמה "Said Rav Mani: But not less than the one made by Moses. And how much? Said Rav Joseph: One cubit." The discrepancy between this size and the dimension of five by five cubits in Exod. 27: 1 is resolved by Abaye, who declares that one square cubit was the size of the hearth. This measure is reached by subtracting from five square cubits the width of the horns, one cubit square on each side, giving three cubits; then subtracting the width of the gangway for the priests, which was one cubit wide all around, leaving one square cubit for the hearth. These dimensions correspond to those given for the Second Temple altar in Mishnah Midoth 3: 1, and can be deduced from Ezekiel's vision in Ezek. 43: 13 - 17; there is a difference of two cubits between the surface of the הראל and that of the עזרה, as between the widths of the steps. Given a size of one square cubit for the actual burning, the ratio between Moses' altar and Solomon's altar would be, according to Rashi, one square cubit to four

hundred square cubits. Hence if one could burn a thousand offerings on a one square cubit altar, one could burn four hundred thousand offerings on Solomon's altar. We need not delve into the attempts to solve this puzzle but can merely note the difficulties created by the resolve to harmonize clearly contradicting biblical quotations, and particularly in this case of the bronze altar which is extraordinarily burdened with so many irreconcilable commands and narratives.

[24] M. Noth, *Könige*, p. 191 draws our attention to the fact that I Kings 8: 5 already records the magnitude, though without indicating the exact number, of the offerings made by Solomon and the people at the occasion of the Temple's consecration. Hence, I Kings 8: 64 refers back to v. 5 as a deuteronomic complement, to emphasize the importance of Jerusalem against Gibeon, where only a thousand animals were sacrificed. Noth also comments that even the consecration of the courtyard space could not practicably contain such a great number of offerings, and that the starting phrase of v. 64, ביום ההוא "on that day," does not denote a typical continuation of the previous verse. One may thus conclude that the verse was interpolated, and hence we must assume that the editor had a particular motive in recording such an improbable situation. In contrast to Noth, I would consider this a later interpolation by a priestly hand, since the terms ואת המנחה ואת חלבי השלמים "the grain offering and the fat of the fellowship offerings" in this verse demonstrate the sophistication of an established cult practice, not yet in force in Solomon's period. The grain offering, the מנחה of Leviticus, is a much later innovation, not earlier than the late pre-exilic period, and appears in Jer. 33: 18 as an independent offering ומקטיר מנחה, probably introduced into the Israelite cult from surrounding cultures. The מנחה as an auxiliary offering together with the burnt offering and peace offering, as in our verse, is a post-exilic adaptation, and has a particular condition כי תבאו אל ארץ מושבתיכם אשר אני נתן לכם "After you enter the land I am giving you [Num. 15: 2]." It does not appear in Leviticus together with the independent grain offerings. The few occurrences of the term מנחה in the earlier writings, such as ויהי בעלות המנחה in Elijah's narrative in I Kings 18: 36 and Elisha's narrative in II Kings 3: 20, are correctly interpreted by the NIV as "at the time of sacrifice," since in these places the term has the generic meaning "offering", " gift". מנחה לעשו אחיו (Gen. 32: 14) and והורידו לאיש מנחה (Gen. 43: 11) have the same generic meaning. J. Gray, *I & II Kings, A Commentary* (London, 1970), p. 217, note a, suggests that only the term מנחה is a later interjection by a deuteronomic redactor. On the other hand, in his comments on the Elijah narrative in I Kings 18: 36 (p. 389, note a), he proposes to consider the phrase ויהי בעלות המנחה as "a gloss in the light of later ritual in the Second Temple." I. Benzinger, *Die Bücher der König*, (Freiburg, 1899), considers the latter phrase a priestly emendation, an adaptation to the priestly codex. The phrase is missing in the LXX, as many scholars have noted. A similar emendation was made by the Chr. editor concerning David's offering at Araunah's altar. In II Sam. 24: 22 we read הבקר לעלה והמרגים וכלי הבקר לעצים "the oxen for the burnt offering, and the threshing sledges and ox yokes for the wood." In the parallel I Chr. 21: 23, we read הבקר לעלות והמורגים לעצים והחטים למנחה "the oxen for the burnt offerings, the threshing sledges for the wood and the wheat for the grain offering." The auxiliary grain offering, as in I Kings 8: 64, is thus seen to be a late post-exilic innovation, and hence the verse consists of a later interpolation. The term חלבי השלמים in this verse is also a later expression; it does not appear, for example, in the Ahaz narrative, which already demonstrates a sophisticated, well-established cult system, with minute

in postulating a reasonable hypothesis concerning the other obscure narrative connected with the מזבח הנחושת: its demotion by Ahaz to a subordinate status and its ultimate disappearance from the formal Israelite cult.[25]

7.1.4 The Poles on the Altar and on the Ark

I have noted that II Chr. 4: 1 does not mention that the bronze altar had poles, items that were supposed to be part of Moses' bronze altar. Similarly, neither in Kings nor in Chr. are such poles mentioned for the שלחן "table" or the מזבח הזהב "golden altar,"[26] two furnishings which were also supposed to have such poles according to the rules in Exod. 25 and 30. This fact stands in blatant contrast to the poles of the ark and their significance, as specifically recorded in I Kings 8: 8 and its almost word-for-word parallel in II Chr. 5: 9:

---

descriptions of the auxiliary grain offering and the libations as well as the blood sprinkling of the peace offerings. This expression appears only in I Kings 8: 64, in the parallel II Chr. 7: 7 and in Lev. 6: 5. Lev. 6: 2- 6 is a late pericope, an extension of the earlier pericopes on burnt offerings, concerning particularly the service upon the altar, the function of the altar and its maintenance. One must observe the parallelism of the details of this pericope with I Kings 8: 64. The burning of the fat is generally missing in Scripture except in the P stratum. The occurrences in Deut. 32: 14 and 38 are considered a P addition to Deut., and the occurrence in Isa. 43: 24 is not conclusive for our purpose, since it appears in Deutero - Isaiah. A more difficult problem is raised by the phrases קטר יקטורון כיום החלב "Let the fat be 'burned'" and יקטרון את החלב "the fat was 'burned'" in I Sam. 2: 15-16, but this is a unique exception. Moreover, the authenticity of the narrative on the sins of the House of Eli is problematic; it may be considered as an aetiological narrative to justify the disappearance of this priestly clan, and its replacement by the Zadokite clan. For a variety of scholarly opinions concerning this matter see Heger, *Incense*, pp. 258 ff. and n. 15.

[25]   The issue of whether the shift was actually accomplished in one stroke by Ahaz, or whether he merely concluded the last stage of a continuous development in this direction, is a matter of speculation. Similarly, I shall deliberate in section 7.2.3 on the issue of whether the function of the bronze altar was replaced by the שלחן, the table which was located in the Temple building.

[26]   It is of no significance to establish the purpose of this golden altar, or whether it refers to the golden table. According to Chr. it certainly refers to the incense altar, decreed in Exod. 30: 1-8: ולמזבח הקטרת זהב מזקק "And the weight of the refined gold for the altar of incense [I Chr. 28: 18 |"; ואהרן ובניו מקטירים על מזבח העולה ועל מזבח הקטרת "Aaron and his descendants were the ones who presented offerings on the altar of burnt offering and on the altar of incense [I Chr. 6: 34 , 6: 49 in KJV]"; and concerning Uzziah's "sin" in offering incense ויבא אל היכל ה' להקטיר על מזבח הקטרת "and entered the Temple of the Lord to burn incense upon the altar of incense [II Chr. 26: 16]." Hence this altar should have poles, as explicitly required in Exod. 30: 5. It is obvious that there are no parallels to these verses in Kings, since there was no incense altar yet.

ויארכו הבדים ויראו ראשי הבדים מן הקדש על פני הדביר ולא יראו
החוצה ויהיו שם עד היום הזה "These poles were so long that their ends
could be seen from the Holy Place in front of the inner sanctuary, but not
from the outside of the Holy Place; and they are still here today."[27] The lack

---

[27] A number of scholars have been engaged with the interpretation of this verse concerning
the relationship between the ark and the shielding cherubim on its top. Cf. Noth, *Könige*,
p. 179. I Kings 6: 23 - 28 indicates the height of the cherubim as ten cubits and their
width, with both wings, as ten cubits. Since the two cherubim stood side by side, the span
of the wings filled the entire width of the Debir - twenty cubits - and touched its two
walls. The Debir was twenty cubits in height, width and depth and hence there remained
ten cubits under the cherubim in which to place the ark. Since the ark was not made by
Solomon, we must rely on the dimensions recorded in Exod. 25: 10: one and one-half
cubits high, two and one-half cubits long and one and one-half cubits wide; it was thus
small enough to stand under the cherubim. Kings does not indicate the thickness of the
cherubim, or whether they were placed perpendicular to the entrance from the Hall, or
along the length of the Debir. One must assume that they stood perpendicular to the
entrance and spanning the width of the entire building, since it is written ותגע כנף
האחד בקיר וכנף הכרוב השני נגעת בקיר השני "The wing of one cherub touched
one wall, while the wing of the other touched the other wall [I Kings 6: 27]"; there was
no wall between the Hall and the Debir, only a door, as we read: ואת פתח הדביר
עשה דלתות עצי שמן "For the entrance of the Debir, he made doors of olive wood [v.
31]." Although we do not have the thickness of the cherubim we must assume that they
were less than twenty cubits thick, otherwise they also would have filled the entire
thickness of the Debir, such a fact is not recorded, as it is for the width. We also do not
know in which direction the ark stood beneath the cherubim: whether its longer side
stood in the same direction as the spread wings of the cherubim, or perpendicular to
them. It is also not clear from Scripture on which side the poles were fixed, whether on
the wide wall of two and one-half cubits, or on the narrower side of one and one-half
cubits; nor do we know the length of the poles. All these questions make it quite difficult
to get at the correct interpretation of the report ויארכו הבדים ויראו ראשי הבדים מן
הקדש על פני הדביר ולא יראו החוצה "These poles were so long that their ends
could be seen from the Holy Place in front of the Debir, but not from outside the Holy
Place [I Kings 8: 8]." Cf. Noth, *Könige*, p. 179, for his vague assumptions, and a
"stretched" interpretation of this peculiar verse. In his opinion, the poles were fixed on
the long sides, leaving a space of one and one-half cubits between the poles; the ark with
its poles was placed in a direction parallel to the entrance and in the same direction as the
cherubim, that is, the length of the poles ran under the length of the cherubim. The
Talmud also attempted to deduce the many unrevealed features. We read in Mishnah
Menahoth 11: 6 כל הכלים שהיו במקדש ארכן לארכו של בית "All the furnishings
of the Temple [were placed] with their length on the long side of the House"; Tosefta
Menahoth 11: 8 and a Baraita in B. T. Menahoth 98a complement the Mishnah with the
following declaration and subsequent deliberation: חוץ מארון שארכו לרחבו של בית
וכך היה מונח וכך היה בדיו מונחין... ובדיו מנלן דתניא ויארכו הבדים יכול לא
היו נוגעין בפרוכת תלמוד לומר ויראו אי ויראו יכול יהו מקרעין בפרוכת
ויוצאין תלמוד לומר לא יראו החוצה הא כיצד דוחקין ובולטין בפרוכת ודומין
כמין שני דדי אשה "...except the ark whose length was [placed] along the width of the
House and so also were its poles [fixed along the width of the ark, leaving a space of two

of any indication of poles on these furnishings cannot be deprecated as evidence *ex silentio*, considering the prominence given to the poles of the ark and the significant comment "they are still here today." This phrase demonstrates the perpetual importance of the poles, and parallels the specific command in Exod. 25: 15 בטבעת הארן יהיו הבדים לא יסרו ממנו "The poles are to remain in the rings of the ark; they are not to be removed." The ark, the table and the other furnishings were all to have poles at their inception in the desert in order to make them portable, and such poles should have been obsolete once these items were transferred to their final destination, and should have been omitted. We nevertheless observe, exclusively for the ark, their continuous existence and utmost significance.[28] This is also corroborated by II Chr. 35: 3, Josiah's command to the Levites concerning the ark: תנו את ארון הקדש בבית אשר בנה שלמה בן דויד מלך ישראל אין לכם משא בכתף עתה עבדו את ה' אלהיכם "Put the sacred ark in the Temple that Solomon son of David king of Israel built. You have no more to carry it on your shoulders,[29] now serve the Lord your God."

---

and one-half cubits between the poles, as is subsequently clarified in the Talmud]....How do we know that the poles were fixed so? Because we have learned from I Kings 8: 8 'These poles were so long.' Could this mean that they did not touch the veil? [No], since it says '[their ends] could be seen.' [If so] could it mean that [the poles] pierced [holes] in the veil and protruded out? [No], since it says 'they could not be seen from outside.' How is that possible? They pushed out the veil and bulged similar to the two breasts of a woman." We observe that the Talmud had the opposite idea from Noth; the poles were fixed on the narrower side of the ark, leaving a larger space between them to allow for four people to carry it. The ark was placed with its length along the width of the Hall and thus the poles protruded into the Hall. Such an interpretation would correspond to the text of v. 8: 8, but would be in contradiction to the above-mentioned 6: 31 stating that there were doors, not a veil, between the Debir and the Hall. The same objection could be raised regarding Noth's postulate, which would allow the end of the poles to be seen only by someone standing near the Debir; that would require the doors between the Hall and the Debir to be left open all the time "that their ends could be seen," and I doubt that this was the case. The Debir was always considered a most holy and mystical chamber, with the ark as the seat or the footstool of the unseen Deity; it was therefore concealed from the public view, with doors in Solomon's Temple and a veil in the Second Temple.

[28] Concerning the transfer of the ark and the Tabernacle, the ancient desert sanctuary, into Solomon's Temple and the possible reason for the poles' significance, see chap. 1 n. 157 and section 5.6.

[29] Tosefta Sotah 13: 1 (Liebermann) and other rabbinic sources interpret this verse to indicate that Josiah commanded that the ark be hidden: אמ' להם גנזו אותו שלא יגלה לבבל כשאר כל הכלים "He said to them [the Levites]: Hide it so that it should not be exiled to Babylonia like the other furnishings." In the continuation of this homily, it is said: ארון נגנז במקומו שנ' ויאריכו הבדים ויראו וגו' ויהיו שם עד היום הזה "The ark was hidden on its spot, as it is said: 'The poles were so long that their ends could be seen...they are still there today.'" In Mishnah Sheqalim 6: 2 a legend confirms this: מעשה בכהן אחד שהיה מתעסק וראה הרצפה שהיא משונה מחברותיה בא

According to this verse, the poles must still have been on the ark, and only on the ark, and Josiah exhorted the Levites to serve the Lord and the people of Israel,[30] since they no longer had to carry the ark on their shoulders. As a result of such textual inconsistencies regarding the poles we must, like previous scholars, express our doubts concerning the existence of those furnishings, other than the ark, described in Exod. 25 - 30. Such doubt is confirmed by the narratives in I Kings 8: 4 - 9 and II Chr. 5: 5 -10, in which the transfer of the ark is vividly and minutely portrayed; nothing is said about the other furnishings made by Moses, though these should also have been transferred on the same occasion.

7.1.5 Additional Inconsistencies

A further inconsistency is found in I Kings 9: 25[31] and II Chr. 8: 12,[32] which suggest that Solomon's altar was probably of stone, and not a bronze altar as appears in II Chr. 4: 1. In these two verses the term בנה is used,[33] in direct

---

ואמר לחברו ולא הספיק לגמור את הדבר עד שיצתה נשמתו וידעו ביחוד ששם
הארון נגנז "It happened that a priest who was busy [in the wood storage shed] observed that the floor showed some irregularity in comparison with the others, and went to tell his friend, but did not succeed in carrying out his intent and passed away; thus they perceived that the ark was hidden there [under that floor]."

[30] This is how Rashi explains this phrase, by connecting it to the following pericope on the Passover offering, at which the Levites played a prominent part. We read in vv. 10 - 11: ותכון העבודה ...והלוים על מחלקותם כמצות המלך...והלוים מפשיטים "The service was arranged...with the Levites in their divisions as the king had ordered...and the Levites skinned [the animals]."

[31] We read there והעלה שלמה שלש פעמים בשנה עלות ושלמים על המזבח אשר בנה לה' "Three times a year Solomon sacrificed burnt offerings and peace offerings on the altar he had built for the Lord." M. Noth, *I Könige*, p. 220 probes the probability of a late origin for this verse, because of the mention of the three yearly sacrifices; he does not comment on the term בנה. M. Rehm, *Das Erste Buch der Könige*, p. 108 suggests that the mention of an altar built by Solomon is intended to remedy the "missing" altar in the list of the furnishings made by Solomon in I Kings chap. 7.

[32] We read there אז העלה שלמה עלות לה' על מזבח ה' אשר בנה לפני האולם "On the altar of the Lord that he had built in front of the portico, Solomon sacrificed burnt offerings to the Lord."

[33] I shall set out a number of examples that support my thesis, and then comment on the few exceptions to the rule. The term בנה in connection with the building of an altar is encountered among other occurrences in Gen. 8: 20; 12: 7, 8; 13: 18; 22: 9; 26: 25; Exod. 17: 15; 24: 4; 32: 5; Num. 23: 1, 14, 29; Deut. 27: 5, 6; Jos. 8: 30; 22: 10, 23, 29; Jud. 6: 24, 26, 28; 21: 4; I Sam. 7: 17; 14: 35; I Kings 9: 25; 18: 32; II Kings 16: 11; 21: 4, 5; Ezra. 3: 2; II Chr. 8: 12; 33: 4, 5, 15, 16; and I Kings 5: 19; 8: 11; 9: 24; II Chr. 2: 3 and 35: 3 with respect to houses and the Temple. In Gen. 13: 4, we read המזבח אשר עשה,

but this refers to the altar recorded as built in 12: 7 ויבן שם מזבח. In Gen. 33: 20 we read ויצב שם מזבח; I have already written about this peculiar expression in chap. 2 n. 114. In Gen. 35: 1 there is again God's command ועשה שם מזבח with no indication as to the type of altar, but v. 7 records Jacob's fulfillment of this mandate as ויבן שם מזבח. The neutral expression הקם מזבח, "set up an altar," is encountered in the prophet Gad's command to David in II Sam. 24: 18 and I Chr. 21: 18, but David's proposal to Araunah and the construction of the altar are recorded with the term בנה in II Sam. 24: 21, 25 and in I Chr. 21: 26. The most difficult problem consists in the use of the term עשה in the ancient law of the altar in Exod. 20: 21 - 22. I propose the following solutions: a) It is plausible that the editor(s) of the early Book of the Covenant had not yet associated the distinctive nuances of the two terms עשה and בנה with the construction of altars of different substances. b) The editor(s) made a subtle distinction between עשה, used for the mounding up of a pile of earth for an altar, and the term בנה, used for the building of an altar of stones. V. 22b therefore states לא תבנה אתהן גזית, while עשה is used in v. 22a for stylistic reasons, to agree with v. 21. The latter use also emphasizes that there is no difference in sanctity and divine approval between a simple earth pile and a stone altar; the use of two different verbs might otherwise have suggested the first as inferior. We may also note that in I Kings 11: 7 אז יבנה שלמה במה "Solomon built a high place" is used for the *bamah*, and similarly אשר בנה שלמה "the ones Solomon...had built" is used in II Kings 23: 13 concerning the destruction of the such *bamoth* by Josiah. In contrast, the term עשה is used in I Kings 12: 33, המזבח אשר עשה, to describe the altar constructed by Jeroboam, and similarly II Kings 23: 15 has אשר בבית אל הבמה אשר עשה ירבעם המזבח to describe its destruction by Josiah. Another oddity is the use of the term קרע to describe damage to this altar in I Kings 13: 3 and 5: הנה המזבח נקרע "the altar will be torn [or split]"; this term is usually used for tearing cloth, or in a metaphorical manner. This is the only use of this term for the destruction or ruin of an altar. It may indicate that the deuteronomic editor was ignorant of the material of which the altar was constructed and therefore used the non-specific terms עשה and קרע throughout for both the construction and destruction; or, what is more likely in my opinion, it may refer to a bronze altar, a presentation table for food offered to the deities, which was the common usage in Mesopotamia. The deuteronomic editor thus attempted to suggest that even the altar made by Jeroboam was an alien type of cult furnishing.

There is a discrepancy between the use of ויבן מזבחות in II Kings 21: 5 for the altars built by Manasseh, and המזבחות אשר עשה מנשה בשתי חצרות בית ה' in II Kings 23: 12 with respect to their destruction by Josiah. It is possible that the redactor through dittography used the same term as for the idolatrous altars in the first part of the verse: אשר עשו מלכי יהודה. It is reasonable to assume that these altars were made of ceramic or other light material, since they were placed on the roofs; we observe in Jer. 19: 13 and 32: 29 the same type of rite, קטרו על גגותיהם, and we must suppose that this refers to censers and not permanent altars. See Heger, *Incense*, pp. 192 ff. In the parallel pericope II Chr. 33: 15, the phrase וכל המזבחות אשר בנה בהר בית ה' is correctly used. W. Zwickel, "Die Altarbaunotizen im Alten Testament", *Biblica* 73-4 (1992), pp. 533-46, approaches the issue of the different terms used for the construction of the altar from another aspect, namely whether the records in Scripture on altar-building denote the establishment of a sanctuary, and whether the building of altars

contrast to the bronze altar for which the term[34] עשׂה in various grammatical forms is used. We should keep in mind that the mention of the three yearly sacrifices in the Kings pericope demonstrates a deuteronomic editing, complemented by precise details in its priestly parallel in II Chr. 8: 13.[35] There is a clear contradiction between these records of the building of an altar by Solomon and the Chronicles account of the large bronze altar made by him, and this contradiction brings up the general question of the distinction between the various narratives concerning Moses' bronze altar and the other furnishings. Whilst the records on the latter tend to demonstrate a similarity and continuation, descriptions of the burnt offerings altar display clear differences, and attempts to reconcile the contradicting data only worsen the dilemma. As stated in the Introduction, we must acknowledge the contradiction between the altar law in Exod. 20: 21- 23 and the command to build a bronze altar; no such alternative structure is provided for any of the other furnishings.

This dilemma is accentuated if we consider the nomadic style of life of the Israelites as portrayed in Scripture: there was no necessity to build a bronze altar in the desert. We read in Exod. 17: 15 that Moses built an altar as a memorial to the miracle[36] of the defeat of the Amalekites: ויבן משה מזבח

---

is an indication of piety on the part of the builder. He consequently reaches different conclusions from his examination. It is not within the scope of this study to contradict his deductions, but I wish nevertheless to comment on one of his postulates. He writes on p. 541, after noting the various terms such as עשׂה, קום, כון and נצב used in connection with the construction of altars: "Zumindestens teilweise scheinen diese Verben sinnidentisches mit בנה zu sein" ("It seems that at least partially they are identical in their sense with בנה"). I agree with this declaration with respect to the creation of a sanctuary, Zwickel's principal thesis, but I believe I have demonstrated that the editors were aware of the differences in nuance between these terms, and used them appropriately to emphasize the distinction between the various types of altars.

[34] In Exod. 27: 1; 30: 1; 35: 16 (in the middle of a long list preceded by the verb עשׂה); 37: 25; 38: 1, 30; I Kings 7: 48; I Chr. 21: 29; II Chr. 1: 5; 4: 1, 19; 7: 7.

[35] We read there ובדבר יום ביום להעלות כמצות משה לשבתות ולחדשים ולמועדות שלוש פעמים בשנה בחג המצות ובחג השבעות ובחג הסכות "...according to the daily requirements for offerings commanded by Moses for Sabbaths, New Moons and the three annual feasts - the Feast of Unleavened Bread, the Feast of Weeks and the Feast of Tabernacles." The detailed list of the well-established fixed sacrifices indicates unequivocally their priestly origin.

[36] Although in other occurrences the traditional commentators interpret נס as "banner" (as does the NIV), on this verse the Mekhilta d'Rabbi Ishmael BeShalah *Parshah* 2 ד"ה ויבן משה states: אמר משה הנס הזה שעשה המקום "Moses said: The miracle that the Deity performed." Rashi, Ibn Ezra and Ramban also interpret the verse this way, and Onkelos translates here דעביד ליה נסין "who made miracles for him." W. Zwickel, "Die Altarbaunotizen im Alten Testament", *Biblica* 73-4 (1992), pp. 533-546, interprets this verse in the same way (p. 535). This interpretation corroborates my thesis that the

ויקרא שמו ה' נסי "Moses built an altar and called it the Lord is my Banner." In Exod. 24: 4, part of the Sinai narrative, we read ויבן מזבח תחת ההר ושתים עשרה מצבה לשנים עשר שבטי ישראל "He [Moses] built an altar at the foot of the mountain and set up twelve stone pillars[37] representing the twelve tribes of Israel." We read similarly in Exod. 32: 5 regarding the altar built for the golden calf: וירא אהרן ויבן מזבח לפניו "When Aaron saw this, he built an altar in front [of the calf]." The law of the altar itself in Exod. 20: 21 specifies an altar of earth, in conformity with the prevailing custom of a nomadic society. Such an altar could be set up everywhere, בכל המקום , "in every place" of the wanderings, easily abandoned - the site did not become sacred - and a new one built at a new location;[38] a portable bronze altar, unlike the ark, was not an absolute necessity for a nomadic way of life. We observe this also in the Balaam narrative, from which we learn that Balak built three times seven altars[39] at separate locations, and we must assume that they were of earth and later abandoned. This was the prevailing practice in that period among the surrounding cultures and in Israel; I have cited many similar narratives concerning Israelite altars built *ad hoc* by various personalities, and they must have been either of earth or of stone. One must ask why Scripture had to invent a portable bronze altar in the desert when on the one hand it was not necessary for the period of desert wandering and on the other hand was apparently not used for burning sacrifices even in the First Temple period, according to a critical analysis of the relevant passages. The attempt to interject[40] the existence of this altar into the narrative from the

---

building of the altar in Rephidim did not constitute the establishment of a sanctuary, but should be considered merely as a gesture of thanks for the divine intervention on behalf of the Israelites in their battle with the Amalekites.

[37] From the text, which distinguishes between the pillars made of stone and the altar, we must deduce that the altar was made of earth, that is, from a substance other than stone.

[38] W. Zwickel, p. 540, referring to Exod. 32: 5 writes: "Der Text ist weiterer interessanter Beleg dafür, dass man an jedem Ort für eine kurze Zeitspanne einen Altar errichten und ein Kultfest feiern konnte" ("This text serves as further interesting evidence that it was possible to set up an altar on any site for a short time and celebrate a cult ceremony").

[39] ויבן שבעה "Build me seven altars here [Num. 23:]"; בנה לי בזה שבעה מזבחת מזבחת "he built seven altars [23: 14]"; and בנה לי בזה שבעה מזבחת "Build me seven altars here [Num. 23:29]."

[40] It is interesting that the Rabbis, who as we have seen usually attempted to harmonize between the various contradictory sources, also abandoned this endeavour on certain occasions. They too had doubts whether the bronze altar actually existed in the Temple in Solomon's period. In a discussion in B. T. Zebahim 60a concerning a dispute between Rabbi Judah and Rabbi Jose on the size of Moses' altar, we read the following reasoning: בשלמא לרבי יהודה היינו דכתיב (מלכים א ח) קידש אלא לרבי יוסי מאי קידש להעמיד בה מזבח בשלמא לרבי יוסי היינו דכתיב קטן אלא לרבי יהודה מאי קטן הכי קאמר מזבח אבנים שעשה שלמה תחת מזבח הנחשת קטן הוה "As for

period of the desert wanderings until the monarchic period merely causes endless perplexities.

7.1.6 Absence of a Bronze Altar in Various Biblical Narratives

According to Scripture and the traditional interpreters Moses' bronze altar was an important element of the portable Tabernacle, and should have been carried together with the other sanctuary furnishings during all of the Israelites' wanderings. In Jos. chaps. 3 and 4, however, where we encounter in the narrative of the crossing of the Jordan a detailed record of the carrying of the ark and the miracles connected with it, the transport of the Tabernacle and its altars is entirely ignored. There is no mention of the Tabernacle even at the eternal stone memorial founded at Gilgal, nor at the performance of the public circumcision and the celebration of Passover during the extended[41] stay at this important and permanent[42] sanctuary. A bronze altar is not

---

R. Judah['s opinion], it is well, as it is written 'consecrated [I Kings 8: 64].' But what does R. Jose make of 'consecrated'? - for [Solomon] to set up the altar on it. As for R. Jose['s opinion], it is well, as it says 'too small [ibid.].' But what does R. Judah make of 'too small'? This is what it means: The stone altar that Solomon made instead of the bronze altar was too small." Rabbi Judah's declaration is understood by the Amoraim to assert that Moses' altar was only three cubits high, as appears in Exod. 27: 1, but ten cubits square; the number of five cubits in Scripture is meant to be measured from the centre of the altar. Rabbi Jose's declaration is understood to affirm that Moses' altar was five cubits square, but ten cubits high. The Gemara states that the statement that the altar was small accords with Rabbi Jose's opinion but not that of Rabbi Judah, then posits that the altar of stone built by Solomon instead of the bronze altar was small. We note that Solomon built a stone altar, not a bronze altar; the contradiction with II Chr. 4: 1, which states that he built a bronze altar, and with Ezek. 9: 2, מזבח אצל ויעמדו ויבאו הנחשת "They came in and stood beside the bronze altar," is resolved in the same way. We read in B.T. Sabbath 55a:הוא ברוך הקדוש להו אמר הוה מי הנחשת מזבח לפני שירה שאומרים ממקום התחילו "Was there [still] a bronze altar [in the time of Ezekiel]? [Answer: what this really means is that] God said to them [the six men]: Start from the place [the altar] in front of which songs are played on bronze instruments [this is Rashi's explanation: the 'bronze' refers to the musical instruments, not to the altar, which was made of stone]."

[41] We read in Tosefta Zebahim 13: 6 אחת חסר ארבעים שבמדבר מועד אוהל ימי שנה עשרי ארבע ובגלגל "The Tabernacle stood in the desert thirty-nine years and in Gilgal fourteen years."

[42] The continuity of this sanctuary is attested in many scriptural records, including: Jud. 2: 1; I Sam. 7: 16; 11: 15; 13: 12; 15: 21. It is interesting to note in this occurrence the significance of the sanctuary in Gilgal. Although it is recorded in I Sam. 15: 7 that the battle with the Amalekites took place in the far south near the border with Egypt, בואך מצרים פני על אשר שור, the captured animals were driven to the distant sanctuary of Gilgal to be offered there as a sign of devotion to the Lord. The sanctuary in Gilgal

mentioned in any of the other sanctuaries recorded in Scripture,[43] except in II Chr. 1: 5,[44] regarding Gibeon, and the latter was interjected with the intention

---

persisted until the late period of the Northern kingdom, as we observe in Hosea 4: 15; 9: 15; 12: 12 and Amos 5: 5.

[43] On the other hand, we encounter talmudic homilies about the altar in Shilo, Nob and Gibeon, where the Tabernacle was located before the inauguration of Solomon's Temple in Jerusalem, as well as debates about the nature of the material of which the altar was built. We read in B. T. Zebahim 61b: אמר רב הונא אמר רב מזבח של שילה של אבנים היה "Said Rav Huna in the name of Rav: The altar of Shilo was of stones." The text continues אבנים שלש פעמים אחד של שילה ואחד של נוב וגבעון ובית עולמים "The word 'stones' is written three times [concerning the altar, once in the altar law of Exod. 20 and twice in the altar law of Deut. 27], hence all three altars in Shilo, Nob - Gibeon and in the Temple were of stone." We observe that certain Sages were concerned only with the law requiring a stone altar to be built, and apparently were not bothered by the divine command to Moses to build a bronze altar, or by the records in Chr. which attested to the existence of a bronze altar in Gibeon and the making of a bronze altar by Solomon for the Temple. Rabbi Nathan was, it seems, sensitive to these contradictions, and his solution is also quoted: רבי נתן אומר מזבח של שילה של נחושת היה חלול ומלא אבנים "Rabbi Nathan says: The altar of Shilo was a hollow made of bronze and filled with stones." Thus the contradictory commands are reconciled; but Ezekiel's altar did not require a bronze overlay, nor did the Second Temple altar have such a characteristic. It is also remarkable that the Rabbis ignore Jud. 20 and the sanctuary in Beth El, where the holy ark was placed, offerings were brought, the oracle was solicited, and Phinehas the Aaronite was the chief priest. The Tabernacle is not mentioned, either in Beth El or in the three locations listed above, because there was none, but from the context one must assume that at that period Beth El was the principal sanctuary, and hence the location of the main altar. We read in Jud. 20:28: ופינחס בן אלעזר בן אהרן עמד לפניו בימים ההם "And Phinehas son of Eleazar son of Aaron ministered before it [the ark] in those days." In B. T. Zebahim 118b we read: כי אתא רב דימי אמר רבי בשלשה מקומות שרתה שכינה על ישראל בשילה ונוב וגבעון ובית עולמים "When Rav Dimi came, he said in the name of Rabbi: In three locations God's glory dwelt upon Israel, in Shilo, Nob-Gibeon and the Temple." Beth El is left out, although we read in Jud. 20 that the Lord had answered the Israelites' questions there; the phrase ויאמר ה' occurs three times, and even divine intervention is recorded: ויגף ה' את בנימן "The Lord defeated Benjamin [Jud. 20: 35]." In B. T. Yoma 73b it is said that the אורים ותומים of the breastplate of the High Priest were in Beth El at that time, and were used by Phinehas to solicit divine guidance in time of war. This was the High Priest's function, as we read in Num. 27: 21: ולפני אלעזר הכהן יעמד ושאל לו במשפט האורים לפני ה' על פיו יצאו ועל פיו יבאו הוא וכל בני ישראל אתו וכל העדה "He is to stand before Eleazar the priest, who will obtain decisions for him by inquiring of the Urim before the Lord. At his command he and the entire community of the Israelites will go out, and at his command will come in." Hence Beth El must have been the principal sanctuary at that period. We observe the difference between the significance of the sanctuary in Beth El and the one in Mizpah. There was no oracle, as in Beth El, and Jephtah and the elders only made an agreement there before the Lord, as they said ה' יהיה שמע בינותינו "The Lord is our witness [Jud. 11: 10]"; this is similar

of "correcting" its absence in Kings, as discussed above. Also perplexing is the command to build a stone altar immediately upon the crossing of the Jordan into the God-given land and to celebrate offerings upon it: at this time the bronze altar made by Moses was supposed to be extant, according to II Chr. 1: 5 and the accepted traditions.

Joshua also built an altar of stone on Mount Ebal[45] for the momentous celebration of the Covenant[46] with the accompanying blessings and curses, and there is no explanation for omitting the bronze altar made by Moses, if it were present at that time.[47] The ark made by Moses, in contrast, was an important element in this ceremony though in fact, according to the command in Deut., the ark had no role in the performance of this Covenant and is not mentioned there at all. One might have connected the two commands in Deut. - the building of the altar and the celebration of the Covenant - merely by the contiguity of the two pericopes and the reference in both to Mount Ebal, but

---

to Jacob's covenant with Laban: הגל הזה עד ביני ובינך "This heap is a witness between you and me today [Gen. 31: 48]." The traditional commentator Radak, on the other hand, was concerned about the contradictions between Jud. 20 and the talmudic homily and proposed a number of hypotheses, among them the assumption that Beth El was close to Shilo. He was also aware of the chronological problem created by the narrative of the concubine in Jud. 19 - 20. If the event reported in chap. 19 occurred according to the chronological order of the chapters in Jud., that is, after the period of Samson narrated in the previous chapters 13 - 17, it would result that Phinehas lived several hundred years, since he ministered as chief priest already in the time of Joshua (Jos. chap. 22), and still had the same position at Beth El after the concubine affair. Radak says that Phinehas lived for more than three hundred years, as a reward for his zeal in killing Zimri and the Midianite woman. God made a promise to him: לכן אמר הנני נתן לו את בריתי שלום "Therefore tell him I am making my covenant of peace with him [Num. 25: 12]." In Mal. 2: 5, which refers to the priests, the prophet says in the name of the Lord: בריתי היתה אתו החיים והשלום "My covenant was with him, a covenant of life and peace." Hence, the covenant with Phinehas assured him of a long life.

[44]　ומזבח הנחשת אשר עשה בצלאל בן אורי בן חור שם "But the bronze altar that Bezalelson of Uri, the son of Hur, had made was [in Gibeon]...."

[45]　Jos. 8: 30.

[46]　As we read in the concluding verse of the blessings and curses in Deut. 28: 69: אלה דברי הברית "These are the terms of the Covenant."

[47]　Num. Rabbah questions this omission, and we read in (Vilna ed.) פרשה יד ד"ה א ביום השביעי: אם בא אדם לומר למה בנה מזבח בהר עיבל כמה דתימא (יהושע ח) אז יבנה יהושע מזבח לה' אלהי ישראל בהר עיבל והלא המשכן היה שם "Someone might question why Joshua built an altar on Mount Ebal, as it states in Joshua 8: 30... since the Tabernacle [with the bronze altar] was [supposed to be] there." The answer is that he built the altar because of the special command by God: ובנית שם מזבח לה' אלהיך מזבח אבנים וגו' "Build there an altar to the Lord your God, and altar of stones [Deut. 27: 5]."

the ark has no part in the ceremony. In contrast, the Jos. narrative joins the building of the altar with a ceremony in which the ark appears to take the dominant place.

The narrative in Jos. 22 concerning the altar built by the two and one-half tribes on the east side of the Jordan also supports the thesis that the bronze altar, among the other Tabernacle furnishings made by Moses in the desert, is a fictional construct,[48] devoid of any basis in reality. We read in v. 10: ויבנו בני ראובן ובני גד וחצי שבט המנשה שם מזבח על הירדן מזבח גדול למראה "The Reubenites, the Gadites and the half-tribe of Manasseh built an imposing altar there by the Jordan." It is evident from the text that they built a large altar, probably of stone, and obviously not a small bronze altar like that of Moses which was supposed to be in the principal sanctuary in Shilo[49] at that time. Their justification for building this altar, which was recognized by the priestly and political authorities who exonerated the tribes from any wrongdoing, was that this altar was not for the purpose of offering but a witness to their unity with the other ten tribes. The mutual resemblance of the altars on both sides of the Jordan was to serve as a symbol of their joint faith: ואמרנו ראו את תבנית מזבח ה' אשר עשו אבותינו לא לעולה ולא לזבח כי עד הוא בינינו וביניכם "Look at the replica of the Lord's altar, which our fathers built, not for burnt offerings and sacrifices, but as a witness between us and you [Jos. 22: 28]." We observe the significance bestowed upon the altar, an element of the sacrificial cult used to express the people's unity;[50] but we must also assume that the large replica built on the east side of the Jordan was similar to the altar in Shilo, which consequently must have been a large built-up altar, and not the small bronze altar of Exod. 27: 1- 8.

The Korah narrative also has a role in undermining the reality of the bronze altar in Scripture. We read in Num. 17: 3 (16: 38 in KJV): מחתות החטאים האלה...ועשו אתם רקעי פחים צפוי למזבח "the censers of the men who sinned...hammer the censers into sheets to overlay the altar." According to Scripture, the Korah rebellion occurred in the desert, and thus it

---

[48] For our purposes, as indicated previously, it is of no significance when this pericope in Jos. was inserted in Scripture, and whether such insertion was made by a deuteronomic or priestly hand. I merely wish to reveal additional textual and logical inconsistencies to substantiate the scholarly assertions concerning the authenticity of the desert sanctuary described in Exodus.

[49] We read in Jos. 19: 51 that the allotment of the land to the tribes took place בשלה לפני ה' פתח אהל מועד "at Shilo in the presence of the Lord at the entrance of the Tent of Meeting."

[50] I must reiterate that for our goal of indicating the many inconsistencies in Scripture concerning the existence of a bronze altar, it is of no significance whether this narrative in chap. 22 of Joshua is purely deuteronomic, or also contains priestly elements.

was the bronze altar made by Moses that was operative.[51] One may assume that an altar made of earth, stone or other material might benefit, practically or aesthetically, from an overlay of bronze sheets,[52] but it would be frivolous and absurd to cover a bronze altar with bronze sheets.[53] Adding to the confusion and perplexities associated with the bronze altar is the odd interpretation in LXX Exod. 38: 22, recording the construction of the altar with the Tabernacle and its furnishings; the statement that the bronze altar was made of the bronze censers used by the Korah rebels[54] is untenable according to biblical chronology.

---

[51] We read in 17: 11 (16: 46 in KJV): ויאמר משה אל אהרן קח את המחתה ותן עליה אש מעל המזבח "Then Moses said to Aaron Take your censer and put fire on it from the altar."

[52] The censers were of bronze, as appears in 17: 4 (16: 39 in KJV), the fulfillment of the divine command: ויקח אלעזר הכהן את מחתות הנחשת "So Eleazar the priest collected the bronze censers."

[53] Cf. J. Liver, "Korah, Datan and Abiram," *Scripta Hierosolymitana* VIII (1961), pp. 189 -217, on p. 191.

[54] οὗτος ἐποίησεν τὸ θυσιαστήριον τὸ χαλκοῦν ἐκ τῶν πυρείων τῶν χαλκῶν ἃ ἦσαν τοῖς ἀνδράσιν τοῖς καταστασιάσασι μετὰ τῆς Κορε συναγωῆς "Then they made the bronze altar from the bronze censers which belonged to the men rebelling in the Korah group." We may perceive this odd record in the LXX as consistent with the view of the translator, who viewed the command to make the "bronze" altar in a manner quite different than commonly interpreted. As we have seen in the analysis of the term מכבר in section 5.4.1, the LXX had a different vision of the bronze hearth and the appendage that extended from under the hearth to the middle of the altar. If we assume, as Wevers did, that initially the LXX editor understood Exod. 27: 2 to imply that the bronze cover was solely for the "horns" while the overall structure of the altar remained of wood, he had to envisage a hearth and a net-like appendage of bronze to protect the body of the altar and allow the burning of fire and coals on a wooden structure. His interpretation of Exod. 27: 4 - 5 would therefore be different from that of the other translators and commentators who assumed that these verses demanded the covering of the entire altar with bronze. However, the altar is called in Scripture מזבח הנחשת, which implies an altar entirely covered by bronze, and there is also God's command to cover the altar with the bronze of the censers of Korah's group. The LXX editor linked all these verses together and created an intelligible outline of the altar, and a reasonable answer to the apparent absurdity of a command to cover a bronze altar with bronze sheets. According to the LXX interpretation, this command was reasonable, since until then only the "horns" had been covered with bronze according to the first command in Exod. 27: 4. While this may be a reasonable solution for this odd LXX text, it does not answer the chronological disorder created by such an interpretation; that is, the linking of the record in Exod. 38 regarding the making of the altar and the Tabernacle's furnishings, together with the much later event of Korah's rebellion. There also remains a further question: God commanded that the altar be covered with sheets of bronze with the following purpose: ויהיו לאות לבני ישראל...זכרון לבני ישראל "Let them be a sign to the Israelites...This was to remind the Israelites [Num. 17: 3 and 5; 16: 38 and 40 in KJV]." It is difficult to justify the later replacement of the bronze altar with a stone altar, in

Another anomaly is the expression יסוד המזבח "the base of the altar," which appears often in the P stratum of the Pentateuch as an indication of where the excess blood was to be poured (Exod. 29: 12 among other instances). The permanent Second Temple altar did have a base within which was a sewage system for the drainage of the blood;[55] but the hollow portable bronze altar described in Exod. 27 had no base at all. Hence the many occurrences of the phrase יסוד המזבח in Exod. and Lev., some of them recording offerings in the desert,[56] must refer to a permanent altar on a base, and not to the bronze altar made by Moses.

I have drawn attention in chap.6 to the complex and vague description of the bronze altar in Exod. 27: 1 - 8. If we compare the portrayal of this altar with the clear and intelligible depiction of the incense altar in 30: 1, we must perceive the real basis of this difference: the golden incense altar was extant at the time of the final redaction of the relevant pericope, in contrast to the bronze altar, of which solely a distant reminiscence of its structure and use persisted. An exact description of the incense altar was therefore possible, while only a vague portrayal of the bronze altar could be devised. Wherever we approach the issue of the bronze altar in Scripture, and in its translations and interpretations, we cannot avoid perceiving inconsistencies, interjections and emendations.[57]

---

violation of God's command that it should serve as an eternal reminder of a grave occurrence and an admonition for proper behaviour in future. This issue, and the deviation of the LXX from the MT text, strengthen the conjecture that each text dealing with the bronze altar adds yet further perplexity to the issue.

[55] We read in Mishnah Midoth 3: 2: ובקרן מערבית דרומית היו שני נקבים כמין שני חוטמין דקין שהדמים הניתנין על יסוד מערבי ועל יסוד דרומי יורדין בהן "And in the south-west corner were two holes, like thin spouts, through which descended the blood which had to be poured on the west and south sides of the foundation." We also have a corroboration of this fact in R. J. H. Shutt, trans., "The Letter of Aristeas," in *The Old Testament Pseudepigrapha*, ed. J. H. Charlesworth, Vol. II, pp. 12-34 (N. Y., 1985), v. 90: "There were many mouths at the base, which were completely invisible except for those responsible for the ministry, so that the large amounts of blood which collected from the sacrifices were all cleansed by the downward pressure and momentum."

[56] Lev. 8: 15; 9: 9. See Z. Zevit, "Philology, Archeology and a Terminus A Quo for P's *hattat* Legislation," in *Pomegranates and Golden Bells: Studies in Biblical, Jewish and Near Eastern Ritual, Law and Literature in Honor of Jacob Milgrom*, pp. 29-38, edd. D. Wright, D.N. Freedman and A. Hurvitz (Winona Lake, 1995), who reaches a similar conclusion that the bronze altar had no יסוד.

[57] We have seen that even the Rabbis who did their best to harmonize all inconsistencies in Scripture had great difficulties with this issue of the bronze altar. The following question and answer is found in B. T. Sabbath 55a: מזבח הנחשת מי הוה אמר להו הקדוש ברוך הוא התחילו ממקום שאומרים שירה לפני "Was there a bronze altar [in Ezekiel's period]? [The answer is]: Start from the place [the altar] in front of which songs are played on bronze instruments" (as Rashi explains this vague wording). This question

7.1.7 Summary of the Evidence

We must conclude that we are facing a concerted effort, not always successful, to hide certain facts about the origin of such a bronze altar, its use, and the reason for its final disappearance from the Israelite sacrificial cult. We cannot ignore its existence altogether, despite the scholarly assertion of the fictitious nature of the desert Tabernacle and its various furnishings, supposedly retrojecting to Moses' time the features of the sanctuary in Jerusalem, its furnishings and the mode of the sacrificial cult. The two quite transparent efforts - in I Kings 8: 64 at Solomon's disqualification and in II Kings 16: 14 at Ahaz' rejection of the bronze altar -[58] to justify the disappearance of something which existed before must induce us to expose the background of this enigma, or at least offer a plausible hypothesis. Such investigation should be based on a re-interpretation of the scriptural records, an analysis of cult practices in the surrounding cultures and an evaluation of archeological findings.

7.2 The Bronze Altar of Ahaz

We have amply deliberated concerning the problems of the "bronze altar" at Solomon's consecration ceremony, recorded in I Kings 8: 64. We must now approach the issue of the "bronze altar" of the Ahaz narrative, and particularly the divergent approaches of Kings and Chr. in this matter. Let us start with the examination of the Kings narrative and its approach to the issue of the bronze altar. The deuteronomic editor(s) ignored the existence of this altar in Kings and in all other writings from Joshua onwards. It appears only in I Kings 8: 64, whose deuteronomic origin may certainly be questioned and a later priestly interjection, at least of some of its elements, assumed. The narrative in II Kings 16: 10 - 16 also demonstrates, as already discussed, a

---

in B. T. Sabbath as to whether there was a bronze altar is based on a declaration in Mekhilta d'Rabbi Ishmael Jethro *Parshah* 11 in which at the end of the discussion we read: אלא ביום שנבנה זה נגנז זה "On the day when this altar was built by Solomon, the other was hidden." This is an interpretation of I Kings 8: 64 that Solomon built a stone altar on the consecrated courtyard and hid [disposed of] the bronze altar made by Moses, on which he offered in Gibeon. I need not demonstrate again the many holes left in this patchwork solution to the inconsistencies in the text regarding Moses' bronze altar.

[58] The bronze altar mentioned in Ezek. 9: 2, ויעמדו אצל מזבח הנחשת, is evidently not the holocaust altar and has no connection with it; the holocaust altar is described in Ezek. 43. I shall revert to this issue and the likely connection of this altar to the tables, שלחנות, in section 7.2.3.

proto-priestly textual intervention. It is the first and probably only[59] occurrence of a systematic daily cult practice in the deuteronomic writings.

---

[59] We encounter in Jos. 22 indications of a well-organized cult practice, such as the use of the terms עולה, זבח and שלמים, as well as particular details regarding the altar's purpose, לבנות מזבח לעלה למנחה ולזבח "building an altar for burnt offerings, grain offerings and sacrifices [22: 29]." There is no evidence, however, of an established daily routine. Moreover, one cannot exclude a priestly hand in the final redaction of this pericope; although the centralization of the cult, a deuteronomic motif, seems to be the main purpose of the narrative, Phinehas the priest is the foremost personality in this pericope. Joshua, according to the chronology, was still the political and spiritual leader and later arranged the Shekhem covenant, yet is entirely ignored. Phinehas, the sole contender for the High Priesthood promised him by God for his zeal in killing Zimri (Num. 25: 12 - 13), captures the entire stage for himself, although his father Eleazar was still living. The latter's death is announced only in Jos. 24: 33, the last verse, and there too Phinehas' importance is emphasized: Eleazar was buried on a portion of his son's estate allotted to him. Cf. H. W. Hertzberg, *Die Bücher Josua, Richter, Ruth*, ATD 9 (Göttingen, 1953). For an extensive discussion concerning the emphasis in Chr. on Phinehas' merits and genealogical entitlement to the priesthood, see Heger, *Incense*, pp. 67ff. In the Joshua narrative Phinehas is sent as the head of the delegation (22: 13); he is supposed to have evaluated the honesty of the tribes' declaration and accepted their response (v. 30), and endorsed their case before the people of Israel (v. 32). This importance bestowed upon Phinehas the priest, on an issue of such consequence as peace and harmony between the different tribes, unequivocally demonstrates a priestly influence. The inconsistent terms used for the various offerings and their different arrangements in vv. 26 - 29 clearly demonstrate an addition by a different hand, probably a priestly emendation of a deuteronomic original. In v. 26 we read עולה and זבח, the latter usually indicating the שלמים, but in v. 27 we read בעלותינו ובזבחינו ובשלמינו, in which they seem to be separate offerings; in v. 28, we again encounter לא לעולה ולא לזבח and in v. 29 לעלה למנחה ולזבח. Cf. R. Rendtorff, *Studien zur Geschichte des Opfers im Alten Israel* (Neukirchen, 1967), p. 50.

The presence in this pericope of נשיא and נשיאי העדה "princes", which are terms used in the P stratum, in contrast to the generally used זקנים or זקני העדה "elders", also demonstrates a late priestly-inspired editing. It seems that with reference to the Gibeonites the term זקנינו (Jos. 9: 11) was left unaltered by the P editor, whose concern for the "correct" term was reserved solely for the Israelites. Nowhere in Deut. do we encounter the title נשיא, whereas the title זקנים occurs on every significant occasion to represent the assembly of the entire community. See, for example, Deut. 27: 1; 29: 9 and 31: 28. Further, we encounter various other titles for the heads of the tribes and the community, such as זקני שבטיכם, זקני ישראל, ראשי שבטיכם, but no נשיא. In Jos. we again encounter the title זקנים at the most important events; we find, for instance, זקני ישראל at the disaster at Ai in 7: 6 and 8: 10, although the narrative describes a tribally organized people. At the ceremonial performance of the blessings and curses in Jos. 8: 33, וכל ישראל וזקניו ושטרים ושפטיו עמדים מזה ומזה לארון, the "elders" again are foremost, and there is no mention of נשיאים "princes". At the end of Joshua's life, at his momentous missive to eternity and the conclusion of the covenant in 23: 2 and 24: 1, "the elders" are similarly in the foreground, and they also took over the leadership after Joshua's death, as we read in 24: 31. In the other deuteronomic writings in Jud. and the books of Samuel and Kings, the ישראל זקני "the elders of Israel" are the chieftains of the people, their delegates at the king's council and the king's advisors. See for example: Jud. 2: 7, 8: 16, 11: 5, 21: 16; I Sam. 4: 3, 15: 30; II Sam. 3: 17, 17: 4; I Kings 8: 3, 12: 13, 20: 8, 21: 8; II Kings 10: 5 and 23: 1. The title נשיא, on the other hand, also occurs in Jos.: in our pericope in chap. 22, in chap. 9 in the narrative of the Gibeonites, and in the statement of Zelophehad's daughters in 17: 4. The term נשיא in the latter is understandable, since this pericope in Jos. refers to the record in Num. 27: 1-11, part of the P stratum of the Pentateuch in which this term is typical.

The story of the Gibeonites in chap. 9 may also have a hidden agenda; it is obvious that this is an aetiological narrative justifying certain special circumstances with the aim of concealing the real events. The massacre of the Gibeonites in Jos. 9 and II Sam. 21 is an issue much debated by a number of scholars; see, e.g. J. A. Soggin, *Joshua*, OTL, transl. R. A. Wilson (Philadelphia, 1972); H. W. Hertzberg, *Die Bücher Josua, Richter, Ruth*, ATD 9, and *I & II Samuel, A Commentary*, transl. J. S. Bowden, (Philadelphia, 1964); M. Noth, *Das Buch Josua* (Tübingen, 1938). The aetiological motive of the narrative and the priestly influence on the final text are common assumptions of these studies, notwithstanding the diverse opinions with respect to the real events concealed in the narrative. The phrase חטבי עצים ושאבי מים לעדה ולמזבח ה׳ עד היום הזה אל המקום אשר יבחר "woodcutters and water-carriers for the community and for the altar of the Lord at the place the Lord would choose [Jos. 9: 27]," and the odd expression וברכו את נחלת ה׳ "so that you will bless the Lord's inheritance [II Sam. 21: 3]" cast a dark shadow on the real circumstances of the relations with the Gibeonites. These people lived in a location where the Great *Bamah* was located, where Solomon went to worship before the building of the Temple in Jerusalem (I Kings 3: 4), and where the Lord appeared to him and granted him discerning wisdom (3: 5- 14). Gibeon was also a town of the Aaronites (Jos. 21: 17), the site of Moses' Tabernacle (according to I Chr. 21: 29 and a talmudic assertion), and the seat of the Zadokite priestly clan (I Chr. 16: 39). A number of modern scholars associate the slaughter of the priests of Nob (I Sam. 22) with the report of the slaughter of the Gibeonites by Saul in II Sam. 21: 1; see e.g. P. Kyle McCarter, Jr., *II Samuel, A New Translation with Introduction, Notes and Commentary*, The Anchor Bible (Garden City, N.Y., 1984), p. 441. The Talmud obviously cannot go so far as to suggest a falsification of scriptural records for the sake of revealing the hidden story behind the "refined" narrative, but has also connected the two accounts. We read in B. T. Yebamoth 78b: וכי היכן מצינו בשאול שהמית הגבעונים אלא מתוך שהרג נוב עיר הכהנים שהיו מספיקין להם מים ומזון מעלה עליו הכתוב כאילו הרגן "Where do we find that Saul killed the Gibeonites? Because he killed the city of priests [at] Nob who provided the Gibeonites with water and food [for their services as woodcutters and water-carriers at the sanctuary and they thus were without means of subsistence], Scripture considers it as if he had killed them."

The אבן הגדולה "the great rock" in Gibeon (II Sam. 20: 8) is evidence of its archaic sanctity. Kiriath Jearim, part of the Tetrapolis of Gibeon, was the site where the ark stood for an extended period, and had a beneficial spiritual influence on all of Israel, from its return by the Philistines (I Sam. 7: 2) until its transfer to the house of Obed-Edom and subsequently to the City of David (II Sam. 6: 10). We also observe the significance of Gibeon in Israelite cult history. The real cause of the humiliation and subsequent annihilation of the Gibeonites might have been a grim and brutal struggle for the control of the *Bamah* in Gibeon, or the rivalry between the Gibeon sanctuary and the Temple in Jerusalem, afterwards concealed under a veil of fanciful fiction as narrated in Jos. 9 and

One may assume a sudden royal decision, inspired by a model inspected in a foreign country, to build an impressive great altar in the king's own Temple, instead of the simple, traditional altar in use until then. On the other hand, it is less easy to accept a sudden radical shift from *ad hoc* cult offerings, the practice of centuries or millennia, to an organized system of daily specific offerings. The narrative in II Kings 16 demonstrates a sophisticated cult

---

II Sam 21. The slaying of Saul's descendants recorded in the latter pericope also has an aetiological purpose, as scholars have argued.

The phrase אל המקום אשר יבחר in Jos. 9: 27, which seems inappropriate here, points to the rivalry with Jerusalem and thus to a deuteronomic influence, but a later priestly revision of the narrative, which would obviously include the prevailing cult centralization, cannot be excluded, and may hint to a struggle between different priestly clans for cult privileges, similar to the fierce contest between the Aaronites and Korahites. Midrash Numbers Rabbah פרשה ח ד"ה ד איש או quotes a homily by Rav Ami in the name of Rabbi Joshua ben Levi which relates to this issue: אחר שאמר לעדה ולמזבח ה' מה צורך לומר אל המקום אשר יבחר אלא תלאו יהושע בדוד "Having said 'for the community and the altar of the Lord [Jos. 9: 27],'" why was it necessary to add 'at the place the Lord would choose'? [Answer] Joshua left the decision to David [whether to accept the Gibeonites into the community of Israel, and it seems that David decided not to accept them, as we read in II Sam. 21: 2 והגבעונים לא מבני ישראל המה "Now the Gibeonites were not a part of Israel.]" I shall discuss in chap. 8 n. 84 scholarly speculations that Gibeon was initially the main central sanctuary, and was downgraded by Solomon, who made Jerusalem the principal sanctuary. This assumption is based on a different reading of II Sam. 21: 6: בגבעון בהר ה' "in Gibeon, on the mountain of the Lord," instead of the MT version "at Gibeah of Saul, the Lord's chosen one." See H. W. Hertzberg, *I & II Samuel*, pp. 380-1. Such circumstances would reinforce the idea that the narratives of Jos. 9 and II Sam. 21 conceal a grim struggle between the clerics of the two sanctuaries and their followers, each contending for supremacy of their holy site.

The unique term נשיאי האבות in I Kings 8: 1 used alongside זקני ישראל also hints at a pericope reworked and emended by a priestly hand. The inconsistency in v. 3, in which "the elders" are mentioned and then abruptly the "priests" הכהנים are introduced as the ark bearers, is well known, and demonstrates that the aim was to emphasize that הכהנים והלוים "the priests and Levites" carried the ark, not the "elders", as probably appeared in the previous *Vorlage*. The repetition of this fact in vv. 3 and 4 confirms that the intent of the editor was to adapt the narrative to the circumstances of his period, in which only the priests were allowed to approach the sanctuary. There is no mention of priests or Levites, in contrast, with respect to the transportation of the ark by David to the City of David (II Sam. chap. 6). Hence, the use of such terms as נשיאי העדה in the Jos. narrative corroborates the priestly influence on the text of this pericope, and explains the appearance of a systematic cult practice.

The problem of the terms נשיא and זקן and their social and legal implications is a much debated issue, like the question of the Gibeonite massacre. It is not within the scope of this study to expand the investigation of these two issues; I merely wished to draw attention to another possible aspect of the Gibeonite narrative - a fierce struggle connected with control of the cult - and to the utilization of the two terms describing the community's leadership as a helpful tool in discerning the origin of the final text editing.

ceremonial; v. 15 sets out an elaborate classification of offerings for king and people (עלת כל עם הארץ and עלת המלך), a daily cycle of diversified offerings (מנחת הערב and עלת הבקר), a grain offering auxiliary to the burnt offering (ומנחתם),[60] and libations (ונסכיהם), which were late additions to the daily offerings.

7.2.1 The New Altar of Ahaz

We must therefore consider the reform of Ahaz in this light. I agree with Cogan[61] and Zwickel[62] that Ahaz acted of his own will and not as a result of

---

[60] We encounter in Gen. 35: 14 a libation by Jacob on a pillar, but this ceremonial act obviously had no connection to the libation offered as an auxiliary together with the grain offering, burnt offerings and peace offerings which appear in our pericope; Jacob's celebration dates from a period before the institution of burnt offerings. The expression ומנחתם ונסכיהם is the same term found in the elaborate sacrificial codex in Num. chaps. 28 - 29 and is the first appearance of regular libations in Kings. It is interesting to note that the Chr. editor, according to the custom in his period, added libations, ונסכיהם וזבחים, in his narrative of David's offerings in I Chr. 29: 21; there is no parallel in Kings or in Samuel. The celebration of נסכים "libations" first appears in Jer. and then only as an alien type of worship: הסך נסכים לאלהים אחרים "and pour drink offerings to other gods [Jer. 7: 18]"; this is reasonable, given that in Mesopotamia, which had political and cultural influence on Judah at that period, the use of libations and incense was common. Cf. Max Löhr, *Das Räucheropfer im Alten Testament* (1927), p.156, who states under the heading "Zweistromland" (Mesopotamia): "Mit der Darbringung von Räucherwerk ist häufig eine Libation verbunden" ("With the offering of incense, a libation is often joined").

[61] There has been much scholarly debate on the issue of why Ahaz built an altar in Jerusalem, as well as literary analysis of the confused text of the pericope. The discussion has comprised the question of whether the altar was Assyrian, Phoenician or Aramaic in type, as well as the more significant issue of whether Ahaz was pressured as a vassal of Assyria to adapt the cult to Assyrian mythology and ceremonial practice, or made the decision of his own accord. The scholarly opinions vary, and I shall briefly quote the assumptions relevant to our study of the bronze altar. M. Cogan, *Imperialism and Religion*, SBL Monograph Series No. 19 (1974) debates most of the earlier theories in his chaps. 1 - 3. He supports the idea that Assyria did not impose the cult of its deities on Judah, a vassal country; such a procedure was applied solely to captured territories incorporated within the Assyrian Empire. Ahaz thus acted of his own will and adapted the cult to the new atmosphere of change which was dominant in the surrounding areas and reached its climax during the reign of Manasseh. Later scholarly publications include M. Rehm, *Das Zweite Buch der Könige*, who shares Cogan's opinion, and E. Würtheim, *Die Bücher der Könige, 1. Kön. 17 - 2. Kön. 25*, Das Alte Testament Deutsch (Göttingen, 1984), who follows H. Spieckermann in considering Ahaz' conduct as a response to Assyrian pressure. Spieckermann postulates a complex stratagem by Ahaz to build a new great altar for the legitimate Yahweh cult and leave the small bronze altar for the

Assyrian pressure. The Assyrian altars were tables used to present food to the gods but not to burn sacrifices. The Assyrian term for altar is in fact *passuru,* "table" [63] (פתורא in Aramaic), and this was a piece of furniture upon which the various foods were exposed for the deities, similar to its use in the home. This fact has been demonstrated by Galling's archeological research on Assyrian altars[64] and confirmed by de Vaux,[65] probably from written documentation. It would therefore be absurd to assume that it was under Assyrian influence that Ahaz built an altar for the burning of sacrifices, at a time when such practice was likely not part of the Assyrian ritual system. The Assyrians had certainly been exposed to the custom of burning sacrifices in other cultures; one may assume that if they did not adopt it, they did not approve of it. On the other hand, they did not oppose such celebrations by their vassals, and even by peoples incorporated within their empire, such as Damascus, wherein stood the altar used as a model by Ahaz. Spieckermann's thesis[66] that the great altar was built for the burning of offerings to Yahweh and the small bronze altar remained dedicated to the Assyrian gods is therefore not plausible. The small bronze altar, according to the text, was originally the main altar in the Temple, before being pushed aside to make place for the great altar, and as I shall demonstrate, was similar to the Assyrian tin altars for exposing food to the deities. It would have been an insult to the Assyrian ruler and deities, rather than a sign of submission, to push aside this Assyrian-type altar in order to make way for another altar dedicated to the Israelite Deity.

I propose, therefore, to accept the assumption of Zwickel and Cogan that Ahaz did not build the altar as a result of Assyrian pressure, but I postulate a different motive than that presumed by these two scholars. While Cogan envisages Ahaz' actions as an estrangement from existing Israelite theology and practice and an adaptation to the "new and progressive" atmosphere in the region, Zwickel in contrast visualizes Ahaz as a pious reformer. In this period, according to Zwickel, the cult in Israel blossomed, and Ahaz took

---

Assyrian cult. This solution does not seem realistic for a number of reasons, which I shall debate in the text of this section, together with W. Zwickel's opinion.

[62] W. Zwickel, "Die Kultreform des Ahas (2Kön 16,10-18)," *SJOT* 7,2 (1993), pp. 250 - 262.

[63] *Theologisches Wörterbuch zum Alten Testament* (Stuttgart), s.v. מזבח and *Reallexicon der Assyriologie,* Ref. "Altar".

[64] K. Galling, *Der Altar in den Kulturen des Alten Orient, Eine Archäologische Studie* (Berlin, 1925), pp. 43-44 and 53 ff.

[65] R. de Vaux, *Ancient Israel, Its Life and Institutions,* transl. J. McHugh (London, 1961), p. 440, writes: "The feature which distinguishes Israelite and Canaanite rituals from those of other Semitic peoples is that, when an animal is sacrificed, the victim, or at least a part of it, is burnt upon an altar. This rite did not exist in Mesopotamia or in Arabia."

[66] H. Spieckermann, *Juda unter Assur in der Sargonidenzeit* (Göttingen, 1982), p. 368.

part in or even assumed the leadership of this trend; he introduced the עולה,
a wholly-burnt offering to the Deity, as a regular sacrifice, and cleansed the
Temple of all symbols and statues of living things. Zwickel refers in his
essay to his elaborate archeological studies,[67] and declares on the basis of
these archeological findings that before Ahaz there were no altars in Israel
specifically for burnt offerings.[68] Burnt offerings were celebrated only *ad
hoc*, where and when warranted by particular events. The many textual
citations concerning offerings in Scripture quoted in this study confirm
Zwickel's archeological deductions. We have seen that in many instances no
altars were built at all, and in others one must assume from the context that a
shapeless heap of earth or stones amassed for the purpose or a large piece of
rock served as the offering locus. I also refer to my comments on the
narrative in I Kings 8: 64, in which we learn that a plethora of offerings was
celebrated on the ground.

7.2.2 Altars for Burning Versus Benches for Exposing

Early worship consisted of exposing food and gifts on a table, either at the
private *bamoth* or in the regional sanctuaries, and in the Temple in Jerusalem.
Archeological findings from the Late Bronze Age[69] and Early Iron Age,[70] as
amply described by Zwickel, reveal platforms and deposit benches in the
sanctuaries for the presentation of food and gifts to the deities. The burning
of fat starts in the Late Bronze Age,[71] but no altars for burning entire animals
were found from this period. Zwickel[72] agrees with Gadegaard's statement[73]
that the large altar found in the court in Stratum X of Tel Arad, dating from
about 900 B.C.E., could not have been used for the burning of animals, and
was dedicated rather to the slaughtering of animals. Zwickel observes on the

---

[67] W. Zwickel, *Räucherkult und Räuchergeräte. Exegetische und Archäologische Studien
     zum Räucheropfer im Alten Testament*, OBO 97 (Freiburg/Göttingen, 1990), and *Der
     Tempelkult in Kanaan und Israel, Ein Beitrag zur Kultgeschichte Palästinas von der
     Mittelbronzezeit bis zum Untergang Judas* (Tübingen, 1994).

[68] Cf. Niels H. Gadegaard, "On the So-Called Burnt Offering Altar in the Old Testament,"
     PEQ 110 (1978), pp. 35-45, who asserts, on the basis of an examination of the physical
     properties of the stone altars found in Israel, that they could not have withstood the fire
     necessary for the burning of the offerings; nor would a wooden altar overlaid with bronze
     have been appropriate for such a task.

[69] *Der Tempelkult in Kanaan*, p. 203.

[70] Ibid. p. 239, Tel Quasile.

[71] Ibid. p. 203.

[72] Ibid. p. 271.

[73] N. H. Gadegaard, "On the So-Called Burnt Offering Altar in the Old Testament," pp. 35 -
     45.

other hand a Phoenician influence on certain artifacts and, what is more important for our purpose, a decrease in the quantity of the offering benches in comparison with the previous strata; he deduces from this a diminished significance of this type of worship,[74] that is, the presentation of food and gifts on benches. The benches disappear entirely in Stratum IX, dating to the middle of the 8th century, the period of Ahaz' reign (742 - 727). That is, the presentation of food and gifts, used extensively as a manner of worship in the Bronze Age and until the 9th century, disappeared in the 8th century.[75] This fact demonstrates unequivocally a drastic shift in the cult system toward the ceremonial of burning animals. Zwickel's interpretation of the archeological findings does not oppose the biblical texts but rather corroborates them.[76]

We must deduce from the biblical narrative that Ahaz actuated a certain ritual reform in the Temple. I do not agree with Zwickel, however, that this reform was motivated by a pious intent, and included the attempt to purify the cult from "any graven images or any likeness of any thing."[77] Verses 17 and 18 of the pericope concerning Ahaz' activities are difficult to decipher, but the negative attitude toward him exhibited by the deuteronomic editor[78] and the explicit and extreme condemnation by the Chr. editor[79] seem to me

---

[74] *Der Tempelkult in Kanaan*, p. 272.

[75] Ibid. p. 282.

[76] I wish to reiterate the point made by W. G. Dever, "Will the Real Israel Please Stand Up?" *BASOR* 297 (1995), pp. 61-80: "... there are a number of points at which datable Iron Age archeological evidence and literary references in the Bible do 'converge' in such a way as to suggest contemporaneity."

[77] This is the translation of the Decalogue phrase פסל וכל תמונה in Exod. 20: 4.

[78] In addition to the stereotypical ולא עשה הישר בעיני ה' אלהיו כדוד אביו "Unlike David his father, he did not do what was right in the eyes of the Lord his God [II Kings 16: 2]," which implies the worship at the *bamoth*, there is in II Kings 16: 3 the accusation וילך בדרך מלכי ישראל "He walked in the ways of the kings of Israel," an expression which at least implicitly suggests idolatrous worship. The same expression, with the addition כאשר עשו בית אחאב "as the house of Ahab had done [II Kings 8: 18]," is found with respect to Joram, king of Judah. Ahaz is also accused (end of v. 3) of "passing his son through the fire." It is interesting that Midrash Tanhuma also compares the two biblical expressions in order to imply that Ahaz and Joram were wicked kings. We read in פרשת ויצא סימן יד ד"ה [יד] ד"א וירא: ביהורם כתיב וילך בדרך מלכי ישראל כאשר עשו בית אחאב באחז כתיב ולא עשה הישר בעיני ה' [אלהיו] כדוד אביו "Regarding Jehoram it is written: 'He walked in the ways of the kings of Israel, as the house of Ahab had done [II Kings 8: 18]'; regarding Ahaz it is written: 'Unlike David his father, he did not do what was right in the eyes of the Lord his God [II Kings 16: 2].'

[79] II Chr. 28: 2 explicitly accuses Ahaz of idolatry: וגם מסכות עשה לבעלים "He also made cast idols for worship to the Baals." In vv. 19 and 22, he is charged with "being unfaithful to the Lord" ומעול מעל בה'. B. T. Sanhedrin 103b accuses Ahaz of making the carved image which Manasseh put in the Temple (II Kings 21: 7). We read there:

irreconcilable with an assumption that he raised the banner of piety and orthodoxy. On the other hand, we observe that notwithstanding the general negative attitude toward Ahaz' religious conduct, the building of the altar after a Damascene model is not censured at all.[80] Uriah the priest, himself a devout personage,[81] takes part in this process of change and celebrates the performance of offerings on this new altar without any objection. We must therefore conclude that the editor(s) did not disapprove of the building of this large new altar. Ahaz accomplished a shift from the prior ritual of presenting food on a table, with sporadic burnt offerings, to a permanent daily burnt offering and a diminution in the significance of food presentation. With this reform, the large permanent altar replaced the small bronze altar.[82]

The presentation of food on an altar was an ancient ritual in Israel, as we may deduce from the numerous biblical references to the patriarchs setting up altars and pillars on which no sacrifice occurs; in some instances, in fact, no presentation of food or anything else is indicated,[83] the altar serving merely as a memorial to a theophany or a miracle, and in other instances libations

---

אחז העמידו בעלייה שנאמר ואת המזבחות אשר על הגג עלית אחז וגו' מנשה
העמידו בהיכל "Ahaz placed it [the image] in the upper room, as it is said [in II Kings 23: 12]...Manasseh placed it in the Great Hall [of the Temple]."

[80] This is probably due to the fact that in the editor's period the permanent stone altar was the customary and legitimate locus of worship upon which the sacrifices were burnt; there was no reasonable motive to disapprove of such an altar. Moreover, Ahaz effected the shift in the Israelite sacrificial cult from the presentation of food and gifts to the burning of the whole or part of the offering, and this was favourably judged by the deuteronomic redactor; see further n. 127. Ahaz was censured for his other discreditable deeds, but not with respect to the building of the stone altar and the replacement of the bronze presentation table. We should also concede that there was a distinction between the adoption of alien forms of worship and ceremonies, which were not denounced, and the adoration of alien gods, which was passionately criticized. There was therefore no disapproval of Ahaz for the building of an altar in imitation of a Damascene model.

[81] Isaiah relies on his trustworthiness, as we read in Isa. 8: 2: ואעידה לי עדים נאמנים את אוריה הכהן "And I will call a reliable witness [like] Uriah the priest."

[82] We do not know Ahaz' real motive in effecting this shift in the performance of the cult, whether he was driven by a pious intention to eradicate the archaic, anthropomorphically tainted custom of feeding the gods, or whether it was his aspiration to introduce an impressive cult in his capital city and his court. The deuteronomic redactor of Kings does not censure him, but certainly does not commend him, and emphasizes his wicked behaviour. The Chr. editor ignores the narrative concerning the change of the altars and criticizes him in a most vehement way; in contrast to the Kings record (II Kings 16: 20) that he was buried in the City of David with his fathers ויקבר עם אבתיו בעיר דוד, we read in II Chr. 28: 27: ויקברהו בעיר בירושלם כי לא הביאוהו לקברי מלכי ישראל "...[he] was buried in the city of Jerusalem, but he was not placed in the tombs of the kings of Israel."

[83] See Gen. 12:8; 13: 4; 26: 25; 33: 20 and 35: 7. Moses too built an altar without sacrificing upon it (Exod. 17: 15).

were poured on pillars.[84] A close reading of I Kings 7: 48 concerning the furnishings made by Solomon provides much elucidation. We read there: ויעש שלמה את כל הכלים אשר בית ה׳ את מזבח הזהב ואת השלחן אשר עליו לחם הפנים זהב "Solomon also made all the furnishings that were in the Lord's Temple: the golden altar and the table on which was the showbread, [also] of gold."[85] The traditional commentators had no problem with this verse;[86] the golden altar refers, in their opinion, to the incense altar and the golden table was dedicated to the showbread. But if we assume, as later scholars do,[87] that the incense altar was not yet an established furnishing in Solomon's period, we must conclude that there were two tables:[88] one

---

[84] See Gen. 28: 18 and 35: 14.

[85] The NIV has ignored the conjunction ו "and" with respect to the table, but the KJV translated the MT text exactly as: "The altar of gold and the table of gold." I have translated the text literally since the emphasis on "and" is important. The LXX (v. 34) also translates τὸ θυσιαστήριον τὸ χρυσοῦν καὶ τὴν τράπεζαν, unequivocally implying two separate and distinct items.

[86] The traditional commentator Radak did have a problem with the use of the singular of this term, since according to II Chr. 4: 8 Solomon made ten tables.

[87] The authenticity of this verse is doubtful; some scholars in fact deny its authenticity. See J. Gray, *I & II Kings, A Commentary* (London, 1964), p.186; B. Stade, *ZAW* 3 (1883), pp. 129 - 177, on pp. 168-9; M. Rehm, *Das Erste Buch der Könige, Ein Kommentar* (Eichstatt, 1979), p. 85; M. Noth, *I Könige* (Neukirchen, 1968), pp. 165-6. Cf V. A. Hurowitz, "Solomon's Golden Vessels and the Cult of the First Temple," in *Pomegranates and Golden Bells, Studies in Biblical, Jewish, and Near Eastern Ritual, Law, and Literature in Honor of Jacob Milgrom*, pp. 151 - 164 (Winona Lake, 1995), who attempts to maintain the authenticity of these verses. On the other hand, he too admits a sweeping development process in the Temple cult, different from the later P rules and regulations. He writes: "Originally beverages were placed on the table in full imitation of pagan practice, in which the deity was thought to have partaken of them secretly and at his leisure." Hence, if we accept such drastic shifts in the cult and its underlying theology, the extent and the pattern of the changes remain a matter of speculation, to be based on the interpretation of supporting biblical narratives, comparison with customs of surrounding cultures, and logical deduction.

[88] This is an appropriate spot to discuss and reject de Groot's assumption of two altars of different types which he envisages in Solomon's Temple; his deductions differ from those which I use to support my hypothesis of two table altars. De Groot formulated his theory based on the perplexing verse II Kings 12: 10 with respect to the placement of the donation chest at the right side of the altar. In chap. 8 n. 102, I have offered another explanation of this dubious text, and as I mentioned in chap. 2 n. 116, most scholars have rejected de Groot's theory on other grounds. De Groot also based himself on II Chr. 6: 12 ויעמד לפני מזבח ה׳ נגד כל קהל ישראל ויפרש כפיו. כי עשה שלמה כיור 13- העזרה חמש אמות ארכו וחמש אמות רחבו ואמות שלוש נחשת ויתנהו בתוך קומתו ויעמד עליו ויברך על ברכיו נגד כל קהל ישראל ויפרש כפיו השמימה "Then [Solomon] stood before the altar of the Lord in front of the whole assembly of Israel and spread out his hands. Now he had made a bronze platform, five cubits long, five cubits wide and three cubits high, and had placed it in the center of the outer court.

dedicated exclusively to the presentation of the showbread, השלחן אשר
עליו לחם הפנים, and the other for the presentation of meat, bearing the
appropriate name מזבח הזהב, etymologically related to the root זבח.[89] We
need not wonder at the fact of two tables, as it was common to have more
than one table-altar; we read in the parallel narrative in II Chr. 4: 19: ואת
מזבח הזהב ואת השלחנות "and the golden altar and the tables," with
"tables" in plural, and it appears in II Chr. 4: 8 that Solomon made ten tables.
It is obvious that Chr. does not have a parallel to I Kings 6: 22, וכל המזבח
אשר לדביר צפה זהב "He also overlaid with gold the altar that belonged to
the inner sanctuary," from which we must understand that the two altars
stood in the Debir,[90] not in the Great Hall; Chr. asserts explicitly in 4: 8 וינח

He stood on the platform and then knelt down before the whole assembly of Israel and
spread out his hands toward heaven." Since the size indicated for this כיור, whose real
character we do not know, corresponds exactly to the dimensions of Moses' bronze altar
in Exod. 27: 1, de Groot deduced that it must be an altar. I have already briefly
commented on this issue in chap. 2 n. 274 and I wish to add that as with his first
argument we must compare this verse in Chr. with its parallel in Kings in order to
apprehend the real motive behind the use of this odd term. We read in I Kings 8: 54- 55:
קם מלפני מזבח ה' מכרע על ברכיו וכפיו פרשות השמים. ויעמד ויברך את כל
קהל ישראל "He [Solomon] rose from before the altar of the Lord, where he had been
kneeling with his hands spread out toward heaven. He stood and blessed the whole
assembly of Israel." We observe that II Chr. 6: 12 and v. 13b are an almost identical
parallel to I Kings 8: 54 - 55, but the circumstantial phrase כי עשה שלמה כיור "Since
Solomon had made a bronze 'platform'" is unequivocally a supplementary explanation of
the Chr. editor, and we must investigate his motive for this additional information. Here
too the editor had to adapt the text to the prevailing conditions of his period. He could not
admit that Solomon, a king but a laic, stood לפני מזבח ה' "before the altar of the
Lord"; in his time, only the priests were allowed to approach the altar. The Chr. editor
therefore added the explanation that Solomon made a special podium to stand on. The
explanation indicates his perplexity with the existing text. If, as de Groot suggests, כיור
means altar, there would have been no need for an explanation or apology for Solomon's
conduct; it would have made no difference which altar he stood on, since in his period it
was prohibited for a laic to stand upon the altar.

89　Given such phrases as לחם פנים לפני תמיד "the bread of the Presence...before me at
all times [Exod. 25: 30]", it is probable that bread was constantly exhibited in the
sanctuaries on a specific table dedicated exclusively to this function, whereas a second
table for the presentation of meat was only sporadically used, when an animal sacrifice
was performed. We observe from the narrative in I Sam. 21: 4-7 that bread was
constantly replaced in the sanctuary of Nob, but no other food was available to give to
David.

90　The traditional but extremely sensitive commentator Radak is also aware of the difficulty
of this verse. He obviously cannot admit that either the altar or the table stood in the
Debir, and it is remarkable that although Scripture states המזבח אשר לדביר, he
interprets this as referring to the table standing in the Great Hall: סמך המזבח לדביר
ואף על פי שלא היה בתוכו אלא בהיכל היה השלחן לפי שהיה מכוון כנגד פתח

בהיכל "and placed [the tables] in the Temple." We also observe in Ezek. that there were many tables in different locations in the Temple, hence the idea of two tables in the Debir before the ark is not extraordinary.

7.2.3 The Connection Between שלחן and מזבח

We may now attempt to systematize the different table-altars. The two golden table-altars for the presentation of the showbread and particular meats, made by Solomon according to the concluding list in I Kings 7: 48, stood in the Debir, as is evident from the detailed record in I Kings 6: 22. The ten tables recorded in II Chr. 4: 8, with no explicit indication of their material, [91] stood in the Great Hall,[92] as is evident from the text. It is at the same time clear that there was only one golden table[93] in the Great Hall in the Second Temple. We must therefore ask why the Chronicles' editor would "invent" ten tables for Solomon's Temple; they did not exist in his period, or in Moses' Tabernacle, and they seem to be useless.[94] We must conclude that there was

---

הדביר "[Scripture] connected the altar with the Debir, although it did not stand inside [the Debir], but the table was in the Great Hall because it faced toward the door of the Debir." Radak also explains the odd expression וכל המזבח, which seems to indicate more than one altar, as meaning that the entire altar, walls and roof, was overlaid with gold.

[91] The attempt of the editor to leave us in ignorance with respect to the substance of which the ten tables were constructed is remarkable. In the preceding v. 7 he indicates that the lampstands were made of gold, ויעש את מנרות הזהב, and in the second phrase of v. 8, following the mention of the tables, we read ויעש מזרקי זהב מאה "He also made a hundred gold sprinkling bowls." A is made of gold, C is made of gold, but the material of B is unspecified.

[92] We read there ויעש שלחנות עשרה וינח בהיכל "He made ten tables and placed them in the Temple."

[93] I Macc. 1: 22 and 4: 49; Josephus, *Ant.* XIV: 72, *War* V: 216 (in *Against Apion* I: 198, no table is mentioned, only the lampstand and the golden altar); Philo, *De Specialibus Legibus* I: 172; *Letter of Aristeas*, 52 - 72; Mishnah Sheqalim 6: 4 שלשה עשר שלחנות היו במקדש "thirteen tables were in the Temple." The Mishnah lists twelve tables which stood outside the Great Hall and their uses, and describes the thirteenth as: ואחד של זהב מבפנים שעליו לחם הפנים תמיד "and one of gold inside [the Great Hall] on which the showbread [was] perpetually [set out]."

[94] We read in Y. T. Sheqalim 6: 3, 50a, after a discussion about the placement of the ten tables: אלא חמשה מימין שלחנו של משה וחמשה משמאלו אף על פי כן לא היה מסדר אלא של משה בלבד שנאמר את השולחן אשר עליו לחם הפנים רבי יוסי בי רבי יהודה אומר על כולם היה מסדר שנאמר ואת השלחנות ועליהם לחם הפנים "Five [tables] stood to the right of Moses' table, and five to its left side; despite [the existence of eleven tables] he set up [the showbread] only on Moses' table,

some recollection in the people's memory of certain tables or benches in the Great Hall,[95] but their use was no longer known; or perhaps as the presentation of gifts and food was no longer appropriate to the custom and theology of the period of the redaction of Chronicles, mention of this function was omitted. The archeological findings quoted above also confirm the existence of many display benches in the early sanctuaries. The many tables mentioned in Ezekiel stood outside the Great Hall, [96] and their material as well as their utilization in auxiliary services to the sacrifices are indicated in the text.

The term שלחן as the designation of the table for the presentation of food to the gods must have been the earliest term, similar to the table in the human dwelling; we have seen that in Akkadian this furnishing continued to be called *passuru*, "table".[97] An unmistakable trace of this use of the table is found in Exod. 25: 29, 37: 16 and Num. 4: 7 with respect to the table utensils, similar to table accoutrements for common human use. We read in Exod. 25: 29 the command ועשית קערתיו וכפתיו וקשותיו ומנקיתיו אשר יסך בהן זהב טהור תעשה אתם "And make its plates and dishes of pure gold, as well as its pitchers and bowls for the pouring out of offerings." According to Scripture, this table served exclusively for the exhibition of the showbread, לחם הפנים[98] or[99] לחם התמיד that was eaten by the priests,[100] and therefore the eating utensils as well as the bowls for libations must have been remnants

---

because it is said 'The table [singular] on which was the showbread [I Kings 7: 48]'; Rabbi Jose son of Rabbi Judah said: He set up [the showbread] on all [the tables], because it is said 'The tables [in plural] and on them was the showbread [II Chr. 4: 19].'"

[95] One may assume that these presentation benches were made of stone, as the archeological findings cited in section 7.2.2 demonstrate, and therefore they, like the simple stone altar which was certainly constructed by Solomon, may have been considered too trivial to be included in the list of Solomon's sumptuous and sophisticated furnishings.

[96] See Mishnah Sheqalim 6: 4 on the tables outside the Great Hall in the Second Temple.

[97] In Ugaritic mythological texts, we encounter the term *tlhn* in connection with the description of food presented to the gods. I shall quote several relevant citations from the tablets of Râs-Shamrah, as published by G. R. Driver, in *Canaanite Myths and Legends*, Old Testament Studies Number III (Edinburgh, 1956). We read in the myth of Baal, B II I 35, among the description of the furnishings for the gods: "a table for a god which is full with varieties of game"; in II iii 14: "the victor Baal, the rider of the clouds complains: Foul meat was set on my table, cheap drink in my cup"; in iv 36, on Athirat: "eat and drink, eat food from the tables, drink wine from the jars." In Rephaim, we read in R III ii 8 - 16: "there Repu-Baal champion of Baal and champion of Anat is to be honoured...the tables are fragrant with vine-blossom, with vine-blossom for kings."

[98] Exod. 25: 30; 39: 36. In I Kings 7: 48 this distinct use of שלחן is indicated explicitly: ואת השלחן אשר עליו לחם הפנים "the table on which was the showbread."

[99] In Num. 4: 7 the table is called שלחן הפנים and the bread לחם התמיד.

[100] Lev. 24: 5 - 9.

of an ancient theology[101] in which food and drink were presented to an anthropomorphic Deity[102] together with the necessary utensils for consumption.[103] I may here reiterate the assumption that rituals often persist long after the theology behind them is rejected and forgotten.

The constant development and sophistication of Israel's theology and ritual engendered refinements and distinctions in the cult, both in the manner of the celebrations and in the appropriate vocabulary. The further development in theology and the repudiation of an anthropomorphic approach to the Deity induced the removal of the food table from the Debir, the Deity's dwelling, to the Great Hall or to the court before it, as an interim stage between the offering of food to the Deity and its sacrificial burning. But we must again consider that these changes did not happen "overnight", nor did they become effective by royal decree; the process was slow, and until the shift was complete the two contrasting theological and ritual systems existed side by side.[104] Ritual terms experienced the same metamorphosis;

---

[101] In some religions, as for example in the Hindu cult, food and flowers are presented to the gods, and are not burned.

[102] The Rabbis were sensitive to this issue and attempted to interpret these utensils in an entirely different way, as the forms used for baking the bread and housing it on the table. For an extensive study of this issue, and a discussion of the talmudic endeavour to dissociate these verses from any anthropomorphic aspect, see Heger, *Incense*, "Excursus", pp. 116 ff.

[103] It is remarkable that we do not encounter in the Book of Ezra any reference to the internal furnishings of the Temple, such as the lampstand and the table. In the Macc. narrative in contrast these items are explicitly emphasized, both at the record of their seizure by Antiochus in I Macc. 1: 22, and at their reconstruction in 4: 49. It is illogical to assume that the construction and placement of these significant holy furnishings were simply and carelessly overlooked in Ezra's report of the building of the Temple and the renewal of the cult. One must assume that as a result of changes in theology and particularly the elimination of anthropomorphic customs the table and its accoutrements were either not made, or were intentionally not mentioned in order to avoid emphasizing their significance; and because the "politically incorrect" table was not mentioned, the lampstand was also left out. The increased vitality of the cult and the priesthood ensuing upon the actions of Ezra and Nehemiah (a matter discussed in section 9.3 in more detail) may have led to the reintroduction of the ancient custom of the showbread and with it a renewed significance for the table. The expression לחם המערכת in Neh. 10: 34, interpreted as the equivalent of לחם הפנים by the commentators, is a term not used before, and appears exclusively in Neh. and in I Chr. 9: 32 and 23: 29; the term מערכת for the showbread also appears only in I Chr. 38: 16, and II Chr. 2: 3; 13: 11 and 29: 18. One must question the motive behind this philological alteration, what the term actually represented, and its practical and theological relationship with the ancient לחם קדש and לחם הפנים in I Sam. 21: 5 and 7.

[104] We must also consider a possible syncretism between the ancient nomadic custom of slaughtering and abandoning the animal, the forerunner of burning, and the Canaanite cult practice of offering food to the gods.

some terms persisted though changing their meaning, while others finally disappeared after a period of co-existence with the new terms. שלחן and מזבח, once distinct, became interchangeable, as we observe in Ezek. 41:22: the מזבח is called זה השלחן אשר לפני ה' "That is the table that is before the Lord."[105] At a later date, these two terms again became distinct, the altar used for burning and the table for the exhibition of the showbread, reminiscent of the primeval cult. The shift in purpose of מזבח is evident in the term itself.[106] It was originally a place for slaughter, as the root זבח implies, but in the P stratum it denotes the place for burning food; it still had some association with זבח because one burned upon it slaughtered animals, but the incense altar, on which the offering of such animal substances is explicitly prohibited, is also called מזבח. I would not exclude the possibility that the incense altar is called מזבח because it was originally the table for the presentation of meat;[107] its purpose was changed with the rejection of this type of worship to serve as a small box-like table for the burning of incense. The שלחן "table" kept its purpose of exhibiting the bread, while its underlying theology changed.[108] The odd prohibition in Exod. 30: 9b against ועלה ומנחה ונסך לא תסכו עליו "...any burnt offering and grain offering, and do not pour a drink offering upon it," referring to an altar made specifically for burning incense, ועשית מזבח מקטר קטרת (v. 1), points to

---

[105] There is a similar interchange between the two terms in Mal. 1: 7: מגישים על מזבחי לחם מגאל ואמרתם במה גאלנוך באמרכם שלחן ה' נבזה הוא "You place defiled food on my altar, but you ask: How have we defiled you? By saying that the Lord's table is contemptible."

[106] Cf. Gadegaard, p. 43, who writes: "Mizbeah is a rather imprecise word....Only the context can tell what kind of an altar is meant."

[107] In the archaic period it was an elevation of earth or stone on which the animal was slaughtered. In the nomadic tradition devotional slaughter was practised and the altar was called *madbah*; in the Mesopotamian cult, where this custom was not practised and food was presented to the gods, the altar was called *passuru*. The influence of both cultures on Israel may also have contributed to the existence of two parallel names for the altar.

[108] I. A. Seligman, מחקרים בספרות המקרא, ed. A. Horowitz et al. (Jerusalem, 1965), pp. 238 ff. writes on a similar topic (free translation) "The terminology remains despite the shift in its essence," and cites as an example the changes in the locus of God's throne: whether the reference was inside the Temple, the Temple itself as the throne, the cherubim as the throne etc., the term כסא "seat /throne" remained unaltered. Other examples are quoted on pp. 178 ff. with respect to the change in function of the כהן, from a diviner who used intermediary oracles such as the אפוד and the אורים ותומים, to the guardian of the sanctuaries and celebrant of sacrifices; though the functions changed dramatically, the title subsisted. The title נביא similarly prevailed unchanged for both the intuitive, clairvoyant ראה and the classical, preaching prophets.

the previous connection of this altar with such rituals, and supports my thesis.[109]

7.2.4 Ahaz' Reform and its Political Background

The burnt-offering altar became the centerpiece of worship, and the presentation table was pushed aside[110] and slowly disappeared; this process is

---

[109] I have drawn attention to this question in Heger, *Incense*, pp. 115ff., and also noted Noth's concerns (n. 40). I now propose an answer to this odd prohibition, which made no sense. On pp. 9ff. of *Incense* I have also drawn attention to the disparate names of this altar in the Pentateuch: in some instances it is called מזבח הזהב, in others מזבח הקטרת without the modifier הזהב, and in some instances composite arrangements, such as מזבח הזהב לקטרת and מזבח מקטר קטרת. I admitted there that I could not find a reasonable explanation for this diversity. I now suggest that my thesis of the shift in the use of this table-altar from a generic use to a specific incense utilization and the probability that also for economic reasons the offering material was changed can explain this oddity; the text may be comprised of the different original sources of the editor, and reflect the various stages of the shifts in the use of this altar.

[110] Many scholars have struggled with the interpretation of II Kings 16: 14-15, and particularly v. 15b ומזבח הנחשת יהיה לי לבקר. It is a common assumption that v. 14 is a later interjection into the original elements of the pericope whose primary sources were royal annals, and 15b is an added adaptation. Some scholars (Rehm, Fricke, Würthwein, Zwickel, Spieckermann) have therefore ignored the linguistic and syntactical difficulties in v. 14, and have mainly concentrated their efforts on explaining the odd phrase יהיה לי לבקר in v. 15 and the type of worship it implies. Rendtorff, *Studien*, p. 48 painstakingly analyzes the literary oddities, proposing various text emendations and consequently an interpretation entirely different from the simple meaning of the existing text. The traditional commentators such as Radak and Ralbag, who do not admit interjections in Scripture, attempted in their own way to solve the irregularities of v. 14. For the purposes of our study it suffices at this stage to demonstrate the shift in the ritual *modus operandi* effected by Ahaz, without the necessity of reconstructing a presumably supplementary and subsequently altered text. With respect to the nature of the altar moved by Ahaz, see E. Würthwein, *Die Bücher der Könige, 1. Kön. 12-2. Kön. 25*, Das Alte Testament Deutsch (Göttingen, 1984), p. 391: "...und den kleineren Tischaltar an die Nordseite rücken liess" ("...and [Ahaz] displaced the smaller **table-altar** to the north side)." I would also like to propose a simple solution to the odd phrase יהיה לי לבקר. This term does not occur very often in the Bible, but in a number of occurrences it expresses an idea of "to look after", "to watch over", "to seek out", "to enquire"- in other words, a general sense of "to care for". The LXX, for example, interprets in Ezek. 34: 11-12 ודרשתי את צאני ובקרתים "I will search for my sheep and look after them" with ἐπισκέψομαι, (כבקרת רעה עדרו) "as a shepherd looks after his herd" with ζητεῖ, and כן אבקר את צאני "so will I look after my sheep" with ἐκζητήσω, and in Ps. 27: 4 לחזות בנעם ה' ולבקר בהיכלו "and seek him in his temple" with ἐπισκέπτεσθαι. The two Greek terms ἐκ-ζητέω ("seek out, enquire") and ἐπισκοπέω ("inspect"), used alternatively for *variatio*, thus imply "to look after."

confirmed by archeological findings, which indicate a gradual decrease in the number of presentation benches in the sanctuaries in the 9th century B.C.E. and their total absence in the 8th century B.C.E.. As suggested above, a royal decree might result in the immediate building of a new altar, but the cessation of an entrenched ritual involving the presentation of food or gifts would take some time. The institution of an elaborate ceremonial of specific offerings would, for its part, also take a long time to evolve. The defined list in II Kings 16: 15 of animal offerings together with their auxiliary grain offerings and libations, so similar to the rules in the P stratum, suggest a later interjection.[111] Such an assumption does not affect my hypothesis concerning the extent of Ahaz' reform, as proposed above.

This reform, the institutionalization of sacrificial worship in Judah,[112] required the building of an impressive altar and the introduction of permanent daily sacrifices. The increased significance bestowed upon the burning of the offerings and its enhanced ceremonial certainly diminished the importance of

---

V. 15 of our pericope consists of the king's command on the organization of sacrificial worship in the new circumstances, i.e. the appropriate division of labour. The first part contains the duties of Uriah the priest concerning the sprinkling of the blood and the burning of offerings on the big altar, and the last phrase indicates the cultic duty of the king to look after the small, bronze presentation table. In this period the king still ministered occasionally, as did David and Solomon; Ahaz himself had also performed at the inauguration of the newly built altar, as we observe in v. 13. On the other hand, it is obvious that the daily offerings were performed by the priests and Ahaz thus imparts the necessary instructions. It is only logical that in order to dignify the new cult procedure, the entire system had to be changed beyond simply the construction of an impressive altar. The performance of the celebrations in a refined manner required professional clerics; the king, who only occasionally performed certain offerings, was not a trained celebrant. We may compare Micah's utterance: ויאמר מיכה עתה ידעתי כי ייטיב ה' לי כי היה לי הלוי לכהן "And Micah said: Now I know that the Lord will be good to me, since the Levite has become my priest [Jud. 17: 13]"; Micah now had a trained celebrant for the offerings. Ahaz thus assigned to the priests the exclusive celebration at the Temple altar in Jerusalem, and left himself the simpler presentation of food and gifts on a table-altar. It is also plausible that with this small step Ahaz initiated unintentionally the great shift in the Israelite cult toward priestly exclusivity in sacrificial celebrations.

[111] Cf. R. Rendtorff, *Studien*, pp. 46ff, who analyzes the literary style of the text and demonstrates the manifold sources intermingled in this pericope.

[112] I emphasized Judah here because it is possible that a permanent sacrifice was instituted in the Northern kingdom at an earlier date. There are two expressions referring to Israelite sanctuaries, which imply a regulated daily ritual in the Northern kingdom: בעלות המנחה, which presupposes an offering in the evening (I Kings 18: 36), and ויהי בבקר כעלות המנחה, a morning sacrifice (II Kings 3: 20), both referring to Israelite sanctuaries. On the other hand there is no indication whether these refer to animal sacrifices, as explicitly indicated in the daily offerings in our pericope, or to the presentation of food and gifts celebrated twice daily. As we have seen, the term מנחה has the generic meaning of "gift" in numerous occurrences in Kings; in II Kings 8: 8 and 17: 3-4, for example, it unequivocally does not designate sacrifices, but gifts.

the presentation of food. Scripture does not tell us where the "bronze altar" stood before it was displaced by Ahaz. We have seen the textual difficulties of II Kings 16: 14; the verse was undoubtedly "rectified", but it seems to me that we can detect in the expression המזבח הנחשת אשר לפני ה' "The bronze altar that stood before the Lord" that this table-altar stood in the Debir, as implied by the specific phrase before the Lord. Such an interpretation would also better explain the remainder of the verse; it would imply that Ahaz moved the altar from the Temple, מאת פני הבית, and placed it in the court near the new altar. This altar, which corresponds to Solomon's וכל המזבח אשר לדביר (I Kings 6: 22) may have still stood in the Debir, or been already in the Hall, a possibility which cannot be excluded, but this would not necessitate any change in my hypothesis.

The same approach is applicable to the מזבח הנחשת of Ezek. 9: 2.[113] It is evident that this cannot be the altar envisaged by Ezekiel in 43: 13 - 18, which is specifically for burnt-offerings (v. 27); nor is it the wooden table-altar מזבח עץ...זה השלחן which stood inside the Great Hall (41: 22). Ezekiel does not inform us of the purpose of this table-altar, and we can only assume from a consideration of other sources that it was dedicated to the exhibition of the showbread. Similarly, Ezekiel does not indicate the purpose of the bronze altar which stood in the court, and we can again deduce its use only from insights gleaned from other sources. We may therefore suppose that this bronze table-altar was the successor to the golden table-altar made by Solomon,[114] which underwent a metamorphosis with respect to use and location, as a result of shifts in theology and custom. The increased significance of burning offerings had a deleterious effect on the practice of exposing food, and consequently the relevant table was degraded in status and moved from the Debir to the Hall, then to the court, until its ultimate demotion.

---

[113] I have already cited in n. 40 the talmudic expression of surprise concerning this altar in B. T. Sabbath 55a: מזבח הנחשת מי הוה "Was there a bronze altar [in Ezekiel's period]?"

[114] The altar mentioned in I Kings 8: 22: ויעמד שלמה לפני מזבח ה' נגד כל קהל ישראל "Then Solomon stood before the altar of the Lord in front of the whole assembly," seems to be an authentic record; it may refer to the table-altar made by Solomon, moved from the Temple into the court for this special occasion, and loaded with gifts for the people to view. We read in B.T. Hagigah 26b: שמגביהין אותו ומראין בו לעולי רגלים לחם הפנים "...the table was raised and the [miracle] of the showbread was exhibited to the pilgrims [it remained fresh after a week of exposure]." The Chr. editor who emended this record by adding in II Chr. 6: 13 the explanation that Solomon made a כיור, probably had a valid reason to assume that this table-altar had the same dimensions as Moses' bronze altar. The circle is thus closed, supporting my thesis about Solomon's table-altar, and my discussion regarding de Groot's assumption of two altars. See n. 85 on de Groot's theory.

It is possible that in Ezekiel's time the custom of exposing food on this table was no longer practised, but the table still stood, similar to many religious rituals which subsist despite their initial theological foundation being long extinct or even forgotten. We may confirm this possibility from the preservation of the table for the exposure of the showbread in the Second Temple period, notwithstanding the certainty that the theological basis for offering food to the Deity had vanished by this time. The many anthropomorphic expressions left in the Pentateuch by its later redactors also confirm this tendency and serve as support for my postulate with respect to Ezekiel's bronze altar.[115]

My postulate concerning the relationship between the table-altar and the bronze altar is not contradicted by the fact that Solomon's two table-altars are stated to be of gold. One may expect that furnishings made by Solomon deteriorated over time and were replaced by substitutes of inferior quality, due to the poverty of some of the kings. Moreover, we know from Scripture that many of the Temple and royal treasuries were either seized by enemies[116] or offered as bribes to foreign powers.[117] There is also textual evidence of changes in the Temple's inventory. I Kings chaps. 5 –7 , narrating the building of the Temple and the fashioning of its furnishings, mentions only

---

[115] It is also possible that this bronze "altar" was one of the eight tables on which the sacrifices were slaughtered (Ezek. 40: 41). Ezekiel does not indicate their substance, in contrast to the additional four tables of dressed stones he records in v. 42. Moreover, we must consider that Ezekiel's prophecy was a visionary description of events to come, without any concrete model before him. We note that his vision does not correspond to the actual circumstances in the Second Temple, neither in its plan nor in its sacrificial system. As discussed in chap. 1 n. 86, the Talmud also detected insurmountable incompatibilities between his vision and the rules of the Pentateuch, in B. T. Menahot 45a: שהיו דבריו סותרין דברי תורה "[Ezekiel's] utterances contradict those of the Torah." On another occasion, in which a contradiction between Ezek. 45: 18 and Num. 28: 11 regarding sacrifices is perceived, Rabbi Johanan answers פרשה זו אליהו עתיד לדורשה "This issue will be resolved by Elijah [who will precede the arrival of the Messiah]." We cannot therefore draw conclusions about the conditions in the First or Second Temple from Ezekiel's imaginative mind, but we may undoubtedly draw conclusions on uses of specific terms in his period, as for example the interchange between the שולחן and מזבח of the Temple's furnishings.

[116] Already in the reign of Rehoboam, Solomon's son, Shishak, king of Egypt, את אצרות בית ה' ואת ארצרות בית המלך ואת הכל לקח "...carried off the treasures of the Temple of the Lord and the treasures of the royal palace. He took everything... [I Kings 14: 26]." This is a very general record, which may or may not include the Temple's furnishings, but later in the reign of Amaziah, Jehoash king of Israel carried away to Samaria כל הזהב והכסף ואת כל הכלים הנמצאים בית ה' "all the gold and silver and all the articles found in the Temple of the Lord [II Kings 14: 14]."

[117] Joash sent a plethora of sacred objects to Hazael (II Kings 12: 19) and Ahaz himself sent gold and silver as bribes to the king of Assyria (II Kings 16: 8).

items of bronze and gold, while in the list of the furnishings seized by
Nebuzaradan in II Kings 25: 15 we read: ואת המחתות ואת המזרקות אשר
זהב זהב ואשר כסף כסף "the censers and sprinkling bowls - all that were
made of gold or silver...." The parallel passage in Jer. 52: 19 also states ואת
הספים ואת המחתות ואת המזרקות ואת הסירות ואת המנרות ואת הכפות
ואת המנקיות אשר זהב זהב ואשר כסף כסף "the basins, censers, sprinkling
bowls, pots, lampstands,[118] dishes and bowls - all that were made of gold or
silver...." In I Kings there is no mention of silver. In Ezra 1: 9 - 11 we also
observe that gold and silver dishes, pans and bowls, articles taken by
Nebuchadnezar from the Temple, were returned to the Judeans by Cyrus. We
should therefore not be surprised that in Ahaz' period a bronze altar was used
for the exhibition of food instead of the gold table made by Solomon. The
absence of the bronze altar in these lists cannot serve as evidence that it was
never made; the golden table for the showbread, which was most certainly
made by Solomon, also does not appear in these lists.[119] Many changes
occurred in the Temple cult and equipment between Solomon's period and
the reign of Ahaz or the fall of Jerusalem to the Babylonians.

But even a royal decision must be made within an accommodating
environment to be effective, and it seems that the period of Ahaz was ripe for
the shift. The Judean kings recognized the significance of the Temple as a
central cult establishment for the development of the city of Jerusalem and
the kingdom as a whole. I have already mentioned that according to
archeological findings Jerusalem enjoyed a period of expansion in the 8th
century. Ahaz' reforms introducing daily sacrifices in the Temple and
building an impressively large altar would not have been possible without a
prior developmental stage preparing the appropriate milieu. I have doubts
whether this shift in theology and custom also embodied a directive to
cleanse the Temple of all symbols and statues of living things, as Zwickel[120]
postulates, but a greater significance bestowed upon burnt offerings is
evident from the utterances of the prophets of this period. In contrast to
Zwickel, I would contend that the devotion to burnt offerings was not the
result of a greater piety, but rather of a mistaken belief that such offerings
would appease the divine wrath, and thus induce forgiveness of the corrupt

---

[118] I call attention to the fact that in Ezek. there is no mention of lampstands in the Temple,
and therefore we may doubt the authenticity of this term.

[119] This table may have been included in the generic expression ויקצץ את כל כלי הזהב
אשר עשה שלמה מלך ישראל בהיכל ה' "and he took away [this is the NIV
interpretation; the term קצץ is commonly used to express the idea of cutting, and the
LXX translates συνέκοψεν "chop off"] all the gold articles that Solomon king of Israel
had made for the Temple of the Lord [II Kings 24: 13]."

[120] "Die Kultreform des Ahas."

deeds of the kings. This erroneous perception, a type of early *indulgentia*, was the trigger for the prophets' censure.[121]

It is possible that Azariah - Uzziah (784-746) started the royal interest in the Temple and the cult celebrations. Nothing of this is reported in II Kings 15: 1 - 7, the record of his reign, but in II Chr. 26 we encounter an extended biography of this king with an account of his great achievements. His powerful army defeated enemies and conquered the southern desert as far as the border of Egypt, and, what is important for our study, he built towers in Jerusalem and fortified them. We observe that he enlarged his country and his capital, Jerusalem. It would be only reasonable that he was eager to enhance the significance of the Temple as a focal point for the prominence of his city as a cult center.[122] His impulse to offer incense as reported in II Chr. may be devoid of precise historical authenticity, but may contain some kernel of truth regarding a royal celebration of offerings in the Temple. Such a practice would resemble and emulate the royal sacrificial celebrations in the surrounding cultures. The Kings editor saw nothing wrong in such a custom, practised by David and Solomon, and therefore did not report it, but the late Chr. editor certainly had strong objections to it, portraying it as a usurpation of the most significant priestly cult celebration in the Second Temple period and as a justification for the divine punishment.[123] It would be unreasonable to assume that the Chr. editor invented a totally false event; it is on the other hand plausible that he presented a real occurrence in a manner suited to his creed and to the circumstances prevailing in his period. It is therefore probable that the shift toward a greater significance for the sacrificial system of burnt offerings in the Temple of Jerusalem, the capital city (from which new intellectual and cultural ideas usually radiate), was initiated by Uzziah and ultimately completed by Ahaz.

Such an hypothesis would imply a careful redaction by the Kings editor to provide a rationale for the disappearance of the bronze altar of Moses. Such a deliberate formulation would explain the lack of any record of the building of an altar by Solomon in I Kings 6 - 7 and the non-specific expression כי מזבח הנחשת אשר לפני ה' in 8: 64, with no indication as to who constructed this altar. The Ahaz narrative reflects the demotion of the bronze altar from its central location to the north of the great altar to a subordinate and occasional role, and again describes the altar in an indeterminate manner (II Kings 16: 14): המזבח הנחשת אשר לפני ה'. The Ahaz narrative serves as an

---

[121] Isa. 1: 11; Jer. 6: 20; 7: 4; 21-23; Hosea 4: 13-15; 6: 6; 8: 11-13; Amos 4: 4; 5: 5; 25; Micah 6: 7-8.

[122] Such an hypothesis would impute to Uzziah the initiation of a politically-based reform, an objective which developed slowly and became fully operative in Josiah's period.

[123] For an extended discussion of the issue of these priestly privileges and their linkage to the Uzziah narrative, see Heger, *Incense*, under the various headings.

ætiological justification for the replacement of Moses' bronze altar with a permanent stone altar, without directly confronting the obscure and delicate issue of the origin of this table-altar and its previous anthropomorphically-tainted use. It is possible that it was Ahaz who eliminated the concept of food presentation, but one cannot exclude the possibility that this might have been accomplished slightly later and been attributed to Ahaz, since he built the great altar for burning sacrifices; it would have been reasonable to assume that at the same time he degraded the table-altar.[124]

The Chr. editor on the other hand seems to have been primarily troubled by the lack of an altar in the inventory of the Temple equipment made by Solomon. In the editor's period the burnt-offering altar had attained momentous significance in the cult, and he had to assume that Solomon constructed a larger altar then the small one made by Moses. He therefore inserted in II Chr. 4: 1 a record of such an altar made by Solomon, and reiterated this in II Chr. 7: 7: מזבח הנחשת אשר עשה שלמה; in the parallel verse in I Kings 8: 64, in contrast, its origin is not indicated. Because of this emendation the Chr. narrative entangles itself in a maze of dilemmas;[125] there

---

[124] We read an interesting homily in Midrash Lamentations Rabbah, פרשה ב ד"ה ג ולא זכר כתיב ויבאו ויעמדו אצל מזבח הנחושת ר' יהודה בר' סימון אמר עד מקום מחיצתו ורבנן אמרי עומד ומזכיר חטאין של אחז דכתיב ביה ומזבח הנחשת יהיה לי לבקר מהו לבקר א"ר פינחס פסלו ועשאו בעלי מומין "It is written: 'They came in and stood beside the bronze altar [Ezek. 9: 2].' Rabbi Judah son of Rabbi Simon said: [They stood] at the edge of the altar's location. The Sages said, [The altar] stood and reminded [them] of the sins of Ahaz, with respect to whom it is written [that he said] 'I will use the bronze altar for seeking guidance [NIV translation of לבקר in II Kings 16: 15].' What is the interpretation of לבקר [a puzzling issue discussed by many scholars]? Said Rabbi Phinehas: He [Ahaz] defiled it [the bronze altar] and polluted [all the sacrifices offered upon it]." The Midrash does not specify the question in respect of which the two solutions above were offered, thus hindering our understanding of the answers. In B. T. Sabbath 55a on the same verse in Ezek., quoted in n. 40, the question is specified: מזבח הנחשת מי הוה "Was there [still] a bronze altar [in the time of Ezekiel]?" The commentators thus assumed that the Midrash was posing the same question. The first answer would be: There was no bronze altar, since it was destroyed by the Babylonians, and Ezekiel refers to its position, that is, where the altar originally stood. The second answer, taking עמד in singular as referring to the altar, declares that the altar stood there [actually or figuratively] to remind people of the sins of Ahaz.

[125] It is regrettable that the Temple Scroll has many lacunae, and we are unable to determine definitely whether its authors attempted to solve the issue of the two disparate altars of bronze and stone. In Col. III it is evident that the editor follows Exod. 27 and perceives the divine command to make a bronze holocaust altar. Occurrences of the term נחושת, whether written in full or in part, are numerous, as is the term מזבח העולה. כסף) is also mentioned among the materials for the Temple and its furnishings, as in Exod. 25: 3; this is entirely missing in the narrative of Solomon's Temple, in Kings; only I Chr. 22: 14

is no justification for the statement in II Chr. 7: 7 that this larger altar was not sufficient for the many offerings,[126] and no explanation for its disappearance and replacement with a permanent stone altar in the Second Temple period. Chr., unlike Kings, does not report the building of an altar by Ahaz and the removal of the bronze altar; this was possibly because it would not have seemed reasonable to move such a large altar as was supposedly made by Solomon. Alternatively, the Chr. editor may have considered the inadequacy of the bronze altar as a sufficient rationalization in itself for the disappearance of this altar from the permanent furnishings of the Temple. He retrojected the substitution of the bronze altar to Solomon, and thus did not

---

lists silver among the materials amassed by David for the Temple building. This corroborates the proposition that the description of the altar in Col. III follows the Exod. text, including the command to build a bronze altar.) On the other hand, the many rules for the offerings on the altar, called מזבח העולה, מזבח ה' or just מזבח, follow the text in Ezek. 43, which unquestionably describes a stone altar with עזרה "ledge", on which the blood of the offering should be smeared. The rule in Col. 23: 12 and 13 ונתן מדמו באצבעו על ארבע קרנות המזבח ועל ארבע פנות עזרת המזבח (as convincingly reconstructed by Yadin, מגילת המקדש, Vol. II (Jerusalem, 1977), corresponds exactly to Ezek. 43: 20 ולקחת מדמו ונתתה על ארבע קרנותיו ואל ארבע פנות העזרה "You are to take some of its blood and put it on the four 'horns' of the altar and on the four corners of the upper ledge...." The bronze altar had no עזרה and there is no mention in the Pentateuch of smearing sacrificial blood other than on the "horns" in Lev. 4. Hence, the Temple Scroll contains a command to construct a bronze altar, like Exod. 27, but the blood-smearing refers to a stone altar as described in Ezek. 43. Yadin (Vol. I pp. 239 ff.) suggests that "the author of the scroll sees a temple with two altars: the small bronze one, which had been used in the Tabernacle, and the main one of stone." Yadin's suggestion generates two different questions: a) whether such a bronze altar existed during the period of the editing of the scroll, and b) whether the editor of the scroll thought that it ought to exist. There is no doubt that such a bronze altar did not exist in the Second Temple; although it is evidence *ex silentio*, I think that the plethora of narratives from so many sources which do not mention such an altar in the Second Temple should satisfy any doubt in this regard. Regarding b) I also wish to express my resolute objection. The Temple Scroll comprises a great number of rules with respect to the use of the altar; some specify the incense altar and others the holocaust altar with the specific mention of the "ledge" עזרה, a characteristic only of the large stone altar. In the description of the bronze altar in Col. III, such elements do not occur, and the bronze altar is also not mentioned in any ordinance for the performance of the offerings. We must thus question the use of this bronze altar. I therefore postulate that similar to the Chr. editor, who left unresolved the question of why the divinely commanded bronze altar was replaced by a stone altar in the Second Temple, but at the same time did not dare to "erase" the order in Exod. 27, the Scroll editor too ignored this apparently grave issue. The D editor also offered no reasonable justification; he simply recorded that Ahaz moved the bronze altar, but this record does not justify the behaviour of the returnees from exile in not making a "bronze" altar, in flagrant defiance of the divine eternal command.

[126] A question asked in B. T. Zebahim 59b and cited above in n. 23.

cite the Kings narrative recording Ahaz' construction of an imitation of the
Damascus altar.[127]

7.2.5 What Altar did Ahaz Move?

It remains now to speculate what type of table-altar was in use in the period
of Ahaz, and why the P editor chose a bronze altar for his visualization of
Moses' altar. There is no indication or hint with respect to the form of
Solomon's tables, the one specifically for meat, called מזבח, and the other
for the showbread with the generic denomination שלחן, except that they
were made of gold. As we observed, however, these tables may have been
changed over the centuries and it would be reasonable to assume that
Assyrian models were copied, given that that nation was the dominant empire
of the region in the 8th century. Scripture does record the copying of a
burnt-offerings altar by Ahaz, since this was connected with a significant
shift in the entire sacrificial system, but one should not expect a record in
Scripture with respect to the remodelling of a presentation table in Jerusalem
in the Assyrian fashion; this was not an event worthy of recording, for the
same reason that the pattern of Solomon's tables was not transmitted. If we
look at Galling's representations and descriptions of Assyrian portable tin

---

[127] The absence of a Chr. parallel to the Kings narrative on the altar copied by Ahaz has also
puzzled others. K. D. Fricke, *Das Zweite Buch von den Königen,* Die Botschaft des Alten
Testaments, 12/II (Stuttgart), pp. 214 ff. suggests that the editor avoided reporting this
because the sacrificial celebrations performed by the king as recorded in Kings would
have constituted a serious violation of the exclusive privileges of the priesthood. I do not
see eye to eye with Fricke on this topic, for a number of reasons. The Chr. editor goes to
great lengths to report Ahaz' misdeeds and thus justify his divine punishment. We are
unaware of why the Chr. editor painted such a dismal picture of Ahaz' misdeeds and
misfortunes, which bears no relationship to its counterpart in II Kings 16: 1 - 20, and has
in fact aggravated the account of Ahaz' relationship with Damascus. Instead of the
neutral report in Kings concerning the building of a Damascene-style altar for worship to
the God of Israel, the Chr. editor accuses Ahaz of a more wicked deed: ויזבח לאלהי
דרמשק המכים בו "He offered sacrifices to the god of Damascus, who had defeated
him [II Chr. 28: 23]." It is thus unclear why this comparatively trivial misdeed of
sacrifice was omitted; including Ahaz' sacrifices would obviously not imply that his
conduct in usurping priestly privileges was correct. The Chr. editor did not similarly
censure reports of sacrificial performances by David (I Chr. 21: 26) or Solomon (II Chr.
5: 6; 7: 4-5; 8: 12), and in fact recorded Uzziah's crime and punishment in an occurrence
similar to our topic (II Chr. 26: 16 - 21), where there was an aetiological motive in
conveying the idea of a severe punishment for violating the priestly privileges. If it was
the element of sacrificial celebration that troubled the editor in the case of Ahaz, he might
have simply omitted this part and recorded the building of the altar. I think that the Kings
editor felt the aetiological necessity of justifying the "disappearance" of Moses' bronze
altar, and therefore had to report the circumstances of its substitution.

table-altars, "Zinnenaltar",[128] we can understand the reason for choosing a portable bronze altar for the desert narrative in the P stratum, and the odd details of its structure in Exod. 27: 1 - 8.

In addition to the similarity of the material, a metal, we find the following comparable features between the bronze altar of Moses and the Assyrian altars:

a) The Assyrian altars are square, a characteristic particularly emphasized in Exod. (27: 1) רבוע יהיה ; this is a tautology, given that the dimensions are already indicated.

b) The upper part is larger than the lower part, and this may have been the reason for the odd and ambiguous כרכב, discussed in the examination of the text.

c) The upper part of the Assyrian altar has a groove-like ornament all around. It is not identical with the מכבר מעשה רשת of the bronze altar in Exod. 27: 4, but it may have served as an inspiration to the P editor. We must consider that he did not have a model before him at the time of his composition of the pericope, and a vague reminiscence or even an equivocally written record of such altars as his source might explain a variation of this kind

d) On top of the upper part of the Assyrian altars we observe indented ornaments, of different depths in the various models. The זר סביב of the ark and the table (Exod. 25: 11, 24), and of the bronze altar in the LXX text, would be a perfect imitation of these indented ornaments. This indenting may also have been the model for the horned altars. The tin altars had, as far as one is able to assume from Galling's sketches of them, three protruding tips on each side, eight in total; such elaborate indenting would have been most difficult on a stone altar, and only four protruding ornamental tips may have remained from the model of the surrounding indented molding on the tin altar's rim. In section 7.2.3 I had envisaged such a possibility, and can now substantiate this with the help of Galling's sketches.

We do not have the dimensions of these altars, and it is difficult to know their correct relation and perspective with the surrounding objects; relative to the trees in sketch number 16, for instance, the altars would have been of substantial size. The P editor had to deduce the dimensions of an altar which could be easily transported but also allowed for the putative burning of an entire animal, and this was the reason for the chosen size.[129] The fact that the

---

[128] K. Galling, *Der Altar in den Kulturen des Alten Orients, Eine Archäologische Studie* (Berlin, 1925), Table 9 and pp. 45-6.

[129] N. H. Gadegaard, "On the So-Called Burnt Offering Altar in the Old Testament," reaches a similar conclusion about the nature of this bronze altar, that it was "intended for the exposition of offering gifts" (p. 43), but he derives his postulate from a practical consideration, namely the unsuitability of a bronze altar for burning animal flesh.

Assyrian altar had an indented molding and the Phoenician altars had "horns" does not imply an absolute dichotomy between them; syncretism is a common feature of cult theologies and custom, and the Israelites may also have combined features in copying alien altars and adapting them to their own conceptions.

7.3 Conclusion

In conclusion, we may suggest that the bronze table-altar replaced by Ahaz, and still kept in some vague memory, served as an imaginary model for the P editor. Such a model served best for a portable furnishing, suited to the narrative of the desert wandering. The poles, which were added to both the table and the bronze altar for portability, were adapted from those of the ark, the ancient sacred symbol whose significance remained vivid in the memory of the people and whose description may also have existed in the archives.

8. Josiah's Reform

8.1 The Relationship Between II Kings 12: 5 - 17 and II Kings 22: 3 - 7

The centralization of the cult attributed to Josiah had far-reaching consequences with respect to the development of the sacrificial cult. The political and social circumstances behind the reform must be ascertained through a careful examination of the relevant texts and their historical context. I shall explore the issue of centralization in this chapter and chap. 9; in this chapter I shall focus in particular on Josiah's repair of the Temple as narrated in II Kings 22, and the methods that may be used to reveal the circumstances behind these repairs.

There is a remarkable similarity between the two texts in II Kings 12 and 22, which narrate the financing and execution of the Temple repairs by Joash and Josiah. This issue has occupied a great number of biblical scholars since Wellhausen.[1] Basing their conclusions mainly on literary and structural analysis, these scholars have been primarily interested in establishing the relationship between the two pericopes, that is, whether II Kings 12 depends on II Kings 22, or vice versa; for the most part they have not focused their investigation on the issue of whether there was only one instance of Temple repair, or two. This chapter will analyze a number of recent scholarly publications on this issue, focusing on the historical authenticity of the two narratives. These will be assessed relative to what is known of the surrounding historical circumstances, a factor that in my opinion was overlooked in previous discussions.

I shall also attempt to determine what may be gained from a comparison with the parallel texts in II Chronicles. It is my opinion that the differences in these texts reveal the changes in ideology and practice that occurred in the period between the editing of the two books; this also offers further insight into the way in which the later editors and their public understood the narratives in Kings. The emendations of and explanations to the text of Kings provide us with a significant substantiation of the emendation process in general, and the particular method used by the biblical editors to adapt their sources to the circumstances of their period. The unequivocal authentication of such a practice allows us a useful working assumption, namely that the same procedure was followed by the redactors of Kings and subsequent biblical editors with respect to their original sources.

---

[1] In F. Bleek, *Einleitung in das Alte Testament* (1878), p. 258 and in *Die Composition des Hexateuchs und der historischen Bücher des Alten Testament* (1963), p. 293.

8.1.1 Scholarly Postulates

Stade,[2] who wrote at the beginning of the century and is quoted by most of the contemporary articles on the subject, concludes that the narrative of chap. 12 depends on that of chap. 22. W. Dietrich,[3] relying on literary analysis, reaches the opposite conclusion; he also declares unhesitatingly that the narrative in chap. 22 is *unhistorisch*, in plain language untrue, and simply represents a transcript of chap. 12.[4] H. D. Hoffmann,[5] on the basis of his literary analysis, reaches the conclusion that II Kings 12 should be considered as a precursor of the Josiah reform in the context of the deuteronomic cult historiography; the narrative in II Kings 22 depends on the detailed report of chap. 12, and would be incomprehensible without it. Hoffmann concurs with Dietrich on the common origin of the two pericopes, quoting Dietrich's assumption[6] that the chap. 22 narrative was included in Kings by the same deuteronomic historiographer who recorded chap. 12, but he does not declare expressly, as Dietrich does, that the narrative of Josiah's repair of the Temple is untrue. Hoffmann's statement that both pericopes are elements of the deuteronomic historiography would not preclude a finding that both pericopes are authentic. His literary analysis merely indicates a stylistic dependence; both pericopes might portray actual repairs performed by both kings, with the redactor using certain stereotypical language parallels in his narrative. The scholarly dispute would then be restricted to a determination of which version was original; alternatively, both versions might be considered as intentional interjections into the setting of the deuteronomic historiography, a procedure often attributed to biblical redactors. Spieckermann[7] analyzes the same literary oddities as Dietrich, but reaches the opposite conclusion. In his opinion, the late deuteronomic redactor attempted to retroject a reform back to Joash, introducing in II Kings 12 the record of a covenant and reform ultimately completed by Josiah. Spieckermann comments that by this procedure the redactor inadvertently minimizes the significance of Josiah's reform and its connection with the

---

[2]   B. Stade and F. Schwally, *The Book of Kings* (London, 1904).

[3]   W. Dietrich, "Josia und das Gesetzbuch," *VT* 27 (1977), pp. 18 - 22.

[4]   He also states: "Der Redaktor hatte eben aus der Josia-Zeit keine Unterlagen über derartige Massnahmen, sondern nur das Quellenstück 2 Reg. XII 5 - 17 aus der Zeit des Joas." ("The [deuteronomic] redactor had no original source concerning such steps [for the Temple repair] from Josiah's period, but solely the source of II Kings 12: 5 -17 from Joash's period.")

[5]   H. D. Hoffmann, *Reform und Reformen* (Zürich, 1980), pp. 192 - 197.

[6]   Note 18.

[7]   H. Spieckermann, *Juda unter Assur in der Sargonidenzeit* (Göttingen, 1982), pp. 179 - 183.

discovery of the book, a result likely not consistent with his general intent. Spieckermann argues mainly about a reform of the cult, under which he includes both the elimination of alien idolatrous elements and the elimination of the *bamoth*; he associates the Temple repairs with the cult "reform". Thus he also considers the record of the repairs made by Joash in chap. 12 as a retrojection of the Josiah narrative of chap. 22. It is Spieckermann's general opinion that the deuteronomic redactor in fact retrojected the initiation of the reform even to the kings Asa and Jehoshaphat. He does recognize that the elimination of the *bamoth* cannot be retrojected to the period of Asa's reign (p. 187), but does not specify to what period it should be attributed; in his opinion, even the connection of the *bamoth* reform to Hezekiah is similarly a deuteronomic retrojection, devoid of any basis in reality.

Ch. Levin[8] performs a minute literary analysis of the pericope II Kings 12: 5 - 17 in apposition to the - in his opinion - original text of vv. 1 - 4 and 18 - 19, and concludes that it represents a later secondary interjection; it underwent additional alterations by priestly redactors, and engendered further inconsistencies. Levin also critically analyzes the II Kings 22: 3 - 7, 9 pericope, and constructs a short and consistent narrative, uncorrupted by later priestly additions and modifications. This, in his opinion, was the original text which served as the *Vorlage* for the story - classified by Levin as Midrash - in II Kings 12 : 5 - 17. We thus observe that scholars arrive at contradictory assumptions from an analysis of the same text, evaluating differently the same oddities in the text. I shall comment on several specific elements brought forward by the scholars in their argumentation.

8.1.2 The Concept of Reform

As noted, Spieckermann includes in his concept of "reform" both the eradication of alien cult elements, such as the מצבות and אשרים, and the elimination of the *bamoth*, that is, the process of cult centralization in Jerusalem. He constructs upon this proposition a theory of an intentional scheme by the deuteronomic redactor to retroject the "reform" to king Asa, right after the first apostates Solomon and Rehoboam. I propose, however, that the deuteronomic "reform" concerned solely the issue of the *bamoth*.[9]

---

[8] Chr. Levin, "Die Instandsetzung des Tempels unter Joasch ben Ahasja," *VT 60*, 1 (1990), 51-88.

[9] Chr. Levin, "Joschija im deuteronomistischen Geschichtswerk," *ZAW* 96 (1984), 351-71 also perceives the "reform" in the same way. He writes on p. 354: "So vehement der Erstredaktor sich für die Kulteinheit verwendet und an ihr als Masstab die Frömmigkeit der Könige von Israel und Juda bemessen hat, so wenig galt der Kultreinheit - den Baal der Omridenzeit und der assyrischen Gestirnkult unter Manasse und Amon ausgenommen - sein Interesse." ("As vehemently as the first redactor of Deuteronomy

We are hampered in our investigation in that we do not know the real "religious" and cultic circumstances in Judah in the monarchic period from David to Josiah; we can only rely on the existing text, supplemented with information from other sources. We are forced to assess this information according to our contemporary understanding of "cause and effect," and to some extent must impute to the various biblical redactors certain motives based on our current comprehension of human thought and actions. In particular, the concept of "reform" is itself a modern one. We must attempt to assess the reaction of the biblical text to a change in policy or in theology; was it considered a drastic and conclusive change from previous conditions, or merely a transitory change in circumstances which produced temporary corruptions and subsequent corrections?

8.1.2.1 The Sin of Idolatry Versus the Sin of *Bamoth*

On the issue of the eradication of alien cult elements, I could not discern in the text any circumstances from which an intention of the redactor might be deduced to retroject a "reform" movement to the period of Asa (905 - 874). One would look for a stable and continuous period of idolatrous worship, in response to which a "reform" movement would be instituted, but no such period can be detected in Judah. In the three hundred thirty-four years from David to Hezekiah,[10] according to the text in Kings only one of the fourteen monarchs, Rehoboam, is expressly accused of having made מצבות ואשרים (I Kings 14: 23).

There are indirect accusations of idolatry, but the language of Kings is careful to distinguish between idolatrous practice and worship at the *bamoth*.[11] For example, Rehoboam's son Abijah is accused only with the

---

pleads for cultic centralization, and judges according to this criterion the piety of the kings of Israel and Judah, so he ignores the issue of the purity of the cult - except the Baal of the Omri period and the Assyrian star worship of Manasseh and Amon.")

[10] David reigned 40 years, I Kings 2: 11; Solomon 40 years, I Kings 11: 42; Rehoboam 17 years, I Kings 14: 21; Abijah 3 years, I Kings 15: 2; Asa 41 years, I Kings 15: 10; Jehoshaphat 25 years, I Kings 22: 42; Jehoram 8 years, II Kings 8: 17; Ahaziah 1 year, II Kings 8: 26; Athaliah 6-7 years, II Kings 11: 4; Joash 40 years, II Kings 12: 2; Amaziah 29 years, II Kings 14: 2; Azariah 52 years, II Kings 15: 2; Jotham 16 years, II Kings 15: 33 and Ahaz 16 years, II Kings 16: 2; in total, 334 years.

[11] The stereotypical expression ויעש הרע בעיני ה' "He did evil in the eyes of the Lord" imputes idolatrous practices (I Kings 14: 22 for Rehoboam; II Kings 8: 18 for Jehoram; II Kings 8: 27 for Ahaziah, as for Ahab in I Kings 16: 30); while לא סר ממנו לעשות or לא כדוד אביו, or the comparable ויעש הישר with the limitation הישר בעיני ה', or the restrictive רק הבמות לא סרו (אך), are used to describe the continuation of worship at the *bamoth* (I Kings 22: 42 - 44 for Jehoshaphat; II Kings 12: 2 - 4 for Joash;

vague וילך בכל חטאות אביו "He committed all the sins his father did [I Kings 15: 3]." Though this declaration tends to suggest idolatry, it is somewhat qualified by the second part of the verse ולא היה לבבו שלם עם ה׳ אלהיו כלבב דוד אביו "His heart was not fully devoted to the Lord his God as the heart of David his forefather was." A similar remark, for example, is used by the redactor to evaluate Amaziah (801 - 785?), who is described as a righteous king, ויעש הישר בעיני ה׳ "He did what was right in the eyes of the Lord [II Kings 14: 3]," with the qualifying רק לא כדוד אביו "but not as his father David did." This ambiguous phrase is further elucidated in the succeeding v. 4: רק הבמות לא סרו עוד "The high places, however, were not removed." Thus the wrongdoing of Amaziah (and Abijah) fit within the scheme of the Kings redactor to credit David for his undertaking to build the Temple,[12] as a counteraction against the *bamoth*,[13] and to denounce those kings who continued to worship at them.[14] Those kings who destroyed the

---

II Kings 14: 2 - 4 for Amaziah; II Kings 15: 2 - 4 for Azariah; II Kings 15: 33 - 35 for Jotham).

[12] Solomon, who built the Temple, continually refers to David his father as its initiator. See, for instance, I Kings 5: 19, in which Solomon mentions God's command to David to build the Temple; I Kings 8: 17, Solomon's oration at the Temple's consecration, in which he asserts his fulfillment of David's request to build the Temple. The designation of David as the primary originator of the Temple is thoroughly documented in Kings, and with even greater emphasis in I Chr. chaps. 28-29; there, in addition to the plans of the Temple and the provision of all the necessary materials, even the organization of the clerics is attributed to David. According to II Chr. 3: 1 David also chose the exact site of the Temple: ויחל שלמה לבנות את בית ה׳ בירושלם בהר המוריה אשר נראה לדויד אביהו אשר הכין במקום דויד בגרן ארנן היבוסי "Then Solomon began to build the Temple of the Lord in Jerusalem on Mount Moriah, where the Lord had appeared to his father David. It was on the threshing floor of Araunah the Jebusite, the place provided by David." But another Midrash is careful to assert that this was an ancient sacred site, and David was told by an angel to choose it. We read in *Pesiqta Rabbati* 43: (וימצא) [ומצא] שם את המזבח שבו הקריב אדם הראשון ובו הקריב נח ובו הקריב אברהם "And he found there the altar to which Adam brought his offerings, and Noah brought his offerings, and Abraham...."

[13] We may note that the prophet who criticizes the altar made by Jeroboam, the rival of the Jerusalem Temple and altar, with the words מזבח מזבח "O altar, altar," emphasizes that it will be a son of David who will destroy it: הנה בן נולד לבית דוד "A son will be born of the house of David [I Kings 13: 2]."

[14] In the first censure against Solomon, worship at the *bamoth* is stated to be contrary to David's statutes. We read in I Kings 3: 3: ויאהב שלמה את ה׳ ללכת בחקות דוד אביו רק בבמות הוא מזבח ומקטיר "Solomon showed his love for the Lord by walking according to the statutes of his father David, except that he offered sacrifices and burned incense on the high places." Censure of worship at the *bamoth* is considered to have been a regulation commanded by David, not a divine dictate. In the portrayal of Ahaz we read: ולא עשה הישר בעיני ה׳ אלהיו כדוד אביו "Unlike David his father

bamoth are distinguished with high praise: ככל אשר עשה דוד אביו "just as his father David did [II Kings 18: 3]" for Hezekiah (727 - 698), who initiated the elimination of the bamoth, and for Josiah (639 - 609), the king who finally eradicated the bamoth, וילך בכל דרך דוד אביו ולא סר ימין ושמאול "...and walked in all the ways of his father David, not turning aside to the right or to the left [II Kings 22: 2]." The expression "as his father David did" became the equivalent of "he destroyed the bamoth," and the opposite of "he continued worship at the bamoth."

With respect to Jehoram (850 - 843) and Ahaziah (843), who are also implicitly accused of idolatry, the redactor attempts to dissociate them from the Davidic dynasty, emphasizing their relationship with the house of Ahab. We read in II Kings 8: 18 regarding Jehoram כי בת אחאב היתה לו לאשה "for he married a daughter of Ahab," and in 8: 27 re Ahaziah כי חתן בית אחאב הוא "for he was related by marriage to Ahab's family"; both verses, it seems, refer to Queen Athaliah, Ahaziah's mother (843 - 837), of the Israelite royal family of Omri.[15] On the other hand, the redactor of Kings does not

---

he did not do what was right in the eyes of the Lord [II Kings 16: 2]"; v. 4 explains ויזבח ויקטר בבמות "He offered sacrifices and burned incense at the high places." Verse 3 here is apparently an interjection, but in any case imputes no idolatrous practice to Ahaz. It is indeed possible that the redactor intentionally made this subtle difference between the structure of his expression in the evaluation of Ahaz and that of the other kings to justify the accusation against Ahaz, since his behaviour was certainly less mischievous than that of the other kings plainly accused of idolatrous practices.

There are, I must admit, one or two exceptions to this thesis of the link between David and the denunciation of the bamoth, but it seems to me that these exceptions do not invalidate the rule, and may be explained. The accusation against Solomon is ויעש שלמה הרע בעיני ה' ולא מלא אחרי ה' כדוד אביו "Solomon did evil in the eyes of the Lord; he did not follow the Lord completely as David his father did [I Kings 11: 6]." Although this verse is placed within the narrative of Solomon's idolatrous practice, it may be divided into two parts by the conjunction ו "and"; the first part refers to idols and the second to the continuation of the bamoth, for which there is also the specific accusation in I Kings 3: 3. Furthermore, the redactor's comparison of Solomon with his father David is appropriate in this specific context and does not affect the understanding of this expression when used with later kings. A similar editorial exigency may have been the motive for the redactor to use the expression כדוד אביו "like his father David" for Asa, in I Kings 15: 11, to emphasize his great achievement in destroying the idolatrous elements in the land, even those belonging to his mother. This earned him the praise כדוד אביו although he did not eliminate the bamoth. To justify this exception, the redactor adds, after his reprimand concerning the bamoth, the commendation רק לבב אסא היה שלם עם ה' כל ימיו "Asa's heart was fully committed to the Lord all his life [v. 14]."

15 There are two apparently conflicting records about Athaliah's parentage. In II Kings 8: 18 we have noted that Jehoram married Ahab's daughter, whereas in II Kings 8: 26 we read ושם אמו עתליהו בת עמרי מלך ישראל "His [Ahaziah, Jehoram's son]

accuse her directly of idolatrous practices; this is again merely implicit in the statement that the people tore down the temple of Baal after her demise (II Kings 11: 18).

We must also consider Solomon's period of idolatry, but it must be noted that the redactor attempts to minimize the seriousness of Solomon's behaviour,[16] suggesting a temporary aberration[17] of short duration.[18] This accusation of Solomon stands in complete contrast to the narratives relating his excellence in all other domains, including the glorification of the Temple built by him, and leads us to the speculation that the account of his stumbling in old age was written as part of a theodicy to justify the tearing of his kingdom from his successors.[19]   One assumes that the editor would have

---

mother's name was Athaljahu, a daughter of Omri, king of Israel." Hence, it is not clear whether she was Ahab's or Omri's daughter. In the following v. 27 we have noted concerning Ahaziah, Athaliah's son, כי חתן בית אחאב הוא "He was related by marriage to Ahab's family." It would appear from this verse that Ahaziah also married a woman from Ahab's family, but we have no other record on this point. We know only that Joash's mother, Ahaziah's wife, was Zibiah from Beer Sheba (II Kings 12: 2). From II Chr. 22: 3, it seems that Ahaziah was not married to a woman from Ahab's family, since we read there of his mother Athaliah גם הוא הלך בדרכי בית אחאב כי אמו היתה יועצתו להרשיע "...encouraged him in doing wrong." We observe that the editor(s) attempted to blame the wrongdoings of the Judean kings on the malevolent influence of their Israelite relations, stressing this at every appropriate occasion, whether warranted or not. The traditional commentators noticed the above discrepancies and reconciled them with the aphorism בני בנים הרי הם כבנים "the sons of the sons are [considered] as sons." The LXX translated in II Kings 8: 18 θυγάτηρ Αχααβ and in 8: 26 θυγάτηρ Αμρι. In 8: 27, however, Rahlfs has chosen the MS with ὁ οἶκος Αχααβ, which includes the meanings "family" and "household", for the translation of the Hebrew חתן בית אחאב; in certain other MSS there appears the term γαμβρός, "someone connected by marriage" (Liddell and Scott).

16   Although we read in I Kings 11: 5 וילך שלמה אחרי עשתרת "And Solomon followed Ashtoreth," the editor has downgraded this apparently grave sin with the use of the mitigating expression in the antecedent v. 4, ולא היה לבבו שלם עם ה' אלהיו כלבב דויד אביו "His heart was not fully devoted to the Lord his God, as was the heart of David his father."

17   Similar to Adam's notorious defence האשה אשר נתתה עמדי "The woman you put here with me [Gen. 3: 12]," we read here ויטו נשים את לבו "and his wives led him astray [I Kings 11: 3]."

18   The phrase ויהי לעת זקנת שלמה "As Solomon grew old [I Kings 11: 4]" implies a short time.

19   We must note the complete contrast between the two reasons given for the split of the kingdom: Solomon's transgression, as announced by God (I Kings 11: 11 - 13) and by the prophet Ahija Hashiloni (vv. 29 - 39), and the political chaos so vividly presented in chap. 12. The redactor attempted to reconcile the justified response of the people in reaction to Rehoboam's arrogant declaration אבי יסר אתכם בשוטים ואני איסר אתכם בעקרבים "My father scourged you with whips; I will scourge you with

preferred to ignore this episode in Solomon's reign,[20] as the editor of Chronicles in fact did.[21]

Thus out of the fourteen kings of Judah only one is explicitly accused of idolatry. Even including those monarchs only indirectly accused of idolatry, the periods of Rehoboam, Abijah, Jehoram and Athaliah amount to 35 years of idolatrous practice out of the 334 years from David to Hezekiah. It seems to me that such a situation is not conducive to a retrojection of a reform outlined by the redactor. With respect to idolatrous practices, his narrative implies short and temporary corruptions in a long line of righteous kings. Circumstances, however, are entirely different when we consider the issue of the *bamoth*; from the above citations we may deduce the redactor's opinion

---

scorpions [12: 14]," and the prophecy, explaining that ולא שמע המלך אל העם כי היתה סבה מעם ה' למען הקים את דברו אשר דבר ה' "The king did not listen to the people, for this turn of events was from the Lord, to fulfil the word the Lord had spoken [v. 15]." But the redactor did not address the second political motive for the split, the old quest for separation and independence by the northern people and their opposition to rule by a king of the southern tribes. We read in v. 16: מה לנו חלק בדוד ולא נחלה בבן ישי לאהליך ישראל "What share do we have in David, what part in Jesse's son? To your tents, O Israel," identical to the manifesto against David, in II Sam. 20: 1. We observe here that a political event, explained as a logical "cause and effect" by Scripture, was interpreted to represent a divine scheme and intervention.

[20] On this point we read an interesting Midrash in B. T. Sabbath 56b: אמר רבי שמואל בר נחמני אמר רבי יונתן כל האומר שלמה חטא אינו אלא טועה שנאמר ולא היה לבבו שלם עם ה' אלהיו כלבב דויד אביו כלבב דוד אביו הוא דלא הוה מיחטא נמי לא חטא אלא מה אני מקיים ויהי לעת זקנת שלמה נשיו הטו את לבבו "Said Rabbi Samuel son of Nahmani in the name of Rabbi Jonathan: Whoever says that Solomon sinned, is mistaken, since it is said: 'He did not follow the Lord completely, as David his father did [I Kings 11: 4]'; [Scripture emphasizes] that he did not do as his father did, but he did not sin. So what does it mean [how do you reconcile this statement with] 'As Solomon grew old, his wives turned his heart [v. 3]'"? The Talmud goes on to offer many ineffectual solutions to this dilemma, and ends the rhetoric with the declaration מפני שהיה לו למחות בנשיו ולא מיחה מעלה עליו הכתוב כאילו חטא "[His failure was really] that because he did not protest against the evil deeds of his wives, Scripture blames him as if he himself had sinned." We observe the talmudic attempt to exonerate Solomon, and we note that the Rabbis too distinguished the dictum כלבב דויד אביו as a particular qualification, whose absence is not identical with sin.

[21] The Chr. editor not only ignored Solomon's misdeeds but also attributed to him a pious act concerning his Egyptian wife: he moved her away from the City of David, to remove her from proximity to the sanctuary. We read in II Chr. 8: 11: כי אמר לא תשב אשה לי בבית דויד מלך ישראל כי קדש המה אשר באה אליהם ארון ה' "For he said: My wife must not live in the palace of David, king of Israel, because the places into which the ark of the Lord have entered are holy." The parallel narrative in I Kings 7: 8 records this event among descriptions of the opulent buildings demonstrating Solomon's wealth; Chr. interprets it as extreme sensitivity to the holiness of the sanctuary and the city.

that David resolved to build the Temple as the unique site of worship but his successors were not loyal to his strategy, allowing the *bamoth* to exist as rivals to what should have been the exclusive Temple in Jerusalem, his capital.

On this topic, we observe a constant and regular interjection of the stereotypical assertion, in different but insignificant stylistic variations, רק הבמות לא סרו עוד, "only the *bamoth* were not removed"; this is used with otherwise righteous kings, described with the attribute ויעש הישר בעיני ה' "He did what was right in the eyes of the Lord." The deuteronomic editor attempted to retroject the elimination of the *bamoth* to David to justify the reform started by Hezekiah and completed by Josiah. This reform provoked extensive opposition from many groups among the public, both laymen and provincial clerics.[22] It was common practice among the biblical and apocryphal authors and redactors to attach their assertions to great leaders of the past. And since Scripture tells us that David initiated the plan to build a Temple in Jerusalem, the "lobby" which realized the political expedience of the cult centralization in Jerusalem retrojected its origin to David, to counteract the opposition to this reform and further its acceptance. I must reiterate that I do not imply that this necessarily represents the actual historical circumstances; it is simply what I understand the intentions of the redactor of the books of Kings to have been. I do not think it necessary to substantiate textually the magnitude of the political and economic advantages resulting to the kingdom of Judah in general, and Jerusalem in particular, from the centralization of the cult.[23] Such a situation is recognizable even in our day, but was far more significant in Josiah's period. There is no doubt that David and Solomon realized the political significance of one unified state and the importance to this union of a central site of worship in the capital, notwithstanding the internal forces which tended to oppose such notions at suitable opportunities.

---

[22] For an extensive discussion of scholarly debate on this issue, see Heger, *Incense*, pp. 194 ff.

[23] It is remarkable that A. C. Welch, "The Death of Josiah," *ZAW 43* (1925), pp. 255 - 260, had already recognized that the primary motive behind Josiah's cult centralization reform was his political interest in making "Jerusalem the religious and political centre of a re-united Israel" (p. 259). On the other hand, V. Maag, "Erwägungen zur Deuteronomischen Kultzentralisation," *VT* 6 (1956), pp. 10 - 18 perceived that the centralization of the cult in Jerusalem was the result of a strong belief that this course of action would fulfil the divine choice and command; only the perfect execution of this divine decree would secure God's favour and support for the total independence of a national state, comprising Judah and the Northern territory liberated from the Assyrian yoke and re-united with Judah. In his opinion, political success was the ultimate goal, but the centralization reform was driven by a genuine pious zeal to obey God's command and secure His protection, just as Hezekiah was miraculously delivered from the Assyrian siege in 701 B.C.E.

These issues of rivalry are again evident when we examine the situation in the kingdom of Israel. Even the redactor of Kings, who attempts to demonstrate that every event is the result of a divine scheme to reward those who obey and to punish transgressors, attributes to Jeroboam (924 - 903) personal and political,[24] not religious, motives for the "establishment" or the "promotion"[25] of the northern sanctuaries as rivals to the Jerusalem Temple. We read in I Kings 12: 26 - 27: ויאמר ירבעם בלבו עתה תשוב הממלכה לבית דוד. אם יעלה העם הזה לעשות זבחים בבית ה׳ בירושלם ושב לב העם הזה אל אדניהם אל רחבעם מלך יהודה והרגני ושבו אל רחבעם מלך יהודה "If these people go up to offer sacrifices at the Temple of the Lord in Jerusalem, they will again give their allegiance to their lord, Rehoboam, king of Judah. They will kill me and return to Rehoboam king of Judah."

The redactor of Kings is pulled between two apparently opposing aims: a) to blame Jeroboam primarily for the institution of rival sanctuaries to the Temple in Jerusalem, and b) to accuse Jeroboam of idolatry. We observe the ambiguity in his numerous references to Jeroboam's conduct. In I Kings 14: 9 Ahijah's accusation is "You have made for yourself other gods," ותעשה לך אלהים אחרים, a non-specific allegation similar to the expression וילך "He בכל דרך ירבעם בן נבט ...להכעיס את ה׳ אלהי ישראל בהבליהם [Omri] walked in all the ways of his father Jeroboam son of Nebat...so that they provoked the Lord, the God of Israel, by their vanities [I Kings 16:26]." These vague pronouncements may be contrasted with the specific accusations made in other instances. Although Ahaziah is accused in I Kings 22: 54 of having "served and worshipped the Baal," v. 53 distinguishes between the

---

[24] A Midrash confirming the political nature of Jeroboam's behaviour can be found in B. T. Sanhedrin 102a: אחר הדבר הזה לא שב ירבעם מדרכו הרעה מאי אחר אמר רבי אבא אחר שתפשו הקדוש ברוך הוא לירבעם בבגדו ואמר לו חזור בך ואני ואתה ובן ישי נטייל בגן עדן אמר לו מי בראש בן ישי בראש אי הכי לא בעינא "[It is written (I Kings 13: 33)] 'Even after this, Jeroboam did not change his evil ways.' After what? Said Rabbi Abba: After God grabbed Jeroboam by his garment and said to him: Repent and I and you and the son of Jesse will stroll in the Garden of Eden! He asked: Who will be first [nearest God? And when he got the answer,] The son of Jesse, [he said] If so, I do not want it."

[25] A Midrash recording the steps instituted by Jeroboam to impede the procession of pilgrims to Jerusalem is found in B. T. Ta'anith 30b and many other rabbinical sources: עולא אמר יום שביטל הושע בן אלה פרוסדיות שהושיב ירבעם בן נבט על הדרכים שלא יעלו ישראל לרגל ואמר לאיזה שירצו יעלו "Ulah says: [The festival of 15 Ab is in remembrance of] the day when the last king of Israel, Hosea son of Elah, removed the guards which Jeroboam instituted on the roads to prevent the people of Israel from making the pilgrimage to Jerusalem, and ordered: They may go wherever they choose [to Beth El or to Jerusalem]."

idolatrous sins of his parents and the wrongdoing of Jeroboam.[26] There is also a distinct difference made in the narrative concerning Jehoram, Ahab's son.[27] We read in II Kings 3: 2 - 3: ויעשה הרע בעיני ה' רק לא כאביו וכאמו ויסר את מצבת הבעל אשר עשה אביו. רק בחטאות ירבעם בן נבט אשר החטיא את ישראל דבק לא סר ממנה "He did evil in the eyes of the Lord, but not as his father and mother had done. He got rid of the sacred stone of Baal that his father had made. Nevertheless, he clung to the sins of Jeroboam son of Nebat, which he had caused Israel to commit." Ahab made a pillar to Baal; although his son Jehoram eliminated it, he is still accused of doing evil in the eyes of the Lord, following Jeroboam. Jeroboam's exact transgression is not specified, but this is obviously not an imputation of idolatry, which is reserved for the worship of the Baal. A similar distinction is observed in the Jehu narrative in II Kings 10: 26 - 29. Although Jehu is accused of continuing Jeroboam's sins, he is still praised for doing what was right in the eyes of the Lord (v. 30). Such a tribute would be inappropriate if Jeroboam's sins, and the persistence of the worship of the golden calves in the sanctuaries of Beth El and Dan, were considered idolatrous celebrations.[28]

The same non-specific accusation, "the sins of Jeroboam," is imputed to all the other kings of Israel except Ahab, and demonstrates the difficulties encountered by the redactor in his quest to impute an idolatrous nature to Jeroboam's sins. At the conclusion of the record of the kings of Israel, after the conquest of Samaria, we encounter again specific accusations of idolatrous practices imputed to Ahab, as well as the non-specific allegations

---

[26] We read in v. 53: ויעש הרע בעיני ה' וילך בדרך אביו ובדרך אמו ובדרך ירבעם בן נבט אשר החטיא את ישראל "He did evil in the eyes of the Lord, because he walked in the ways of his father and mother and in the ways of Jeroboam son of Nebat, who caused Israel to sin," and in the succeeding v. 54: ויעבד את הבעל וישתחוה לו ויכעס את ה' אלהי ישראל ככל אשר עשה אביו "He served and worshipped Baal and provoked the Lord, the God of Israel, to anger, just as his father had done." The text distinguishes in the first part of v. 53 between the ways of his father and mother, and the ways of Jeroboam.

[27] We observe a definite distinction between the sins of Jeroboam and those of Ahab in I Kings 16: 31.

[28] It is not the purpose of this paper to elaborate on the issue of the connection between the narrative of the idolatrous golden calf in Exod. 32 and Jeroboam's calves. It is obvious that at some stage, the phrase אלה אלהיך ישראל אשר העלוך מארץ מצרים "These are your gods, O Israel, who brought you up out of Egypt," a "pejorative exaggeration of the original circumstances" depicting the calves "as an image of the God who has brought Israel up out of Egypt (Exod. 32: 8 and I Kings 12: 28)" was "purposely introduced with polemical intent" (M. Noth, *Exodus*, p. 247). The calves were thus invested with an explicit idolatrous significance, in contrast to their original function "merely as pedestals for the God who is imagined to be standing invisibly upon them" (ibid.). As demonstrated, the Kings editor did not explicitly accuse Jeroboam of idolatrous deeds.

ascribed to Jeroboam. In Micah's grim chastisement of Israel in chap. 6, the prophet bases himself strictly on Ahab's sins, not those of Jeroboam.[29] We must conclude that Jeroboam's "sins" were not considered *a priori* of an idolatrous nature, but consisted of an illicit rivalry against the Jerusalem Temple, like that of the local *bamoth* in Judah. The redactor of Kings judges the *bamoth* as a transgression of a divine law, but their political effect as a hindrance to the unity of all the tribes of Israel is obvious. Their existence as local shrines also challenged the claim for exclusivity of the Jerusalem Temple. In effect, there was no "religious" difference between the sanctuaries in Beth El and Dan, and the *bamoth* in Judah; neither was considered idolatrous, but both opposed "David's legacy" of the uniqueness of the Temple in Jerusalem. The redactor of Kings, in his attempt to discriminate in favour of the Judean kings, used different literary styles to describe the same royal behaviour depending on the origin of the king; kings of Judah are judged positively, 'ויעש הישר בעיני ה "He did what was right in the eyes of the Lord," though with the qualifier רק הבמות לא סרו "only the *bamoth* were not removed," whereas the kings of Israel are described with ויעש הרע בעיני ה' "He did evil in the eyes of the Lord." The specific idolatrous practices of Ahab, as we have seen, are distinguished from the "sins" of Jeroboam, and Jehu is praised with לעשות הישר בעיני "accomplishing what is right in my eyes," notwithstanding that he followed the ways of Jeroboam.

In the prophecy of Amos there is firm substantiation of the thesis that the northern sanctuaries were not considered idolatrous. Amos was active in the period of Jeroboam II (785 - 745), son of Joash, king of Israel (800 - 785) (Amos 1: 1), who is censured in II Kings 14: 24 with the stereotypical charge ויעש הרע בעיני ה' לא סר מכל חטאות ירבעם בן נבט אשר החטיא את ישראל "He did evil in the eyes of the Lord and did not turn away from any of the sins of Jeroboam son of Nebat, which he had caused Israel to commit." However, as a divine messenger he condemned the social misdeeds of the ruling classes, not the existence of the northern sanctuaries, rivals to the Jerusalem Temple. On the contrary, he warned that as punishment for social corruption the sanctuaries would be destroyed by God, and the sacrifices offered there would not save from destruction either the sanctuaries themselves or the kingdom;[30] we find similar prophecies with respect to the

---

[29] We read in Micah 6: 16: וישתמר חקות עמרי וכל מעשה בית אחאב ותלכו במעצותם למען תתי אתך לשמה וישביה לשרקה וחרפת עמי תשאו "The statutes of Omri are being observed and all the practices of Ahab's house, and you have followed their traditions. Therefore I will give you over to ruin and your people to derision; you will bear the scorn of the nations."

[30] See Amos 3: 14; 4: 4; 5: 5; 7: 9 and 8: 14.

Temple in Jerusalem.[31] It is not within the scope of this study to interpret Amos' theology concerning the sacrificial cult, but I think that his attitude toward the northern sanctuaries is for our purposes evident.

8.1.2.2 The Political Background of Josiah's Reform

The economic significance of one sanctuary in Jerusalem is clear; it was certainly obvious to the kings of Judah, and probably to the Jerusalem priestly group, who attempted to enforce its exclusivity. The religious duty to make a pilgrimage to Jerusalem three times yearly is forcefully commanded in Deut. chap. 16: 1 - 17.[32] The slaughter of the Passover "sacrifice", an obligation whose transgression is punished by "being cut off from the people [Num. 9: 13],"[33] was a boon for the city of Jerusalem; [34] an even greater boon

---

[31] We read in Jer. 7: 4 ff.: אל תבטחו לכם אל דברי השקר לאמר היכל ה' "Do not trust in deceptive words and say: This is the Temple of the Lord," and in Micah 3: 11: ועל ה' ישענו לאמר הלוא ה' בקרבנו לא תבוא עלינו רעה "Yet they lean upon the Lord and say: Is not the Lord among us? No disaster will come upon us."

[32] The rule requiring a pilgrimage to Jerusalem on the three feasts does not appear in Exod. 23: 14 - 17, in the earlier Book of the Covenant, or in Exod. 34: 23 - 4, part of the J redaction; in the latter pericope, only a visit to a sanctuary is required. M. Noth, *Exodus*, pp. 190 ff. and 264, draws attention to the fact that the festivals are still mentioned in Exod. 23: 14 - 16 with their old meaning and names and without the mention of the exodus from Egypt. Noth maintains that Exod. 34: 24, in which a pilgrimage to a distant location is implied, is a deuteronomic addition to the original text. I am somewhat sceptical of this statement, because in my opinion, a deuteronomic editor who added the concept of going to a unique central locus of worship would also have attached the stereotypical deuteronomic phrase "to the place He will choose," as appears in similar occurrences. There were many important sanctuaries before the centralization of the cult, and the pilgrims had to leave their homes and fields to travel to them. With respect to Elkanah we read: ועלה האיש ההוא מעירו ... להשתחות ולזבח...בשילה "...[he] went up from his town to worship and sacrifice...at Shilo [I Sam. 1: 3]," and there were certainly other important sanctuaries at that time, as for example in Shekhem (Jos. 24: 26), Beth El (Jud. 20: 18, 27), Gilgal (I Sam. 10: 8 ff, 11: 15; Hos. 4: 15) and Nob (I Sam. 21: 2ff).

[33] It does not matter for our purposes whether the command in Num. is of a later origin than that in Deut. The importance of Passover as a family feast was certainly well-established and the deuteronomic command only changed its site to Jerusalem instead of the individual's place of residence.

[34] This command is in apparent opposition to the rule in Exod. 12: 46 בבית אחד יאכל "It must be eaten inside one house." The traditional sources were aware of this contradiction; we read in Tosefta Pesahim 6: 11 and in other rabbinical sources מה ת״ל בבית אחד יאכל בחבורה אחת "What does it mean 'It must be eaten inside one house?' Among one group [of people]." The term בית was interpreted as "group", and the Rabbis offer a

was the command to celebrate seven days of feasting in Jerusalem, in the euphoric period after the harvest, together with all one's family (Deut. 16: 11). Another significant rule was promulgated by the deuteronomic author(s), namely the obligation to eat the tithes, the first fruits and the firstborn[35] of the animals in Jerusalem,[36] as we read in Deut. 14: 23: ואכלת לפני ה׳ אלהיך במקום אשר יבחר לשכן שמו שם מעשר דגנך תירשך ויצהרך ובכרת בקרך וצאנך "Eat the tithes of your grain,[37] new wine and oil, and the firstborn of your herds and flocks in the presence of the Lord your God at the place he will choose as a dwelling for His name."[38] Practical methods to overcome the possible difficulties in fulfilling this precept are communicated in the subsequent verses 24 - 26;[39] this is exceptional advice, demonstrating the significance of the precept and the desire of the author to facilitate its

---

number of elucidations on this issue. The traditional commentators Rashi and Ibn Ezra explain the scriptural text accordingly.

[35] See also Deut. 12: 17 - 18; 15: 20; 26: 2.

[36] See G. von Rad, *Deuteronomy, A Commentary*, The Old Testament Library, transl. D. Barton (Philadelphia, 1966), p. 94, regarding the issue of whether "only Jerusalem could be intended by 'the place which Y. will choose.'"

[37] According to the rule in Deut. 12: 18, the Levite too is counted among the members of one's family group and should eat the tithes in Jerusalem: אתה ובנך ובתך ועבדך ואמתך והלוי אשר בשעריך "...you, your sons and daughters, your menservants and maidservants, and the Levites from your towns." On the other hand, we read in Deut. 14: 28 - 29: מקצה שלש שנים תוציא את כל מעשר תבואתך בשנה ההוא והנחת בשעריך. ובא הלוי... והגר והיתום והאלמנה ...ואכלו ושבעו "At the end of every three years, bring all the tithes of that year's produce and store it in your towns so that the Levites...and the fatherless and the widows...may come and eat and be satisfied," a rule that suggests that one may eat the tithes in the towns, in contrast to Deut. 14: 23. The Rabbis deduced from these verses that only the tithes of every third year are donated to the underprivileged and may be eaten in the towns. Rashi dissects the verse and interprets: ובא הלוי ויטול מעשר ראשון והגר והיתום ויטלו מעשר שני "...'the Levite' will take the first tithe, and the 'alien and the fatherless' will take the second tithe." Thus according to rabbinic regulation, the "first tithe" is given every year to the Levites, and the "second tithe" is to be eaten in Jerusalem by the family group in the first, second, fourth and fifth years of the seven year cycle, and is reserved for the underprivileged in the third and sixth years. There are no tithes in the seventh year when the land remains unplowed (Exod. 23: 11).

[38] Similar commands are encountered in Deut. 12: 5 - 28; 15: 20; 16: 15 and 26: 2. See von Rad, pp. 89 ff., who also compares and contrasts the law of the centralization of the cult in Deut. chap. 12 with the law of the altar in Exod. 20.

[39] We read there ונתתה בכסף צרת הכסף בידך והלכת אל המקום אשר יבחר ה׳ אלהיך בו "Then exchange your tithe for silver, and take the silver with you and go to the place the Lord your God will choose [v. 25]."

performance. Jerusalem was also instituted as the exclusive legal and cultural center of the entire kingdom, as we read in Deut. 17: 8 - 10 and 31: 10 - 11.[40]

Pilgrimage to sanctuaries was an ancient and common custom in Israel; we observe, for instance, the habit of Samuel's parents, who were accustomed to perform a pilgrimage every year (I Sam. 1: 7). In Deuteronomy, however, there are two fundamental differences: a) a duty to perform a pilgrimage three times yearly, in contrast to the Samuel narrative, in which one has the impression that pilgrimage was merely a custom of Elkanah, not a duty, which he performed once yearly, and b) an obligation to set aside ten percent of the harvest and consume it in Jerusalem.[41] The economic and political advantages bestowed by these particular statutes are obvious.[42] From recent archeological results, we learn that in contrast to Samaria, which enjoyed early on a period of great urban development, Jerusalem remained underdeveloped in the first period of the united

---

[40] We read in Deut. 17: 8 - 9: כי יפלא ממך דבר למשפט בין דם לדם בין דין לדין ובין נגע לנגע דברי ריבת בשעריך וקמת ועלית אל המקום אשר יבחר ה׳ אלהיך בו. ובאת אל הכהנים הלוים ואל השפט אשר יהיה בימים ההם ודרשת והגידו לך את דבר המשפט "If cases come before your courts that are too difficult for you to judge - whether bloodshed, lawsuits or assaults - take them to the place the Lord your God will choose. Go to the priests, who are Levites, and to the judge who is in office at that time. Inquire of them and they will give you the verdict." In 31: 10 - 11, we read with respect to the cultural dominance of Jerusalem: ויצו משה אותם לאמר מקץ שבע שנים במעד שנת השמטה בחג הסכות. בבוא כל ישראל לראות את פני ה׳ אלהיך במקום אשר יבחר תקרא את התורה הזאת נגד כל ישראל באזניהם "Then Moses commanded them: At the end of every seven years, in the year for cancelling of debts, during the Feast of Tabernacles, when all Israel comes to appear before the Lord your God at the place He will choose, you shall read this law before them in their hearing." I do not exclude the possibility that particularly in Deut. 17: 8 - 10 some priestly hand made suitable additions to emphasize the significance of the cult officials.

[41] It is not within the scope of this study to elaborate on the issue of the tithes, which has been much debated by both rabbinical sources and modern scholars. It suffices for our purpose to observe that this pericope in Deut. does not harmonize with the P laws, as they appear in Num. 18: 8 - 32. The Rabbis interpreted this pericope as including מעשר שני (see n. 37), to be eaten by the owners in the first, second, fourth and fifth years of the seven year cycle, and מעשר עני, to be given to the economically underprivileged in the third and sixth years. They thus attempted to separate the two pericopes: that in Num. refers to the priests and Levites, and that in Deut., which also mentions הגר והיתום והאלמנה "the aliens, the fatherless and the widows [14: 29]" refers to the socially disadvantaged. Modern scholars consider each pericope to have originated in a different period, and to be addressed to different interest groups. Cf. G. von Rad, *Deuteronomy, A Commentary*, pp. 102-3.

[42] The economic importance of the pilgrimage is also emphasized by S. Safrai, העליה לרגל בימי הבית השני (Tel Aviv, 1965), pp. 9-10.

monarchy, and increased in size only around 700 B.C.E.[43] It was therefore in the interest of the Judean kings to augment the importance of Jerusalem,[44] and the glorification of its central sanctuary, the Temple, was a primary element of this policy.

Spieckermann[45] notes that Wellhausen doubted Hezekiah's reform, since it left no mark; he concurs with this doubt, considering the biblical narrative part of the deuteronomic historiography. I do not dispute that this might be the case, but this need not imply that Josiah then had to repeat the same action. It is quite possible that Hezekiah attempted to centralize the sacrificial worship in Jerusalem for political and economic reasons,[46] but did not

---

[43]   M. Broshi, "The Expansion of Jerusalem in the Reigns of Hezekiah and Manasseh," *IEJ* 24 (1974), pp. 21-26 writes: "The chronological and historical evidence is still incomplete, but one can claim with certainty that around 700 B.C. the city had expanded to three to four times its former size" (p. 21). And on p. 23 he states: "The above evidence makes it clear that Jerusalem at about 700 B.C. had mushroomed, historically speaking, overnight." Broshi assumes that this growth was due to mass migrations from the Northern kingdom after the fall of Samaria, and from the Judean provinces ceded by Sennacherib to the Philistines after 701 B.C. An exact date would be impossible to determine for such an occurrence as the expansion in size of a city, since such increase could not have happened overnight; it is possible that Broshi assumed the mass migrations as the cause of the increased building activity, and therefore was inclined towards a date "around 700," the period of Hezekiah's reign. In chap. 9, I shall postulate the thesis that Ahaz (742 - 727) had already recognized the political importance of an impressive cult center in Jerusalem, his capital, probably to support a central royal hegemony against provincial autonomous interests. In addition to the appeal of majestic cult ceremonies, he may have also undertaken steps to encourage the immigration of larger numbers of people to Jerusalem. Thus, Broshi's assumptions correspond with my thesis, and support the idea of the influence of cult issues on political and economic development.

[44]   Based on archeological findings, D. W. Jamieson-Drake, *Scribes and Schools in Monarchic Judah*, JSOTS 109 (Sheffield, 1991), writes on p. 138, with respect to the circumstances at the end of the 8th century and the 7th century: "The presence of a broad range of functions had its centre exclusively at Jerusalem."

[45]   p. 174.

[46]   Although we cannot authenticate the Ravshaqeh's speech, we may accept as valid the remarks concerning Hezekiah's command to centralize the sacrificial worship in Jerusalem. There would have been no valid reason for the deuteronomic redactor to include such an imaginary passage in the Ravshaqeh's harangue, had it been entirely devoid of any real basis. It is interesting to note that the Ravshaqeh gives significance to the altar, not to the Temple in Jerusalem; we read: לפני המזבח הזה תשתחוו בירושלים "You must worship before this altar in Jerusalem [II Kings 18: 22]." H. Niehr, "Die Reform des Joschija," in *Jeremia und die Deuteronomistische Bewegung*, B. B. B. Band 98, pp. 33 - 55, ed. W. Gross (Weinheim, 1995), wonders that in the record of Josiah's "reform" in II Kings chap. 23 we encounter only the vague ויבא את כל הכהנים מערי יהודה "He brought all the priests from the towns of Judah [v. 8]." This phrase demonstrates in my opinion a cohesiveness with the Hezekiah narrative in II

succeed because of the political situation at his time; Josiah completed the centralization within a more favourable political climate.

For a substantial period of Hezekiah's reign, most of Judah was occupied by the Assyrians; hence the king did not possess the requisite power to impose the destruction of the *bamoth*, against the likely opposition of the local clerics and other interested parties. Moreover, the Judean people, who would not be prepared to abstain from sacrificing at the *bamoth*, could easily have gone to the prominent sanctuaries in Samaria, such as the nearby Beth El, which was under the dominion of the Northern kings and later under Assyrian rule. In Josiah's period the political situation was entirely more propitious for reform and cult centralization. The Northern kingdom no longer existed, and Assyrian power was already in decline at that time. Josiah could therefore enter into the Northern territory and destroy the sanctuary of Beth El and all the *bamoth* in Samaria.[47] We must observe the prominence conferred by the redactor upon Josiah's destruction of the Beth El sanctuary, the particular emphasis on the altar instituted by Jeroboam,[48] the many repulsive details concerning its desecration, and the brutal conduct against the local priests. We must also note the significance of Josiah's entering into a "foreign" territory, and proceeding there as if it were his own.[49] The elimination of the *bamoth*, constant rivals to the centrality of Jerusalem, would have been useless as long as there were other sanctuaries in the former Northern kingdom.[50] What Hezekiah was unable to achieve, due to political

---

Kings 18: 4, הוא הסיר את הבמות "He removed the high places"; the editor, who had already credited Hezekiah with the removal of the *bamoth*, could commend Josiah only with a supplementary act toward the same goal, the ultimate termination of worship at the *bamoth*.

[47] II Kings 23: 19.

[48] We read in II Kings 23: 15: וגם את המזבח אשר בבית אל הבמה אשר עשה ירבעם בן נבט "...even the altar at Bethel, the high place made by Jeroboam." The particular emphasis on this altar, in contrast to the general record of the destruction of the other *bamoth* in 23: 19, demonstrates the political importance granted to the destruction of that altar and the invalidation of Jeroboam's acts.

[49] According to II Chr. 34: 6, 7 and 33, Josiah performed his cleansing operations מכל הארצות אשר לבני ישראל "from all the territories belonging to the Israelites" ועד נפתלי "as far as Naphtali." A. Malamat, ישראל בתקופת המקרא (Jerusalem, second revised edition 1984), p. 230, declares that Josiah enlarged his domain to all the territory of Samaria. With respect to the issue of whether the areas covered by Josiah's reform matched his territorial dominion, see M. Noth, *Übelieferungsgeschichtliche Studien 1* (Halle, 1942), p. 178.

[50] One may assume that people from Judah went to worship at the ancient and venerable sanctuary of Beth El, aetiologically and certainly mythically linked to the Patriarchs. Thus the exclusivity of the Jerusalem Temple could only be secured through the sanctuary's destruction. Similarly, it is possible that people from the Northern kingdom went on pilgrimages to Jerusalem. We learn from Scripture that Jeroboam was concerned

circumstances, Josiah was able to accomplish. Further, we note again that the accusations against the Northern kings concern mainly their rival sanctuaries. There is no indication that Josiah destroyed altars of alien gods or idols in Beth El; only במות and אשרה are mentioned.[51] In Judah and Jerusalem there were many more idolatrous artifacts, which were eradicated by Josiah, but their priests were not treated so brutally;[52] only the Beth El priests were slaughtered, since they were considered a major menace to the centralization of the cult. Such blatant discrimination could not have been religiously motivated and must have been the result of political zeal, shrouded in the guise of piety.

---

about such behaviour, but there is no indication that he promulgated any prohibition in this respect, or that he possessed the necessary bureaucracy and organization to ensure the strict adherence to such an edict. The Midrash quoted above in n. 25, which declares that Jeroboam established guards to prevent the pilgrimage of Northerners to Jerusalem, recounts that the pious people invented tricks to deceive the guards and bring their first fruits to Jerusalem. This also demonstrates that there was nothing to prevent people from crossing the border and buying an animal in Judah for an offering in the Jerusalem Temple. We also find in Amos 5: 5: ואל תדרשו בית אל והגלגל לא תבאו ובאר שבע לא תעברו "Do not seek Beth El, do not go to Gilgal, do not journey to Beer Sheba," which would indicate that Northerners made pilgrimages to the Southern sanctuary in Beer Sheba; there is a question, however, whether this verse refers to Beer Sheba in the Negeb, or to a locality with such a name in Galilee, as implied by the context of a citation in Josephus, *War II*, 20: 6.

[51] Although the *asherah* is an illicit cult element, we must concede that the redactor of Kings distinguishes between the Baal, manifestly an idol, and the *asherah*, a somewhat ambiguous artefact, denounced in less severe terms than the Baal. Spieckermann calls the three elements, *bamoth, asherah* and *masseboth*, the *Trias*, implying that these three elements share something in common and are distinct from the more evil Baal. I have noted in section 8.1.2.1 the distinction made by the Kings redactor between the sin involved in worshipping at the *bamoth* and that involved in worshipping the Baal.

[52] We read in II Kings 23: 5: והשבית את הכמרים אשר נתנו מלכי יהודה ויקטר בבמות בערי יהודה ומסבי ירשלם ואת המקטרים לבעל לשמש ולירח ולמזלות ולכל צבא השמים "He did away with the pagan priests appointed by the priests of Judah to 'burn incense' on the high places of the towns of Judah and on those around Jerusalem - those who 'burned incense' to Baal, to the sun and moon, to the constellations." This pericope obviously refers explicitly to priests who celebrated idolatrous worship. The sanctions against them are expressed with the ambiguous והשבית, which does not indicate whether they were actually killed, or just relieved of their priestly privileges, in contrast to the priests of the *bamoth* who still enjoyed financial advantages. In comparison, the priests of the Beth El *bamoth*, though not accused of idolatrous practices, were brutally slaughtered. This difference in treatment must be due to a political strategy, and not to religious zeal.

8.2 The Temple Repairs

8.2.1 The Repairs as Interjections

Chr. Levin posits that the records in our pericope and in a number of earlier texts, which mention grants bestowed by the various kings on the Temple treasury, are later interjections. He deduces this idea from the fact that such grants, קדשים, do not occur in Deuteronomy, and must be of priestly origin, since similar types of endowments appear in the P stratum. I do not think that an *ex silentio* argument can serve as evidence in this specific case; royal gifts for the temples were a common custom in the surrounding cultures, and one may assume that such a custom was also adopted by the Israelite kings. It was not necessary to create a command in the legal codex for such a voluntary act, and its absence from the deuteronomic code does not indicate its absence in practice. Further to his thesis that these verses describing the king's grants were intentionally added with an ideological purpose, Levin deduces that the reason that the money brought by the people (II Kings 12, II Chr. 24) was not spent to make Temple artifacts was to save such artifacts from being taken away to pay bribes to the king of Aram. The money spent for repairs was thus saved for a good aim. Evidently Levin has assumed that such a motive may have been interjected in editorial hindsight.

I doubt whether this peculiar fact should lead us to such a speculation. The entire pericope is laden with many bizarre occurrences, for which we have no reasonable explanations; they were also puzzling to the redactor of Chr., who attempted to emend certain records in order to make them more plausible. The issue of not using the collected money for Temple furnishings is reversed in II Chr. 24: 14, as Levin himself notes.[53] The Chr. redactor understood the expression in II Kings 12: 11, כי רב הכסף to mean that there was much money, and was even more precise: ויאספו כסף לרב "and they collected a great amount of money [II Chr. 24: 11]." The implication, therefore, either from the text in Kings or from another *Vorlage* with a similar text, was that there was a surplus of money, and it was inconceivable to the Chr. editor that no furnishings should have been made with this surplus. He saw no hidden stratagem underlying the absurd report, and thus changed it, or alternatively had another original text with a different record.

Further, Levin's explanation that no furnishings were made for the Temple in order to save them from Hazael is illogical. Scripture does not inform us how the bribes were assessed: did Hazael request the entire contents of the royal and Temple treasuries, or was an exact quantity of precious metals imposed? An analysis of the various bribes or ransom payments by the Israelite kings does not reveal a uniform system; in certain occurrences

---

[53] Note 14.

everything was taken away[54] or offered,[55] and in others a fixed quantity was requested and paid.[56] On one occasion, elements of the building itself were also given,[57] and therefore Joash's supposed stratagem would not have solved the problem. Moreover, if we assume that Hazael demanded and received all the precious objects and materials, we must ask why the king did not use the resources of the royal and Temple treasuries to execute the repairs, and instead waited for the priests to collect the moneys. One must assume that gifts for the Temple's treasury were dedicated *a priori* for its maintenance; thus if they were used for the Temple's repair, nothing would have been left for Hazael, if we follow Levin's theory. I propose that whenever the text indicates that "everything" was taken, this does not imply an "absolute";[58] it simply means that "much" was taken, and the quantity given was negotiated in advance, as with Hezekiah's payment in II Kings 18: 14 -16,[59] or the Judean king assumed that the amount given would satisfy the adversary or the king whose military help he sought.

---

[54] ולקח את כל הזהב; "[Shishak] took everything [I Kings 14: 26]"; ואת הכל לקח "[Jehoash, king of Israel] took all the gold and silver and all the article [from Amaziah, king of Judah] [II Kings 14: 14]"; ויצא משם את כל ...והכסף ואת כל הכלים "[Nebuchadnezzar] removed all the treasuries [II Kings 24: 13]." With respect ...אוצרות to Ahaz' redemption payment to the Assyrian king in II Kings 16: 8, the term הכל "everything" does not occur, but from the context, one may assume that he emptied both the royal and Temple treasuries. Most scholars deduce this circumstance from the narrative in vv. 16 and 17, in which we are told that Ahaz cut the panels and removed the Sea from the bronze bulls to obtain bronze, since his treasury was totally emptied. Cf. W. Zwickel, "Die Kultreform des Ahas (2 Kön 16,10-18)," *SJOT* 7,2 (1993), pp. 250-262, who proposes that the verses refer to a cult reform to eliminate images.

[55] Asa sent to Ben-Hadad "all the silver and the gold that was left in the treasuries" כל הכסף והזהב הנותרים באוצרות (I Kings 15: 18).

[56] Hezekiah offered to pay what Sennacherib demanded, and did so after receiving his precise request (II Kings 18: 14 -16); Pharaoh Neco imposed on Jehoiakim a fixed fine of gold and silver (II Kings 23: 33); Menahem of Israel gave to king Pul of Assyria one thousand talents of silver (II Kings 15: 19).

[57] Hezekiah stripped the gold off the Temple doors and door posts and gave it to Sennacherib (II Kings 18: 16).

[58] There is substantiation for this assumption in II Kings 14: 14, where we read that Jehoash took כל הזהב והכסף ואת כל הכלים הנמצאים בית ה' "all the gold and silver and all the articles found in the Temple"; we must assume that all the articles made by Solomon were taken away. But in II Kings 24: 13 we read that Nebuchadnezzar "took away all the gold articles that Solomon had made." Taking both verses literally, the contradiction is evident; Solomon's articles were no longer in the Temple in Nebuchadnezzar's period.

[59] Hezekiah said: את אשר תתן עלי אשא "I will pay whatever you demand of me."

8.2.2 Analysis of II Kings Chaps. 11 and 12

There seems no logical reason that the priests would not follow the king's command, especially since Jehoiada was both the Chief Priest and a leading figure in the court. From the text in Kings, one must conclude that the king's order was given to the Jerusalemite priests,[60] and they of all groups should have been most interested in enhancing the splendour of the Temple, the site of their service and source of income. It is also odd that after being reprimanded[61] the priests were willing to give up their privilege of collecting money, lest they be compelled to use it for the Temple repair,[62] yet did receive money for the guilt and sin offerings (II Kings 12: 17; v. 16 in KJV).[63] The key issue, of course, is why Joash, out of all the kings before

---

[60] We read in II Kings 12: 5: כל כסף הקדשים אשר יובא בית ה' "all the money brought as sacred offerings to the house of the Lord," a term used exclusively for the Temple in Jerusalem.

[61] Levin (p. 64) considers this pericope as favourable to the priests; he takes Joash as inquiring why the priests did not execute the repairs themselves and left them to the workmen. I do not think that the context allows for such an interpretation; as we see in II Kings 12: 12 - 13, skilled professionals were necessary to execute the repairs, and it is unlikely that the king would expect the priests to possess the necessary skills. Verse 6b clearly links the command והם יחזקו את בדק הבית "let them repair what is necessary" to the antecedent vv. 5 and 6a, which explicitly refer to the collection of the necessary funds. The fact that Chr. changed the text to shift the blame from the priests to the Levites also affirms the common interpretation that this pericope is a reprimand.

[62] In II Kings 12: 9 Scripture uses the term ויאתו, from the root אות, a term which appears apart from this instance only in the discourse between the sons of Jacob and the people of Shekhem concerning their circumcision. In both cases it represents a consent given with a condition; we read in Gen. 34: 15 אך בזאת נאות לכם "We will give our consent to you on one condition only." The same conditional agreement appears in the following vv. 22 and 23. In our case, the priests consented not to collect any money, on condition they be relieved from the duty to repair the Temple.

[63] Levin compares this verse to the money that was to be paid at the *Asham* in Lev. 5: 15, assuming that such payment was also due with respect to atonement for sin. I do not think it is possible to reconcile this verse with the final pericopes in Lev. 4 and 5 concerning the *Asham* and *Hattat* offerings. Although the phrase בערכך כסף שקלים " of the proper value in silver" in Lev. 5: 15 is ambiguous, according to its plain meaning the text requires both the payment of compensation plus twenty percent, and the bringing of a ram for an *Asham* offering. Elliger, *Leviticus*, p. 77, agrees with the traditional interpretation proposed by Rashi that the ram must have a value of at least two *sheqalim*, since this word is expressed in plural; Elliger suggests that the number two was somehow omitted from the text. He also connects our verse in II Kings with the payment of the fine. Cf. Noth, *Leviticus*, pp. 45-46, who does not agree that the verse indicates the value of the ram; he considers the money as a substitute for the sacrifice of the ram. Noth must therefore address the question of the difference between the offerings indicated in chaps. 4 and 5, which do not allow for a money substitution, and the *Asham* offering, which is to be replaced by money. Noth suggests that the earlier custom was to bring a sacrifice, and

him, decided to repair the Temple two hundred years after its construction. The Chr. redactor, who wrote his record relatively close to the deuteronomic redactor and presumably had more insight into the latter's method of thought and theological purpose, had no logical answer to these oddities; he changed the facts and composed a more rational narrative. He proposed a reason for

---

this was later replaced by a more "progressive" monetary restitution. Noth's assumption seems to me entirely inconsistent with the text. Lev. 5: 15 and 16 clearly require both an offering and a payment, as noted above. Further, chap. 7 contains precise rules on the *Asham* sacrifice (among others), and we would have to assume, according to Noth's speculation, that this pericope too was of an earlier origin and had become obsolete, to be replaced by a money offering. Noth's proposal would also require us to consider our verse in II Kings, in which money for *Asham* and *Hattat* is mentioned, to be of a later origin than the pericope in Lev. 5: 14 - 26. There is also the issue of why only the *Asham* sacrifice was to be replaced with a pecuniary penalty, and not the other offerings. Moreover, Noth does not contemplate a money substitute for the sin offering, which also appears in our verse in Kings, and which Levin attempts to join together with the *Asham*. Rendtorff, in *Studien zur Geschichte des Opfers im Alten Israel*, pp. 53ff, is more cautious, admitting that the text does not allow us to draw a decisive conclusion regarding its meaning; it might be interpreted as money for "sins and wrongdoing." It is plausible that prior to the institution of the specific *Asham* and *Hattat* sacrifices, two late offerings not mentioned in the earlier writings, the people would offer money to the priests for the Temple service, to assuage their guilt for some wrongdoing. Rendtorff correctly states that the term אשם in I Sam. chap. 6 does not presuppose a sacrifice. I do not exclude the general scholarly opinion that this verse is a later interjection of priestly origin, but it may reflect an earlier stage of the development of these offerings; we observe in Neh. 10: 33 the institution of a duty to pay a third sheqel for the various Temple services, including חטאות "sin offerings," likely public ones. One must assume that previously such amounts were brought voluntarily to the Temple. A guilty conscience originally induced people to bring offerings to the Deity, and this must have also been the motive for bringing monetary gifts to the Temple. We read in our pericope in II Kings 12: 5: כל כסף אשר יעלה על לב איש להביא בית ה' "the money brought voluntarily to the Temple"; some likely brought gifts expecting some future benefit, and some wished to relieve a guilty conscience. Finally, we may note the rabbinic explanation of this odd verse. We read in Mishnah Sheqalim 6: 6: זה מדרש דרש יהוידע כהן גדול אשם הוא אשום אשם לה' זה הכלל כל שהוא בא משום חטא ומשום אשמה ילקח בו עולות הבשר לשם והעורות לכהנים נמצאו שני כתובים קיימים אשם לה' ואשם לכהנים ואומר כסף אשם וכסף חטאות לא יהיו לכהנים בית ה' יובא. "This Midrash was expounded by Jehoiada the Chief Priest: 'It is a guilt offering; he has been guilty of wrongdoing against the Lord [Lev. 5: 19].' This is the general principle: any offering brought for sin or guilt, is used to purchase burnt offerings, the flesh for God and the hides for the priests. Thus the two scriptural verses stand together; '...a wrongdoing against the Lord [Lev. 5: 19]' and '...to the priest as a guilt offering {Lev. 5: 18].' It [also] says {II Kings 12: 17]: 'The money from the guilt offerings and sin offerings was not brought into the Temple of the Lord; it belonged to the priests.'" In essence, this Midrash attributes to Jehoiada the rule that the surplus left over from money dedicated for a guilt or sin offering must be used to offer an *Olah*, whose flesh is to be burnt on the altar and whose hide is awarded to the priests; this is the meaning of the phrase "it belonged to the priests."

the repair (II Chr. 24: 7), and shifted the blame for the failure to collect the money to the Levites. He entirely exonerated the priests from any wrongdoing, and also omitted the odd record concerning the money for the sin and guilt offerings. Narrating events in light of his period and its circumstances, the Chr. editor also changed the building materials from the wood in Kings to the iron and bronze used in his time for the Temple building.

Josephus also tried his hand at rationalizing this narrative. Although in many instances he follows the Chr. record, he introduces several innovations, which confirm the thesis that each biblical redactor and ancient historian interpreted Scripture in light of the circumstances in his period. Since they would not consider the possibility of developmental changes in the divine rules and customs, they assumed that these had always been the same, and simply omitted by previous writers. Josephus,[64] for example, assumed that the king asked Jehoiada to send the priests and Levites to collect the half sheqel that everyone was required to pay for the Temple according to Exod. 31: 12. This was a late P rule, in force in Josephus' period, which probably superseded the previous rule of a third sheqel established by Nehemiah (Neh. 10: 33).[65]

There is no doubt that our pericope raises many questions and demonstrates the many minds and hands that attempted to present a picture suitable to their *Weltanschauung*. In order to delve beneath the surface of the narrative and attempt to detect, as far as possible, the real situation which the redactor tried to interpret in accordance with his credo, we must investigate the political climate in the relevant period, in contrast to those whose investigation has concentrated mainly on literary analysis. There is no doubt that in the period of J(eh)oash the kingdom of Judah underwent great political upheaval. In contrast to the Northern kingdom, in which kings were often overturned and new dynasties emerged, the Davidic house had a stable foothold in Judah, with the exception of three instances of conspiracy;[66] each

---

[64] *Ant*. IX: 161-165. On the other hand, Josephus runs into a logical flaw. He records that Jehoiada did not follow the king's command to send the priests and Levites to collect the half sheqel, because he understood that the people would not disburse it. This conflicts with his report that the people were delighted with the new collection system, the box, and donated eagerly, there being so much money available that many kinds of Temple furnishings could be prepared with the leftover funds.

[65] The traditional commentators, who do not admit changes in the divine rules, interpret this third sheqel levy as additional to the half sheqel.

[66] There are few details in Scripture regarding the killing of Amon (II Kings 21: 23 - 24), but one cannot escape the similarity between the pericopes in our study, with two cases of Temple repairs effected by two kings with similar names, ‏י(ה)ואש‏ and ‏יאשיהו‏, and the only two insurrections in the Judean court. Joash was proclaimed king by the people

monarch was succeeded by a member of the same family. Our period indicates protracted unstable circumstances.[67] We must ask the reason for Athaliah to kill all her grandsons,[68] and how she attained the necessary power. One might have thought that as the sister of Ahab (or Omri), she intended to reunite both kingdoms under the reign of that family, but she destroyed the Davidic royal family after Jehu's revolution (843)[69] and the assassination of all Ahab's descendants.[70] The text states that Athaliah acted in this way "when she saw that her son was dead," but this adds no insight into the real motive for her preposterous behaviour.[71] Regarding the second issue, we find no other indication that the queen mother exercised any political power,[72] and we may assume that women in general did not enjoy

---

after the lawless annihilation of the legitimate throne contenders, and similarly Josiah was made king by the people of the land who killed all the plotters.

[67] Ahaziah's successors were killed (843), his son J(eh)oash was killed by conspirators (837?), and his son Amazjahu suffered the same fate. A. Malamat, ישראל בתקופת המקרא (Jerusalem, second revised edition 1984), pp. 229 ff. asserts that the assassinations were the result of a struggle between pro-Assyrian and pro-Egyptian groups in Judah in that period. Later, in the time of Ahaz (742 - 727), we learn from Isa. 7: 6 that the Israelite king Pekah plotted to depose Ahaz and put Ben Tabael on the throne of Judah. We have no clue as to who this individual was, nor do we know his actual name, but we must assume that he was a Judean aristocrat who collaborated with the forces of Pekah and Rezin. We observe from this narrative that there were elements inside Judah who conspired against the Davidic dynasty. The traditional commentators Rashi and Radak as well as the Y.T. quote various homilies regarding Tabael's identity; in one of them, it is suggested that the reference is to Pekah himself.

[68] For speculation on this topic, see H. Schulte, "Die Rettung des Prinzen Joas. Zur Exegese von II Reg 11, 1-3," ZAW 109/4 (1997), pp. 549-56.

[69] II Kings 11: 1.

[70] II Kings 10: 11.

[71] II Chr. offers no explanation in the parallel verse 22: 10, and repeats the Kings text. On the other hand, we may find an explanation in II Chr. 24: 7. We read there that Athaliah's sons profaned the Temple's furnishings; this narrative, which does not appear in Kings, seems to be a misguided interjection. We read in Kings that Athaliah killed all the royal family; Chr. adds "of Judah." Hence, there were no sons left to perform this despicable act. Possibly these were children from a previous marriage, yet it is not likely that a Judean king would marry a woman with children from another man; moreover, they would have been killed together with Athaliah, and there is no mention of this. One should note that in II Kings 11: 1 there is a Ketib וראתה "and she saw," not appropriate in the context, and this may indicate a deletion from the original text which may have given us the real reason for her action. Josephus was aware of the dilemma and attempted to understand her behaviour as a psychological reaction geared to ensuring that neither her dynasty nor David's should prevail; a similar attitude is encountered on the part of one of the prostitutes disputing rights to a baby in I Kings 3: 26: גם לי גם לך לא יהיה "Neither I nor you shall have him."

great authority in that period. Athaliah must have had assistance from political groups who attempted to overturn the Davidic dynasty, or at least change their policy, and ultimately also killed Joash; they were only subdued by his son Amazjahu, after he gained political strength.[73]

---

[72] It is not within the scope of this study to elaborate on this specific issue, which is the subject of scholarly dissent; see e.g. H. Donner, "Art und Herkunft des Amtes der Königmutter im Alten Testament," in *Festschrift Johannes Friedrich*, pp. 105 - 144, ed. R. von Kienle et al. (Heidelberg, 1959). I shall, however, briefly comment on Donner's article. Donner formulates his theory on two bases: the use of the term גבירה for the king's mother in some biblical quotations, and a probable influence from Ugarit. The masculine parallel for גבירה appears in Scripture twice with reference to Isaac's blessings of Jacob (Gen. 27: 29, 37); in v. 29 the meaning of הוה גביר לאחיך is that Jacob is in a preferred position to his brothers (Masoretic punctuation). We must similarly consider the term גבירה to refer to the preferred position in Court of the new king's mother, until then just one of many of the late king's wives, In Kings, we therefore encounter the name of the new king's mother after his investiture as king, and not at her marriage to the prior king. It is only natural that the new king honoured his mother, possibly by conferring upon her a specific title, similar to Dowager or Queen Mother in England. There is, however, no evidence that the honourary title endowed her with any political or other power. She might have had a personal influence on the king as his mother, subject to the relations between them, but no real power. Bathsheba was asked by Adonijah to intercede on his behalf with Solomon, but alas! with fatal results (I Kings 2: 15 -23).

Regarding Ugaritic influence, I would emphasize in general that while Israel was certainly influenced by the surrounding cultures, we must agree that many of the ideas and customs were changed and adapted to Israelite tradition and culture before their assimilation into Israelite heritage. Were this not the case, it would be inconceivable that Israel would have generated a revolutionary doctrine and belief so different from the culture of its neighbours. I would argue that this proposition is also relevant to our topic. The term מלכה "queen" is not used in the Bible for any Israelite king's wives or mothers, in contrast to the other ancient cultures, in whose literature we find many such personalities. The title מלכה is used in the Bible for the alien queen of Sheba (I Kings 10: 1 - 13), and for Esther, the Persian queen; in the latter case, the king's preferred wife was nominated queen (Esth. 2: 17). The Israelite kings may have bestowed perks on their favoured wives, but did not confer upon them any title or special powers. After the king's death, מלכה was no longer applicable, and so the new king honoured his mother with the preferential title of seniority, גבירה. It is interesting that in the N. T. the term βασίλισσα "queen" appears in Matthew 12: 42 and Luke 11: 31 with reference to the Queen of Sheba, in Acts 8: 27 for an Ethiopian queen, and in Rev. 18: 7 as a metaphor for Babylon. I hope to do more elaborate research on this interesting topic in a separate essay.

[73] We encounter here one of the few politically grounded declarations in Scripture: ויהי כאשר חזקה הממלכה בידו ויך את עבדיו המכים את המלך אביו "After the kingdom was firmly in his grasp, he executed the officials who had murdered his father the king [II Kings 14: 5]."

8.2.3 The Motives of the Kings Redactor

All the above issues suggest that the purpose of the redactor (or redactors) was to downplay the real motives behind the events and portray a set of circumstances reflecting certain ideological conclusions. They saw in every event a divine intervention, founded on a system of reward and punishment, not the result of historical cause and effect. Athaliah of the house of Omri, similar to all her extended family,[74] was therefore an evident malefactor,[75] and was duly punished. Joash, enthroned by the people after the murder of his father and the annihilation of his brothers, was the pious king, and like Josiah was installed by the masses, "the people of the land," after the conspiracy against his father Amon (642 - 640).[76] As often happens, some narratives escaped the attention of the redactor, and the real causes and effects are evident in Scripture. In the case of Amazjahu, we do not find any issue of theodicy regarding his demise, since "he did what was right in the eyes of the Lord [II Kings 14: 3]."[77] From the context, we may deduce that the conspiracy against him was in fact caused by his catastrophic and frivolous war with Jehoash, king of Israel. However, in v. 21 there appears the stereotypical allegation that the people persisted in their loyalty to the Davidic dynasty: "all the people of Judah" enthroned Azariah, his son.

Aside from this "theological formulation" of historical events, we must consider another factor that may affect our ability to assess the authenticity of the two narratives on Temple repairs. The annals from which the Kings redactor formulated his narrative were not based on an orderly chronological system, such as for example our current system, or the Greek computation grounded on the Olympic Games cycle. We observe that the chronology of the kings is based on a relative method of correlation (synchronism) between the reigns of kings of Judah and those of the kings of Israel.[78] Such a system cannot ensure a precise and infallible dating.[79] To make matters worse, the

---

[74]   I Kings 22: 53; II Kings 8: 18 and 27.

[75]   She killed all the throne pretenders and was likely an idolater; though in II Kings 11: 18 we read only that after her death, the people destroyed the Baal sanctuaries, with no information on who built them, II Chr. 24: 7 is more specific, attributing to her sons the desecration of the Temple furnishings and their use for the Baal.

[76]   II Kings 21: 24.

[77]   The Chr. redactor corrected this flaw overlooked by the Kings redactor, and relates that Amaziah "brought back the gods of the people of Seir" and worshipped them (II Chr. 25: 14). Thus the theodicy issue was reinstated.

[78]   For example: ובשנת שמנה עשרה למלך ירבעם בן נבט מלך אבים על יהודה "In the eighteenth year of the reign of Jeroboam son of Nebat, Abijah became king of Judah [I Kings 15: 1]."

[79]   We read in II Kings 8: 17: בן שלשים ושתים שנה היה במלכו ושמנה שנה מלך בירושלם "[Jehoram] was thirty-two years old when he became king, and he reigned in

names of the kings are often repeated,[80] and pass across from one kingdom to the other.[81] The theophoric element יהו is sometimes used as a suffix[82] and in other instances as prefix,[83] sometimes with the character ה and sometimes without it, creating another confusing factor in the correct identification of the various kings.[84] It is little wonder, therefore, that errors and interchanges occur. It is thus possible to hypothesize that the redactor encountered only one record concerning the repair of the Temple, during the period of a king with the name יאשיהו or יהואש, or perhaps connected with both names, and had no means of attributing the record to one or the other. Both kings had reputations of piety, both succeeded unworthy fathers who were killed by

---

Jerusalem eight years." This record is repeated in II Chr. 21: 20. But in II Chr. 22: 2, we read: בן ארבעים ושתים שנה אחזיהו במלכו "Ahaziahu [his son] was forty-two years old when he became king," hence he would have been born two years after his father's death, as Joram became king at thirty-two, reigned eight years, and died at the age of forty. In II Kings 8: 26 it is recorded that Ahaziahu was twenty-two years old. This anomaly was observed by the Rabbis, who attempted to harmonize all the books of Scripture, and the question is asked and answered in Tosefta Sotah 12: 3. Scholars consider this discrepancy as a copy error between כב and מב, which are similar characters, but raise other questions concerning the chronologies in Kings. Cf. Rehm, *Das Zweite Buch der Könige*, pp. 89 - 92, and John Gray, *I & II Kings*, Introduction and chap. 3, pp. 55ff., who writes: "But on the sole evidence of Kings these precise figures often confuse rather than elucidate chronology, which in consequence is one of the notorious problems of Old Testament scholarship" (p. 56). He also quotes de Vaux "that the synchronism in Kings set a problem which is perhaps insoluble" (p. 58). See also Gray, p. 495, regarding the discrepancy between the accession accounts for Ahaziah in II Kings 8: 25 and 9: 29.

[80] There are several kings with the same names: Ahaziah, J(eh)oram, Jehoahaz.

[81] Ahaziah, Jehoahaz, Joash and Jehoram. The kings Jehoram reigned at the same time, inducing some scholars (see Rehm, p. 89) to speculate that there was only one king of that name, who ruled both kingdoms. According to II Kings 13: 10, two kings with the name J(eh)oash reigned simultaneously in Judah and Samaria: "In the thirty-seventh year of Joash king of Judah, Jehoash son of Jehoahaz became king of Israel"; in II Kings 12: 1 we read that Joash king of Judah reigned forty years, hence for three years two kings of the same name reigned in Judah and Israel. On the other hand, we read in II Kings 13: 1: "In the twenty-third year of Joash son of Ahaziah king of Judah, Jehoahaz son of Jehu became king of Israel in Samaria, and he reigned seventeen years." According to this record, Joash son of Jehoahaz king of Israel became king only in the fortieth year of Joash king of Judah, that is, in the year of his death, and not three years before.

[82] אחזיהו and יאשיהו.

[83] יהואש and יהואחז; these names have the same root with the theophoric addition יהו.

[84] One must note that the Kings redactor is more careful in this respect; but both redactions show a number of such interchanges. Ahaziahu, king of Judah and son of Jehoram in II Kings chaps. 8 - 14, is called Jehoahaz in II Chr. 21: 17 and again in 25: 23, but Ahaziahu in chap. 22; in 22: 6, he is called Azariahu. In II Kings 15: 1, 17, 23 and 27, the king of Judah is called Azariah son of Amaziah; in verses 6, 8 he is called Azariahu, but in vv. 13, 30, 32 and 34 as well as in II Chr. chap. 26, he is called Uzziah[u].

conspirators after a short reign; therefore the redactor might have decided to split the narrative and credit both kings with the type of good deed one might expect from such virtuous kings. This would explain the similarity in the narratives in II Kings 12 and 22. We cannot know which personal traits the redactor discovered in the annals, and whether he added such traits as would have been expected. A portrayal of two kings who were pious and dedicated to the glorification of the Temple fits well into the general philosophy of the deuteronomic editor to magnify the piety of the Judean kings and their devotion to the Temple in Jerusalem.

It is highly coincidental, however, that in the long period (about 350 years) between Solomon's construction of the Temple and Josiah, only two kings with a similar or even identical name - if we assume the interchange of the theophoric addendum as a prefix or suffix - thought to repair the Temple, and acted in like manner. According to the Kings narrative most of the Judean kings were pious, and one must thus wonder at their ongoing negligence concerning the Temple's condition. M. Haran states[85] that after Solomon's reign the entire cultic system in the Temple was in decline. We must therefore come to the conclusion that only one king performed these repairs, and it remains to be analyzed, from an historical perspective, which king is the more likely candidate.

The centralization of the cult was a revolutionary idea, totally inconsistent with the prevailing custom in Israel and the surrounding cultures.[86] The complete preference bestowed upon one sanctuary to the exclusion of the

---

[85] *Encyclopaedia Biblica*, Vol. IV, s.v. כהונה ("Priesthood").

[86] Such a centralization of the cult in one place and the elimination of the individual worship common in those days was anomalous. It is probable that this was the trigger for the establishment in Israel of the surrogate בית כנסת "House of Meeting," synagogue, in the later Hellenistic period. This was an innovative institution, unknown before in Israel and in the surrounding cultures, where it was not needed; an ample number of sanctuaries were spread over the land. We observe that in the Second Temple period, organizational steps were undertaken to create a symbolic participation in the cult celebrations in Jerusalem, by selected groups of laics acting on behalf of the rest of the people. Mishnah Ta'anith 4: 2 asks the question: How is it possible to bring an offering at the Temple when the offerer is not present? To alleviate this problem, the Mishnah tells us, the population was divided into twenty-four groups, and every week the representatives of one group went up to Jerusalem and attended the sacrificial service in the Temple, while the rest of the group gathered in their towns and read the Torah. Thus all the people symbolically took part in the sacrificial system, as a compromise between the desire of the people to participate in the worship and the impossibility of everyone attending in Jerusalem after the cult centralization. I shall write further on this issue in section 9.6. Cf. R. P. Merendino, *Das Deuteronomische Gesetz*, who notes on pp. 388 - 9 speculations that a simple centralization formula designating one sanctuary as the main one is of ancient origin. This status may have been bestowed upon Gibeon in ancient times, until Solomon designated Jerusalem. At any rate, Merendino also concedes that it was only Josiah who effected the complete centralization of all cult celebrations.

bamoth was an act that drew opposition from the local clerics, for financial reasons, and from the people attached to their customary places of worship.[87] We should also not exclude "local patriotism," a factor of great relevance even in our day. A fundamental competition existed between the Jerusalem Temple and the local *bamoth*; the enhancement of the status of one caused the absolute erosion of the status of the others. Joash, like the other kings before and after him, had no valid reason to grant privileges to and elevate the status of the Temple in Jerusalem to the disadvantage of the *bamoth*, and enter into a power struggle with the vested interests and preferences of various groups.

Josiah, on the other hand, who dared to execute the reform and invalidate the *bamoth*, did have incentive to enhance the status of the Temple by raising money for its repair, and probably its embellishment. I wish to postulate that Josiah possibly also enlarged the size of the Temple;[88] beyond simply a repair of the existing construction, this was a radical change to the Temple's relatively[89] small dimensions and appearance.[90] The wealth and variety of the

---

[87] See. M. Weinfeld, מיהושע עד יאשיהו (Jerusalem, 1992), pp. 156ff. and Heger, *Incense*, p. 195, n. 15 for additional scholarly references concerning the practical consequences of Josiah's reform.

[88] It is understandable that the redactors of Kings and Chr. would not assume that a later king should have changed the form and the dimensions of the Temple planned by David and constructed by Solomon.

[89] Solomon's palace was one hundred cubits by fifty cubits (I Kings 7: 2), and thus larger than the size of the Temple, which was only sixty by twenty (I Kings 6: 2), and that included the Debir. He also needed thirteen years for the construction of this palace (I Kings 7: 1), against seven years for the building of the Temple (I Kings 6: 38). The size of Solomon's Temple and its pattern were fashioned, as archeologists maintain, after Northern Syrian sanctuaries, such as in Ein-Daraah and Taynat; for example, the hall of the first was about sixteen meters square (see J. H. Monson, מקדש שלמה והמקדש בעין דארא שבסוריה *Qadmoniot* 29/1 (1996), pp. 33 - 38), that is, about two hundred and fifty square cubits, and Solomon's היכל had approximately the same surface. These dimensions were suitable for local temples, but not appropriate for a central sanctuary.

[90] I establish my hypothesis based on the following: Solomon's Temple was of moderate dimensions, as described in I Kings 6: 2: sixty cubits in length, twenty cubits in width and thirty cubits in height. According to Ezra 6: 3 the returning exiles built their Temple sixty cubits wide and sixty cubits high; no length is indicated, but we must assume, given the greater width and height, a length of at least sixty cubits, as in Solomon's Temple. In fact, the commentator Ibn Ezra claims that the length was not indicated because it was identical to the length of Solomon's Temple, sixty cubits, thus forming a perfect cube. However, though this Temple was thus larger than Solomon's, we read evidence from a contemporary witness, the prophet Haggai, of how the people who remembered the First Temple regarded the Second: הלוא כמהו כאין בעיניכם "Does it not seem to you like nothing [Haggai 2: 3]?" We must therefore assume that the Temple destroyed by Nebuchadnezzar was larger than Solomon's Temple, and we can only propose that it was Josiah who rebuilt it to that size; there is no other king (unless we assume that Joash also

materials[91] and the skilled specialists[92] employed in the assignment also tend to suggest something more than a maintenance project. With such a program,[93] Josiah might induce the people to come to the Temple and admire its splendour,[94] to experience a feeling of reverent excitement, and to feel a part of its grandeur by donating funds for its adornment.[95] It is logical to assume that Josiah had to expand the size of the Temple[96] and its court to adapt to the increased numbers of worshippers expected, as a result of the change in status of the Temple from one among many to the single sanctuary of the country. He must also have made efforts to attract people from the previous Northern kingdom to come to Jerusalem on pilgrimage,[97] and thus

---

repaired the Temple) to whom one can attribute this work, on either textual or historical evidence. It is interesting to note that Ezekiel also envisaged a larger temple than Solomon's (Ezek. 41: 12ff.); while it is beyond the scope of this study to examine the debate concerning Ezekiel's complex plans and dimensions for the Temple, we may assume that his vision must have been influenced by the proportions of the Temple before its destruction. Josephus also addresses the issue of the Temple's size. In *Ant.* XI: 81 he refers to Haggai's narrative and emphasizes that the Second Temple, recently constructed, fell short of the earlier Temple, which had been "very great and costly," μεγιστόν τε καὶ πολυτελέστατον. In *Ant.* XI: 99 he describes the size of the Temple built by the returnees using the terms in Ezra 6: 3, that is, without indicating the length. Herod's Temple was even larger, as indicated by Josephus in *Ant.* XV: 391 and Mishnah Midoth 4: 6.

[91] Timber and dressed stones in II Kings 12: 13 and 22: 6.

[92] Carpenters and builders, masons and stonecutters in II Kings 12: 11 - 12; carpenters, builders and masons in II Kings 22: 6. In II Chr. 24: 12 workers in iron and bronze are added.

[93] Such a program would answer the question posed by both the Chr. redactor and modern scholars, concerning the reason for the repairs.

[94] This may explain the question of why the king insisted that all money be spent on the decoration of the Temple: it was to be made an impressive sight for the pilgrims. The addition of a few sprinkling bowls, trumpets and similar accessories would not attain this goal.

[95] This possibility may explain why the king did not use the money in the Temple treasury for the repairs.

[96] We do not possess reliable data concerning the specific cult celebrations performed in the Temple itself, and whether laics were allowed to enter it. We must assume that they were not allowed to enter the Debir, the location of the ark, but we cannot exclude the possibility that in Solomon's period laics could enter the Temple and display their offerings on the tables; the phrase בבוא איש בית ה' "as one enters the Temple [II Kings 12: 10]," a verse which I shall discuss in n. 102, tends to confirm that laics were allowed to enter the Temple. Hence the small size of Solomon's Temple would not be suitable for the modified circumstances.

[97] Kings is silent about the effort of the Judean kings Hezekiah and Joash to attract the Northerners to Jerusalem; in Chr., however, we do find such evidence, and as with other occurrences we must assume that there is a kernel of truth in the narrative. We read in II Chr. 30: 1 that Hezekiah wrote letters על אפרים ומנשה "to Ephraim and Manasseh"

attempt to reunite[98] the two kingdoms under the Davidic dynasty. The same idea that inspired Jeroboam to use his cult "reform" to sustain the division between the Northern and Southern tribes induced Josiah to achieve their unification. These historical circumstances, based on the text in our hands, lead us to consider Josiah's enhancement of the Temple as within his broad political scheme[99] to expand the significance of Jerusalem. This thesis would explain why Josiah, of all kings, aspired to the repair of the Temple.

לבוא לבית ה' בירושלם "to come to the Temple of the Lord in Jerusalem." The confusion in Chr. with reference to the actions of Hezekiah and Josiah with respect to the reform is well known, and we should therefore assume that the appeal to the Northerners to come to Jerusalem for sacrificial worship was made rather by Josiah. We read in II Chr. 30: 10 that the people of Ephraim and Manasseh as far as Zebulun were not amenable: ויהיו משחיקים עליהם ומלעגים בם "...but the people scorned and ridiculed them." There were some exceptions (v. 11): אך אנשים מאשר ומנשה ומזבלון נכנעו ויבאו לירושלם "...[some] men from Asher, Manasseh and Zebulun humbled themselves and went to Jerusalem." Though we read in II Chr. 31: 1: וינתצו את הבמות ואת המזבחות מכל יהודה ובנימן ובאפרים ומנשה עד לכלה "...they pulled down the high places and the altars throughout Judah and Benjamin and in Ephraim and Manasseh," this seems unlikely given the popularity of the *bamoth* in this region, and at a time when it was occupied by the dominant Assyrian power. The emphasis in 30: 25 is on the people of Israel who came to Jerusalem, as we read there: וישמחו כל קהל יהודה והכהנים והלוים וכל הקהל הבאים מישראל והגרים הבאים מארץ ישראל והיושבים ביהודה "The entire assembly of Judah rejoiced, along with the priests and Levites and all who had assembled from Israel, including the aliens who had come from Israel and those who lived in Judah"; but this stands in unmistakable contradiction to the previously cited circumstances in v. 10. According to the chronological order of II Chr. all this happened at the apex of Assyrian might, before Sennacherib's invasion of Judah, which is recorded in chap. 32 with the preamble in v. 1: אחרי הדברים והאמת האלה "After these things and the establishment thereof."

[98] The fact that cultic motives underlie political policies is not new, and we have encountered such an approach in Jeroboam's decision to enhance the significance of the Northern sanctuaries, and even to establish a different date than that prevailing in Jerusalem for the most important festival, the Feast of the Ingathering (I Kings 12: 32 - 33). See also E. Würthwein, *Das Erste Buch der Könige, Kapitel 1 - 16* (Göttingen, 1977), pp. 89ff. who postulates that David transferred the ark, sacred to the Northern tribes, to the City of David in order to inspire their loyalty to his new capital, although his tribe adored the Cherubim.

[99] Josiah was a king with great political vision; he attempted to establish Judah as a regional power playing off between Assyria and Egypt. With this objective in mind, he sided with Assyria, whose international power was already debilitated, against Egypt, a venture that ultimately cost him his life (II Kings 23: 29). Kings does not indicate any reason for Josiah's military venture against Neco of Egypt, but II Chr. 35: 21 - 25 records a remarkable discussion between the two kings. Neco attempted to divert Josiah from his intent to oppose him, asserting that he had not come to fight Josiah but only to combat Assyria. This narrative would confirm my assumption that Josiah's fight against Neco was not a defensive action against an aggressive occupying force, but a deliberate action to assert his independence and the inviolability of his territory. Chr. records Neco's

Josiah was assisted in the achievement of his project by three important social elements: a) the local priesthood, who realized the great advantage they would enjoy from the centralization and the dominance of Jerusalem in cult and law, b) the local landowners and the entire population of Jerusalem, who would enjoy the great prosperity resulting from the pilgrims who would come and spend time and money in Jerusalem, and c) the scribes, who introduced suitable divine commands in the Book of the Law, the Deuteronomy. I do not agree entirely with Chr. Levin's assertion that Josiah's cult centralization was a result of the king's desire to control the cult,[100] which would imply a conflict of interest between the king and the priesthood. I think that the Jerusalemite priesthood had a common interest with the king, and fully co-operated with him to achieve this goal. The provincial priests and the Levites,[101] on the other hand, would have been adversely affected by these new rules, and it is their reactions that might be reflected in the narrative of II Kings 12, concerning the reluctance of the priests, and the complementary II Chr. 24: 5 - 6, concerning the obstinacy of the Levites. The redactors, as we have seen in other instances, interpreted their *Vorlage* in the light of their understanding of how matters "ought" to

---

arguments with an interesting style: ואלהים אמר לבהלני חדל לך מאלהים אשר עמי "God has told me to hurry; so stop opposing God [v. 21b]." This argument may have been added to justify Josiah's death; that is, though he was a pious king, he did not heed God's mandate as conveyed by Pharaoh. The Rabbis give two opposing interpretations of this biblical phrase "God has told me," one that Neco referred to his idol deity, and the other that he referred to the God of Israel. We read in B.T. Ta'anith 22b: מאי אלהים אשר עמי אמר רב יהודה אמר רב זו עבודה זרה "What does it mean 'God who is with me [II Chr. 35: 21]?' Rav Judah said in the name of Rav: This is an idol." We then read: מפני מה נענש יאשיהו מפני שהיה לו לימלך בירמיהו ולא נמלך "Why was Josiah punished? Because he should have asked advice from Jeremiah and did not do so." In Lamentations Rabbah Parshah 1: 53 ד"ה צדיק הוא we read: ולא שמע אל דברי נבו מפי אלהים זה ירמיהו שאמר ליאשיהו כך מקובלני מישעיה רבי (ישעיה י"ט) וסכסכתי מצרים במצרים ולא שמע לו "He did not listen to God's utterances pronounced by Neco, that is, what Jeremiah said to Josiah: This is what I received by tradition from Isaiah my teacher: 'I will stir up Egyptian against Egyptian [brother will fight against brother - Isa. 19: 2],' and Josiah did not heed him." That is, Josiah had no valid reason to fight the Egyptians and was punished because he did not heed Jeremiah's advice.

[100] Chr. Levin, "Joshija im deuteronomistischen Geschichtswerk," *ZAW* 96 (1984), pp. 351 - 71, writes (p. 352): "Die Konzentration in der Hauptstadt unterwarf die offizielle Religionsausübung des ganzen Landes dem unmittelbaren Zugriff des Königs" ("The concentration [of the cult] in the capital city placed the official practice of the national religion directly under the control of the king").

[101] The Levites, a guild of clerics, had initially no functions in Jerusalem, and wandered over all of Israel, offering their cultic services. See Heger, *Incense*, pp. 262-64 and nn. 26 - 28 on the subject of the Levites and their activities.

have been,[102] or to convey what they considered to be the true tradition concerning the divine will.

8.2.4 The Emendation System of the Biblical Editors and Redactors

The scribes presented the theological justification for the exceptional and anomalous new regulation. The king's political interest in centralizing the cult activities in Jerusalem,[103] to enhance its status and expand its economic advantages, was ingeniously presented to the people as a divine command; Jerusalem was the one and only locality chosen by the Deity for the "dwelling of His Name,"[104] and the unique site for sacrificial worship. The

---

[102] Just as the Chr. editor attempted to correct the Kings text and blame the Levites for the delay in the collection of the money, we observe the same attempt to adapt the text to current conditions concerning the much-discussed issue of the site of the collection box. In II Kings 12: 10, we read ויתן אתו אצל המזבח בימין בבוא איש בית ה' ונתנו שמה הכהנים שמרי הסף את כל הכסף המובא בית ה' "He placed it beside the altar, on the right side as one enters the Temple of the Lord. The priests who guarded the entrance put into the chest all the money that was brought to the Temple of the Lord." The text of this verse, and specifically the term בימין, is equivocal, giving rise to much debate from ancient times until today; see Chr. Levin's report of these discussions, pp. 60ff. In II Chr. 24: 8 - 10, the description of the location of the box and the handling of the money is different. We read there: ויתנהו בשער בית ה' חוצה...ויביאו וישליכו לארון עד לכלה "He placed [the chest] outside at the gate of the Temple of the Lord...[all the people] brought their contributions, dropping them into the chest." I do not intend to enter into a discussion concerning the term בימין and I do not think that it poses a real problem, if we consider the changed circumstances between the periods of Kings and Chronicles. In the period of the First Temple, individuals were allowed to enter the Temple; therefore, the collection box was placed at the right side of the altar, or at the right of the person entering the Temple. I suspect that v. 10b in II Kings 12, recording that the priests put the money in the box, is a later interjection, to adapt the text to the period when laics were no longer allowed to enter the sanctuary. The text in Chr., of a later date, was written when this prohibition was already quite established; the box was specifically placed "outside the gate of the Temple" and therefore the people themselves put the money in the box.

[103] Cf. Y. Suzuki, "A New Aspect of Occupation Policy by King Josiah, Assimilation and Codification in View of Yahwism," *AJBI* 18 (1992), pp. 31 - 61, who writes on p. 34: "The central figure who made the 'deuteronomic code' is nobody else but King Josiah."

[104] There are an impressive number of occurrences of this phrase in Deut. chaps. 12 - 16. The deuteronomic redactors of Chronicles implied that Jerusalem was chosen by God even before David's election, and interjected this topic in a sloppy way in Solomon's address at the Temple's inauguration. I Kings 8: 16 records Solomon's oration: מן היום אשר הוצאתי את עמי ישראל ממצרים לא בחרתי בעיר מכל שבטי ישראל לבנות בית להיות שמי שם ואבחר בדוד להיות על עמי ישראל "Since the day I brought my people out of Egypt, I have not chosen a city in any tribe of Israel to have a

question of whether myth or theological justification succeed acquired custom and ritual in order to rationalize them, or whether theology or myth serve as the foundation for the creation of ritual, is a much debated issue concerning "the making of Religions."[105] In our case, I postulate that the scribes rationalized and justified the king's intentions by skillfully introducing numerous dictates in a version of a "Book"[106] found in the Temple and attributed to divine origin.[107] It is commonly accepted that the laws and statutes of the Pentateuch came into being to serve concrete necessities, as is persuasively argued by O. Kaiser.[108]

We must distinguish in our analysis between the work of three generations or strata of sources, in their chronological order: the Pentateuch (in our case the Book of Deuteronomy in particular), the books of Kings, and the books of

---

Temple built for my Name to be there, but I have chosen David to rule my people Israel." We observe the apparently odd structure of this verse: part *b* refers to the choosing of a city, whereas part *c* refers to the choosing of a person, a ruler of the people. The traditional commentators were aware of this irregularity in the text, and attempted to adjust it. Radak asks: למה שהקדים לא בחרתי בעיר היה לומר ואבחר בירושלם "Since [the verse] starts with the utterance 'I have not chosen a city' it should have then declared 'I have chosen Jerusalem'"; the commentator then proposes a lengthy addition to rectify the inconsistency. In II Chr. 6: 6, the editor was not compelled to amend an existing text, and had the liberty of expressing his new doctrine in a clear way: ואבחר בירושלם להיות שמי שם ואבחר בדויד להיות על עמי ישראל "I have chosen Jerusalem for my Name to be there, and I have chosen David to rule my people Israel." Rashi in his commentary to this verse connects it with the Kings verse, and uses it to explain the oddity in the Kings verse. For our purposes we observe that Solomon's address did not mention at all the choosing of the city of Jerusalem, merely the divine selection of his father David, and the latter's plan to build the Temple; the subsequent editors interjected, without adequate care, the divine choice of Jerusalem.

[105] See A. N. Whitehead, *Religion in the Making* (New York, 1926).

[106] Or parts of a book, since we do not know exactly which elements were assumed to have been found at that event. See I. A. Seligman, מחקרים בספרות המקרא, 2nd edition (Jerusalem, 1996), p. 108 concerning the various strata and origins of Deuteronomy. For our purposes, it is not necessary to debate which deuteronomic pericopes were of earlier or later origin. From the context of the Kings narrative on the centralization of the cult, we can definitely deduce that the relevant utterances on the choice of Jerusalem and the pertinent statutes and regulations were deliberately introduced into the "discovered" Book.

[107] The Kings narrative is not explicit about the origin of the "Book", but the divine origin of its content is certainly implied. In II Chr. 34: 14, it is explicitly identified as ספר תורת ה' ביד משה "the Book of the Law of the Lord that had been given through Moses."

[108] Otto Kaiser, *Einleitung in das Alte Testament* (Gütersloh, 1969), p. 55: "...dass Rechtsreihen, Rechtsbücher und Kultordnungen in der Regel aufgrund konkreter Bedürfnisse und nur in seltenste Fällen aus prophetisch- oder philosophisch-utopischer Absicht entstehen." (in free translation: "...legal statutes, legal codices and cult ordinances are devised to serve concrete necessities, and only in the most rare cases do they result from some prophetic or philosophical-utopian aim.")

Chronicles. Because there are parallel narratives in Kings and Chronicles which may be compared and contrasted, it is relatively easy to construct reliable assumptions on the development of customs and beliefs between the two periods. There are no such definite parallels between Kings and the Pentateuch, and here we must rely on a variety of elements, such as critical literary and structural analysis, historical circumstances and possible foreign influences, to construct a plausible hypothesis. Matters are yet more indecisive when we analyze pentateuchal texts, for which there is no written *Vorlage*,[109] and we must rely exclusively on textual analysis, historical circumstances known from other sources (which are not trustworthy for the study of the development in the cult), and on archeological findings concerning material culture in Israel. As with all general schemes, exceptions are possible, and this should be kept in mind when assessing the validity of deductions reached on the basis of this three-strata assumption.

The Chronicles redactors adapted their narratives to the circumstances of their period, to conform with their ideas and doctrines, and their assumptions of how "it ought to have been." They achieved this goal in different ways: sometimes with the addition of a few words, sometimes with explanatory phrases, and occasionally by attaching an entirely distinct event, which has no parallel in Kings.[110] The relapse of Joash demonstrates the unmistakable philosophy of the Chronicles' redactor to deviate from the plain understanding we reach from the Kings narrative concerning the period of the kings Ahaziah, Joash and his son Amaziah. The Kings record reflects unstable political conditions in Judah, with conspiratorial assassinations and coups, whereas the Chronicles account implies that Joash was punished because of his moral and religious wickedness. The same alteration is applied to the fate of Amaziah. Kings implies that his doom was the result of poor political decisions, but in II Chr. 25: 14 - 16 his doom is the result of a divine scheme to punish him for his idolatrous sins.

Similar corrections were also carried out by the Kings redactors; there were also interjections of additional phrases or changes by later P redactors. As we have no comparative parallels to their *Vorlage*, however, we must rely on literary analysis, examination of historical circumstances, and logic to

---

[109] In some instances we may rely on narratives in the earlier books, such as Judges and Samuel, but here too we must be aware of the possible interjections by later redactors, to adapt the text to the circumstances in their period.

[110] The instances are manifold; I shall quote such occurrences relevant to our study. In II Chr. 34: 14, the "Book" found in the Temple is attributed explicitly to Moses, in contrast with the Kings narrative. An explanatory addendum is encountered in II Chr. 24: 7 clarifying that the Temple repair was necessary because of the break-in into the Temple by Athaliah and her son. An entirely new event is recorded in II Chr. 24: 17 - 22 concerning Joash's relapse into idolatrous worship and the killing of Zechariah, Jehoiada's son.

assess how far these texts seem to deviate from the probably trustworthy court annals and other documentation on which they were based. The redactors interpreted such sources and traditions so as to correct assumed lacunae in the Pentateuch, adapt the narratives to the actual circumstances of their period, and convey to the people their message and inculcate them in correct behaviour. The transmission of an unadulterated historiography was not their aim,[111] although I do not suggest that they invented events out of their own imagination; they simply interpreted matters as they understood them to have been.

Thus we may assess the apparently strange accounts in our pericopes. They appear to be the result of a theological interpretation of political events likely introduced into existing objective records of events. I have drawn attention to a number of these occurrences in our text; we may now turn to the obvious interjections effected by the later P redactors concerning the status and activities of Jehoiada. Having established the period of our pericope as politically unstable, rife with conspiracies and assassinations, we must assume that Jehoiada was a courtier who sided with a certain political group against Athaliah and who probably had the support of the clerics in the Temple. The title כהן was awarded to him by the king[112] to compensate him for his loyalty to the Davidic dynasty and his military actions in restoring the throne to Joash. A priest dedicated to the sacrificial service, as we know from the P section of the Pentateuch, would not have been the appropriate person to give orders to the army, having neither the requisite authority, nor obviously the necessary skills to devise the efficient military strategy found in II Kings 11: 5 - 8. In fact, the first time Jehoiada is mentioned in 11: 4, he is without the title כהן;[113] it is only in v. 9 that he appears with that title. The textual confusion concerning Jehoiada's title כהן is overwhelming[114] and clearly demonstrates a clumsy manner of interjection. The single mention of his title הכהן הגדול in II Kings 12: 11 affirms its anachronism.[115]

---

[111] Cf. M. Noth, *The History of Israel*, transl. A. and C. Black (London, 1960), pp. 43 ff.

[112] At that period, the title and status of כהן was not yet a genealogical privilege, but an honourable rank awarded by the king to his friends and supporters. See Heger, *Incense*, pp. 261 ff. and 273 ff. for the substantiation of this postulate.

[113] It is remarkable that in II Chr. 22: 11, in which Jehoiadah is mentioned for the first time in the Chr. narrative as Joash's uncle, he appears with the title כהן, but in 23: 1, the parallel to II Kings 11: 4, he is mentioned without the title, as in the text in Kings. On the issue of Jehoiada's priesthood, see further Appendix III.

[114] In addition to the inconsistency between vv. 4 and 9 regarding Jehoiada's title כהן, we find in the remainder of chap. 11 certain occurrences of his name without the title, certain with the title, and in some instances only the denomination כהן without his name.

[115] This title was definitely not yet in force at that period, and the "chief" priest was still under the king's authority. We observe that in the later period of Ahaz, the king ordered Uriah, who was probably his "chief" priest, to build the altar and perform the sacrifices

There are several reasons that might have induced the redactors to characterize Jehoiada as a priest. As suggested above, he might have received this title from the king after his enthronement; therefore the court annals which described this procedure[116] were suitably altered, as such a system of naming a priest stands in stark opposition to the P narrative. We also observe in the Kings narrative that Joash was hidden by Jehosheba in בית ה', "in the Temple of the Lord," and later on we read that Jehoiada took the weapons from the Temple of the Lord (II Kings 11: 10). Moreover, many military activities were performed in the Temple, and in the Temple court. The redactors may thus have deduced that Jehoiada must have been a priest, otherwise he would not have been allowed to enter the Temple, according to the later P rules; consequently, we observe the (inconsistent) interjection of the title כהן to adapt the narrative to the current laws.[117] Another motive may have been to demonstrate the piety and good deeds of the priesthood, caring for the Temple,[118] obeying God's dictates and inducing king[119] and people to fulfil them,[120] and upholding the divine promise by supporting the perpetuity of the Davidic dynasty.[121] Any or all of these motives may have induced the

---

according to his commands, and Uriah submitted to the king's order: ויעש אוריה הכהן ככל אשר צוה המלך אחז "And Uriah the priest did just as king Ahaz had ordered [II Kings 16: 16]." Uriah is not mentioned with the title הכהן הגדול, although we must assume that he had the highest rank among the priests at that time, being responsible for the cult system and organization in the Temple, and thus it was to him that the king gave his orders. The Chr. editor corrected this flaw in Kings and changed the title; in the parallel verse II Chr. 24: 11 he calls Jehoiada כהן הראש, "the head priest." This is apparently an administrative title, judging from the use of the term in Jer. 52: 24, which we may consider authentic.

[116] Similar to David's procedure in II Sam. 8: 16 - 18, and the actions of Solomon in I Kings 2: 27 and 35.

[117] II Chr. "corrected" the Kings narrative, identifying the soldiers who went into the Temple as priests and Levites (23: 4) and then emphasizing this in v. 6 to avoid any doubt: ואל יבוא בית ה' כי אם הכהנים והמשרתים ללוים המה יבאו כי קדש המה "No one is to enter the Temple of the Lord except the priests and Levites on duty; they may enter because they are consecrated."

[118] Jehoiada was involved in such activities, as appears in II Kings 12: 10, 11 and 12.

[119] II Kings 12: 3: ויעש יהואש הישר בעיני ה' כל ימיו אשר הורהו יהוידע הכהן "Joash did what was right in the eyes of the Lord all the years Jehoiada the priest instructed him."

[120] "Jehoiada made [renewed] the Covenant between God, the king and the people, to be God's people [that is, to obey His commands] [II Kings 11: 17]."

[121] The Kings redactor takes this for granted, but the Chr. editor confirms it explicitly in II Chr. 23: 3, in which Joash is presented to the people by Jehoiada: ויאמר להם הנה בן המלך ימלך כאשר דבר ה' על בני דויד "The king's son shall reign, as the Lord promised concerning the descendants of David."

P redactor[122] to step in and "improve" the original text to what "ought to be." The probability of a number of subsequent emendators, each with his own ideas, might explain the perplexing and equivocal text we find today.

8.3 Conclusion

We may thus conclude that the Temple repairs effected by Josiah were part of his overall program of cult centralization. The creation of the Jerusalem Temple as the sole legitimate locus of sacrifice had a profound impact on the sacrificial cult, as we shall see in chap. 9.

With respect to the relationship between II Kings chaps. 12 and 22, I arrive at the same conclusion as Stade, Spieckermann and Chr. Levin, but from an entirely different perspective. I have added historical elements to the investigation, which are essential for the verification of the literary analysis. As we have seen in the expositions of Spieckermann and Dietrich, it is possible to reach opposite conclusions using only a purely literary analysis of the same text. I have also attached great significance to the comparison between the narratives in Kings and Chronicles, a method that offers us substantial insight into the method of thought and consequent literary activities of the redactors of these books.[123] Their perception of events, which we are often able to apprehend by this comparison, is a valuable tool, since it reflects the views of intelligent and erudite people who lived and created close to the recorded events. Analysis of their accounts also contributes to a thorough assessment of the circumstances of their period. I wish to reiterate

---

[122] With respect to the priestly interjections in the pericope II Kings 12: 5 - 17 see also R. Rendtorff, *Studien zur Geschichte des Opfers im Alten Israel*, Wissenschaftliche Monographien zum Alten und Neuen Testament (Neukirchen, 1967), p. 54.

[123] Although the Chr. editor at the beginning of the narrative praises Joash's behaviour and his interest in the repair of the Temple, his extremely pejorative account of Joash's later deeds, missing in Kings, leads us to assume that it was founded on some negative report on this king. A rabbinic homily in Midrash Tanhuma פרשת וארא סימן ח goes even further and accuses Joash of presenting himself as a god, based on the wording of II Chr. 24: 17, באו שרי יהודה וישתחוו למלך "the officials of Judah came and prostrated themselves before the king"; as his due punishment, he was abused as a homosexual object by the Arameans, with the phrase ואת יואש עשו שפטים "judgment was executed on Joash" in v. 24 being interpreted as "sexually abused." Such denigrating accounts in Chr. and the rabbinic literature do not seem to befit a king who worked so intensively to repair the Temple; this lends further credence to the idea that there might have been additional records, or that there were doubts (similar to those of modern scholars) on the authenticity of the report in Kings about Joash's repairs. Such considerations add some support to the thesis that the narrative in II Kings 12 is a duplicate of the "authentic" one in II Kings 22.

here the caution that while we possess a fairly convincing system to explore the distinctions between the texts of Kings and Chronicles and their implications, the critical analysis of the Kings text is less reliable and relies on less realistic methods. Nevertheless, I believe I have substantiated my thesis on both literary and historical grounds, and constructed a plausible hypothesis.

9. Developments in the Sacrificial Cult in Practice and Theology

9.1 Introduction

It is my conviction that there is a constant interaction between cult practice and theology, though without a defined pattern of cause and effect: sometimes it is the change in theology which spurs a shift in the manner of cult celebrations, and in other instances an alteration in cult practice, due to external influence, furthers an ideological adjustment. It is therefore of no significance for our purpose to determine which element preceded and which was its consequence; it suffices to demonstrate the remarkable and meaningful shifts that occurred from the early customs of nomadic and farming peoples, through protracted developmental stages of increasing sophistication and institutionalization, until the ultimate materialization of recitation and prayer after the destruction of the Second Temple. In my study of the altar laws I have illustrated, sometimes directly (mainly in chaps. 1 and 2) and in other cases by inference, the changes in the sacrificial cult until the end of the Second Temple; as is generally accepted, sacrifice was not practised after the Temple's destruction.[1] I shall now discuss the radical shift in Israelite theology that accompanied this cessation of the sacrificial cult and its replacement with the recitation of relevant biblical periscopes, ultimately combined with prayer. I shall not discuss the anthropological origins of the sacrificial cult, an issue amply debated by many scholars of all disciplines, or the corresponding Israelite theological concepts as revealed by scholars through textual analysis and other methodologies. I shall thus limit my study

---

[1] The question whether sacrifices were offered in Jerusalem in the period 70 - 135 C.E., that is, after the destruction of the Second Temple and the Second Revolt, is an issue in which many scholars have been involved. K. W. Clark, "Worship in the Jerusalem Temple after A.D. 70," in *The Gentile Bias and Other Essays*, selected by J. L. Sharpe III, pp. 10 - 20 (Leiden, 1980), recapitulates various scholarly opinions in this respect, and concludes that the definite cessation of sacrifices occurred only after 135 C. E.; some offerings were performed at the Temple between 70 and that date. It is not the purpose of this study to critically analyze Clark's assumption, but in the course of my examination of the theological changes with respect to the sacrificial cult, I shall postulate that no such sacrifices were performed after 70 C.E. At any rate, it is of no crucial significance for our study of change in the sacrificial theology whether the cessation of offerings occurred in 70, or in 135 C.E.

exclusively to the changes in the cult practice in Israel, and in its underlying theology.

9.2 From Archaic Food Offerings to the Gods to Loftier Concepts

From the first periods for which we possess historical evidence,[2] food[3] and gifts for the gods[4] constituted the scope of offerings. In some cultures the gift was explicitly donated to the deities to secure their favour[5] or minimize their hostility,[6] while in others this consideration is not evident. A critical analysis

---

[2] It is not my intention to dispute the totem theory of Robertson Smith and his followers regarding the origin of sacrifices. I shall avoid the anthropological issues and concentrate on following the changes revealed through analysis of the texts, and what they show of earlier custom and ideologies.

[3] See F. Thureau-Dangin, "Le Rituel du Temple d'Anu, Uruk," in *Rituels Accadiens*, (Paris, 1921), pp. 98-9, and the many mentions of "le grand repas" and " le petit repas"; the extended and precise list of foodstuffs to be presented to the Babylonian gods, in F. Blome, *Die Opfermaterie in Babylonien und Israel* (Rome, 1934) and the general discussion on p. 13 headed "Opfer als Speise Gottes." See also G. A. Barton, "A Comparison of Some Features of Hebrew and Babylonian Ritual," *JBL* 46 (1927), pp. 79 - 89: "... Hebrews had regarded sacrifices as food offered to God" (p. 80); and B. A. Levine and W. W. Hallo, "Offerings to the Temple Gates at Ur," *HUCA 38* (1967), pp. 17 - 58. If we assume that the sacrificial meal had the purpose of a communion with the Deity, this implies a common meal in which both parties, man and god, each received his dedicated share. A later sophistication may have considered the Deity's share not as food, but simply as the god's share in everything.

[4] The issue of whether offerings also had a propitiatory or expiatory background is not significant for our study, which is limited to the shifts in Israelite sacrificial theology. See R. J. Thompson, *Penitence and Sacrifice in Early Israel Outside the Levitical Law. An Examination of the Fellowship Theory of Early Israelite Sacrifice* (Leiden, 1963), pp. 26 ff. who quotes the different scholarly opinions on these background issues.

[5] I shall quote several examples: G. Eglund, "Gifts to the Gods," in *Gifts to the Gods*, Proceedings of the Uppsala Symposium 1985, ed. T. Linders and G. Nordquist (Uppsala, 1987), pp. 57-64, writes on pp. 61 ff. on "reciprocal giving" in the Egyptian cult. Walter Burkert, "Offerings in Perspective," ibid. pp. 43 - 50, states, "Odysseus can claim divine help because he has given sacred things to the gods more often than other men." We read in the *Iliad*, Book 12: 6-9: "To the gods they gave no hekatombs that might have won them to guard the wall as shield..."

[6] The pleasant aroma of Noah's offering after the deluge (Gen. 8: 21), a narrative with Mesopotamian parallels, induced God to adopt a forgiving and more positive attitude towards nature and mankind. We read there ויאמר ה' אל לבו לא אסף לקלל עוד את האדמה בעבור האדם כי יצר לב האדם רע מנעריו "...Never again will I curse the ground because of man, even though every inclination of his heart is evil from childhood." A rabbinical homily elevates the simple interpretation to a more sublime idea; we read in Genesis Rabbah, *Parshah* 34: 9: וירח ה' את ריח הניחוח הריח ריחו

of biblical texts reveals archaic expressions, left unexpurgated, which verify that early sacrifice served as food for the Deity. Expressions such as קרבני לחם "... the food for my offerings made by fire [Num. 28: 2],"[7] לחמי לאשי פנים לפני תמיד "... the bread of the presence ... before me at all times [Exod. 25: 30]," את לחם אלהיך הוא מקריב "... they offer up the food of your God [Lev. 21: 8]," and the numerous occurrences of ריח ניחוח לה'[8] substantiate this proposition. The denial of the Deity's requirement of food in such pronouncements as אם ארעב לא אמר לך כי לי תבל ומלאה "If I were hungry I would not tell you, for the world is mine, and all that is in it," and האוכל בשר אבירים ודם עתודים אשתה[9] "Do I eat the flesh of bulls or drink the blood of goats? [Ps. 50: 12-13]" merely confirms the general belief

---

של אברהם אבינו עולה מכבשן האש וירח ריח של חנניה מישאל ועזריה עולין מכבשן האש "'God perceived the pleasant odour' - the odour [surrounding] Abraham as he climbed up from the furnace [a midrashic homily] and the odour of Hananiah, Mishael and Azariah climbing up from the furnace [into which they were thrown for their belief in God (Daniel 1: 6 and 3: 19 - 27), and this was the reason for His change of attitude towards mankind]."

[7] The Rabbis were sensitive to these anthropomorphic expressions, and attempted to interpret them in a homiletic manner. We read in Tosefta Menahot (Zuckermandel) 7: 9: בזמן שישראל ברצון לפני המקום מה נאמר בהם את קרבני לחמי לחמי כבנים שמתפרנסין מאביהן בשעת תוכחות מהו אומר לאישי ריח ניחוחי כל קרבנות שאתם מקריבין אינן אלא לאש "When the Israelites are in a state of benevolence before God, it is said of them: '... the food for my offerings made by fire [Num 28: 2],' like children who are fed by their father [God provides them with His bread], but when they are admonished, it is said : 'by fire, as an aroma pleasing to me [ibid.],' all your offerings are solely for the fire [burned in vain]."

[8] Onkelos changed the interpretation of this expression to ומתקבל ברעוה קדם ה' "accepted with pleasure before God." A similar explanation is given in Sifrei on Num. Pisqa 143, ד"ה כמנחת הבקר, in which we read: אשה ריח ניחוח לה' נחת רוח "... [the interpretation of ריח ניחוח is] satisfaction before me - I have spoken and My desire is done." Instead of the usual translation as "an aroma pleasing to the Lord," a different etymological interpretation is offered, and the expression ניחוח is derived from the phrase נחת רוח "satisfaction"; God is pleased that the Israelites fulfill His commands. In the late regulations of the incense cult in Exod. 30 1 - 9 and 34 - 38 there is no mention of ריח ניחוח, although one would expect it with respect to a performance which is primarily intended to spread a pleasant odour (See Heger, Incense, p. 50).

[9] The Rabbis connect this verse with the expression לרצנבם תזבחהו "You shall offer it at your own will [Lev. 19: 5]." We read in B. T. Menahoth 110a: לא אמרתי אליכם זבחו כדי שתאמר אעשה רצונו ויעשה רצוני לא לרצוני אתם זובחים אלא לרצונכם אתם זובחים שנאמר (ויקרא י"ט) לרצונכם תזבחהו "I did not command you to offer that you should say: 'I will comply with His wish and let His wish be fulfilled! You are not offering to fulfill My wish but you are doing it because you wish to do so, as is said 'You shall offer it at your own will.'"

of the populace, as condemned by the author of the hymn. The table with its showbread and eating utensils[10] (Exod. 25: 23 - 30), the equivalence of the terms שלחן and מזבח in Ezek. 41: 22,[11] and the possible use of the bronze altar (Exod. 27: 1 - 8) as a presentation table for food and gifts (as postulated in the antecedent chapter), all bear additional witness[12] to archaic cult observances associated in their external forms with the presentation of food to the Deity.

Old customs persist long after their underlying theology ceases to be relevant. The presentation of food ceased and was ultimately replaced by the burning of animal parts[13] or entire offerings; but the exhibition of the showbread subsisted, and traces of the archaic language survived in the later priestly texts. The burning of the offering reflected a dissonance between the concept of providing food to the gods and more sophisticated and abstract notions. I have cited Galling's postulate that the burning of the offerings is a later sophistication in the sacrificial system;[14] a worshipper far from the

---

[10] For an extensive exposition of the relevant biblical texts and the forced talmudic interpretations attempting to dissociate them from their simple anthropomorphic definition, see Heger, "Excursus: The Table and its Accoutrements," in *Incense*, pp. 116 ff..

[11] Here too the Rabbis present a homily to reconcile what seemed to them to be a contradiction between מזבח and שלחן. We read in B. T. Berakhoth 55a: וידבר אלי זה השלחן אשר לפני ה' פתח במזבח וסיים בשלחן רבי יוחנן ורבי אלעזר דאמרי תרווייהו כל זמן שבית המקדש קיים מזבח מכפר על ישראל ועכשיו שלחנו של אדם מכפר עליו "[It is written] 'And he said to me: This is the table before the Lord [Eze 41: 22].' [Why did] he start with [the term] table and finish with [the term] altar? Both Rabbi Johanan and Rabbi Eleazar said: While the Temple existed, the altar atoned for the sins of the Israelites, but now man's table atones for his sins."

[12] Since I limit myself at this point to textual evidence, I refrain from quoting archeological evidence with respect to platforms and deposit benches in the sanctuaries for the presentation of food and gifts to the deities. See section 7.2.1 and the sources cited in the respective footnotes on the archeological evidence from the Late Bronze Age and Early Iron Age.

[13] It is interesting to note that the rabbinical language carefully avoided any anthropomorphic association even with respect to the animal parts burned on the altar. The term למזבח "to the altar" is utilized instead of לה' for the Deity. I shall cite one example from Mishnah Menahoth 6: 2: מנחת כהנים ומנחת כהן משיח ומנחת נסכים למזבח ואין בהם לכהנים בזה יפה כח המזבח מכח הכהנים שתי הלחם ולחם הפנים לכהנים ואין בהם למזבח ובזה יפה כח הכהנים מכח המזבח "The *Minhah* of the priests, and of the anointed [High] Priest, and of the auxiliary offering goes to the 'altar', and nothing [goes] to the priests; [thus] in these cases, the 'altar' is more privileged than the priests. The two breads [offered on the Feast of Weeks - Lev. 23: 17] and the showbread all go to the priests and nothing [goes] to the 'altar', and in this case the priests are more privileged than the 'altar'."

[14] Section 1.3.1, especially n. 136.

location of his deity burned the offering and created a smoke rising up to heaven, to be united in this symbolic way with his deity. A similar perception is encountered in the Hindu Scriptures, the Rig Veda:[15] the flame of the sacrifices, going straight up, made a connection between the ritual sacrificer and the gods in heaven through the mediation of Agni, the Vedic god of fire.

We encounter other lofty motives for offerings,[16] such as the ancient Arab custom of abandoning the slaughtered animal as a symbol of surrender or submission,[17] and the giving away of a precious possession or a part of oneself, such as the *Aquiqa*, the burning of one's hair.[18] Philo states in *The Special Laws* I that offering is symbolic,[19] with man presenting himself as a victim; purged and cleansed in body and soul, he comes to the sanctuary.[20] Therefore, Philo declares, there is no difference what gift he brings, whether ox or dove, since the aim and purpose of the sacrifice is for man to offer himself. The shift in Israelite sacrificial cult from the presentation of food and gifts to the burning of the whole or part of the offering is supposed by Scripture to have been effected by Ahaz (II Kings 16), as postulated in chap. 7.[21] We may also deduce another significant aspect of Ahaz' cult reform, the shift from a simple, informal and spontaneous cult,[22] grounded in nomadic

---

[15] Nicol MacNicol, "To Agni," in *Hindu Scriptures* (London, 1938), pp. 1, 6, 36-37.

[16] R. Money-Kyrle, *The Meaning of Sacrifice* (London, 1930), offers a variety of scholarly opinions on this topic (abstract, p. 259).

[17] H. Lammens, *L'Arabie occidentale avant l'Hégire* (Beyrouth, 1928), p.126: "On honorait ces *ans'ab* par des visites et par des sacrifices périodiques...; la chair des victimes demeurant abandonée aux oiseaux et aux fauves du désert" ("One honoured these pillars by visits and periodic sacrifices...; the flesh of the victims remaining abandoned to the birds and wild animals of the desert.") J. Henninger, *Arabica Sacra*, notes among the various theories in his Conclusion, "Le sens du sacrifices chez les Arabes": "...ou bien hommage à un être de puissance supérieure qui n'a pas besoin d'un don" (...or, a payment of tribute to a superior being, who does not need a gift.")

[18] J. Henninger, "Zur Frage des Haaropfers bei den Semiten, "*Arabica Sacra*, pp. 286 - 306.

[19] *The Special Laws* I: 272, transl. F. H. Colson (London, 1929 - 1962): "In bringing themselves they offer the best of sacrifices, the full and truly perfect oblation of noble living."

[20] Ibid. I: 257.

[21] The editor of Kings could obviously not credit Ahaz with the accomplishment of this meritorious reform, since he certainly rejected the notion that the bronze altar was initially a table for the presentation of food to the Deity. For a discussion of the nuances of kingly epithets, see E.J. Revell, *The Designation of the Individual* (Kampen, 1996), especially p. 153.

[22] We observe a constant tension in Judah between the ancient nomadic tradition and the elaborate Canaanite practice in all aspects of life, private and public. David, the first wealthy king, remained in his heart a shepherd, a simple man, with common manners. His wife Michal, the daughter of a king, was used to refined conduct at the palace, and could not tolerate David's plebeian and vulgar behaviour during the transfer of the ark to

Jerusalem. In the narrative of their altercation (II Sam. 6: 16, 20 and 23) it is remarkable that although we already know that Michal married David (I Sam. 18: 28), the editor particularly emphasizes that she was Saul's daughter, מיכל בת שאול, and does not mention that she was David's wife; in I Sam. 19: 11, the other narrative recording their relationship, in which Michal saves David's life, she is called מיכל אשתו "Michal his wife," with no mention of her being Saul's daughter. These different identifications of Michal seem to emphasize the core of their controversy, the divergent opinions of a royal daughter and a shepherd concerning correct behaviour, versus Michal's loyalty to David as her husband. I wish to postulate that David's simple ideals (and his attachment to the ancient nomadic simplicity) were the real motives for his failure to build the Temple. There are a number of different aetiological justifications in Scripture for this deficiency: (1) David's initial aspiration to build a Temple, and God's reluctance, transmitted by Nathan the prophet, as narrated in II Sam. 7: 1 - 29, and its parallel in I Chr. 17: 1 - 27; (2) Solomon's letter to Hiram, recorded in I Kings 5: 17 - 19 and its parallel in II Chr. 2: 2 - 5; and (3) Solomon's oration at the Temple's consecration, reported in I Kings 8: 16 - 20 and II Chr. 6: 4 - 10. There is also one further account in I Chr. 22: 7 - 16, without a parallel in Kings. Let us now compare and contrast the seven versions of the motive justifying David's failure to build the Temple. God's recommendation not to build the Temple in the two pericopes of (1) are not very clear, and one has the impression that He preferred the customary nomadic tent and did not show a desire for a fixed house: הדבר דברתי את אחד שבטי ישראל אשר צויתי לרעות את עמי את ישראל לאמר למה לא בניתם לי בית ארזים "Did I ever say to any of their rulers whom I commanded to shepherd my people Israel: 'Why have you not built me a house of cedar?' [II Sam. 7: 7 and I Chr. 17: 6]." For a literary analysis of this pericope see H. W. Hertzberg, *I & II Samuel*, pp. 281 ff, who quotes among others M. Noth, and L. Rost, *The Succession to the Throne of David*, transl. M.D. Rutter and D.M. Gunn (1982). In I Kings 5: 17 of group (2), Solomon states in his letter to Hiram: אתה ידעת את דוד אבי כי לא יכול לבנות בית לשם ה' אלהיו מפני המלחמה אשר סבבהו "Because of the wars waged against my father from all sides, he could not build a Temple for the name of the Lord his God," justifying in this way David's failure to build. This statement is clearly contradicted in II Sam 7: 1, which asserts that David contemplated building the Temple: וה' הניח לו מסביב מכל איביו "[After] the Lord has given him rest from all his enemies around him." The parallel in II Chr. 2: 2 - 5 offers no such justification, since this would contradict its own narrative in I Chr. chap. 22, recording David's preparation of plans and amassing of building materials; this indicates that he had no military problems to prevent him from accumulating building materials and hence from building the Temple. Moreover, this report in II Chr. does not really offer any justification for David's omission to build the Temple, and in fact the simple interpretation of the text contradicts all other records of this topic. II Chr. 2: 2 confirms that Hiram had sent cedar wood to David, as reported in I Chr. 22: 4, but that these were used for building his own private house: כאשר עשית עם דויד אבי ותשלח לו ארזים לבנות לו בית לשבת בו "As you did for my father David when you sent him cedar to build a palace to live in." In group (3), Solomon's oration, there is no contradiction between Kings and Chr., and both records follow the obscure rationale of group (1). The final justification in I Chr. 22: 8 introduces a unique apologetic: ויהי עלי דבר ה' לאמר דם לרב שפכת ומלחמות גדלות עשית לא תבנה בית לשמי כי דמים רבים שפכת ארצה לפני "But this word of the Lord came to me: 'You have shed much blood and have fought many wars. You are not to build a house for my Name, because you have shed much blood on the earth on my side.'" This statement stands in evident contradiction to the divine communication transmitted by Nathan in II Sam. 7: 1 - 29 and I Chr. 17: 1 - 27. It is also entirely contrary to I Kings 5: 17; both have in common the circumstance of war, but in Kings the hindrance is simply the practical impediment of David's military involvement, whereas in Chr. God forbids David to build Him a Temple from a moral perspective - because he has "shed much blood." Kings attempts to retroject the centralization of the cult and the consequent rule to destroy the *bamoth* to David (see section 8.1.2.1); I Chr. (chaps. 22 and 23) further elaborates and credits David with all preparations for the building of the Temple - its structural plans, the accumulation of all the necessary materials and the organization of its functions. It is thus no wonder that the editors were hard pressed to explain David's failure to realize his plans, and ventured to exculpate him by any means. The many conflicting justifications for David's failure to build the Temple provide solid evidence of an effort to conceal the real motive, if it was known, or to explain this incomprehensible phenomenon. One has the impression that the various editors were not satisfied with the explanations they had received from previous editors, and attempted to improve upon them, or offer a justification in line with their philosophical - theological convictions.

I postulate that in fact the editors had good reason to absolve him. David did not contemplate building a lavish Temple; he remained a simple man who preferred the ancient spontaneous worship, not confined to any place or date or other rules of an established institutionalized cult. We have seen his simple and impulsive personal conduct, and we can observe the same attitude toward sacrificial worship. He did not build any altars during the translocation of the ark, merely offering sacrifices every six steps (II Sam. 6: 13) on temporary heaps of earth or stones, and probably on a similar temporary site before the tent with the ark (6: 18). As I have already noted in chap. 1 n. 115, we must assume that the altar built by David on Araunah's threshing floor (ויבן שם דוד מזבח, II Sam. 24: 25) was also a simple *tumulus*, since there is no record of any materials brought or bought for the construction of an elaborate altar. In contrast to Solomon, David did not go to the Great *Bamah* in Gibeon (I Kings 3: 4) to offer sacrifices, nor have we a record of his pilgrimage to any other established sanctuary; he worshipped spontaneously whenever and wherever he felt a spiritual exigency. The editor I Chr.could not accept that David repudiated the most revered sanctuary in Gibeon, as described in 21: 30: ומשכן ה' אשר עשה משה במדבר ומזבח העלה בעת ההיא בבמה בגבעון "the Tabernacle of the Lord, which Moses had made in the desert, and the altar of burnt offering were at that time on the high place at Gibeon [v. 29]"; he thus came up with a bizarre excuse: ולא יכל דויד ללכת לפניו לדרש אלהים כי נבעת מפני חרב מלאך ה' "But David could not go before it to inquire of God, because he was afraid of the sword of the angel of the Lord."

One must assume that a great part, if not the majority, of the Israelite public concurred with David on this topic and preferred the informal spontaneous cult, had it been otherwise, David, evidently the shrewd politician, would have followed the *vox populi* and built the Temple. For similar reasons of political expediency he moved his royal seat from Hebron, where he was anointed king by all the elders of Israel including those from the Northern tribes, to Jerusalem, in the center of the land and close to the Northern tribes. Solomon, the son of a king, with refined desires and tastes who took pride in marrying Pharaoh's daughter, persisted in building an opulent Temple, similar to the sanctuaries of other kings in the area, but did not dare to change the simple sacrificial cult rooted in the ancient nomadic tradition; he did not build an elaborate altar, but continued the custom of offering sacrifices on the ground or on a rock in the Temple court. He thus

tradition,[23] to a sumptuous, permanently institutionalized formalism,[24] copied from the Damascene court. One must assume that although this innovation is

---

devised a compromise to the tension between nomadic versus "settled" (or Babylonian) traditions. Ahaz accomplished the second step in the adaptation of the cult to a fashion appropriate for a settled people with a state organization in political and cult issues; he built a large sophisticated altar, and introduced a fixed, institutionalized system of sacrificial celebrations, an imitation of the Damascene ceremonial system.

The problems attested in this pericope in II Sam. 7 with respect to literary structure, composition, and the strained association with the theme of succession, have provoked many scholarly discussions; see, e.g. G. von Rad, *Old Testament Theology*, Vol. I, transl. D. M. G. Stalker (New York, 1962), p. 61; V. W. Rabe, "Israelite Opposition to the Temple," *CBQ 29* (1967), pp. 228 - 230; and A. Weiser, "Die Tempelbaukrise unter David," *ZAW* 77 (1965), pp. 153 - 67. There are obviously different nuances to the assumptions of each of these scholars with respect to the circumstances and origin of the different literary elements of the pericope, but all consider the narrative as evidence of a struggle between those elements which insisted on maintaining the traditional nomadic customs, represented by Nathan, and that segment of society which promoted the construction of an innovative and refined temple, a contest finally resolved only by Solomon. The structure of the Shilo sanctuary is also a matter of debate in this respect, and I wish to add here that Tosefta Megilah (Lieberman) 1: 17 portrays this structure as still possessing features of a nomadic cult: the lower part was of stone, but the upper element consisted of curtains (like the Tabernacle, Exod. chap. 26). It is doubtful whether an internal faction would have been able to impose its will on David (Absalom's rebellion is of a totally different nature), and induce him to change his plans to enhance the cultic status of his capital subsequent to the transfer of the most holy ark, which was effected for just that purpose. I attempted to present a slightly different picture, suggesting that it was David's own character and upbringing which inclined him against copying the temples of the surrounding cultures. Since later generations strove to attribute to David, the charismatic figure and founder of the eternal Israelite dynasty, the introduction of the cult in Jerusalem as practised in their period, they had to bring forward convincing excuses to account for his failure to build the Temple.

It seems that in the Northern kingdom, the influence of the settled Canaanite society had eradicated somewhat earlier the nomadic customs, which may not have been so entrenched in those tribes initially; stable and enduring altars were built, or taken over in the many sanctuaries seized from the previous inhabitants and adapted to the worship of Yahweh. Most if not all the ancient sanctuaries of note were situated in the territory of the Northern tribes, including Benjamin. We observe that Jeroboam (924 - 903), in contrast to Solomon, built an altar in Beth El (I Kings 12: 33) which was still functioning about three hundred years later, when Josiah (639 - 609) destroyed it: וגם את המזבח אשר בבית אל הבמה אשר עשה ירבעם בן נבט אשר החטיא את ישראל גם את המזבח ההוא ואת הבמה נתץ "Even the altar at Beth El, the high places made by Jeroboam son of Nebat, who had caused Israel to sin - even that altar and high place he demolished [II Kings 23: 15]." It is remarkable that Solomon built only *bamoth*, not altars, even for the idols of his women (I Kings 11: 7), and these were destroyed by Josiah (II Kings 23: 13). The only altars destroyed by Josiah were those more recently built on the roof of Ahaz' room and those built by Manasseh (II Kings 23: 12).

[23] As asserted in the previous note, Solomon built an opulent Temple under the influence of the surrounding cultures, but did not change the simple, traditional character of the sacrificial cult.

described as a distinct and singular royal decision, it was made possible by a slowly developing ideological change.[25] One must similarly presume that the two patterns of offerings, the presentation of food and the burning, were performed concurrently for a period both before Ahaz' ruling and after.

The parallel celebration of old and new rites is not only reasonable and historically confirmed, but is also in this case attested in textual evidence. II Kings 16: 14 - 15 indicates that Ahaz imposed a subordinate status on the bronze table-altar, rather than an absolute eradication of the previous manner of worship. There is, on the other hand, ample evidence from early writings such as Judges[26] and Samuel of holocaust offerings before Ahaz' period. As is well known, there are divergent mythological traditions in the south and north, even with respect to such crucial issues as the Sinai or Shekhem Covenant, and these were amalgamated at a certain stage in the common tradition.[27] We may similarly assume that both Babylonian and Canaanite cult patterns influenced the nomadic Israelite tribes, and it is not appropriate to insist on a single model as the origin of Israelite sacrificial rites. The Babylonian cult was based mainly on a great variety of food types presented to the gods according to precise and minutely-described rules.[28] The Ras-Shamra documentation confirms the existence of the holocaust offering, Šrp, in Ugarit,[29] hence the burning of the entire animal. Bedouin custom,[30] involving the abandonment of the slaughtered animal and the burning of

---

[24] The precise list of the various offerings and their characteristics and the precise timing of the different celebrations (II Kings 16: 15) unmistakably indicate an effective formalism, and a total alienation from a spontaneous cult.

[25] A. Malamet, ישראל בתקופת המקרא (Jerusalem, 1983) refers to a telescopic view: a number of events occurring at different times are compressed into a single action and retrojected to a simple episode, instead of the complex stages which ultimately effected the end result.

[26] For example, Jud. 6: 26; 11: 31; 13: 16; I Sam. 6: 14; 7: 9; 13: 9; II Sam. 6: 18; 24: 22.

[27] We have another striking example of the co-existence of two dissimilar, if not opposite, traditions: the ark is considered as the container of the two tablets, and as the throne of the Deity. See J. Morgenstern, *The Ark, the Ephod and the Tent of Meeting* (Cincinnati, 1945), p. 78.

[28] See H. Zimmern, *Beiträge zur Kenntnis der Babylonischen Religion* (Leipzig, 1901), pp. 94-5.

[29] R. Dussaud, "Le sanctuaire et les dieux phénicien de Ras Shamra," *RHR* CV-CVI (1932), pp. 285-86. In *Les decouvertes de Ras Shamra et l'Ancien Testament* (Paris, 1937), pp. 110-113, Dussaud declares that the borrowing by the Israelites from the Canaanites already took place at an early stage, in the time of the Patriarchs.

[30] J. Henninger, "Esquisse de la Religion bédouine préislamique, *"Arabica Sacra*, pp. 19 - 33 writes on p. 27: "Il arrivait aussi que les animaux tués étaient abandonnés aux animaux sauvages et aux oiseaux de proie." ("It also occurred that the animals killed were abandoned to wild animals and birds of prey.")

one's hair and nails, is only a short step away from the concept of burning the offering as the absolute surrender of part of one's possessions or body.

9.2.1 Influence of Monotheism on the Sacrificial Cult

The disappearance of the concept of feeding the gods was either generated by a new theology or was itself the cause of a radical shift in the conception of the relationship between God and man. The lack of explicit texts with respect to ideological changes in Israelite society in this period makes it impossible to reach a decisive conclusion in this respect; yet we may still be allowed to speculate. The shift from the idea of one God, greater and stronger than the others, to the monotheistic concept of a unique God, Creator of the universe and omnipotent, had a radical influence on the philosophy underlying the offerings. The Israelite Deity had been since early times an unseen God with no human likeness to man, and hence with no physical representation of his various aspects (as for example in the Greek mythological imagination). The affinity of Israelite thought and custom with nomadic Arab belief and habits is instructive. The pre-Islamic Arab pillar, 'nsab, is identical to the Hebrew מצבה; both represent a shapeless stone, symbolizing the site of God's presence and dwelling, but not his image. Such a belief is a great step toward a more sophisticated credo of an abstract Deity. Henninger[31] speculates that the nomadic way of life in the vastness of the desert, and its reliance on Allah as the supreme provider of rain rather than on other symbols of fertility, subverted any urge to create icons representing the various powers thought among farming cultures to dominate the world, and contributed significantly toward the crystallization of the monotheistic faith. One may thus consider the similar nomadic traditions of the Israelite tribes as influencing the birth of the monotheistic faith among them.

---

[31] Ibid. The nomadic way of life in the vastness of the desert and its exclusive dependence on rain perceives *Allah* as the patron of rain (p. 26), the supreme and uncontested master, the creator of the world (p. 30) and the god of heaven (p. 35); the nomadic religion represents the most primitive form of the Semitic religion (p. 16); the oldest form of the Semitic religion is considered as pure monotheism, and *El*, the common, primitive god, is probably unique to the Semites (p. 18); nomadic religion is a religion of promise, as the nomad does not live by a cycle of sowing and reaping (p. 42); the patriarchal god of heaven is the typical supreme being of the nomadic shepherd, in contrast to the matriarchal agricultural society in which mother earth is the supreme deity (p. 36). For these reasons it seems to me that no pantheon of deities was created corresponding to the various powers of nature, nor idols in the model of man.

9.2.2 The Shift in the Relationship between God and Man and its Effect on Sacrifices

The idea of an omnipotent Creator of the world who wants for nothing must also induce a shift in the relations between God and man, and specifically with respect to the cultic practice surrounding offerings. Offerings could no longer be conceived as something done by man for God's benefit to satisfy His necessities; it had to be transformed theologically to reflect something done for the advantage of man. This concept may be seen in the two verses quoted in section 9.1 from Ps. 50. The prophets Isaiah,[32] Hosea[33] and Micah,[34] who were active during the reign of Ahaz, the assumed period of the cult reform, also denounced the people's attitude to the sacrifices.[35] Their criticism was not directed solely against the priority bestowed upon sacrifice by the ignorant, versus their disregard of just and compassionate social behaviour;[36] it also reflects a radical theological reform: God does not need the sacrifices, they are not purveying His necessities, and His commands and rules are not for His advantage,[37] but for the benefit of human society.[38] The

---

[32] Isa. 1: 11: למה לי רב זבחיכם יאמר ה' שבעתי עלות אילים וחלב מריאים ודם
פרים וכבשים ועתודים לא חפצתי "The multitude of your sacrifices - what are they
to me? says the Lord. I have more than enough of burnt offerings, of rams and the fat of
fattened animals. I have no pleasure in the blood of bulls and lambs and goats."

[33] Hos. 8: 13: זבחי הבהבי יזבחו בשר ויאכלו ה' לא רצם "They offer sacrifices given
to me and they eat the meat, but the Lord is not pleased with them." This NIV translation
follows the LXX προσδέξεται "accepts favourably," but literally it is "The Lord does
not want them"; Rashi translates this phrase accordingly as כי איני רוצה אותם
"because I do not want them."

[34] Micah 6: 7: הירצה ה' באלפי אילים ברבבות נחלי שמן "Will the Lord be pleased
with thousands of rams, with ten thousand rivers of oil ?"

[35] Cf. J. Wellhausen, *Prolegomena to the History of Ancient Israel*, transl. M. Black (1957),
pp. 56 ff. on this topic.

[36] R. de Vaux, *Ancient Israel; Its Life and Institutions* (London, 1973), pp. 454 - 55 writes:
"The Prophets are opposed to the formalism of exterior worship when it has no
corresponding interior dispositions," an interpretation which one must assume is
informed by a christological viewpoint. R. S. Hendel, "Prophets, Priests, and the Efficacy
of Ritual," in *Pomegranates and Golden Bells, Studies in Biblical, Jewish, and Near
Eastern Ritual, Law, and Literature in Honor of Jacob Milgrom*, pp. 185 - 198 (Winona
Lake, 1995), characterizes the tension between the priests and prophets from another
aspect, and writes: "Whereas the priests see a correspondence and mutuality between
ritual and ethics, the classical prophets contrast the ethical with the ritual." See also M.
Weiss, "Concerning Amos' Repudiation of the Cult," idem., pp. 199-214 on this topic.

[37] We obviously do not encounter in Deuteronomy a divine reward for sacrifices, or a
punishment for failure to sacrifice or for improper performance. Yet it is remarkable that
we also do not encounter any such system even in the P stratum of the Pentateuch. There
is the punishment of כרת, being "cut off," for failure to celebrate the Passover (Num. 9:

13); but as I demonstrate in section 9.5.4.1, this celebration cannot be considered a "sacrificial offering," since according to the pentateuchal precept no part of the animal was offered to the Deity on the altar. The blessings and curses in Lev. 26 are exclusively linked to the observance of the divine precepts, with particular emphasis on abandoning idols and honouring the Sabbath. Similarly, in Deut. 7: 12 - 8: 20, the blessings in 11: 13 - 25, and in the great pericope of curses and blessings in 27: 15 - 28: 69, the sacrificial system is entirely omitted. Most of the records of sacrifices in Israelite writings indicate that they are performed as thank offerings after a successful battle. The odd narrative of the sacrifices offered by Saul at Gilgal before Samuel's arrival (I Sam. 13: 8 - 14), apparently before an anticipated battle, is not linked even implicitly to an offering performed in supplication for a victory in combat. Samuel's instructions to Saul to wait seven days for his arrival to offer the sacrifices has no connection whatsoever to a battle (I Sam. 10: 8). This is in contrast to the explicit manipulation of the deities through offerings in Greek and Egyptian ceremonial (see n. 5). The prophetic censures by Haggai and particularly by Malachi (cited in section 9.3.3) with respect to the neglect of the sacrificial celebrations seem to be an exception, and may demonstrate the depressed spiritual conditions at that specific period. There is another exception in Gen. 28: 20 - 22, in which it is recorded that Jacob promised to create God's house from the pillar he set up if he returned safely from his escape, but it seems that this was not the main purpose of his pledge; the declaration of faith, the utterance והיה ה' לי לאלהים "then the Lord will be my God," is the primary vow, and the devising of God's house was only the secondary consequence of his pledge. Josephus the priest added his personal approach to this event, stating in *Ant.* I: 284: θύσειν ἐπ' αὐτῶν "to sacrifice upon them [the stones]." Josephus deviates totally from the biblical text on this occasion; he does not mention the setting up of the pillar as a house of God, and we should thus not concern ourselves with his particular view. We observe that at Jacob's most dangerous trial, in fear and distress before his encounter with Esau, he prayed and offered supplication to God on the basis of His commands to return to his homeland and His promise to make him prosper, but did not make a pledge for anything in compensation for his deliverance. On the other hand, one cannot exclude the possibility that any manipulative intentions with respect to the offerings were "censured" by later redactors from earlier *Vorlagen* in which they occurred, but in view of our general experience it does not seem possible that on this particular issue the redactors succeeded in completely eradicating every trace of such conduct. See also Josephus, *Contra Apionem* II: 23, who explains the purpose of the sacrifices; he declares that one must not ask God for personal favours at the presentation of the offerings - God grants us His benefaction by His grace - but one prays to be fit to receive His grace.

[38] Isaiah concludes the above pericope by proclaiming God's command in 1: 17: למדו היטב דרשו משפט אשרו חמוץ שפטו יתום ריבו אלמנה "Learn to do right, seek justice, encourage the oppressed. Defend the cause of the fatherless, plead the case of the widow." Hosea declares in the name of God (6: 6): כי חסד חפצתי ולא זבח ודעת אלהים מעלות "For I desire mercy, not sacrifice, and acknowledgement of God rather than burnt offerings." Micah proclaims God's will in 6: 8: הגיד לך אדם מה טוב ומה ה' דורש ממך כי אם עשות משפט ואהבת חסד והצנע לכת עם אלהיך "He has showed you, O man, what is good. And what does the Lord require of you? To act justly and to love mercy and to walk humbly with your God." The later Jeremiah continued preaching the same theology concerning God's aim, stating: כי אני ה' עשה חסד משפט וצדקה בארץ כי באלה חפצתי נאם ה' "...that I am the Lord, who exercises

prophets contested the idolatrous belief that the gods created mankind[39] to serve them, declaring that God's wish consists rather in ensuring to humans, His creatures, a meritorious life[40] in a righteous[41] and compassionate society.[42] Such prophetic utterances could not co-exist with a notion that the

---

kindness, justice and righteousness on earth, for in these I delight [Jer. 9: 23; v. 24 in KJV]," and דן דין עני ואביון אז טוב הלא היא הדעת אתי נאם ה' "He defended the cause of the poor and needy, and so all went well. Is that not what it means to know me [my wishes]? declares the Lord [22: 16]."

[39] Contrasting views are evident with respect to the creation of woman. Hesiod, in "The Theogony" (Creation of Woman), states that the creation of a female was an evil thing for mankind, whereas Scripture says that God created Eve to be עזר כנגדו "a suitable helper [Gen. 2: 18]."

[40] It would certainly not be erroneous to assume that this particular Israelite belief of a compassionate God, whose primary object is the well-being of His creatures, prepared the ground for the later Christian credo that God went so far as to sacrifice His own son for the sake of humans. I do not intend to enter into the well-known debate as to whether the Jewish faith considers God as immanent or transcendent. Scripture and post-biblical Jewish literature unmistakably assert divine involvement in all matters of the world, including the idea of a personal providence, השגחה פרטית, in the late writings. It seems to me that in rabbinic literature the most disparaging epithet for a sinner is אפיקורוס "Epikouros", who denied divine interest and involvement in worldly matters. Although there is a discussion in B. T. Sanhedrin 99b as to what this appellation represents, it seems to me that its original meaning had already been forgotten, and the Sages therefore assumed it referred to some sort of wicked behaviour which had nothing in common with Epikouros and his philosophy.

[41] E. O. James, *Origins of Sacrifice* (New York, 1971), p. 262 introduces another aspect of the post-exilic approach to sacrifice and its relationship with ethical behaviour. He writes: "...the ethical righteousness of Yahweh demands above all things and side by side with objective worship, rightness of conduct....Henceforth the ritual in Israel was invested with an ethical and spiritual content." A well-known rabbinical homily similarly bases the plea for ethical human conduct on *imitatio Dei*. We read in B. T. Sabbath 133b: "ואנוהו הוי דומה לו מה הוא חנון ורחום אף אתה היה חנון ורחום." [It is written in Exod. 15: 2: 'He is my God] and I will praise him'; [this means] be like Him: as He is compassionate, you too be compassionate, as He is gracious, you too be gracious."

[42] Monotheism by its very nature engendered a new approach to relations between man and God, and also a philosophical basis for a moral attitude between humans. In polytheistic mythology each deity has its own particular desires and interests which often compete with those of the other gods, provoking aversion against them and consequently disregard in general for the requirements and fates of all others, gods and men alike. The monotheistic Deity, a single, omnipotent God with no competitors who created all *ex nihilo*, has on the other hand no egocentric interests except the preservation of His creation, the world, and its pre-eminent element, humankind. He provides sustenance for all His creatures, נתן לחם לכל בשר כי לעולם חסדו "Who gives food to every creature, His love endures forever [Ps. 136: 25]," and is concerned for their well-being, exercising kindness, justice and righteousness in the management of the world (Jer. 9: 23): כי אני ה' עשה חסד משפט וצדקה בארץ. He therefore commands humans to

gods need food to be provided by man. The burning of the offerings could now be interpreted as the satisfaction of human spiritual necessity for numinous devotion and exaltation, achieved through ritual celebrations, a symbol of submission and adoration. The prophecies of Isaiah, Hosea and Micah with respect to the sacrificial cult and its significance are suited to Ahaz' period, and the shift from the presentation of food to the deity and its underlying archaic theology to the method of burning the offerings and its opposing philosophy; the "center of gravity" of the sacrifices had shifted from the Deity to man. This doctrine, grounded in the reinterpretation of the previous notion, was the profound intellectual element which engendered the institution of the sin offering,[43] a sacrifice for man's catharsis;[44] such an offering had no place in the prior notion of the offering as food for the deity.

---

behave similarly, with compassion and fairness toward all of God's creatures, human and animal, כי באלה חפצתי נאם ה' "for in these I delight."

[43] The first occurrences of the חטאת, sin offering, are in Ezekiel. The occurrence in Ezra 8: 35, צפירי חטאת שנים עשר שנים עשר הכל עלה לה' "twelve male goats as sin offering, all this was a burnt offering to the Lord," is confusing, since the sin offering is called עולה; the sin offering is eaten by the priests while the עולה in entirely burnt. Sifra *Parshah* 2 *Pereq* 3 and other rabbinical sources discuss this problem: אפשר חטאת עולה אלא מה עולה לא נאכלת אף חטאת לא נאכלת רבי יהודה אומר על עבודה זרה הביאום "Could a sin offering be a holocaust? [This] sin offering, like the holocaust offering, was not eaten, [as] Rabbi Judah said: It was brought as a sin offering for the sin of idolatry by all the people [and as such it is entirely burnt like the עולה]." This answer reflects a rabbinical attempt to reconcile between Lev. 4: 13 - 21, in which an ox is required for the חטאת, and Num. 15: 22 - 26, in which an ox for the עולה and a male goat for the חטאת are required; Sifrei BeMidbar *Pisqa* 111 resolves the problem by stating that the Num. pericope refers exclusively to the sin of idolatry, for which the sacrifice is different than that for other transgressions. See chap. 1 n. 15 for another aspect of this issue. In a recently published essay by Z. Zevit, "Philology, Archeology and a *Terminus A Quo* for P's *hattat* Legislation," in *Pomegranates and Golden Bells, Studies in Biblical, Jewish, and Near Eastern Ritual, Law, and Literature in Honor of Jacob Milgrom*, pp. 29 - 38 (Winona Lake, 1995), the author also assumes from the mention of the יסוד in the ordinances that the pericope of sin offering rules in Lev. chap. 5 reflects a post-Ahaz period; but he speculates that a different version of the sin offering may have existed at an earlier period.

[44] Similar to all divine commands which are for man's benefit, the sin offering, with its particular spiritual state of mind of repentance and resolve to avoid sinning in future, is for man's advantage. We encounter an interesting homily in B. T. Eirubin 69b: מן הבהמה להביא בני אדם הדומין לבהמה מכאן אמרו מקבלין קרבנות מפושעי ישראל כדי שיחזרו בתשובה "[It is written] 'from an animal [Lev. 1: 2],' [this means] 'from men resembling animals.' From this we deduce that one accepts sacrifices from Israelite apostates so that they might repent." The spiritual agitation associated with offering the sacrifice will influence their thoughts and cause them to abandon their wicked conduct.

On the other hand, the burning of the sacrifices enhances their ceremonial significance, a factor utilized in later developments of the sacrificial system by intelligent "statesmen" who understood its potential in the promotion of their political goals.

Cult and theology are two closely joined and mutually influential aspects of the religious element of culture.[45] Changes in the celebration of rituals and in the underlying theology are a constant feature of religion, occurring sometimes more slowly and sometimes more quickly, and it is seldom possible to discern which preceded the other. It suffices therefore for our purpose to have established, philosophically and historically, the mutual changes in the sacrificial cult and its theology.

9.3 The Ezra and Nehemiah Narratives

9.3.1 Ideological Dissension Among the Returnees from Exile

9.3.1.1 Rebuilding the Temple

This re-evaluation of the role of sacrifices must also have generated an erosion of the veneration of the sacrificial system in general. It was certainly a factor within the larger issue of the minimal concern for the renewal of the Temple and it sacrificial cult, exhibited by a significant element of Israelite society after the return from exile, and its importance is thus difficult to appreciate. The centralization of the cult and the consequent exclusion of laics from the actual performance of the sacrifices may also have effected some weakening in the attitude of the people.[46] There were obviously many factors[47] in Israelite society [48]at that time which influenced the complex of

---

[45] Cf. R. Rendtorff, "Der Kultus im Alten Israel," in *Gesammelte Studien zum Alten Testament*, Theologische Bücherei, Band 57 (München, 1975), pp. 88 ff. concerning the various influences on the development of Israelite cult and theology.

[46] The repercussions of this reform will be discussed later in section 9.5.1.

[47] Zoroastrian custom and thought, particularly the almost total lack of animal sacrifices in the Achaemenid period, may also have influenced some of the Israelites in this respect. Although the Greek historians report sacrifices by the Iranians (see *Passages in Greek and Latin Literature relating to Zoroaster & Zoroastrianism*, transl. by W. Sherwood Fox and R.E.K. Pemberton [Bombay, 1928], the Iranian literature on the cult practices does not absolutely confirm this. J. Duchesne-Guillemin, "The Religion of Ancient Iran," in *Historia Religionum*, Vol. I: *Religions of the Past* (Leiden, 1969), pp. 323 - 376, writes on p. 353: "Zarathustra seems to have disapproved of a certain sacrificial rite, but it is by no means certain that he condemned blood-sacrifices as such." On the other hand, we read in Mary Boyce, ed. and trans., *Textual Sources for the Study of Zoroastrianism*

attitudes toward the rebuilding of the Temple. Those who returned from the exile certainly had a different point of view than those who had remained;[49] the segment of the people that remained in Judah[50] and did not attempt to rebuild the Temple or to revive the sacrificial cult on an altar without restoring the Temple, so as not to provoke the opposition of the Babylonians, must have retained their own specific views. We should also not disregard the probable differences of opinion between the people of Judah and those who remained in Galilee.[51] The Ezra narrative[52] about the vague צרי יהודה

(Chicago, 1984), p. 16: "As part of Western respect for Zarathushtra, it was supposed that the prophet had rejected all devotional observances except prayer." We note precise rules in the Iranian religious literature for the various cult rituals of the fire worship and other ceremonies with offerings of food and flowers, but no rules for animal sacrifices; see *Textual Sources* and K. P. Mistree, *Zoroastrianism* (Bombay, 1982). We must therefore assume that some syncretistic cult practices may have been sporadically performed after Zarathustra, but they were not an official element of that religion. We read in C.J. Adams, ed., *A Reader's Guide to the Great Religions*, 2nd ed. (N.Y., 1977), p. 64: "To decide what Achaemenid religion actually was, the historian must reconcile the stipulation of observances in the Iranian literature with the practices reported by Greek and Roman writers."

The Persian political authorities granted and even encouraged freedom of religion among the conquered peoples, and did not require conversion to their faith; there were, however, Persian cultural influences on Israelite religion, and one cannot exclude a similar cultural influence with regard to the celebration of sacrifices. On the issue of Iranian influence on Israelite custom and thought, see D. Winston, "The Iranian Component in the Bible, Apocrypha, and Qumran: A Review of the Evidence," *History of Religion* 5 (1965-6), pp. 183-216.

[48] Cf. S. Japhet מחקרים בתולדות ישראל בתקופת in עם וארץ בתקופת שיבת ציון הבית השני, ed. D. Schwarz (Jerusalem, 1996), pp. 127 - 145, who examines the political attitude of the various groups in Israelite society during the period of the return from exile.

[49] There might have been fundamental emotional and theological differences between these groups. Some may have felt the lack of the Temple and were eager to renew it, as it is common to long for something one does not possess or has lost. Others may have concluded that the Temple and its celebrations were no longer necessary for the survival of the Israelite people and its unique faith, as they had remained loyal to this faith in Babylon despite the lack of the Temple cult. Still others may have been entirely disillusioned and frustrated with the Israelite creed and its rituals because of its failure to avert the destruction of the sanctuary and the seizure of the land.

[50] People from the previous Northern kingdom, משכם משלו ומשמרון (Jer. 41: 5), brought offerings to Jerusalem.

[51] I am avoiding any discussion of the political and religious circumstances surrounding the creation of the distinct Samaritan community, another element of Israelite society, as the conflicting documentation and opinions on this issue do not allow for a definite answer.

[52] It is not within the scope of this study to discuss the many literary and chronological inconsistencies in the books of Ezra and Nehemiah, and their contrast with the Apocryphal books of Ezra, a subject amply researched and debated by various scholars. I have concentrated my study of this period exclusively on the influence of these two

ובנימן and עם הארץ[53] (4: 1 - 4) who tried to disrupt or prevent the rebuilding of the Temple unequivocally demonstrates strong dissension within Israelite society.

9.3.1.2 Sabbath Laws and Marriage with Foreign Women

We observe similar disagreements[54] among the various segments of society with respect to other significant traditions or divine precepts, such as the extent of the labour restrictions on Sabbath, and the prohibition against intermarriage.[55] While for the first issue one could assume that Nehemiah limited himself to interpreting in a novel, restrictive way the extent of the prohibited מלאכה, he evidently promulgated new rules contrary to the pentateuchal decrees with respect to the latter subject (Deut. chap. 23).[56] We observe that not only the common people practised intermarriage, but also the priestly aristocratic families;[57] one must therefore assume that the latter were convinced that this was lawful and would not attract public objection.

Moreover, the reasons for the biblical prohibition against absorbing Moabites into Israel and the historical narratives with respect to the actual relations between Israel and Moab are a maze of inconsistencies, which reflects a variety of conflicting political circumstances. We may note, for

---

personalities on the theological and political changes in Israelite society, based on a broad analysis of the contents of the two books bearing their names.

[53] There are many scholarly speculations about the meaning of these vague terms, but it seems to me that the editor intentionally obscured the identification of these groups so as to portray an internally cohesive community, intimidated only by external sects or nations.

[54] I suspect that then as today divergent opinions with respect to the origin of the laws and rituals were common in intellectual circles, influencing their authority and consequently their performance.

[55] To facilitate the expeditious reading of the main issue, I have transferred the elaboration of these two topics, the extention of the labour restrictions on Sabbath and the prohibition against intermarriage, to Appendix II.

[56] See Appendix II.

[57] השיבו נשים נבריות מבני ישוע בן יוצדק ואחיו "[The following] had married foreign women; from the descendants of Jeshua son of Jozadak and his brothers [Ezra 10: 18]." We must assume from the various citations of this individual's activities that he was the most important priest at the time of the return from exile, although he is not called by the title High Priest. In Neh. 13: 28 we read: ומבני יוידע בן אלישיב הכהן הגדול חתן לסנבלט החרני "One of the sons of Jehoiada son of Eliashib the High Priest was son-in-law to Sanballat the Horonite." The High Priest, it seems, did not object to this marriage, though Nehemiah drove him away, as we see from the text. In Ezra 10: 18 - 44 we find a long list of presumably prominent families whose members married foreign women.

instance, the stated justification that Moab did not provide food and water to the Israelites (Deut. 23: 5), and its discrepancy with Deut. 2: 28 - 29 which implies that the Moabites did sell them these provisions.[58] There is no mention that the Ammonites did not act similarly. Furthermore, we read in Deut. 2: 9 God's command to Moses: אל תצר את מואב...כי לבני לוט נתתי את ער ירשה "Do not harass Moab...because I have given Ar to the descendants of Lot as a possession." In 2: 19 we read the same exhortation regarding the Ammonites. The later revulsion against these two peoples, for apparently trivial behaviour, does not harmonize, to say the least, with the divine guaranty to safeguard their inheritance and prohibit Israelite revenge for their indecorous attitude towards them.[59] An additional perplexity is raised by the narrative in Gen. 19: 30 - 38 regarding the incestuous birth of Ammon and Moab. One must ask the purpose of this biblical narrative within the overall framework, and one must conclude that its aim is to denigrate these people as descended from an "abomination" and thus to reject them forever from inclusion within pure Israelite society. This motive is implied in the deuteronomic pericope detailing the people to be rejected from inclusion among the Israelites. Deut. 23: 3 starts with the ממזר, born of an illicit relationship, and follows with the Ammonites and Moabites. The almost exact parallelism with regard to these two types of persons - גם דור עשירי לא יבא לו בקהל ה' "[No one born of a forbidden marriage]...may enter the assembly of the Lord, even down to the tenth generation" in v. 3 with respect to the ממזר, and גם דור עשירי לא יבא להם בקהל ה' עד עולם "[No Ammonite or Moabite]...may enter the assembly of the Lord, even down to the tenth generation" in v. 4 on the Ammonites and Moabites, demonstrates the affinity between the two ideas. It is remarkable that although Scripture suppressed here this motive of incestuous origin, a homily in B. T. Nazir 22b implies such a connection.[60]

---

[58] We read in Deut. 2: 28 - 9: כאשר...אכל בכסף תשברני ואכלתי ומים בכסף תתן לי עשו לי בני עשו הישבים בשעיר והמואבים הישבים בער "Sell us food to eat and water to drink...as the descendants of Esau, who live in Seir, and the Moabites, who live in Ar, did for us."

[59] An unidentified traditional commentator raised another fundamental question: Why did the Israelites need to buy food while they still had the manna? We read in Exod. 16: 35: את המן אכלו עד באם אל קצה ארץ כנען "They ate manna until they reached the border of Canaan." Jos. 5: 12 also explicitly mentions that the manna was available inside the "border of Canaan" after the crossing of the Jordan, stating: וישבת המן ממחרת באכלם מעבור הארץ ולא היה עוד לבני ישראל מן "The manna stopped the day after they ate this food from the land; there was no longer any manna for the Israelites."

[60] We read there: לא יבא עמוני ומואבי בקהל ה' דרש רבא ואיתימא רבי יצחק מאי "No דכתיב לתאוה יבקש נפרד בכל תושיה יתגלע לתאוה יבקש נפרד זה לוט Ammonite or Moabite may enter the assembly of the Lord [Deut. 23: 4, KJV 23: 3].'

Nehemiah also used this flexible topic of Israelite - Moabite relations, adjusting it to the circumstances of his period and adding a novel, previously unknown motive to support his regulation against marrying foreign women. In addition to repeating the biblical justifications for the specific prohibition of intermarriage with the seven peoples and the absorption of Ammonites and Moabites, Nehemiah introduced a politically-rooted nationalistic motive to promote his ideas and reach his objectives. The survival of the Hebrew language seems to have been his main concern; this is stated first, which indicates its prominence.[61] The literary and structural analysis of the relevant pericope in chap. 13 confirms this: The first verse (13: 23) portrays Nehemiah's awareness of the circumstances גם בימים ההם ראיתי את היהודים השיבו נשים אשדודיות עמוניות מואביות "Moreover, in those days I saw men of Judah who had married women from Ashdod, Ammon and Moab." The next verse indicates his objections to their behaviour: ובניהם חצי מדבר אשדודית ואינם מכירים לדבר יהודית וכלשון עם ועם "Half of their children spoke the language of Ashdod and did not know how to speak the language of Judah, as every other people."[62] In the third verse of the pericope Nehemiah indicates how he terminated this conduct: ואריב עמם ואקללם ואכה מהם אנשים ואמרטם ואשביעם באלהים אם תתנו בנתיכם לבניהם ואם תשאו מבנתיהם לבניכם ולכם "I rebuked them and called curses down on them. I beat some of the men and pulled out their hair.[63] I made them take an oath in God's name and said: 'You are not to give your daughters in marriage to their sons, nor are you to take their daughters in marriage for your sons or for yourselves.'"

The three verses in Nehemiah's address to God summarize all his activity with regard to the issue of the foreign women. The additional verses 26 - 27,

---

Rava, or possibly Rabbi Isaac, interpreted: What does it mean 'Through desire a man, having separated himself, seeketh and intermeddleth with all wisdom [KJV translation of Proverbs 18: 1]'? [This refers] to Lot [who separated himself from Abraham, and slept with his daughters out of lust]." Cf. G. von Rad, *Deuteronomy, A Commentary*, transl. D. Barton (Philadelphia, 1966), p. 146, who considers cultic issues as the determining factor distinguishing the Ammonites and Moabites from the other alien nations.

[61] Nehemiah's national political aim is also obvious from the fact that his first activity in Jerusalem was the rebuilding of the walls (Neh. 2: 17); this actually was his initial reason for travelling to Judah (1: 3). Nehemiah, coming from the Diaspora, was probably aware of the danger of the assimilation of the Israelite people as a result of the linguistic acculturation.

[62] The phrase וכלשון עם ועם is missing in the LXX. My interpretation follows the commentator A. Kahane, כתובים, ספרי עזרא ונחמיה (Tel Aviv, 1930). The NIV translates: "Or the language of one of the other peoples," and the KJV's interpretation is similar.

[63] According to a narrative in the Morashu tablets, this was a common form of punishment.

which indicate a further justification for his actions,[64] are superfluous; there
was no purpose in reporting to God how he justified his deeds before the
people, particularly since this was untruthful.[65] It is not within the scope of
this study to elaborate upon this distinctive topic, but I would like to
comment briefly on the inconsistencies of the text, which hint at the problems
encountered by Nehemiah in imposing his regulations on the various
segments of society. Vv. 13: 1 - 3 are in the nature of a record of events, not
included in Nehemiah's report to God. The reading in public of the biblical
prohibition against absorbing Ammonites and Moabites into the Israelite
community is indicated as the trigger which stimulated the people, willingly,
to banish all the foreign women[66] from their midst. In vv. 23 - 25, in contrast,
Nehemiah indicates the survival of the language of Judah as the motive
behind his opposition to all foreign women, including those from Ashdod;
what is more astonishing, the people did not accede willingly to his request,
and he was forced to impose it with brutal and strange measures.[67] Moreover,
he did not divulge his concern to them, but indicated to them a different
justification for his actions, namely the danger of "religious" corruption by
their foreign women.

9.3.1.3 Variations between the Ezra and Nehemiah Narratives

Ezra portrays a different picture of the circumstances regarding the foreign
women; here too inconsistencies both within the text and as compared to the
narrative in Nehemiah abound. In Neh. 13: 1 - 3 the issue arose following a
reading in the Torah prohibiting the absorption of Ammonites and Moabites
into Israel, and as the result of Nehemiah's own observation of such
marriages with women from Ashdod, Ammon and Moab (v. 23); Ezra, in
contrast, became aware of marriages between recalcitrant leaders and a great

---

[64] The avoidance of bad influence, as we read in Neh. 13: 26: גם אותו החטיאו הנשים
הנכריות "Even he [Solomon] was led into sin by foreign women."

[65] The survival of the language was Nehemiah's concern (v. 24), yet he indicated the danger
posed by the wicked influence of the women as the reason for his decision (v. 26).

[66] We read in Neh. 13: 3: ויבדילו כל ערב מישראל "They excluded from Israel all who
were of foreign descent." I did not cite Neh. 9: 2, ויבדלו זרע ישראל מכל בני נכר
"Those of Israelite descent had separated themselves from all foreigners," because the
correct interpretation of this event is a matter of dispute. The traditional commentators
relate the event to the separation from the foreign women narrated in Ezra 10: 1 - 17, but
the LXX translates ἐχωρίσθησαν οἱ υἱοὶ Ισραηλ ἀπὸ παντὸς υἱοῦʼ ἀλλοτρίου "The
sons of Israel were withdrawn from all the sons of the others [foreigners] [Esdras II 19:
2]," which implies a separation between the Israelites and the other peoples living in
Judah and has no connection to the issue of marrying foreign women.

[67] Neh. 13: 25.

variety of foreign women.[68] Ezra's reaction to the situation is also different from that of Nehemiah. Both pulled hair, but while Nehemiah pulled the (ואמרטם) of those who married women from Ashdod (Neh. 13: 23), Ezra pulled his own hair in despair: ואמרטה משער ראשי וזקני ואשבה משומם "I pulled hair from my head and beard and sat down appalled [9: 3]." Ezra at first suggests a willingness on the part of all the people[69] to send away their foreign women and their offspring, but a following verse then implies that

---

[68] We read in Ezra 9: 1: וככלות אלה נגשו אלי השרים לאמר לא נבדלו העם ישראל והכהנים והלוים מעמי הארצות כתעבתיהם לכנעני החתי הפרזי היבוסי העמני המאבי המצרי והאמרי "After these things had been done, the leaders came to me and said: The people of Israel, including the priests and the Levites, have not kept themselves separate from the neighbouring peoples with their detestable practices, like those of the Canaanites, Hittites, Perizzites, Jebusites, Ammonites, Moabites, Egyptians and Amorites." This verse contains many problems, textual and conceptual. The first issue is the expression העם ישראל; the simple interpretation would imply that all of the people of Israel were acting wrongly, but such an understanding would not harmonize with the context of the succeeding narrative, which relates that a number of God-fearing people, כל חרד, gathered around Ezra in support (v. 4). If on the other hand it refers to only a part of the people, we would have expected העם בישראל. The LXX translates ὁ λαος Ισραηλ, " the people of Israel," which implies all the people. Ibn Ezra also questions the unusual expression, and suggests that it should have been העם עם ישראל. The second part of the verse is more difficult; certain of the peoples mentioned correspond to the biblical prohibitions, one group is explicitly not forbidden, and the women of Ashdod, especially emphasized in Neh., are missing. Deut. 7: 1 enumerates seven nations to be destroyed and with whom one must not intermarry, but in our verse the Hivites of that list are missing. The prohibition with respect to the Ammonites and Moabites corresponds to Deut. 23: 4, but the Egyptians, included in Ezra's list, are the subject of positive legislation in Deut. 23: 8 (v. 7 in KJV): לא תתעב מצרי "Do not abhor an Egyptian." The women of Ashdod, of Philistine origin, are correctly omitted in Ezra's list. Moreover, this verse does not specify whether the type of wrongdoing involved was a social and cultural intermixing between the Israelites and the gentiles, as expressed in Neh. 9: 2, or actual intermarriage. V. 1 seems to be an accusation against social fraternization with people other than Israelites, provoking the imitation of their abominable practices, but the succeeding verse, starting with the subordinate conjunction כי, seems to explain the character of the wrongdoing as intermarriage.

[69] Although in Ezra 10: 1 it seems that only part of the people agreed with Ezra's objective (נקבצו אליו מישראל קהל רב מאד) "a large crowd of Israelites gathered around him"), the subsequent v. 5 attempts to include all of Israel in the consensus: ויקם עזרא וישבע את שרי הכהנים הלוים וכל ישראל לעשות כדבר הזה וישבעו "So Ezra rose up and put the leading priests and Levites and all Israel under the oath to do what had been suggested, and they took the oath." It is possible that this verse meant to indicate that the leader of all Israel took the oath, an interpretation which would be appropriate in the context of the narrative, but one cannot exclude the possibility that here too the intent of the writer was to portray the cohesive community characteristic of the Book of Ezra.

this grim and painful decision was due to the warning of severe consequences to those who would not comply with the ultimatum.[70] This demonstrates two important features of the circumstances at that time: first, Ezra had only a spiritual influence over the people,[71] and some were willing to embrace his ideas, whereas Nehemiah with his political power coerced[72] others unwillingly to obey his commands; second, the people were not unified, and various opposing ideas circulated among them.

9.3.2 Ezra's New Religious Concepts

Ezra, the spiritual preacher, introduced an original and revolutionary concept of a holy lineage, זרע הקדש, σπέρμα τὸ ἅγιον (9: 2), which must not be mingled with other peoples.[73] Ezra does not cite Torah passages to explain and justify his attitude with respect to the desired relationship between Israelites and gentiles, presenting instead two particular motives for the isolation of the Israelites: to avoid imitation of the gentiles' detestable behaviour,[74] and to maintain the perfection of the "lineage".[75] Ezra also

---

[70] We read in Ezra 10: 8: וכל אשר לא יבוא לשלשת הימים כעצת השרים והזקנים יחרם כל רכושו והוא יבדל מקהל הגולה "Anyone who failed to appear within three days would forfeit all his property, in accordance with the decision of the officials and elders, and would himself be expelled from the assembly of the exiles." It is no wonder that all the people heeded the dictate and gathered in Jerusalem, as described in the succeeding verse 9.

[71] Cf. W. Th. in der Smitten, *Esra. Quellen, Überlieferung und Geschichte* (Assen, 1973), p. 88, who perceives a tension between Nehemiah the politician and the theory-oriented priest Ezra.

[72] We observe that Nehemiah's dictate to separate the foreign women, effected before his departure to Persia according to Ezra 10: 17 and Neh. 13: 3, was neglected during his absence (Neh. 13: 23 - 24) and had once again to be enforced (Neh. 13: 25).

[73] It is probable that Ezra's concern (much like the contemporary situation) was the national survival of Israel, seemingly endangered by the great number of intermarriages, but this motive is not mentioned. Nehemiah's fear for the cultural survival of the national language, on the other hand, is more directly indicated.

[74] We read in Ezra 9: 1: כתעבתיהם "like their detestable practices." The list of different nations that are incompatible with the biblical pericopes is therefore not problematic; the two motives offered by Ezra are pertinent to all foreign people, and are not intrinsically connected to the prohibitions with respect to the seven nations or to the Ammonites and Moabites.

[75] We read in Ezra 9: 2: והתערבו זרע הקדש "and have mingled the holy lineage." This concept is entirely new and remains unique in the Bible; elsewhere we encounter only the expressions זרע ישראל, זרע אברהם, זרע ברך ה'. The phrase זרע קדש מצבתה "the holy lineage will be the stump" is found in Isa. 6: 13, but this phrase is missing in the LXX and therefore may be considered a later interjection. We find in Mal. 2: 15 the

instituted a novel ecstatic attitude of awe toward numinous utterances and precepts, כל חרד בדברי אלהי ישראל "everyone who trembled at the words of the God of Israel [9: 4]," [76] an approach which changed the character of Israelite religion and influenced its future development. [77] The introduction of this emotional element of awe in the fulfillment of the divine commands allowed the extension of these commands to hitherto unprohibited peripheries in order to ensure the avoidance of any erroneous transgression. The concept of סייג לתורה "a [wide] fence to [the core] of the Torah," so elaborated by the rabbinical schools, was instituted by Ezra, ideologically and practically. The two leaders Ezra and Nehemiah were thus able to widen the application of the Sabbath laws and the prohibitions against intermarriage beyond their previous limits, through suitable interpretations, [78] and to impose such

---

obscure term זרע אלהים. Sifra יג פרק ט ד"ה פרשה מות אחרי connects this phrase with Mal. 2: 11: ובעל בת אל נכר "married the daughter of a foreign god," and with the condemnation by Ezra and Nehemiah of wedlock with foreign women. Thus the term זרע אלהים refers to the Israelites. This prophetic admonition does not contradict my thesis that Ezra and Nehemiah endeavoured to enforce the notion in practice; a law is instituted to serve a necessity. D. L. Petersen, *Zechariah 9 - 14 and Malachi* (Louisville, Ky, 1995) interprets זרע אלהים as "Israel as holy offspring."

[76] We also encounter this distinct expression in Ezra 10: 3: והחרדים במצות אלהינו "...and of those who fear the commands of our God," and in Deutero- Isa.: וחרד על דברי "...and trembles at my word [66: 2]," שמעו דבר ה' החרדים אל דברו "...you who tremble at his word [66: 5]." The Greek language, it seems, had not coined a particular term to express this specific type of awe for the word of God. The LXX therefore translates this expression in Ezra 9: 4 as διώκον λόγον θεοῦ, "follower of the word of God," in 10: 13 as φοβέρισον "frightened", and in Isa. as τρέμοντα "trembling".

[77] This novel idea of fearing the word of God is utilized today as the identifying attribute of the ultra-orthodox Jewish groups (חרדים).

[78] We read in Neh. 8: 8: ויקראו בספר בתורת האלהים מפרש ושום שכל ויבינו במקרא "They read from the Book of the Law of God, making it clear and giving the meaning, so that the people could understand what was being read." Ezra came to Judah with the intent of imposing the law on the Israelites according to his interpretation of the Torah. We read in Ezra 7: 10: כי עזרא הכין את לבבו לדרש את תורת ה' ולעשות חק ומשפט וללמד בישראל "For Ezra had devoted himself to the study [i.e. an understanding of the correct meaning = interpretation] and observance of the Law of the Lord, and to teaching its decrees and laws in Israel." In B. T. Sabbath 123b, after a discussion of a specific Mishnah with respect to the Sabbath laws, we read: אמר רבי חנינא בימי נחמיה בן חכליה נשנית משנה זו דכתיב בימים ההמה ראיתי ביהודה דרכים גתות בשבת ומביאים הערמות "Said Rabbi Hanina: In the days of Nehemiah son of Hakaliah was this Mishnah learned, as is written [Neh. 13: 15]: 'In those days I saw men in Judah treading winepresses on the Sabbath and bringing in grain.'"

extensions: the one by his theological preaching and the other by his political power. Only a combination of these two elements had a chance of success.[79]

I have enlarged the scrutiny of these two subjects and the roles played by Ezra and Nehemiah[80] in order to illustrate the circumstances in Judah after the return of the exiles; the texts in our possession on these two topics clearly show the dissension in Israelite society. On other subjects, and specifically the cult issue that is the main topic of our study, the texts are not so straightforward, and one has the impression that the prevailing circumstances in this respect were intentionally obscured. Minute examination will, however, allow us to detect the same disagreements at the core of the community.

The Book of Ezra attempts to portray an eager and resolute community poised to build the Temple, start the sacrificial cult and rigorously obey all divine commands. We shall investigate the authenticity of that representation. The first pericope at once delineates its principal theme, the rebuilding of the Temple. Cyrus declares והוא פקד עלי לבנות לו בית בירושלם "He [God] has charged me to build a Temple for him in Jerusalem [1: 2]," and this is repeated for further emphasis in v. 3. Although v. 1 refers to the event as the fulfillment of the word of the Lord spoken by Jeremiah, Cyrus' edict does not correspond faithfully to Jeremiah's prophecy. Jeremiah proclaimed in chap. 29, in v. 10[81]and particularly v. 14,[82] the return of the exiles from all nations. The building of the Temple according to the divine command, apparently the

---

[79] I do not contend that all the reforms were instituted and effected by Ezra and Nehemiah. It is probable that a number of ordinances were introduced later and attributed to these great personalities, to enhance their prestige. Ezra and Nehemiah did, however, lay the foundation for this shift in Israelite religion. The Rabbis compare Ezra to Moses, as we read in Tosefta Sanhedrin 4: 7: ר' יוסי אומ' ראוי היה עזרא שתינתן תורה על ידו אילמלא קידמו משה "Rabbi Jose says: It would have been fitting for the Torah to have been handed down by Ezra, had not Moses preceded him"; as is common in rabbinical discussions, a number of parallel expressions in biblical verses referring to Moses and Ezra substantiate this equation.

[80] Since this study is not a critical analysis of the Books of Ezra and Nehemiah but rather an examination of their respective influence on the sacrificial cult, I have bundled together their records and deeds. Both books were originally unified under the name of Ezra, and the book of Nehemiah also records Ezra's activities; I thus see nothing wrong in the joint portrayal of their religious and political accomplishments.

[81] We read there: כי לפי מלאת לבבל שבעים שנה אפקד אתכם והקמתי עליכם את דברי הטוב להשיב אתכם אל המקום הזה "When seventy years are completed for Babylon, I will come to you and fulfill my gracious promise to bring you back to this place."

[82] We read there: וקבצתי אתכם מכל הגוים ומכל המקומות אשר הדחתי אתכם שם נאם ה' והשבתי אתכם אל המקום אשר הגליתי אתכם משם "I will gather you from all the nations and places where I have banished you, declares the Lord, and will bring you back to the place from which I carried you into exile."

sole[83] motive of Cyrus' proclamation, is not mentioned in Jeremiah's prophecy. Ezra shifts the focus of the momentous event of deliverance, from the return of the exiles to their homeland and its political consequences to the building of the Temple, the renewal of the cult, and the elaboration and imposition of the religious laws.

It is remarkable that the Apocryphal Esdras shows a better literary structure than the Book of Ezra. Its contents parallel the Book of Ezra, with the exception of one episode,[84] but what is significant for our purpose is the addition of chapter 1, which starts at king Josiah's period. The Book of Ezra is composed of two main divisions, chaps. 1 - 6 narrating the return from exile and the overcoming of adversities until the building of the Temple and its consecration, and part two recording Ezra's activities. Chapter 6 concludes the first part with a report of the celebration of the Passover feast and sacrifice, and that is the theme of chapter 1 of Esdras that starts with the Passover celebration of Josiah. It is not within the scope of this study to investigate the relative authenticity of the two similar books, and what induced the canonists to prefer the one to the other, but one must assume that both editions were in circulation at that period. I wish to postulate that from the literary point of view, Esdras presents a better choice; it starts with the Passover sacrifice as its prologue, and concludes the cycle with the same subject as its epilogue. This substantiates the leading objective of the narrative: the return from exile is dedicated to the building of the Temple and the resumption of the sacrificial cult. Jeremiah's prayer השיבנו ה' אליך ונשוב חדש ימינו כקדם "Restore us to yourself, O Lord, that we may return; renew our days as of old [Lam. 5: 21]," was thus understood as fulfilled, and his prophecy concluded.[85]

9.3.3 Comparison and Contrast between Ezra and the Prophets Haggai and Malachi

Ezra paints in broad strokes an idyllic picture of unity[86] in Israelite society, great enthusiasm for the renewal of the sacrifices[87] and the building of the

---

[83] From the text of Cyrus' cylinder we determine that he also ordered the return of the exiles to their homeland; the biblical record of the proclamation conceals this element, and conveys the impression that the building of the Temple was the sole motive of Cyrus' decree.

[84] The episode that induced the king's permission for resumption of the Temple construction: in Esdras the royal banquet and Zerubabel's victory replace the retrieval of an archival document in Ezra.

[85] In Jer. 29: 10 and 14, cited above.

[86] We read in Ezra 3: 1: ויאספו העם כאיש אחד "The people assembled as one man." S. Mowinckel, *Studien zu dem Buche Ezra-Nehemia III* (Oslo, 1965), also perceives a bias

Temple,[88] and eagerness to provide the necessary financial means.[89] Only the slander of the neighbouring nations[90] and the ensuing royal edict to halt the Temple's construction[91] caused the extended[92] interruption of the building activity. Before investigating the inconsistencies in the text of Ezra itself, let us examine the utterances of Haggai and Malachi, in which a conflicting scene to Ezra's representation is clearly evident. We read in Hag. 1: 2: העם הזה אמרו לא עת בא עת בית ה' להבנות "These people say 'The time has not yet come for the Lord's house to be built,'" and in v. 4 God through Haggai remonstrates with the people: העת לכם אתם לשבת בבתיכם ספונים והבית הזה חרב "Is it a time for you, yourselves to be living in your paneled houses, while this house remains a ruin?" There is no indication of any slander and outside repression hindering the building of the Temple, as so vividly described in Ezra; it is solely that the people prefer to be concerned with their own personal enjoyment than with the building of the Temple, as the prophet says: יען ביתי אשר הוא חרב ואתם רצים איש לביתו "Because of my house which remains a ruin, while each of you is busy with his own house [1: 9]." Nor is their hesitation a result of poverty; they possess the means to indulge in luxury, building expensive paneled houses. Their defense that "the time has not yet come" is a manifest misrepresentation, and because they grant preference to their own assets, God will punish them in the same

---

in Ezra's portrayal of the religious circumstances in Israel. He writes on p. 33: "Er sucht soweit wie möglich zu idealisieren und erbaulich zu schildern." ("He [Ezra] tries as much as possible to portray an edifying and ideal description.")

[87] They built the altar and offered sacrifices כי באימה עליהם מעמי הארצות "despite the fear of the peoples around them [3: 3]."

[88] We read in 3: 11: וכל העם הריעו תרועה גדולה בהלל לה' על הוסד בית ה' "And all the people gave a great shout of praise to the Lord, because the foundation of the house of the Lord was laid."

[89] We read in 1: 6: וכל סביבתיהם חזקו בידיהם בכלי כסף בזהב ברכוש ובבהמה ובמגדנות "All their neighbours assisted them with articles of silver and gold, with goods and livestock, and with valuable gifts," and in 2: 68 - 9: ומראשי האבות בבואם לבית ה' אשר בירושלם התנדבו לבית האלהים להעמידו על מכונו. ככחם נתנו לאוצר המלאכה זהב דרכמונים שש רבאות ואלף וכסף מנים חמשת אלפים וכתנת כהנים מאה "When they arrived at the house of the Lord in Jerusalem, some of the heads of the families gave freewill offerings toward the rebuilding of the house of God on its site. According to their ability they gave to the treasury for this work sixty-one thousand drachmas of gold, five thousand minas of silver and one hundred priestly garments."

[90] Ezra 4: 6 - 7.

[91] Ezra 4: 23 - 24.

[92] From the second year of Cyrus' reign (537), the initiation of the building (Ezra 3: 8), until the second year of Darius' reign (520), the resumption of building (4: 24).

measure; they will have no success in any of their economic activities.[93] The prophet urges the people: עלו ההר והבאתם עץ ובנו הבית "Go up into the mountains and bring down timber and build the house [1: 8]." I do not envisage how this exhortation and the state of affairs recounted in and castigated by Haggai can be harmonized[94] with the generally approving picture described in Ezra, and specifically with the record in 3: 7[95] that the people gave money for cedar wood, or with the record in 2: 68 - 69 of the significant donations for the Temple.

We can also detect holes in Ezra's admirable illustration itself with respect to the financing for the construction of the Temple. Contrary to the portrayal described above, we observe that only "some of the heads of the families" ומראשי האבות (2: 68) donated resources for the Temple building. Further, though it is stated that the Israelites had given money for the purchase of the timber from Lebanon and for the preparation of stones etc. (3: 7), the financing came from the Persian king, as we read in 6: 4: נדבכין די אבן גלל תלתא ונדבך די אע חדת ונפקתא מן בית מלכא תתיהב "...three courses of large stones and one of timbers. The costs are to be paid by the royal treasury." We have no way of confirming the authenticity of this supposed Persian archival document that established the exact size of the Temple and the specific details of the construction of its walls, but we must hesitate to assume that Cyrus the Persian king was engaged in the resolution of such minute details. The same hesitation applies to the subsequent royal edict to comply with the document's instructions (chap. 7), and one must ask oneself

---

[93] We read in Hag. 1: 10: על כן "Therefore", and in the succeeding 1: 11: ואקרא חרב על הארץ ועל ההרים ועל הדגן ועל התירוש ועל היצהר ועל אשר תציא האדמה ועל האדם ועל הבהמה ועל כל יגיע כפים "I called for a drought on the fields and the mountains, on the grain, the new wine, the oil and whatever the ground produces, on men and cattle, and on the labor of your hands."

[94] The traditional commentator Radak in his commentary to Jer. 29: 10 attempted to harmonize the conflict between the eagerness to build the Temple expressed in Ezra and the statement "the time has not yet come" in Haggai 1: 2. He referred to a rabbinical dissertation in B. T. Megilah 11b on the correct interpretation of the seventy years predicted by Jeremiah 29: 10, repeated several times in various forms and particularly specified in II Chr. 36: 21 - 22, which came to an end only in the second year of Darius' reign. This was the meaning of the statement "the time has not yet come"; that is, the pledged period of seventy years was not yet fulfilled.

[95] We read there: ויתנו כסף לחצבים ולחרשים ומאכל ומשתה ושמן לצדנים ולצרים להביא עצי ארזים מן הלבנון אל ים יפוא "Then they gave money to the masons and carpenters, and gave food and drink and oil to the people of Sidon and Tyre, so that they would bring cedar by sea from Lebanon to Joppa." We must assume that according to this report they had already received some materials to begin the construction of the Temple (v. 8), and had made sufficient progress to give an outline of its ultimate proportions (v. 12).

the reason why the Jews did not finance the building of the Temple themselves,[96] particularly considering that they were wealthy and had the resources to build luxurious "paneled houses" for their personal enjoyment, as Haggai affirms.[97] We must assume that, as with respect to the Sabbath laws, not all the people had the same commendable disposition toward the restoration of the Temple and its purposes.

The sacrificial celebrations were the most significant if not the sole purpose of the Temple, and concerning these we observe similar circumstances. In contrast to the portrayal in Ezra 3: 1 - 6 of the eagerness for the renewal of the sacrifices, notwithstanding feared harassment from the surrounding peoples, we encounter a totally opposite picture in the utterances of the prophets. In Zech. 3: 1 - 4[98] and strongly in Mal. 1: 6 - 14; 2: 1 - 9[99] we

---

[96] In *Ant.* XII: 139 - 141 Josephus records that Antiochus the Great offered the Jews funds for offerings and assistance for the repair of the Temple; but as Josephus portrays it this was a special occurrence, a clear reward for their assistance against the Ptolemies, and likely also to ensure their future cooperation in this respect. Moreover, as is evident from Josephus, the city and the Temple were damaged in the course of the fighting, and one must assume that as a result the land too was impoverished; it was only natural that the Seleucids, eager to have the Jews as their allies, would help them in the reconstruction of their country and sanctuary. These particular circumstances did not exist in Darius' reign, and one may doubt whether Cyrus' edict contained the instructions to finance the building of the Temple; we observe, according to the narrative in Ezra 3: 7, that in his time the Jews themselves financed the purchase of wood and stones, and brought "the cedar logs by sea...as authorized by Cyrus king of Persia." The Jews thus financed the purchase, and the king's authorization was limited to the transportation. The king's donation for the offerings at the Temple, on the other hand, seems more authentic, since such a custom was considered appropriate. Demetrios' offer to Jonathan of financial assistance for the Temple repairs, among other items recorded in *Ant.* XIII: 57, was evidently promised to gain Jonathan's badly needed military help, as is obvious from the ensuing battle.

[97] Lester L. Grabbe, in his recently published *Ezra-Nehemiah* (London, 1998), critically examines the authenticity of these narratives, and poses certain of the same questions that I have posed in my study. This is not to be wondered at, as the inconsistencies in the records are too obvious to be ignored by any critical observer.

[98] The nature of Joshua the priest's sin expressed in the metaphor in v. 3: לבוש בגדים צואים "dressed in filthy clothes" is not clear, but a censure of the priesthood is indicated, and we may look for complementary facts from Mal. The Rabbis, probably following Targum Jonathan, also questioned this, and we read in B. T. Sanhedrin 93a: וכי דרכו של יהושע ללבוש בגדים צואים אלא מלמד שהיו בניו נושאים נשים שאינן הגונות לכהונה ולא מיחה בהן "Would Joshua habitually wear filthy clothes? [No], but it teaches us that his sons married [foreign] women inappropriate for the priesthood, and he did not protest." But Ibn Ezra contends that speculation on the marriage of his descendants must have been much later than Zechariah's prophecy. He therefore interprets this pericope as the prophet's criticism of the lack of decorum on the part of the priest, and the absence of the other precious furnishings, because the Temple was not yet constructed.

observe a gross negligence bordering on contempt with respect to the offerings. The prophets' censures apply to the people and the priests; both segments of the population are accused of outrageous lack of reverence with respect to the sacrificial celebrations. And as with the financing of the Temple building, the king of Persia had to contribute the provisions for the sacrifices, including the trivial cost of salt (7: 22).[100] Such inconsistencies

---

[99] Because of the great number of relevant pericopes, I shall quote only key phrases. We encounter הכהנים בוזי שמי "O, priests who show contempt for my name [1: 6]"; מגישים על מזבחי לחם מגאל וכי תגישו "You place defiled food on my altar [v. 7]"; ואתם מחללים פסח וחלה "When you sacrifice crippled and diseased animals [v. 8]"; אתו באמרכם שלחן אדני מגאל הוא "You profane it by saying of the Lord's table 'It is defiled' [v. 12]." The above accusations refer both to the people who bring the debased animals and to the priests who offer them on the altar. The censure and exhortations in chap. 2 are addressed to the priests; we read there: אם לא תשמעו ואם לא תשימו על לב לתת כבוד לשמי אמר ה' "If you do not listen, and if you do not set your heart to honor my name, says the Lord [v. 2]"; וזריתי פרש על פניכם "I will spread upon your faces the offal [v. 3]"; ואתם סרתם מן הדרך "You have turned from the way [v. 8]"; and וגם אני נתתי אתכם נבזים ושפלים "So I have caused you to be despised and humiliated [v. 9]."

[100] It is possible, as some scholars suppose, that the Persian kings assumed the obligation of the former Israelite kings to provide for the sacrifices at the main Temple. I do not intend to confirm or dispute this assumption, but I would like to point out that there is no explicit affirmation of such a custom in Scripture. The fact that the biblical narratives record royal sacrifices does not automatically exclude offerings by other people. There are also several instances in which the people's offerings are recorded, as for example in I Kings 8: 5, at the transfer of the ark: והמלך שלמה וכל עדת ישראל...מזבחים צאן ובקר "And king Solomon and the entire assembly of Israel...sacrificing so many sheep and cattle," and also at the Temple's consecration, in v. 62: והמלך וכל ישראל עמו זבחים זבח לפני ה' "Then the king and all Israel with him offered sacrifices before the Lord." The authenticity of II Kings 16: 15 on the sacrifices listed by Ahaz is problematic, but there too one must suppose that the עלת כל עם הארץ, "the burnt offering of all the people of the land," was not donated by the king. In II Chr. 29 it is explicitly stated that the people brought the offerings; we read in v. 21: ויביאו פרים "They brought bulls," and in v. 31: ויביאו הקהל זבחים ותודות וכל נדיב לב עלות "So the assembly brought sacrifices and thank offerings, and whose hearts were willing brought burnt offerings." The narrative in II Chr. 30: 24 is even more remarkable. We read there: כי חזקיהו מלך יהודה הרים לקהל אלף פרים ושבעת אלפים צאן "Hezekiah king of Judah provided **for the assembly** a thousand bulls and ten thousand sheep." The king and the princes donated animals for the people to sacrifice, probably as שלמים to be eaten (though Scripture does not indicate the purpose of these donations), not as sacrifices for themselves. In Ezra we observe that the people of the first immigration donated the sacrificial offerings, and did not wait for the Persian king's grant. We read in Ezra 3: 3 - 5: ויעל עליו עלות לה' עלות לבקר ולערב...ועלת יום ביום...ואחרי כן עלת תמיד ולחדשים ולכל מועדי ה' ...ולכל מתנדב נדבה לה' "...and sacrifices burnt offerings

with regard to the Temple and the sacrifices demonstrate fluid circumstances and great dissension between different segments of society. It seems impossible to assume that the people and the priests unanimously displayed carelessness or opposition to the building of the Temple and the revival of the cult, as Ezra and Nehemiah would not then have succeeded in so drastically reversing the trend and creating a theocratic state. On the other hand, the passages above serve as indisputable evidence of such disregard; we must therefore assume some measure of dissension among various groups of society. The fact that Ezra required a Persian royal edict to force obedience to דתא די אלהך "the law of your God" with the threat of such harsh punishments as הן למות הן לשרשו הן לענש נכסין ולאסורין "death, banishment, confiscation of property, or imprisonment [Ezra 7: 26]," also bears witness to the "religious" attitude of at least some segments of Israelite society at that period.

9.3.4 Similarity of Political Objectives between Josiah's Reform and the Reform of Ezra/Nehemiah

The broad cooperation between Ezra and Nehemiah, each with his specific contribution, succeeded in imposing[101] their concepts of Judaism on Israelite

---

to the Lord, both the morning and evening sacrifices...burnt offerings for each day...and after that the regular burnt offerings, the New Moon sacrifices and for all the appointed feasts of the Lord...and freewill offerings to the Lord." Nehemiah too arranged for public contribution for the financing of the sacrifices, and did not rely on the king's donation. It is possible that the Persian king had to provide for the sacrifices in a period of crisis, before Nehemiah's decree; one may also doubt the authenticity of this record, perhaps appended to the biblical narrative to praise the Persian king and to indicate his great reverence for the Israelite Deity and His Temple. We might also consider in the same light the financing of the Temple building by the Persian king. While it is true that from I Kings chap. 6 it would appear that Solomon built the Temple from his own resources, we observe that king Joash (II Kings 12: 4 - 16), or king Josiah (II Kings 22: 3 - 7), (or both), approached the public for donations to repair the Temple, and did not bear the costs themselves.

[101] In addition to the repression by Nehemiah of mixed marriages, they used Persian authority to enforce all the laws according to their own interpretation, as we read in Ezra 7: 25 - 26: מני שפטין ודינין די להון דאנין לכל עמה די בעבר נהרה לכל ידעי דתי אלהך ודי לא ידע תהודעון. וכל די לא להוא עבד דתא די אלהך ודתא די מלכא אספרנא דינה להוא מתעבד מנה הן למות הן לשרשו הן לענש נכסין ולאסורין "Appoint magistrates and judges to administer justice to all the people of Trans-Euphrates - all who know the laws of your God. And you are to teach any who do not know them. Whoever does not obey the law of your God and the law of the king must surely be punished by death, banishment, confiscation of property, or imprisonment." The legislative, judicial and executive powers were all concentrated in one person, Ezra the priest.

society, creating a theocratic state with the priests at its spiritual summit and at its pragmatic helm.[102] They realized the significance of the single Temple and its elaborate cult ceremonies for the cohesion of the Israelite people in Judah, and its sense of unity with the increased Diaspora population. The centralization of the cult introduced by Josiah was thus bolstered and finally effected;[103] Josiah utilized the sacrificial ceremonial to foster his political

---

[102] The circumstances which led to the disappearance of the political authority of the descendants of the Davidic dynasty and the unification of "church and state" under one priestly authority in the Second Temple period are still unclear. One may consider that the utmost significance bestowed upon the punctilious performance of the religious precepts and cult celebrations had an important, if not a decisive, influence on this peculiar development: the advancement of religion above all other institutions also elevated its leadership to a position beyond that of the political leader, and might have contributed to the total disappearance of the latter.

[103] Recent scholarly opinion questions the authenticity of Josiah's "reform" as recorded in II Kings 23; see, e.g. Chr. Uhlinger, "Gab es eine Joshijanische Kultreform?" [Was there a Reform effected by Josiah?] in *Jeremia und die Deuteronomistische Bewegung*, B. B. B. Band 98, pp. 57- 89, ed. W. Gross (Weinheim, 1995) .Although the issue does not directly affect my thesis with respect to removal of the *bamoth*, an operation in which Josiah was undoubtedly a principal performer, I wish nevertheless to convey some relevant comments. In our speculations about the authenticity of a text, our first consideration should be whether the editor had a strong incentive to portray events and circumstances other than those that actually occurred, or were retrieved from previous sources. In our case, I do not perceive any valid reason for the deuteronomic editor to credit Josiah with a decisive and virtuous reform, if this were devoid of any kernel of truth. It is true that the biblical editors did not conceive of a developmental process, and assessed the spontaneous acts of a king as either righteous or wicked shifts of conduct, and therefore may have credited Josiah alone with a great array of virtuous deeds; we must agree, however, that their decision in this respect was founded on certain factual events. Against the background of such superlative deeds there arises the problem of theodicy; we observe that the editor has great difficulty in justifying the destruction of the kingdom despite the king's impeccable behaviour. Such a resolution does not reflect the habitual divine way, and is in utter conflict with the view expressed in Jeremiah's later prophecy in Jehoiakim's reign (26: 3): אולי ישמעו וישבו איש מדרכו הרעה ונחמתי אל הרעה אשר אנכי חשב לעשות להם מפני רע מעלליהם "Perhaps they will listen and each will turn from his evil way. Then I will relent and not bring on them the disaster I was planning because of the evil they have done." An unknown prophetess had to be devised to foretell such undeserved destruction. And although Josiah was spared to see his kingdom ruined, his personal life did not come to a peaceful end, as the prophetess foresaw: ונאספת אל קברתיך בשלום "I will gather you to your fathers and you will be buried in peace [II Kings 22: 20]." One would have expected a different outcome as a reward for Josiah's deeds. The editor's problem to justify the destruction of Jerusalem was even more aggravated in that he had no evidence of any "religiously" wicked deeds committed by Josiah's successors. To overcome this theological problem, he interjected among his record of their rebellious policies (the authentic causes of their downfall) the vague stereotypical phrase ויעש הרע בעיני ה' ככל אשר עשו אבתיו "He did evil in the eyes of the Lord, just as his fathers had done." This phrase was invoked for all the succeeding kings (II Kings 23: 32, 37; 24: 9, 19, with variations),

ambitions of uniting the people in the northern and southern parts of Israel, and Ezra and Nehemiah acted similarly for the sake of uniting the people in Israel and the Diaspora. The connection between the two reforms is evident not only in chap. 1 of Esdras, but also in the specific emphasis on the Passover celebration by Josiah and by Ezra. And as Josiah "refashioned the Passover,[104] Ezra and Nehemiah reoriented the Feast of Tabernacles.[105] They instituted public meetings[106] for the teaching of the Law and its

---

instead of the previous stereotypical accusation with respect to the *bamoth*, in order to justify the divine punishment. The editor even overlooked the fact that Josiah, the pious king, was the father of Jehoaz and Jehoiakim, and the phrase "as his fathers had done" in their cases is patently misplaced. It is remarkable that in contrast to the Kings approach, which imputed to the kings the evil idolatrous behaviour of the people, Jeremiah seems mainly to accuse the people of such misdemeanours, and blamed the kings, Josiah's successors, primarily for their social misconduct and political miscalculations. We must therefore assume that Josiah's reform had an enduring effect with respect to the cessation of worship at the *bamoth* and official idolatrous practices. The centralization of the sacrificial cult in one place must generate, by default, a standardization of the ceremonies, an effective method for the exclusion of deviant practices. I speculated in *Incense*, pp. 194 ff. that the destruction of the *bamoth* and the cessation of the local sanctuaries induced the spread of private ceremonies of incense-burning on the roofs (Jer. 19: 13; 32: 29). If the reform had been accomplished only in exile, we must also ask what theological advantage the editor would attain by the retrojection of the reform to the pre-exilic Josiah. His theological doctrine that the destruction of the Temple constituted divine punishment for wicked deeds would be better served by a roster of evil kings before the debacle, and the portrayal of the rebuilding of the Temple as a divine reward for the return to the Lord and heartfelt obedience to all His commands. Such an account would utterly harmonize with the text in Deut. 30: 1 - 10. I therefore postulate that the deuteronomic editor felt compelled by reality to record Josiah's virtuous deeds, despite the theological difficulties created with respect to his general philosophy. The extended developmental process started before Josiah and continued after his period, ignored by the deuteronomic editor; but Josiah's role in this process must have been of such significance that the editor credited him with the ultimate accomplishment of the reform.

[104] We read in II Kings 23: 22: כי לא נעשה כפסח הזה מימי השפטים "Not since the days of the judges, had any such Passover been observed." This archaic spring festival acquired another mythological definition and a distinct character. From a family feast celebrated in the local dwelling (Exod. 12: 21 - 28), it became a testimony to history celebrated in Jerusalem.

[105] We read in Neh. 8: 17: וישבו בסכות כי לא עשו מימי ישוע בן נון כן בני ישראל עד היום ההוא "They lived in the booths. From the days of Joshua son of Nun until that day, the Israelites had not celebrated it like this." From the previous agricultural feast חג האסף, "Feast of the Ingathering" in the Book of the Covenant (Exod. 23: 16), and the unspecified but well-identified החג, "**the** festival", celebrated by Solomon (I Kings 8: 65) and even in Ezekiel's period (Ezek. 45: 23), it became the historical holiday linked to the Exodus mythology.

[106] We read in II Kings 23: 2: ויעל המלך בית ה' וכל איש יהודה וכל ישבי ירושלם אתו והכהנים והנביאים וכל העם למקטן ועד גדול ויקרא באזניהם את כל דברי ספר הברית הנמצא בבית ה' "He went up to the Temple of the Lord with the men of

interpretation[107] according to their thoughts and purposes, and to ensure the people's acceptance[108] of its precepts and prohibitions. Like Josiah, Ezra and Nehemiah emphasized the exalted status of Jerusalem,[109] and political[110] as

---

Judah, the people of Jerusalem, the priests and the prophets - all the people from the least to the greatest. He read in their hearing all the words of the Book of the Covenant, which have been found in the Temple of the Lord." In Neh. 8: 1- 3 we read: ויאספו כל העם כאיש אחד...ויביא עזרא הכהן את התורה...ויקרא בו "All the people assembled as one man...Ezra the priest brought the Law...and he read it."

[107] We read in Neh. 8: 8: ויקראו בספר בתורת האלהים מפרש "They read from the Book of the Law of God, making it clear and giving the meaning." It seems that at that period the people understood Hebrew, the language of the Bible; hence there was no need for a translation as in later generations, but only for the interpretation and meaning that Ezra considered correct and appropriate.

[108] We read in II Kings 23: 3: ויעמד המלך על העמוד ויכרת את הברית...ויעמד כל העם בברית "The king stood by the pillar and renewed the covenant...all the people pledged themselves to the covenant." We encounter a similar phrase in Neh. 8: 4, ויעמד עזרא הספר על מגדל עץ "Ezra the scribe stood on a high wooden platform," and in 10: 1 the making of the covenant is called כרתים אמנה. The LXX translates ברית as διαθήκη "will, arrangement between two parties, and covenant in O.T. and N.T." and אמנה as πίστις "assurance, pledge of good faith and similar" (Liddell and Scott).

[109] Similar to other socio-linguistic innovations in this period, as indicated above, Jerusalem had bestowed upon it the attribute עיר הקדש, "the holy city." This expression appears only in this period: Neh. 11: 1, 18; Deut-Isa. 52: 1, and with stylistic variations in 48: 2, 64: 9; Dan. 9: 16: הר קדשך and 9: 24: עיר קדשך; Zech. 8: 3: הר הקדש. We also encounter בציון הר קדשי והיתה ירושלם קדש in Joel 4: 17, but the period of this prophet is in dispute and some attribute it to the Second Temple era. It is not within the scope of this study to debate the dating of this prophet, but the fact that Joel utilizes this specific expression, not employed elsewhere in Scripture except in the period of the Second Temple, may assist scholars in their relevant arguments.

[110] Josiah's reforms in this respect, as described earlier, were reinvigorated by the decree to increase and maintain a stable population in Jerusalem. We read in Neh. 11: 1: וישבו שרי העם בירושלם ושאר העם הפילו גורלות להביא אחד מן העשרה לשבת בירושלם עיר הקדש "Now the leaders of the people settled in Jerusalem, and the rest of the people cast lots to bring one out of ten to live in Jerusalem, the holy city." The parallel with the scope of Josiah's reform is remarkable in this respect. The leaders are compelled or encouraged to settle in Jerusalem, recalling Josiah's institution of the city as the legal center; similarly, the rules requiring the bringing to Jerusalem of the first-fruits, first-born, offerings, wine and oil, and tithes of the crops (Neh. 10: 36 - 40; 35 - 39 in KJV) mark the city as the cultic center. The phrase ומעשר אדמתנו ללוים והם הלוים המעשרים בכל ערי עבדתנו (10: 38, v. 37 in KJV) records that the Levites "collect the tithes in all the towns where we work," but does not indicate where the tithes were ultimately brought for distribution. Neh. 13: 12: וכל יהודה הביאו מעשר הדגן והתירוש והיצהר לאוצרות "All Judah brought the tithes of grain, new wine and oil into the storerooms," again does not specify where these storerooms were located, whether in Jerusalem for central distribution under the supervision of the committee, as

well as cult procedures,[111] including a systematic organization of the clergy, were instituted[112] toward the realization of this goal. Necessary legislation was promulgated to guarantee provision of funds and combustibles for the Temple and the cult,[113] and the ensuing financial friction between the various

---

would appear from the ensuing verses 13 and 14, or in various storerooms spread over the land.

[111] A precise sacrificial system was instituted: עלות לבקר ולערב "burnt offerings morning and evening [Ezra 3: 3]" instead of עלת הבקר ואת מנחת הערב "the morning burnt offering and the evening grain offering [II Kings 16: 15]," established by Ahaz. This ordinance is identical to the final rule in the sacrificial codex, Num. 28: 3 - 4. The sacrifices for the various holidays were also established, as we read in Ezra 3: 5: ואחרי כן עלת תמיד ולחדשים ולכל מועדי ה׳ "After that [they presented] the regular burnt offerings, the New Moon sacrifices and the sacrifices for all the appointed sacred feasts of the Lord." "After that" should be interpreted that after the Feast of the Tabernacles they offered the various sacrifices established for each event. Rashi interprets it thus, fitting the context, while the LXX translates ὁλοκαυτώσεις, in future: "You shall bring burnt offerings [each at its proper time]."

[112] The various duties in the Temple were classified and divided between the priests and the Levites. We read: ויעמידו את הלוים מבן עשרים שנה ומעלה לנצח על מלאכת בית ה׳ "and appointed Levites twenty years of age and older to supervise the building of the house of the Lord [Ezra 3: 8]"; הכהנים מלבשים בחצצרות והלוים בני אסף במצלתים "the priests in their vestments and with trumpets, and the Levites the sons of Asaph with cymbals [3: 10]"; והקימו כהניא בפלגתהון ולויא במחלקתהון על עבידת אלהא "And they installed the priests in their divisions and the Levites in their groups for the service of God [6: 18]"; ויפקדו השוערים והמשררים והלוים "the gatekeepers and the singers and the Levites were appointed [Neh. 7: 1]," and are subsequently counted; ואעמידה משמרות לכהנים וללוים איש במלאכתו "I assigned duties to the priests and Levites, each to his own task [13: 30]." A full-fledged organization is evident.

[113] A sophisticated mixed financial system was instituted: a yearly universal head tax of שלישית השקל "a third of a shekel [Neh. 10: 33; v. 32 in KJV]," and contributions of wood for the altar, whose periodic cycles were determined by casting lots: והגורלות הפלנו על קרבן העצים "...we have cast lots to determine...a contribution of wood [10: 35; v. 34 in KJV]." Precise plans were established for the use of the money: ללחם המערכת ומנחת התמיד ולעולת התמיד "for the showbread, for the regular grain offering and burnt offering [10: 34; v. 33 in KJV]." There is no doubt that the well-developed organization contributed to the success of the enterprise and ensured its long existence throughout the entire Israelite Diaspora. We read in Neh. 12: 47 of its immediate institution: וכל ישראל בימי זרבבל ובימי נחמיה נתנים מניות המשררים והשערים דבר יום ביומו ומקדשים ללוים והלוים מקדשים לבני אהרן "So in the days of Zerubabel and of Nehemiah, all Israel contributed the daily portions for the singers and gatekeepers. They also set aside the portion for the other Levites, and the Levites set aside the portion for the descendants of Aaron." The entire complex scheme functioned perfectly according to this verse; we would have to assume that the contradictory narrative in 13: 10, cited in the next note, consists of the record of a prior

clerical classes was regulated.[114] The results of these concerted efforts were the shift of political power to the High Priest, and the perfection and sophistication of the sacrificial system, as is reflected in the P stratum of the Pentateuch.[115] Ezra preached the new theology, and Nehemiah ensured the fulfillment of its practical consequences with the help of his political authority. The process of diminution of the sacrificial system, which had been initiated with shifts in practice and theology and further exacerbated by the destruction of the Temple, was entirely reversed.[116] Thanks to the double-pronged, systematic intervention of the two leaders, the sacrificial system was renewed with unusual vigor; thus was closed another cycle in the

---

occurrence. There is also ample evidence from various outside sources that the tax, later increased to half a shekel, was collected in the Israelite communities in the Roman Empire and transferred to Jerusalem until the destruction of the Temple, when it was replaced by the *Fiscus Judaicus*, imposed by the Romans. On the latter see *War* VII: 218, and *Pro Flacco* 67 regarding the judicial case before the Senate in 59 B.C.E; in this case Cicero defended the Roman procurator accused by the Jews for his prohibition against transferring to Judah the gold of the half shekel tax collected by them throughout the Roman Empire.

[114] We read in Neh.13: 10 of a conflict regarding the distribution of the contributions: ואדעה כי מניות הלוים לא נתנה ויברחו איש לשדהו הלוים והמשררים עשי המלאכה "I also learned that the portions assigned to the Levites had not been given to them, and that all the Levites and singers responsible for the service had gone back to their own fields." For an extensive discourse on this problem of the economic struggle between the priests and Levites, see Heger, *Incense*, p. 212, n. 81. Nehemiah reacted vigorously and in the best bureaucratic tradition; he first reprimanded those in charge: ואריבה את הסגנים "So I rebuked the officials [v. 11]," and then appointed a tri-party commission to impartially decide the shares to be distributed to each of the two competing classes of clerics: ואוצרה על אוצרות שלמיה הכהן וצדוק הסופר ופדיה מן הלוים ועל ידם חנן בן זכור בן מתניה כי נאמנים נחשבו ועליהם לחלק לאחיהם "I put Shelemiah the priest, Zadok the scribe, and a Levite named Pedaiah in charge of the storerooms and made Hanan son of Zaccur, the son of Mattaniah, their assistant, because these men were considered trustworthy [v. 13]." A similar situation took place during Josiah's reform, as we read in II Kings 23: 9: אך לא יעלו כהני הבמות אל מזבח ה' בירושלם כי אם אכלו מצות בתוך אחיהם "Although the priests of the high places did not serve at the altar of the Lord in Jerusalem, they ate unleavened bread with their fellow priests." We must assume that like Nehemiah after him, Josiah decided how to distribute the priestly remuneration between the two classes of clerics.

[115] O. Eissfeldt, *The Old Testament, An Introduction*, transl. P. R. Ackroyd (New York, 1965), declares on p. 207 that the P stratum portrays the most developed cult system, and hence it represents the latest stage of the sacrificial development.

[116] It is probable that even before the joint deeds of Ezra and Nehemiah certain elements of Israelite society already held the sacrificial cult in great reverence, and sided with the authority of the High Priest. It would otherwise have been impossible to impose rules and opinions against the inclination of the entire people; yet Ezra and Nehemiah managed the triumph of this attitude despite the existence of divergent opinions.

long path of development of the ritual and theological history of Israelite culture.

These leaders recognized the political significance of the cult ceremonial[117] and its centralization, as the focal point of the Israelite people; they pursued and strengthened this particular character of the Israelite cult, initiated by Josiah,[118] creating the basis for further revolutionary developments within the framework of Josiah's reform and its far-reaching consequences. I would further suggest that in a certain sense Ahaz' reform facilitated Josiah's reform. Ahaz built a large, impressive altar in the Temple at Jerusalem, and as it seems, only at Jerusalem, thus emphasizing the definite prominence of this sanctuary.[119] This special event laid the

---

[117] The fact that the ceremonial impression made by a burnt offering on a large elaborate altar is much superior to the display of food and gifts on presentation benches or small tables was recognized by Ahaz (see section 7.2.2). Rendtorff, "Kult, Mythos und Geschichte im Alten Israel," in *Gesammelte Studien*, p. 110, quotes Mowinckel's statement: "Das alle Lebensbereiche Israels, jedenfalls in der älteren Zeit, in sakralen, kultischen Ordnung wurzlen." ("All aspects of the life of Israel, certainly in older times, have their roots in the sacral cult system.")

[118] One aspect of Josiah's reform may have been reversed; whereas in his period king and Jerusalemite priests had a common interest - both benefited from the centralization of the cult - the increased power of the priesthood in the Second Temple period may have contributed, as hinted above, to the decline and subsequent demise of its rival, the political authority.

[119] As noted in chap. 8 n. 43, the importance of establishing Jerusalem as a cult center so as to enhance its political and administrative significance was probably already recognized by Ahaz, who instituted the distinction between the primitive secondary provincial altars and the refined principal altar in Jerusalem. Since it is likely that the "divine" command for a unique site of worship was not yet "published" in Ahaz' period, we must assume that political expedience induced Ahaz to imitate the imposing Damascene sacrificial ceremonies. I also hinted at the possibility that king Azariah - Uzziah (784 - 746) had already had the same objective in mind, by instituting Jerusalem as the site of royal sacrificial ceremonies instead of Gibeon; his personal burning of incense (II Chr. 26: 16 - 20), probably the newly-introduced, highly valued frankincense, may serve as evidence for such an assumption. See the previous arguments on this act (chap. 7, text at n. 122) and Heger, *Incense*, p. 200 on the political circumstances which facilitated Azariah's procurement of frankincense. The archeological evidence quoted by H. Niehr, "Die Reform des Joschija," in *Jeremia und die Deuteronomistische Bewegung*, B. B. B. Band 98, pp. 33 - 55, ed. W. Gross (Weinheim, 1995), indicates (p. 46) that after the 9th century one finds far fewer artifacts from provincial sanctuaries in Judah, suggesting that at this time the Jerusalem sanctuary was beginning to achieve a priority status. In Niehr's opinion, the Judean kings focused their efforts positively in enhancing the status of Jerusalem, but only Josiah also acted negatively in eliminating the other sanctuaries. The thesis of a developmental process in the cult centralization is thus also suggested by this scholar. He also perceives (ibid., p. 43) the possibility that an administrative structure was already in place in Judah in Uzziah's reign, though this is usually attributed to Josiah. We see the simultaneous development of the cult and of the political structures.

foundation for the next stage, the concentration of the sacrificial celebrations in Jerusalem,[120] and ultimately its proclamation by Josiah as the uniquely designated sacrificial site. We have thus established the long line which links the reform of Ahaz to Josiah and to Ezra and Nehemiah.

9.4 Renaissance of Priestly Theology and Subsequent Political Struggles

The interruption of the sacrificial celebrations due to the destruction of the First Temple produced a certain indifference, as we have seen, toward the whole system, and its revival by Ezra and Nehemiah caused an unprecedented invigoration. We have no records to establish whether this renaissance embraced all the people, but it certainly bestowed great power on the priestly class, who dominated both the spiritual and political scene. We can only determine these circumstances from the consequential outcome: the enormous influence of the P stratum of the Pentateuch, created and refined by the priestly class, the disappearance of dynastic political leadership, and the concentration of the religious, legislative and political power in one person, the High Priest.

The priestly editors created an elaborate cult system with specific rites for every event and occasion, for the community and the individual. To ensure its acceptance by skeptics or ideological opponents, the editors retrojected the

---

See also H. M. Niemann, *Herrschaft, Königtum und Staat*, FAT 6 (Tübingen, 1993), p. 205 in this regard.

[120] II Kings 16 does not record any building of idolatrous altars by Ahaz, but from II Kings 23: 12, ואת המזבחות אשר על הגג עלית אחז, we may deduce that the altars destroyed by Josiah were built by Ahaz. The Hebrew text here is corrupt grammatically in the expression הגג עלית אחז, and its context is also problematic. The simple translation implies that the altars were built on the "top of the upper chamber of Ahaz which the kings of Judah had made" as the KJV interprets, in line with the LXX. But it is not clear who these "kings of Judah" were who built the altars after Ahaz had built his upper chambers. It could not have been Hezekiah or Manasseh, because the destruction of the altars follows immediately after this phrase, and we have no record that Ammon built any additional altars. It seems that due to this problem the NIV interpreted "near the upper room of Ahaz," evidently contrary to the text which specifies על, "on". J. Gray, *I & II Kings, A Commentary*, writes on p. 670 that the phrase עלית אחז is a gloss influenced by II Kings 20: 11. In II Chr. 28: 24 we read concerning Ahaz: ויעש לו מזבחות בכל פנה בירושלם "He set up altars at every street corner in Jerusalem." The traditional commentator Radak also suggests that Ahaz built the altars recorded in II Kings 23: 12. II Kings 21: 3 does not specify where Manasseh built the altars of Baal, but from the subsequent vv. 4 - 7 the emphasis is clearly on his wicked deeds in Jerusalem. Hence we observe that the kings following Ahaz concentrated their "religious" activities in Jerusalem.

initiation of this system to the mythological era of the wanderings in the desert and its leading personalities Moses and Aaron. Ancient narratives, written and oral, were readapted and modified to correspond with the current ideological doctrine and its practical requirements, as seen and understood by the clerical leadership. The greatest sanctity was imputed to the impeccable performance of the sacrificial celebrations, and an excellent organization with a regulated division of labour and appropriate remuneration was set up for a smooth operation. An elaborate legal foundation was devised and promulgated to ensure the exclusive cult privileges of the clerical caste, with draconian punishments, divine[121] and human,[122] against possible usurpers and transgressors. The intensity and efficiency of the legal admonitions in this respect were enhanced by pertinent narratives about the punishments inflicted in the historical past[123] upon those who dared to infringe these priestly privileges.

These two factors, the great concentration of political and economic power and the minutely particularized details of the rituals, must logically have engendered two decisive consequences. Unlimited power brings corruption, and rigidly established permanent rituals annihilate the spontaneous spiritual excitement of the worshipper, by their tendency to formalism. We know this outcome generally from historical experience, but the paucity of written evidence of the period between Ezra and Nehemiah and the Maccabees,[124] the only record of the circumstances, limits us to bare speculation. We may hypothesize on the manner by which the political power of the descendants of the Davidic dynasty declined, and totally disappeared from the national stage for a long period. Zechariah prophesied the exalted future of Jerusalem and the people under the authority of the two leaders, the priest and the prince in perfect harmony: ועצת שלום תהיה בין שניהם "And there will be harmony between the two [Zech. 6: 13]." The prophet's auspicious augury indirectly implies that contemporary conditions were opposite. Moreover, the fact that every bit of information with respect to the circumstances of the disappearance of the prince of Judah and his descendants from the public stage was so effectively "censored" hints at an intentional concealment of the real cause of this disappearance. A speculation that the priestly class, which

---

[121] We read in Num. 4: 20: ולא יבאו לראות כבלע את הקדש ומתו "They must not go to look at the holy things, even for a moment, or they will die."

[122] We read in Num. 3: 10: והזר הקרב יומת "Anyone else who approaches the sanctuary must be put to death."

[123] For instance, the fate of the Korah rebels (Num. 16), and of Uzziah king of Judah (II Chr. 26: 16 - 20).

[124] Some of the apocryphal books may have been written in the later part of this period, but scholars disagree on their exact dates; moreover, I do not think that their contents radically change the postulated circumstances in Judah.

ultimately consolidated both the religious and political hegemonies, overpowered the political authority of the aristocratic royal descendants and grasped it for itself is therefore plausible.[125]

---

[125] I am aware of the time span between the building of the Temple, accomplished in 515 B.C.E. (the sixth year of the reign of Darius I), and the arrival of Ezra in 458; we have no indication of the date when Zerubabel or his descendants disappeared from the public scene, and we must assume that the absence of such information is intentional. An interesting phrase in Neh. 12: 47 attempts to suggest that at the time of Zerubabel the financial arrangement for the remuneration of the Temple clerics was already set up, a fact which is not mentioned earlier, and which seems to be in contradiction with the record in the preceding v. 44 that only at "that time," that is, at the time of Nehemiah (445 - 425), was an efficient organization for the collection of the tithes set up. The narrative in 13: 10 ff. also points against the existence of orderly conditions with respect to the tithes and their distribution. Moreover, one must hesitate to agree with the chronological order of the narratives in the books of Ezra and Nehemiah; we have seen with respect to some topics that they were either erroneously transmitted or intentionally blurred. We read in Ezra 4: 5 "they hired counselors [to obstruct the building of the Temple] during the entire reign of Cyrus...and down to the reign of Darius." Cyrus conquered Babylon in 539 and Darius I started his reign 522. But in v. 6, we read "At the beginning of the reign of Xerxes [486] they lodged an accusation against the people of Judah and Jerusalem." Verse 7 complicates matter further, since it records that "In the days of Artaxerxes [probably I, 464 - 423] ...Bishlam...wrote a letter to Artaxerxes." All these hostile approaches are supposed to have happened before the permission granted by Darius to build the Temple, in the second year of his reign (520) as subsequently recorded in Ezra 4: 24. In 6: 15, we read that "The Temple was completed...in the sixth year of the reign of king Darius [516]," but in v. 14 it is reported that "They finished building the Temple according...to the decrees of Cyrus, Darius and Artaxerxes [539 - 486, the first year of the latter's reign]." Either the different dates of the events are confused, or the names of the kings are confounded. A similar perplexity is evident in the names and titles of the presumed Davidic heir. In Ezra 1: 8 the political leader is Sheshbazzar, with the title הנשיא ליהודה, but in 5: 14 he is called פחה. It is assumed that Zerubabel is the Hebrew name of the same Sheshbazzar, which is his Persian name, but there is no logical explanation for this interchange of names. In Haggai, Zechariah and Nehemiah we encounter only the name Zerubabel, and in Hag. 1: 1 and 2: 21 his title is indicated as פחה. Nehemiah 12: 47, "So in the days of Zerubabel and of Nehemiah, all Israel contributed the daily portions for the singers ....," leaves us in perplexity; what happened in the interim period between Zerubabel, the time of the first migration (537) and Nehemiah's arrival in 445, or was there no great interval between the rule of Zerubabel and the dominion of Nehemiah? The confusion on these issues is evident, and cannot serve as a basis for historical examination. Even if we assume that certain actions by Zerubabel were deemed insurgent by the Persian authorities, this would justify his personal dismissal and replacement by another more loyal Israelite personality, a customary Persian solution to such crises in other parts of the Empire; it would certainly not be in the interests of the Persian authorities to concentrate all power in one hand in a conquered land. It therefore seems logical to exclude Persian influence in the consolidation of all power in the hand of the High Priest; we must assume this to be the result of internal circumstances, successfully concealed from future generations. A rabbinical homily in B. T. Sanhedrin 38a confuses the names and dates even further; we read there: זרובבל שנזרע בבבל ומה שמו נחמיה בן חכליה שמו "[His nickname

I also wish to hypothesize concerning the cessation of prophecy in Israel, and reiterate that this is based solely on analysis of the historical record of similar conditions, and on the examination of apparently oddly-timed circumstances. It is possible that the pre-eminence bestowed upon the sacrificial cult over and above righteous conduct, as well as its formalism, engendered reproach by "would-be prophets," with messages similar to some of the pre- and post-exilic prophets;[126] these were, however, probably silenced by the authorities, who disliked criticism of their most cherished vocations and doctrines; they would have acted in the same manner as certain of the kings who were also criticized by the prophets. The fact that prophecy ceased inexplicably just at that period[127] must lead us to contemplate that this sudden disappearance of a long tradition in Israel was not due to pure chance but was a consequence of particular conditions.

9.4.1 Decadence of the Priestly Class

As noted above, we have no textual evidence from the period between Ezra and Nehemiah and the Maccabees to enlighten us as to the practical and theological circumstances of the sacrificial system and its developmental stages and changes, except the P stratum of the Pentateuch and traces of

---

was] Zerubabel, because he was conceived [from the Hebrew root זרע 'semen'] in Babylon, but his [real] name was Nehemiah son of Hakaliah."

[126] See Zech. 7: 9 -14, in which the prophet declares that social evils were the reason for the destruction of the First Temple, and Mal. 3: 5.

[127] We encounter an interesting homily in Tosefta Sotah 13: 3: משמתו נביאים האחרונים חגי זכריה ומלאכי פסקה רוח הקודש מישראל ואע״פ כן היו משמיעין להן על בת קול "After the death of the last prophets, Haggai, Zechariah and Malachi, the holy spirit ceased [to be active] in Israel, but nevertheless [God] caused them to hear a *Bat Qol* [an inspiration from heaven, instructing on how to decide uncertain issues of the Law]." It is remarkable that prophecy is called here the "holy spirit"; after its cessation, the Rabbis had the assistance of a spiritual enlightenment. There is no amazement at or explanation for the cessation of prophecy, but another homily may implicitly offer an answer. We read in Y. T. Maqoth 2: 6, 32b: אילו ה׳ דברים שחסר מקדש אחרון ממקדש ראשון ואילו הן אש ארון אורים ותומים שמן המשחה ורוח הקודש "These five elements from the First Temple were missing in the Second Temple: The [perpetual] fire [on the holocaust altar, originally from heaven], the ark, the *Urim* and *Thumim*, the anointing oil, and the Holy Spirit." As we have observed from the previous homily, prophecy is linked to the holy spirit, and from this homily we may speculate that the absence of the ark, the throne of the Deity, caused the disappearance of the holy spirit, the source of prophecy. Cf. E. M. Meyers, "Second Zecharia and the 'End' of Prophecy," in *Pomegranates and Golden Bells, Studies in Biblical, Jewish, and Near Eastern Ritual, Law, and Literature in Honor of Jacob Milgrom*, pp. 713 - 723, who postulates that the teaching priest replaced the prophet in Judean society.

priestly editing of the other biblical segments. These writings indicate the prevailing situation, as postulated above. We may therefore refrain from elaborating on that period, and speculate about the conditions in Judah in the period just before the Maccabean revolt. As we observe from the Maccabean texts, and from recent historical research,[128] the crisis in Judah was not solely the result of the forced imposition of Hellenistic culture and rituals by the foreign governing authorities, but also the outcome of inner dissension within the Israelite community concerning the appropriate political, cultural and religious direction the people of Israel should embrace;[129] the Hellenizing faction was then supported by the Seleucids. We must also be astonished by the fact that the aristocracy of the priesthood, the High Priest and the Jerusalemite priestly clan, were so solidly infested with alien cultural influences.[130] The cynicism of the High Priests and the neglect of the sacrifices on the main altar in the Temple by the priests[131] cannot be reconciled with the great reverence toward the sacrificial ceremonies implied in the P stratum of the Bible. We must therefore assume that the corruption of the priestly class as a result of their unlimited power, and the accentuated formalism which overwhelmed the sacrificial system, engendered this cynicism and nihilistic attitude of the dominant group. This supposition obviously does not exclude that other interests,[132] as well as motives of both intellectual and political expediency, were also essential elements of this abatement in Israelite faith and traditions. I think, however, that the altered attitude toward the sacrificial system on the part of the priestly class, so emphasized in the Books of Maccabees, must be considered as a significant cause of the general shift in the heart of Israelite creed and custom.

---

[128] See: K. Bringmann, *Hellenistische Reform und Religionsverfolgung in Judäa* (Göttingen, 1983), pp. 97 - 140; E. Bickermann, *Der Gott der Makkabäer* (Berlin, 1937); M. Stern, יהדות ויוונות בא"י במאות השלישית והשנייה לפנס"ה, מדינת החשמונאים לתולדותיה על רקע התקופה ההלניסטית, קובץ מאמרים, ed. U. Rappaport and I. Ronen (Jerusalem, 1994), pp. 55 - 74, pp. 72 - 74.

[129] See I Macc. 1: 11 - 15, II Macc. 13: 4, and *Ant*. XII: 247, 252 and 384.

[130] The Book of Ecclesiasticus, which demonstrates great respect for the priestly functions and conduct, and was probably written before the Hasmonean revolt, does not serve as contrary evidence. According to M. Stern, p. 68, the Hellenization process in Judah was initiated only around 200 B. C. E.

[131] See II Macc. 4: 14 - 15.

[132] M. Stern, מרד החשמונאים ומקומו בתולדות החברה והדת היהודית, in מדינת החשמונאים pp. 507 - 517, asserts (p. 508) that the well-known House of Tobiah, which had noteworthy connections with the Judean aristocracy (Neh. 6: 17) and family liaisons with the High Priest (Neh. 13: 4 - 8), was one of the main promoters and agitators on behalf of the Hellenization process in Judah.

9.4.2 Maccabean Rebellion and the Restoration of Pious Sacrificial Celebrations

It is therefore no wonder that the counter-reaction to these conditions was headed by a subordinate provincial priestly family[133] and by simple and underprivileged[134] farmers, who adhered to the traditional values[135] and customs. These were the people far from the political and cult center in Jerusalem, who persisted in "the ways of their fathers,"[136] a phrase utilized by Josephus to express the tradition and laws of the Torah. Their first action after the liberation of Jerusalem was the resumption of the sacrificial cult; the new perpetual holiday in remembrance of the event was called ἐγκαινισμοῦ τοῦ θυσιαστηρίου "the consecration of the altar" (I Macc. 4: 59), not the consecration of the Temple.[137] Their passionate deliberations with respect to the fate of the holy stones of the old altar defiled by the Hellenists (4: 43 - 47) demonstrate the reverence bestowed upon the sacrificial cult and its furnishings. The Temple and the sacrificial ceremonies regained or even surpassed the previous significance and public reverence accorded them, and became the focal point of all the Jewish people in Israel and the Diaspora.

There are countless texts confirming this postulate, and I shall therefore limit myself to quoting some of the characteristic records. The *Letter of Aristeas*,[138] whose principal goal is the glorification of the Israelite faith and its source, the Torah, by illustrating the Ptolemeian king's interest in the Torah's translation, found it necessary to exalt the Temple and the most excellent manner of the sacrificial ceremonies performed there.[139] The king expressed his tangible appreciation for the translation of the Torah by

---

[133] See *Ant.* XII: 265, which emphasizes Modiin as some uncertain village, τις οἰκῶ ἐν Μωδαΐ κώμη.

[134] We read in I Macc. 2: 29 of those who joined the rebellion ζητοῦντες δικαιοσύνην καὶ κρίμα "seeking justice and judgment."

[135] In Macc. and more often in Josephus' writings, we encounter a new concept, τῶν πατρίων νόμων "the custom of the fathers," emphasizing tradition rather than the divine origin of the Law.

[136] Τοῖς πατρίοις ἔθεσι (*Ant.* XIV: 213); πάτριος νόμος (*Ant.* X: 11, XI: 231, XII: 300). Philo too uses the term πάτριος to express the traditional divine laws (*Ad Gaium* 117).

[137] It is remarkable that in the letter written by Demetrius to Jonathan (I Macc. 11: 34) the Jews are defined as τοῖς θυσιάζουσιν εἰς Ἱεροσόλυμα "those offering in Jerusalem"; this is their particular characteristic.

[138] I am aware that the dating of this letter is a matter of scholarly discussion, and some assumptions place it in the period before the Hasmonean revolt.

[139] *Letter of Aristeas*, 84 - 99.

fashioning and sending particularly luxurious furnishings for the Temple,[140] and funds for offering sacrifices.[141] When Herod attempted to pacify his people and earn their respect and friendship, he built a sumptuous Temple, and in consideration of the significance bestowed upon it by the people, he constructed the new Temple before destroying the old one to avoid any disruption in its ceremonies.[142] Philo dedicates parts of *The Special Laws* and *Moses* II[143] to an exact description of the sacrificial ceremonies and their allegorical significance and purpose. He also records that great amounts of donations were contributed to the Temple[144] from all over the Roman Empire.[145] Josephus also mentions[146] Diaspora contributions to the Temple, and the Roman extraordinary permit granted to the Jews. Jerusalem became the center of the Jewish people and the destination for great numbers of pilgrims,[147] or immigrants who came to live near the Temple.[148] Following in the steps of Josiah, the Hasmoneans entirely demolished the city of Samaria,[149] and its temple,[150] to ensure the exclusivity of the one and only Temple in Jerusalem.[151] The Sanhedrin, the highest court, was also in Jerusalem[152] in the Temple precinct, confirming Jerusalem as the religious,[153] political, legislative[154] and administrative[155] center.

---

[140] Ibid., 52 - 81.

[141] Ibid., 33.

[142] *Ant.* XV: 380 - 425.

[143] Philo, *The Special Laws* I: 66 - 75 (on the Temple); 79 - 161 (on the priests, Levites and their remuneration); 162 - 298 (on the sacrifices).

[144] ibid., 76 - 78; *Ad Gaium* 156 and 157.

[145] Philo, *Ad Gaium* 156, Cicero, *Pro Flacco*.

[146] *Ant.* XIV: 112 and 227; XVI: 166 and 312.

[147] See Philo, *The Special Laws* I, 69 - 70; *Ant.* XIV: 337, XVII: 214, XX: 106; *War* I: 253, II: 40 about חג השבועות; *War* II: 10, VI: 423 - 425 about פסח ; II : 515 about the Feast of Tabernacles.

[148] See Acts 2: 5 - 11.

[149] *Ant.* XIII: 281.

[150] Josephus does not explicitly record here the destruction of the Samaritan temple, but it is understood from the context. We know that there was severe competition between the two temples; *Ant.* XIII: 74 - 79 records the bitter quarrel before the Ptolemeian king regarding legitimacy, and its grim outcome.

[151] The prominence bestowed by the Hasmoneans upon the exclusivity of the Temple in Jerusalem, and its political undertone, are also evident from the narrative in *Ant.* XIII: 54. In Demetrios' letter to Jonathan on practical and political issues, he associates in one clause the annexation of three additional toparchies to Judah with the idea that no Jew should have another Temple than that in Jerusalem.

[152] The exact date of its institution is a matter of debate, but it was certainly not before the Hasmonean period.

9.4.3 Textual Evidence from the Apocrypha and Temple Scroll

The great significance of the sacrificial cult and the priesthood are emphasized in the apocryphal books of that period. In *The Testaments of the Twelve Patriarchs*, and particularly in *The Testament of Levi*, the angels also offer sacrifices to the Deity,[156] and Levi the son of Jacob was brought up into heaven and promised the priesthood.[157] In *The Book of Jubilees*, the sacrificial system as it appears in the P stratum of the Pentateuch[158] is retrojected to Noah[159] and to the Patriarchs,[160] to impute to it a primeval origin and an even greater significance than in the Bible. Most of the dissension between the Pharisees and Sadducees, as recorded in the Talmud,[161] refers to issues of the cult in the Temple, and demonstrate the significance granted to the sacrifices. Josephus also reports that the sacrificial celebrations in the Temple were performed according to the Pharisaic interpretation of the biblical rules,[162] and even when the Sadducees were in

---

[153] Mishnah Sanhedrin 11: 2 records three courts in the precinct of the Temple, with hierarchical authority. The highest court sat in the *Gazit* Chamber, לבית דין הגדול שבלשכת הגזית שממנו יוצאת תורה לכל ישראל "...from which the [final decision on how to interpret the] Torah went out to all of Israel." Jesus too taught in the Temple court, as we encounter so often in the N. T. (Matt. 21: 23; Mark 14: 49; Luke 20: 1; 21: 37).

[154] Hyrcanus presided over the Sanhedrin trying Herod for political murder (*Ant.* XIV: 168 - 70). According to B. T. Sanhedrin 14b, the establishment of the legislative center in Jerusalem was based on Josiah's command in Deut. 17: 8: וקמת ועלית אך המקום אשר יבחר ה' אלהיך בו "take them to the place the Lord your God will choose."

[155] We read in Tosefta Sheqalim 1: 1 that the representatives of the court were commissioned to repair the roads damaged by the rains and prepare them for the safe passage of the pilgrims before the holidays.

[156] *The Testament of Levi* 3: 6.

[157] Ibid., 5: 1 - 2.

[158] There is a distinction between the sin offering, a goat, of which only the fat is burned, and the *Olah*, the holocaust offering of other animals and birds. The auxiliary grain offering and libations as well as the addition of salt are recorded for Noah's offerings, exactly as in the P stratum of the Pentateuch, but are obviously absent in the parallel biblical account of Noah's sacrifice. The addition of incense mentioned in *The Book of Jubilees* (see next note) must have been the custom at special occasions, as practised by the sect of which the writer of this book was a member.

[159] *The Book of Jubilees* 6: 2 - 3. Adam and Enoch offered incense, as appears in 3: 27 and 4: 25.

[160] Ibid., 13: 4 and 9. In Gen. 12: 7 and 8 we read that Abraham built altars, but no sacrifices are mentioned.

[161] See J. Le Moyne, *Les Sadducéens* (Paris, 1972), Chapitre IX, "Domaine Liturgique et Rituel concernant l'Ensemble du Peuple," pp. 177 - 218.

[162] *Ant.* XVIII: 15.

power the Temple's ceremonies were carried out according to the Pharisaic rule.[163] The interpretation of the biblical rules on the sacrificial celebrations became a matter of great dissension in Israelite society[164] and we observe that *The Temple Scroll*, an entire codex, similar in language and structure to the Pentateuchal text, was created by members of a sect who so vehemently disputed the official interpretation of the biblical sacrificial rules that they devised this codex as the original divine text. One cannot exclude that the sacrificial issue was the reason for their split with the majority of the people. Josephus records in *War* I: 150 that at Pompeii's conquest of the Temple, the priests did not stop the celebration of the daily perpetual offerings despite the flood of arrows and stones, which killed them at the site of the altar. In *War* VI: 5,[165] he records that some priests died in the fire at the burning Temple; there is a marked difference between the self-sacrifice of the priests in this period and their neglect of the sacrificial celebrations preceding the Hasmonean rebellion. Finally, we may also observe the significance of the sacrificial system from The Epistle to the Hebrews.[166]

9.5 Sublimation and Substitution

9.5.1 Historical Roots

The utmost significance of the sacrificial cult with respect to practice and doctrine in the period preceding the destruction of the Second Temple is obvious from the above arguments, and it is therefore astonishing how briskly and successfully this cult was replaced in Israelite society by the unique custom of prayer; the established sacrificial ceremonial with its

---

[163] *Ant.* XVIII: 17. Y. T. Yoma 1: 5, 39a, confirms this phenomenon, and heightens its impact with a story of a Sadducee High Priest who performed the incense rite on the Day of Atonement according to the Sadducean rule, despite his father's admonition, and died in a horrible way after a few days.

[164] On the dissension between the Pharisees and Sadducees regarding the most important rite of the High Priest's annual entry into the Holy of Holies with the smoke of the incense, see Heger, *Incense*, pp. 216 ff.

[165] See also *Ant.* XIV: 65 - 68 in which Josephus quotes alien evidence in this respect.

[166] Heb. 4: 14 ; 5: 10; 6: 11 - 28; 9: 11 - 14, 23; 10: 14. The importance of the sacrifices is not put in question, or denied; on the contrary, it is enhanced in its significance by the exalted nature of the most perfect sacrifice, the synthesis of the High Priest and the sacrificial offering, generating a perpetual sacrifice of the highest order, thus making superfluous the continuous daily offerings. The function of the sacrificial rite in the relations between the Deity and humans remains unchanged, simply shifting to another format.

obligatory adjustments appropriate for particular days and events was smoothly and swiftly replaced by a parallel recital ceremonial. The subsequent segment of our study will attempt to comprehend the basis of this seemingly inconceivable evolution. Pursuing my previous thesis of a continuous line in the developmental stages of the sacrificial cult and its various ramifications from Ahaz through Josiah until Ezra and Nehemiah, I wish to proceed further in the same direction, and postulate that Josiah's reform facilitated the last stage of the sacrificial cult, and that is its disappearance. Every step in this long line of changes caused further modifications in the system and its underlying theology, and facilitated their approval by Israelite society in the respective periods.

The shift in the sacrificial system to the burning of offerings, accomplished by Ahaz, constituted the first step toward the sophistication of the process, through the conception of an alternative or replacement for the offering of food. However we consider this shift, we must conceive it as a revolutionary theological insight with respect to the essence of the Deity and the relations between God and man. The first breakthrough into ingrained beliefs and opinions is the most difficult, but then the way is open for further sophistication and refinement. The centralization of the cult carried out by Josiah had to undergo a much tougher logical and theological modification. Scholars[167] have argued about the purpose of this reform, its difficulties, chances for success, and its implications on the development of the cult.[168] Before the centralization, one must assume that the offerer himself performed all or part of the sacrificial celebration, as is clear from many scriptural narratives;[169] this included the slaughtering, to some extent, although this is the least significant element of the celebration.[170]

The centralization of the cult, the institution of a professional class of clergy for the ceremonial celebration of the sacrifices, and the consequent exclusion of laics from the actual performance of the sacrifices, had

---

[167] M. Noth, *The History of Israel*, transl. from German and revised by P. R. Ackroyd (London, 1960), pp. 276-7; G. Hölscher, "Komposition und Ursprung des Deuteronomiums," *ZAW* 40 (1922), pp. 161-255; K. Budde, "Das Deuteronomium und die Reform König Josias," *ZAW* 44 (1926), pp. 177-244.

[168] See Moshe Weinfeld, מיהושע עד יאשיהו (Jerusalem, 1992), pp. 156ff., and Heger, *Incense*, pp. 194 ff. on the implications of Josiah's reform.

[169] For an extended list of biblical quotations in this respect, see Heger, *Incense*, pp. 203-4, nn. 47 - 54.

[170] We read in Lev. 1: 5: ושחט את בן הבקר לפני ה' והקריבו בני אהרן הכהנים את הדם וזרקו את הדם על המזבח "He is to slaughter the young bull before the Lord, and then Aaron's sons the priests shall bring the blood and sprinkle it against the altar." See also R. Rendtorff, *Studien zur Geschichte des Opfers im Alten Israel*, Wissenschaftliche Monographien zum Alten und Neuen Testament (Neukirchen, 1967), p. 111.

obviously caused some erosion in the attitude of the people to the reformed sacrificial system. It had suddenly deprived the individual worshipper of his hitherto spontaneous and intimate numinous experience, to which he was accustomed at his offerings. A modified rationale and theology had to be provided to remedy this deficiency in the *modus operandi*. The revolutionary concept of performance by proxy in religious and cult matters, one of the most crucial reforms in religious behaviour and history, was successfully adapted[171] and applied to the sacrificial system,[172] and from there to an ever-increasing array of religious duties.[173] But at the same time the concept

---

[171] It is not within the scope of this study to examine when and where this substitution system was "invented". It seems to me that there is no indication of any such solution in the carrying out of any divine precept in the early scriptural writings, while the sacrificial code of the P stratum of the Pentateuch is evidently grounded on this principle. We read in Tosefta Ta'anith 3: 2: צו את בני ישראל ואמרת אליהם את קרבני לחמי לאשי "[It is written:] אי איפשר לומ' כל ישראל אלא מלמד ששלוחו של אדם כמותו 'Give this command to the Israelites and say to them: See that you present to me the food for my offerings made by fire [Num. 28: 2].' This is impossible [because the Israelites are not allowed to present the offerings themselves], but it teaches us that the delegate of a person is equal to himself." The earlier biblical narratives on offerings record their performance by the offerer himself.

[172] I do not believe that the anthropological notion of the sacrifice of an animal as a surrogate for the offerer should be considered in our study, since this conception does not apply to the period of our examination. As I declared at the beginning, I am not exploring the anthropological origins of the sacrifices.

[173] In some instances, a deed performed for someone by a delegate was deemed to absolve him from his personal duty. In other instances one act replaced another, see the passage cited in n.193, in which R. Tarfon considered the consumption of *Terumah* equal to the celebration of a sacrifice.

Like every new concept that widens its scope with time, this idea of substitution progressed and expanded. I shall indicate two noted examples: God commanded every father to circumcise his sons and so Abraham did (Gen. 17: 23; 21: 4); but now this rite is performed by a professional. Scripture commanded the sounding of the trumpets on the Feast of the Trumpets, ובחדש השביעי באחד לחדש מקרא קדש יהיה לכם יום... תרועה יהיה לכם "On the first day of the seventh month hold a sacred assembly...it is a day for you to sound the trumpets [Num. 29: 1]." The Rabbis in Mishnah Rosh Hashanah 4: 9 declare: כשם ששליח צבור חייב כך כל יחיד ויחיד חייב "Just as the 'Leader in Prayer' is obliged to blow the *shofar*, so is each individual"; however, רבן גמליאל אומר שליח צבור מוציא את הרבים ידי חובתן "Rabban Gamaliel says: the 'Leader in Prayer' discharges the public from their obligation." Jewish communities adopted Rabban Gamaliel's edict, illustrating the use of the principle which enables one person to perform a divine precept for another. The entire Jewish system of prayer in public is still based on the ancient custom of a "Leader in Prayer" who absolved the public from having to recite all the prayers. The people merely confirmed their association with the contents of the hymns and benedictions by the utterance *amen*. We read, in fact, in B.T. Berakhoth 53b the declaration of a Tanna that the proclaiming of *amen* is actually preferred to the saying of grace: רבי יוסי אומר גדול העונה אמן יותר מן המברך

of individual duty and deed was not suppressed or canceled or totally replaced in all respects by the actions of certain special clerics; the two systems existed together in a certain tension, as is the case with other issues. With respect to the sacrificial system, we observe that the professional clerics, the priests, with the assistance of a concept of a divinely-chosen genealogy, gained the upper hand and barely left to the offerer the slaughtering of the offering,[174] the most insignificant aspect both theologically and emotionally in that period. The priesthood developed into an intermediary body between God and the people, a notion totally incompatible with Israelite tradition and consciousness; a solution to this distressing condition would have to be devised.

9.5.2 Tension in Israel between the Individual and the Collective

The above-mentioned tension between the act of the individual and that of his representative or intermediary has a parallel with the conspicuous tension in Israel between the general duties and responsibilities of the individual and those of the collective. The divine decrees are usually directed to the people as a whole, but it is understood that the accomplishment of God's commands depends ultimately on the correct behaviour and performance of each individual member of the community. Israelite religion is a complex system; it is simultaneously a religion for the perfection of the individual and the perfection of the Israelite people, and one is totally dependent on the other.[175]

"Rabbi Jose says: The one who utters *amen* [when someone else pronounces the blessing after the meal] is more favoured than the one who pronounces the blessing." I would assume that the Christian Mass celebrated by the priest for the entire congregation is also related to the same principle of substitution.

[174] We do not need to elaborate on the issue of whether the sprinkling of the blood or the burning on the altar was considered the most lofty element of the sacrificial ceremony; it was certainly not the slaughter.

[175] Buddhism, as a contrasting example, is a religion exclusively adapted for the individual. Christianity has a universal messianic vision, but not to the extent of a definite responsibility of each person for the deeds of his brethren. This undivided and inevitable collective reward and punishment in the Israelite case is implicitly obvious from the style of the biblical text, and was explicitly declared in a homily in Song of Songs Rabbah, *Parshah* 7: ד"ה א [ח] זאת: כל ישראל ערבין אילין באילין דכתיב וכשלו איש באחיו"All Israelites are responsible one for another, as it is written 'They will stumble over one another [Lev. 26: 37].'" Another homily in Elijah Rabbah, *Parshah* 12 vividly and concretely portrays this abstract principle and compares it to ...לספינה שנקרעה בה בית אחד אין אומרים נקרע בית אחד בספינה אלא נקרעה כל הספינה כולה שנאמר הלוא עכן בן זרח מעל מעל בחרם ועל כל עדת ישראל היה קצף והוא איש אחד לא גוע בעונו "...a ship in which a part was torn off; one does not say that one part was torn off, but that the whole ship is damaged. The same is said [in Jos. 22:

The constant shifts in the biblical literary style between the singular אתה and the plural אתם in the divine addresses to the people should not be interpreted solely as a reminder of different origins, but as a manifestation of the dual character of God's commands to and expectations from both corporate and individual Israel. The conduct of the individual influences the fate of the community and vice-versa. This duality creates a constant tension in Israelite thought, and spurred many measures to alleviate or decrease the tension between the two apparently opposite poles.

It was therefore only natural that also with respect to the sacrificial *modus operandi* a dual system slowly evolved: the individual and the public offerings, to take into account both exigencies. I do not speak here of the communal sacrifices performed in the towns on special occasions, as for example in the presence of Samuel: זבח היום לעם בבמה "the people have a sacrifice at the high place [I Sam. 9: 12]"; these are not comparable at all to the public offerings of the daily *Tamid*, and similar fixed public offerings for every specific date and occasion. We do not know exactly when these public offerings, paid for by the public and performed for the whole of Israel, or the world,[176] were instituted, but we encounter the first signs of public financing of the sacrifices in Neh. 10: 33 - 34,[177] much after the centralization of the

---

20:] 'Akhan son of Zerah acted unfaithfully regarding the devoted things, did not wrath come over the whole community of Israel? He was not the only one who died for his sin.'"

[176] We read in B. T. Sukkah 55b: הני שבעים פרים כנגד מי כנגד שבעים אומות "What do the seventy oxen [offered during the seven days of the Feast of Tabernacles] represent? [They are offered for the sake] of the seventy nations [the *oikoumene*]." Rabbi Johanan further explains: בזמן שבית המקדש קיים מזבח מכפר עליהן "At the time of the Temple, the [sacrifices upon the] altar atoned for their sins." Another homily in Aboth of Rabbi Nathan ד א נוסח goes even further and declares: כל זמן שעבודת בית המקדש קיימת העולם מתברך על יושביו וגשמים יורדין בזמנן... ובזמן שאין עבודת בית המקדש קיימת אין העולם מתברך על יושביו ואין הגשמים יורדין בזמנן "As long as the celebration in the Temple continued, the world and its inhabitants were blessed and the rains fell in the appropriate period... but when there is no celebration in the Temple, the world and its inhabitants are not blessed and the rains do not fall in the appropriate period."

[177] These verses on the collection of the third shekel for the financing of the sacrifices were cited in n. 112. We observe that the prior passage on sacrifices in Ezra 3: 3 - 5 contains no indication of who offered the animals, but this does not imply that they were purchased through a public contribution, as in Nehemiah. One has the impression that the animals were donated; we may speculate that the ראשי האבות "heads of the families" who "gave freewill offerings" in the preceding pericope (Ezra 2: 68 - 69), also provided the animals *in naturalis*. The offerings of the kings, such as those of Solomon in Gibeon (I Kings 3: 4) or at the Temple's consecration (I Kings 8: 63) were their own sacrifices, not made on behalf of the public. The king's duty and right to celebrate the sacrifices, the more magnificent the better, was the custom in the surrounding cultures, particularly in

cult. The sophisticated public offering system, and its financing through a fixed and equal tax collected without distinction from every Israelite, was instituted principally to grant the people the sensation that they still participated personally in the sacrificial celebration. The centralization of the cult in Jerusalem and the shift of its performance from the offerer to the priest diminished the excitement of the sacrificial celebration for the individual who came to Jerusalem for that purpose, and eliminated any emotional devotion for those who could not come in person to the Temple from their distant homes. The surrogate public offerings were considered the right solution, but as further developments demonstrate, this was not to be the case.

Egypt, which was the model the king sought to emulate. At the Temple's consecration, the text specifies that the king's sacrifices and those of the people are entirely distinct. We read in I Kings 8: 62: 'והמלך וכל ישראל עמו זבחים זבח לפני ה "Then the king and all Israel with him offered sacrifices before the Lord." The list of Ahaz' sacrifices in II Kings 16: 15 does not contradict this postulate. As I have indicated in section 7.2, especially n. 110, scholarly opinion doubts the authenticity of this verse, and assumes it to be a post-exilic interjection; regardless of its origin, however, the text does not imply a public offering financed by the people. The expression in II Kings 16: 15: ואת עלת כל עם הארץ the burnt offering of all the people of the land," should rather be interpreted as an offering on behalf of the people, donated by the king, parallel to the עלת המלך "the burnt offering of the king," also donated by the king and celebrated according to the king's orders (בעל המאה הוא בעל הדעה or *Pecunia una regimen est rerum omnium*, Publilius Syrus, Sententiae). Even at the time of Ezekiel, the people donated land for the sanctuary, for the housing of the priests and the Levites, for the city, and for the prince (Ezek. 45:1 - 8). In the latter case the people were to offer a percentage of their animals and produce to the prince: זאת התרומה אשר תרימו "This is the special gift you are to offer [45: 13]," and it is later specified: כל העם הארץ יהיו אל התרומה הזאת לנשיא בישראל "All the people of the land will participate in this special gift for the use of the prince in Israel [45: 16]." But it was the prince, not the people, who donated the sacrificial offerings: ועל הנשיא יהיה העולות והמנחה והנסך בחגים ובחדשים ובשבתות בכל מועדי בית ישראל הוא יעשה את החטאת ואת המנחה ואת העולה ואת השלמים לכפר בעד בית ישראל "It will be the duty of the prince to provide the burnt offerings, grain offerings and drink offerings at the festivals, the New Moons and the Sabbaths - at all the appointed feasts of the house of Israel. He will provide the sin offerings, grain offerings, burnt offerings and fellowship offerings to make atonement for the house of Israel [45: 17]." It is interesting to note that according to a talmudic interpretation of *Megilat Ta'anith* in B. T. Menahoth 65a (I personally am not convinced of its authenticity), the Sadducees contested the Pharisaic decision that an individual could not donate the daily public *Tamid* offering. The Sadducees may have attempted to persist in an old tradition whereby the "aristocrats", like the "heads of families" noted in Ezra 2: 68 above, also contributed to the daily sacrifices.

9.5.3 The Distinction between the Roman and the Israelite Sacrificial Cults

It is not surprising that the impressive public ceremonials *en vogue* in the Roman world should have influenced the Israelite cult, and they certainly did so with respect to the external character of the Temple, its structure and furnishings, and the majestic celebrations of the sacrifices with all appropriate pageantry.[178] The many testimonies from rabbinical sources,[179] Josephus,[180] Philo[181] and the *Letter of Aristeas*[182] confirm this influence. We must observe, on the other hand, the great distinction between the Jewish and Roman philosophies underlying the sacrificial system, to understand the different paths in their particular development. Roman sacrificial ceremonies, as generally with the pagan cult, were closely tied to the state, serving exclusively to unify the people at special events; participation at the celebrations "turned into a symbol of political loyalty, especially because of its emperor worship."[183] The Roman sacrifice was entirely a public ceremony, requiring no spiritual emotion on the part of the individual who participated in the general celebration, whereas the individual Israelite offering intensified the offerer's inherent enthusiasm. Even the Israelite public sacrifice, given its primeval origin in an individual offering, was supposed to manifest the numinous excitement of all Israelites, who had donated the funds for it. The introduction of the sin offering into the Israelite cult, a sacrifice unknown in the Roman world, may also have been instigated by a similar purpose, to grant the individual Israelite an appropriate ritual for personal spiritual exaltation.[184]

This significant difference in the philosophical perspective toward the sacrificial celebrations conditioned the divergent course of sacrifice in the

---

[178] Mishnah Tamid 7: 3 portrays the completion of the daily *Tamid* ceremony as involving the waving of flags, blowing of horns, playing of musical instruments, and songs by the Levite chorus. The climax of the ceremonial on the Day of Atonement, with the participation of the people and the splendour of the High Priest's special garments, is described in Mishnah Yoma chap. 3.

[179] We read in B. T. Sukkah 51b: מי שלא ראה בית המקדש בבנינו לא ראה בנין מפואר מעולם "Whoever has not seen the Temple standing has never seen a magnificent building."

[180] *War* V: 184 - 237.

[181] Philo, *The Special Laws* I: 72; *Ad Gaium* 157, 191.

[182] Particularly 83 - 99.

[183] D. Rokeah, *Jews, Pagans and Christians in Conflict* (Leiden, 1982), p. 15.

[184] The introduction of this unique Israelite offering may also have been induced by the desire to grant the priests the entire body of the sin offering, in contrast to the burnt offering; with respect to the latter, the priests received only the hide, according to a later decree referring to the *asham* in Lev. 7: 8.

two cultures. The Roman sacrificial system continued its rituals despite the loss of its pagan religious vitality,[185] whereas the Israelites discontinued the sacrificial celebrations after the destruction of the Temple, but in a period of heightened spiritual awareness and enormous religious creativity. This apparent paradox can be explained: the shallow Roman ritual disappeared entirely with the downfall of its executive system, the source of its implementation, but the Israelite ritual, founded on an ingrained emotionally-driven tradition, survived in its inherent essence, and was replaced solely in its external manifestation, by recital and prayer. The previous stage of substitution in the sacrificial system, the equalization of the prime mover, the donor of the offering, with the actual performer, slowly developed to a more subtle and almost abstract conception: the spiritual identification with a religious performance along with relevant oral expression become equivalent to actual performance by the celebrant, and provide the devotee with the same inner exaltation as the actual celebration. These evidently were the stages of development in the Israelite cult, from the reform of Ahaz until the ultimate substitution by the Sages of prayer for sacrifice.[186] In order to better understand the last radical stage, a number of issues should be examined.

9.5.4 Were There Sacrifices after the Destruction of the Second Temple?

Although the examination of this issue is chronologically out of order, it is imperative to first verify that in fact the sacrificial cult was not performed in Israel after the destruction of the Temple, and that this was due to an internal decision of the rabbinical authorities, and not imposed by the Roman conqueror. Following the destruction of the Temple, no Roman edict was enacted barring the Jews from Jerusalem, as in the later period of the Bar-Kokhba rebellion. The offering of sacrifices was certainly not prohibited by the Roman authority at that period after the Temple's destruction; however, the discussion is not based solely on *ex silentio* argument but is

---

[185] Julian the Apostate (Roman emperor 361 - 363 C. E.) reintroduced the pagan sacrificial cult, after its cessation through Christian influence and Constantine's declaration of Christianity as the official Roman religion. In his polemic treatise *Contra Galileos*, Julian confutes Christianity's abolition of the sacrifices, and affirms that the Jews still adhered to sacrifice in principle, though not in practice as they were deprived of the Temple (D. Rokeah, *Jews, Pagans and Christians in Conflict*, pp. 27 - 33).

[186] We read in Num. Rabbah, *Parshah* 18: 21: ד"ה ונשלמה פרים שפתינו אמרו ישראל
רבש"ע בזמן שבהמ"ק קיים היינו מקריבים קרבן ומתכפר ועכשיו אין בידינו
אלא תפלה "'That we may offer the fruit of our lips [Hos. 14: 3; v. 2 in KJV].' Israel said to the Lord of the World: When the Temple was standing, we offered a sacrifice and were forgiven, but now we have only prayer [to achieve the same purpose]."

confirmed by a number of rabbinical narratives[187] whose authenticity we have no reason to doubt. Scholars have also vigorously debated[188] whether sacrifices continued to be performed in Jerusalem. Those scholars who answer in the affirmative base their position on two points: the fact that there was no restriction imposed by the Romans on the performance of sacrifices on the one hand, and the logical assumption that sacrifices should continue to be celebrated by the Jews because of the great significance of the sacrificial cult.[189] I wish to add to the debate by noting a rabbinical statement that one may offer sacrifices without a permanent Temple,[190] as well as a specific and explicit scriptural record that the returnees from exile had in fact done this.[191] I nevertheless contend, as do many others,[192] that the rabbinical authority deliberately discontinued the sacrificial cult. We have no explicit declaration that sacrifices should not be performed, but neither is there any record that they were celebrated. The evidence to prove positively that something was accomplished must, in principle, be stronger than a negative postulate that something was not done. The lack of such evidence in itself should tip the scale toward the assumption of the absence of sacrifices in the period under discussion, but we also possess many indications from various narratives and rabbinical rules which indirectly but circumstantially attest to such absence.

---

[187] See S. Safrai, העליה לרגל לירושלים לאחר חורבן בית שני in פרקים בתולדות ירושלים בימי בית שני, ספר זיכרון לאברהם שליט pp. 376 - 393, who quotes rabbinical rules and narratives on carrying tithes to Jerusalem and visits of pilgrims after the destruction of the Temple. We also encounter in Aboth of Rabbi Nathan נוסחא א פרק ד the comments of Rabbi Johanan ben Zakkai and Rabbi Joshua, Tannaim living at the time of the destruction of the Temple, who visited Jerusalem, and saw it in ruins. There is a similar narrative in Sifrei Deut. *Pisqa* 43 about Rabban Gamaliel, Rabbi Joshua, Rabbi Eleazar ben Azariah and Rabbi Akiba, who visited the Temple Mount, viewed the desolation and saw a fox running out from the site of the Holy of Holies.

[188] See n. 1.

[189] K. W. Clark writes on p. 11: "It would be inconceivable that Jews would make no effort to return to Temple worship at the end of the First Revolt."

[190] We read in B.T. Zebahim 62a: שלשה נביאים עלו עמהם מן הגולה אחד שהעיד להם על המזבח ואחד שהעיד להם על מקום המזבח ואחד שהעיד להם שמקריבין אף על פי שאין בית "Three prophets returned with them [the exiles] from the exile, one who testified about the [structure] of the altar, one on its [exact] site, and one who testified that sacrifices are offered even if there is no Temple [yet built]."

[191] Ezra 3: 6: מיום אחד לחדש השביעי החלו להעלות עלות לה' והיכל ה' לא יסד "On the first day of the seventh month they began to offer burnt offerings to the Lord, though the foundation of the Lord's Temple had not yet been laid."

[192] See S. Safrai, ארץ ישראל מחורבן בית in התאוששות היישוב היהודי בדור יבנה שני ועד הכיבוש המוסלמי, היסטוריה מדינית, חברתית ותרבותית (Jerusalem, 1982), Vol. I, pp. 18 - 39, with particular emphasis on the cessation of the sacrificial cult (pp. 28-29).

There is, for example, textual evidence that the priests received and ate the special priestly tithe *Terumah*,[193] and this was perceived as if they had offered the daily perpetual *Tamid* sacrifice. This evidence indicates that a) the cult routine other than the sacrifices, such as the priestly privileges, was effective for a certain time after the destruction of the Temple, and is documented in the rabbinical literature, and b) the *Tamid* offering was not performed, and the priestly consumption of the *Terumah* was considered a substitute.

9.5.4.1 The Particular Character of the Passover Sacrifice

Some scholars[194] have attempted to deduce from a passage in Mishnah Pesahim 7: 2[195] that at least the Passover lamb continued to be sacrificed after the Temple's destruction; G. Allon,[196] however, has already demonstrated that this citation refers to the preparation of a roasted kid for consumption on

---

[193] There are a number of talmudic narratives about Rabbi Tarfon, a priest who lived during and after the Temple's destruction, who ate *Terumah*. From these narratives we gain a perspective on how *Terumah* was perceived. We read in Sifrei Zuta, *Pisqa* 18: אמרו עליו על רבי טרפון שהיה אוכל תרומה בשחר ואומר הקרבתי תמיד של שחר ואוכל תרומה בין הערבים ואומר הקרבתי תמיד של בין הערבים "They recounted about Rabbi Tarfon that he ate *Terumah* at dawn and said: 'I have offered the *Tamid* [the daily perpetual offering of Num. 28: 4] of the morning,' and ate *Terumah* in the evening and said: 'I offered the *Tamid* of the twilight.'" There is another record to the same effect in Tosefta Hagigah 3: 33, and an even more remarkable narrative in B. T. Pesahim 72b-73a: מעשה ברבי טרפון שלא בא אמש לבית המדרש לשחרית מצאו רבן גמליאל אמר לו מפני מה לא באת אמש לבית המדרש אמר לו עבודה עבדתי אמר לו כל דבריך אינן אלא דברי תימה וכי עבודה בזמן הזה מנין אמר לו הרי הוא אומר עבדת מתנה אתן את כהנתכם והזר הקרב יומת עשו אכילת תרומה בגבולין כעבודת בית המקדש "It occurred that Rabbi Tarfon had not come to the college the day before. Rabban Gamaliel [the chief of the college] met him and asked him the reason for his absence the day before. He replied: I performed priestly duty. Said Rabban Gamaliel: Your statement is bizarre; is there any priestly performance at this time [without the Temple]? He answered: It says: 'I am giving you the priesthood as a gift. Anyone else who comes near the sanctuary must be put to death.' The eating of the *Terumah* in the provinces is made equal to the celebration in the Temple." The Rabbis thus attempted to interpret a biblical verse to substitute the priestly consumption of the tithe for the offering of sacrifices.

[194] K. W. Clark, pp. 272ff.

[195] We read in Mishnah Pesahim 7: 2: מעשה ברבן גמליאל שאמר לטבי עבדו צא וצלה לנו את הפסח על האסכלה "It happened that Rabban Gamaliel said to his servant Tabi: Go and roast for us the Passover [kid] on the grill."

[196] G. Allon, תולדות היהודים בא"י בתקופת המשנה והתלמוד (Tel Aviv, 1967), pp. 164 - 166.

Passover eve, solely as a memorial of the real sacrifice, similar to the eating of matzoth and bitter herbs on that occasion.[197] The various rabbinical discussions on this roasted kid demonstrate that the Rabbis were extremely careful to avoid suggesting that the preparation of the kid be considered a Passover sacrifice,[198] whose performance they had prohibited. This attitude stands in contrast to other specific ceremonies in the Temple, such as the sounding of the *shofar* and the taking of the *lulav* on Sabbath; regarding these, Rabban Johanan ben Zakkai decreed that one might act in Yabneh in the same way one acted in the Temple. It was only with respect to the preparation of a kid on Passover that the sages were extremely careful to avoid any similarity to the Temple offering, so as to dissociate this rite from the idea of sacrifice.

One must doubt in any event whether the Passover communal meal should be perceived as a regular sacrifice. According to the pentateuchal decrees[199] the eating of the Passover lamb is a purely communal affair, and there is no indication of a celebration at a sanctuary with the usual sprinkling of blood and burning of fat on the altar;[200] only in Deut. do we encounter the

---

[197] It is obvious from another rabbinical narrative on the same topic that Rabban Gamaliel did not intend to demonstrate by his conduct that one is required to roast such a kid to fulfill the divine precept; he thought on the contrary that one is allowed to do so if one wishes in order to exhibit on the festive table the three principal components of the Passover saga. We read in Mishnah Beitzah 2: 7: אף הוא אמר שלשה דברים להקל ...ועושין גדי מקולס בלילי פסחים וחכמים אוסרין "He [Rabban Gamaliel] also proclaimed three lenient dicta ...one roasts a kid on the eve of Passover, but the Sages prohibit [it]." As the Sages contradicted Rabban Gamaliel's decision, we must assume that the people acted according to their resolution, since law and custom are determined by the opinion of the majority against the views of an individual Rabbi, whatever his status. Another discussion on this issue in B. T. Beitzah 23a confirms that this "roasted kid" was eaten in the Diaspora, but was certainly not considered as the Passover sacrifice, which had to be eaten only in Jerusalem (Deut. 16: 1 - 7). We read there that Todos of Rome advised the Roman community to eat a roasted kid on Passover eve, and was criticized for this because שאתה מאכיל את בני ישראל כעין קדשים בחוץ "You make them eat something similar to the holy sacrifices outside [Jerusalem]."

[198] According to rabbinical interpretation, the blood of the Passover sacrifice had to be sprinkled on the altar and its fat burned upon it. See Mishnah Pesahim 5: 6 and 10.

[199] Exod. 12: 1- 28, 43 - 50; 23: 18; 34: 25; Lev. 23: 5-8; Num. 9: 1 - 14; 28: 16 - 25; Deut. 16: 1- 8.

[200] Although in Ezra 6: 20 we encounter for the first time the attendance of priests at the Passover celebrations, a fact which is not surprising after the centralization of the cult in Jerusalem, there is as yet no mention of any sprinkling of blood and burning of fat; only the slaughtering by the priests and Levites is recorded. H. Albeck in his Commentary to the Mishnah ששה סדרי משנה, סדר מועד (Tel Aviv - Jerusalem, 1952), p. 139, assumes that from the narrative in II Chr. 35: 14, כי הכהנים בני אהרן בהעלות העולה והחלבים עד לילה "Because the priests, the descendants of Aaron, were

command to perform the sacrifice "in the place he will choose as a dwelling for his Name."[201] We do not know when, if ever, the rabbinical rule to sprinkle the blood and burn the fat was applied, and therefore we must consider it as a celebration *sui generis*, which did not affect other, real sacrifices. It is remarkable that the Samaritans, who also abolished the offering of sacrifices after the destruction of their temple on Mount Gerizim, still celebrate the Passover celebration in this place, their understanding of "the place the Lord will choose" in Deut. 16: 2. It is not perceived as a regular sacrifice, for whose performance an altar is required; they simply slaughter the animals and roast them on the fire before eating, without any sprinkling of blood or burning of fat. Even in rabbinical literature we note some hesitation in considering the Passover celebration as a regular sacrifice.[202] Therefore any attempted deduction from the Passover celebration

---

sacrificing the burnt offerings and the fat portions until nightfall," one may deduce that the offered fat originated from the Passover animals, but I am contesting such an assumption. The relevant pericope in II Chr. 35 also records donations of cattle by the king (v. 7) and by the officials (vv. 8 - 9). Scripture does not inform us of the use of these cattle, which according to the rules in Exod. 12: 3 - 5 and 21, are not appropriate for the Passover (though in Deut. 16: 2, on the other hand, we read that the Passover animal should be slaughtered צאן ובקר "from your flock or herd"). At any rate, though some of the animals must have been utilized for the burnt offerings (v. 12), I suggest that some were definitely offered as *Shelamim*, just to feed the masses with meat. We read in v. 13: ויבשלו הפסח באש כמשפט והקדשים בשלו בסירות ובדודים ובצלחות ויריצו לכל בני העם "They roasted the Passover animals over the fire as prescribed, and boiled the holy offerings in pots, cauldrons and pans and served them quickly to all the people." We observe two distinct types of offerings and two explicitly different methods of cooking. Hence, we must assume that the קדשים boiled in pots and pans, a process not appropriate for the Passover animal, refer to *Shelamim*, whose meat was served to the people, and whose fat was burnt on the altar according to Lev. 3: 3. It is this fat that is mentioned in the above-cited v. 14, not the fat of the Passover. There is no scriptural suggestion of the sprinkling of the blood and burning of the fat of the Passover animal. The traditional commentator Ramban in his comments to Deut. 16: 2 also interprets the expression והקדשים in II Chr. 35: 13 as referring to animals slaughtered to provide meat to feed the masses.

[201] In II Kings 23: 21 - 23 it is explicitly recorded that such a Passover in Jerusalem was celebrated for the first time since the time of the Judges.

[202] Tosefta Pesahim 4: 14 and B. T. Pesahim 66a record a dilemma of the Rabbis concerning whether one is allowed to supersede the Sabbath law for the slaughtering of the Passover animal when the fourteenth of Nisan occurs on Sabbath. They asked Hillel: כלום אתה יודע אם הפסח דוחה את השבת אם לאו "Do you know whether the Passover supersedes the Sabbath?" And his answer was: מה מועדו האמור בתמיד דוחה את השבת אף מועדו האמור בפסח דוחה את השבת "Just as the term 'at the appointed time' appears with respect to the *Tamid* [Num. 28: 2], and [this offering] supersedes the Sabbath, similarly the same term which appears at the Passover [Num. 9: 2] affirms that it supersedes the Sabbath." We need not assume the full authenticity of the narrative, but

with respect to the continuation of sacrifices after the Temple's destruction would be groundless. We must conclude that those rules which had some connection to the Temple and its rituals and which continued to be practised after the Temple's destruction[203] are discussed in the rabbinical literature, but the offering of sacrifices was totally abolished, and therefore we find no record in this literature.

9.5.5 Rabbinical Perspective after the Temple's Destruction - Jerusalem Versus Yabneh

We should now approach other aspects of the rabbinical attitude toward Jerusalem as a cult center after the Temple's destruction. Rabbi Johanan ben Zakkai, the governing נשיא, Patriarch, at the time of its destruction, was primarily responsible for laying the foundation of Jewish life and practice in all its political and religious aspects, including the attitude to Jerusalem, the Temple and its ceremonies. We should therefore examine his viewpoints, based on the rabbinical narratives of his actions and accomplishments, and his rules *ex cathedra* with respect to the religious status of Jerusalem and all that it represented in Jewish faith and procedure. His first and foremost action, which brought him to the leadership of the people of Judah, was his platform to end the war and negotiate a compromise with the Romans, or rather a *modus vivendi* in the light of the new conditions. B. T. Gittin 56a-b describes how he was smuggled out of the besieged city of Jerusalem, his encounter and dialogue with Vespasian which gained him the Roman commander's goodwill, and his three petitions which were granted. These are well known: תן לי יבנה וחכמיה ושושילתא דרבן גמליאל ואסוותא דמסיין ליה לרבי צדוק "Grant me Yabneh and its Sages, and [save] the dynasty of Rabban Gamaliel, and [provide] physicians for Rabbi Zadok." The ideological implications of the first request on the future development of the Jewish people, whether as a regular national entity or as a religious

---

it obviously demonstrates the difference between the Passover celebration and the regular offerings in the view of the Rabbis, and the hesitation against profaning the Sabbath for its slaughtering.

[203] As we have seen above the *Terumah* was eaten by the priests, and from many citations we note that the strict laws of purity were observed long after the Temple's destruction. See, e.g. Tosefta Demai 2: 2; B. T. Sabbath 43a; Pesahim 34a. We have no record that the Red Heifer was prepared after the Temple's destruction, though its preparation would not in itself attest to the continuation of regular sacrifices, being *sui generis*; but the Rabbis still had a supply of the purifying water. We read in Mishnah Parah 7: 6 that a man came three times to Yabneh to inquire about the suitability of some element for the purifying solution, that had not been handled properly; it was finally cleared for use, through a special procedure, probably because of its scarcity.

community with purely spiritual goals, are much debated, and are not of concern in our study.

On the other hand, the immediate impact of these requests on the status of Jerusalem and its hub, the Temple and the cult, is of considerable interest. We need not presume that the details of the story of the meeting are authentic, but they do indicate how the Rabbis perceived Rabban Johanan's objective. He aspired to show the Romans that there were Jews who wished to stop the fighting, and to obtain from them some concessions. His pleading for the Gamaliel dynasty had a political undertone, since the acting Nasi, Rabban Simeon ben Gamaliel, was perceived by the Romans as a leader of the rebellion and was executed. The request for Yabneh and its Sages was not to save their lives - no such peril endangered them - but also contained a political purpose, the survival of an autonomous legal system; in view of the prevailing conditions in Judah, this also ensured the continuation of authority on the religious status and future development of Judaism. From the examination of Rabban Johanan's edicts, we observe that he walked a very fine line. On the one hand, he attempted to preserve a reminiscence of the previous rituals connected to the Temple, but on the other hand he promulgated practical regulations to strengthen Yabneh as the main spiritual and legal center, without temple and ceremonies, over the prior dominant status of Jerusalem.[204] These were the theories and procedures of Rabban

---

[204] We find a great number of rules and regulations enacted by Rabban Johanan in this respect. Mishnah Rosh Hashanah 4: 1 tells us that previously one sounded the *shofar* only in the Temple when the New Year occurred on a Sabbath day; after the Temple's destruction, it was decreed by Rabbi Johanan that the *shofar* could be sounded in every town in which there was a court (or only in Yabneh, according to another opinion). It is interesting to note the forcefulness used by Rabban Johanan to impose his ideas against the opposing opinions of other Rabbis, who were probably unwilling to agree to such a sweeping replacement of Jerusalem with Yabneh. We read in B. T. Rosh Hashanah 29b: פעם אחת חל ראש השנה להיות בשבת אמר להם רבן יוחנן בן זכאי לבני בתירה נתקע אמרו לו נדון אמר להם נתקע ואחר כך נדון לאחר שתקעו אמרו לו נדון אמר להם כבר נשמעה קרן ביבנה ואין משיבין לאחר מעשה "It happened that Rosh Hashanah occurred on a Sabbath day [and before the Temple's destruction it was prohibited to sound the *shofar* on a Sabbath day, except in the Temple, and one did not know how to proceed in Yabneh]; Rabban Johanan said to the sons of Beteirah [of the Nasi's clan]: Let's sound [the *shofar*]! [But] they said: Let's discuss it! He said to them: We shall sound first and then discuss. After sounding [the *shofar*], they said: Let's discuss! He said: One has already heard the *shofar* in Yabneh [on a Sabbath day] and it is now a *fait accompli*, and there is no need to discuss it anymore." As recorded in B. T. Sukkah 41a, he also ruled according to the same principle regarding the use of the *lulav* "palm fronds" (Lev. 23: 40) on the Feast of Tabernacles when it occurred on a Sabbath day. In Tosefta Parah 7: 4 we learn: הלכה זו עלו עליה בני אסייה שלשה רגלים ליבנה ברגל השלישי הכשירו להן "People from Asia went on three pilgrimages to Yabneh to inquire about a legal matter, and at the third pilgrimage it was declared suitable." The term שלשה רגלים is utilized in this passage and in others, possibly

Johanan, which effected the cessation of the sacrificial system, without an explicit declaration to this effect. This paradox, the equating of the symbol to the actual ritual and the creation of realistic reforms to replace such ritual in practice, is a continuation of the previously applied theory of substitution, and the pillar of Jewish religious philosophy and custom. The ancient traditions were thus preserved,[205] but daily conduct was adapted to the current necessities of life in its political, economic and spiritual aspects. We must at the same time comprehend that Rabban Johanan, who accomplished this consequential reform at one of the most critical periods in the development of Israelite religious thought and conduct, had no power and authority to constrain all the spiritual leaders of the people to accept his philosophy. Thus although generally this line of thought prevailed, both extreme shifts and slight modifications did occur from time to time.

---

implying that people went three times yearly as pilgrims to Yabneh, instead of as previously to Jerusalem. We also observe a socio-linguistic adaptation to the enhanced status of Yabneh. In many occurrences in the Talmud we encounter such expressions as כך היינו נוהגין ביבנה "This is what we practised in Yabneh [Tosefta Rosh Hashanah 2: 11]," כך פרשו חכמים ביבנה "This is how the Sages interpreted [it] in Yabneh [B. T. Nidah 15a]," or לא היינו נוהגין כן ביבנה "We did not so proceed in Yabneh [Y. T. Rosh Hashanah 4:6, 59c]." The religious-legal decisions taken in Yabneh were put in the foreground, indicating its prominent status.

[205] As we have seen, the observance of many precepts continued, including the sounding of the *shofar* and the taking of the *lulav* זכר למקדש "as a remembrance to the Temple [B. T. Sukkah 41a]." But the Sages also took care to preserve the hope of rebuilding the Temple, and promulgated appropriate regulations. In B. T. Rosh Hashanah 30a we read that after the destruction of the Temple, it was prohibited to eat from the new harvest during the entire day when the wave offering of the sheaf used to be brought to the Temple, although the ceremony was no longer performed, and its consumption should have been permitted at dawn. This was done because מהרה יבנה בית המקדש ויאמרו אשתקד מי לא אכלנו בהאיר מזרח עכשיו נמי ניכול "...soon the Temple will be built, and they [the people] may say: Didn't we eat already at dawn [from the new harvest]? Let us also eat now!" That is, if the Temple were operational consumption would not be permitted before the offering was performed, and therefore to avoid the possibility of such an erroneous consideration, Rabban Johanan decreed this regulation. Other rules were pronounced with the same justification; for instance, B. T. Beitzah 5b concerning an egg laid on a holy day; Keritoth 9a concerning dedicating money for a proselyte's sacrifice. In other instances, ancient customs were maintained with the above justification זכר למקדש "as a remembrance to the Temple" – for instance, in addition to the *shofar* and *lulav*: keeping the High Priest awake the night before the Day of Atonement (Tosefta Yoma 1: 9), the custom of eating matzah and bitter herbs together (B. T. Pesahim 115a), and the counting of the days of the *omer* (B. T. Menahoth 66a). In B. T. Rosh Hashanah 30a an obligation to perform deeds in remembrance of the Temple is derived from a midrashic interpretation of Jer. 30: 17.

9.6 The Replacement of Sacrifices

Though we may understand in theory the rabbinical philosophy with respect to the abolition of the sacrifices, we are still left in amazement at the speed, seemingly instantaneous, with which the Rabbis succeeded in obtaining the consent of the people to the cessation in practice of the sacrificial worship, so revered until then, and its replacement with symbolic performance. I wish to postulate a double-pronged thesis: a) the substitution theory in its different aspects and manifestations was already an established facet of Israelite religious fashion, and b) the organization required for the implementation of such substitution with respect to sacrificial ritual was already in place. I need not elaborate on the substitution theory, amply argued in section 9.5, and I shall therefore limit myself to demonstrating this additional step in its enhancement and refinement, which laid the foundation for the creation of the synagogue and the final vanishing of the sacrificial ritual and its replacement with a symbolic routine. Scholars admit that we have no textual or other valid evidence on either the philosophical basis or development in practice of the synagogue, other than the late rabbinical literature. We rely on speculations grounded on logical interpretation of texts and events from preceding and succeeding periods. I shall thus propose a plausible set of circumstances to explain the roots of this extraordinary phenomenon, the institution of daily fixed prayers in Israelite religion.

9.6.1 Recitals of Corresponding Biblical Verses in the Synagogues

Nehemiah's idea that donations might substitute for the individual's excitement at his personal offering of a sacrifice was not effective, and we read in Mishnah Ta'anith 4: 2 the question וכי היאך קרבנו של אדם קרב והוא אינו עומד על גביו "Is it conceivable that a person's sacrifice is offered and he does not stay near it?" Therefore, declares the Mishnah, the ancient prophets[206] divided the land and the people into twenty-four districts and corresponding assemblies for the organization of the sacrificial worship in the Temple, and further: הגיע זמן המשמר לעלות כהנים ולוים עולים לירושלם וישראל שבאותו משמר מתכנסין לעריהן וקוראין במעשה בראשית "When the [allocated] time of each assembly arrived, the priests and Levites went up to Jerusalem, and the [corresponding] Israelites of the assembly gathered in their towns and read [the biblical pericopes about] the creation of the world."

---

[206] We certainly do not have to assume the authenticity of this utterance, which follows the common custom of retrojecting later adaptations and attributing them to earlier personalities.

The Gemara asks the reason for this particular reading, and makes the creation of the world contingent upon the offering of sacrifices. A homily follows, declaring that God promised Abraham at the Covenant of the Dismembered Animals (Gen. 15) to act with consideration toward his descendants after the Temple's destruction: כבר תקנתי להם סדר קרבנות כל זמן שקוראין בהן מעלה אני עליהן כאילו מקריבין לפני קרבן ומוחל אני על כל עונותיהם "I have already set up the order of the sacrifices; whenever they [will] read them, I will consider it as if they offer the sacrifices [in practice] and will pardon their sins." The groups thus read the pericopes of the sacrifices and of the creation. We observe the Rabbis' doctrine that the offering of sacrifices could be replaced by the recitation of the corresponding biblical pericopes. It is the same principle that induced them to organize the people in assemblies during the time of the Temple to recite the appropriate biblical pericopes, and thus gain the same spiritual excitement as if they had been actually present at the ceremony.[207] As summarized in the rabbinic homily on ונשלמה פרים שפתינו (Hos. 14: 3, cited in section 9.5.4), the performance of the recital[208] was equated to the performance of the sacrifice, and offered the perfect solution for the new circumstances.[209]

---

[207] We encounter in Midrash Tanhuma *Parshah* 96 *siman* 14 צו ד"א (יד) ד"ה ד"ה a number of homilies connecting the recital of biblical pericopes with sacrifice. The following is representative: למה אמר זאת תורת העלה ירצה לומר קריאת תורה ראו כמה חביבה קריאת תורה לפני הקב"ה... שיאמרו לבני ישראל ויתעסקו בקריאת העולה שאע"פ שמקריבין עולה היו בקריאתה כדי שיזכו בקרבן עולה ובקריאתה "Why is it written: 'These are the regulations [the homily is on the term *torah*] for the burnt offering [Lev. 6:2; v. 8 in KJV]'? This means: the reading of the Torah; look how the reading of the Torah is loved by God...the Israelites should be told that they should be engaged with the reading of the *Olah* [pericope] at the same time as they offer the sacrifice, so that they will benefit from both the offering and the reading."

[208] This custom could be connected to the ancient manner of reciting mythical epics at the sanctuaries, on the occasion of feasts and days of remembrance. We should also consider the power of the spoken word in Israelite mythology. In Genesis God created the world, not by deed but by utterance; creation starts with the expression ויאמר אלהים יהי אור ויהי אור "And God said: Let there be light, and there was light [Gen. 1: 3]," and so on with respect to each further step. (At the completion of the creation this term could not be used for philological reasons, and we read [1: 31]: וירא אלהים את כל אשר עשה "God saw all he had made [by His utterances]"; here it was necessary to use the term עשה "to do.") An interesting homily in Genesis Rabbah, *Parshah* 17, (יח) ד"ה ב declares: בעשרה מאמרות נברא העולם ויאמר "...with ten utterances the world was created," and enumerates them; a similar idea is found in Ps. 33: 6: בדבר ה' שמים נעשו וברוח פיו כל צבאם "By the word of the Lord were the heavens made, their starry host by the breath of his mouth." God's intervention in the world is also performed through his word, as evidenced by the following expressions in Ps. 147: השלח אמרתו

9.6.2 A Delayed and Unexpected Consequence of Josiah's Reform

The organization of the assemblies or synagogues - the existing meeting places - and the ceremonies performed there were in full operation at the time of the Temple's destruction. The underlying philosophy had acquired, with time, its mature vitality, and therefore the cessation of the sacrifices had no detrimental effect on the religious disposition of the people.[210] The dominant theory of substitution prevented any traumatic sense of the loss of the ritual center, and assisted the reorganization of the people as a religiously guided community. It is evident that the Rabbis did not attempt to renew the sacrificial cult;[211] they would have done so had it been their goal,[212] and it is

---

ארץ "He sends his command to the earth [v. 15]," and ישלח דברו וימסם "He sends his word and melts them [v. 18]."

[209] In Midrash Tanhuma (see n. 207) we read: אמר הקב"ה לישראל אע"פ שבה"מ עתיד ליחרב והקרבנות בטלין לא תשכחו עצמכם לסדר הקרבנות אלא הזהרו לקרות בהן לשנות בהן ואם תעסקו בהן אני מעלה עליכם כאלו בקרבנות אתם עוסקים "God said to the Israelites: Although the Temple will be destroyed and the sacrifices abolished, you should not forget the order of the sacrifices, but be careful to repeat them, and when you engage [in reading them], I will consider it as if you were engaged in their offering."

[210] Cf. I. Elbogen, התפלה בישראל בהתפתחותה ההיסטורית, transl. from the 3rd German ed. by J. Amir, ed. J. Heinemann (Tel Aviv, 1972), p. 178, who quotes Bousset, *Die Religion des Judentums*.

[211] We find a remarkable homily in Lev. Rabbah, *Parshah* 22, ד"ה [ח] ר' פינחס which demonstrates a somewhat negative attitude toward the concept of sacrifices. On the verse איש איש מבית ישראל אשר ישחט "Any Israelite who sacrifices [Lev. 17: 3]," a parable with an apparently apologetic purpose is cited by Rabbi Phinehas: A mentally disturbed son of a king used to eat the carcasses of decayed animals; the king ordered such abominable food to be set before him all the time, so that he might ultimately give up this senseless habit. Similarly, the Jews were used in Egypt to offer sacrifices to the idols, and so God said: יהיו מקריבין לפני בכל עת קרבנותיהן באהל מועד והן נפרשים מעבודה זרה והם ניצולים "Let them offer their sacrifices all the time to me in the Tabernacle, and so they will separate from idolatrous practice, and [thus] shall be saved." This apologetic for the practice of sacrifice is quite similar to that of Maimonides (1138 - 1204 C. E.) in *The Guide of the Perplexed*, III: 32, transl. S. Pines (Chicago, 1963).

[212] As already noted, there were periods of good relations between the rabbinical leadership and the Roman authorities. The infamous *Fiscus Judaicus* was modified in 96 C. E.; see F. Bruce, "Nerva and the Fiscus Judaicus," *PEQ 96* (1964), pp. 34ff. Even after the Bar Kokhba rebellion and the persecutions, extremely friendly relations existed between Rabbi the Nasi and the Roman authority (latter half of the 2nd century); there are a great number of talmudic narratives evidencing the familiarity between Rabbi and emperor Antoninus, whose exact identity is not established (possibly Antoninus Caracalla). In Y. T. Megilah 1: 11, 72b, there is a discussion of whether or not Caesar Antoninus converted to Judaism, and in Leviticus Rabbah, *Parshah* 16 ד"ה ח אמר רבי we read:

even doubtful whether they were interested in the rebuilding of the Temple[213] with its prior character and purpose. In a long and tortuous way Josiah's reform, which out of necessity induced the creation of the substitution theory with respect to the sacrificial ritual, ultimately created the conditions for the abolition of sacrifice from Jewish practice.[214]

9.6.3 The Addition of Prayers as an Expansion of the Synagogue's Primary Purpose

The synagogues, the meeting places, were initially instituted for the recital by each group of the prescribed pericopes at the time of the offering of the sacrifices in the Temple. As is characteristic of every established institution, only later [215] was its purpose expanded beyond its initial function to teaching,

---

"אנטונינוס אמר לרבינו הקדוש צלי עלי"Antoninus said to Rabbi the Holy [Rabbi's surname]: Pray for me." Given also the favourable attitude of the Romans toward sacrificial ritual, the emperor would not have objected to its restoration.

[213] We do not possess authentic information from Jewish sources with respect to the Jewish attitude toward Julian the Apostate's scheme to build the Temple. We find, on the other hand, a remarkable report in Gen. Rabbah, *Parshah* 64: ד"ה (כט) אם תעשה בימי ר' יהושע בן חנניה גזרה מלכות שיבנה בית המקדש "In the period of Rabbi Joshua son of Hananiah, the [occupying] government decreed that the Temple must be built." As in the Ezra narrative, the *Kutim* (a byword for Samaritans) slandered the Jews, and as the result of a legal trick the Temple could not be built. The Jews were disappointed, the story continues, and were on the brink of rebellion against the Romans. Desiring to avoid rebellion, the Rabbis sent Rabbi Joshua ben Hananiah, a Tanna who lived at the period of the destruction of the Temple, to pacify the masses, which he did with a suitable parable. The authenticity of the narrative is doubtful, but the implicit message is that the Rabbis did not encourage the building of the Temple. The expression used for the government's edict to build the Temple is unusual; the term גזרה from the root גזר is utilized, which denotes a harmful decree (as in B. T. Ta'anith 18a: שפעם אחת גזרה מלכות הרשעה שמד על ישראל שלא יעסקו בתורה "Once the wicked government decreed apostasy for Israel, that it should not study the Torah") or the enactment of a prohibition or a restrictive measure. Such an expression, repeated twice in the narrative, is definitely unusual in this context, and may demonstrate, whether intentionally or not, the attitude of the Rabbis toward the building of the Temple.

[214] M. Weinfeld, *Deuteronomy and the Deuteronomic School* (Oxford, 1972), observed a similar reversal in theology in the Josianic reform, from God's actual dwelling in the Temple to causing "His name" to dwell in the Temple: "It is interesting to note that the very book which elevates the chosen place to the highest rank of importance in the Israelite cultus should at the same time divest it of all sacral content and import" (p. 197).

[215] I. Levin, בתי כנסת in בית הכנסת בתקופת בית שני - אופיו והתפתחותו עתיקים, ed. A. Oppenheimer, A. Kasher, U. Rappaport (Jerusalem, 1987), p. 11 - 29, writes on p. 11 that "the status and the performance of the synagogue of the period after the Temple's destruction are not necessarily identical to those before its destruction."

preaching and prayer.[216] We must keep in mind the distinction between songs and other recitals to praise God,[217] and prayers, usually understood as

---

Levin also quotes many sources which confirm that the synagogue was dedicated initially to the reading of Scripture, not for prayer. On p. 24 he draws attention to the fact that the earlier synagogues did not face Jerusalem because they were not intended for prayers; only after their dedication to prayer did people face the Holy City and the site of the Temple, the divine dwelling, and direct thither their supplications. In a more recent publication, בית הכנסת בארץ ישראל: ראשיתו ואופיו בראייה מחודשת in *Tehillah le-Moshe, Biblical and Judaic Studies in Honor of Moshe Greenberg*, ed. M. Cogan at al. (Winona Lake, 1997), pp. 143 - 162, Levin expresses himself more unequivocally, saying that before 70, i.e. the Temple's destruction, המוקד היה קריאת התורה וההפטרה ודרשות ("the focal purpose [of the synagogues] was the reading of the Torah and the Haftaroth [the pertinent prophetic pericopes] and the homilies").

[216] There is no definite evidence as to when the synagogue as a meeting place was instituted. Daily prayers with an established text were certainly instituted in Yabneh after the Temple's destruction, as we read in B. T. Berakhoth 28b: שמעון הפקולי הסדיר שמונה עשרה ברכות לפני רבן גמליאל על הסדר ביבנה "Simeon of Pequli arranged eighteen blessings before Rabban Gamaliel in Yabneh." The prayers on fast days, which may have been instituted during the time of the Temple, cannot be considered as fixed prayers. We read in Mishnah Ta'anith 2: 2 that in fact on a fast day twenty-four blessings were said, eighteen daily blessings and an additional six. This Mishnah thus refers to a period after the institution of the eighteen daily blessings. J. Heinemann, התפלה בתקופת התנאים והאמוראים (Jerusalem, 1965), writes on p. 29 that initially the prayers were a creation of the people; they were not imposed from above, that is, arranged by the Sages and conveyed to the people, but on the contrary were a grassroots creation, in different forms and patterns. Only much later were they edited and unified by the Sages in order to achieve a uniform order of prayer for all the people, similar to their goal in imposing a uniform legal codex. I. Levin, p. 14, affirms (free translation): "... the synagogue was initially a mixed institution, without any definite manner and purpose; the public of each community established its character and purpose, according to their needs." The fact that there are two interchangeable names for the synagogue, προσευξή and συναγωγή, whose roots are unrelated to any concept of prayer, may also confirm this assertion. On the other hand, we find in Dan. 6: 11: וזמנין תלתה ביומא הוא ברך על ברכוהי ומצלא ומודא "...and three times daily he knelt and prayed and gave thanks," and in Ps. 55: 18: ערב ובקר וצהרים אשיחה "Evening, morning and noon I cry out in distress," which would hint at fixed prayers thrice daily. I suggest, however, that these two citations do not indicate fixed prayers; they were not public prayers but individual supplications for God's succor, with no fixed style. Three daily prayers were not meant to replace sacrifice, especially as the Sages maintained that the evening prayer was not obligatory; if the three prayers in Dan. and Ps. were an established order, the Sages would not have rendered a contradictory decision. The three prayers, evening, morning and noon, should rather be interpreted as symbolizing a continuous, perpetual appeal to God, thanking and blessing the Deity for his benevolence, and requesting future compassion. In his commentary to Eccl. 5: 1, Ibn Ezra states that man should thank God every minute to honour God for his grace and mercy in keeping us alive, but because man is engaged in his worldly chores (to earn a living), fixed times were established for such thanksgiving at evening, morning and noon. This is evidently the spirit of the phrase in Ps., and could be similarly applied to Daniel's pious behaviour.

supplications for relief. Most of the daily prayers, even today, consist of blessing God, and declarations of faith. Only in the eighteen blessings arranged after the Temple's destruction[218] were supplications included.[219] We observe from Mishnah Ta'anith, cited above, which we may consider as an

---

[217] The "prayers" of the priests in the Temple were only songs of praise and benediction, as well as biblical pericopes consisting of proclamations of faith, as we observe from Mishnah Tamid 5: 1: אמר להם הממונה ברכו ברכה אחת והן ברכו קראו עשרת הדברים שמע והיה אם שמוע ויאמר ברכו את העם שלש ברכות אמת ויציב ועבודה וברכות כהנים "The supervisor told them: Say one blessing, and they did; they read the Ten Commandments and three biblical pericopes; [the traditional commentators interpret the next phrase as] they said **with** the people three benedictions: a proclamation of faith, a prayer to God to accept the sacrifices, and the priestly blessing of the people [Num. 6: 24 - 27]." The Levites sung different chapters of Psalms every day (Mishnah Tamid 7: 4).

[218] See note 207. Even this prayer with supplications is called שמונה עשרה ברכות, as we read in B. T. Berakhoth 28b. Only in the late Middle Ages was it called תפלת עמידה, the standing prayer, because one must perform it while standing. I have found the first mention of this name, now commonly used, in the Responsa of Rabbi Moses of Trani (1500 C. E.) דלשון תפלה בלשון, who explains: חלק ב סימן עה ד"ה תשובה כיון חכמים אינו אלא תפלת עמידה שהם י"ח ברכות "because the term תפלה 'prayer' in the language of the Sages concerns the standing prayer, which consists of the eighteen blessings." He relies on a rabbinical homily in B. T. Berakhoth 26b, interpreting Gen. 19: 27 to mean that Abraham had instituted the morning prayer: וישכם אברהם בבקר אל המקום אשר עמד שם את פני ה' ואין עמידה אלא תפלה "'Early the next morning Abraham got up and returned to the place where he had stood before the Lord,' and [the term] עמידה 'standing' can only be understood as praying."

[219] It is remarkable that prayers and even confessions (חטאנו etc.) are all in plural, which demonstrates their origin in the routine of the public meetings, whereas the Psalms, which can be perceived as prayers, are all in singular form and represent the prayer of the individual, each with a different content appropriate to the specific circumstances and mood of the suppliant. Even those Psalms apparently composed by a group, as for example לבני קרח מזמור, are expressed in singular form, indicating their primary origin as an individual prayer. The prayers of the people at the time of the incense celebration, as in Luke 1: 9 - 11, appear to be individual prayers, each person expressing his personal petition at the propitious time of the incense celebration. The rabbinic homily which equates prayer to the incense celebration (Sifrei Num. *Pisqa* 41 ד"ה ולעברו) originates from Ps. 141: 2: תכון תפלתי קטרה לפניך "May my prayer be set before you like incense," a psalm composed in singular, indicating its origin as an individual and particular prayer. A homily in Midrash Tehilim (Buber) on this verse also characterizes prayer as a substitute for the incense celebrations discontinued after the Temple's destruction. We read there: כך אמר דוד רבוני כשהיה בית המקדש קיים היינו מקטירים לפניך קטורת עכשו אין לנו לא מזבח ולא כהן גדול תקבל תפלתי ותקרע הרקיע ותכנם תפלתי לכך נאמר תכון תפלתי וגו' "So said David: Lord, when the Temple existed we burned incense before you, but now as we have no altar or High Priest, accept my prayer and rend the heavens and let my prayer enter; that is what is meant by his utterance: 'May my prayer etc.'"

authentic explanation for the division of the land and the people into groups, that the groups were instituted to secure the identification of the people with the sacrificial system; there is no mention that prayers were performed at these meetings. The addition of Psalms, praising God for His righteousness and generosity, and biblical verses witnessing God's uniqueness and accepting His unequaled sovereignty, were a natural complement to the recitals at the time of the sacrifices.[220] Narratives from the New Testament also confirm that the synagogues were dedicated to teaching and preaching,[221] not to prayers.[222] The concept that prayers serve as a substitute

---

[220] It is only natural that the Qumran sects, which did not perform or share spiritually in the sacrifices celebrated in Jerusalem, and practised a rigorous communal way of life, created a sophisticated liturgy to recite at their daily meetings. They effected the last step, the replacement of sacrifice with recitals, at the time of the Temple, while the Rabbis instituted this replacement after the Temple's destruction. The priests conducted all the ritual ceremonials, and hymns and prayers were recited at the time of the sacrificial celebrations. See E. Hazon, חיי הרוח של כת מדבר יהודה, in על מגילת ספר, מאמארים על מגילות מדבר יהודה (Jerusalem, 1997), pp. 85 - 97. From the analysis of the various fragments relevant to their liturgy, we observe that these consisted mainly of benedictions. Their daily prayers (4Q503) comprised different benedictions for each day of the month. See G. Vermes, *The Dead Sea Scrolls in English* (reprinted with revisions London, 1968), pp. 231-37, and L. H. Schiffman, הלכה, הליכה ומשיחיות בכת מדבר יהודה (Jerusalem, 1993), pp. 230-31 and relevant notes.

The Qumran community followed the established pattern of the Temple ceremony, in which thanksgiving and praises to the Lord and blessings of the people were performed daily by the priests at the completion of the sacrificial celebrations, and songs were sung by the Levites (Mishnah Tamid 5: 1, 7: 2 and 7: 3). I do not intend to intrude into the heated scholarly discussion on the issue of whether the Damascus Rule and the other Qumran texts originate from the same group or sect. I merely wish to draw attention to the fact that the Damascus Rule (CD), which embodies a number of rules and ordinances with respect to the sacrificial worship and performances, does not contain any reference to prayers, hymns or blessings, though these do apppear in the Community Rule 1QS. In the latter, "the spirit of holiness of the Community" - not prayer or hymns - atones for sins, "without the flesh of holocausts and the fat of sacrifices. And prayer rightly offered shall be as an acceptable fragrance of righteousness, and perfection of way as a delectable free-will offering." (Translation by G. Vermes, *The Dead Sea Scrolls in English*, p. 74.)

[221] We read in Matt. 4: 23: διδάσκων ἐν ταῖς συναγωγαῖς καὶ κηρύσσων τὸ εὐαγγέλιον "teaching in their synagogues, and preaching the good news." Other occurrences mention either or both of these activities. For example, in Luke 4: 15, 6: 6, 13: 1, only teaching is recorded, using the term διδάσκω, while in Mark 1: 39, Luke 4: 44, Acts 9: 20, 13: 5 and 15: 21, the term κηρύσσω "to proclaim" is utilized; in Acts 13: 5, we read: κατήγγελλον τὸν λόγον τοῦ θεοῦ "they proclaimed the word of God," and in 13: 14 - 15 it is recorded that they read in the synagogue "from the Law and the Prophets," with no mention of prayers. Individual prayers were said in solitary places, as we read in Mark 1: 35, and the public recited prayers near a river, as we read in Acts 16: 13, or at the seashore, as attested in *Ant.* XIV: 258. Josephus records in *Ant.* XIV 190 - 267 a great number of special privileges granted to Jews in the Roman Empire, and from the texts of the relevant edicts we learn that the Jews had the right to organize and meet in special

for sacrifices[223] as well as atonement[224] was a later development,[225] to exalt their religious significance; other righteous deeds were similarly encouraged, as substitutes or equivalents to the sacrifices.[226]

---

places, to perform their religious duties and common meals. Prayer is not mentioned as a purpose of these meetings, with the possible exception of one unclear record (260-1). The purpose of προσευχή in *Life*: 280 is also unclear, that is, whether it represents a meeting or a prayer house. From the context, one may assume that it refers to a meeting house, since the Jews of Tiberias were summoned there, and they did not know the reason for their summons. Josephus uses the term synagogue several times, but its utilization is also unclear. In *War* II: 285 it is only indicated that the Jews met there on Sabbaths, but we have seen that they also met for reading the Torah. In VII: 44 - 45 its use is quite bizarre, since Josephus mentions that they had votive offerings of bronze there, which would be strange for a prayer house; in addition, Josephus calls it τὸ ἱερὸν "the temple" in v. 45. In *Ant.* XIX: 300 - 305 we read Ἰουδαίων συναγωγήν, but again without any indication of its use. Philo uses the term προσευχή in *Ad Gaium* 132 - 137 to describe the damaged meeting houses of the Alexandrian Jews, also without any precise indication of their use. But in 156 he specifies their utilization, and we read there: ...προσευχὰς ἔχοντας... "they have 'houses of prayer' [Colson's transl.] and meet together in them, particularly on the sacred sabbaths when they receive as a body a training in their ancestral philosophy." A similar confirmation of the scope of the προσευχὰς occurs in 157. We observe that even the προσευχή, commonly translated as relevant to prayer, was in fact dedicated to meetings and teaching, as we have also learned from the New Testament.

[222] Evidence that praying in the synagogues was not the common custom may be deduced from the censure of Matt. 6: 5, which states that only hypocrites pray in the synagogues; it would not be appropriate to criticize such behaviour if it were customary procedure.

[223] See n. 186 regarding a homily in Num. Rabbah, *Parshah* 18 on the verse ונשלמה פרים שפתנו.

[224] In Song of Songs Rabbah *Parshah* 4: 5 ד"ה ד"א שערך, the recital of biblical verses is equated to the red thread which was tied to the scapegoat and to the door of the Great Hall on the Day of Atonement, and which turned white as a sign that the sins were expiated (Mishnah Yoma 6: 8 and Sabbath 9: 3). We read there: אמר להם כחוט השני שפתותיך רחישת פיך חביבה עלי כחוט השני של זהורית "[God] said to them [the Israelites]: 'Your lips are like a scarlet ribbon [Cant. 4: 3]' - I love the whisper of your mouth like the red thread [on the scapegoat]." Again there is an explicit analogy between the recital and the corresponding deed which it has absolutely replaced.

[225] There is nowhere in Scripture any obligation at all for prayer, let alone a rigorous system of texts to be recited daily at fixed times. As I noted, I do not wish to elaborate on the issue of prayer, a topic which requires a separate study, but I would like to draw attention to a few odd circumstances in Scripture with respect to "prayer". The root of the term most often used to express "prayer" is פלל, which has no relation to prayer (it is interpreted as "judge" or "mediate" in I Sam. 2: 25; "judged" in Ezek. 16: 52; "expected" in Gen. 48: 11 and "intervened" in Ps. 106: 30). Only in the *Hitpa'el* התפלל is it interpreted according to the context as "he prayed." We find a remarkable homily in Sifrei Num., *Pisqa* 26 which states: עשרה לשונות נקראת תפלה "Prayer is expressed in ten terms," and these are then enumerated with suitable biblical citations: זעקה שועה נאקה קריאה רנה נפול פלול עתירה עמידה תחנה. We observe that there was not even an established and stable term for prayer as we know it, and therefore many terms,

As the meetings and the recitals were established daily at the fixed times
of the corresponding sacrifices, so the later-instituted prayers[227] were added

---

each with its particular nuance suited to the context or mood of the worshipper or
supplicant, are utilized; the existence of these various terms is the utter antithesis of the
concept of fixed prayers. We should also wonder why Scripture does not record prayers
or supplications in many instances in which one would expect them. I shall quote a few
examples: Abraham did not pray for children for himself, though he did pray for
Abimelekh, in whose household every womb was closed (Gen. 20: 17 - 18). One would
also have expected Abraham to supplicate God for his own and Sarah's salvation when
he sensed danger in his wanderings to Egypt and Gerar, yet he only searched for a trick to
save himself. When Rachel did not bear children, Jacob said to her "Am I in the place of
God"; yet he did not pray to God, as he did at Beth El (Gen. 28: 20 - 22) and before his
encounter with Esau (Gen. 32: 9 - 13). The incident at the Waters of Meribah is also
puzzling. In Num 20: 12 - 13, it seems that Moses accepted God's severe punishment for
his oversight without any attempt to supplicate for mercy and pardon, whereas in the
parallel narrative in Deut. 3: 23 - 26 we read: ואתחנן אל ה' בעת ההוא לאמר "At
that time I pleaded with the Lord"; the plea did not help him, and we read: ויתעבר ה'
למענכם ולא שמע אלי ויאמר ה' אלי רב לך אל תוסף דבר אלי עוד בדבר הזה
"But because of you the Lord was angry with me and would not listen to me. That is
enough, the Lord said. Do not speak to me anymore about this matter." These are serious
issues, in my opinion, which deserve thoughtful consideration.

[226] We read a homily in B. T. Hagigah 27a: בזמן שבית המקדש קיים מזבח מכפר על
אדם עכשיו שלחנו של אדם מכפר עליו "When the Temple stands, the altar atones
for man, now it is his table which atones for him." In B. T. Sukkah 49b we read: אמר
רבי אלעזר גדול העושה צדקה יותר מכל הקרבנות שנאמר עשה צדקה ומשפט
נבחר לה' מזבח "Said Rabbi Eleazer: Doing charity is greater than [offering] all the
sacrifices, as it is said: 'To do what is right and just is more acceptable to the Lord than
sacrifice [Prov. 21: 3].'" Midrash Tanhuma, *Parshah* Zav, *siman* 14 ד"א צו (יד) ד"ה
זאת התורה לעלה למנחה goes even further and entirely re-interprets a biblical verse:
ולחטאת ולאשם ולמלואים ולזבח השלמים אל תקרי כן אלא זאת התורה לא
לעולה ולא למנחה ולא לחטאת ולא אשם ולא מלואים ולא זבח השלמים אלא
היו עוסקים בתורה ויהיה חשוב לפני כאלו אתם מקריבים לפני כל הקרבנות "[It
is written in Lev. 7: 37] 'These, then, are the regulations for the burnt offering, the grain
offering, the sin offering, the guilt offering, the ordination offering and the fellowship
offering.' Don't read it this way, but 'This is the Torah, not for the burnt offering, not for
the grain offering, not for the sin offering, not for the guilt offering, not for the ordination
offering and not for the fellowship offering, but study the Torah, and I will consider it as
if you were offering all the sacrifices.'" Similarly, we read in Aboth of Rabbi Nathan
א"ל בני אל ירע לך יש לנו כפרה אחת שהיא כמותה ואיזה זה :נוסחא א פרק ד
גמילות חסדים שנאמר כי חסד חפצתי ולא זבח "He said to him: Son, don't be
perturbed, we have another way of atonement [besides sacrifice] which is equal to it; and
this is charity, as it is said: 'For I desire charity not sacrifice [Hos. 6: 6].'"

[227] It is not within the scope of this study to determine which songs, blessings and prayers
were instituted during the period of the Temple and which were introduced later. It
suffices for our purpose to postulate a process of interchange between the various types
of ritual. For further debate on this specific issue, see E. Fleischer, לקדמוניות תפילות

to the same fixed schedule: in the morning, at the time of the morning *Tamid*, and in the afternoon, at the time of the twilight *Tamid*. The timing observed was that of the actual offerings in the Temple, and it is natural that the same timing was later upheld with respect to the recitals, in substitution for the actual sacrifices, and with respect to the prayers that became combined with them. The recitals were initially an interchange of one type of ritual, sacrifice, with another, the recital of the relevant pericopes; both rituals existed side by side. After the Temple's destruction, recital became a substitute. The Sages effected the transformation of a priestly-controlled, concrete ritual into a sophisticated conceptual and intellectually-guided ritual,[228] another momentous step in the constant adaptation of ritual to prevailing circumstances. And, like all rituals, this developed in function and in style, following the same course as the sacrifices: from a primitive, spontaneous, occasional and informal ritual to a sophisticated, stable, regular and elaborate ceremony with defined rules of performance.

The later-instituted *Ma'ariv*, "sunset" prayer, has no connection to the sacrifices, and the Rabbis thus decided[229] that it is not an obligation but only a permitted act. On the other hand, the *Musaf* prayer was instituted as a substitution for the additional sacrifices offered on the Sabbath, New Moon and other holy days. The notion that prayers were a substitute for sacrifices is the commonly acknowledged motive; in fact, however, these prayers were an outgrowth of the recitals of the relevant biblical pericopes detailing the requirements for each sacrifice, and these recitals became the core of the prayers. Thus, in the wake of the sacrificial system, a unique and unusual

---

החובה בישראל *Tarbiz* 59 3 / 4 (1990), pp. 397 - 441, who contends that there is no hint in the talmudic literature of obligatory prayer at the period of the Temple and that such prayers were introduced by Rabban Gamaliel after the Temple's destruction; and the opposing arguments presented by H. Fox, תשובות לשני מדהפכנים *Sinai 114* (1994), pp. 162 - 170, who postulates that in the Second Temple period, and particularly after the Hasmonean revolt, obligatory public prayer was instituted, while the individual obligation was established after the Temple's destruction.

[228] A similar if not identical sophistication in development is encountered in Christian doctrine with respect to the *hostia* and the vine at the Eucharist celebration: from the actual sacrifice of Jesus' flesh and blood, through the dogma of a concrete participation in His flesh and blood (John 6: 51 - 58), to Zwingli's reformed doctrine of a symbolic act.

[229] We read in B. T. Berakhoth 27b of a dissension between two Tannaim as to whether this evening prayer is an obligation or not, but as we read in Maimonides Hilkh. Tefilah 1: 6: ואף ע"פ כן נהגו כל ישראל בכל מקומות מושבותיהם להתפלל ערבית וקבלוה עליהם כתפלת חובה "And nevertheless, all Israelites are accustomed to pray the evening prayer in all their communities, and have accepted it as an obligatory prayer." But even this voluntary prayer is justified by a connection with sacrifice, as Maimonides declares on the basis of a rabbinical utterance: שהרי איברי תמיד של בין הערבים מתעכלין והולכין כל הלילה "...because the limbs of the evening *Tamid* offering burned all night [upon the altar] until they turned into ashes."

manner of worship in the form of an arrangement of established prayers at fixed times[230] was generated in Israelite faith, and gained a dominant status in Western civilization. The reasons for the additions of prayers at the occasion of the meetings, initially instituted for another purpose, and the stages of their development, require a separate extensive study, which is not within the framework of our examination; it suffices for us to have established the thread which connected Josiah's reform of the sacrifices to their replacement by recitals, and to have explained the conceptual foundation and historical events which enabled this apparently inconceivable metamorphosis.

---

[230] Shortly after their institution, we apprehend a concern that prayers at fixed times might become a habit rather than an exciting experience. We read in Mishnah Aboth 2: 13: רבי שמעון אומר הוי זהיר בקרית שמע ובתפלה וכשאתה מתפלל אל תעש תפלתך קבע אלא רחמים ותחנונים לפני המקום ברוך הוא "Rabbi Simeon [a disciple of Rabban Johanan ben Zakkai, hence living close to the time of the destruction of the Temple and the institution of prayer] says: Be careful [to perform] the reading of Shema [the declaration of God's oneness] and prayer; and when you pray do not make your prayer a fixed habit, but [implore for] grace and mercy from God the Blessed." Similarly, we read in Mishnah Berakhot 4: 3 in the name of R. Eliezer, and in Midrash Tannaim for Deut. 3: 23: העושה תפלתו קבע אין תפלתו תחנונים "If one makes his prayer a habit, it is not a supplication." Rabbi Shimlai, a later Amora known for his ethical homilies, therefore recommends in B. T. Berakhoth 32a: לעולם יסדר אדם שבחו של הקדוש ברוך הוא ואחר כך יתפלל "One should always proclaim first the praise of God the Blessed, and then pray [for one's own requirements]."

10. Conclusion

I have listed in the Introduction a number of topics relevant to the three biblical altar laws, and to the shifts which occurred in the sacrificial system until its ultimate cessation, and I shall now refer to these topics again in order. I would nevertheless like to emphasize at the beginning the three main aims of the study: a) the substantiation of the developmental process at work in the sacrificial cult, b) the validation of the scholarly assertion discrediting the existence of a "bronze altar" in the desert Tabernacle, and c) the elucidation of the conceptual process by which the ideological and practical replacement of the sacrificial system with an entirely different type of cult, recital and prayer, was effected. I believe I have achieved these aims, through three phases of research: 1) a meticulous examination of the biblical pericopes relevant to the altars with respect to their philological, literary and structural problems, demonstrating their diversity and their particular oddities, 2) the comparison and contrast of these passages with other more or less conflicting quotations, and 3) a consideration of the outcome of this analysis in light of the political and economic circumstances in each period.

The first issue of my study was the examination of the relation between the two apparently similar commands to build altars in Exod. 20: 21 - 23 and Deut. 27: 2 - 8. The literary and structural analysis of the respective texts verified their evident diversity, and demonstrated their origin in different periods and historical settings. This review substantiates the developmental process in the cult, with respect to such issues as the necessity of a dedicated site for the sacrificial worship, the nature of the equipment required, and the features associated with its celebrations.

The Exod. pericope, which favours the most simple mound of earth, or a pile of stones, originates in the conditions of life of a nomadic society, when worshippers would set up a temporary site for the performance of a sacrifice and believed that God would appear and bless them wherever it might be. The mound-altar turned into God's dwelling, and therefore a homicidal tool was not to be associated with it, just as the nomad's home offered a safe haven to anyone seeking it. The Deut. pericope reflects the settled society of a later period, but maintains the archaic tradition of the simple altar, as substantiated by a number of biblical citations. This tradition persisted until the period of Ahaz, who built an impressive copy of a Damascene altar.[1]

The mythological significance of stone, the Deity's dwelling, is substantiated in biblical and post-biblical quotations, and prevailed in

---

[1]   II Kings 16: 10 - 16.

Israelite society until Josiah's reform; this reverence explains the prohibition against splitting the stones used in construction. The custom of not splitting the stone prevailed, as is usual, after its underlying theology had been repudiated, and ceased to be observed only in Ezekiel's period. At the time of the command in Deut. 27, the stones for the altar still had to be used whole, but their surface could be smoothed by iron implements; such an aesthetic enhancement did not blemish their "wholeness" or "perfection", their obligatory character of אבנים שלמות. I have quoted and critically analyzed various scholarly propositions, some of which viewed a correlation between the Exod. and Deut. pericopes. I dedicated in particular an extensive philological argument to dispute the recent publication on this issue by S. M. Olyan, who suggests that the term חלל in Exod. 20: 22 is an antonym to the term תמים/שלם in Deut. 27: 5-6, and therefore one pericope complements the other. I demonstrated that the term חלל is an abstract concept connoting sacrilege applied mainly within the cultic system, and with respect to altars appears exclusively in the Exod. pericope. This confirms the distinctive character and motive of the prohibitive decree in Exod., versus the positive command in the Deut. pericope to use only אבנים שלמות, "whole - perfect stones," for the building of an altar. The numinous quality of stone in ancient Israelite mythology and custom is corroborated in the study through a comparison with nomadic Arab custom, as well as by a great number of biblical citations. The connection between the term צור "rock" and the metaphorical power of the Deity is also amply documented in biblical quotations. I also analyzed the occurrences of צור in two odd narratives connected to the circumcision of the male's sexual organ, reflecting in this case the phallus as a numinous symbol; the comparison of the different historical settings of the two pericopes, supported by their disparate language and style, confirms that there was an extended period of time between them. Citations from Josephus and rabbinic sources are also quoted and discussed in the course of the study.

Having confirmed the absolute separation of the two altar laws of Exod. 20: 21 - 23 and Deut. 27: 2- 8, I was then able to propose the fundamental principles, not elucidated in Scripture, that logically lay behind the specific requirements and restrictions of each pericope.[2] This also shed light on some

---

[2] The prohibition against using dressed stones on which a sword, a homicidal implement, was used, is explained in Scripture. The prohibition against climbing up the steps of the altar is also justified in Scripture, but is questioned by the traditional commentators and scholars according to their various perspectives. According to the command in Exod. 28: 42-43 the priests must wear linen undergarments to cover the body, לכסות בשר ערוה, precisely to avoid exposure of their nakedness (the same term ערוה is used in Exod. 20: 23 לא תגלה ערותך); hence the prohibition in Exod. 20 would be pointless. My proposition offers a reasonable solution to this dilemma.

of the more inexplicable decrees, such as the prohibition against going up on the altar on steps, the command to build the altar of large and perfect stones ordained in Deut. 27, and the strange narrative in I Kings 6: 7.

I then examined whether a correlation can be perceived between the pericope in Deut. and those of I Kings 5: 31- 32, 6: 7 and 7: 9 - 11; the latter contain apparent literary similarities to the Deut. pericope with respect to the use of iron tools on the stones for the Temple building, and have been associated with the deuteronomic decree in the rabbinic literature, and implicitly by some scholars. I have critically analyzed this allegation, as well as the rabbinic solutions proposed to harmonize all three altar laws and the Kings narratives. I have demonstrated the irrationality of the rabbinic proposition, and illustrated the improbability of any connection between the altar law of Exod. 20 and the Kings narratives.

No definite resolution, on the other hand, can be made between two other conjectures: a) The possibility that the Kings record has an affinity with the decree of Deut. 27, with respect to their common motif of a reverence for stone; this attitude led to a prohibition against splitting the stone used in construction, but allowed the refinement of its surface with metal or any other tools; b) The possibility that the Kings record does not refer to any prohibition with respect to the treatment of the stones; the verses contain superlative descriptions of the enormous dimensions of the stones, their elaborate surfaces and their great cost simply with the aim of impressing the reader with the marvelous elements of the Temple, and the king's piety in not sparing any expense for its magnificence. The study also offers an interpretation of the apparently odd record that "no [noise] of iron tools was heard at the Temple site." I conclude that there is no textual or other evidence to allow a clear preference of one possibility over the other; the philosophical postulates underlying each retain the support of quotations from biblical and other relevant sources.

I then investigated whether the archeological findings of altars in Israel could offer definite verification or contradiction of the results of the textual and literary scrutiny effected by scholars and specifically my conclusions postulated above. I enumerated the obstacles hindering the incontestable identification of the altars uncovered in Israel, and particularly the association of these altars with the relevant biblical rules. I quoted a number of disagreements between noted archeologists on the correct identifications of findings at certain archeological sites in order to demonstrate the fragility of archeological assertions, at least on the topic of the altars, and their dependence on a scrupulous interpretation of the relevant biblical texts in all their minutiae. I cited the completely opposing opinions with respect to the classification of archeological findings at Mt. Ebal and Meggido by noted archeologists such as Zertal, Shanks, Ussishkin and Stern, and questioned their interpretation of the texts upon which they formulated some of their identifications and conclusions.

I conferred additional attention upon the dissension between Yadin and Aharoni regarding the Beer Sheba excavation, and critically analyzed their interpretation of the biblical texts and their efforts to accommodate these texts to their conjectures based upon their archeological findings. The fact that two such experts as Yadin and Aharoni disagree on the identification of such a well-known excavation with extremely well-preserved artifacts demonstrates my thesis that only a comprehensive and proficient examination and interpretation of biblical texts together with the archeologist's expertise can serve to ensure the most accurate investigation of the past as possible. In particular, I critically scrutinized Yadin's interpretation of the phrase in II Kings 23: 8 ויטמא את הבמות...מגבע עד באר שבע "...and [Josiah] desecrated the high places from Geba to Beer Sheba," utilized by him in his dispute with Aharoni as evidence for the existence of a *bamah* in Beer Sheba and its destruction by Josiah. Finally, the archeological findings of altars from the late monarchic period constructed of both unworked and ashlar stones support my thesis that the archaic custom of building primitive altars of unworked stones was no longer considered mandatory, and permanent shrines were constructed of dressed stones.

The third law of the altar in Exod. 27: 1 - 8, ordering the construction of a bronze altar, was minutely examined. The indecipherable description of the bronze altar in Exod. 27: 2 - 8 with the term כרכב, which has no parallel in Scripture and whose interpretation is crucial to an understanding of the altar's structure, is only one of the many enigmatic aspects of this law. The propositions of Cassuto and Haran, as well as the rabbinic efforts to portray the altar's structure based on the MT text, were amply discussed and their deficiencies exposed. Other textual difficulties of the pericope were examined, as well as the odd term בדים for the poles, and the use of the סירתיו and יעיו "pots and shovels." Both oddities hint to an archaic origin of certain elements of the text. The pots and the forks remind us of the narrative in I Sam 2: 13, and the use of the term בדים, more appropriate to connote a simple branch, suggests a vestige of a nomadic period. The ark, a sacred item, was kept by tradition in its original state with its customary simple carrying rods, and thus its association with the term בדים is appropriate in the Kings narrative; by extension, these rods were also assumed to have been utilized for the carrying of the other sacred furnishings, such as altars and table.

The totally divergent text of the LXX was amply discussed and on the basis of this text I proposed a functional description of this altar. Without taking a position, at this stage, on the question of whether there ever was such an altar, one must assume that the LXX editor or translator had just such a functional description in mind. Yet the many oddities of the MT text do cast doubt on the reality of the altar's existence.

An Excursus was dedicated to a review of the issue of the "horns" of the altar, mentioned only in the law of the bronze altar and not in the laws of Exod. 20 and Deut. 27. I postulated considering them metaphorically as a symbol of totality, rather than as representing the strength of a bull, or of the deity, as argued by some scholars, or as a remnant of the pillars, as suggested by others. I argued against the association of the altar's קרנים with "animal horns," noting the distinction between the dual קרנים, which alludes to animal horns that are always in pairs, and the plural קרנות, alluding generally to the totality of the subject with which they are associated. In the case of the altar, the קרנות are associated with the number four, and allude metaphorically to the four corners of the world. My proposition is supported by the fact that both in Scripture and in the literature of that period in the surrounding cultures the four corners symbolized the totality of the world; this totality is also suggested by the ceremonial smearing of blood on the four קרנות during the sin-offering. My proposition is further confirmed by the absence of scriptural evidence granting any particular significance to bull's horns. I thus conclude that the "horns" of the altar denoted the Deity's seat dominating the entire universe, symbolized by the four corners of the world.

The biblical narratives in which the term קרנות המזבח occurs were then examined and explained in light of the above hypothesis. A host of passages in both the Bible and Josephus are cited in support of the thesis that the קרנות were actually protruding elements of the altar. Analysis of archeological findings confirms that the protruding elements did not have the slightest similarity to animal horns. I consider it probable that the protruding elements on the four corners of the later altar constituted a remnant of the rim or molding on the earlier type; this had already been discarded on the metal table-altar, on which it had once had a practical purpose. The rim and molding, זר and מסגרת, on the Temple's table, and the absence of the מסגרת "rim" on the golden incense altar, support such a conjecture.

The scholarly skepticism with respect to the authenticity of the narrative in Exod. 25: 2 - 30: 38 describing the Tabernacle and its furnishings, including the bronze altar,[3] is well known and generally accepted. Scholars have therefore not looked to Scripture for additional evidence to corroborate this fact by a thorough analysis of the biblical texts regarding the various furnishings. Since my study is dedicated to the altars, I had the opportunity to review all the pericopes in which one would expect the mention of the bronze altar if it were actually in use, and to draw attention to them. This absence further substantiates the scholarly postulate that the rules of the sacrificial

---

[3]   Chap. 29 describes the consecration of Aaron and his sons for their priestly duties.

cult and its appropriate furnishings were retrojected to the period of Moses, the greatest prophet and founder of the Israelite creed. On the other hand, if such a bronze altar was never in use, and it is evident that the Second Temple had a stone altar, one must ask why the P editors envisioned a bronze altar in Moses' Tabernacle. We must also wonder at the fact that of all the furnishings of the Second Temple, and probably also of the First Temple, only the holocaust altar was completely different in its substance from Moses' altar.

The Kings' editor, whether a deuteronomist or of priestly origin and whether from an earlier period or later, attempted to explain the disappearance of the bronze altar. We encounter a passage in I Kings 8: 64 recording that it was too small, and a report in II Kings 16: 14 that Ahaz moved it. But the question remains why the bronze altar was "devised" at all, thus creating an enigma that had later to be untangled with dubious success. The Chr. editor struggled in a different way to solve other oddities connected with the bronze altar, and left entirely open the question of its disappearance and replacement by a stone altar. The Sages attempted, in their predictable way, to harmonize all biblical pericopes, and I critically analyzed these endeavours and indicated their flaws. I then postulated an hypothesis to explain the enigma of this altar and its metamorphosis during an extended period in which the underlying theology also underwent dramatic changes. Assisted also by an examination of the interchange at a certain period of time between the biblical terms שלחן and מזבח, I proposed to consider Ahaz' reform as the final stage of separation between the custom of presenting food to the Deity and the more lofty idea of burning the offerings. The bronze altar displaced by Ahaz represents the previously utilized presentation table, and its replacement represents the concrete execution of a crucial reform of the cult. This fundamental shift both induced and promoted the institutionalization of the cult, an essential modification with significant future consequences. My proposition is supported by a thorough analysis of various biblical texts, the evaluation of archeological findings, the examination of the political circumstances during Ahaz' period, and a comparison with Mesopotamian presentation tables. I am confident that I have offered a feasible solution to the many questions with respect to the bronze altar raised by scholars, and to the additional issues I have noted.

Ahaz' reform induced both the subsequent institutionalization of the sacrificial cult and a modification in the nature of the altar; the magnificent structure of the Jerusalem altar and its elaborate ceremonial in turn emphasized the prominence of the Jerusalem Temple, and thus created the basis for further reforms, including that of king Josiah. The changes in the altar's structure were either the cause or the effect of radical alterations in the manner of the sacrificial ceremonial and its underlying theology. My analysis of these significant shifts included a review of Josiah's crucial reform of the sacrificial system. As this event is of such importance to the understanding of the ultimate development of the Israelite cult, it was necessary to analyze in depth the concealed motives behind this unique and revolutionary transformation. The study discussed scholarly assumptions with respect to the well-known issue of the almost identical language of the two passages recording repairs to the Temple, by Joash in II Kings 12 and by Josiah in II Kings 22, and the question of their authenticity. A thorough investigation of Josiah's activities, as recorded at length in Scripture, and the association of these deeds with deuteronomic laws and regulations, support the thesis that the repair of the Temple was performed by that king. The political circumstances of his period, and his objective to reunite the previous Northern kingdom under the rule of the Davidic dynasty explain his pragmatism in increasing the significance of Jerusalem as the unique cult centre.

Josiah attempted to reverse Jeroboam's policy of constructing separate sanctuaries so as to avoid the reunification of the two kingdoms. The eradication of the local sanctuaries, the *bamoth*, the utter destruction of the competing sanctuary in Beth El and the brutal slaughter of its priests were all systematic steps to achieve this goal. It is thus likely that Josiah performed the repairs, and probably also an expansion of the size of the Temple, since the magnificence of the Temple constituted a significant element of his overall policy. Though the centralization of the cult was totally inconsistent with the prevailing custom in Israel and the surrounding cultures, Josiah was assisted in the implementation of this unique reform by those elements of society who expected to benefit socially and economically from it, such as the Jerusalem population and its priests, and by the scribes, who introduced suitable divine commands in the Book of the Law, the Deuteronomy. The study examines those deuteronomic statutes and regulations which had as their purpose the formulation of a theological justification for the Deity's election of Jerusalem and its sanctuary as the divine seat. The establishment of Jerusalem as the exclusive ceremonial, legal, political and economic center with the assistance of those newly promulgated rules ensured the pre-eminence of Jerusalem from that time until today. Josiah's cult reform also had far-reaching consequences on the further development of the Israelite cult and ritual. Though his reform was instituted to effect the centralization of the Israelite cult in Jerusalem, the divinely-chosen city, it unexpectedly achieved, or at least indirectly facilitated, the opposite outcome. As demonstrated in section 9.5.1, the ultimate result was the abolition of any requirement of a designated holy place for the performance of the cult, and the institution of cult rituals, albeit of a different character, which could be performed anywhere; no site was preferable to another.

This radical change must have been the cause, or the effect, or both, of momentous shifts in Israelite theology in general, and in the beliefs underlying the sacrifices in particular. The study illustrates the transition from the primeval idea that it is man's task to feed the gods to the sublime belief that God has no need for gifts and sacrifices. An omnipotent Creator of the world has no need for anything, and therefore the offerings could no longer be conceived as something done by man for God's benefit to satisfy His necessities; it had to be transformed theologically to an act performed for the advantage of man. Quotations denouncing the previous creed with respect to the sacrificial cult and its significance, from Psalms and from the prophets Isaiah, Hosea and Micah who were active during the reign of Ahaz, substantiate this thesis. The "centre of gravity" of the sacrifices shifted from God to man; they were dedicated to providing man with the benefit of spiritual exaltation, rather than as offerings for the pleasure of the Deity.

This momentous ideological shift was linked to the simultaneous evolution of a more subtle monotheistic creed, as is evident in the relevant prophetic citations of this period; this linkage in turn created the philosophical foundation for consecutive stages of further sublimations of the cult. Josiah's reform resulted in a radically new concept - performance by proxy in cult matters; this concept was possible only after Ahaz' first step of a more spiritually abstract attitude toward the sacrifices. Josiah's reform was consequently facilitated by the previous reformer, king Ahaz, who possibly executed the first revolutionary shift in the manner of offerings in the Israelite cult, and who opened the door to a more sublime and sophisticated sacrificial cult. I thus analyzed the impact of Ahaz' reform in its various aspects, and its consequences are perceived as the first step in a line of reforms and modifications extending to the ultimate cessation of the sacrificial cult.

The exile to Babylonia had important consequences on the development of Israelite custom and religion, and therefore I granted much prominence to an analysis of the relevant circumstances in Judah after the return from exile, and the accomplishments of the great reformers Ezra and Nehemiah. Their overall theology was portrayed in order to explain the impact of their operations on the cult. The shift from the previous manner of worship, performed for the sake of the Deity, to a procedure designed for man's spiritual exaltation, as well as the centralization of the cult and consequent exclusion of laics from the actual performance of the sacrifices, may have induced a certain indifference among the people toward the sacrificial system. Critical analysis of the books of Ezra and Nehemiah and the juxtaposition of their statements with the prophetic remonstrances of Haggai and Malachi demonstrate the careless attitude of some elements of the populace with regard to the Temple and the sacrificial cult. Ezra and Nehemiah attempted to address the problematic attitude, both by good-natured persuasion and by the use of repressive measures, within the framework of their beliefs regarding the characteristics of the Torah, God's word, and their sweeping interpretations of this word. Due to the utmost significance of their reform with respect to the future development of the Israelite creed and particularly the manner in which the divine rules were obeyed, the study elaborates on a number of other elements of Israelite national and religious life, particularly the circumstances in Judah in this period and the interpretive system of Ezra and Nehemiah.

I have also demonstrated the relevance of the tension between the individual and the collective with respect to the sacrificial system, and the way in which this tension was resolved by Ezra and Nehemiah. The perspective that donating money for the cult would equal actual performance was a further sophistication in cult practice. Ezra and Nehemiah thus achieved a twofold payoff: they ensured a constant inflow of money for the Temple's cult and other activities, and offered the people the same spiritual exaltation as if they had performed the offerings themselves. Ezra and Nehemiah followed in the path of Josiah, and enhanced the status of Jerusalem as the religious center of the Israelite people. Josiah had utilized the sacrificial ceremonial to foster his political ambitions of uniting the people in the northern and southern parts of Israel, and Ezra and Nehemiah acted similarly for the sake of the union of the Israelite people in Israel and the Diaspora. In establishing their theocratic state, they organized the various classes of clergy and ensured their remuneration through appropriate laws allocating the expenses for the maintenance of the Temple, its sacrificial ceremonies and the sustenance of the Temple's servants. The organized system in which all the people shared in the financing of the sacrifices was the origin of the concept of performance by proxy, and solved the deficiency created by Josiah's centralization of the cult in Jerusalem as an exclusive privilege of the priesthood. A sophisticated theology was created whereby the individual, through his donation, was granted the prospect of a spiritually exciting experience, as if he were sacrificing the offering himself. There is no adequate evidence to ascertain whether this idea was initially included in Nehemiah's rule for the general contribution to the Temple services, or whether it was a consequence of it; but I think that the Israelite concept of fulfilling divine precepts by proxy originated in that time, and was thereafter broadly applied wherever logical and feasible. The division between public and individual sacrifices was also instituted as a result of this change in practice and theological thought.

The utmost significance bestowed upon the sacrifices and its assignment to a select aristocratic oligarchy concentrated momentous power, religious, legal, economic and political, in the hands of the High Priest. This led to two opposing consequences. On the one hand, it inspired the significant P stratum of the Pentateuch, and influenced its final redaction; on the other hand, as is common in human behaviour, it engendered the corruption of the eminent priestly clans, who neglected the sacrificial service and with their power and money attempted to impose alien custom on the Israelite people. But the devotion of the simple people and the lesser priestly clans to the original Israelite way of life and sacrificial ceremonial succeeded in restoring control over the Temple and its celebrations. The sacrificial ceremonies in Jerusalem again became the focal point of all the Jewish people, both in Israel and the Diaspora. Though this process is not explicitly described in Scripture, logical reflection on the relevant biblical pericopes establishes a sound basis for these conjectures.

At a later point it seems that the donation of money for sacrifices was no longer perceived as sufficient to satisfy the individual's spiritual needs. We learn from Mishnah Ta'anith that to remedy this deficiency the land and the people were divided into twenty-four districts; when the priests and Levites of each district went up to Jerusalem to offer sacrifices, according to their turn, the people assembled in their locations to read biblical pericopes. A further sublimation of the sacrificial cult was thus accomplished: the recital of the biblical text describing the daily *Tamid* was made equal to its actual performance. A full-fledged organization of meeting places and gatherings of devotees was thus in full operation at the time of the Temple's destruction, and was ready to replace the sacrifices after their cessation. Thanks to the previously entrenched concept of the replacement of actual offerings with recitals, the ultimate shift was not drastic and was able to be smoothly implemented. The study postulates that prayers were attached later to the now firmly-established recitals; as the recitals were performed at fixed schedules, in harmony with the corresponding sacrifices, so too were the newly instituted public prayers.

For this last step of the cult reform, the cessation of actual performance of the sacrifices and their replacement with recitals of the relevant biblical pericopes, there are no biblical sources, and I availed myself of quotations from various post-biblical sources. I examined the proposition proffered by some scholars concerning the probable continuation of sacrificial worship after the Temple's destruction, and demonstrated the opposite, substantiating my assertion with talmudic citations; I illustrated the deliberate policy of the Sages, the spiritual leaders of the people, not to renew the sacrifices after the Temple's destruction. I believe I have thus offered a reasonable explanation for the commonly held but hitherto unexplained assumption that sacrifices were replaced with prayer.

I proposed to distinguish between the concept of prayer as a petition for a desired result, and the recital of biblical passages, and postulated the following: The continuous sublimation of the sacrificial cult and the system of substitution, continually refined and sophisticated, achieved as its end result the equalization of the recitals of the relevant biblical pericopes with the performance of the offerings. It was thus the recitals of the pertinent verses, and not the later-added prayers, which replaced the sacrifices. I substantiated my thesis through citations from primary and secondary sources, and through an examination of the many biblical terms, commonly perceived to express the concepts of prayer and supplication. The great diversity in the words used for these concepts reflects the manifold experiences of man's dialogue with the Deity in Israelite tradition, in stark opposition to a system of established prayer at fixed times. The later prayers were an outgrowth of a long-established and institutionalized use of a sacrificial "surrogate". In defence of this later manifestation, we must acknowledge that the greatest part of these so-called prayers actually consists of praises, benedictions of the Deity, and thanksgiving for benefits received, with only a small part representing supplications.

I believe that my theory illustrates the phases in the development of the ideology of substitution, and explains other enigmatic and complex issues: a) the foundation of the unique rite of established prayers, b) the absence of traumatic consequences with the loss of the ritual center after the Temple's destruction, and c) the reorganization of the Israelite people as a religiously guided community. The Sages' efforts were thus responsible for various paradoxical outcomes, a common phenomenon in religious thought. Josiah's reform set up the centralization of the cult in one holy site; yet in the end this led to the creation of synagogues for the performance of ritual ceremonies all over the world, with no special sanctity attached to them prior to their dedication by the people as a site for prayer. Josiah's reform concentrated the execution of the cult ceremonials in the hands of a small and select group, descended from an imaginary "forefather", but ultimately the opposite result obtained: simple rituals of recitation and prayers, which could be performed by everyone, became the essence of the cult, and an intellectual leadership was created without any requirement of a special lineage.

The Sages sustained an even greater paradox: they convinced the people that the cessation of the hitherto most significant sacrificial cult was not fatal to the continuation of Israel and the fulfillment of the divine precepts in order to preserve the particular relation between God and Israel; yet at the same time they kept alive the hope and expectation that the cult in its previous form would eventually be reinstated. The daily prayers for the rebuilding of the Temple in holy Jerusalem and the resumption of the sacrificial ceremonies, along with the recital of the relevant biblical and post-biblical pericopes, confirm their success in harmonizing these extremes.

Appendices

Appendix I. I Kings 6: 17 - 22: A Comparison Between The MT and LXX Texts

The golden altar is mentioned three times in I Kings chaps. 6 and 7, in the list of the Temple's furnishings made by Solomon. The first occurrence is in 6: 20: ויצפהו זהב סגור ויצף מזבח ארז "He overlaid the inside with pure gold, and he also overlaid the altar of cedar." Although it is not specified to which altar this refers, one must understand from the context that it concerns the altar (table?) inside the Temple, and not the outer altar, where sacrifices were burned. The second occurrence is in 6: 22: וכל המזבח אשר לדביר צפה זהב "He overlaid with gold the altar that belonged to the inner sanctuary," and here there is explicit reference to the inner golden altar. The third occurrence, in 7: 48, is found in the concluding pericope recapitulating all that Solomon made: ויעש שלמה את כל הכלים אשר בית ה' את מזבח הזהב ואת השלחן אשר עליו לחם הפנים זהב "Solomon made all the furnishings that were in the Lord's Temple: the golden altar; the golden table on which was the showbread." The authenticity of a number of verses in these passages describing the Temple furnishings has been a matter of discussion among scholars. The LXX has significantly different texts for certain verses, and attests to the inherent textual problems in the MT passages. Let me set out the relevant pericope in chap. 6 and review several of the issues.

וארבעים באמה היה הבית הוא ההיכל לפני. וארז אל הבית פנימה מקלעת פקעים ופטורי צצים הכל ארז אין אבן נראה. ודביר בתוך הבית מפנימה הכין לתתן שם את ארון ברית ה'. ולפני הדביר עשרים אמה ארך ועשרים אמה רחב ועשרים אמה קומתו ויצפהו זהב סגור ויצף מזבח ארז. ויצף שלמה את הבית מפנימה זהב סגור ויעבר ברתיקות זהב לפני הדביר ויצפהו זהב. ואת כל הבית צפה זהב עד תם כל הבית וכל המזבח אשר לדביר צפה זהב

The main hall in front of this room was forty cubits long. The inside of the Temple was cedar, carved with gourds and open flowers. Everything was cedar; no stone was to be seen. He prepared the inner sanctuary within the Temple to set the ark of the covenant of the Lord there. The inner sanctuary was twenty cubits long, twenty, and twenty high. He overlaid the inside with pure gold, and he also overlaid the altar of cedar. Solomon covered the inside of the Temple with pure god, and he extended gold chains across the front of the inner sanctuary, which was overlaid with gold. So he overlaid the whole interior with gold. He also overlaid with gold the altar that belonged to the inner sanctuary.

Verse 6: 17 ends with the word לפני "before" or "in front", which does not fit either stylistically or contextually. The LXX has entirely omitted verse

18 and connected the end of verse 17 with verse 19, changing the indefinite ודביר to a definite location, לפני הדביר κατὰ πρόσωπον τοῦ δεβιρ, making the text logical and understandable: "The main hall before the Debir [the inner sanctuary] was forty cubits long; he prepared the House, the middle of [the Debir], to set there the ark of the Covenant of the Lord." Again, however, the two first words of verse 20 ולפני הדביר "And before the Debir" make no sense in the context, since they are followed with the measure of the Debir, and nothing which would logically follow "before". The LXX omits this phrase, and thus places the dimensions of the Debir in logical continuation after its description - first its purpose and then its dimensions. The second part of v. 20 in the MT, ויצף מזבח ארז, is also out of place; there was no mention that an altar was made, yet now we are informed that it was overlaid with gold. The LXX changed the text to read καὶ ἐποίησεν θυσιαστήριον "and he made an altar." It seems that this interjection was already made before the Greek translation, because it represents an odd interpolation of the making of an altar between the description of the building, the היכל, and that of the דביר; the making of an altar is entirely out of context. MT verses 21 and 22 seem an unnecessary repetition, and therefore the LXX has changed the text and placed v. 21 as a continuation of the end of v. 20, referring to the altar, in contrast to the MT text in which v. 21 relates to the main hall. The odd addition at the end of MT v. 22 referring to the altar, וכל המזבח אשר לדביר צפה זהב, though the beginning of the verse refers to the interior of the Temple, was also omitted by the LXX.

Noth[1] and Rehm[2] examine these verses, and although there are some differences of opinion concerning certain parts of the verses, they agree that this pericope was extensively modified, with some verses interpolated before and some after the translation of the LXX. For our purpose it suffices to demonstrate the obvious "manipulations" in this pericope, a fact which should support the same assertion for I Kings 8: 64 concerning the holocaust altar, a matter directly related to our study. Later changes of the texts concerning the sacrificial cult in all its aspects, including the Temple furnishings, which were made for ætiological purposes, are evident in these chapters. There is one particular issue I wish to elaborate upon, relating to I Kings 6: 22.

Both Noth and Rehm suggest that the second part of v. 22, וכל המזבח אשר לדביר צפה זהב, which is missing in the LXX, is a later interpolation with the purpose of somehow clarifying the preceding verses. I would propose considering this verse as just the opposite. This verse attests to the fact that the altar overlaid with gold was placed in the דביר, that is in the

---

[1]   M. Noth, *Könige*, Biblischer Kommentar Altes Testament IX/1 (Neukirchen, 1968), p. 101.

[2]   M. Rehm, *Das Erste Buch der Könige, Ein Kommentar* (Eichstatt, 1979), pp. 65-6.

Holy of Holies, and this was certainly not the case in the Second Temple period, where we read in Exodus that the golden altar stood in the היכל, the Great Hall; therefore, the term ולפני "in front" was interpolated at the beginning of v. 20.[3] This prior declaration that the golden altar stood in the Debir may represent the situation in the First Temple, when a golden table on which food was laid out was offered to the Deity in the Debir before the ark, the seat of the Deity, on the Cherubim.[4] It is possible, therefore, that some late editor changed the term המזבח from plural into singular; the adjective וכל "and all" requires the plural המזבחות, but since according to tradition there was only one golden "incense" altar in the Temple, the text was changed. In fact, we may deduce from the above-quoted I Kings 7: 48 that at least two tables stood in the Debir, one for the exhibition of the showbread and the other for meat. Offering food to the gods was a general custom in the surrounding cultures,[5] and would explain the odd command in Exod. 30: 36 requiring Moses to put fragrant substances לפני העדת "in front of the Testimony," the ark; this would correspond to "in the Debir" in our verse, where one might expect such offerings to be put on a table. The odd location of the golden altar לפני הפרכת אשר על ארן העדת לפני הכפרת אשר על העדת "in front of the curtain that is before the ark of the Testimony - before

---

[3]   Prof. J. Revell expressed his general hesitation against the common attitude of Bible critics who postulate interpolations made by the ancient editors, but at the same time denounce them as unfitting, literally or conceptually. Why, in other words, would the editors insert something in a sloppy way; could they not have contrived an addition that would make sense? In light of this valid question, I shall attempt to defend the Bible critics and my specific postulate regarding the interpolation of the phrase ולפני הדביר. As I have argued in sections 8. 2. 3 and 8. 2. 4, the redactors interpreted their *Vorlage* according to their understanding of how matters "ought" to have been, or to convey what they considered to be the true tradition concerning the divine will. Doctrinal issues to bring the text in line with current circumstances and beliefs motivated the editors to execute emendations and additions, and this goal was considered superior to any literary consideration. The editors could not leave unaltered a text that would imply that the golden altar was in the Holy of Holies, and had to add a phrase to correct this assumed error in transmission. It is also plausible to assume that the editors were more likely to add words, a common procedure with respect to ancient manuscripts, than to erase passages of the text, a system which may have made it easier to effect reasonable emendations. The deemed holiness of the text, as well as a natural human preference for adding rather then erasing text, may explain the sometimes odd and apparently senseless interpolations. Each case must be analyzed on its own merits; there are instances in which the interpolations are logically and literarily appropriate, and only historical evidence reveals them as later additions.

[4]   The attribute ישב הכרבים is attested in this period from a number of citations: I Sam. 4: 4; II Sam. 6: 2; II Kings 19: 15 and Isa. 37: 16.

[5]   See G. A. Barton, "A Comparison of Some Features of Hebrew and Babylonian Ritual," *JBL 46* (1927), pp. 79 - 89; H. J. Hermisson, *Sprache und Ritus im Altisraelitischen Kult* (Neukirchen-Vluyn, 1965), p. 22.

the atonement cover that is over the testimony [Exod. 30: 6]" would also indicate that this altar was to be located "in front of the ark" in the Debir, as verse 22b must be understood from a plain reading.

The interchange between מזבח and שלחן is documented in Ezek. 41: 22, a matter amply discussed in chap. 7; this interchange supports the above thesis that a table once stood "in the Debir," in front of the ark,[6] on which food and fragrant substances were presented, but not burned. Noth[7] comments that the mention of the altar in the MT text of I Kings 6: 20 and 22 is not in its place, since in chap. 6 we encounter only the particulars of the building, and not of the furnishings, which appear only in chap. 7. He speculates that this golden altar, which is located "before" the ark, is not appropriate for burning, and he therefore assumes that the altar mentioned in chap. 6 corresponds to the table on which the showbread was laid, in 7: 48. He too considers there to be an equivalence between the table and the altar. It is thus plausible that 22b - with the notion that a table- altar, *Altartisch* in the lexicon of the German biblical scholars, stood in the Debir, in front of the ark - was actually an ancient element of the pericope, and was left untouched by the later editor. We do not know what occasion provoked the shift of the table from the Debir to the Great Hall, and the linguistic division between the מזבח and שלחן, as a result of the separation of their purposes. The development and the sophistication of the cult generated such modifications in the use of the furnishings and in their nomenclature, but in the transition period both names were interchangeable.

It is now impossible to reconstruct the original text of this pericope, and the *Vorlage* the LXX translator found before him. It is possible that he already had the corrupt text as it now appears in the MT, and attempted merely to make order in the text and render it intelligible; or it is possible he had a straightforward text, exactly like the translation, which was corrupted later. The issue is even more complex, since in the LXX the entire narrative concerning Solomon's building of the Temple differs from the MT text to a great extent. As Prof. J. W. Wevers has enlightened me, it was common procedure for the LXX editor to correct texts that were in his opinion flawed. The following is a simple example. I Kings 11: 32 and 36 in the MT text read respectively והשבט האחד and שבט אחד, that is, a single tribe. The LXX translates in both instances δύο σκῆπτρα, two sceptres, to correct the

---

[6]   The inappropriate verse division in Ezek. 41: 22 (its dependence upon the end of v. 21 - see Zimmerli, *Ezekiel*, p. 384) and the cryptic introduction to the altar-table in v. 21 (ופני הקדש) may conceal some emendations regarding the site of the table. It is also plausible that in Ezekiel's period the table had already been moved from the דביר into the היכל.

[7]   p. 122.

apparent discrepancy with respect to v. 31, which indicates עשרה השבטים;[8] subtracting one tribe from twelve would result in eleven, not ten. In summary, it suffices for our purpose to doubt the authenticity of the verses in I Kings relating to the building of the Temple and its furnishings, and to add further evidence to the thesis of the interchange of שלחן and מזבח in the biblical language of the monarchic period.

---

[8]   For another solution of this apparent discrepancy, see P. Heger, *Incense Cult*, pp. 282 - 286, Appendix V, "A Study on the Hermeneutics of שבט."

Appendix II. The Hermeneutical Method of Ezra and Nehemiah with Respect to Labour Restrictions on Sabbath and the Prohibition Against Intermarriage

The "Restrictions" of Ezra and Nehemiah

I use the term "restrictions" to coincide with the rabbinic concept of making a "fence", to expand the extent of the precepts and prohibitions so as to further insulate the core of the law from the possibility of transgression. At the end of the first Mishnah of Aboth, the significant declaration of how the Torah given to Moses on Sinai was transmitted to the Rabbis, we read the maxim ועשו סייג לתורה "Make a 'fence' to the Torah." In this occurrence, as in many others, the Aramaic term סייג is used, but the Hebrew term גדר is also found in this respect. The verse ופרץ גדר ישכנו נחש "Whoever breaks through a wall may be bitten by a snake [Eccl. 10: 8]" is interpreted as follows in Sifrei Num. *Pisqa* 48: ד״ה (כב) כי: ופורץ גדר ישכנו נחש הא כל הפורץ גדרם של חכמים לסוף שפורענויות באות עליו "Whoever breaches the fence of the Sages, in the end he will suffer punishment."

Extension of Labour Restrictions on Sabbath

We read in Neh. 13: 15: בימים ההמה ראיתי ביהודה דרכים גתות בשבת ומביאים הערמות ועמסים על החמרים ואף יין ענבים ותאנים וכל משא ומביאים ירושלם ביום השבת ואעיד ביום מכרם ציד "In those days I saw men in Judah treading winepresses on the Sabbath and bringing the grain and loading it on donkeys, together with wine, grapes, figs and all other kinds of loads. And they were bringing all this into Jerusalem on the Sabbath. Therefore I warned them against selling food on that day." This is the NIV interpretation, which suggests that there were Jews working on Sabbath, but the Hebrew text does not confirm this. The KJV interprets "saw I in Judah," with no indication as to who was doing the work. The LXX also translates the phrase with the non-specific ἐν Ιουδα (Esdras II 23: 15). The correct interpretation of this phrase is crucial to the understanding of the problem of the institution of the Sabbath laws, an issue debated by scholars; we may understand that the work of treading the winepresses and bringing the staples to Jerusalem was effected by non-Jews, while the Jews simply bought these provisions. The pericope in Jer. 17: 21 - 22, כה אמר ה' השמרו בנפשותיכם ואל תשאו משא ביום השבת והבאתם בשערי ירושלם. ולא תוציאו משא מבתיכם ביום השבת וכל מלאכה לא תעשו וקדשתם את יום השבת כאשר צויתי את אבותיכם "This is what the Lord says: Be careful not to carry a load on the Sabbath day or bring it through the gates of Jerusalem. Do not bring a load out of your houses or do any work on the Sabbath, but keep the Sabbath day holy, as I commanded your forefathers," is considered by

scholars to be a deuteronomic interjection, as they are of the opinion that the
Sabbath laws are a post-exilic institution. In the opinion of W. L. Holladay,[9]
for instance, the Sabbath laws date "most likely from the last half of the fifth
century."[10] W. Thiel[11] demonstrates that the text of Jer. 19 - 27 unmistakably
represents a deuteronomic literary style;[12] the context of the promise in vv.
24 - 26 confirms an exilic origin, and the theme of vv. 21 - 22 and the
additional activities prohibited on Sabbath reveal a post-exilic origin in
Nehemiah's period.[13] M. Grinberg[14] disputes this view and illustrates on the
basis of various biblical pericopes that the Sabbath was already sanctified in
the pre-exilic period. It is not within the scope of this study to discuss the
literary analysis of these verses in Jer. and their affinity with deuteronomic
texts, but I wish to point out another aspect of the issue. The Sabbath was
certainly an ancient holy day, as we must deduce from early writings such as
II Kings 4: 23: היום לא חדש ולא שבת "It is not the New Moon or the
Sabbath"; II Kings 11: 7, recording the changing of the guards in the Temple
on Sabbath: כל יצאי השבת "those who go out on the Sabbath"; Hosea 2: 13
(2: 11 in KJV): והשבתי כל משושה חגה חדשה ושבתה וכל מועדה "I will
stop her celebrations: Her yearly festivals, her New Moons, her Sabbath days
- all her appointed feasts"; and Isa. 1: 13: חדש ושבת קרא מקרא לא אוכל
און ועצרה "New Moons, Sabbaths and convocations - I cannot bear your
evil assemblies."

The point of contention in Israelite society was the extent of the
prohibitions. One may ask in particular the meaning of the new terms utilized
in the later writings - קדש for the hallowing of the Sabbath (Jer. 17: 22, 24,
27; Neh. 9: 14, 10: 32, 13: 22) and חילול for the desecration of the Sabbath
(Neh. 13: 17, 18) - and what precise activities these terms included. These
terms do not occur in the earlier writings, but are prominent in post-exilic
writings with respect to the veneration of the Sabbath; we also encounter in
these writings additional activities which are now forbidden on the Sabbath.

---

[9]   *Jeremiah 1, A Commentary on the Book of the Prophet Jeremiah Chapters 1 - 25*, ed. P.
      D. Hanson (Philadelphia, 1986).

[10] W. Gross in the Introduction to *Jeremia und die Deuteronomistische Bewegung*, B. B. B.
      Band 98, (Weinheim, 1995) summarizes the recent scholarly opinion regarding the origin
      of the Book of Jeremiah that it was formulated or reworked into its current form in exile
      by deuteronomic editors.

[11] *Die Deuteronomistische Redaktion von Jeremia 1 - 25* (Neukirchen, 1973).

[12] Jeremiah's utterances are remarkably similar to those of the later Isaiah; see 56: 2-6 and
      58: 13.

[13] As with other cases of changes in belief and ritual, the move toward a more strict
      application of the Sabbath laws may have begun earlier, but Ezra and Nehemiah were
      responsible for its ultimate implementation.

[14] עיונים בספר ירמיהו in פרשת השבת בירמיהו Vol. II, pp. 23 - 52 (Tel Aviv).

Nehemiah criticizes the evil habit of engaging in commerce and business transactions on Sabbath. We read in 13: 19: לא יבוא משא ביום השבת "No load could be brought in on the Sabbath day," referring to Nehemiah's regulation forbidding the sales activity described in the antecedent verse 16: וכל מכר ומכורים בשבת לבני יהודה ובירושלם "...all kind of merchandise and selling them in Jerusalem." It does not seem reasonable that the nobles of Judah whom Nehemiah rebuked (v. 17) did not respect the Sabbath; it is simply that they did not consider the practice of commerce a prohibited activity, included in the concept of מלאכה "work". Jeremiah's above-cited admonition has a complete affinity with Nehemiah's censure of and covenant with the Israelites: וכל שבר ביום השבת למכור לא נקח מהם בשבת וביום קדש "We shall not buy merchandise [brought in] for sale on Sabbath or in any holy day [Neh. 10: 32]." This verse unequivocally corroborates the thesis that the dissension between Nehemiah and the people and nobles of Judah was not about the holiness of the Sabbath, since it is included with the other holy days, which were most certainly recognized; his purpose was to prohibit trading on those days. It is possible that in the Northern kingdom, trading was already considered a prohibited activity on Sabbath. We read in Amos 8: 5: לאמר מתי יעבר החדש ונשבירה שבר והשבת ונפתחה בר להקטין איפה ולהגדיל שקל ולעות מאזני מרמה "[...those that swallow up the needy] saying: When will the New Moon be over that we may sell grain, and the Sabbath be ended that we may market wheat"; it seems that selling was a prohibited activity in the Northern kingdom on the holy days, New Moon and Sabbath, and the business people waited for their passing to recommence their insidious activities. This interpretation is based on the assumption that the term שבת refers to the weekly Sabbath day, as the LXX translates τὰ σάββατα; but Jonathan interprets this as ושמטתא, the seventh year resting of the land (Lev. 25: 2-7), and some traditional commentators follow the Targum.

Nehemiah's perspective on the character of the Sabbath appears in other pericopes of the same period, which employ the same novel terms קדש and חלל with respect to the Sabbath (Ezek. 20: 12, 13, 16, 20, 21, 24; 22: 8; 23: 38; 44: 24; Isa. 56: 2; 58: 13). This commonality confirms the later origin of this new ideological disposition toward the Sabbath and the extension of its functional codex. The dissensions were not about the concept of the Sabbath as a day of rest, but with respect to what activities were included in the term מלאכה and thus to be avoided. It seems that a significant sector of the Israelites did not consider business transactions to be prohibited on the Sabbath, because they were not "toil" like the usual work in the field. Nehemiah had a different perception of the veneration of the Sabbath, a day hallowed by God, as written in Exod. 20: 11: על כן ברך ה׳ את יום השבת ויקדשהו "Therefore the Lord blessed the Sabbath day and made it holy"; every profane activity was considered to defile its divine sanctity. The enhanced glorification of the Sabbath probably started in exile, as a means of separation from the general Babylonian society, as we may observe from the numerous citations emphasizing its pre-eminence in Ezek. and Deutero-Isaiah. The Sabbath constitutes the אות "sign" between God and Israel (Ezek. 20: 12), and the crucial element of the covenant between God and proselytes (Isa. 56: 4). The desecration of the Sabbath is compared to the defilement of the Temple (Ezek. 22: 8 and 23: 38). Ezra and Nehemiah translated the abstract spiritual vision of these prophets into pragmatic and concrete reality. Holladay concludes his thesis on the above-qoted verse of Jer.: "It is not, we conclude, a word from Jrm [Jeremiah], but it is a word that helped to shape the outlook of the postexilic community....[Nehemiah's] zeal helped to assure the survival of the community."

Extension of Prohibition against Intermarriage

a) Differences of Opinion in Israelite Society

I refer to the relevant narratives in Ezra 10: 2 - 44, Neh. 9: 2; 10: 31; 13: 1- 3 and 23 - 28. It is obvious that on this issue also significant segments of the people had not considered intermarriage a transgression of the divine law. Without going into a detailed discussion, I shall note several passages that confirm this viewpoint. Well-established mythological tales found in Scripture include Joseph's marriage to an Egyptian (Gen. 41: 45), and Moses' marriage to a Midianite (Exod. 2: 21) and a Cushite (Num. 12: 1). Solomon's marriage into the Egyptian royal family is recorded to demonstrate his great international prestige; there is no hint of any censure (I Kings 3: 1). The story of Ruth, the Moabite whose descendant was king David, also corroborates this thesis; even if it is a late document, composed to counteract Nehemiah's legislation, it certainly serves as evidence of dissension in this respect on the part of at least one group of intellectuals.

b) New Rules Contrary to Pentateuchal Decrees

Scripture explicitly prohibits intermarriage with both males and females only with respect to members of the seven peoples who inhabited the Promised Land; the reason indicated is to avoid exposure to evil idolatrous influence (Deut. 7: 1 - 4). The prohibition against absorbing Ammonites and Moabites into the Israelite community appears in Deut. 23: 4 - 5, and Nehemiah repeats in 13: 2 the deuteronomic motive for this exclusion: כי לא קדמו את בני ישראל בלחם ובמים וישכר עליו את בלעם לקללו "because they had not met the Israelites with food and water but had hired Balaam to call a curse down on them." Nehemiah extends his opposition to marriage with women from Ashdod (13: 23), obviously Philistines, who are not mentioned in any other biblical prohibition. We must assume that in v. 25 he was implicitly extending to all peoples the prohibition in Deut. 7: 3 against intermarriage only with members of the seven peoples. Ezra also objected to intermarriage with all foreign women; v. 10: 2 mentions נשים נכריות מעמי הארץ "foreign women from the people around us," while other occurrences refer simply to נשים נכריות, not specifically Moabites and Ammonites. It is interesting to note certain rabbinic homilies and dicta with respect to this issue of intermarriage, which are in total opposition to Nehemiah's dictate. We read in Mishnah Yebamoth 8: 3 עמוני ומואבי אסורים ואיסורן איסור עולם אבל נקבותיהם מותרות מיד "Male Ammonites and Moabites are eternally prohibited [from being absorbed into the Israelite community], but their females are permitted immediately." Moreover, in Mishnah Yadayim 4: 4 we read of a male Ammonite who desired to be converted to Judaism and be incorporated into the Jewish people, and the assembly of the Sages decided to accept him, against the opposition of Rabban Gamaliel the President, because they declared: כבר עלה סנחריב מלך אשור ובלבל את כל האומות "Sennacherib king of Assyria had intermingled all the peoples [by his exchange of conquered populations]."

Appendix III. The Priesthood Of Jehoiada

The approach of Chronicles to the issue of the High Priesthood of Jehoiada is remarkable, and is characteristic of the confusion generated by the attempt to harmonize the different biblical citations with a predetermined concept - in this case, that the High Priesthood started with Aaron and that all successive High Priests were his descendants.

Jehoiada does not appear in the list of the twenty-three High Priests from Aaron to Jehozadak enumerated in I Chr. 5: 29 - 41 (6: 3 - 14 in KJV). Jehozadak was not in fact a High Priest, since we read in II Kings 25: 18 and Jer. 52: 24: ויקח רב טבחים את שריה כהן הראש ואת צפניה[ו] כהן [ה]משנה "[The commander] took as prisoners Seraiah the High priest, Zephaniah the priest next in rank"; hence Seraiah's son was not consecrated as a High Priest, since the celebrations at the Temple were discontinued with its destruction. Jehozadak appears again in Ezra and Nehemiah as the father of Jeshua, the High Priest. On the other hand, though the genealogy of Aaron's descendants in I Chr. 5 does not explicitly declare that all were acting High Priests, one must implicitly assume that they were. A partial list of the same personalities appears in I Chr. 6: 35 - 38, following the introduction ואהרן ובניו מקטירים ...לכל מלאכת קדש הקדשים "But Aaron and his descendants were the ones who presented offerings...in the most Holy Place [6: 34 in MT, 6: 49 in KJV]," which demonstrates the duties carried out by these kinsmen. The traditional commentator Mezudath David was concerned with the absence of Jehoiada in the above genealogical list; as he could not admit an error in Scripture, he proposed that Johanan, the father of Azariah, might have been Jehoiada. He identified Azariah, the son of Johanan/ Jehoiada, as the Azariah mentioned in I Chr. 5: 36, and as the כהן הראש "Chief Priest" Azariah at the time of king Uzziahu / Azariah in II Chr. 26: 17 - 20; it would thus be possible that Jehoiada's son Azariah served as a High Priest during a part of the reign of Joash (29 years, according to Scripture), the reign of his son Amaziah, and the reign of Azariah - Uzziah (I refrain from quoting calendar years, since there are no reliable scholarly dates for the period of these kings). It seems, however, from I Chr. 5: 36 (6: 10 in KJV) that this Azariah was considered by the Chr. editor as the High Priest during the period of Solomon, when he built the Temple. We read there: ויוחנן הוליד את עזריה הוא אשר כהן בבית אשר בנה שלמה בירושלם "Johanan the father of Azariah, it was he who served as priest in the Temple Solomon built in Jerusalem." The simple interpretation of this pericope is thus that it opens with the first High Priest, Aaron; v. 36 starts the list of the High Priests who served in the Temple built by Solomon and concludes with the last priest in v. 41 (6: 15 in KJV),ויהוצדק הלך בהגלות ה' את יהודה) וירושלם ביד נבכדנאצר "Jehozadak was deported when the Lord sent Judah and Jerusalem into exile by the hand of Nebuchdnezzar." Tosafoth in their comments to B. T. Yoma 9a also interpreted this pericope in this way. We also read in I Kings 4: 2: אלה השרים אשר לו עזריהו בן צדוק הכהן "And these were his [Solomon's] chief officials, Azariah son of Zadok, the priest....," but in the above genealogical list in I Chr. 5, Zadok was the father of Ahimaaz, Ahimaaz the father of Azariah, Azariah the father of Johanan and Johanan the father of Azariah, who served as priest in the Temple; hence there were two generations between Zadok and the first Azariah, and four generations between Zadok and the second Azariah. We must remember that Zadok was nominated as a priest by Solomon in place of Abiathar (I Kings 2: 35), and thus the Chr. genealogy describing Azariah as serving at Solomon's Temple does not facilitate the resolution of the various conflicting biblical records.

The phrase in I Kings 4: 4, וצדוק ואביתר כהנים, "And Zadok and Abiathar - priests," after the narrative of Abiathar's deposition in I Kings 2: 35, complicates this issue even further. This may be an automatic repetition of the same phrase from II Sam. 20: 25, a record of David's officials, but the traditional commentators Radak and Ralbag considered it a contradiction and attempted to find solutions. Radak proposed that this Abiathar in I Kings 4: 4 was not the one deposed and deported by Solomon, but another priest with the same name. Ralbag postulated that Abiathar remained as a priest in reserve, to serve at the Temple when Zadok was prevented from discharging his priestly duties when unclean or through a similar impediment. On the other hand, there is unquestionable corroboration from II Sam. 18: 19 that Zadok, David's priest, had a son Ahimaaz, a record that matches the genealogical list in I Chr. 5; but this would put in question the possibility that his grandson Azariah, son of Johanan, served at Solomon's Temple as is recorded in I Chr. 5, especially if Zadok himself still served Solomon. Rabbi Yekutiel of Worms, a member of the Tosafoth group, suggests in his comments on B. T. Yoma 9a that the Azariah of I Chr. 5: 36 did not actually serve at the Temple in Solomon's period; v. 36 refers to Azariah who served at the time of Uzziah. Scripture grants him the same honour as if he had served at the Temple's consecration because he risked his life and position by censuring Uzziah for offering incense. The commentators were well aware of the confusion, and attempted to devise some solution.

Returning now to a general analysis of the above genealogical list in Chr., we observe that in contrast to Jehoiada, whose name is missing, we are able to corroborate the identity of the other High Priests in this list from different scriptural citations. In addition to Zadok the first and Ahimaaz, mentioned above, we find Amariah as a High Priest in the period of Jehoshaphat in II Chr. 19: 11; Azariah as High Priest in Uzziah's period in II Chr. 26: 20; Hilkiah as Josiah's High priest in II Kings 22: 4; Seraiah as the High Priest killed by the Babylonians (II Kings 25: 18 and Jer. 52: 24). A question arise with respect to the Azariah who served in Uzziah's period, namely, with which of the three Azariah's of I Chr. 5 he is to be identified. It is not the last of the three, the father of Seraiah, since his father Hilkiah served in the period of Josiah, who reigned much later (639 - 609) than Uzziah. It is also not the

Appendices

second Azariah, who served at Solomon's Temple, some two hundred years before king Uzziah, and it certainly cannot be the first Azariah, Johanan's father and the second Azariah's grandfather.

Ezra 7: 1 - 5, which traces Ezra's lineage from Aaron, conforms to the sequence of the generations in the genealogical list of I Chr. 5; this is likely not coincidental, considering the scholarly opinion that both books had the same editors. In Ezra, however, a block of six persons - Johanan, Azariah, Ahimaaz, Zadok, Ahitub and Amariah - are missing between Meraioth and Azariah in the Chr. list, possibly due to haplographic oversight. There are no other occurrences of the priests Abishua, Bukki, Uzzi, Zerahia, Meraioth, Amariah and Ahitub enumerated in the Chr. genealogy between Phinehas and Zadok. According to a Midrash in Elijah Rabbah (ed. Ish Shalom) *Parshah* 12, the High Priesthood was removed from Phinehas' descendants because of his unfortunate handling of the Concubine of the Hill affair, and granted to Ithamar's descendants; Eli's sons of the Ithamar clan then corrupted the priesthood, and therefore they lost it. Solomon removed Abiathar of this clan from the High Priesthood, and reinstated Zadok, of Phinehas - Eleazar lineage, to this high office. This would explain the absence of Ahimelech and Abiathar from the lists in Chr. and Ezra, since these lists record only the priestly Eleazar lineage, and do not mention Ithamar's descendants. Josephus repeats this Midrash in *Ant.* VIII: 11, and explains that these descendants of Phinehas served as common priests during the period in which Ithamar's descendants were the High Priests. Josephus, however, is not meticulous in transmitting exact data, and there are differences between the names in *Ant.* V: 361 - 362 and VIII: 11 - 12. The Samaritans also believe that Eli was of Ithamar's lineage: "Eli came of the Ithamar branch of the priesthood, and the Samaritans ever since his time have rejected the claims of that branch in favour of the sons of Phinehas."[15]

The above arguments demonstrate the general difficulties and perplexities in sorting out the genealogical issues connected with the office of the כהן in the records of the monarchic period. Through a critical analysis of hidden clues in the text, we may attempt to reveal some residues of the actual appointment process of the bearer of the title כהן in the early period, before the aetiological historiography of the P stratum of the Pentateuch. One must consider the probability that kings, priests and military commanders had special names. We observe, for example, that the names of the first and foremost kings, such as David and Solomon, do not recur, but many names of the later kings are repeated in Judah and Israel, sometimes with insignificant changes. We have, for example, three occurrences of Jehoahaz (Ahaz), two of Jeroboam, two of Jehoram, two of Joash, and Ahaziah with the theophoric

---

[15] John MacDonald, *The Theology of the Samaritans*. New Testament Library (London, 1964), p. 17.

suffix instead of Jehoahaz with the same prefix. We encounter similar circumstances in the priestly clan: the names of Aaron, Eleazar and Ithamar, the "founding" priests, do not occur in "later" generations, but the names Ahitub, Zadok and Ahimelech, for example, repeat themselves, and generally do not appear as common names. Although Ahitub is recorded as Ithamar's descendant in I Sam. 14: 3 בן פינחס בן עלי כהן ה' , and in I Sam. 22 as the father of Ahimelech, a priest in Nob, we also encounter Ahitub as Zadok's father in II Sam. 8: 17 and as a member of Phinehas' descendants in Ezra 7: 2; Neh. 11: 11; I Chr. 5: 33, 34, 37, 38; 6: 37; 9: 11 and 18: 16. In I Chr. 5, we encounter Zadok twice, once as Ahimaaz' father in v. 34, and a second time as Shalum's father in v. 38. We encounter Ahimelech the priest as son of Ahitub in I Sam. 22: 9, and another priest Ahimelech as son of Abiathar in I Chr. 24: 6. These and other recurrences of specific names of kings and priests should induce us to consider it plausible that these specific names went with the titles, similar to the current custom of kings and pontiffs who assume particular names when attaining these high offices. The name thus carries an affinity with the title.

An interesting support for this postulate, for which I am indebted to Prof. H. Fox, may be deduced from Mishnah Sheqalim 5: 1. We read there אלו הן הממונין שהיו במקדש "These were the appointed officers in the Temple," and then a list of their names and functions. It is understandable that Y. T. Sheqalim 5: 1, 48c, questions why only these names are mentioned, since there were many officers with the same functions during the existence of the Temple. As is common, there are two opposing solutions proposed by the Amoraim, and different explanations of their answers by the commentators. The scholar Ch. Albeck in his commentary to *Seder Mo'ed* [16] prefers the interpretation that all the officers of the Temple appointed for these functions acquired the same name with the assignment, possibly because these were the names of the first appointees. This interpretation seems to me the most logical, and is supported by a deduction based on Mishnah Midoth 1: 4 in which the various gates of the Temple court are enumerated. We read there: שבמזרח שער נקנור ושתי לשכות היו לו אחת מימינו ואחת משמאלו אחת לשכת פנחס המלביש ואחת לשכת עושי חביתין "On its east side [was] the Nicanor Gate which had two [attached] chambers, one to its right and one to its left; one [was] the chamber of Phinehas the Dresser and one the chamber of the *habitin* makers." We observe that the chamber in which the garments for the priests were kept bore permanently the name of Phinehas, who probably founded or was the original holder of this office, and hence we must assume that the same title Phinehas the Dresser prevailed for the respective officials performing the same function.

---

[16] *Commentary to the Mishnah*, Vol. 5: סדר מועד (reprinted Jerusalem, 1952).

We may similarly propose that the name Jehoiada is associated with a
military title. Benaiah son of Jehoiada appears countless times in Samuel,
Kings and Chronicles as a hero, a military commander and a confidante of
the king; his loyalty was exclusively to the king, for whom he performed
many deeds, repulsive and otherwise, similar to a *Samurai* in Japanese
tradition. One may assume that he was duly compensated for these services
with titles and honours at the court. Benaiah son of Jehoiada was one of
David's mighty men, as appears in II Sam. 23: 22 and I Chr. 11: 22. From the
Sam. narrative we have no hint as to when Benaiah started his career as one
of David's mighty men, but from the Chr. record one may assume that he
was one of David's first followers before he became king. According to I
Chr. 12, thirty mighty men came to Ziklag to support David against Saul.
Although Benaiah is not mentioned in that chapter, we read in v. 27 ויהוידע
הנגיד לאהרן ועמו שלשת אלפים ושבע מאות "Jehoiada leader of the
family of Aaron, with three thousand and seven hundred men." We might
therefore ask whether the Benaiah who served Solomon was the same person
who served David, or another with the same recurring name. We read in II
Sam. 23: 20 and I Chr. 11: 22 that Benaiah came from a courageous family
and his father was בן איש חי[ן]ל] רב פעלים. I Chr. 27: 34 mentions a certain
Jehoiada son of Benaiah, nominated a counsellor at David's court after
Ahithophel; was this Jehoiada the son of Benaiah the military hero, whose
own son Benaiah eventually served Solomon, or was it another person by the
same name? We have no way of knowing for sure, but we see recurring
names of high officials in court. Also remarkable is that a certain Abiathar, a
name that appears exclusively as that of a priest in Scripture, is also
mentioned as a counsellor together with Jehoiada the son of Benaiah. We
observe here the possible affinity between the title of priest and counsellor to
the king, and we must consider other scriptural hints, mainly in Chr., with
regard to the relationship between the title כהן and military services, a fact
which would explain Jehoiada's military intervention at Joash's
enthronement and his subsequent nomination as a כהן.

We have noted in I Chr. 12: 27 that Jehoiada of Aaron's descendants was
a military commander, and we observe from v. 28 that Zadok of the same
extraction was נער גבור חיל ובית אביו שרים עשרים ושנים "a brave young
warrior with twenty-two officers from his family." In I Chr. 27: 5 we
encounter again the association between the office of military commander
and the priesthood. We read there שר הצבא השלישי לחדש השלישי בניהו
בן יהוידע הכהן ראש ועל מחלקתו עשרים וארבעה אלף "The third army
commander, for the third month, was Benaiah son of Jehoiada the priest. He
was chief and there were twenty-four thousand men in his division." In v. 17
we find Zadok as an unspecified leader of the tribe of Aaron לאהרן צדוק,
and in 29: 22 he is nominated as a priest by David, ולצדוק לכהן. Benaiah
son of Jehoiada is mentioned numerous times in Sam. and Kings as a military
person, but never as a priest, or connected to priesthood; in those occurrences

in which priests are mentioned in the same verse, Scripture emphasizes him specifically as a military personality. Only in I Chr. 27: 5 does Benaiah appear connected to the priesthood. (In I Chr. 15 and 16 a certain Benaiah occurs as a Levite, but there is no further identification to connect him to Benaiah son of Jehoiada). Similarly, Jehoiada is not mentioned as a priest in Sam. or in Kings, before our subject narrative in II Kings 11 and 12, but again he is connected to the priesthood in I Chr. 12: 28 and 27: 5. We must therefore conclude that king Joash granted Jehoiada, the military commander and court confidante, the title כהן, and from that period onward we find priests by the name of Jehoiada in Kings, in Jer. 29: 26, and in Neh. chaps. 12 and 13 as יוידע without the ה. The returnees from exile accepted the genealogical lineage of the priestly clans of the last period of the Temple as coming from Aaron's stock, and therefore Jehoiada was considered a legitimate priest. As would be expected, the titles כהן, כהן הראש or הנגיד לאהרן were added to Jehoiada in the various occurrences of this name in Chr., and in the narratives in Kings and Chr. which relate to Jehoiada's military operation to ensure Joash's enthronement, to adapt these references to the idea prevailing at that time that all priests derive their lineage from Aaron.

Bibliography

Abbreviations

ANET   *Ancient Near Eastern Texts*, J.B. Pritchard, ed.
BAR   *Biblical Archeology Review*
BASOR   *Bulletin of the American Schools of Oriental Research*
BZAW   *Zeitschrift für die alttestamentliche Wissenschaft, Supplements*
IEJ   *Israel Exploration Journal*
JBL   *Journal of Biblical Literature*
JSOT   *Journal for the Study of the Old Testament*
VT   *Vetus Testamentum*
ZAW   *Zeitschrift für die alttestamentliche Wissenschaft*

Adams, C.J., ed. *A Reader's Guide to the Great Religions.* 2nd ed. New York, 1977.
Aharoni, Y. "Excavations at Tel Arad. Preliminary Report on the Second Season, 1963." *IEJ 17* (1967), pp. 233-49.
- "Arad: Its Description and Temple." *The Biblical Archeologist* 31 (1968), pp. 2-32.
- "Preliminary Report of the Fifth and Sixth Season 1973-74. Excavation at Tel Beersheba." *Tel Aviv* 2 (1975), pp. 54 - 156.
Albeck, Ch. *Commentary to the Mishnah.* 5 vols. Reprinted Jerusalem, 1952.
- מבוא למשנה Tel Aviv, 1959.
Albright, W. F. "The Babylonian Temple-Tower and the Altar of Burnt-Offering." *JBL* 39 (1920), pp. 137 - 142.
- "The Date and Personality of the Chronicler." *JBL* 40 (1921), pp. 104 – 124.
Alon, G. תולדות היהודים בא״י בתקופת המשנה והתלמוד Tel Aviv, 1967.
Alpert Nakhai, Beth "What's a Bamah? How Sacred Space Functioned in Ancient Israel." *BAR* 20/3 (May/June 1994), pp. 18-29, 77-8.
Altheim, F. and R. Stiehl, eds. *Die Araber in der Alten Welt.* I. Band. Berlin, 1964.
Anbar, M. "The Building of an Altar on Mount Ebal." In *Das Deuteronium. Entstehung, Gestalt und Botschaft.* Bibliotheca Ephemeridum Theologicarum Lovaniensium LXVIII, pp.304 - 309. Edited by N. Lohfink. Leuven, 1985.
The Assyrian Dictionary. Chicago, 1982. Vol. 13, s.v. "qarnu".

Bar-Efrat, S. שמואל ב. עם מבוא ופירוש. מקרא לישראל, פירוש מדעי

למקרא 9 Edited by M. Greenberg and S. Ahituv. Jerusalem, 1996.

Barton, G. A. "A Comparison of Some Features of Hebrew and Babylonian Ritual." *JBL* 46 (1927), pp. 79 - 89.

Beeby, H. D. *Grace Abounding. A Commentary on the Book of Hosea.* International Theological Commentary. Edinburgh, 1946.

Benzinger, I. *Die Bücher der Könige.* Kurzer Hand-Commentar zum Alten Testament, Abt. IX. Freiburg, 1899.

Ben Zvi, Ehud. "A Gateway to the Chronicler's Teaching." *JSOT* 7/2 (1993), pp. 216 -249.

Biblia Sacra iuxta latinem vulgatam versionem ad codicum fidem iussi Pii. Deutsche Bibelgesellschaft. 3rd ed. Stuttgart, 1983.

Biblisches Reallexikon. 2nd edition revised. Tübingen, 1977. S.v. "Altar", by A. Reichert.

Bickermann, E. *Der Gott der Makkabäer.* Berlin, 1937.

Bleek, F. *Einleitung in das Alte Testament.* Berlin,1878.

Blome, F. *Die Opfermaterie in Babylonien und Israel.* Rome, 1934.

Bodley, John H. *Anthropology and Contemporary Human Problems.* 2nd ed. Palo Alto, Ca., 1976.

Bousset, W. *Die Religion des Judentums.* Berlin, 1903.

Boyce, Mary, ed. and trans. *Textual Sources for the Study of Zoroastrianism.* Manchester, 1984.

Broshi, M. "The Expansion of Jerusalem in the Reigns of Hezekiah and Manasseh." *IEJ* 24 (1974), pp. 21-26.

Bringmann, K. *Hellenistische Reform und Religionsverfolgung in Judäa.* Göttingen, 1983.

Bruce, I.A.F. "Nerva and the *Fiscus Iudaicus*." *PEQ* 96 (1964), pp. 34-45.

Budde, K. "Das Deuteronomium und die Reform König Josias." *ZAW* 44 (1926), pp. 177-244.

Burkert, Walter. "Offerings in Perspective." In *Gifts to the Gods, Proceedings of the Uppsala Symposium 1985*, pp. 57-64. Edited by T. Linders and G. Nordquist. Uppsala, 1987.

Cassel's New Latin English, English Latin Dictionary. London, 1959. S.v. "cornu".

Cassuto, M. D. פירוש על ספר שמות Jerusalem, 1952.

Chajes, H. P. Commentary to Amos in *Biblia Hebraica, Prophetae, Liber Duodecim prophetarum.* Edited by A. Kahana. Kiev, 1906, reprinted Jerusalem, 1969.

Clark, K. W. *The Gentile Bias and Other Essays.* Selected by J. L. Sharpe III. Leiden, 1980.

Cogan, M. *Imperialism and Religion.* Society of Biblical Literature Monograph Series No. 19. Missoula, Montana, 1974.

de Groot, Johannes. *Die Altäre des Salomonischen Tempelhofes.* Stuttgart, 1924.

de Tarragon, J. M. *Le Culte à Ugarit.* Paris, 1980.

de Vaux, R. *Ancient Israel, Its Life and Institutions.* 2nd ed. London, 1973.

Dever, W. G. "Will the Real Israel Please Stand Up?" *BASOR* 297 (1995), pp. 61-80.

Dietrich, W. "Josia und das Gesetzbuch." *VT* 27 (1977), pp.18 - 22.

Dillmann, A. *Die Bücher Numeri, Deuteronomium und Joshua.* Kurzgefasstes exegetisches Handbuch zum Alten Testament, XIII. 2nd ed. Leipzig, 1886.

- *Die Bücher Exodus und Leviticus.* Kurzgefasstes exegetisches Handbuch Zum Alten Testament, XII. 3rd ed. Leipzig, 1897.

Diez Macho, A., ed. *Neophyti, Targum Palestinense*, MS de la Biblioteca Vaticana. Madrid, 1971.

Donner, H. "Art und Herkunft des Amtes der Königmutter im Alten Testament." In *Festschrift Johannes Friedrich, Zum 65. Geburtstag gewidnet*, pp. 105-44. Edited by R. von Kienle et al. Heidelberg, 1959.

Driver, S.R. *Deuteronomy.* The International Critical Commentary on the Holy Scriptures of the Old and New Testaments. 2nd ed. Edinburgh, 1896.

- *Notes on the Hebrew Text and the Topography of the Book of Samuel.* Oxford, 1913.

Duchesne-Guillemin, J."The Religion of Ancient Iran." In *Historia Religionum. Handbook for the History of Religions.* Vol. I: *Religions of the Past*, pp. 323-76. Leiden, 1969.

Dussaud, R. "Le sanctuaire et les dieux phנnicien de Ras Shamra." *RHR* CV-CVI (1932), pp. 285-86.

- *Les decouvertes de Ras Shamra (Ugarit) et l'Ancien Testament.* Paris, 1937.

Edwards, C. *The Hammurabi Code and the Sinaitic Legislation.* London, 1921.

Eichrodt, W. *Theologie des Alten Testaments.* 2 vols. Stuttgart, 1957-61.

Eissfeldt, O. *The Old Testament, An Introduction.* Translated by P. R. Ackroyd. New York, 1965.

Eglund, G. "Gifts to the Gods." In *Gifts to the Gods, Proceedings of the Uppsala Symposium 1985*, pp. 57-64. Edited by T. Linders and G. Nordquist. Uppsala, 1987.

Elbogen, I. התפלה בישראל בהתפתחותה ההיסטורית Translated from the 3rd German ed. by J. Amir. Edited by. J. Heinemann. Tel Aviv, 1972.

Elliger, K. *Leviticus.* Handbuch zum Alten Testament, Erste Reihe 4. Tübingen, 1966.

Enciclopedia delle Religioni. Roma, 1970. S.v. "Pietre".

Encyclopaedia Biblica. Jerusalem, 1962.

S.v. כהונה by M. Haran.

S.v. מיתות בית דין by S. Loewenstamm.

The Encyclopedia of Islam. New edition, Leiden, 1965. S.v. "Radjm" by M Gaudefroy-Demombynes (T. Fahd).

The Encylopedia of Religion. Edited by Mircea Eliade. London, 1987. S.v. "Stones" by C. M. Edsman.

Fleischer, E. לקדמוניות תפילות החובה בישראל *Tarbiz* 59/3-4 (1990), pp. 397-441.

Fox, H. שמחת בית השאבה *Tarbiz* 55/2 (1986), pp. 173-216.

תשובות לשני מהפכנים *Sinai* 114 (1994), pp. 162-70. -

Sherwood Fox, W. and R.E.K. Pemberton, trans. *Passages in Greek and Latin Literature relating to Zoroaster & Zoroastrianism.* Bombay, 1928.

Fricke, K. D. *Das Zweite Buch von den Königen.* Die Botschaft des Alten Testaments, 12/II. Stuttgart, 1972.

Fritz, V. *Tempel und Zelt, Studien zum Tempelbau in Israel und zu dem Zeltheiligtum der Priesterschrift.* WMANT 47. Neukirchen, 1977.

Galling, K. *Der Altar in den Kulturen des Alten Orient, Eine Archäologische Studie.* Berlin, 1925.

Gadegaard, Niels H. "On the So-Called Burnt Offering Altar in the Old Testament." *Palestine Exploration Quarterly* 110 (1978), pp. 35-45.

Gesenius' Hebrew Grammar. Edited by E. Kautzsch. 2nd English edition revised by A.E. Cowley. London, 1970.

Grabbe, Lester. *Ezra-Nehemiah.* London, 1998.

Gray, J. *I & II Kings, A Commentary.* Old Testamant Library. Revised edition. London, 1970.

Gray, John, ed. *Joshua Judges and Ruth.* The Century Bible. London, 1967.

Gressmann, Hugo. *Die Ausgrabungen in Palästina und das Alte Testament.* Altorientalische Texte zum Alten Testament 133. Tübingen, 1908.

Grinberg, M. עיונים בספר ירמיהו In פרשת השבת בירמיהו, Vol. II, pp. 23 - 52. Edited by B-Z. Luria. Tel Aviv.

Gross, W., ed. *Jeremia und die Deuteronomistische Bewegung.* B. B. B. Band 98. Weinheim, 1995.

Gunkel, H. *Genesis.* 7. Auflage. Göttingen, 1966.

Hadas, M., ed. and trans. *Aristeas to Philocrates.* New York, 1974.

Halivni, David Weiss. *Midrash, Mishna and Gemara.* Cambridge, 1986.

Hallo, W. W."The Origins of the Sacrificial Cult." In *Ancient Israelite Religion, Essays in Honor of F. M. Cross,* pp. 3 - 13. Edited by P. D. Miller, Jr., P. D. Hanson, S. D. McBride. Philadelphia, 1965.

Handbuch der Altarabischen Altertumskunde, in Verbindung mit Fr. Hommel und Nik. Rhodokanakis. Edited by D. Nielsen. I. Band: *Die*

Altarabische Kultur. Kopenhagen, 1927.

Hazon, E. על מגילת ספר, מאמרים על In חיי הרוח של כת מדבר יהודה
מגילות מדבר יהודה, pp. 85-97. Jerusalem, 1997.

Heger, P. T*he Development of Incense Cult in Israel. BZAW* 245. Berlin,
1997.

Heinemann, J. התפלה בתקופת התנאים והאמוראים Jerusalem, 1965.

Hendel, R.S. "Prophets, Priests and the Efficacy of Ritual." In *Pomegranates
and Golden Bells: Studies in Biblical, Jewish and Near Eastern Ritual,
Law and Literature in Honor of Jacob Milgrom*, pp. 185-98. Edited by D.
Wright, D.N. Freedman and A. Hurvitz. Winona Lake, 1995.

Henninger, J. *Arabia Sacra.* Orbis Biblicus et Orientalis 40. Göttingen,1981.

- "Zum Verbot des Knochen-zerbrechens bei den Semiten." In *Studi
Orientalistici in Onore di Giorgio Levi della Vida*, I, pp. 448 -458. Rome,
1956.

Hermisson, H. J. *Sprache und Ritus im Altisraelitischen Kult.*
Neukirchen-Vluyn, 1965.

Herodotus. *The Histories.* The Loeb Classical Library. 4 vols. Translated by
A.D. Godley. London, 1920-1925.

Hertzberg, H.W. *I & II Samuel, A Commentary.* The Old Testament Library.
2nd revised edition. Translated by J.S. Bowden. Philadelphia, 1960.

- *Die Bücher Joshua, Richter, Ruth.* ATD 9. 3rd ed. Göttingen, 1965.

Herzog, Ze'ev, et al. "The Israelite Fortress at Arad." *BASOR* 254 (1984), pp.
1-34.

Hesiod. "Theogony." In *Greek Literature. An Anthology*. Edited by R.
Lattimore. London: Penguin Classics, 1973.

Hoffmann, D. *Leviticus.* Berlin, 1905.

- *Das Buch Deuteronomium.* 2 parts. Berlin, 1922.

Hoffmann, H. D. *Reform und Reformen.* Zürich, 1980.

Holladay, W. L. *Jeremiah 1, A Commentary on the Book of the Prophet
Jeremiah Chapters 1 - 25.* Edited by P. D. Hanson. Philadelphia, 1986.

Hölscher, G. "Komposition und Ursprung des Deuteronomiums." *ZAW 40*
(1922), pp. 161-255.

Homer. *Iliad.* Translated by R. Fitzgerald. New York, 1974.

Hooke, S. H. *Babylonian and Assyrian Religion.* Oklahoma, 1963.

Houtman, C. *Exodus.* Historical Commentary on the Old Testament, Vol. I.
Kampen, 1993.

- "Der Altar als Asylstätte im Alten Testament." *Revue Biblique* 103/3
(1996), pp. 343-366.

Hurowitz, V. *I Have Built You an Exalted House.* JSOT/ASOR Monograph
Series 5, Supplement Series 115. Liverpool, 1992.

- "Solomon's Golden Vessels and the Cult of the First Temple." In
*Pomegranates and Golden Bells: Studies in Biblical, Jewish and Near
Eastern Ritual, Law and Literature in Honor of Jacob Milgrom*, pp.

151-64. Edited by D. Wright, D.N .Freedman and A. Hurvitz. Winona Lake, 1995.

in der Smitten, W. Th. *Esra. Quellen, Überlieferung und Geschichte*. Assen, 1973.

The Interpreter's Dictionary of the Bible. New York, 1962. S.v. "altar" by K. Galling.

James, E. O. *Origins of Sacrifice*. New York, 1971.

Jamieson-Drake, D. W. *Scribes and Schools in Monarchic Judah*. JSOTS 109. Sheffield, 1991.

Japhet, S. מחקרים בתולדות ישראל In עם וארץ בתקופת שיבת ציון השני הבית בתקופת, pp.127 - 45. Edited by D. Schwarz. Jerusalem, 1996.

Jastrow, M. *A Dictionary of the Targumim, the Talmud Babli and Yerushalmi, and the Midrashic Literature*. New York, 1985.

Josephus, *Jewish Antiquities*. Loeb Classical Library. 10 vols. Edited and translated by H. St. J. Thackeray, R. Marcus, and H. Feldman. London, 1926-1965.

- *Against Apion*. Loeb Classical Library. Translated by H. St. J. Thackeray. London, 1926.

- *The Jewish War*. Loeb Classical Library. 2 vols. Translated by H. St. J. Thackeray. London, 1928.

Joüon, P. A *Grammar of Biblical Hebrew*. Subsidia Biblica 14/I, 14/II. Translated and revised by T. Muraoka. Rome, 1993.

Julian. *Contra Galilaeos*. Edited by E. Masaracchia. Rome, 1990.

Kaiser, Otto. *Einleitung in das Alte Testament*. Gütersloh, 1969.

Kahana, A. ספר תרי עשר, חגי וזכריה Tel Aviv, 1930.

Keil, C.F.and F.D. Delitzsch. *Biblical Commentary on the Old Testament*. 4 vols. Translated from German by J. Martin. 1969.

Kempinski, A. "Joshua's Altar - An Iron Age Watchtower." *BAR* 12/1 (Jan./Feb. 1986), pp. 43-9.

Kluckhohn, Clyde "Myths and Rutuals. A General Theory." In *Reader in Comparative Religion, An Anthropological Approach*, pp. 66-77. Edited by W.A. Lessa and E.Z. Vog. N.Y., 1979.

Knohl, I. מקדש הדממה Jerusalem, 1993.

- יחס המקרא לאלילות של הנוכרים *Tarbiz* 64/1 (1995), pp. 5-12.

- "Two Aspects of the 'Tent of Meeting.'" In *Tehillah le-Moshe. Biblical and Judaic Studies in Honor of Moshe Greenberg*, pp. 73-9. Edited by M. Cogan et al.Winona Lake, 1997.

Koch, K. *The Growth of the Biblical Tradition*. Translated from the second German edition by S. M. Cupitt. New York, 1969.

- "Gefüge und Herkunft des Berichtes über die Kultreform des Königes Josia." In *Alttestamentlicher Glaube und Biblische Theologie, Festschrift für H. D. Preuss,* pp. 80-92. Stuttgart, 1992.

Lammeñs, H. *L'Arabie occidentale avant l'Hégire.* Beyrouth, 1928.

Le Moyne, J. *Les Sadducéens.* Paris, 1972.

Levin, Chr. "Joshija im deuteronomistischen Geschichtswerk." *ZAW* 96 (1984), pp. 351-371.

- "Die Instandsetzung des Tempels unter Joasch ben Ahasja." *VT* 60 (1990), pp. 51-88.

Levin, I. בתי כנסת In בית הכנסת בתקופת בית שני - אופיו והתפתחותו עתיקים, pp. 11-29. Edited by A.Oppenheimer, A. Kasher and U. Rappaport. Jerusalem, 1987.

- בית הכנסת בארץ ישראל: ראשיתו ואופיו בראייה מחודשת In *Tehillah le-Moshe. Biblical and Judaic Studies in Honor of Moshe Greenberg,* pp. 143-62. Edited by M. Cogan et al. Winona Lake, 1997.

Levine, B. כיפורים *Eretz Israel* 9 (1969), pp. 88-95.

Levine, B. A. and W. W. Hallo. "Offerings to the Temple Gates at Ur." *HUCA 38* (1967), pp. 17 - 58.

Lexicon der Ägyptologie. Edited by W. Helck und W. Westendorf. Wiesbaden, 1985. Band VI, s.v. "Todesstrafe".

Liver, J. "Korah, Datan and Abiram." *Scripta Hierosolymitana* 8 (1961), pp 189-217.

Lods, A. *Israel, Des Origines au Milieu du VIIIe Siècle,* Hebrew translation M. Halamish, ישראל קדמוניות העם והארץ Tel Aviv, 1960.

Löhr, Max. *Das Räucheropfer im Alten Testament.* Schriften der koniglichen Gelehrten Gesellschaft. Halle, 1927.

Maag, V."Erwägungen zur Deuteronomischen Kultzentralisation." *VT* 6 (1956), pp. 10-18.

MacDonald, John. *The Theology of the Samaritans.* New Testament Library. London, 1964.

MacNicol, Nicol, ed. *Hindu Scriptures.* London, 1938.

Maimonides. *The Guide of the Perplexed.* Translated by S. Pines. Chicago, 1963.

Malamet, A. ישראל בתקופת המקרא Jerusalem, 1983.

May, H. G. and R. M. Engberg. *Material Remains of the Meggiddo Cult.* Chicago, 1935.

Mays, J. L. *Hosea, A Commentary.* London, 1969.

McCarter, P. Kyle Jr. *II Samuel, A New Translation with Introduction, Notes and Commentary.* The Anchor Bible. Garden City, N.Y., 1984.

Merendino, R. P. *Das Deuteronomische Gesetz.* Bonn, 1969.

Meyers, E.M. "Second Zecharia and the 'End' of Prophecy." In *Pomegranates and Golden Bells: Studies in Biblical, Jewish and Near*

Eastern Ritual, Law and Literature in Honor of Jacob Milgrom, pp. 713-23. Edited by D. Wright, D.N. Freedman and A. Hurvitz. Winona Lake, 1995.

Mistree, K. P. *Zoroastrianism*. Bombay,1982.

Money-Kyrle, R. *The Meaning of Sacrifice*. London, 1930.

Monson, J. H. מקדש שלמה והמקדש בעין דארא שבסוריה *Qadmoniot* 29/1 (1996), pp. 33-38.

Morgenstern, J. *The Ark, the Ephod and the Tent of Meeting*. Cincinnati, 1945.

Mowinckel, S. *Studien zu dem Buche Ezra-Nehemia III*. Oslo 1965.

Niehr, H. "Die Reform des Joschija." In *Jeremia und die Deuteronomistische Bewegung*. B. B. B. Band 98, pp. 33 - 55. Edited by W. Gross. Weinheim, 1995.

Niemann, H. M. *Herrschaft, Königtum und Staat*. FAT 6. Tübingen, 1993.

Noth, M. *Das Buch Josua*. Tübingen, 1938.

- *Übelieferungsgeschichtliche Studien 1*. Halle, 1942.

- *The History of Israel*. Revised and translated by P. R. Ackroyd. London, 1960.

- *Exodus, A Commentary*. The Old Testament Library. Translated by J. S. Bowden. London, 1965.

- *Leviticus, A Commentary*. The Old Testament Library. Translated by J.E Anderson. London, 1965.

- *Numbers, A Commentary*. The Old Testament Library. Translated by J. D. Martin. Philadelphia, 1968.

- *Könige*. Biblischer Kommentar, Altes Testament IX/1. Neukirchen, 1968.

Obbink, H. Th."The Horns of the Altar in the Semitic World, Especially in Jahwism." *JBL* 56 (1937), 43 - 49.

O' Leary, De Lacy. *Arabia before Muhammad*. London, 1927.

Olyan, Saul M. "Why an Altar of Unfinished Stones? Some Thoughts on Exod. 20,25 and Dtn 27,5 - 6." *ZAW* 108 (1996), pp.161 - 171.

Osumi, Y. *Die Kompositionsgeschichte des Bundesbuches Exodus 20,22b – 23, 33*. Orbis Biblicus et Orientalis 105. Göttingen, 1991.

Paul, S.M. תורה לתורה מדעי פירוש, לישראל מקרא .אמוס. Edited by M.Greenberg and S. Ahituv. Jerusalem, 1994.

Petersen, D. L. *Zechariah 9 - 14 and Malachi*. Louisville, Ky, 1995.

Philo. *The Embsassy to Gaius*. Loeb Classical Library. Translated by F.H. Colson. London, 1968.

- *On the The Special Laws*. Loeb Classical Library. 2 vols. Translated by F.H. Colson. London, 1968.

- *Questions and Answers on Exodus*. Loeb Classical Library. Translated by

R. Marcus. London, 1970.

Pritchard, J.B., ed. *Ancient Near Eastern Texts Relating to the Old Testament* 3rd edition with Supplement. Princeton, 1969.

Rabe, V.W. "Israelite Opposition to the Temple." *CBQ* 29 (1967), pp. 228-30.

Reallexicon der Assyriologie. Edited by E. Ebeling and B. Meissner. Berlin, 1932. S.v. "Altar" by E. Unger.

Rehm, M. *Das Erste Buch der Könige, Ein Kommentar*. Eichstatt, 1979.

- *Das Zweite Buch der Könige*. Eichstatt, 1979.

Die Religion in Geschichte und Gegenwart. Handwörterbuch für Theologie Und Wissenschaft. Tübingen, 1957. S.v. "Altar. II. In Israel" by K. Galling.

Rendtorff, R. *Studien zur Geschichte des Opfers im Alten Israel*. Wissenschaftliche Monographien zum Alten und Neuen Testament. Neukirchen,1967.

- *Gesammelte Studien zum Alten Testament*. Theologische Bücherei, Band 57. München, 1975.

Revell, E.J. *The Designation of the Individual. Expressive Usage in Biblical Narrative. Contributions to Biblical Exegesis and Theology* 14. Kampen, 1996.

- "The Repetition of Introductions to Speech as a Feature of Biblical Hebrew." *VT* 47 (1997), pp. 91-110.

Richter, H.F. "Geschlechtlichkeit, Ehe und Familie im Alten Testament und seiner Umwelt." *BET* 10 (1978), I25f.; II,20ff

Rokeah, D. *Jews, Pagans and Christians in Conflict*. Leiden, 1982.

Rosenthal, Franz. A *Grammar of Biblical Aramaic*. Wiesbaden, 1961.

Rost, L. *The Succession to the Throne of David*. Translated by M.D. Rutter and D.M.Gunn. Sheffield,1982.

Rudolph,W. *Hosea*. Kommentar zum Alten Testament. Gütersloh, 1966.

Ryckmans, G. "Das Opfer in der altsüdarabischen Hochkulturen. Addenda et Corrigenda."In *Arabia Sacra*. Orbis Biblicus et Orientalis 40, pp. 240-53. Göttingen,1981.

Safrai, S. פרקים בתולדות In העליה לרגל לירושלים לאחר חורבן בית שני ירושלים בימי בית שני, ספר זיכרון לאברהם שליט pp.376 - 393. Edited by A. Oppenheimer, U. Rappaport and M. Stern. Jerusalem, 1991.

- ארץ ישראל וחכמיה בתקופת In מעמדו ומעשיו של יוחנו בן זכאי המשנה והתלמוד, pp. 181-208. Jerusalem, 1983.

- התאוששות היישוב.In ארץ ישראל מחורבן בית שני ועד הכיבוש היהודי בדור יבנה המוסלמי Vol. I, pp. 18-39. Jerusalem, 1982.

Sakowitz, Y. ספר הברית מבאר את ספר הברית - תופעת הבומרנג In *Texts, Temples and Traditions, A Tribute to Menahmen Haran*, pp. 59 - 64.

Edited by M. V. Fox et al. Winona Lake, 1996.

Sarna, N. *Exodus* שמות. The JPS Torah Commentary. Philadelphia, 1991.

Schiffman, L. H.יהודה מדבר בכת ומשיחיות הליכה, הלכה Jerusalem, 1993.

Schmidt, Werner H. *Exodus*. Biblischer Kommentar Altes Testament II3. Neukirchen, 1974.

Schulte, H. "Die Rettung des Prinzen Joas. Zur Exegese von II Reg 11, 1-3." *ZAW* 109 (1997), pp. 549-56.

Schwienhorst - Schönberger, L. *Das Bundesbuch*. BZAW 188. Berlin, 1990.

Seitz, G. *Redaktionsgeschichtliche Studien zum Deuteronomium*. Stuttgart, 1971.

Seligman, I. A. המקרא בספרות מחקרים Edited by A. Horowitz et al. Jerusalem, 1965.

Shanks, H. "Two Early Israelite Cult Sites Now Questioned." *BAR* 14/1 (Jan/Feb. 1988), pp. 48-52.

Shutter, R.J.H. "Letter of Aristeas." In *The Old Testament Pseudepigrapha*, Vol. II, pp. 712-34. Edited by J.H. Charlesworth. N.Y., 1985.

Smith, W. Robertson. *The Religion of the Semites*. N. Y.: Schoken Paperback, 1972.

Soggin, J. A. *Joshua, A Commentary*. The Old Testament Library. Translated by R. A.Wilson. Philadelphia, 1972.

- *Judges, A Commentary*. The Old Testament Library. Translated by J. Bowden. Philadelphia,1981.

Sokoloff, M. *A Dictionary of Jewish Palestinian Aramaic*. Ramat Gan, 1990.

Spieckermann, H. *Juda unter Assur in der Sargonidenzeit*. Göttingen, 1982.

Stade, B. "Der Text des Berichtes uber Salomos Bauten. I Ko. 5-7." *ZAW* 3 (1883), pp. 129-177.

Stade B. and F. Schwally. *The Book of Kings*. London, 1904.

Stäubli, Thomas. *Das Image der Nomaden im Alten Israel und in der Ikonographie Seiner Sesshaften Nachbarn*. Orbis Biblicus et Orientalis 107. Göttingen, 1991.

Stendebach, F. J."Altarformen im kanaanäisch-israelischen Raum." *Biblische Zeitschrift* 20 (1976), pp.180 - 196.

Stern, E."Limestone Incense Altars." In *Beer Sheba I. Excavations at Tel Beer Sheba 1969-1971 Season*, pp. 52-53. Edited by Y. Aharoni. Tel Aviv, 1973.

- "Schumacher's Shrine in Building 338 at Meggido, A Rejoinder." *IEJ* 40 (1990), pp. 102 - 107.

Stern, M. יהדות ויוונות בארץ ישראל במאות השלישית והשנייה לפנה״ס מדינת החשמונאים לתולדותיה על רקע התקופה ההלניסטית, קובץ In מאמרים., pp. 55 - 74. Edited by U. Rappaport and I. Ronen. Jerusalem, 1994.

- מרד החשמונאים ומקומו בתולדות החברה והדת היהודית In idem, pp.

507 - 517.

Suzuki, Y. "A New Aspect of Occupation Policy by King Josiah, Assimilation and Codification in View of Yahwism." *AJBI* 18 (1992), pp. 31 - 61.

Swanson, D. *The Temple Scroll and the Bible, The Methodology of 11QT.* Leiden, 1995.

Tal, A. ed. התרגום השומרוני לתורה 2 vols. Tel Aviv, 1980 - 1982.

Theologisches Wörterbuch zum Alten Testament. Stuttgart, 1973.

S.v. מזבח by C. Dohmen.

S.v. סקל by A.S. Kapelrud.

S.v. קרן by B. Kedar-Kopfstein.

S.v. צור by W. Thiel.

Thiel, W. *Die Deuteronomistische Redaktion von Jeremia 1 - 25.* Neukirchen, 1973.

Thompson, R. J. *Penitence and Sacrifice in Early Israel Outside the Levitical Law. An Examination of the Fellowship Theory of Early Israelite Sacrifice.* Leiden, 1963.

Thureau-Dangin, F. *Rituels Accadiens.* Paris, 1921.

Uehlinger, Chr. "Gab es eine Joshijanische Kultreform?" In *Jeremia und die Deuteronomistische Bewegung.* B. B. B. Band 98, pp. 57- 89. Edited by W. Gross. Weinheim, 1995.

Ussishkin, D. "Schumacher's Shrine in Building 338 at Meggido." *IEJ* 39 (1989), pp. 149-172.

Van Seters, J. "Cultic Laws in the Covenant Code (Ex. 20,22 - 23 - 33) and Their Relationship to Deuteronomy and the Holiness Code." In *Studies in the Book of Exodus, Redaction - Reception - Interpretation.* Bibliotheca Ephemeridium Theologicarum Lovaniensium, CXXVI, pp. 319 - 346. Edited by M. Vervenne. Leuven, 1966.

Vermes, G. *The Dead Sea Scrolls in English.* Reprinted with revisions, London, 1968.

von Mutius, H. G. *Der Josua-Kommentar des Tanchum Ben Josef ha-Jeruschalmi.* Hildesheim, 1983.

von Rad, G. *Old Testament Theology.* Vol. I. Translated by D.M.G. Stalker. N.Y., 1962.

- *Deuteronomy, A Commentary.* The Old Testament Library. Translated by D. Barton. Philadelphia, 1966.

- *5. Buch Moses.* 2. Auflage. Göttingen, 1968.

Weinfeld, M. *Deuteronomy and the Deuteronomic School.* Oxford, 1972.

- "The Emergence of the Deuteronomic Movement: The Historical

Antecedents." In *Das Deuteronium. Enstehung, Gestalt und Botschaft*, pp 76-98. Edited by N. Lohfink. Leuven 1985.

- מיהושע עד יאשיהו. Jerusalem, 1992.

Weiser, A. "Die Tempelbaukrise unter David." *ZAW* 77 (1965), pp. 153-67.

- *Das Buch der Zwölf Kleinen Propheten, I.* Das Alte Testament Deutsch. 5. verbesserte Auflage. Göttingen, 1967.

Weiss, M. "Concerning Amos' Repudiation of the Cult." In *Pomegranates and Golden Bells: Studies in Biblical, Jewish and Near Eastern Ritual, Law and Literature in Honor of Jacob Milgrom*, pp. 199-214. Edited by D. Wright, D.N Freedman and A. Hurvitz. Winona Lake, 1995.

Welch, A. C."The Death of Josiah." *ZAW* 43 (1925), pp. 255 - 260.

Wellhausen, J. *Prolegomena to the History of Ancient Israel*. New York, 1957

- *Die Composition des Hexateuchs und der historischen Bücher des Alten Testament*. Berlin, 1963

Westermann, Claus. *Genesis*. Biblischer Kommentar Altes Testament. 3 vols. Neukirchen-Vluyn, 1974-82.

Wevers, J. W. *Ezekiel*. The Century Bible. London, 1969.

- *Notes on the Greek Text of Exodus*. Septuagint and Cognate Studies 35. Atlanta, 1990.

- "The Composition of Exodus 35 to 40." In *Text History of the Greek Exodus*. Mittelung des Septuaginta Unternehmens XXI, pp. 117 - 146. Göttingen, 1992.

Whitehead, A. N. *Religion in the Making*. New York, 1926.

Wiegand, A. "Der Gottesname צור und seine Deutung in dem Sinne Bildner Oder Schöpfer in der alten jüdischen Litteratur." *ZAW* 1 (1881), pp. 85 – 96.

Wildberger, H. *Jesaia*. Biblischer Kommentsar Altes Testament. Neukirchen, 1974.

Winston, D. "The Iranian Component in the Bible, Apocrypha, and Qumran. A Review of the Evidence." *History of Religion* 5 (1965-6), pp. 183-216.

Wolf, H. W. *Dodekapropheton 1, Hosea*. Biblischer Kommentar, Altes Testament. 3. verbesserte Auflage. Neukirchen, 1976.

Woudstra, Marten H. *The Book of Joshua*. Grand Rapids, Michigan, 1981.

Würthweim, E. *Das Erste Buch der Könige, Kapitel 1 - 16*. Göttingen, 1977.

- *Die Bücher der Könige, 1. Kön. 17 - 2. Kön. 25*. Das Alte Testament Deutsch. Göttingen, 1984.

Yadin, Y. "Beer-sheba: The High Place Destroyed by King Josiah." *BASOR* 222 (1976), pp. 5-17.

- *The Temple Scroll*. English version. Jerusalem, 1983.

Zertal, Adam. "Has Joshua's Altar Been Found on Mt. Ebal?" *BAR* 11/1

(Jan./Feb. 1985), pp. 26-43.

Zevit, Z. "Philology, Archeology and a *Terminus A Quo* for P's *hattat* Legislation." In *Pomegranates and Golden Bells: Studies in Biblical, Jewish and Near Eastern Ritual, Law and Literature in Honor of Jacob Milgrom*, pp. 29-38. Edited by D. Wright, D.N Freedman and A. Hurvitz. Winona Lake, 1995.

- "The Earthen Altar Laws of Exodus 20: 24-26 and Related Sacrificial Restrictions in their Cultural Context." In *Texts, Temples and Traditions, A Tribute to Menahem Haran*, pp. 53-62. Edited by M.V. Fox et al. Winona Lake, 1996.

Zimmerli, W. *Ezekiel 2, A Commentary on the Book of the Prophet Ezekiel, Chapters 25-48.* Translated by J. D. Martin. Philadelphia, 1983.

Zimmern, H. *Beiträge zur Kenntnis der Babylonischen Religion.* Leipzig, 1901.

Zwickel, W. "Die Altarbaunotizen im Alten Testament." *Biblica* 73/4 (1992), pp. 533-546.

- *Räucherkult und Räuchergeräte. Exegetische und Archäologische Studien Zum Räucheropfer im Alten Testament.* OBO 97. Freiburg/Göttingen, 1990.

- "Die Kultreform des Ahas (2Kön 16,10-18)." *JSOT* 7,2 (1993), pp. 250-262.

- *Der Tempelkult in Kanaan und Israel, Studien zur Kultgeschichte Palästinas von der Mittelbronzezeit bis zum Untergang Judas.* Forschungen zum Alten Testament 10. Tübingen, 1994.

Citations Index

21: 1-8 99
21: 4 55
21: 7 54-5, 98, 99
21: 8 323
21: 9 98, 99, 101
21: 23 55
23: 5-8 375
23: 16-21 129
23: 17 324
23: 34-43 129
23: 39 129
23: 40 378
23: 42-3 129
24: 5-9 268
24: 14 97, 100, 105
24: 16 97, 102, 105
24: 23 97, 105
25: 2-7 409
chap. 26 331
26: 1 28, 89, 120
26: 37 368

Numbers
3: 10 358
chap. 4 197
4: 6 84, 118, 200, 201
4: 7 181, 268
4: 10 199
4: 12 199
4: 13 180, 181, 185, 199
4: 13-14 193
4: 14 177, 178, 181, 184, 185, 196
4: 15 201
4: 20 358
6: 17 24
6: 24-7 385
7: 84 20
7: 87 20
9: 1-14 375
9: 2 376
9: 13 294, 331
10: 10 24
12: 1 410
13: 23 9, 199
14: 10 98, 100, 105
15: 2 237, 242
15: 3-16 237

15: 18-21 237
15: 19 237
15: 22-26 21, 324
15: 35 100, 102
15: 35-6 97, 105
15: 38 223
15: 39 223
chap. 16 358
chaps. 16-17 184
17: 3 253, 254
17: 4 183, 254
17: 5 254
17: 11 254
18: 8-32 296
19: 2-13 129
20: 7-13 109
20: 8 109
20: 12-13 388
21: 14 96
22: 28 212
22: 32 212
22: 33 212
23: 1 246, 249
23: 14 246
23: 29 246, 249
25: 4 107, 108
25: 5 107
25: 6 85
25: 8 85
25: 9 107
25: 12 252
25: 12-13 257
25: 14-15 85
27: 1-11 258
27: 21 251
chaps. 28-9 59, 260
28: 2 323, 367, 376
28: 3-4 354
28: 4 374
28: 11 274
28: 16-25 375
28: 26 129
chap. 29 19
29: 1 367
29: 16 19
33: 52 120
35: 11-28 221-2

453

Subject Index

adultery 97, 98-9, 101n

Ahab
  altar 133
  as idolater 292-3

Aharoni, Y. See archeological evidence

Ahaz
  changes to sacrificial canon 3, 10-11, 12, 134-5, 218-9, 231, 262, 264, 325-8, 325-9, 366, 396, 398
  demotion of bronze altar 10, 237, 256, 275-9, 329, 396
  elaborate altar 134-7, 218-9, 259-64, 272-3, 279, 328n, 356-7, 396
  political motives 297n
  transgressions 263-4n, 279n, 286-7n, 357n

Ahaziah, as idolater 287, 291

altars
  ad hoc 59n, 71-2, 74-5, 117-8n, 249, 262
  archeological evidence See archeological evidence
  as bamoth See bamoth
  as tables 268-75, 324n, 396, 405-6
  bronze See bronze altar
  building terminology 246-8
  comparisons of biblical laws See Pentateuchal altar laws compared; Pentateuchal altar laws and First Temple construction
  earthen (Exod. 21:21) 4, 14,21, 22-32
  First Temple See First Temple
  golden See incense altar
  holocaust See holocaust altar
  incense See incense altar
  memorials 264
  of Ahab See Ahab
  of Ahaz See Ahaz
  of David See David
  of Elijah 80, 119, 133-4
  of Gideon 133

altars, cont'd
  of Jeroboam See Jeroboam
  of Moses 248-9
  of Noah 72n, 132
  of Patriarchs 77-8, 132-3
  of Samuel 133
  of Solomon See Solomon
  on east side of Jordan 132, 253
  on Mount Ebal 39-47, 61-2, 115-6, 165-6, 252-3
  on Mount Gerizim 40-2, 45-7
  seat of Deity 213, 214, 222
  Second Temple See Second Temple
  steps 63-72, 125n, 127, 130, 165
  stone See also stone
    (Deut. 27: 2-8) 4-5, 14, 23, 33, 36, 38-47
    (Exod. 21: 22) 4, 14, 32-8

anthropomorphism 126, 130, 181, 268-9, 323n, 324n, 334

archeological evidence
  altars
    Aharoni, Y. 8, 154-6, 164-5, 394
    extrapolation from bronze altar dimensions 135-6, 155, 156, 166-9
    Shanks, H. 8, 166n, 393-4
    Stern, E. 169-70, 393-4
    Ussishkin, D. 8, 169-70, 393-4
    Yadin, Y. 8, 154-7, 163-5, 394
    Zertal, A. 8, 165-9, 393-4
  horns 155-6, 207, 228-30
  table-altars 169-170, 262-3, 268, 272

ark
  hidden 94-5, 245-6n
  location in Debir 244-5n
  poles 10, 198, 199, 243-6, 280
  structure 203
  transport 68n, 74-5, 11708n, 175, 199, 250

Asa, role in cult reform 284

asherah 89n, 93, 284, 285, 299n

DATE DUE

JUL 29 20X			
SEP 8 2004			
AUG 18 2004			
Mayzo, 2005			
MAR - 1 2013			
GAYLORD			PRINTED IN U.S.A.